Forecast Scheduling

with Microsoft® Project 2010

Best Practices for Real-World Projects

Eric Uyttewaal, PMP, Microsoft MVP for Project
President ProjectPro Corporation

Published by ProjectPro Corporation

Publishing Notice

Copyright © 2010 ProjectPro Corp.
ISBN 978-0-9867339-0-1
Uyttewaal, Eric.
Forecast Scheduling with Microsoft® Project 2010: Best Practices for Real-World Projects / By Eric Uyttewaal
1. Microsoft Project 2. Project Management--Computer programs, I. Title
Dewey decimal classification number: 658.404

This publication contains information obtained from authentic and highly regarded sources. Reprinted material is used with permission, and sources are indicated. Reasonable effort has been made to publish reliable data and information, but the author and the publisher cannot assume responsibility for the validity of all materials or for the consequences of their use.

Notwithstanding the previous disclaimer, we would like to show you that we have given it all we have to make this book flawless. Herewith, we promise a reward to those who uncover errors or omissions in this book. We will pay $20 to the first person who reports each technical error or serious omission to us. For this purpose, we have created a public, online database for this book where you can check if an item has been reported already and where you can also leave positive comments about the book:

www.projectprocorp.com/fs.php

This database is accessible to everybody and also serves as a continuously updated list of errata for the book. *Nothing is perfect – even this statement!*

Direct all inquiries to:
Eric Uyttewaal, PMP, MCITP, Microsoft MVP for Project
President ProjectPro Corp.
EricU@ProjectProCorp.com
Tel. 613-692-7778

Who Is the Author?

Eric is one of the foremost authors, trainers and consultants on the use of project, resource and portfolio management applications from Microsoft. Eric has authored the best-selling book *Dynamic Scheduling with Microsoft Office Project 2003*, as well as the 2002 and 2000 editions in the same series.

He is a project management practitioner and carries the following designations:

- Microsoft *MVP* for Project, a most-valuable-professional designation by Microsoft for those who have served the community of Microsoft Project users. The designation is evaluated and awarded on a yearly basis for contributions made in the previous year.
- *MCITP* (Microsoft Certified Information Technology Professional), a designation by Microsoft for those who have passed all three exams in Microsoft Project and Project Server 2007.
- *PMP®* (project management professional), a designation by PMI, the Project Management Institute.
- *MS Business Administration* from the University of Groningen, The Netherlands
- *BS Engineering* from the Higher Horticultural College in Utrecht, The Netherlands

You will find that this book has an attitude, and you may be interested in how that attitude came about. I will tell my story in the first person.

In September 1993 I became the first Canadian to be certified by Microsoft in MS Project. At that time, the current version was 3.0. When Project 4.0 came out, I recertified immediately. My career was progressing well, and I started to get contracts in MS Project, but it was part-time.

The Project Management Institute (PMI) certified me as a Project Management Professional (PMP) in March of 1994. In 1996, I founded ProjectPro Corporation and incorporated it federally in Canada. I put myself on ProjectPro's payroll.

In 1998, I eagerly awaited the certification exam for Project 98 … and waited … and waited. It was never released. I realized that I was probably not the only person who was looking for it. In the same year, I developed advanced courses in MS Project and approached the International Institute of Learning (IIL) to market them. I was contracted to be their *Director of MS Project Certification*, while remaining on the payroll of my own company, ProjectPro, which slid into the background. Since then, IIL has held many MS Project certification classes in North America and in Europe. In those early workshops, I had the pleasure of working with some of the finest project managers and project schedulers in the world. I remember this time fondly.

I observed that many people were wasting much valuable work time trying to learn MS Project on their own. I realized that organizations, therefore, needed a meaningful training curriculum so that they could implement MS Project more quickly and thoroughly. Training is only thorough if it measures the outcome of the training and if passing the benchmark comes with a certificate that is meaningful in the marketplace. To address the need for training and certification in the marketplace, I developed the certification curriculum with the "belts" at IIL: the White, Orange, Blue and Black Belt in Microsoft Project. I developed all course content and tests and managed the certification curriculum. I selected, trained and led the team of instructors. This team eventually consisted of about thirty instructors in seven different countries.

In 2004, IIL promoted me to *Executive Director, Microsoft EPM Division*, but in July of 2005, IIL terminated its agreement with my company, ProjectPro. We went our own way with the *Dynamic Scheduling* book, courses and course materials. I decided to return ProjectPro to the foreground and grow it as much as I can. To that end, I will continue with this book under its new title, *Forecast Scheduling*, and focus on offering courses and consulting to people who use MS Project, Project Web App and Project Server.

During the slow time in 2009 and 2010, ProjectPro diverted into building add-in solutions, because we found that previous editions of this book pointed out several omissions in MS Project but failed to provide an automated way to resolve them.
For example:

- The factors that break a Critical Path just begged for an automated solution to repair it. Resource-constrained projects begged for a solution to identify the Resource-Critical Path in an automated fashion. We developed the add-in *Complete Critical Paths* to address these issues. We are selling this solution on our website www.ProjectProCorp.com.
- I never chose to write about Earned Value in MS Project, because its algorithms were, and still are, wrong. Together with Rod Gill, another Project MVP, we built an add-in that can generate correct and reliable Earned Value numbers and charts. This add-in works around the issues in MS Project. We are selling this solution on our website www.ProjectProCorp.com.
- We also built a solution for program managers to help them model and manage hundreds of cross-project links between subprojects. This solution is also able to automatically identify the Critical Path going across the subprojects in a large program schedule. We do not sell licenses to this solution, but we use this solution to be efficient in our consulting on projects that have more than one thousand tasks and, thus, need to be divided into subprojects.

- We have future plans for creating a schedule evaluation application that will perform about 70% of the checks published in this book in an automated fashion.

We feel that for the first time we left no open ends in this edition of the book.
All previous editions had open ends where we could only conclude with: *This is what the tool does, and from here you are on your own.* We think we now provide the complete package: theories, insights, best practices, checklists to build best-practice schedules and automated solutions to address weaknesses in the Microsoft Project application and in the Critical Path technique.

ProjectPro Corporation

ProjectPro specializes in consulting and training in Microsoft Project, Project Web App and Project Server. The training is provided through onsite or public courses and delivered as self-paced training, live training on the web, or traditional classes on site. ProjectPro can customize the training to your organization. We commit to you, the client, that:

- **As our client, you are our reason for being**
  At ProjectPro, we are committed to your satisfaction. We acquire clear understanding of your expectations, and we commit to meeting, if not exceeding, those expectations.
- **You will always receive advice from us that is in your own best interest without consideration for ours**
  We will always give you the best advice we know. We are not afraid to give you advice that makes our services redundant if that advice serves you best. We would always like you to become self-sufficient in the quickest way possible. No matter how much we like you as our client, we do not like to stick around.
- **You will receive unbiased information**
  We will give you objective information in our courses and consulting; we like to talk straight. If there is a bug, we will tell you (and Microsoft, of course). We will provide a workaround when available. If other software is better suited to your needs, we will tell you.
- **You will receive the best materials possible**
  At ProjectPro, we strive to create the best content possible on project, resource and portfolio management software from Microsoft. The content is always well-researched, up-to-date, tested and true.
- **You can learn the way you want**
  Whether you are an auditory, visual or kinesthetic (hands-on) learner, we always make sure that your learning style is well served. We also provide several options for learning:
  - from learn-when-you-can courses to scheduled, instructor-led classes
  - from learn-wherever-you-are, web-based courses to face-to-face classes

- ◇ from learn-on-your-own, self-paced courses to live-and-interactive training
- ◆ **You can measure what you learned**
  We believe that training is not just a perk for employees, but the means to realize targeted changes within organizations. We like to see that organizations measure what was learned in order to track progress on achieving the targets. Measuring is of particular importance for those organizations that are trying to adapt quickly but thoroughly to new technology, business processes, and realities.
- ◆ **You can learn where you want**
  We have an international focus; we reach out to the entire world through web-based training, self-paced training and through partnering with organizations abroad.
  We have our ACT-program for Associate Certified Trainers, in which we train associates and then make our course and instructor materials available to them so they can work with their own clients. The people we are looking for are:
  - ◇ Candidates with hands-on experience in managing projects.
  - ◇ Candidates that use MS Project on an almost daily basis.
  - ◇ Candidates that have the *Project Management Professional* (PMP) designation by *PMI*.
  - ◇ Candidates that have the *MCTS* (Microsoft Certified Technology Specialist) or *MCITP* (Microsoft Certified IT-Professional) designation from Microsoft.
  - ◇ Candidates that have earned credentials in training groups in MS Project.

  Candidates need to go through a train-the-trainer process in which they teach the course back to the lead trainer. If you are interested in becoming an ACT instructor, please send us your resume at *EricU@ProjectProCorp.com*.

Download Files that Accompany this Book

Free added-value materials are available at:

www.ProjectProCorp.com

At ProjectPro, we are committed to providing today's professional with practical, hands-on tools that enhance the learning experience and give readers an opportunity to apply what they have learned. That is why we offer free, additional materials available for download. The steps to download these files are:

1. Open your Internet browser and navigate to: www.ProjectProCorp.com.
2. In the sidebar on the left, click the **Log in** button at the bottom. You are now prompted for your **Log in** data.
3. If you bought the book on our website, you have your log in password already and you can **Log in**. If you bought the book elsewhere, you need to create a new log in account using **Create your Login Account**.
4. After you log in, you are taken to the **My Account** page with the **My Download Page** section, where you can find the links to the download files.

The download files that are available to all readers of this book consist of (subject to modification without prior notice):

- Evaluation version of Complete Critical Paths 2.0 to help you find the most critical path in your schedule
- Solution files for the Relocation Project exercises
- Filters to check the quality of your own schedules
- Files with views, tables and filters described and recommended in this book
- Approximately one hundred examples of schedules that we have certified.

There is also a *solutions manual*, with the answers to all review questions as well as the questions embedded in the Relocation Project exercises. This solutions manual is designed and written for professors. However, the solutions manual is only available to those professors who make the book mandatory reading for their students in their courses. Professors need to contact the author, Eric Uyttewaal, first at: *EricU@ProjectProCorp.com*. Then they may be given access to the solutions manual that can be retrieved from our website.

Short Table of Contents

Join the dialog about this book and about scheduling at the *LinkedIn Group* called *Forecast Scheduling*.

Long Table of Contents

Dedication

I dedicate my fourth book on Project 2007 to my late colleague, Rebecca Munn. Rebecca, it was a true pleasure working with you. Your inspiration and ideas are wandering throughout the book. You must know your book was entirely written; it is just a pity that it was never published as a textbook.

I dedicate my fifth book and first edition of *Forecast Scheduling with Microsoft Project 2010* to the guys and gals at Microsoft who have, indeed, built the best release of MS Project so far and … for doing this at a time I could, once again, enjoy my fundamental right to freedom of speech in this wonderful "free" world. I have tried to match your efforts and hope that people will embrace this as "*the best book on the best release of MS Project*".

What Is New in This Edition of the Book?

Join the dialog about this book and about scheduling at the *LinkedIn Group* called *Forecast Scheduling*.

Forecast Scheduling shows you how you can forecast your project with just the schedule – even without advanced techniques like *Earned Value* or *Monte Carlo Simulation*. It builds onto the author's principle of *Dynamic Scheduling*, which explained how to minimize the effort spent on a schedule. In this book, the author goes to the next level by showing you how to make your schedule forecast by itself.

Forecast scheduling is built on four premises:

- The scheduler uses the *deadline dates* and the *baseline schedule* to capture promises made. Too many schedulers use the schedule itself to reflect their promises, and then they desperately want to keep their schedule static, thereby killing it. In our approach, the schedule will be a living document.
- The scheduler minimizes the time spent on scheduling by setting up the schedule properly with all dependencies and as few as possible date constraints (introduced by the author as *Dynamic Scheduling* in previous books). The scheduler uses the *checklist* in this book to ensure that the schedule is a valid, dynamic and robust model of the project.
- The scheduler updates the schedule properly, rather than merely entering actual progress. In order to forecast, you need to capture revised forecasts from your team members as well. Once team members have started working on a task, they have a much better idea how long the remainder of their own tasks and other tasks will take.
- The scheduler will be brutally honest to the scheduling tool and to the project stakeholders and enter all factors into the model that affect the forecasts the schedule produces – even if these factors do not reflect well on the scheduler, such as errors and omissions. The scheduler should correct errors and enter omissions as soon as they become apparent.

Apart from this main message, other things are new as well:

- We added the qualifier "*robust*" to the definition of a schedule and added more emphasis on forecasting as the main purpose of scheduling. The definition of the term *schedule* is now: *A schedule is a valid, dynamic and robust model of the project built to forecast the project*.
- The following standards released by PMI® have been incorporated into this book:
  - The Project Management Body of Knowledge (PMBOK®), 4th Edition, 2008

  - ◇ The Practice Standard for Scheduling, 1st edition, 2007, as well as the exposure draft of the 2nd edition published in October 2010.
  - ◇ The Practice Standard for Work Breakdown Structures, 2nd edition, 2006
  - ◇ The Practice Standard for Project Configuration Management, 1st edition, 2007
  - ◇ The Practice Standard for Earned Value Management, 1st edition, 2005
  - ◇ The Standard for Program Management, 2nd Edition, 2008
  - ◇ The Standard for Portfolio Management, 2nd edition, 2008

  This book contains guidelines on how to adhere to these standards. If you wondered how to apply all the standards from PMI with Microsoft Project, this book is perfect for you.

- All text has been reviewed and changed to work with the 2010 release of Microsoft Project. The new features of Project 2010 are discussed throughout and indicated with a 2010 icon to make them easy to find (as shown in the left margin). Most notably, you will find discussion of the new views Team Planner and Timeline, as well as new features like manually scheduled tasks, also marked with the 2010 icon. All screenshots and button images have been updated to reflect changes in the MS Project and Project Web App interfaces.
- We kept the 2007 icons in this book, which indicate what was new in the 2007 release and provide guidance for people upgrading from 2003. We removed older icons to avoid clutter.
- In this edition *Earned Value Management* is discussed for the first time in detail. Because more and more organizations are moving towards *Earned Value*, this edition provides a detailed explanation of how to do Earned Value with MS Project. We show you the Earned Value reports. We provide clear procedures for maintaining the integrity of your baseline and corresponding *Planned Values*. We will provide workarounds for weaknesses in MS Project's calculation of Earned Value, as well as an add-in solution to automate the workarounds and create the Earned Value charts easily.

- Project Server has a more prominent place in this edition, since many organizations are moving towards implementing enterprise project management. Project managers who are using Project 2010 in combination with Project Server will find the things they need to know in this book. People who are using Project 2010 as a standalone application are well served by this book as well. Where needed, you will find alternative procedures for standalone and enterprise use. The enterprise-specific procedures are marked by the *Pro* and *2010 Pro* icons in the margin of this bullet point, noting what is unique to any version of Project Professional (Project Server) and what is new in the 2010 version, respectively.
- The checklist of guidelines for valid and dynamic schedules in the Summary Chapter has been updated. Several checks and corresponding filters have been added and many were modified for clarity. We have made several changes to the checklist:
  - ◇ All checks in the list are now numbered, so you can more easily refer to a particular check. The numbering system is also a step towards standardization.

  - ◇ The checklist items refer back to the pages in the book where they are discussed in more detail and with more elaborate procedural steps provided.
- ◆ We have added several updating exercises. Project managers really need to know how to update their schedule efficiently during project execution, which is a very busy time. Updating the schedule is what they do most during their project; only at the start of the project do they create a dynamic model of the project. With the added exercises they will be able to develop hands-on skill and good habits for updating the model efficiently.
- ◆ You will find that the book has a more international character. We have inserted more examples from other countries. For example, in this edition there is information on how calendars and workweeks differ from country to country.
- ◆ We added a ton of cross-references. A robust series of steps is described in one place, then referenced wherever needed. This allowed us to add a lot of content to this book while keeping the total number of pages under 800.

Foreword by Doc Dochtermann

Microsoft Project is a project management software program, developed and sold by Microsoft, which is designed to assist project managers in developing plans, assigning resources to tasks, tracking progress, managing budgets and analyzing workloads. There are currently over 20 million copies of Microsoft Project in use throughout the world today. Unfortunately, most users of Project however, I dare say, do not have a good grasp on how to properly utilize this wonderful tool.

This book, entitled *Forecast Scheduling* with Microsoft Project 2010, by Eric Uyttewaal, PMP, MVP, provides users with everything they will need to learn to more easily and effectively manage projects to a successful conclusion. Eric's new book is based on the new release of Project 2010 and illustrates step-by-step processes to follow with a real-life project. The book includes web-based access to a repository of sample schedule templates, checklists for good models, filters to check your own project – and is based on research from over 1,000 real-life schedules.

Forecast Scheduling is not just another "tool" book either. *Forecast Scheduling* shows you how you can forecast your project performance with just the schedule – even without advanced techniques like Earned Value. It builds on Eric's original principle of Dynamic Scheduling (described in his first three books) that demonstrates how to minimize the effort spent on a schedule. In this new edition, Eric clearly takes scheduling to the next level by showing you how to create a model of the project; and how to *Forecast it Dynamically!*

I first met Eric back in 2004 at MCI Business Systems. Little did I realize how much I was about to learn about the art and science of creating and maintaining good schedules. Through our journey together at MPUG, PMI, the International Institute of Learning (IIL), Project-Pro Corp., PMICOS, and Microsoft, I have come to fully realize the depth of Eric's expertise. He is a true "Maven" in the full sense of the word, as defined by Malcolm Gladwell in his book, *The Tipping Point.* Gladwell describes Mavens as, *"those who are intense gatherers of information and impressions and so are often the first to pick up on new or nascent trends"*. Wikipedia defines a Maven as *"a trusted expert in a particular field, who seeks to pass knowledge on to others"*. Regardless of whose definition you choose, Eric is a world renowned expert scheduler with over 20 years of experience using and teaching Microsoft Project.

Doc Dochtermann, PMP, PMI-SP, MCITP, CISSPS
Project Portfolio Management Specialist
Microsoft Corporation

Acknowledgements

I would like to thank all the people whom I have had the pleasure of meeting during my MS Project and Project Server courses and consulting. Our discussions provided valuable input for this book. Many people have opened my eyes to remarkable insights. Where I thought an individual made a particularly valuable contribution, I have recognized the person individually in this book. Unfortunately, I have forgotten the origin of many thoughts and insights. To all of those who feel they should have been mentioned, I apologize.

Some people were very actively involved in creating this edition of the book and deserve special recognition. First of all, I would like to thank the technical editors for their contributions to the accuracy of the text. Because of their help, I have used the word "we" throughout the book when making recommendations. The recommendations are really a culmination of experiences and insights from this team, many of whom are instructors at ProjectPro. Let me thank them individually here:

- Doc Dochtermann: You caught some big picture items. Thank you for the foreword!
- B. Sai Prasad: Your analytic and logical thinking straightened out my spaghetti thoughts in several places.
- Kevin Watson: Your practical examples from your EPM work experience made this book a richer experience for the readers.
- Jim Cox: Your broad experience in installing Project Server and keeping it going has eradicated many small technical errors.
- Chuck Magee: The thoroughness of your review and feedback forced me to make many changes. The book is a much better book because of you!
- Ellen Lehnert: You helped the reader a great deal by making me define words and concepts when they first appear in this book, resulting in many cross-references.
- Cindy Goehring: You helped me call the screen elements by their right names. The technical steps are clearer and more teachable thanks to you!
- Lathif Masood: Your examples from your training and consulting experience have made this book richer. Thank you!
- Aviva Carmen: You provided some great insights gleaned from your real-world experience in applying these principles to large programs!

Other people who contributed in their own ways:

- Diane Donaldson: You designed a stunning cover page that visually captures the idea of forecast scheduling.
- Paul Mason: You created all the wonderful cartoons based on my little stories. You have a real talent for making abstract concepts visual and funny.
- Barbara Petoskey: Thank you for your pragmatic English language editing. Technical steps are already difficult enough to understand.

- Rina van Adrichem: Thank you for your help with the logistics and the screenshots.
- Justin McLean: You helped me find my way in printing this book as a first-time publisher. Thank you for your patience.
- Donna Moore: You helped me find my way in distributing this book as a first time publisher. Thank you for your patience.

Last but not least, thanks to you, the reader of this book. I hope you will find the time reading this book to be well spent. If you have any questions, comments or suggestions, please send them by e-mail to *EricU@ProjectProCorp.com*. I always enjoy hearing from you!

Introduction

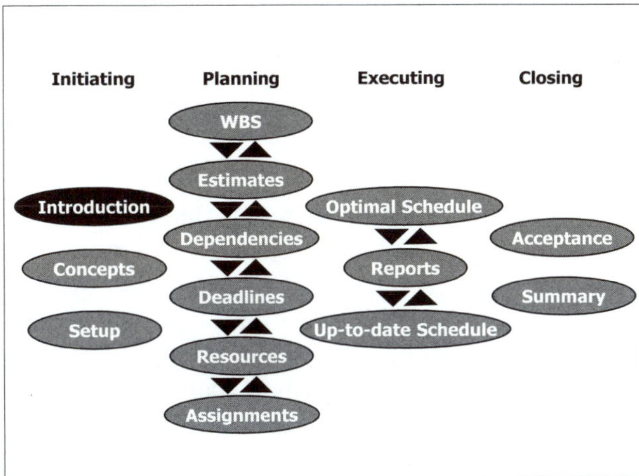

In this chapter, we will introduce the new features in the 2010 release of Microsoft Project and Project Server. We will introduce the book and discuss what you can expect from it and what not. We will introduce the principle of *forecast scheduling*. Finally, we will introduce the conventions used in this book.

Microsoft Project 2010

Project 2010 is a software application that helps you create a computer model of your project. It helps you create all the different representations of your project that are commonly used: *Gantt Charts*, *network diagrams*, *workload histograms*, *project budgets* and *forecast reports*. It will allow you to tailor the reports to your needs. The strengths of the software are:

- Ease of use for novice users as well as advanced features for power users
- Flexibility and feature-richness in scheduling and re-scheduling tasks
- Powerful *algorithms* that recalculate all dates of the project model within split seconds.
- Powerful reporting features: With Project 2010 you can extract almost any information from the project database and present it in concise reports.
- *Collaboration* features that help the project manager communicate with team members via Intranet or Internet, which is ideal for project teams that are dispersed around the globe. You will need to use Project 2010 in conjunction with SharePoint or Project Server for this.

Project 2010 is a powerful tool that has grown in its usefulness for professionals. Like all tools, correct use requires knowledge and skill. The software is not a magic bean that will grow a successful project by itself. Experience and research shows that a successful project results from a combination of executive support, competent project management, a committed team and … the right tools.

What Is New in Microsoft Project 2010?

- **Ribbon** (or *Fluent User Interface*)
  There are 6 ribbons in Project: **File, Task, Resource, Project, View** and **Format**. This book will call them ribbons, because that is what they look like. *Fluent User Interface* is Microsoft's term. If you have used previous versions of MS Project, there is nothing "fluent" about learning this new interface. The ribbons replace the classic menu bar and all the toolbars. This new interface may annoy you at first, but when you start to find your way around in it, you may like it. Microsoft has put the buttons you may use most often first on the ribbon starting on the left. Buttons of related features are logically grouped. Microsoft made the buttons you may use most often bigger than the others within the same group. All ribbons are context sensitive, meaning that buttons will be enabled or disabled depending on where you clicked (primarily when you click on a task or a resource). Depending on the view you are in, the back ground color of the **Format** ribbon will change, which communicates

better than ever before the context-sensitivity of the **Format** ribbon. The view you are in will also determine the items available on the **Format** ribbon. If you do not agree with Microsoft's ribbon choices, which are based on usage research, you can easily add buttons to the ribbons.

- **Quick Access Toolbar** (QAT) in the title bar of windows
  2010 The Quick Access Toolbar (QAT) is always visible, unlike each ribbon. Buttons you put on the QAT are always accessible with one click.
- Microsoft Office *Backstage* (**File** ribbon)
  2010 The backstage can be accessed by clicking **File**. It contains the file management features and all features of secondary use, which may appeal more to advanced users. The **Options** can now be found in the backstage.
- 2010 *Keyboard shortcuts*
  The ribbon design comes with new keyboard shortcuts, which bring two advantages over previous versions:
  - ◇ Shortcuts for every button on the ribbon.
  - ◇ Shortcuts that often require fewer keys.

  The new shortcuts also have a new name: *KeyTips*. Press ALT to make the KeyTips appear for all ribbon tabs and Quick Access Toolbar commands. Then press the KeyTip for the tab you want to display; for example, press H for the **Home** tab, as shown here. This makes all the KeyTips for that tab's commands appear. Then press the KeyTip for the command you want. You get to Backstage view in roughly the same steps you used to open the **File** menu: For example, Alt + F opens the **File** ribbon; Alt + F + A opens the **Save As** dialog.
- 2010 Status bar at the bottom of the screen:
  The status bar now provides more feedback and has some new interactive buttons as well as the popular zoom slider for zooming the timescale in or out.
- *Manually scheduled tasks*
  2010 Manually scheduled tasks have a pushpin icon in the indicators column. This is the new default replacing *Auto Scheduled* tasks. Manually scheduled tasks give you the flexibility of Excel but the power of Project and allow you to start entering data into your MS Project schedule as soon as you receive them without having to complete the schedule. Your schedule can be your notepad much earlier during the planning phase. Manually scheduled tasks do not automatically move out when they have dependencies and will keep their dates as you entered them. Manually scheduled tasks even allow you to enter notes in **Start** and **Finish** date fields, for example: *discuss with Harry*. But please, do not let this feature seduce you into entering agreed-upon dates into the **Finish** date field instead of the **Deadline** date field. Eventually, dates need to be calculated by MS Project. After all, it is scheduling software; it schedules for you. If you do not want to use it that way, you may as well stick to Excel.

- Team Planner
  The Team Planner view is a workload chart in which you can easily drag workloads around. The bars depict workloads for the resource. Their position in the timescale represents when the workloads are scheduled.

- Time Line view
  The Time Line view provides an overview of all important milestones and tasks of your choice. The view is easy to manipulate. Best of all, you can paste it into a PowerPoint slide as a Microsoft Drawing object that you can continue to manipulate in PowerPoint. If only all views were like that!

- Resource Graph view
  The Resource Graph view can now also chart proposed work, availability and cumulative numbers.

- Sync to SharePoint
  You can synchronize the tasks from within a project plan into a SharePoint tasks list, or open a SharePoint task list directly in MS Project. You can even have team members update their tasks through a SharePoint site, and all without Project Server.

- *Paste* is improved
  Tasks copied between MS Office applications now keep their formatting (e.g., bolding). An indented task list copied from MS Word will also keep its indentation structure in Project 2010. *Paste* is the most frequently used feature in many Office applications, and Microsoft has paid attention to this usage data. A thank-you to all of you who allowed Microsoft to collect usage information in an automated fashion.

- *Move Project*
  Move Project is a new feature found on the **Project** ribbon. When you move a project, MS Project adjusts all the hard dates in the schedule relative to the new project start date you enter. This feature lets the schedule travel through time when a new project start date is entered and adjusts actual dates if you approve this when asked, making it useful for working with templates.

- 64-bit version of MS Project
  If you track large projects, you will end up with a large schedule. File sizes greater than 2 GB are now possible with the 64-bit version of Project 2010. However, you cannot install the 32-bit and 64-bit Office side-by-side on the same machine. Also, the 64-bit version is not compatible with 32-bit versions of ActiveX Controls and some third-party add-ins. You may need to obtain a new version of these extensions, which may not be immediately available. For these reasons, Microsoft recommends running 32-bit Office 2010 even on 64-bit Windows operating systems for better compatibility unless you have a really large schedule and need the power.

- Create PDF files without Adobe Acrobat
  Microsoft has been touting for a long time its own what-you-see-is-always-what-you-get file format, called *XML Paper Specification* or *XPS,* as can be seen in the print dialog as a virtual printer called **Microsoft XPS Document Writer**. Still, people continue to use the PDF format that they have come to love. Microsoft now

allows printing directly to PDF files, which spares you from having to buy the pricy Adobe Acrobat. Question to Bill Gates, did you have to buy a license from Adobe for this?

- Collaboration and multi-user authoring of Office documents
Projects often require many documents to be produced, and in the past contributions needed to be scheduled in serial. Now most editing can be scheduled in parallel, and multiple users can simultaneously edit Office documents in Word, PowerPoint and OneNote if the documents are stored on a SharePoint 2010 or Windows Live site. This sharing maintains only one version of the document so that a painful merging of revised copies is no longer necessary. No waiting for your turn, no checking in and out, just get your hands into it. Even though MS Project does not allow this multi-user access yet, it is in the future of MS Project and will be a great feature for project teams who are often working against tight deadlines. What you can use already is this: Projects often require many Word and PowerPoint documents to be produced, and in the past contributions needed to be scheduled in serial. Now most editing can be scheduled in parallel. As this new feature in other tools affects MS Project users, you will have to rethink your dependencies in your schedule!

What Is Gone From this Release of Project 2010?

- The menu bar and all toolbars: I knew the menu and toolbars in previous versions like the back of my hand. Yes, it took effort to find the features I knew via the ribbons. We definitely do not need both.

- Data entry bar
The entry bar has disappeared, making room for the ribbon (even though it can still be displayed through **File,** Options **, tab Display**.) You now use in-place editing only: You edit in the cell you are in, which is made easier by automatic word wrapping of long task names and automatic adjusting of the row height.

- *View Bar*: the view bar became redundant with the arrival of the ribbon. Different views are now as easily accessed through the **View** ribbon. The View Bar is still available but hidden.

- *Project Guide*
The Project Guide held the great promise of capturing and exposing your entire project management methodology inside MS Project, and allowing project managers to access it where and when it was needed. However, I have rarely seen an implementation that took real advantage of the possibility of this feature. The technology of the Project Guide turned out to be too complex and custom guides were hard to roll out, so the Project Guide may not be missed. Custom Project Guides are still supported.

- *Gantt Chart Wizard:* Most of it functionality was transferred to the Format ribbon.

- *Copy Picture to Office Wizard:* Microsoft now relies on the new Timeline view to make beautiful pictures in PowerPoint.

- *Custom forms:* Project 2010 does not support creating or using custom forms. Instead, Microsoft now encourages you to use the much more versatile Visual Basic for Applications (VBA) to create custom forms.

- The **Graphs** on the **Assign Resources** dialog box
  The graphs have been replaced with the Resource Graph displayed as the bottom view. It can only handle one resource at a time. Microsoft encourages people to use the new **Team Planner** view.

- Add-ins and sample macros
  Project 2010 does not include add-ins and sample macros. The following add-ins and sample macros are no longer available: PERT Analysis, Format_Duration, ResMgmt_TaskEntry, Rollup_Formatting, Toggle_Read_Only, and Update_File. However, the following add-ins have been converted into out-of-the-box features in Project 2010: Copy Picture, Adjust Dates, Compare Project Versions.

- Excel PivotTable reports
  In Project 2007, you could save your project as an Excel PivotTable file.
  In Project 2010, you can use Visual Reports instead.

- Dialog boxes with multiple rows of tabs
  Good riddance; I always clicked myself silly in those dialogs, not being able to keep track of which tab I had already searched for something! For example, the ribbon **File**, tab **Info**, button **Organizer** dialog box now only has one row of tabs. Some tabs are gone because of the ribbons.

Microsoft Project Server 2010

This book is not a complete reference on Project Server. It only describes the minimum you need to know as a project manager when you work in a Project Server environment. A detailed course and course binder are available to you if you need to know all. See the course *Managing Projects* and *Configuring Project Server* at *www.ProjectProCorp.com*.

Project Server is the *Enterprise Project Management* (*EPM*) platform for organizations that want to get serious about project management and to gain competitive advantages through project management. When organizations improve their project management practices, they lower the cost of managing projects. Organizations that have projects as their core business, like construction and consulting firms, can benefit greatly, as can departments that handle mostly projects, like IT departments.

Project Server facilitates the communication between the project manager and other project stakeholders:

- The project manager can easily send out timesheets and textual status forms to team members, have forms completed and submitted by team members, and then transfer the timesheet data back into the project schedule.

- The project manager needs only to save and publish the schedule; executives can immediately see the latest updates on their portfolio of projects, check on any problems arising, and develop what-if scenarios to find solutions.
- Project managers can communicate the number of resources needed by skill. Resource managers can fill those needs in the web-based interface for Project Server, *Project Web App*.

The project manager needs Project Professional 2010 to connect to the Project Server database, whereas other project stakeholders only need *Internet Explorer* and a license for the web-based application *Project Web App* to access Project Server. Project Server allows the following applications to communicate with each other and acts as *middleware* between them: *MS Project, Outlook, Excel, Internet Explorer, SQL Server database server, SQL Server analysis server, SharePoint Server*, and *IIS Web Server*.

Project Server is more than just a postal service between project stakeholders. By using Project Server you can enjoy the following benefits in the areas of project management, resource management and portfolio management:

- Standardization across the enterprise on templates, calendars, views, performance indicators (fields) and workflows to manage the governance around projects.
- Better *collaboration* between project stakeholders
  The project manager can collaborate with team members on creating new tasks, assignments, issues, risks and documents. Project Server creates a two-way street between project managers and their team members. Team members and their resource managers can collaborate on vacation day requests. Portfolio managers can collaborate with resource managers on authorizing and staffing projects.
- Better visibility of the status and forecasts of the project for the project sponsor and clients as well as other groups of stakeholders.
- The ability to optimize the project schedule, utilization of resources and the balance in the portfolio of projects using advanced features like *what-if scenario* analysis in MS Project, automatic *resource substitution* for utilization maximization and *efficient frontier* analysis for the project portfolio.

What Is New In Project Server and PWA 2010?

- *Project Web Access* is now called *Project Web App*
  Microsoft made this change across all other Office 2010 applications as well, emphasizing the increasingly rich feature set included with PWA beyond simply accessing data. For example, you can now make simple edits to your project schedule in PWA. PWA also uses the new ribbon interface.

- Project Server 2010 is now entirely built on SharePoint Server 2010.
  SharePoint Server brings a powerful platform that can:
  - Help you access sophisticated reports and create flashy dashboards.

- ◇ Allow you to control document review and approval through workflows.
- ◇ Facilitate search across the enterprise and enhance communication through wikis, blogs, discussion forums and social networking sites, all of which are easily accessible to the project manager.

- ◆ Microsoft has united project and portfolio management in Project Server 2010 by merging Project Portfolio Server 2007 into Project Server 2010. The portfolio management has been enhanced as follows:
  - ◇ Standardized data collection for different project types: each type of project can now have its own business case forms, workflow, project template and workspace template.
  - ◇ Departmental portfolio management: Portfolio management can now more easily be done for each line of business instead of centrally.
  - ◇ Project prioritization: the portfolio of projects can now also be optimized under time-phased resource constraints in addition to strategic value, financial indicators and risk.
  - ◇ Better capacity planning using generic resource demand and availability projections, which facilitates headcount decisions.

- ◆ Timesheets: single entry mode for task updates and time reporting.
  There is now one place where team members can enter their actual hours (for both project and administrative tasks) and the remaining hours on project tasks and send them to HR for attendance, to accounting for billing and to the project manager for updating the schedule. Microsoft redeemed itself.

- ◆ Web-based project editing: Even though not all aspects of the schedule can be changed, Microsoft is well on its way to create a true web-based project scheduling engine.

- ◆ Improved approval workflows are now much more versatile and easier to customize. The workflow interface is improved, and approvals are consolidated in the so-called Approval Center interface. The privilege to approve can now be delegated during absence.

- ◆ Exchange Server integration: Team members could already receive and update their tasks in Outlook, but now they can also do it in Outlook Web App, the web-based MS Outlook. Tasks can now be grouped by project. The Outlook ActiveX add-in is no longer required, removing installation and security problems.

- ◆ Enhanced reporting and business intelligence using Excel Services, PowerPivot for Excel 2010, Performance Point Services, Visio Services and SQL Reporting Services, which put the quirky Data Analysis views of 2007 in the past forever. There are many best practice templates available. Reports are easier to customize in the familiar Excel. Reports can be shared easily with people inside or outside the organization using Excel Server. Excel reports can be pulled together as web parts into dashboards; the dashboards can be individualized. Cubes can be departmentalized for the business lines and will refresh faster. Cubes now also contain all portfolio level information. Few limitations are left on reporting.

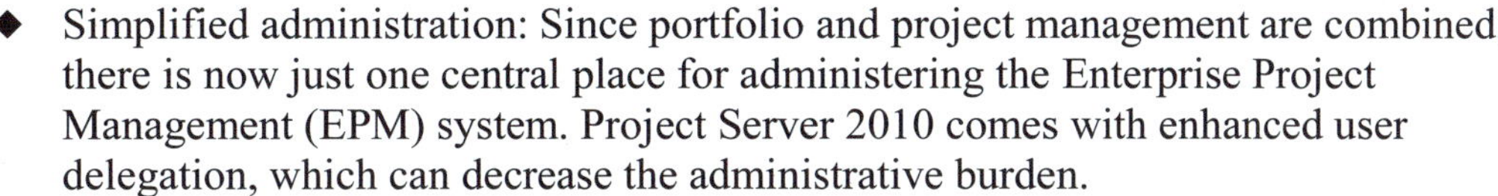

- Simplified administration: Since portfolio and project management are combined, there is now just one central place for administering the Enterprise Project Management (EPM) system. Project Server 2010 comes with enhanced user delegation, which can decrease the administrative burden.

- Integration with Visual Studio Team Foundation: Connect the world of application development with project and portfolio management, and you have a one-stop place for any software development group.

What Is Gone From this Release of Project Server 2010?

- Data analysis views: these views were based on Office Web Components and required an ActiveX object to be installed on every machine. This approach was not secure and often led to installation problems. Good riddance!
- ActiveX for Outlook: Few will shed a tear.

Is This Book for You?

This book is different from other books written on Project 2010. It not only shows you how to use MS Project, but also adds insights and experiences from the trenches, the real-life management of projects. You will learn how to manage projects with Project 2010, not just how to click the ribbon buttons and access the features. The book is primarily aimed at the busy, practicing project manager who needs to get up-to-speed quickly using MS Project and needs to learn the best practice habits with MS Project.

When I use the word "*you*" in this book, I am addressing readers as if they were practicing project managers. If you are not a practicing project manager, please imagine yourself as one while reading this book. The book is intended for the following target groups:

- Project managers who use Project 2010 on a day-to-day basis
  This book targets novice to intermediate users of MS Project, whereas advanced users will definitely find worthwhile bits and pieces as long as they do not mind reading selectively. Advanced users will learn better ways to work with MS Project and best practices of scheduling that are unique to MS Project. If you help your colleagues with scheduling, you will discover better terms, ways and metaphors to explain the tool.
- People who schedule and manage a single project
  This book focuses on managing a single project at a time with MS Project and will

not delve deeply into multi-project management issues. ProjectPro offers other courses like *Managing Programs* and *Managing Portfolios* that address those needs.[1]

- Students and professors at colleges and universities
  For effective delivery of (post)graduate courses, we added:
  - Hands-on exercises at the end of each chapter. The case study for these exercises is an office relocation project that will be followed from cradle-to-grave across the chapters of this book.
  - Review questions for self-evaluation of understanding at the end of each chapter

  All readers have access to the solutions of the first item. Professors who make this book mandatory reading in their courses can request a solutions manual from us for the second item.

What You Will Find in This Book

This book presents the most beneficial features of MS Project for the efficient creation of effective project schedules. At ProjectPro, we constantly ask our customers and course participants what features they use, why they use them and how. In this book, we have captured their insights that provide guidance to you on how to run your projects in practice.

We have consulted and trained people from a wide variety of sectors: information technology, telecommunications, banking, automotive, construction, manufacturing, pharmaceutical, international development and government. As a result, this book does not cater to one sector in particular but instead provides a wide variety of examples. I personally think that the principles in this book are universally applicable across all industries.

This book is based on and consistent with the Fourth Edition of the PMBOK® Guide published by the PMI. We will refer to the concepts of the PMBOK® in detail. If you have not read the Fourth Edition of the PMBOK®, I recommend that you read it first or, at least, keep it nearby.

We have kept the text as succinct as possible. Less text is better in our mind. Too many words waste your precious time, and too much language can obscure a simple point. We have inserted illustrations throughout the text wherever they would save words. We have added many cross-references so we did not have to repeat the same procedures.

---

[1] See www.ProjectProCorp.com for detailed course outlines.

This book has an attitude. It is not a complete description of the features of Project 2010, nor is it meant to be a complete reference for MS Project. It is meant, instead, to be a complete reference of features in MS Project that are useful for managing projects. I will recommend certain features, and I will argue against using other features. A key criterion I use for my recommendations is that the schedule you build with Project 2010 should be a *valid, dynamic and robust model* of your project built to forecast the project; see page 23 for a detailed explanation of this definition.

In this book we will cover two main configurations of MS Project that are currently in use: Project Standard 2010 used as a standalone tool and Project Professional 2010 used with *Project Server*.

What You Will Not Find in This Book

You will not find the following in this book:

- An explanation of all the features in Project and Project Server 2010. The features we discuss in this book are those that will most benefit users when managing a single project. This book is not a complete reference on Project 2010.
- An explanation of all scheduling concepts. We only discuss the concepts we have found to be most valuable, practical and feasible.
- An explanation of all approaches to scheduling projects. We do not discuss Critical Chain, Agile or SCRUM. We do discuss Critical Path, Resource-Critical Path and Monte Carlo Simulation.
- An explanation on how to manage many small, short-term projects with MS Project. Small, short-term projects are for example: maintenance projects of software or hardware, technical support projects (that require more than just a phone call), or information request projects (common in government agencies or standards organizations). Even though many recommendations in this book will also apply to small projects, some will be different or even opposite. For example, in small, short-term projects, there is relatively much more scheduling effort per project. The recommendations will, therefore, be focused in those small projects on how to minimize the effort on modeling these many projects. We often recommend managers of small projects to put all projects into one file and schedule their tasks by drawing and dragging task bars in the timescale, which is something we recommend against in regular projects, because it creates too many scheduling constraints (hard dates). Furthermore, there are specific issues in many small projects and corresponding features in MS Project to handle many small projects that we do not discuss in detail in this book; we could write a separate manual on how to manage these with MS Project.
- An explanation on managing very large, integrated program schedules that consist of multiple subproject schedules. Instead, we recommend our courses *Forecasting*

Programs with Microsoft Project and *Managing Programs with Microsoft Project Server* for program managers and project office staff. We have written separate manuals for these courses that are sent to you when you register for the public web-based courses.
- An explanation of managing portfolios of projects. Instead, we recommend our course *Managing Portfolios with Microsoft Project Server* for portfolio managers and project office staff. Our separate course manual on managing portfolios will also be sent to you when you sign up for this course.

Even though this book does not elaborate on programs or portfolios, studying this book is an essential first step on your way towards gaining control over programs or portfolios. The schedules for each project may end up in the program schedule. The project and program schedules are components of the portfolio schedule. You need to be able to build a solid model of a single project before venturing into modeling multiple projects of a program or portfolio. Only when you build valid, dynamic and robust models of single projects will your program schedules and portfolio schedules be manageable and controllable. Only with good schedules of single projects can you develop what-if scenarios with program schedules or entire portfolios and find the optimal program and portfolio schedule.

The Author's Perspective on Scheduling

In my years of consulting and training project managers, I have had the following experiences and made these observations:

- Some large schedules did not have a Work Breakdown Structure (WBS). All tasks were on the first (and only) indentation level. Imagine if this book did not have a hierarchy of sections, chapters and paragraphs. A well-known automotive company used a template schedule like this in the year 2000 to develop new cars. (Sorry, no names!) It was just a list of 900 items without any groupings or indentation levels. This organization was not using the basic concept of logical and hierarchical Work Breakdown Structures. Their schedules were difficult to explain to anyone who only wants to see the high-level schedule — like executives.
- Some project managers create schedules that are as complex as the project itself. It takes weeks to understand these schedules. I am always afraid to ask these project managers how long it took them to create monsters like that. If the *model* of the project is as complex as the reality itself, the model is not a model. A complex model does not give you a better handle on the reality. Modeling is, by definition, replicating and simplifying the reality to better understand and manage it. Too many project managers seem to forget this. If you cannot explain your project schedule to your team, the schedule is too complex. If your team understands it, you get much

more value from your schedule and scheduling efforts. If other stakeholders can also understand your schedule, even better.

- Many schedules created by "experienced" project managers turned out to have only a few dependencies (links between tasks). Of over 1,000 schedules we evaluated, 90% had incomplete network logic and needed to be revised in order to be certified. Not surprisingly those schedules had many date constraints that held the task bars captive to their dates. Constraints, however, make the schedule very rigid. Every time a change occurs, the entire schedule needs to be reviewed and updated before the project is again well depicted, reminiscent of the time when we printed our schedules on paper to hang them on our walls. Such schedules are nice charts of the project, but they are definitely not useful, dynamic models of the project. These managers spend too much time on scheduling at a time when they do not have a moment to spare — during project execution. Needless to say, they would inevitably stop updating their schedules after a few weeks into the execution phase of their projects.
- Many organizations invest in creating schedules, but abandon them when the project execution starts. Of over 1,000 schedules we evaluated, 70% were out of date and had to be updated before being certified. The chance that updating will be abandoned increases with the size of the schedule and the lack of dependencies (i.e., the abundance of constraint dates). One aerospace company admitted to me in 2001 that it had never been able to keep any of its schedules alive during project execution. After the company had one project manager trained in our program, this person managed to do that for the first time in the history of the company. (Sorry for this plug.) Project managers tend to get very busy fighting fires after the project kicks off. To control your project you need your model to forecast constantly. If you do not update your schedule, you do not have accurate forecasts. A dynamic schedule is easy to maintain and continuously provides forecasts.
- Many project managers do not enter resources into MS Project. And even if they do, they often do not check if they overallocated their resources. The unleveled schedule may show finish dates that executives like and may result in swift approval, but when the workloads are leveled it becomes painfully clear that the promised dates are not feasible. Resources that are narrowing in availability are driving the schedule in more and more projects.
- Many IT departments share their resources across all their projects but do not have a central resource pool. These IT departments will likely miss many deadlines, because each overallocated resource impacts every project it is involved in. IT resources tend to be expensive and always in short supply. The individual project managers assume they will get the resources when they need them and will forecast dates that executives like. When the project execution begins, project managers start stealing each other's resources in order to meet their own deadlines, because that will be the topic of their performance appraisals. Stealing each other's resources wreaks havoc with deadline accomplishment across the entire IT portfolio. If the

total workload of the resources has not been modeled accurately in each project and aggregated through a shared, central resource pool, the date forecasts shown by individual schedules are likely all too optimistic. In 2006, we assessed an IT department in which 735 of the 750 schedules had serious overallocations (workloads greater than 48 (!!) hours per week). With *Project Server* you can set up a shared resource pool that can eliminate this issue.

- The Standish Group survey hundreds of IT managers from many different industries and publishes reports regularly on the performance of IT projects. In 1994, only 1 in 8 IT projects was delivered successfully. In 1996 the number had improved to 1 in 4 because the shock wave of the first report led to faster cancellation of dead-end projects. I am convinced that project management can successfully be applied to IT projects; however, many IT project managers are either not applying the principles or not applying them properly for some weird reason. I admit that in certain areas it is necessary to adjust the techniques used. In that respect, a relatively new concept is explained in this book for resource-constrained projects, the Resource-Critical Path. Most IT project managers will have to find the Resource-Critical Path in their schedule instead of the Critical Path.
- Last but not least, many people do not know about the *baseline schedule* and confuse the *schedule* with the *baseline schedule*. Most people treat the schedule as the contractual dates they need to meet, but they could capture those contractual dates in the baseline schedule. If you store the agreed upon schedule in the baseline schedule instead, the schedule can now be used as a forecast model that you update easily and can regularly compare against the baseline.

If you have made similar observations in your organization and you want to resolve them, you should read this book from cover to cover. It will provide you with the insights and techniques to address these problems.

The skills of MS Project users are currently low and need to be elevated to improve the accuracy of the forecasts their schedules provide. We think that applying the principles in this book will result in more successful projects in the following ways:

- Work Breakdown Structures will make more sense to every stakeholder and reflect a meeting of minds (the agreement or contract).
- Schedules will need little maintenance during the project execution phase, when you are very busy as a project manager. Your schedule will stay alive during execution of the project.
- Your team members will experience fewer schedule conflicts, more reasonable workloads and less burnout.
- Forecasts will be more accurate and reliable for deliverables, particularly in resource-constrained schedules. Executives will start to trust the forecasts from their project managers more and more, and will be less inclined to simply impose ridiculous deadlines based upon flimsy gut-feelings or wishful thinking.

- Managing projects will cost less and result in more projects delivered on time and within budget.

In summary, if the major recommendations from this book are implemented consistently, the competitiveness of your organization will increase in the global marketplace. For non-profit organizations, the efficiency and, hence, the legitimacy of your organization will increase.

A Schedule is a Valid, Dynamic and Robust Model to Forecast

To address the problems we observed, we introduced the concept of treating a schedule as a valid, dynamic and robust model of the project to forecast it. There are five aspects to this approach of scheduling:

- **Valid**
  A *valid* schedule is a schedule that produces accurate forecasts reliably. Most project managers create schedules to better forecast their projects.
- **Dynamic**
  A dynamic schedule is a schedule that updates itself as much as possible. A dynamic schedule is set up to come as close as possible to realizing the principle of dynamic scheduling: when one thing changes in the project, you need to make only one change in the schedule, then all forecasts in the entire schedule are immediately recalculated by the software and are accurate again. There are several reasons why we need schedules to be *dynamic*:
  - Only dynamic schedules can keep up with the changes in projects.
    Changes happen so frequently in projects that it is hard to keep up with them. If your schedule is not as dynamic as it can be, you will have to review the future part of the schedule whenever you make one change. You will spend too much time keeping it alive and likely stop updating it sometime during project execution.
  - A *dynamic* schedule updates itself when a change is entered.
    After you have indicated to MS Project how all components of the schedule relate to each other and should interact with each other, MS Project can do most of the hard work for you.
  - Dynamic schedules save time.
    We have made an attempt to quantify the amount of time saved when working with a dynamic schedule instead of a rigid schedule. For a project of 100 tasks and 3 months, we calculated that you will save about 50 hours of effort if you create a dynamic schedule in the first place (see page 205).
  - Dynamic schedules facilitate scenario development.
    In order to explore *what-if scenarios* to solve problems, the schedules need to be

dynamic models. If there are many constraint dates in the schedules, it is hard to assess the impact of proposed solutions. In a typical project, many slippages need to be compensated for with what-if scenarios.

- ◇ Dynamic models of subprojects are required for programs.
  Schedules of subprojects need to be dynamic *models* when you want to roll them up into a master schedule. Otherwise, you will spend too much time making changes in the master schedule – so much time that you will stop doing it or not even consider it. When dynamic models are rolled up, problems become visible in the master schedule and can also be addressed in the master schedule.
- ◇ Dynamic models are required for schedule simulation.
  In order to perform schedule *simulation* for quantitative *risk analysis*, you will need dynamic models. *Monte Carlo schedule simulation* is essential to provide forecasts with their probability to executives and clients.

- **Robust**
  There is an extra level of sophistication when building a forecast model. A forecast model is alive and responds to changes, but how well does the model respond to those changes? Project models only survive changes well if they are set up in such a way that they respond in the proper way to a wide variety of changes. A robust model is a model that can survive as many changes as possible, even extreme circumstances, with as few necessary adjustments as possible.
- **Model**
  A model is a deliberate and smart simplification of the reality. A schedule should be an intentional and intelligent simplification of the project. If you try to replicate the complex reality of the project inside scheduling software, you will end up with a large monstrosity of a schedule to manage a complex project. The art of scheduling is capturing only what is important in the project. Do this and you will end up with a schedule that is workable and that forecasts the project well.
- **Forecast**
  The schedule is a model built to forecast the project. Schedules are built for other reasons as well, but we believe that the biggest benefit is using your schedule to continuously forecast your project. Stakeholders are interested in accurate forecasts.

The judicious application of features is critical in using MS Project. Thousands of practitioners have helped us to determine which features in MS Project are most beneficial. With this book, we are working towards a universally accepted body of knowledge for scheduling projects using MS Project.

Introduction to this Book

Learning Objectives

The following are the learning objectives we aim to accomplish with this book. After reading this book you will:

- ◆ Understand project management terminology from the Fourth Edition of the PMBOK® Guide [2]
- ◆ Be able to create a valid, dynamic and robust model of your own project:
  - ◇ Choosing the options and setting up the project calendar
  - ◇ Entering tasks, estimates, dependencies, deadlines, constraints, resources and assignments
- ◆ Be able to assess if you implemented the best practices of scheduling that were based on research of over 1,000 real-life schedules
- ◆ Know how to optimize the schedule to meet deadlines and budget restrictions while keeping the workloads of the resources within their availability
- ◆ Be able to create custom reports and views for the project that allow you to monitor the project and meet all information needs of the project stakeholders
- ◆ Know how to efficiently update the schedule when the project is running to continue forecasting the project cost and finish date

In general, after reading this book you should feel comfortable with Project 2010 and have a good understanding of what the tool expects from you as well as how the tool functions and behaves. This understanding will enable you to efficiently and effectively manage your project(s).

---

[2] See the *PMBOK® Guide*, Fourth Edition, published by the PMI.

Outline of This Book

First you initiate the project and then you plan it. After your plan is approved, you execute the plan. When you have finished the execution, you formally close out the project. You monitor and control the project throughout its life. The illustration shows these five process groups as distinguished by the Project Management Institute (PMI) in the Fourth Edition of the Guide to the Project Management Body of Knowledge (PMBOK® Guide). The PMBOK® Guide details each process group into individual processes, like *Develop Project Charter* as the first process (*Initiating* process group) and *Close Procurements* as the last process (*Closing* process group). Not all processes from the PMBOK® Guide were relevant when explaining how to schedule and manage with MS Project. Some processes fell outside of the scope of this book. The schedule is just one of the deliverables of the process groups; therefore, not all PMBOK® processes were applicable.

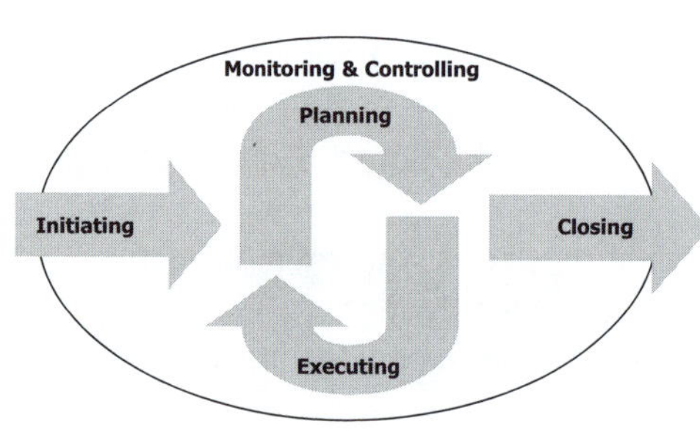

Fourth Edition PMBOK® Guide

The PMBOK® Guide contains the following Planning processes that relate to scheduling and managing a project: *Create WBS, Define Activities, Sequence Activities, Estimate Activity Resources, Estimate Activity Durations*, and *Develop Schedule*. The Executing processes that relate to scheduling are: *Acquire Project Team* and *Distribute Information*. The Monitoring & Controlling processes that relate to scheduling are: *Verify Scope, Control Scope, Control Schedule, Control Costs* and *Report Performance*. All of these processes are covered in this book. Even though we could have taken these processes verbatim and structured this book with them, we felt this book needed to focus more on the results you want from MS Project, and so we have made our chart more results-oriented rather than process-oriented.

We decided to treat creating a schedule and managing a project with MS Project as a mini project by itself. We structured this project with the process groups from the PMBOK® Guide. The result can be seen in the next illustration. As you can see, the process groups have been broken down into the next level of detail, the results (gray ellipses) or outputs of project scheduling. If you deliver these results, you will do well in terms of *scheduling* and PMBOK's *project time management*. To improve the flow for readers, we added chapters at the front (*introduction* and *concepts* of project management) and the back (*summary* chapter) that are depicted as white ellipses. Each ellipse represents a chapter in the book.

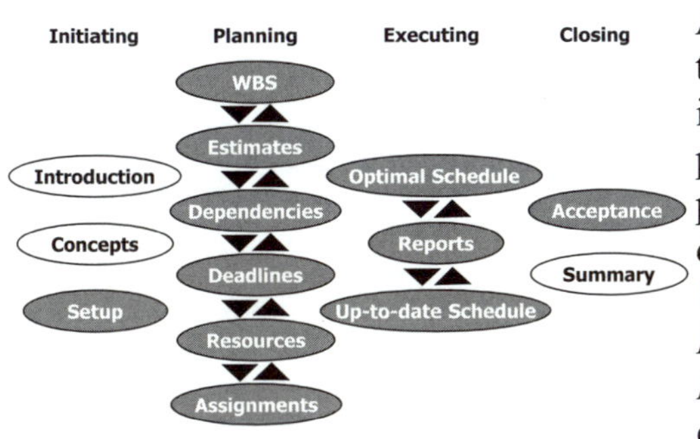

As you can see in the illustration on the left, the *Initiating* process group is broken down into *Introduction* of the book, *Concepts* of project management and *Setup* of a new project. The *Planning* process is broken down into the components of a schedule: *WBS (Work Breakdown Structure), Estimates, Dependencies, Deadlines, Resources* and *Assignments*. If you enter all of these into MS Project, you basically have a first draft of your schedule. The *Executing* process group is broken down into the deliverables of finding the *Optimal Schedule*, creating custom *Reports* and continuously maintaining the schedule to achieve an *Up-to-date Schedule*. These deliverables have to be produced repeatedly at each status cycle during project execution. The *Closing* process group is broken down into the deliverable *Acceptance* by the client or project sponsor and the *Summary* of the book.

The previous illustration provides an overview of all the chapters of this book. It will be shown at the start of every chapter to indicate where we are in the overall process. Hopefully it will put you, as the reader, back into overview mode before we delve into the details of the next chapter.

Many people have asked us for a good process to follow for creating schedules and managing their projects with the schedules. The chapters of the book correspond to the process steps and reflect the order of the steps to follow. To clarify this point, I have transcribed the results-oriented chapter titles to process verbs in the following table:

Chapter Title	**Corresponding Process Sentences**
Setup	Set up a new schedule and configure its options.
WBS	Create the Work Breakdown Structure.
Estimates	Estimate task durations or efforts (work) and enter them.
Dependencies	Create a complete and correct network of dependencies to create a dynamic model of the project.

Chapter Title	Corresponding Process Sentences
Deadlines	Enter deadlines and perhaps some constraints or task calendars.
Resources	Define and enter the resources.
Assignments	Assign resources to the detail tasks.
Optimal Schedule	Optimize the schedule so it meets its targets and then re-optimize it at each status period.
Reports	Customize reports to the needs of project stakeholders once, and then generate them at each status period.
Up-to-date schedule	Set the baseline once, maintain it if needed, and update the schedule so it forecasts the project at all time.

We recommend that you, as a project manager, use this process as your own business process to create schedules and manage your projects. Many in your profession have tried it, tested it and found the process tacit and true.

Initiating

Introduction

You are here. We introduced the new features in Project 2010 and Project Server 2010, as well as the topics and learning objectives of this book, and the author's perspective on scheduling. We will still discuss the conventions used in this book.

Concepts (Chapter 1)

In this chapter we will explain some basic concepts of project management. Because this book is not meant to be a theory book on project management, we will provide as few concepts as you need to utilize Project 2010 effectively. We will also explain the different purposes for using Project 2010 and our maturity model for scheduling.

Setup (Chapter 2)

In this chapter we will introduce the Project 2010 interface. We will discuss file management, templates and views. Then we will discuss creating a new project including naming the project and entering the project start or finish date. We will invite you to think about the default settings that are active in Project 2010, because some important options need to be set at this stage before any tasks are entered. We will create the project calendar at this stage.

Planning

In this section we will develop and enter all the schedule data into Project 2010. This step involves most of the effort in creating the forecast model of the project. There are six types of data that Project 2010 needs in order to produce a schedule for you. We will discuss each of these in the next six chapters.

Work Breakdown Structure (Chapter 3)

The Work Breakdown Structure (WBS) answers the question: *What needs to be done?* The task list is developed from the deliverables that, together with the tasks, form the Work Breakdown Structure. The structure can have several hierarchical levels, as in an organizational chart. In MS Project the levels are called outline levels and can be seen as indentation levels. This chapter will explain how to create and enter the Work Breakdown Structure in Project 2010. We will also discuss how to reorganize the task list by moving and copying.

Estimates (Chapter 4)

Estimates answer the question: *How long will the task take?* Estimates can be made in business days (duration) or in person days (work). There are many factors to consider when estimating. We will provide a process in this chapter that will hopefully make estimating easier. We will also discuss the human side that may bias the estimates. We will discuss some difficulties that occur in practice. We will suggest how to handle these biases and difficulties.

Dependencies (Chapter 5)

Dependencies answer the question: *How will the tasks impact each other?* Dependencies are the logical cause-and-effect relationships between tasks that are very important for creating forecast models of projects. Scheduling software does not require the user to enter dates for each task, even though many people do so. By entering dependencies instead, you can build a very powerful, forecast model of the project that calculates the dates. If you change the duration of one task, Project 2010 will reschedule all affected dependent tasks. It will do this on every change you make. The core secrets of dynamic scheduling will be revealed in this chapter.

Deadlines (Chapter 6)

Deadlines answer the question: *What dates did you promise or commit to?* They are dates you promised to stakeholders in your project. In this chapter we will also discuss constraints and task calendars. Constraints and task calendars can be used for restricting MS Project's freedom to schedule tasks to make the schedule more realistic. The Gantt Chart can be finalized after this chapter, and we will also show you how to create a printout of it.

Resources (Chapter 7)

Resources are the answer to: *Who will do the work?* Resources can be human resources, facilities, machines, materials or cost resources. In this chapter, we will discuss all these types of resources and how to enter them into Project 2010. We will explore the cost side of managing projects in this chapter. We will conclude with how to print the list of resources.

Assignments (Chapter 8)

This last type of schedule data answers the question: *Who does what?* Tasks and resources have a many-to-many relationship: multiple resources can be assigned to work on one task, and many tasks can be assigned to one resource. An assignment is the combination of one task and one resource.

Human resources do the work and need to be assigned to the appropriate tasks. We will discuss the mechanics of assigning human resources. We will also discuss assigning material resources, which is often done to model the cost of the project.

Project 2010 does its own thing when you work with assignments. Behind the screens it uses a formula to recalculate data you may have entered when you assign or change assignments. We will explain the when and how and provide you with the insight to help you predict what Project 2010 will do. From then on you will be in the driver's seat and make the tool do what you want it to. The goal of this chapter is to make Project 2010 work for you instead of you working for the tool. If you found that MS Project did not do what you wanted, this is the chapter to read.

Executing

Optimal Schedule (Chapter 9)

After entering all the data, Project 2010 shows a schedule that ends before or after the project deadline. The schedule may be under or over the budget. The first draft of the schedule hardly ever meets its time and cost constraints. Scenarios may have to be developed to find ways to stay within the deadline, the budget or the availability of resources; this is called optimizing the schedule and the result is the *optimal schedule*.

We will present three different approaches for optimizing schedules. You should choose the approach that best fits your project always keeping scope and quality in mind as well:

- Optimizing for Time
- Optimizing for Time and Cost
- Optimizing for Time, Cost and Resources

In *Optimizing for Time* we will explain the Critical Path method briefly and show how to highlight the Critical Path in your schedule. Sometimes the Critical Path is incomplete, and we will show you how to make it complete so that it explains the entire duration of the project again. We will then present many different ways in which you can reduce the duration of your project.

In *Optimizing for Time and Cost* we will make the optimization a bit more complex (or more interesting, in my professionally deformed opinion) by incorporating the cost dimension of projects. We will explore the methods available to bring down the cost without compromising too much on scope, quality or time.

Optimizing is more complex when you also want to ensure that the required resources are available and that they are not overloaded with work. Overallocating resources can compromise the quality of the deliverables and will often lead to missing deadlines. In the section on *Optimizing for Time, Cost and Resources* we will start to look at the workloads and how to level any overallocations. We will introduce the new concept of a Resource-Critical Path. The Resource-Critical Path allows you to find the tasks that truly drive the finish date of the project in a *resource-constrained schedule*. Thus, the Resource-Critical Path allows you to shorten your schedule, just as the Critical Path allows you to do this in schedules not constrained by resources.

After reading this chapter, the schedule will meet its deadline, be within the budget and have reasonable workloads. It is ready for reporting.

Reports (Chapter 10)

In this chapter we will not change the data in the schedule; we will only create different outputs from the schedule database designed for the respective stakeholders. Visual reports, views or Project Server can be used to communicate with project stakeholders. Filters can hide certain tasks and display other tasks, and can be used to provide the overview to executives or the detail of a specific problem to team members. Tables can be used to communicate certain data by inserting or deleting fields. The task or resource records can be grouped by any commonalities found in the data. Different formats can be applied to lead the eye of the reader to the important parts of the report. The first reports of the project will be used to obtain project approval. After that, project managers typically produce status reports on a periodic basis.

Up-to-date Schedule (Chapter 11)

As soon as the project is approved, a copy of the approved schedule is created, the *baseline schedule*. The baseline schedule serves as the standard of comparison to track progress. Progress information has to be entered into MS Project, which is known as *updating* the plan and the result is an up-to-date schedule. If you really want the most out of MS Project and obtain accurate forecasts, you would also collect to-complete estimates and enter those. An updated schedule shows the actual performance compared to the baseline. Updating should be done on a regular basis, just like bookkeeping.

In case there is slippage, you may need another round of optimizing. During project *execution*, status and forecast reports will support the decision-making in the project. They will also support the decision-making about the project (i.e., rework, approval of the next deliverable, stage or phase, cancellation, or suspension).

During the executing of the project, many cycles will be made through the last three project management activities of optimizing, reporting and updating. Delivering a project involves many cycles of making progress (updating), monitoring the progress (reporting) and taking corrective actions (optimizing).

Closing

Acceptance (Chapter 12)

Ideally each project results in acceptance by the client, which can also be an internal sponsor of the project. It is also important to take some time to look back and see what went well, what went wrong and why. In this chapter, we will discuss what to evaluate in your project and how. Evaluating your projects is the only way to become a better project manager. It can prevent you from running into the same traps with your next project.

Summary (Chapter 13)

In this chapter, you will find two things: a checklist to troubleshoot your schedule and a checklist for creating a *valid, dynamic* and *robust* model of your project to forecast it, as discussed throughout the book. These checks reflect the results of our search for best practices in well over 1,000 real-life schedules. You can use this chapter as a handy reference to the appropriate pages if you need more explanation on specific topics.

Appendix: Files Available For Download

This appendix describes the 100 examples of excellent real-life schedules that reflect our best practices of scheduling with MS Project. You will find schedules here from a wide variety of industries. The schedules are listed with the names of the people who created them and generously allowed us to publish them. The schedules are available for download at www.ProjectProCorp.com (see page vi for the procedure to access these files).

Exercises and Their Solutions

You will find exercises at the end of each chapter.

- Review questions
  These questions are meant to evaluate the knowledge you gained in each chapter. They review the theoretical concepts. Most answers can be found explicitly in the text of the book itself.
- **Hands-on exercises for the Relocation Project**
  You can test yourself to see if you can create a schedule with Project 2010 in the *Relocation Project* exercises. The relocation project is an imaginary office move that you will lead as the project manager. You will be moving about 100 co-workers to a yet-to-be found new location that needs to accommodate 150 workers. The solutions to these exercises are available for download at www.ProjectProCorp.com. These exercises provide a chance for you to develop your skills and see what you have learned.

Professors can acquire a separate solutions manual that contains all of the answers to the review questions and the questions posed in the Relocation Project exercises. This solutions manual is only available to professors who use this book as mandatory reading in their courses; please contact us at 613-692-7778. The solutions manual will be available for download at www.ProjectProCorp.com.

Conventions in This Book

Symbols and Typeface

The light bulb shows a tip or recommendation to the user. It may be a time saver or a way of achieving better project control information.

An exclamation mark shows a warning to the user of Project 2010. Heeding the warnings may keep you out of trouble and avoid unexpected results, loss of data or quirks in Project 2010.

The *Pro* icon indicates that these features are only available in the Professional Edition of any version of MS Project.

The *2010* icon indicates that the feature is new in the *Project 2010* release, in both the *Project Standard 2010* and the *Project Professional 2010* edition. For people who are upgrading to Project 2010 from Project 2007 and just want to focus on new features, this is the icon to look for.

The *2010 Pro* icon indicates the features that are new in only the professional edition of Microsoft *Project Professional 2010*.

The *2007* icon indicates the features that were new in the *Project 2007* release.

The *2007 Pro* icon indicates the features that were new in the Project 2007 Professional release.

File Words in bold type can literally be found on your screen in MS Project — either as a ribbon button or as a label or phrase in a dialog box.

Quote Italicized words are literal references. These can be literal quotes from people, data you literally need to enter into MS Project or literal words from the index at the back of the book. The indexed keywords are italicized so that you can find them easily in the text.

<file name> Any text enclosed within the arrow brackets is text that should not be taken literally, because it refers to another thing. For example, <file name> refers to the name of the project file you currently have opened.

Use of the Words "*We*" and "*You*"

When I write "*we*" in this book, I refer to my team of MS Project and Project Server instructors and consultants at ProjectPro Corp, as well as the team of technical editors who worked on past editions or this current edition. They come from a variety of industries and countries.

When I use the word "*you*" in this book, I am addressing you as the reader as if you are a practicing project manager. If you are not a practicing project manager, please imagine you are one while reading this book.

Word Choice in Procedural Steps

You will notice I use the words *MS Project* and *Project 2010* often. I typically use the term *MS Project* when the feature was already available in previous releases. I use the term *Project 2010* only when it is a feature that is new in Microsoft Project 2010.

We have not used creativity in formulating the step-by-step instructions. In fact, we have followed very rigid guidelines to be as clear and consistent as possible in this respect. We know it is difficult enough to interpret technical books; consistent formulation of steps might help. These guidelines are:

- To display a particular ribbon, we always use the verb "*Click*" as in:
  Click ribbon **File**.

- For buttons on the ribbons and in dialog boxes, we always use the verb "*Click*" as in:
  Click Save
- For tab pages in dialog boxes, we always use the verb "*Click*" with the name of the tab as in:
  Click tab **Advanced** (in the ribbon **File,** Options dialog)
- For shortcut key combinations on your keyboard, we always use the verb "*Press*":
  - For a single keystroke: Press F2.
  - For two keystrokes: Hold down Alt and press F.
  - For three keystrokes: Hold down Alt + Shift and press →.
- For entering text with your keyboard into fields that have a name, we always use "*Key in*" as in:
  Key in the name of the file in the field **File Name**.
- For check boxes that are checked or not and where the user can choose one or more, we always use the verb "*Check*" to select or "*Clear*" to de-select. We display the resulting check box as in:
  Check ☑ **Display Help on Startup**
  Clear ☐ **Display Help on Startup**
- For radio buttons where the user has to choose only one option from two or more mutually exclusive options, we always use the verb "*Select*" and display the resulting radio button as in:
  Select ⦿ **Automatic.**

Alternative Options or Alternative Steps

Whenever you have two options that do different things I have separated them with a lowercase "*or*". For example:
*Click ribbon **File**,* button ***Save** to save current changes into the same file, or click ribbon **File**,* button ***Save As** to save them in a different file.*

If you have two alternative step procedures that accomplish the same goal, I have separated them with an uppercase "*OR*" that is always on its own separate line. For example:

press F3
OR
*select the item **[No Filter]** from the list* Filter:

Screenshots and Illustrations

We used many illustrations in this book. Most illustrations only show a small part from a larger schedule. This allowed us to keep the illustrations concise and to the point.

The procedural steps include screenshots of dialog boxes that are inserted in the steps right at the place where you should encounter them. This is to ensure that you are in the right dialog box before proceeding with the next step. Otherwise, you could easily get lost in intricate steps.

Where screenshots of MS Project are shown, we have tried to show only the relevant portion of the screen.

We have annotated the screenshots with blue callouts and lines, so you can easily find the option or field referred to in the text. If we added arrows, you need to read the annotations in the direction of the arrows. The annotations may even contain extra tips, so you may still find them worthwhile reading as well.

Meet the Cartoon Characters…

Throughout this book you will find little stories with cartoons at the start of each chapter. One of the main characters in these stories is Bob, a very dynamic and successful project manager. This is Bob (any resemblance to actual people is purely coincidental):

As you can see, the man is busy communicating in several different ways at the same time. The smile on his face radiates success. Notice the certificate on the wall.

The second project manager looks rather confused and overwhelmed. His name is Nob (any resemblance to actual people is, again, purely coincidental):

As you can see Nob has not mastered the latest communication technology. For him, the computer monitor is just a bulletin board for yellow stickies.

Bob and Nob will share their project adventures with us at the start of each chapter. I hope you will enjoy them during this serious project management stuff. Every time I received a new batch from the creator, Paul Mason, I had some good laughs.

Paul and I discussed what the characters' genders should be. There was no way we could come out unscathed by using a male and a female project manager. Was the successful project manager going to be a man and the loser a woman, or vice versa? We realized it was a lose-lose situation, and eventually we decided to make both of them men. I apologize to those women who would have liked to see the successful project manager be female. The stories that come with the cartoons apply to both genders.

Throughout the book I tried to randomly use *he* or *she* in my examples.

Chapter 1 Concepts of Project Management

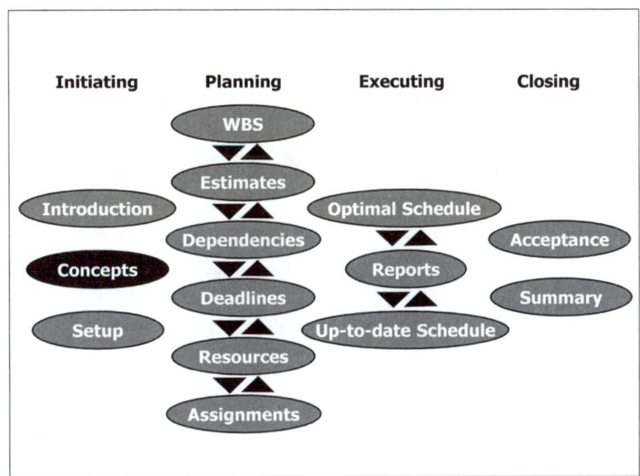

In *Initiating*, we will discuss the *concepts* of project management (see the black ellipse above). We will make sure every reader is aware of some important definitions. Many concepts in this chapter are taken straight from the Fourth Edition of the Guide to the Project Management Body of Knowledge (PMBOK® Guide) by PMI, the Project Management Institute.

After reading this chapter you will:

- be aware of the Fourth Edition of the PMBOK® Guide
- understand how projects relate to programs, portfolios, corporate strategy and enterprise project management
- start to see a schedule as a forecast model of the real world project
- be able to recognize and analyze the driving forces in projects
- be able to determine the purpose of the schedule you are about to create
- know what project management software can do for you

Things come in Cans, not in Can'ts

Nob and Bob are pouring over Nob's schedule, which currently indicates the project deadline will be missed by several weeks. Nob: "I don't know what to do! I can't drop a requirement; the client will not approve. I can't ask my resources to work more weekends; they will never want to be on my team again! I can't ask the sponsor for more money because this project will make a loss!"

Bob: "Okay, okay ... you can't, you can't, but ... things come in cans, not in can'ts! So, let's see what is possible! Do you remember all knowledge areas from the PMBOK?" "Yes, I do!"

Bob: "So, let's see, which one is the most important area that you cannot compromise on?" Nob: "They are all equally important!" Bob: "Well, if that is the case, you have to start writing your resignation letter! What is the least important area then?" Nob: "Perhaps we can make some compromises in quality; we wanted to impress the client with this slick algorithm that does a much better job! I suppose we could drop it, but it is dear to my heart and painful to drop."
Bob: "How hard is the deadline itself, the time? Would it be reasonable to propose to the client that they can have it on time as per the original requirements, or later with the slick algorithm included? Would they be willing to pay extra for the new algorithm?"

Nob: "That would make the time or cost area more flexible. I am going to try that!"

Projects

A project is *a temporary endeavor undertaken to create a unique product, service or result.*[3] A project is the management vehicle to create change, any type of change. Project teams create unique deliverables. When all deliverables are ready and approved, the project is over.

A project has the following characteristics:

- A project is *temporary* by definition.
  The end date of the project is forecasted before the project begins. A temporary team creates the deliverables of the project.
- The objective is to create a *unique* product, service or result.
  Each project has a verifiable objective that is a relatively new or unique challenge for the organization(s) in the sense that it has not been done to those specifications before. The project product can be divided into *deliverables* that are components of the project product or support components (*interim deliverables*), like research reports, test reports, trained employees, handbooks or spares.
- *Progressive elaboration*
  The project plan is elaborated progressively, which goes hand-in-hand with the unique nature of a project and the looming time constraint. The plan is developed in increments.

Some organizations have projects as their core operations, like research, construction, aerospace and consulting companies. There are full-time project managers in these companies. In other organizations, projects are often used to create new products (high-tech), implement changes (like relocations and reorganizations) or create new systems (such as information and financial systems). The line manager of today often has one or more projects in progress. MS Project can be a helpful tool to create a solid schedule and budget to manage any project.

Examples of Projects

We will give many examples of projects from different industries.

- Organizational change projects

---

[3] See the *PMBOK® Guide*, Fourth Edition, published by the PMI.

  - ◇ Implementing a new financial system (*ERP*)
  - ◇ Implementing a *Six Sigma quality system*
  - ◇ Implementing supply chain management
  - ◇ Designing and implementing a project management methodology
  - ◇ Business process re-engineering
  - ◇ Designing and implementing a new job classification system
- ◆ Regulations implementation projects
  - ◇ Nuclear power plant application approval
  - ◇ Projects to meet new environmental policy standards
  - ◇ Implementation of equal opportunity regulations in the workplace
  - ◇ Airport security projects
- ◆ Event projects
  - ◇ Relocating the office
  - ◇ Organizing a conference
  - ◇ Writing the yearly financial report
  - ◇ Organizing a press conference
- ◆ New product development
  - ◇ Developing a new pharmaceutical drug
  - ◇ Developing new computer hardware
- ◆ Research projects
  - ◇ Developing ways to heal sickness by manipulating genes in human DNA
  - ◇ Developing a way to transfer electric power through radio waves
- ◆ Information systems projects
  - ◇ Programming a desktop application
  - ◇ Implementing a LAN or WAN
  - ◇ Developing the company's e-commerce website
- ◆ Construction projects
  - ◇ Designing and constructing buildings, bridges or roads
  - ◇ Constructing a new plant
  - ◇ Assembling a new manufacturing line
- ◆ Education projects
  - ◇ Developing and testing new courseware
  - ◇ Organizing training workshops across several sites
- ◆ Maintenance projects

  Maintenance project managers often deal with many small projects or "jobs". Sometimes the maintenance project is huge and can stop an entire plant, as is the case when a condenser needs to be replaced in a coal-fueled power plant. Such a project can take up to five weeks, during which operations are suspended. Every day late has huge financial consequences. Therefore, the project needs to be planned carefully.

As you can see projects are everywhere. There probably is not an organization today that does not have one or more projects running. Projects are the vehicles executives use for change. Organizations implement their strategies with projects.

Portfolios, Programs and Projects

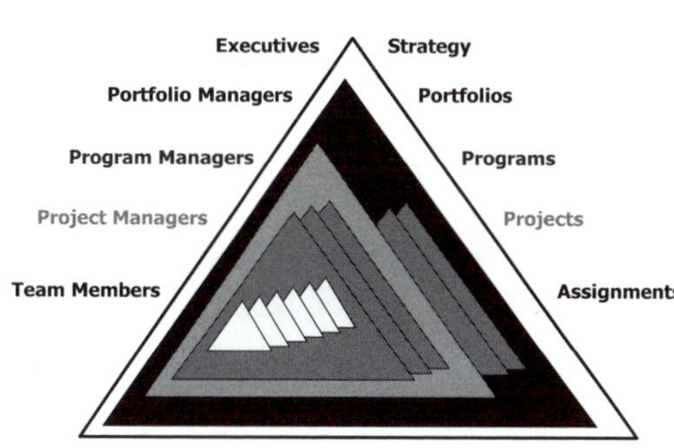

A *portfolio* is a *collection of projects or programs and other work that are grouped together to facilitate effective management of that work to meet strategic business objectives*.[4] Portfolios consist of initiatives that share the same resources. When resources are shared, the initiatives will impact each other because of limited availability of resources. *Portfolio management* is the *centralized management of one or more portfolios, which includes identifying, prioritizing, authorizing, managing, and controlling projects, programs, and other related work, to achieve specific strategic business objectives*. Portfolios are typically set up for each line of business, division or geographic market.

A *program* is *a group of related projects managed in a coordinated way to obtain benefits and control not available from managing them individually*.[5] There are always dependencies among the related projects, and the resulting schedule is therefore often called an *integrated program schedule*. Projects can be integrated into programs for a variety of reasons:

- A need for overall reporting on all related projects in the program
- A need to model the logical impacts each project has on other related projects (*cross-project dependencies*)

This book will deal with managing a single project only and will not address issues related to programs or portfolios.[6] However, unless you know how to plan and manage

---

[4] *The Standard for Portfolio Management*, 2nd Edition, published by the PMI

[5] *The Standard for Program Management*, 2nd Edition, published by the PMI

[6] ProjectPro offers other courses, please visit www.ProjectProCorp.com and follow the link *Forecasting Programs*, *Managing Programs* or *Managing Portfolios*.

a single project effectively, there is very little hope of gaining control over programs or portfolios! Projects are the building blocks of programs and portfolios.

Project Server and Enterprise Project Management

Project Professional 2010 can save projects in a central Project Server database. Microsoft Project Server provides the capability to implement *Enterprise Project Management* (*EPM*).

EPM aims at effectively managing portfolios, resources and projects within an organization. The vision of enterprise project management is that:

- The authorization and closing of projects is strictly governed by portfolio management processes.
- The performance of the project portfolio is monitored on a regular basis.
- The enterprise resources are listed and maintained in a central, shared resource pool.
- All authorized projects are captured in resource-loaded schedules.
- The project schedules are stored in a central repository.
- The resource capacity needed for projects is planned for a long-term look-ahead window based on the total demand for resources on authorized projects.
- The resource workloads are monitored regularly in a short-term look-ahead window and leveled if needed.
- All schedules are always up-to-date: all actual progress is scheduled in the past, and all remaining work is scheduled in the future.
- All data are easily accessible online.

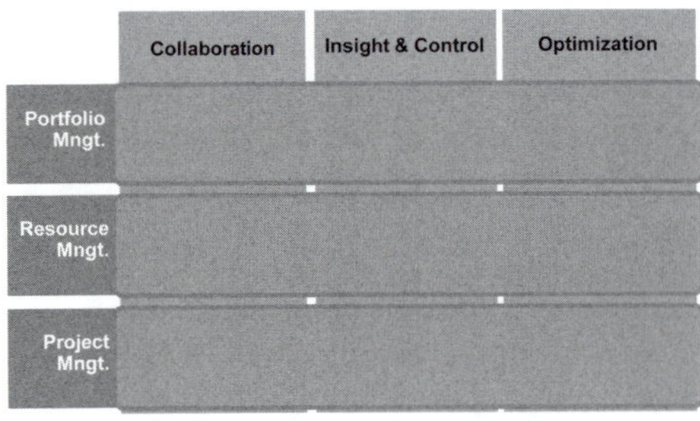

A well-deployed EPM system allows executives to find out the status of their portfolios, programs and major projects within minutes before they meet with clients, suppliers, financial analysts or shareholders.

Often in practice, only certain projects are stored in the central repository and the word '*Enterprise*' actually refers to a subset of the organization (e.g., the IT department). In that case, one cannot proclaim to do enterprise project management, but rather departmental project management.

EPM typically consists of the following areas:

- *Portfolio management* to support the strategic direction of the organization.
- *Resource management* to use the resources optimally
- *Project management* to help project managers with their projects. The system provides ways for the project manager to collaborate with team members and other stakeholders. For simplicity sake, we include *program management* under this label, even though a distinct body of knowledge is taking shape for programs.

Within these three areas, the objectives for an EPM implementation can be aimed at improving:

- Collaboration between portfolio, resource and project stakeholders
- Insight into and control of the portfolios, resources and projects
- Optimization of the strategic value of the portfolio, the utilization of resources and the delivery of projects.

All three areas are closely intertwined. In fact, they are even dependent upon one another.

- If the portfolio managers do a bad job and do not prioritize their projects, the resource managers and the project managers will experience difficulties. The resource managers will not know which projects are important and need their best resources. The project managers just want to meet their own deadlines and will fight fiercely among themselves and with the resource managers to get the best resources on their project.
- If the resource managers drop the ball and, for example, do not plan the resource capacity well, then the portfolio managers do not know how many projects they can staff and therefore authorize. The project managers cannot rely on getting the right resources and getting them exactly when they need them. They will start lobbying and fighting to get the best resources.
- If the project managers do a bad job and do not deliver projects successfully, the portfolio managers will have a portfolio that does not realize the enterprise strategy they established. If project managers do not model the workloads properly, the resource managers will be in the dark as to what their resources are really doing and will be unable to monitor resource utilization.

As you can see, in order for the enterprise to be successful, all three roles have to be performed by competent people. An EPM system is only as strong as its weakest players!

Guide to the Project Management Body of Knowledge

The Project Management Institute (PMI) has issued the Fourth Edition of the Guide to the Project Management Body of Knowledge, or PMBOK® Guide. The PMBOK® Guide has become a global standard on project management. Most multi-national companies have embraced the PMBOK® Guide as their reference and glossary. Each project has to deal with all nine knowledge areas as specified in the PMBOK® (see the illustration on the left). This book is based on and aligned with the fourth edition of the PMBOK® Guide published by the PMI. If you have not read the PMBOK®, I recommend you read it first or, at least, keep it nearby while you read this book.

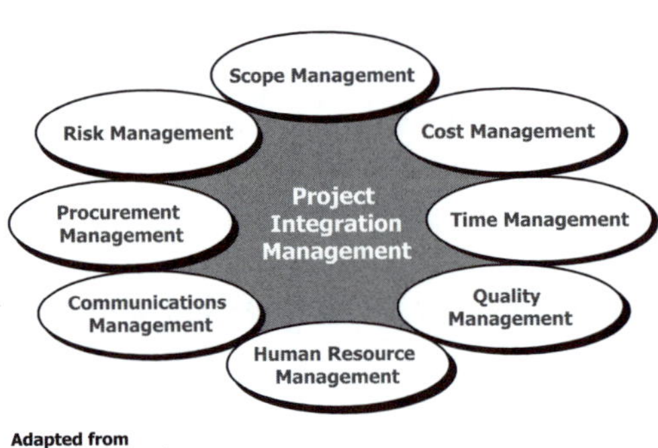

Adapted from
PMBOK® Guide, 4th Edition

The PMBOK® Guide describes project management as "t*he application of knowledge, skills, tools, and techniques to project activities to meet the project requirements.*"

The Pulling Forces of a Project

The PMBOK® Guide discusses knowledge areas in which project managers need to have knowledge and skills. These areas can also be seen as forces that pull at the project, as shown in the illustration on the left. The forces pull the project in opposite directions, and they can be traded off with each other. Deciding what trade-offs to make is one of the biggest challenges of *Project Integration Management*. For example, when time is short, you can try to remove quality requirements (quality) or deliverables (scope). You can try to get more money (cost) or people (resources), spend more time on managing stakeholder expectations (communications). You can assume, avoid, decrease or deflect adverse effects (risk), or subcontract to vendors for extra capacity (procurement).

The four knowledge areas from the PMBOK® Guide that can be well managed with *Project 2010* as a standalone application are:

- *Scope*: what to accomplish
- *Time*: the deadlines
- *Cost*: the budget
- *Resources*: availability (or capacity) and workloads of the resources, but only up to about 50 resources in a resource pool shared across projects (not an enterprise resource pool) with MS Project as a standalone tool (for a more detailed discussion, see page 410).

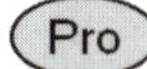

Project Server 2010, when used in combination with *Project Professional 2010*, enhances resource management, allowing you to build much larger shared resource pools of thousands of resources encompassing the entire enterprise (a.k.a. *enterprise resource pools*). Furthermore, Project Server covers the following knowledge areas from the PMBOK® Guide:

- *Communication* is a flow of information from the project manager to the project stakeholders. While MS Project provides many flexible reporting features as a standalone application, Project Server really facilitates communication with project stakeholders.
- *Risk management* includes risk and issue management features and primitive risk quantification (probability-impact).

The following knowledge areas from the PMBOK® Guide are not currently supported by the Microsoft toolset as it is out-of-the-box:

- *Procurement management*
  Here you want to create and track your contracts. There is no feature designed to manage contracts, but you can store the contract documents in the online project workspace and apply configuration management to them. Often the *accounting system* (*ERP*) has contract management capabilities.
- *Quality management*
  Quality control activities can be created as tasks in the schedule, but the tool does not capture quality requirements or acceptance criteria for deliverables. Neither software is a *quality management* system. Even though the tools do not provide quality management features, as a project manager you must ask yourself if a change to the schedule or budget will also have an impact on quality, and you must keep your eye on quality at all the times. The quality dimension of projects is often managed with separate tools, like *Team Foundation Server* (Microsoft) for software development projects, or *Rational DOORS* (IBM) for *new product development* projects.

Even though these knowledge areas are not supported by MS Project and Project Server, the supporting technology of SharePoint Server provides easy-to-customize lists (which are essentially tables in a database) that can be used to create interfaces for simple procurement and quality management. SharePoint also has workflow features that allow you to model business and governance processes for quality and procurement.

If you look at all dimensions covered by MS Project and Project Server, you can see that Microsoft has all the foundational software and is well on its way to creating a fully featured project management suite.

How Strong Are the Forces in Your Project?

We will now explore the field of forces that surrounds your own project. This will help us to model the important aspects of it. One of the first things a project manager needs to do is determine the strength of each of the forces. Recognizing the dominant force and modeling the project accordingly can determine the success of the schedule early in the project life cycle. For example, if a nuclear power station has to be renovated, it is clear that the *scope* and the *quality* cannot be compromised, because of the immense consequences of an error (see the large arrow for scope in the illustration). Meeting the quality standards of the International Atomic Energy Agency (IAEA) would be a dominant force, even if this leads to higher cost than budgeted or to a later completion of the project than promised.

Remodeling a Nuclear Power Station

For most projects, however, the dominant force is less obvious. Sometimes two forces seem to be equally important. Therefore, a good question to ask yourself and your stakeholders before starting is: *Which force is dominant?* If that question is difficult to answer, ask yourself: *Which force is least important?* All forces are never equally important. Project managers who think that all forces are equally strong cannot effectively manage their projects, because they cannot make trade-off decisions. Project managers must prioritize these forces through effective communication with their stakeholders.

Depending on whether scope, time, cost, quality or resources is relatively dominant, you will set up your schedule in a different way and the resulting schedule will then be different. For example:

- If a target date is very hard, you may want to enter it as a constraint date into the model, add multiple interim deadlines to get your team going quickly and schedule regular status meetings. If the deadline is soft, you may choose to let the schedule float freely and enter the target date as a deadline instead of as a constraint.

- If the budget is very tight, you want to model all expenses in detail and use the cost management features in MS Project.
- If the resource availability is very limited, you want to capture all workloads, level them and find the Resource-Critical Path instead of the Critical Path (see page 499).
- If quality is the dominant force, you could add more testing tasks and set deadlines on them.

As you can see, being aware of the dominant force in your project before creating the schedule is important.

Why Do We Schedule?

At this point we have to ask ourselves: *Why do we create a schedule of our project?* There are four goals people can have when scheduling their projects:

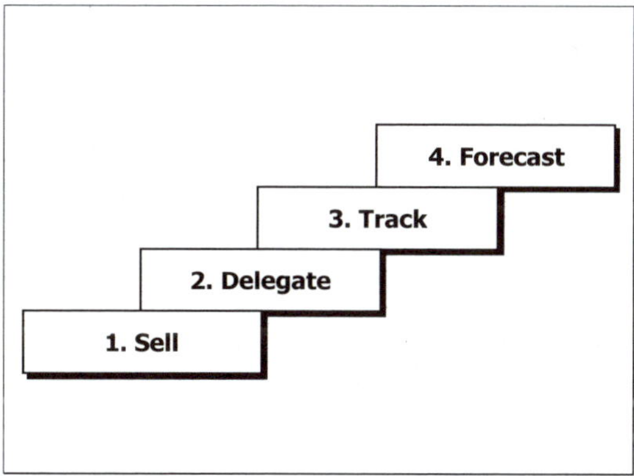

The goals can be ranked by level of challenge with the least challenging first:

1. **Sell**
   Project managers may want to sell an idea to upper management in order to start a new project and manage it. Or, a consulting firm may try to sell a new project to a client. The selling is often supported by making a slick, high-level schedule in MS Project to help estimate the duration and cost. Selling requires the least amount of detail in your schedule. The expected result would be that you win the contract or receive approval for the project.
   If you adopt this goal, you only need to be able to paint a nice *Gantt Chart*: tasks represented as bars over time. To achieve this, read the following sections in this book: entering tasks (see page 138), drawing task bars in the timescale in the Gantt

Chart by dragging with your mouse and printing the Gantt Chart (see page 277). Alternatively, you could use a new feature in Project 2010 and create an attractive *Timeline* chart (see page 582).

2. **Delegate**
   When you add a detailed Work Breakdown Structure (WBS), including activities, you can delegate by assigning detailed tasks to individual team members. In this case the schedule is used as a vehicle to coordinate and manage commitments from team members. The benefits of a schedule as an instrument of delegation are that everybody knows what to do and when to do it. The expected result is a sense of direction in your project.

   This goal is now well supported in Project 2010 with the new and easier to use features of manually scheduled tasks (see page 96), entering tasks (see page 138), entering resources (see page 303), assigning resources with the *Team Planner* view (see page 362), synchronizing with *SharePoint* task list and updating the schedule through SharePoint (see page 628). If delegating is your only goal, we recommend you follow the listed page references and focus primarily on these features.

3. **Track**
   You can track your project by entering the current status into your MS Project schedule. The output of tracking is a status report, which shows what has been accomplished (*actuals*) and when tasks were finished. Tracking a project helps you know your team members better and immediately learn from past mistakes. If you do not track, you will lack the facts to learn from. The main benefit of tracking is to improve management of future projects and, to a lesser degree, the current project. In order to track a project, you need to read almost the entire book except for Chapter 11 on Updating, where you can restrict yourself to only entering actuals.

4. **Forecast**
   You can use MS Project to model your project so that you continuously forecast its end date and total cost. Forecasting projects requires two things:
   - ◇ Using the features of deadlines and baselines to capture promises made to stakeholders, while ensuring that the schedule stays alive as a dynamic model.
   - ◇ Enter the actuals (tracking) but also enter revised forecasts from your team members scheduling them in the future when you update the schedule.

   The main benefit of forecasting is gaining control over the future of the project that you are currently managing. With a dynamic forecast model of the project you will be able to get answers for the following questions:
   - ◇ When will the remaining deliverables be available?
   - ◇ When will the resources be needed?
   - ◇ When will the entire project be done?
   - ◇ What will be the total cost of the project?

If you want to forecast your project, you will need to read the entire book with emphasis on using deadlines versus constraints (see page 255), the principle of dynamic scheduling (see page 205), creating complete and correct network logic (see page 239), optimizing the schedule (see page 413), using baselines (see page 605) and updating the schedule properly (see page 677). Throughout the book we make recommendations for how you can make MS Project forecast better.

The four levels above are listed in order of increasing challenge or difficulty. The farther down the list (or the higher up the staircase), the more ambitious you are with MS Project. Forecasting is the most ambitious goal you can have when using scheduling software. If you want to continuously forecast your project, you have to set up your schedule in a particular way. For example, you have to enter all the dependencies between the tasks. We will provide you with all the guidelines to help you set up schedules that will give you this continuous forecasting power. The summary chapter of this book contains the complete checklist of guidelines. Forecasting is what most project managers aspire to accomplish with MS Project. Forecasting is what most executives expect from their project managers. That is also why we titled the book *Forecast Scheduling*.

Dwight Was Right, But Is He Still?

We need to deal with a well-known saying about planning. In the era of President Dwight Eisenhower (1890-1969), project plans only existed on paper. Paper plans are static in nature and dead as soon as they are written. They are a snapshot of the project that captures the vision of the project when the plan was written. A plan printed on paper is a project-plan-of-the-past. At best, paper plans are "*history-books-written-ahead-of-time*". In his time, Dwight was right.

> "In preparing for battle, I have always found that plans are useless, but planning is indispensable."
>
> **President Dwight D. Eisenhower (1890-1969)**

With the advent of computers, we can now create schedules that are alive and dynamic. Start thinking of a project plan as an online database that contains the originally approved schedule (*baseline schedule*), as well as the most current version of the schedule that is always up-to-date and forecasts the project. The database also contains all other project artifacts that are all living documents governed by automated business processes of creation, review and approval (a.k.a. *workflows*). This project-plan-of-the-future is an up-to-date electronic model of your project in all its aspects that allows you to produce relevant artifacts and make accurate forecasts at any time during the life of the project.

Such a project-plan-of-the-future is a powerful tool for project managers. We like to think, if Dwight were still alive, he would likely agree.

Scheduling Is Modeling

Ideally, the project manager has a schedule that is always up-to-date and that provides accurate forecasts at any time. We have found that this is possible as long as you create a dynamic model of your project. You should not draw a beautiful chart that you hang on your wall that is just nice to look at. Nice charts are useful for selling purposes, but not for managing purposes. The differences between a *static chart* and a *dynamic forecast model* of your project are:

- **A model is a deliberate and smart simplification of the reality.**
  Architectural models are small, three-dimensional versions of the final building and are built at a fraction of the final cost. Similarly, models of projects should be simple versions of large, complex realities. Models should be built at a fraction of the total effort and cost of the project. When modeling, we try to approach reality as closely as possible, but with as little effort as possible. Simplifying is both legitimate and essential when modeling. For example, we can simplify the schedule by focusing on *deliverables*, instead of putting to-do list items in the schedule.
- **A forecast model provides predictive power.**
  Schedules need to forecast the finish date and often the final cost of the project. Schedules also need to be a vehicle to quickly forecast what-if scenarios. A model will only have predictive power if the following conditions are met:
  - **The model is kept up-to-date.**
    A schedule that is not maintained is static and will be useless soon after it is ready. Project models are never finished; they are living documents and should be kept alive and up-to-date until the project ends. If they cannot be kept alive (i.e., up-to-date), they do not deserve the label *forecast model.*
  - **The model is dynamic and responsive.**
    In order for schedules to be easily kept up-to-date, they need to be responsive. A responsive model updates itself as much as it can. Schedules can do this if they are created as dynamic models with as many dependencies as needed and as few fixed dates as possible. Fixed dates are known as *constraints* in MS Project. Constraints are stronger than dependencies and will interfere with what dependencies need to do. A responsive model also supports what-if analysis.
  - **The model is robust.**
    A model is robust when it can handle a variety of changes with minimal input. If you often have to change the structure of the model (i.e., the WBS, dependencies in a schedule) while updating, the model is not robust. If you have to change many cells to capture one change request, your model is not very

robust. Treating dependencies as *cause-and-effect relationships* instead of as task sequencers is one example of how project models can become more robust.

- **A forecast model is accessible online all the time to stakeholders.** *Project Server* allows stakeholders to check the status of the projects they need to monitor on any day and at any time. Project Server allows stakeholders to slice and dice the schedule data in any way they choose in order to find problems, then drill down into the schedule to see lower level detail that caused the problem. These powerful and dynamic features are accessible through a user-friendly, web-based interface. Stakeholders can do their own analysis and what-if scenario development using data that is as up-to-date as possible in real time. Best of all, with Project Server's web-based access, paper project reports are no longer needed at agreed-upon dates and in agreed-upon formats. The latest status can be viewed at any time and any place where there is intranet or internet access. Stakeholders can thus keep a closer eye on the project and shorten feedback cycles.

In the chapters that follow we will show you how to create a forecast model of your project — a model that meets all the criteria of a forecast model as just explained.

Scheduling Software

When you want to schedule any project, the following seven questions are important:

1.	*What needs to be done?*	Deliverables (summary tasks) and Tasks (detail tasks)
2.	*How long will it take?*	Duration Estimates or Work Estimates
3.	*In which causal order?*	Dependencies
4.	*When should it be done?*	Deadlines, Constraints, Calendars, Baseline
5.	*Who is going to do it?*	Resources and Assignments
6.	*When will it happen?*	Start and Finish Dates
7.	*How much will it cost?*	Rate * Assignment Effort

The user will have to enter the answers to the first five questions, and Project 2010 will automatically answer the last two questions by creating the *schedule* and the *budget*. If you do this, you are using Project 2010 as scheduling software – software that calculates dates.

When you schedule electronically, you should not enter start or finish dates for tasks. If you use MS Project to simply capture dates and only dates, you may as well use *Microsoft Excel* instead. With MS Project, you enter durations and dependencies instead of dates to create a *forecast model*. The software then calculates the start and finish dates by itself, based upon those durations and dependencies. A schedule with dependencies knows how to update other tasks automatically and is a dynamic model. Entering dates on **Auto Scheduled** tasks leads to rigid schedules with many constraint dates.

2010 In Project 2010, Microsoft added **Manually Scheduled** tasks, which allow you to enter dates and have the duration be calculated by MS Project instead of the other way around. You can opt for that as long as you eventually add the dependencies into the schedule as well and switch the **Manually Scheduled** tasks over to **Auto Scheduled** tasks; otherwise, the schedule will never be a forecast model of the project. From that point on, MS Project will calculate the **Start** and **Finish** dates for you and you are taking advantage of MS Project's power as scheduling software.

Scheduling Maturity

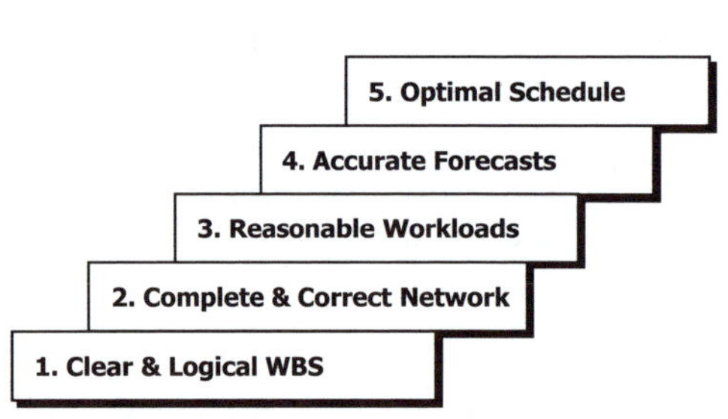

Over the years, we have learned to quickly assess how mature an organization is in terms of scheduling. We use the model as shown in the illustration for this assessment. You can also use it to self-assess your organization by comparing it to the criteria we present below.

You can check if your organization meets the criteria of each level starting with the lowest level in the staircase:

1. Clear & Logical WBS (Work Breakdown Structure)
   With a clear and logical WBS, the commitments are clear and the resources are focused. The majority of projects in your organization have a WBS that:
   - has multiple levels of indentation,
   - is logically grouped by deliverables,
   - has all deliverables needed (as per the contract),
   - has a milestone for each deliverable,
   - has neither too few, nor too many items, and
   - is clear to the stakeholders.
2. Complete & Correct Network
   Your organization will benefit from complete and correct network logic (dependencies between activities) because the schedules will need little maintenance. A solid network also reveals a reliable Critical Path, the tasks that determine the project duration. To assess the network logic:
   - The network is complete if all detail tasks have a predecessor, except tasks that are independent from all other tasks listed.
   - The network is complete if all detail tasks have a successor, except the project finish milestone.
   - The network is correct if the *high-level schedule* or *timeline* looks correct, if the *Critical Path* seems correct, if no tasks seem to have an unreasonably large

amount of buffer (field **Total Slack**) and if the scheduling by the dependencies is not jeopardized by hard constraint dates.

3. Reasonable Workloads
   Reasonable workloads put reasonable demands on employees and facilities, which make the forecasts in the schedule feasible. The majority of projects in your organization have reasonable workloads if:
   - ◇ All resources needed have been identified and no overlaps exist between resources (e.g., *Bill Murray* and *William Murray* may be the same person).
   - ◇ The availability of each resource has been modeled accurately.
   - ◇ The efforts of the resources have been estimated and modeled accurately on each task.
   - ◇ The aggregated effort stays within the availability of the resources (no serious *overallocations*).

4. Accurate Forecasts
   Your organization will benefit from accurate forecasts by being able to better communicate with clients, prevent last-minute surprises and keep clients satisfied. The majority of projects in your organization have accurate forecasts if:
   - ◇ The schedules are updated regularly.
   - ◇ All actuals are scheduled in the past.
   - ◇ All remaining effort is scheduled in the future.
   - ◇ At the start of the projects, the majority of projects are forecasted in terms of duration, effort and cost within a 10% margin, which seems to be the commonly accepted margin for reasonable overruns.

5. Optimal Schedule
   Project managers need to find the optimal schedule continuously. Continuously optimized schedules provide savings of time and cost. If you have met all previous levels, you have a forecast model of your project with which you can find the optimal schedule quickly in most circumstances. When things happen, you can easily identify the best solution and keep your schedule optimal.

All these levels build on top of one another. If you do not have a clear and logical WBS (level 1), it will be hard to find the dependencies in your project (level 2). If you do not have a complete and correct network (level 2), the workloads may not be scheduled accurately and you will not be able to assess whether you have reasonable workloads (level 3). If you cannot check the workloads, your forecasts will not be reliable or accurate (level 4). If the model of your project is not updated regularly or correctly (level 4), it is not suitable for what-if analysis to continuously find the optimal schedule (level 5). You cannot skip a level and still reach the top level of the scheduling maturity model. Mountain climbers have to trot each yard of elevation.

Review Questions

1. What are the three main ways in which projects differ from programs, portfolios, operations, task forces, committees, work groups and departments?
2. Are there organizations that never have any projects?
3. Are there organizations that only have projects?
4. What is the difference between project management and program management?
5. Which knowledge areas does the PMBOK® cover?
6. What are the forces that pull your project in different directions and that you constantly need to trade off as a project manager?
7. What are the differences between a *static chart* and a *dynamic model* of your project?
8. Why do you intend to create a schedule of your current project? Is it for selling, delegating, tracking or forecasting purposes?
9. What is the difference between tracking a project and forecasting a project?
10. What is the minimum data you need to enter into MS Project to generate a complete and dynamic schedule?
11. Which levels of scheduling maturity do you distinguish? Name at least one criterion for each level.

Chapter 2 Setting Up a New Project

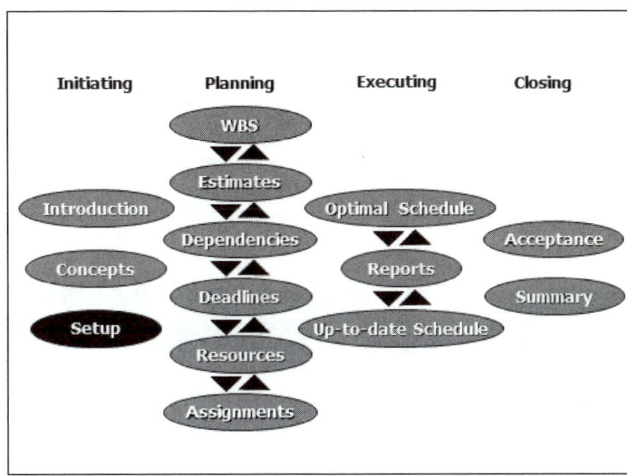

Now that we have reviewed the terminology and some basic concepts, we are ready to explore the application interface of MS Project and set up a new project. After reading this chapter you will:

- be familiar with the MS Project interface
- understand what data MS Project stores and where:
  - understand MS Project as a relational database application
  - be aware of the main data-entities of the relational database: projects, tasks, resources, assignments
  - be familiar with the Global.MPT template file
- be able to set up a new project:
  - know how to find project templates and know how to use them
  - choose the appropriate options
  - be able to review the project calendar, and to modify it when you use MS Project as a standalone tool
- know the best practices for setting up new project schedules

Get to the Core Fast and Forecast

It is a Friday afternoon and the sounds of work are winding down. Nob decides to relax in Bob's office for a moment before going home. They start talking about why they create schedules, and, in a flurry of frankness, Nob admits that he only creates schedules because management wants him to.

Bob: "Did you ever ask management what they want from the schedules?" "I must admit, I never did!" Bob decides to explore the topic further: "So, what do you show in your schedule updates?" Nob: "Oh, I did not bother updating the schedule until they started asking for updates. Now, I just show them what we have accomplished so far." "But Nob, do you know what management really wants to know? They want to know what your latest and best forecast is on the project." "Well, I can assure you that I have never given them that because I just enter actuals and don't revise the future projections. Only if they compare carefully the rate of progress to the planned rate will they be able to tell if my project will be early or late!" Bob: "I think that management could have done a better job in explaining what they really want!"

Microsoft Project 2010 Standard and Professional

2

MS Project comes in two editions: *Microsoft Project Standard 2010* and *Microsoft Project Professional 2010*. The professional edition can connect to a Project Server database which provides the capability to implement *Enterprise Project Management* (*EPM*).

When working with project schedules, there are differences between using Project Professional with Project Server and using Project Standard by itself as a standalone tool. To complicate things further, even Project Professional 2010 can be used as a standalone tool. We will use the term *standalone* for all situations in which you can use Project Standard or Project Professional by itself without Project Server.

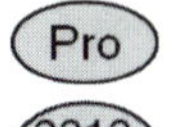

All steps that require Project Professional to be connected to Project Server are marked with the *Pro* icon shown in the margin of this paragraph. If the steps require Project Professional 2010, then the icon has the text *2010 Pro*, which indicates a new feature in the Professional edition of the 2010 release.

Working with Files in Project 2010 as a Standalone Tool

File Types

MS Project can store its data in project files and *project template* files among other file types. Project templates are like regular project files, but with an added protection against accidental changes. The protection is that when you open a template, the template first copies itself and you continue to work with the copy. The original template stays the same. Templates are commonly used in organizations that run similar projects over and over, like construction companies. A template is a standardized schedule.

Microsoft has thoroughly thought out the file extensions:

- A project file has an **.MPP** extension, which stands for **M**icrosoft **P**roject **P**roject.
- A template file has an **.MPT** extension, which stands for **M**icrosoft **P**roject **T**emplate.

Project files (.MPP) and project template files (.MPT) can contain:

- *Schedule Data*:
  - ◇ tasks, estimates, dependencies, dates, deadlines, constraints, task calendars, resources, resource calendars, assignments and baselines
  - ◇ project-specific options
    Project-specific options relate to one project only and are stored in the individual project schedule. You can easily recognize which options are stored in the file in the **Project Options** dialog – click ribbon **File**, [Options] and click tab **Schedule**. Where the section heading starts with **<type of> options for this project <name of project>**, the option is specific to the project and stored with the project.
- *Objects*: views, reports, modules (Visual Basic), tables, filters, calendars, maps, fields and groups. You can see these in the **Organizer** dialog; click ribbon **File**, [Info]. The **Organizer** allows you to transfer objects between files.

A special template exists, called *Global.MPT*, which is the default template file. When MS Project is started, this *Global.MPT* is opened. The *Global.MPT* is always open when MS Project is running. It contains all the default objects, like views, tables and filters that you use for reporting purposes.

The difference between a *project template* and the *Global.MPT* template is that the *Global.MPT* cannot contain *schedule data*, for example tasks.

The *global options* and the default project-specific options are stored in the *Windows Registry* – a database on your computer with your personal settings.

2

Opening a Project File in Project 2010 Standalone

1. Start MS Project.
2. Click ribbon **File**, click [Open] – the **Open** dialog appears:

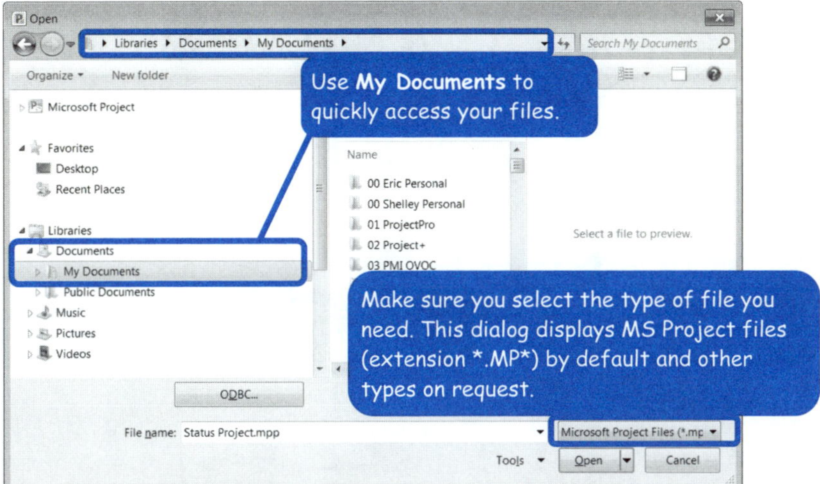

3. Navigate to the file to open.
4. Double-click on the name of the file to open.
   OR
   Single-click on the file name and click [Open ▾]. The drop-down list of the button also allows you to **Open read only** or **Open as Copy**.

If the file was open recently, you can more easily open it: Click the **File** ribbon and click [Recent] and then double-click the file to open. You can even pin a file to the top of the list by clicking its pushpin button [pushpin] behind the file name.

Saving Changes in an Existing MPP File

1. Click ribbon **File** and click [Save].
2. If your file exists already, the file on your hard disk will be updated with the changes. If the file does not exist, the **Save As** dialog will appear automatically.

There is an **Auto Save** option that saves your schedule every so many minutes, which you can indicate in ribbon **File**, [Options], tab **Save**.

Saving a New File with MS Project Standalone

1. Click ribbon **File** and click Save, and you are prompted for a file name in the **Save As** dialog:

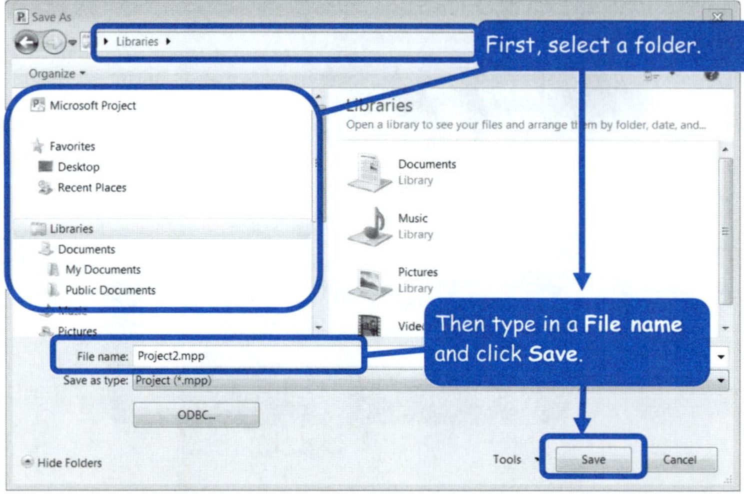

2. Click Save. Each project file will be saved with the extension **.MPP** by default.

Closing a File

1. Click ribbon **File** and click Close. If you have made changes to an open project, MS Project will prompt you to save the changes and the **Microsoft Project** dialog appears.

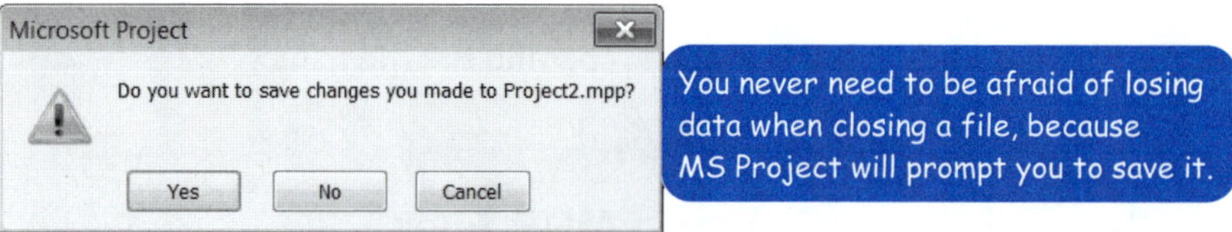

2. To save your changes, click Yes, and the **Save As** dialog appears if the project has not been saved before.
   To discard changes, click No
   To interrupt closing the file, click Cancel

Working with Schedules in the Project Server Database

When you use MS Project in standalone mode, the projects are stored as separate files in your file directory system. When you use *Project Server*, the projects are stored into one *SQL Server* database that we will also refer to as the *Project Server database*.

We prefer using the word *schedule* rather than *file* in the context of the Project Server database, since the SQL Server database contains all the schedules that do not exist as separate files. It is better to use the word *schedule*.

MS Project as a Relational Database Application

At first glance, the MS Project application bears a striking resemblance to a spreadsheet application, since it has columns and rows. However, if you look at the *schedule data*, MS Project is more like a relational database application. The (simplified) data model for the Project Server database is shown in the next illustration. A relational database has several different tables that are related to each other through fields they have in common. In MS Project, these common fields are the ID fields.[7] You can see this in the illustration. The tasks and assignments tables have a so-called one-to-many relationship, since one task can be assigned to multiple resources. Similarly for resources, one resource can be assigned to multiple tasks. It is the one-to-many relationships in the data that are hard to manage within a spreadsheet application, but easy in a database. Instead of looking upon MS Project as a spreadsheet, we suggest you think of it as an application to access a relational database. There are three reasons for seeing the application as a relational database application:

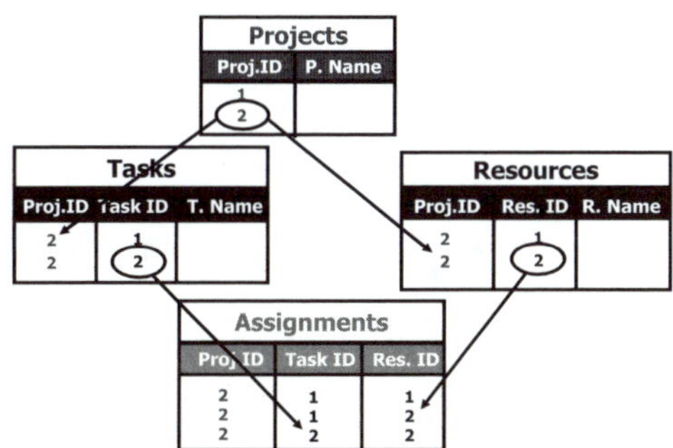

1. **There are multiple types of schedule data (data-entities).**
   The four main types of *schedule data*, or *data-entities*, in the database are: projects, tasks, resources and assignments. In a spreadsheet table, you typically monitor only one type of data.

---

[7] In fact, the **Unique ID** field contains the unique identifiers, because the **ID** values are just row numbers that constantly change when items are inserted or moved.

2. **Each data-entity is stored and viewed separately.**
   - ◇ *Projects* can be seen in the Project Center in PWA.
   - ◇ *Tasks* can be found in any of the task views in MS Project.
   - ◇ *Resources* can be seen in the resource views in MS Project.
   - ◇ *Assignments* do not have separate views in MS Project. Assignments can be found in between the tasks in the *Task Usage* view or in between the resources in the *Resource Usage* view.

3. **The data-entities have one-to-many relationships.**
   The data-entities are related and have one-to-many relationships between them:
   - ◇ Projects: one project can have many tasks and many resources.
   - ◇ Assignments: one resource can be assigned to many tasks and one task can be assigned to many resources.

   You can see in the previous illustration that the projects and the assignments have one-to-many relationships with tasks and resources.

It is too hard to manage multiple data-entities that are related with a spreadsheet application. Project Professional 2010 acts as the user interface to retrieve projects from the Project Server relational database.

Entering an Account to Connect to the Project Server Database

Project Server is a web application on top of the *SQL Server* databases. The Project Server administrator manages this application and determines who can open schedules in the database. This is done through login accounts in the Project Server database that are used to securely establish a connection between Project 2010 and Project Server. Project 2010 will then be able to open schedules from the Project Server database and save changes back into the database.

Here are the steps to configure MS Project with an account to access the database:

1. In Project Professional 2010, click ribbon **File** and click Info, button **Manage Accounts**, and, if needed, select item **Configure Accounts** from the drop-down menu. The **Project Server Accounts** dialog appears.

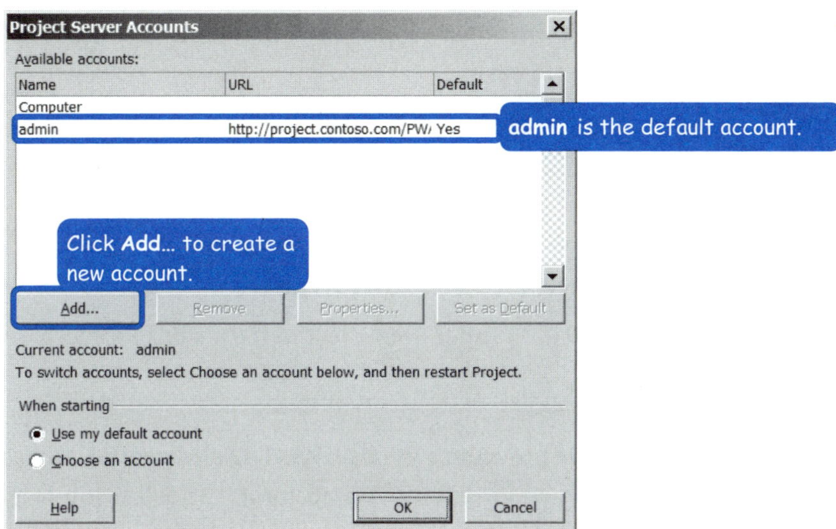

2. Click Add... – the **Account Properties** dialog appears:

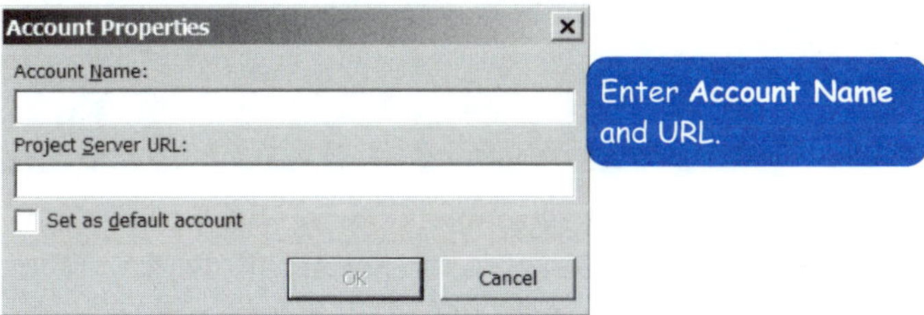

3. Enter the **Account Name**, which is a descriptive name of your own choice.

4. Enter the **Project Server URL** following the syntax:
   http:// <server>/<project web app site> where:
   <server> is the name (like *Dell08*) or the IP address (like *63.118.100.55*) of the computer on which Project Server is installed.
   <project web app site> is the name given to Project Web App site during installation
   To select this account as your default account, select ☑ **Set as default account**. As you can see the account is not really a login account, MS Project just needs to know where the Project Server database is.

5. Click [OK] and you are back in the **Project Server Accounts** dialog. You can select ◉ **Use my default account** if you do not want to be prompted for which account to use when you start Project Professional. If you will always connect to Project Server and have only one Project Server account, you could select this to start the system more quickly. If you need to take your schedule on travel and want to work on it offline, we recommend you select ◉ **Choose an account**, which allows you to work offline more easily.

6. Click [OK] and click ribbon **File,** [Exit] to close MS Project. We have now created an account to connect to Project server while offline. Restart Project Professional to use an account and connect to the Project Server database.

Connecting to the Project Server Database

1. Start Project Professional 2010. In order to connect to the secure Project Server database, you need to identify yourself using a valid account, which is typically your normal computer login account and is transparent to the user.

2. If you selected in the previous procedure ◉ **Use my default account,** the **Login** dialog is skipped. If you selected ◉ **Choose an account**; the following **Login** dialog appears.

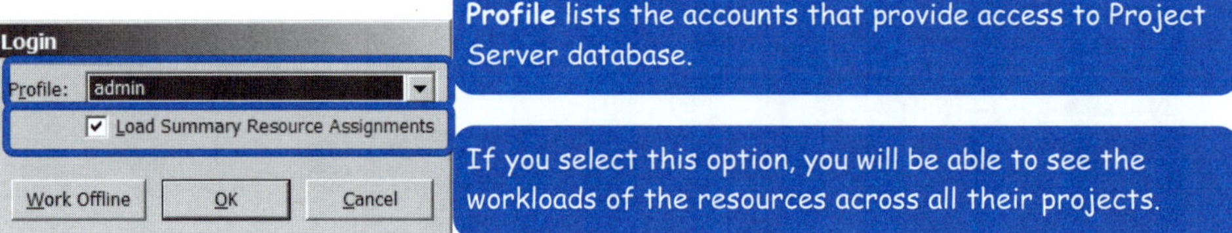

If you select **Computer** from the **Profile** list, you do not connect to Project Server at all. The option ☑ **Load Summary Resource Assignment** allows you to see if resources are available for work on your tasks across all projects the resources are involved in. Selecting this option makes MS Project a bit slower.

3. Click [OK] and you are now connected to the Project Server database.

If you want to work with your Project Server schedules offline (without a connection to the *Project Server* database), you can click [Work Offline]. This allows you to work on your schedules while on a plane or wherever you do not have access to the server.
In order to have your project schedules accessible offline, you first need to check out the schedule from the database. You can do this by opening it ◉ **Read/write** and selecting ◉ **Keep project checked out** when closing the schedule.

Opening a Project Schedule from the Project Server Database

1. Click ribbon **File**, click Open and the **Open** dialog appears:

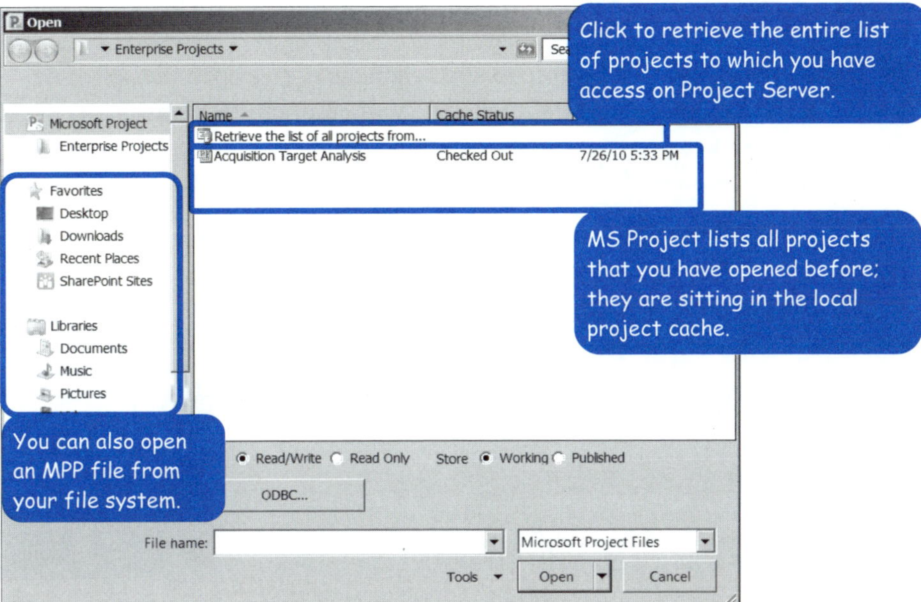

2. Upon opening, the dialog will list only those projects in the *local project cache* that you have opened before. The local cache is a spooler that processes all transactions with the Project Server database in the background, so you can more quickly continue working. You can access projects in different places:
   ◇ You can ask for a complete list of projects available to you in the Project Server database by double-clicking the item **Retrieve the list of all projects from Project Server**.
   ◇ There are draft schedules saved in the **Store** called ◉ **Working**. Draft schedules cannot be seen by other people. There is also a store called ◉ **Published**. Published schedules are schedules that your stakeholders can see. If you switch **Store**, you may see different listings.
   ◇ If you want to open an MPP file from your file system, click **Documents** in the left-hand pane.

3. To quickly open the schedule read/write, you can double-click the project name in the list and it will open right away.
OR
Select the project to open with a single click and choose whether you want to open the project:
◉ **Read/write**: you will be able to save changes if you open the schedule read/write. Opening a schedule read/write will automatically check out the schedule. Only one person can have the schedule checked out at a time.
◉ **Read-only**: you will not be able to save changes to Project Server.
Then click Open ▾.

Saving a Project to the Project Server Database

1. Click ribbon **File** and click Save As – the **Save to Project Server** dialog appears:

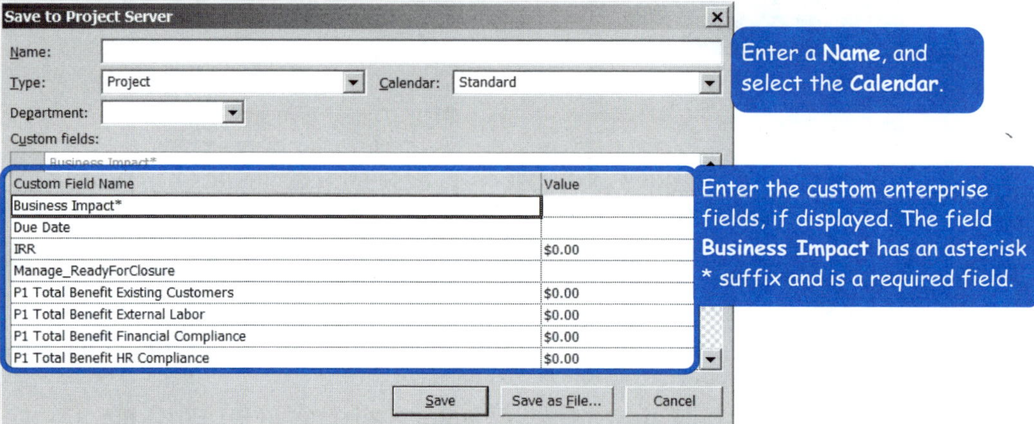

2. In the field **Name**, enter a descriptive name for the project that will be clear to you and the project managers. If you enter a name that already exists in the database, you will receive a warning; you have to give it a unique name across all projects in the database.

3. Under **Type**, select to save the project as a **Project** or as a **Template**. To save templates you will need to have the appropriate rights in Project Server.

4. Under **Calendar**, select one of the enterprise calendars your project should be based on.

5. Under **Custom Field Name**, there can be one or more custom fields to describe your project in more detail. Some fields may require you to enter data; the fields that are required have an asterisk * suffixed to their name.
6. Click Save – if you forgot to enter a value in a required field you will be prompted. You must then find the fields with an asterisk and enter values.

When you save a project, it ends up in the *local project cache* on your computer, and any changes you made are sent to the Project Server Queue for sequential processing and updating of the Project Server database. If you want to check on the status of the saving, look at the bottom status bar on the right, which will display a **Save job ...% complete** message. When done, it displays **Save completed successfully**.

Publishing the Project in Project Server

In Project Server, you can keep your schedule for your eyes only when it is still in draft and saved in the **Working** store. You have to choose the moment when you wish to show the project to the other stakeholders (particularly executives and team members) in Project Web App by publishing the project. The project is then saved in the **Published** store.

The steps to publishing a project are:

1. Click ribbon **File** and click Publish. A prompt to save the schedule may appear if your latest changes were not saved yet. Then the **Publish Project** dialog appears:

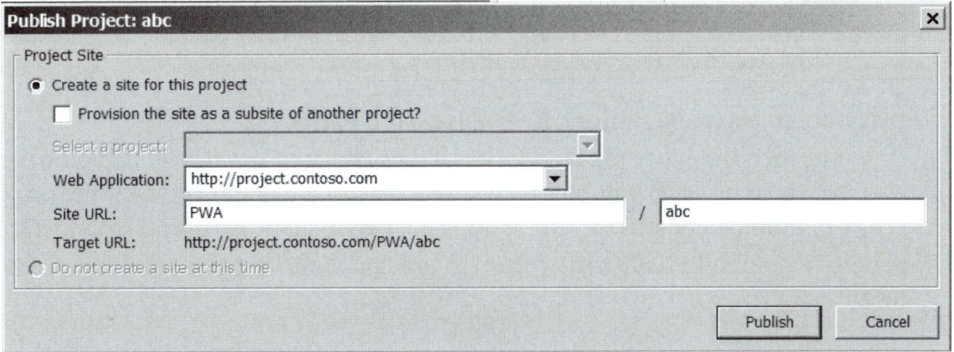

2. By default, MS Project creates a site for the project; these default settings are configurable by the *Project Server Administrator*. The option ⦿ **Create a site for the project** creates a SharePoint website for the project that provides several different *collaboration* options, like a pin board for messages, a calendar (to capture

project events), a list of team members, discussion groups, and a central storage space for project-related documents, issues, risks, deliverables (things to be handed off between projects). The site is entirely customizable, and you can display any other information, such as a workflow view (to monitor the status of the project in the portfolio governance process), a dashboard (to display the performance of the project), and so forth.

After making more changes to the project, you can save the changes for your eyes only (**Working** database) or you can communicate those changes by clicking ribbon **File**, button **Publish** again (which copies it into the **Published** database). For example, you need to do this when:

- You added new tasks.
- You made changes in the assignments to the team members.
- The project duration or cost changed significantly, and executives may want to know.

Closing a Schedule in Project Server

1. Click ribbon **File** and click Close – the **Close** dialog will appear:

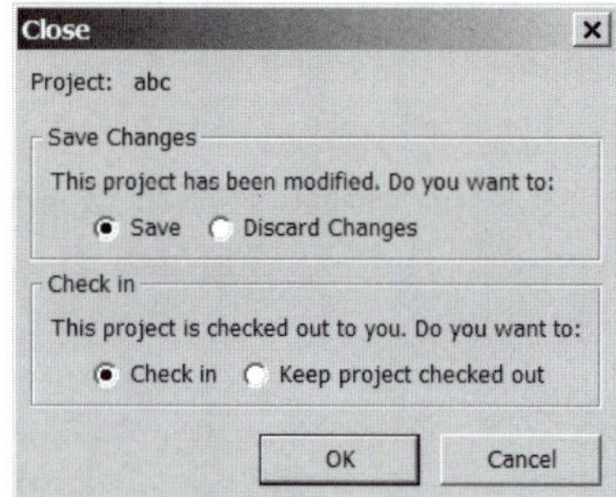

2. Select to ⦿ **Save** the project or ⦿ **Discard Changes**.
   If you opened the schedule read/write, it was checked out to you. If you have checked out a project, you will be prompted as to whether you want the project checked into the database again. If so, select ⦿ **Check in**; doing so will allow other people to open it in read/write mode (if they have these rights) and make changes to it.

Note that when Project 2007 was first released you had to be careful clicking the button that closes the application because it wrecked the queue. This issue was taken care of in cumulative updates for Project 2007 and is not an issue in Project 2010.

The Microsoft Project 2010 Interface

The Main Screen

MS Project has many different screen areas that pop up when they are needed (and sometimes when they are not). In order for you to follow our procedural steps, you have to know the names of these screen parts, which are labeled in the next screenshot.

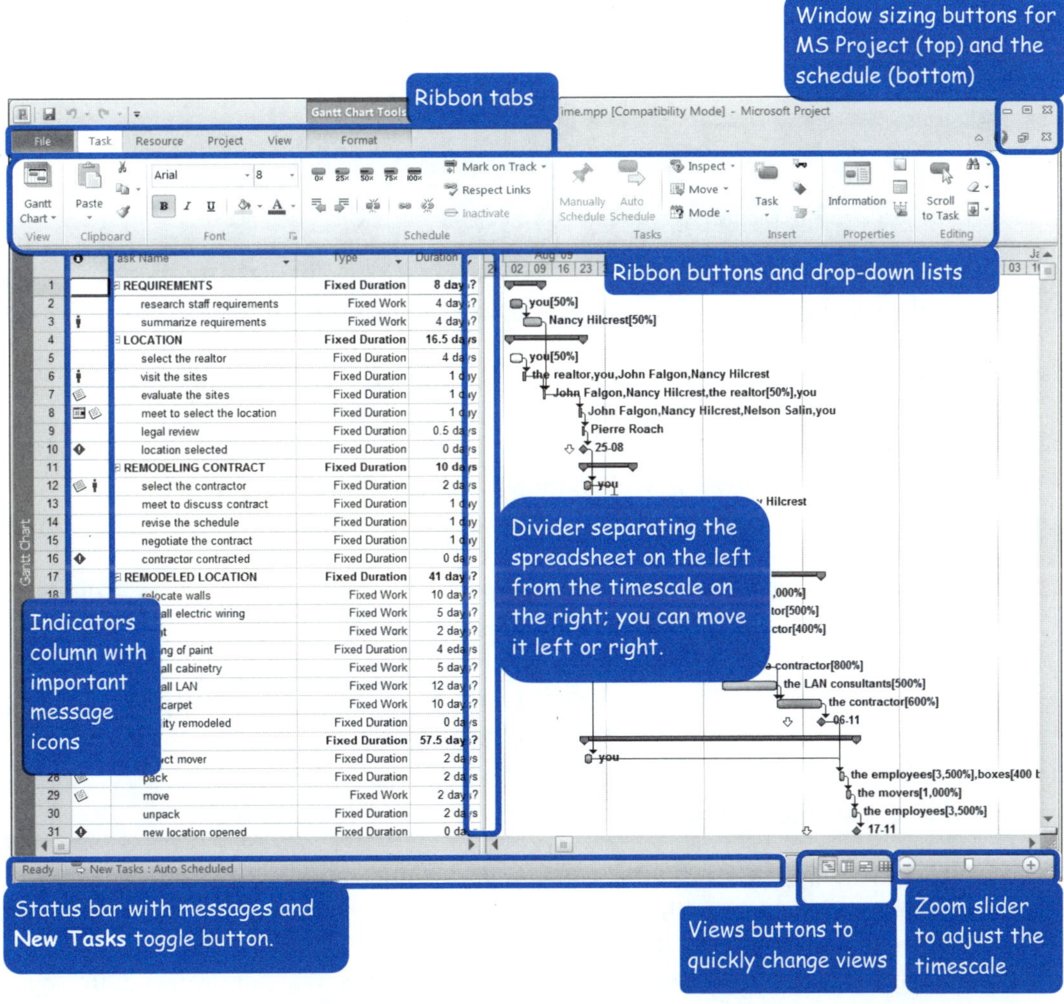

The Ribbon

The ribbon is a new interface that makes Project 2010 more intuitive. Frequently used features have bigger buttons in a more prominent place on the ribbon.

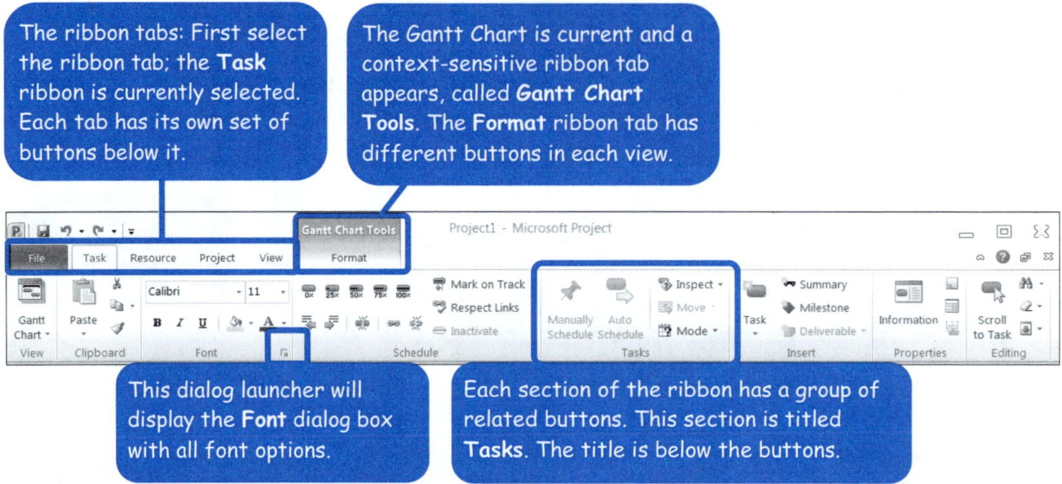

- *Ribbon Tabs*: Each tab looks like a ribbon, and that is what we will call it. The **Format** ribbon is view-specific.
- *Ribbon Groups*: Each section on a tab displays a group of related items. Each group has a title that is displayed at the bottom of the section.
- *Ribbon Commands*: A ribbon command can be a *button* or a *drop-down list*. Lists can be recognized by a triangle button [▾] or [▾]. A button will immediately execute an action, whereas a list will require an extra click to select an item from the list and trigger an action.
- *Ribbon dialog launcher*: When the ribbon does not display all buttons, a dialog launcher button [ ] will allow you to display a dialog that provides all options.
- *Ribbon backstage*: The **File** ribbon is special; it gives you access to the so-called backstage that has all file commands (save, open close, new, print) and also the help system, the options, the organizer, the templates and Project Server accounts.

Working with the Ribbon

People who are used to the 2007 menu structure will not feel comfortable soon in Project 2010. The culprit is the new ribbon interface that replaces the menu structure in previous releases. Microsoft did publish a very helpful reference guide that will tell you how to do something in Project 2010 if you know what to click in Project 2007. With their permission, we provide that guide to you as the file *Ribbon bar reference guide for*

Project 2007 users - Microsoft.xls in the download files that come with this book. See page vi for the procedure to access these files.

To invoke the action of a ribbon button, click it with the primary mouse button – the left mouse button if you are right-handed.

If you are not sure which ribbon button you need, place the mouse pointer on top of a button without clicking, and a screen tip will explain what that button does.

To invoke a ribbon button with the keyboard, just press the Alt key and the *shortcut keys* are superimposed on the tabs for each ribbon (a.k.a. *KeyTips*). Press the key on your keyboard for the ribbon you want to use, and another set of KeyTips appears for the buttons on the ribbon you chose.

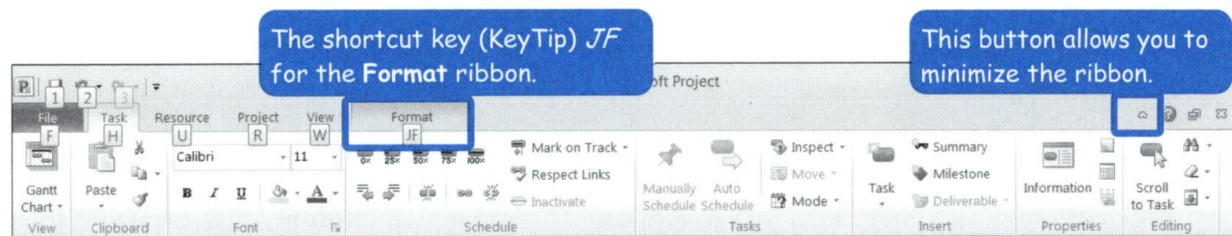

If you need the space that is occupied by the ribbon, you can minimize the ribbon by double-clicking on the ribbon tabs. Or right-click on a ribbon and select **Minimize the Ribbon** from the popup menu or click the button as indicated in the screenshot above.

Customizing the Ribbon

Each ribbon can be customized by right-clicking on it and selecting the item **Customize the Ribbon**. You can:

- Create a new ribbon, click New Tab in the bottom right of the dialog.
- Create a new group (section) in the new ribbon or in an existing one, select a tab in the list on the right and click New Group. Notice you can only change the default ribbons by first adding a group (section) to it.
- Add an item: First select a category in the list **Choose commands from** at the top left. Note:
  - The item **Commands Not in the Ribbon** allows you to add features back to Project 2010 that you knew from previous releases.
  - The item **Macros** allows you to run macros you recorded with one click. Then select the item to add from the list on the left and click Add >> or simply drag it to where you want it in the list on the right.

- Remove an item: From the list on the right, select a ribbon, group or button to remove and click << Remove
- Rename any item: From the list on the right, select the tab, group or button and click Rename... . This button also allows you to add an image to the button.
- Share your custom ribbon with other people: Click Import/Export ▾ and select **Export all customizations**. To install someone else's custom ribbon, click Import/Export ▾ and select **Import customization file**. The customization file includes the *Quick Access Toolbar* (QAT) customizations as well.
- Return to the default ribbon: Click Reset ▾ and select ◉ **Reset only selected ribbon tab** or ◉ **Reset all customizations**.

Working with the Quick Access Toolbar (QAT)

The *Quick Access Toolbar* (QAT) is in the top left of the screen and looks like this by default:

Unlike the ribbon buttons, the QAT buttons are always visible on the screen and allow you to trigger an action with just one click. Therefore, we recommend you use it to make the tools you use most often the most accessible, for example, the tools to open and close a schedule. The QAT can be customized by right-clicking on it and clicking **Customize Quick Access Toolbar**. The dialog works similarly to customizing ribbons as discussed above. Alternatively, the QAT can quickly be customized by clicking the ▾. We recommend you consider adding the following buttons using the **All commands** list:

- **Scroll to task** to move bars or numbers into view
- **Zoom in** and **Zoom out**
- **Advanced Document Properties** to see the **Properties** dialog
- **Project Statistics** to see project-level data
- **Print Preview**
- **Insert Page Break**

If you like your custom QAT a lot, you can display it below the ribbon: **Show below the Ribbon**. (QAT is pronounced the same as *cat*. Does it not sound funny to click with your mouse on the QAT?)

Right-Mouse Clicks and Double-Clicks

The mouse button under your middle finger (the secondary mouse button – right mouse button for the right-handed) can pop up shortcut menus that relate to the object. We will call pressing this mouse button right-clicking. You can *right-click* on all the objects and areas that are labeled in the previous illustration. This is a stylized version of a Gantt Chart; you can make many more right-clicks in other views.

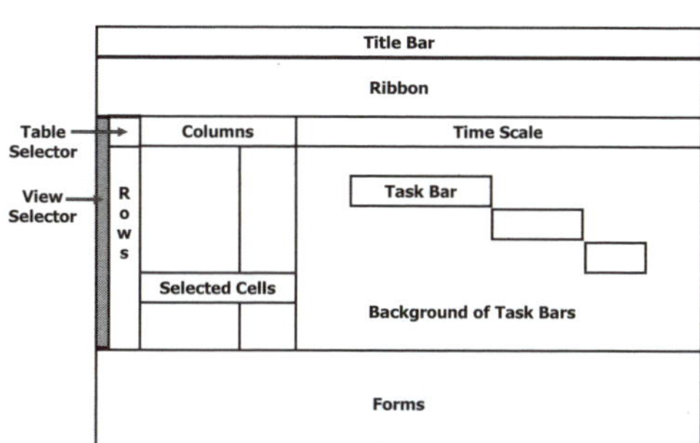

Alternatively, you can *double-click* in some of these places; this will take you to the most likely shortcut for that area and display a dialog box right away.

In Project 2010, the right-click displays a mini toolbar in addition to the shortcut menu. An example is when you right-click a task in the spreadsheet:

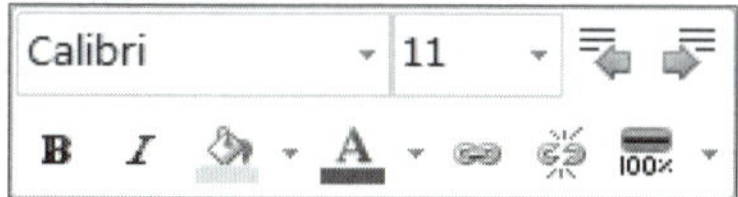

The Revamped Status Bar

The MS Project status bar at the bottom of your screen (just above the Windows task bar if you locked it there) is more informative than ever before. If you right-click on it, you will get a list with all the notifications that you can choose to display in the status bar:

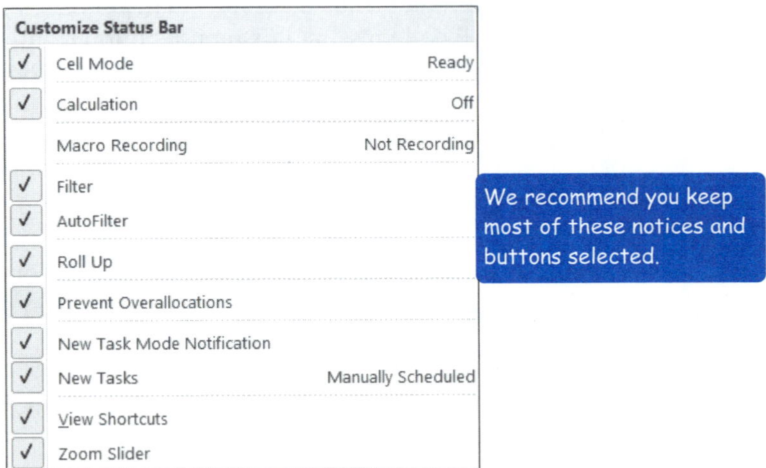

Cell Mode reveals if you are in the middle of a cell **Edit** (which prevents you from doing anything but edit) or if you are **Ready** with it (after keying [Enter ↵]) and can proceed in clicking ribbon buttons. We recommend you look at the status bar to check if **Filter** or **AutoFilter** is on; the latter is hard to see otherwise. In a departure from previous versions, the status bar now even has veritable buttons; by clicking **New Tasks** you can now easily switch the default **Task Mode** for the tasks. Also, the **View Shortcuts** and **Zoom Slider** are buttons. Microsoft transformed the status bar from bare land into cropland.

Project Professional has an extra item, **Online Status,** that tells you if you are logged into Project Server or not (in case you lost your memory since you did that), and the hoover-over screen tip will show you into which account.

Working with Scroll Bars

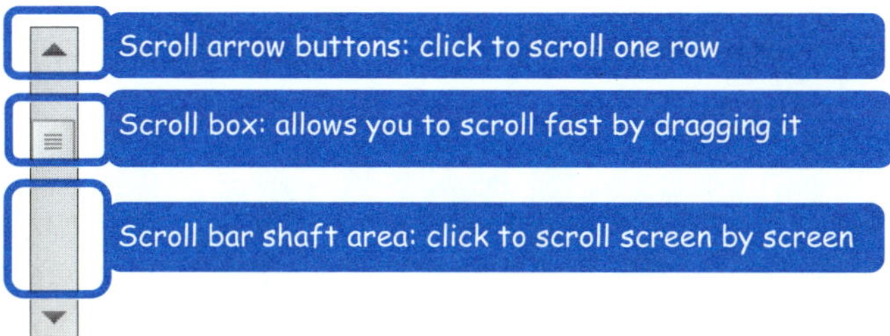

The scroll bar consists of three parts: scroll arrow, scroll box and scroll bar shaft. As you are dragging the timescale scroll boxes, you will see a feedback box pop up that will tell you where you will land. The vertical scroll box shows the ID number of the task you are browsing to:

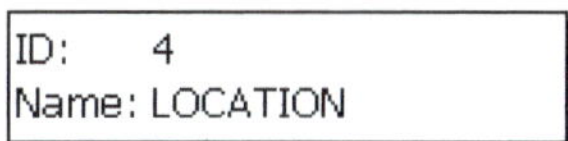

The horizontal scroll box in the timescale tells you the date you are traveling to:

8/15/12 11:46 PM

To View the Whole Project or Selected Tasks in the Timescale

You can make all task bars visible in the timescale by clicking the **View** ribbon. In its section **Zoom,** click Entire Project (may also appear as Entire Project).

2010 Alternatively, you can display the task bars of a certain number of tasks by selecting them first and then clicking Selected Tasks (may also appear as Selected Tasks).

To Zoom the Timescale to Certain Time Units

Click the **View** ribbon and find its section **Zoom**, which contains the **Timescale** drop-down list:

This list allows zooming the bottom tier of the timescale to a particular time unit ranging from **Hours** to **Years**.

Alternatively, you can use the zoom slider at the bottom right of the screen; it looks like:

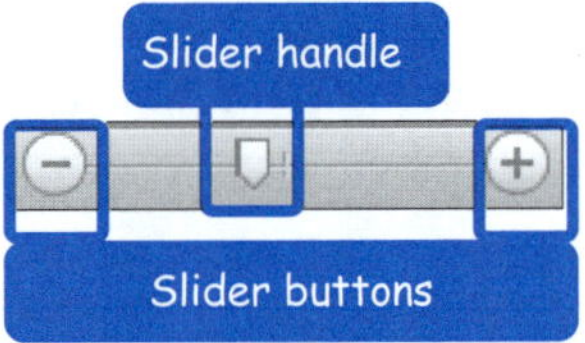

Drag its slider handle or click the slider buttons.

To Zoom Using the Timeline View

1. Switch to the Gantt chart and display the *Timeline view* by clicking the **View** ribbon, finding its **Split View** section and selecting ☑ Timeline.
2. Make the timeline view as small as possible by clicking its **Format** ribbon and clicking

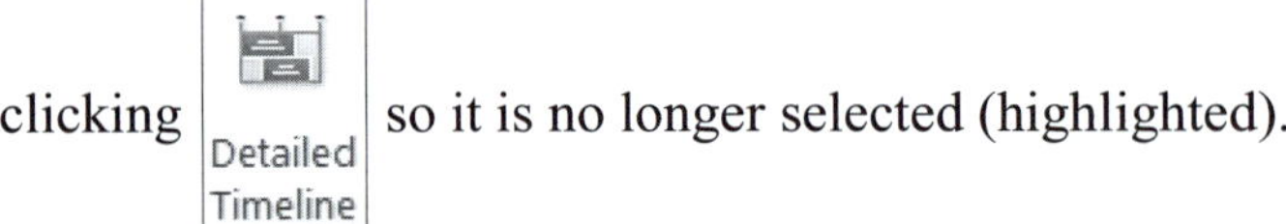

so it is no longer selected (highlighted).

3. The timeline view will now be small at the top of the screen:

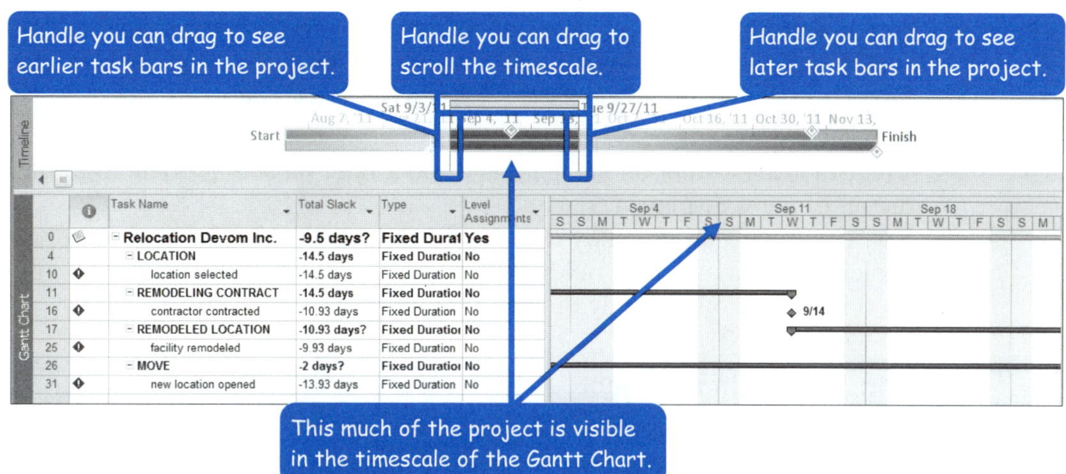

4. Make sure the pan & zoom option is selected; click **Format** ribbon, ☑ Pan & Zoom. The timeline view now has a scroll window as annotated in the screenshot above that you can drag to scroll. You can also widen the window to see earlier or later task bars.

The timeline view provides an easy way to keep the overview of the entire project timescale and zoom into a detailed period. For more on this view, see page 582.

Sorting, Filtering and Grouping Rows Quickly

Each column heading has a triangular button shown here for the task name column:

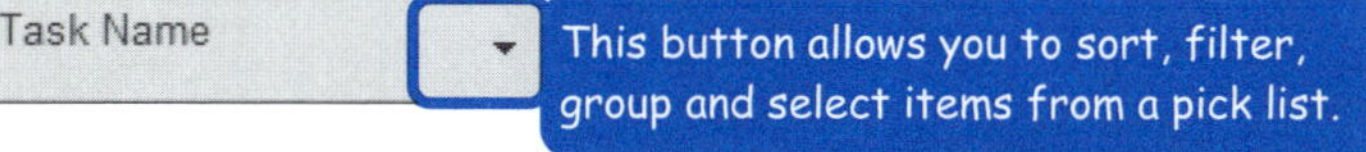

When a filter is in effect you will see the triangular button change to a funnel button as shown here: Task Name — The triangle turned into a funnel.

To remove a filter and redisplay all tasks, press F3.

When a sort is in effect, the only indicator will be that the ID numbers of the list are no longer sequential.

Remarks:

- When you sort using this feature, Project 2010 sorts the summary tasks on outline level 1 first, then outline level 2, etc. (a.k.a. **Keep outline structure**). It does not sort all detail tasks. To do that, use the ribbon **View**, the button **Sort** and the item **Sort By**, making sure to clear the ☐ **Keep outline structure** check box.
- You can apply a filter and then sort the subset of items displayed by the filter.
- You can apply a filter on one field and add a filter on another field to further narrow the set of items displayed.
- You can apply a grouping by clicking **Group by**. For the **Task name** column, choices of other available fields are offered to group by. For other columns, **Group on this field** or other handy options are provided.

Moving Around in a Project

The following convention is used: [Alt] + [→] means hold down [Alt] and press [→].

Note that in Project 2010, the [Alt] key displays the shortcuts (*KeyTips*) for each ribbon after a small time delay.

Move to	By keyboard	By mouse
Cell in next row	[Enter ↵] or [↓]	Click the cell
Cell in next column	[Tab] or [→]	Click the cell
Display next minor time unit in the timescale, or Display previous	[Alt] + [→] [Alt] + [←]	Click the arrow button ▶ on the scroll bar of the timescale, or click ◀
Next screen in timescale	[Alt] + [Page Up] or [Alt] + [Page Dn]	Click to the left or right of the scroll box [IIII] in the horizontal scroll bar
The start date of the project	[Alt] + [Home]	Left align the scroll box [IIII] in the horizontal scroll bar
The end date of the project	[Alt] + [End]	Right align the scroll box [IIII] in the horizontal scroll bar

Move to	By keyboard	By mouse
The first task of the project	Control + Home	Drag the vertical scroll box to the top
The last task of the project	Control + End	Drag the vertical scroll box to the bottom
A specific task and task bar, resource or date	F5 OR Control + F	Click ribbon **Task**, click Find
The other view in a split window	F6	Click in the other view to make it active
Move the timescale to a task bar	Control + Shift + F5	Click ribbon **Task**, click Scroll to Task

Moving Around in a Dialog Box

The following convention is used: Alt + Tab means hold down Alt and press Tab.

Action	By keyboard	By mouse
Move to next field in a dialog box, or Move to previous field	Tab Shift + Tab	Click in the field
Move to any field in a form	Alt + press underlined letter of the field name	Click in the field
Increase or decrease value in a field	↑ ↓	Use the spin button

Action	By keyboard	By mouse
Move between tabs in a dialog with tabbed pages	Tab to the tab title first, then move to another tab by pressing an arrow key: ←, →	Click on the tab

Selecting Data

Select	By keyboard	By mouse
An entire row or record (task or resource)	Shift + space bar	Click on a row heading
An entire column	Control + space bar	Click on a column heading

When you select an entire row as explained in the previous table, all the fields of a task (hundreds!) are selected, even if they are not visible. It is important to select a task in its entirety before moving or copying it. Remember that MS Project is a relational database application, as discussed on page 63.

Project 2010 Views

The *View* of a project is a predefined layout that presents the project from a certain angle. The views allow you to enter or edit data, review or report your project. You can access the views by clicking the **View** ribbon.

View	View Ribbon Button	Shows
Gantt Chart	Section **Task Views**, Gantt Chart of Gantt Chart, **Gantt chart**	The tasks and their task bars over time, plus spreadsheet columns
Tracking Gantt	Section **Task Views**, Gantt Chart of Gantt Chart, **Tracking Gantt**	Two bars for each task in this view: The most recent update of the schedule and the original schedule (baseline) if the baseline is set.
Task Usage	Section **Task Views**, Task Usage of Task Usage, **Task Usage**	Tasks with their assigned resources and the effort or cost over time
Network Diagram	Section **Task Views**, Network Diagram	The network of dependencies between tasks (dependencies are shown as arrows)
Calendar	Section **Task Views**, Calendar	The tasks shown as bars on a calendar
Timeline	Section **Task Views**, Other Views, Timeline	The Timeline view can display phases and milestones on one timeline bar to summarize the project. It appears as the top view.

View	View Ribbon Button	Shows
Team Planner	Section **Resource Views**, [button] of Team Planner	The Team Planner view facilitates allocating tasks to resources while keeping an eye on their workloads.
Resource Usage	Section **Resource Views**, Resource Usage	Resources with their assigned tasks with the workloads or cost over time
Resource Sheet	Section **Resource Views**, Resource Sheet	The spreadsheet with resource information
Resource Graph	Section **Resource Views**, Other Views, Resource Graph	The workloads for resources in a bar chart format

Single View versus Combination View

A *single view* is a one-view screen. The views shown on the previous pages are single views. A *combination view* is a screen with two views. A combination view consists of a top and a bottom view.

The bottom view only shows information pertaining to the tasks (or resources) that you selected in the top view. This interaction between top and bottom view can be very useful for data entry with a sheet view in the top and a form view in the bottom. Form views allow you to enter detail information.

2

Here is an example of a combination view, the **Task Entry** view. This view displays the **Gantt Chart** in the top and the **Task Form** in the bottom:

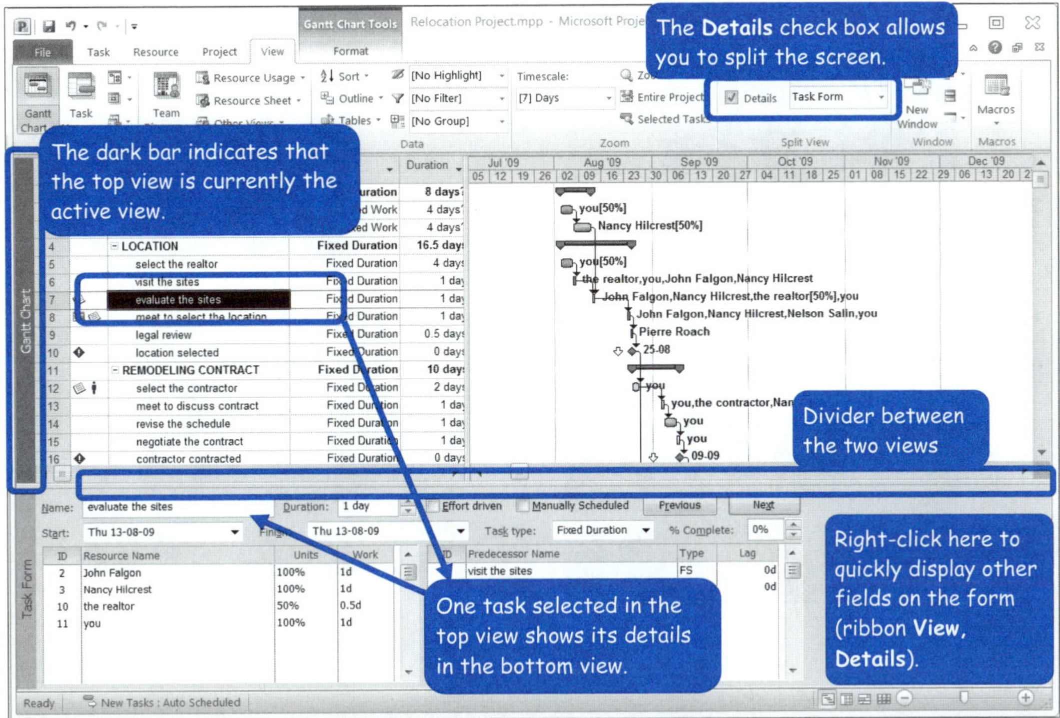

This view allows you to enter detailed information on tasks. You can enter resource assignments and predecessors. The task you select in the top view, the *Gantt Chart*, is shown in detail in the bottom view, the *Task Form*. The top and bottom views interact; whatever you select in the top is shown in more detail in the bottom. This interaction makes combination views well suited for analyzing schedules as well:

- With a task view in the top and a resource view in the bottom (or vice versa), you can view assignments.
- With a resource view in the top and a task view in the bottom you can view overallocations (ribbon **View**, section **Resource Views**, button **Other Views**, item **More Views**, item **Resource Allocation**).

We show the latter in the next screenshot:

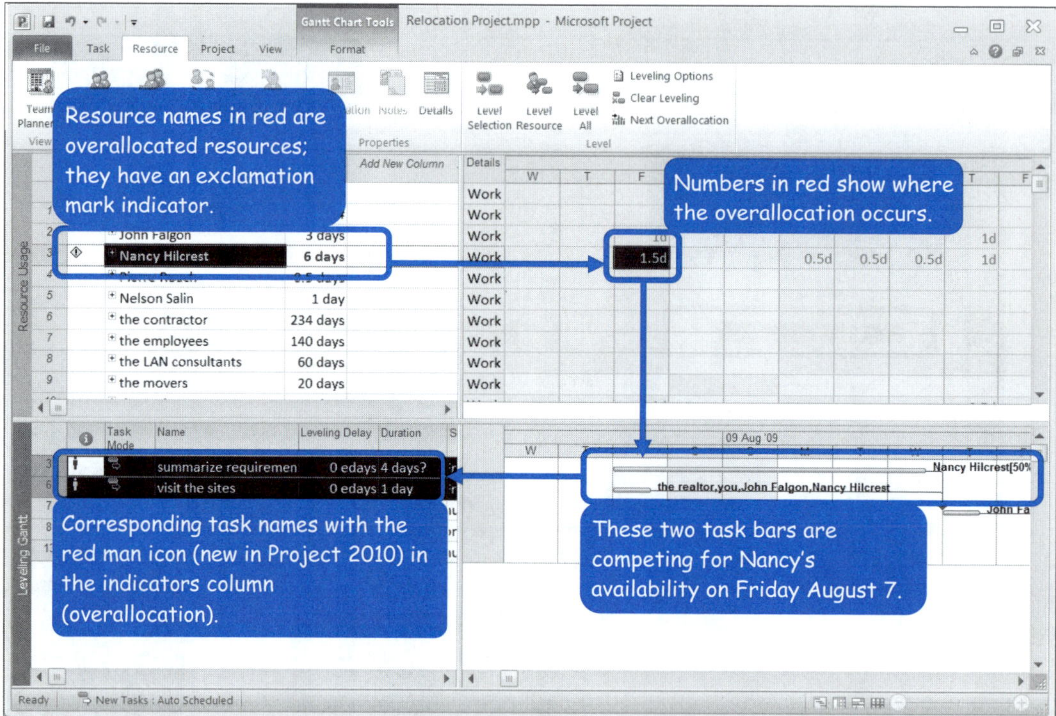

The **Resource Allocation** view has the **Resource Usage** in the top view and the **Leveling Gantt** view in the bottom. This combination view allows you to analyze and resolve overallocations. The interaction between the top and bottom view is such that selecting a resource in the top view displays its assignments in the bottom view.

To Create a Combination View

1. Click ribbon **View** and find its section **Split View**.

2. Select ☑ Details and the default bottom view appears (i.e., the **Task Form** for any Gantt Chart). Select from the list to the right of the **Details** check box the view you want to display in the bottom. Note that the view you select in the ☑ Details list always appears as the bottom view. If you click on any view button in the **Task Views** or **Resource Views** sections on the **View** ribbon, it will always appear as the top view.
   Also note that not all views can be in the bottom of a combination view; for example, the *Team Planner* view cannot be in the bottom (except when the Task

Sheet is in the top). Also, the Team Planner view can only have a form or sheet view in the bottom.

OR
Right-click in the timescale and select **Show Split**.

OR
You can point with the tip of the mouse pointer to the sliding window handle at the bottom right of your screen (the tiny horizontal bar under the scroll down button).

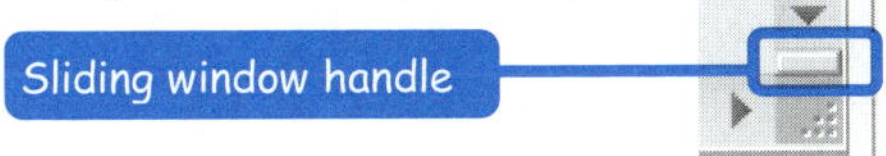

The mouse pointer will become a double-headed arrow ⇳. Drag it up or double-click on it to display the bottom view. You now have two views on the screen, one in the top and one in the bottom. You can change the size of each view by pointing to the divider line between the views; the mouse pointer should change to ⇳. Hold down the primary mouse button and drag the divider line as desired. To move the cursor between the views, press F6 or click in the other view.

To Switch Back to a Single View

Drag the horizontal divider line between the views to the bottom (or to the top depending on which view you want to keep) using the mouse pointer ⇳.
OR
Double-click on the divider line when you see the mouse pointer ⇳ to keep the top view.
OR
Click ribbon **View** and uncheck ☑ Details to keep the top view.

Setting Up a New Project Schedule

We suggest the following process for preparing a new project schedule. We will provide an overview here and discuss the steps in more detail on the indicated pages:

1. Creating a new project schedule from the ground up or from a project template (see next section)
2. Describing the project (see page 90 and following):
   ◇ In the dialog box: ribbon **File**, tab **Info,** list button **Project Information** (on the right side of the screen), item **Advanced Properties**, tab **Summary**: enter the title and manager of the project

- ◇ In the screen: ribbon **File**, tab **Info** (on the right side of the screen)
  OR
  In the dialog box: ribbon **Project**, button **Project Information**: enter the start date for the project.

3. Setting the schedule options (see page 90 and following). Options to consider are:
   - ◇ Date order
   - ◇ Ribbon **Resource**, button **Leveling Options**
   - ◇ **Team Planner** view, **Prevent Overallocations** button
   - ◇ Ribbon **File**, button **Options**
   - ◇ **Manually Scheduled** tasks or **Auto Scheduled** tasks
4. Setting the *project calendar* in ribbon **Project**, button **Change Working Time** button (see page 99 and following):
   - ◇ Working hours
   - ◇ Business days
   - ◇ Holidays

Creating a New Project Schedule

Click ribbon **File** and click New – the following screen appears:

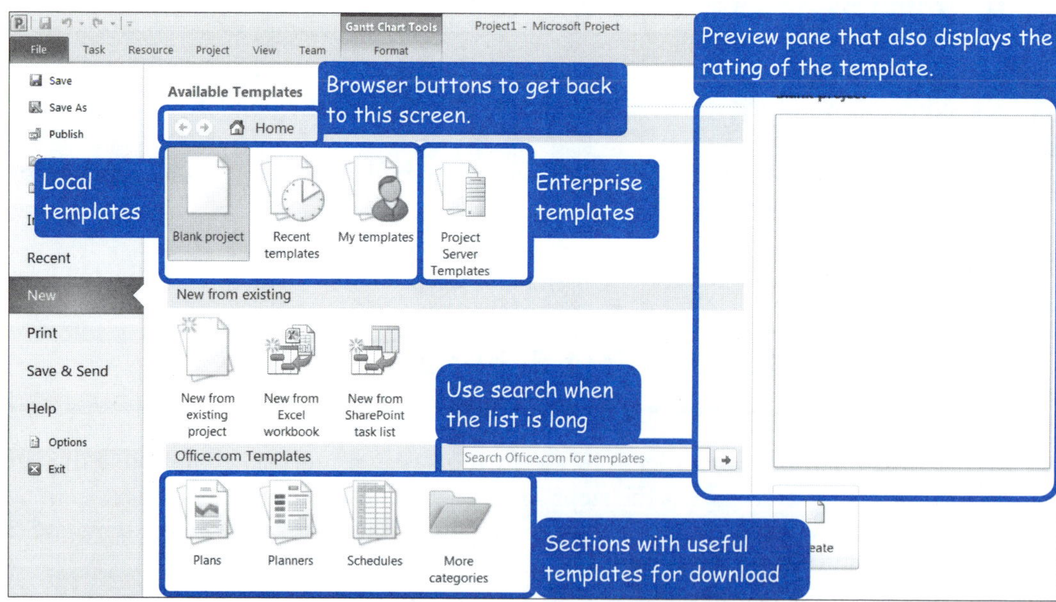

You can create a new **Blank Project** or jump start your project with:

- ◆ **Recent templates**: templates you have recently accessed
- ◆ **My templates**: templates you have downloaded from Office.com.

2

- **New from existing project**: reuse an existing project. Note that MS Project will not offer to strip out the baseline or actuals.
- **New from Excel workbook**: this requires you to create a map to tell MS Project in which fields the data from Excel need to be loaded. You can also copy straight from Excel, then lay out the columns similarly in MS Project and paste.

- **New from SharePoint task list**: Note that you can also create a new project from a SharePoint task list in Project Professional, but, at the time of sending this book to press, SharePoint did not allow:
  - ◇ indented task lists within one view,
  - ◇ Auto Scheduled tasks,
  - ◇ sorted task lists,
  - ◇ generic resources,
  - ◇ assigning multiple resources to one task,
  - ◇ duration or work estimates, or
  - ◇ work updates.

  We will therefore not discuss using a SharePoint task list in detail for creating a new project schedule. We expect the SharePoint functionality will evolve quickly and will provide an update on its capabilities in a download file called *Updating through SharePoint – ProjectPro.doc* available at www.ProjectProCorp.com (see page vi for the procedure to access these files).
- **Office.com Templates**: Unlike previous releases, Project 2010 does not come with out-of-the-box templates, but the list of templates on Office.com will keep growing.

Project templates are useful as a jumpstart on your project plan. If you run similar projects over and over again, templates are particularly useful. Templates can be created centrally by your *project management office* to promote consistent *Work Breakdown Structures*, common project options, standard views and shared project calendars.

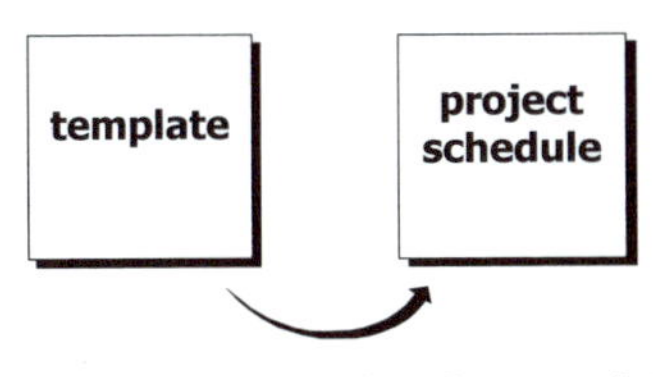

Open template copies the template

Templates are protected from accidental changes, so they stay the same and can be reused. The way the templates are protected is simple. When you open a project template, MS Project copies it; you never open the template itself. When saving the template, you will always be asked for a (new) file name or schedule name. This way the templates are safe and can be used by many different people. Template files have the extension **.MPT** (which stands for Microsoft Project Template).

Solid templates typically have tasks, dependencies, estimates, *generic resources*, assignments, *project-specific options* and a *project calendar* and may even contain custom views. Templates should not contain constraint dates, deadlines, baselines or actuals.

Describing the Project

Project Properties

1. Click ribbon **File** and click Info – the following screen appears:

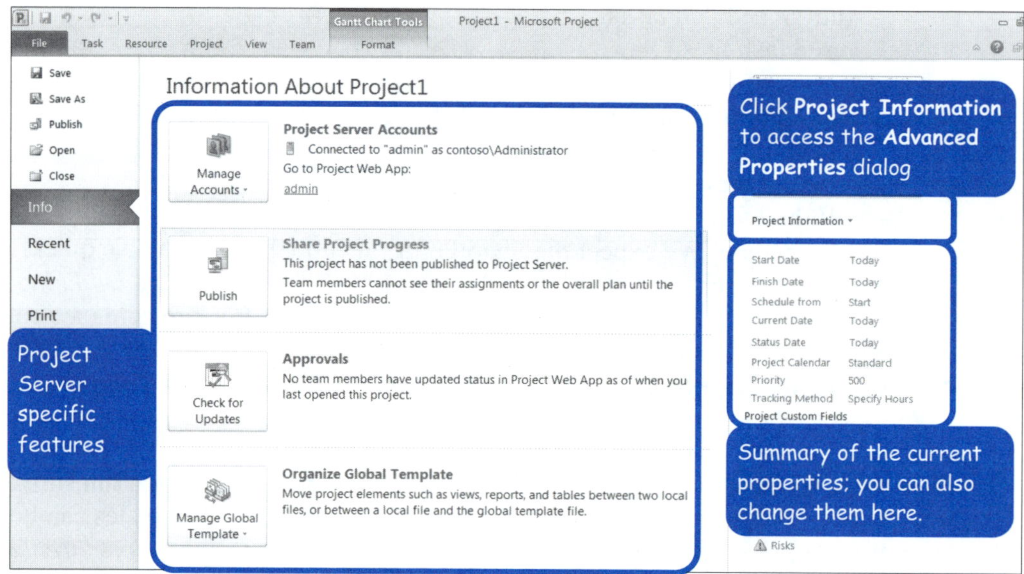

2

2. Click list button **Project Information** (on the right side of the screen) to display its drop-down menu and select **Advanced Properties** – the following dialog appears:

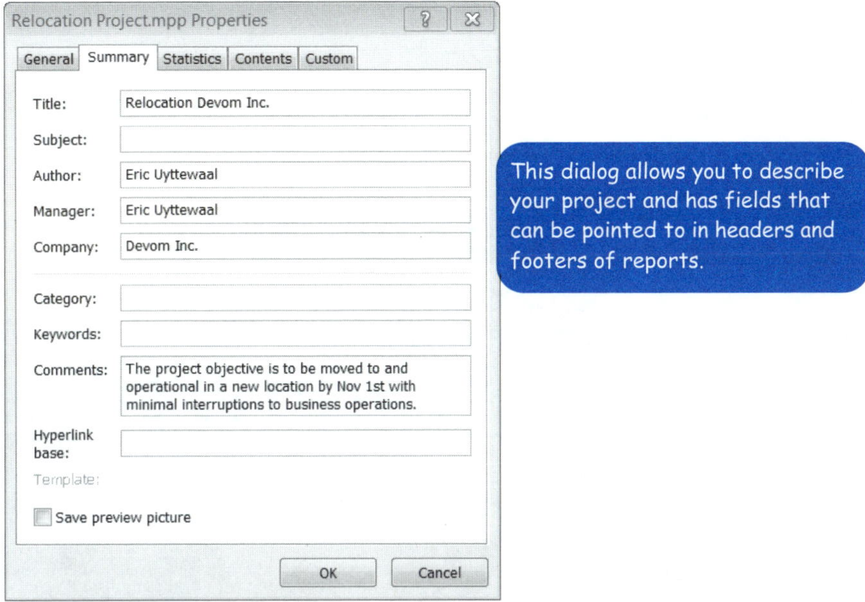

3. Click the tab **Summary** and in this dialog:
   - ◇ In the field **Title**, enter the name of the project
   - ◇ Enter your name as the **Author** and/or **Manager** and
   - ◇ In the **Comments** field, enter the project objective or a description of the final project product. Try to develop a single sentence that captures the essence of your project. Having such a sentence prepares you for short encounters with executives. The text you enter here will also be visible as a note on task 0 (zero: the Project Summary Task) visible in the indicators ❶ column.
4. Click [OK].

The entries in the **Properties** dialog can be used in the headers and footers of each report you create by referring to them. These links save time; for example, if the title or manager changes, all of your ten reports are updated automatically. They also provide consistency.

Entering the Project Start Date

1. Click ribbon **File**, tab **Info** and enter the **Start Date** on the right side of the screen.
   OR

   Click ribbon **Project** and click Project Information – this dialog appears:

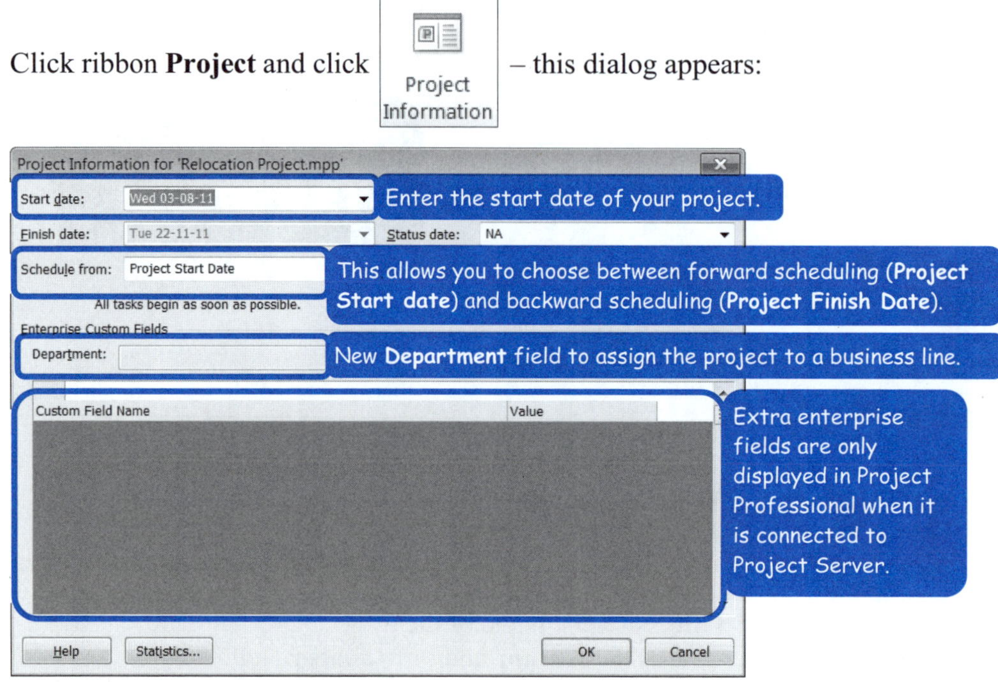

2. Enter the basic project information in this dialog. There are two choices in the list **Schedule from**:
   - ◇ **Project Start Date** (*forward scheduling*): enter the **Start Date** and MS Project will schedule all tasks *As Soon As Possible* (ASAP) after the project start date. After you have entered all the data, MS Project will show what the earliest finish date will be for the project.
   - ◇ **Project Finish Date** (*backward scheduling*): enter the **Finish Date** and MS Project will schedule all tasks *As Late As Possible* (ALAP) working backward from the project finish date. After you have entered all the data, MS Project will show what the target start date of the project should be.

The choice you make depends on what you know most certainly about your project: the start date or the finish date. Neither approach will guarantee that the initial schedule will not turn out too long. You usually have to squeeze the project into the time available for it. This makes the choice between entering the start or the finish date less important, and most people use the default, scheduling from the project start date forward.

Setting the Options

Date Order Option

The date order (ddmmyy or mmddyy) cannot be set inside Project 2010. You have to set it in the Windows *Control Panel*. This means that it will affect the date order in all of your Windows applications.

1. In Windows 7, click the start menu , **Control Panel, Clock Language and Region, Region and Language**.
2. Click tab **Formats** and select the date order from the list **Short Date**.
3. Click OK – all lists in Project 2010 that provide choices for date formats will now only show items in the date order you chose in the Control Panel.

Schedule Options in the Backstage

There are two types of options

- *Global options* that take effect in **All New Projects**: these options are stored in the *Windows Registry*. The Windows Registry is a user-specific database of Windows and application settings. When you create a new, blank project, the Windows Registry is consulted.
- *Project-specific options* that affect the active project only: you can recognize these because they start with a section heading showing the name of the project schedule. These options are stored in the project file.

To access the options:

1. Click ribbon **File** and click [Options] – the **Options** dialog appears:

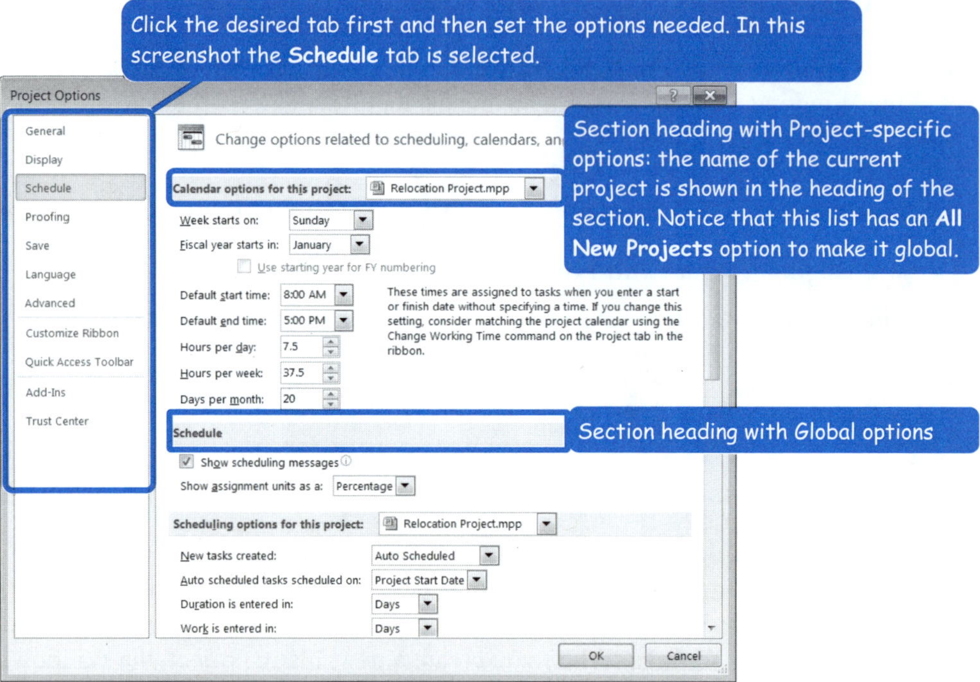

2. Select the category of options by clicking one of the tabs.
3. Select the section heading and decide if the options you want to set are project-specific or global. In the latter case, you first need to select the item **All New Projects** in the section heading list.
4. Set the options.
5. Click [OK] to accept the changes and close the dialog.

This table indicates the most important options you should review at this point:

Tab	**Set to**
General	**Date Format:** *Jan 28 '09* To avoid confusion about dates in international projects, choose a date format with the month spelled out, i.e., Jan 28 '09. Americans will interpret a date like 7-8-2009 as July 8, 2009. Europeans, South Americans and Québécois (Canada) will interpret it as August 7th and think they have an extra month.

Schedule	Section **Calendar options for this project** **Hours per Day** MS Project uses this number to convert estimates expressed in days into hours. This number should represent the hours worked by a *Full-Time Equivalent* (FTE) employee. If it does not, the schedule will not be accurate. **Hours per Week** MS Project uses this to convert estimates expressed in weeks into hours. The setting should be aligned with what you entered under *Hours per Day*. **Days per Month** MS Project uses this number to convert estimates expressed in months into days. This number should reflect your situation.
	Section **Schedule:** ☑ **Show Scheduling Messages** will give helpful messages when it notices a problem in the schedule.
	Section **Scheduling options for this project** **New tasks created: Manually Scheduled** or **Auto Scheduled**. See discussion below this table.
	Section **Calculation**: **Calculate project after each edit:** ◉ **On**; This will ensure that you see the effect of the last changes immediately.
Advanced	☑ **Advice from Planning Wizard** Meant for novice users; clear if it does not help or annoys you.

Hours per Day Conversion Factor

Before entering any tasks, you have to specify how many work hours in a workday by using the option **Hours per Day** on the tab **Schedule** (ribbon **File**, [Options]). MS Project uses this setting to convert between time units; it is the *time unit conversion factor*. All durations will be recalculated when you change this option. For example, if the **Hours per Day** option is set to 8 hours and you enter a duration of 5 days, MS Project knows this equals 8 * 5 = 40 hours. If you then change the **Hours per Day** setting to 7, MS Project changes the duration to 5.71 days (= 5 * 8 / 7). If you start with the wrong conversion factor, MS Project will interpret the durations you enter incorrectly, which may result in a schedule that is too optimistic or pessimistic in its forecasts.

There is workaround to keep the current durations without having to re-enter all durations when you change the **Hours per Day** setting. Before changing the **Hours per Day**, copy all durations to one of the extra fields (**Duration1** for example), then change the **Hours per Day**. Make sure you have the task field **Type** set to **Fixed Units** for all tasks (see page 170). Then copy the durations from the **Text1** field back into the **Duration** field.

Leveling Options

Workload leveling is making sure the workloads stay within the availability of the resources. We recommend you keep MS Project from continuously leveling the workloads, which will make your schedule dance in front of your eyes when MS Project moves tasks back and forth in response to changes you make to the schedule. It will do this with every little change you make. There are two places you need to make sure the default settings are still intact:

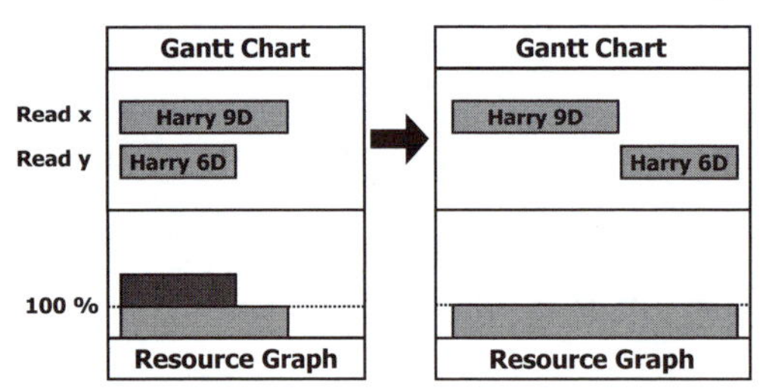

- Ribbon **Resource**, button **Leveling Options**: select ◉ **Manual Leveling**.
- **Team Planner** view, the **Prevent Overallocations** button: If the button is highlighted orange when the mouse is off it, the automatic leveling is on and you need to click it once. If the button is not highlighted orange, the automatic leveling is off.

These recommended settings do not make it impossible to have MS Project level the workloads but we will address this at a time of our choice, see page 468 for a detailed discussion on leveling.

Manually Scheduled or Auto Scheduled: User-Controlled Scheduling

The new **Manually Scheduled** scheduling option makes Project 2010 behave more like a spreadsheet application, thus inviting Excel users to switch to MS Project. This feature uses a new task-related field called **Task Mode,** in which you can choose **Manually Scheduled** or **Auto Scheduled**. When creating a new project schedule, **Manually Scheduled** will allow you to control the scheduling. You can:

- Prevent MS Project from calculating the Duration, Start and Finish date of the task. You can even enter text, like *TBD* (To Be Determined) or *late June* into these fields.

- Keep dependencies from continuously pushing tasks out to later dates by turning off the option ☐ **Update Manually scheduled tasks when editing links** (ribbon **File,** Options, tab **Schedule**, section **Scheduling options for this project**).
- Stop summary tasks from summarizing their detail tasks.

You can set the default task mode for the entire project and all new projects in one of the following three ways:

- Click ribbon **File** and click Options and tab **Schedule**, or
- In the bottom left of the screen click on New Tasks : and select **Manually Scheduled** or **Auto Scheduled**, or
- Click ribbon **Task**, click Mode and select **Manually Schedule** or **Auto Schedule**.

You can override the default task mode and switch one particular task between **Manually Scheduled** and **Auto Scheduled** in one of the following ways:

- Right-click on the task number and select **Manually Schedule** or **Auto Schedule**, or
- Click in the **Task Mode** cell and select from its list.
- Select the task(s) and click 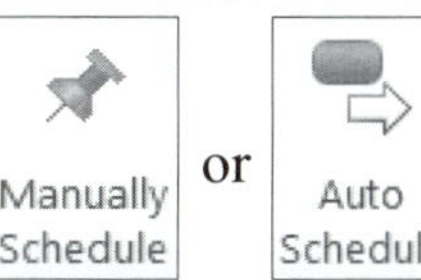

 on the **Task** ribbon.

We think that manually scheduled tasks are very useful when you are creating a draft schedule quickly. In the preliminary stages of planning a project, you may have some data but not all data to complete a final schedule. A small example of such a draft schedule is:

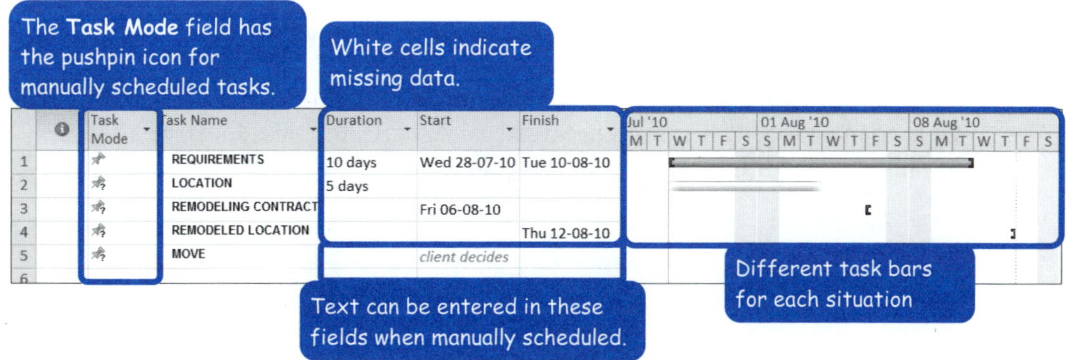

Notice that:

- When you create a new, manually scheduled task, the cells **Duration, Start** and **Finish** are left blank, whereas a new, auto scheduled task will immediately get a default **Duration** of *1 day?* and a default **Start** and **Finish** date.
- In the timescale, the task bars are different when certain information is missing.
- You can enter text in any empty cell for a manually scheduled task.

Manually Scheduled tasks can also lead to sloppy schedules that will require much more effort than necessary to maintain. The temptation is great to start entering dates for manually scheduled tasks. Instead of entering dates, we recommend you switch most tasks to **Auto Scheduled** after entering the dependencies and let MS Project calculate dates; after all, scheduling software is supposed to schedule (i.e., determine dates and maintain them!).

Setting the Project Calendar

Calendar Types

Calendars created by human beings follow the sun (*solar calendars*), the moon (*lunar calendars*) or both (*lunisolar calendars*)

In the ribbon **File,** Options on the tab **Display**, there is a **Calendar Type** field that is set to **Gregorian Calendar** by default. This solar calendar was named after Pope Gregory XIII, who decreed this calendar in 1582.[8] This calendar is regarded as a simple and precise calendar today and is currently in use in most of the world. Its precursors are the Roman calendar and the Julian calendar (Julius Caesar, 46 B.C.E.), respectively. Alternatives for the Gregorian calendar are:

- **Hijri Calendar** (Islamic/Muslim): a lunar calendar of about 354 days per year starting with Gregorian year 622.
- **Thai Buddhist Calendar**: a lunisolar calendar of 360 days per year starting with the Gregorian year 544. It is used in Southeast Asia: Cambodia, Laos, Thailand, Myanmar and Sri Lanka.

---

[8] See www.Wikipedia.com

Microsoft uses the Gregorian calendar as its default and generally follows the ISO 8601 standard for date and time notations (instead of the Astronomical notation that has an extra year, called 0).

Setting the Project Calendar

The **Change Working Time** dialog (**Project** ribbon) allows you to set the *project calendar*:

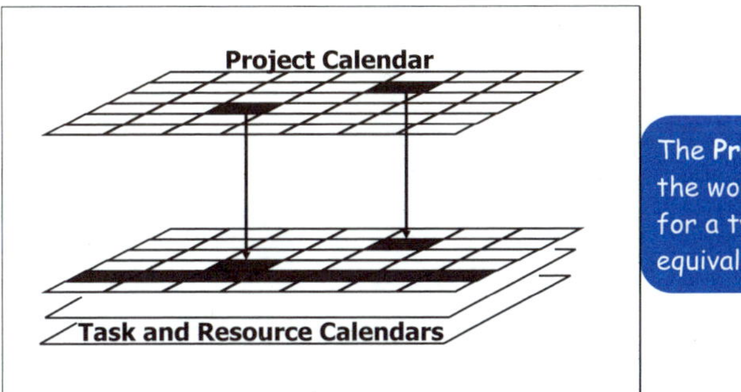

The **Project Calendar** models the workweek and the holidays for a typical full-time equivalent resource.

The default project calendar is called *Standard (Project Calendar)*. On the project calendar you indicate:

- *Workweek*
  - The *Working days (business days)* and *nonworking days* in the *workweek* – which days are the business days in a regular workweek?
  - The *Working times* on the business days – what are the typical working hours for full-time project team members?
- National and corporate *holidays* are technically called *Exceptions* in MS Project – what days are nonworking days throughout the year for the entire country or your company?

In addition to the project calendar there are:

- *Task calendars*
  These can be assigned to individual tasks and used to schedule these tasks. For example, outdoor construction tasks can only take place when the weather permits, and a task calendar could be created for all tasks affected by winter weather. An office-move task can only take place during the weekend. We will discuss task calendars on page 273.
- *Resource calendars*
  These are calendars for each individual person. A resource calendar typically contains individual working days and vacations; sometimes the working hours are individualized as well. We will explain resource calendars on page 311.

The business days, working hours and national holidays of the project calendar will be copied to all resource calendars. The changes you make on the project calendar apply to every task and every resource in the project (unless you have overwritten those settings with individual task or resource calendars). At this point, we will only edit the project calendar; later we will create task calendars and resource calendars. All tasks will be scheduled using the project calendar unless:

- They have their own task calendar attached, or
- They have resources assigned; the resource calendar takes effect.

The task and resource calendars override the project calendar

In summary, the project calendar has two functions:

- It is used to schedule tasks without a task calendar or resources assigned.
- It is a time-saving device to change all resource calendars.

MS Project Schedules Tasks in a Two-Step Process

The two steps are:

1. When you enter an estimate expressed in days, weeks or months, MS Project interprets the estimate by converting it to hours using **Hours per day** and **Hours per week** settings in ribbon **File,** Options **,** tab **Schedule**.
2. MS Project schedules the number of hours required (estimate) using the applicable calendar: *task calendar*, *resource calendar* or *project calendar* listed in order of precedence.

Step 1:
For example, if you enter an estimate of "2w" in the **Duration** column for a task, MS Project recognizes that you entered a duration expressed in weeks and it interprets this number by converting it to hours. The conversion factor is set in ribbon **File,** Options **,** tab **Schedule, Hours per day** and **Hours per week** settings. If, for example, the setting is currently 40 hours per week, MS Project knows that you have entered 2 weeks * 40 hours = 80 hours that need to be scheduled. MS Project will even store the number of minutes and the time unit that you used originally ("w"); in this way it always knows to display the estimate in the same format you entered ("2w").

Step 2:
Now that MS Project knows how many hours it needs to schedule, it retrieves the applicable calendar. It uses:

- The *task calendar* if there is a task calendar assigned to the task; the field **Task Calendar** is filled in.

- The *resource calendar* if there is a resource assigned to the task (the field **Resource Names** has at least one resource name), but no task calendar.
- The *project calendar* if there is no task calendar and no resource assigned to the task (the field **Resource Names** is empty).

MS Project then schedules the task by filling in the number of hours needed for the task (estimate) on the calendar, while taking into account the working times each day, national holidays, weekends, and so forth. For **Auto Scheduled** tasks, MS Project then calculates the date and time that the task will finish. It now has all it needs to build the schedule: start date and time, duration and finish date and time of the task.

Why is all of this important? Firstly, if the **Hours per day** setting is not right, MS Project will convert and interpret all your estimates incorrectly and create an incorrect schedule. This is an important setting to review and revise before entering any tasks. Secondly, the conversion factors need to be aligned with the project calendar; otherwise MS Project will not determine the correct finish dates and times for tasks. Thirdly, calendars are essential in the scheduling process and need to be filled in correctly.

If you change the number of **Hours per Day** in ribbon **File,** Options **, tab Schedule**, MS Project does not update the working times in the project calendar by itself. This has to be done manually, which surprises many people. The **Hours per day** setting needs to be aligned manually with the working hours in the project calendar.

What If Resources Have Different Working Times?

For example, you entered an estimate of 40 hours of effort on an **Auto Scheduled** task. As the illustration shows, 40 hours of effort for a *full-time resource* will take 5 business days (Monday–Friday), and the duration of the task will be 5 days.

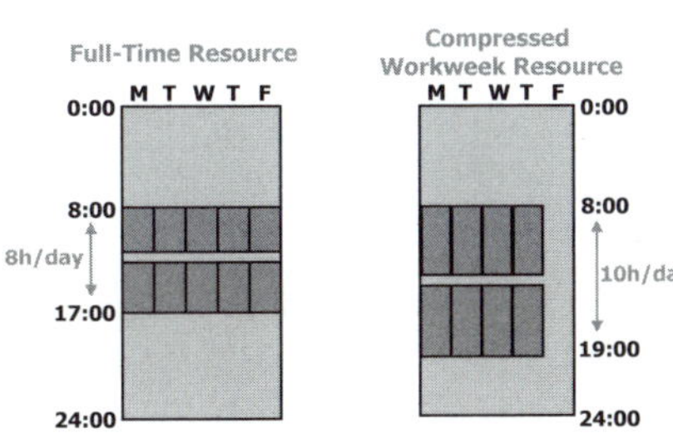

Forty hours of effort for a *compressed workweek* resource who works 10 hours a day will only need 4 business days (Monday – Thursday in the illustration), and the duration of the task will be 4 days.

You can see that MS Project uses the resource calendars for **Auto Scheduled** tasks to calculate durations when there is a resource assigned to the task.

Entering the Workweek: Working Days and Times

The default *standard project calendar* has a 5-day workweek from Monday through Friday that is used in most of the world. The workweek is different in the Middle East:

- Algeria and Saudi Arabia: a workweek of 5 days from Saturday through Wednesday
- Egypt and Israel: 5 days from Sunday through Thursday
- Iran: 6 days from Saturday through Thursday

To create calendars like these:

1. Click ribbon **Project** and find its section **Properties**.
2. Click Change Working Time – the **Change Working Time** dialog appears.
3. You can set the working days of the *workweek*. Select at the top of the dialog in the list **For** the item **Standard (Project Calendar)**; this is the calendar that acts as the default project calendar.

4. Click the tab **Work Weeks** – the dialog looks like:

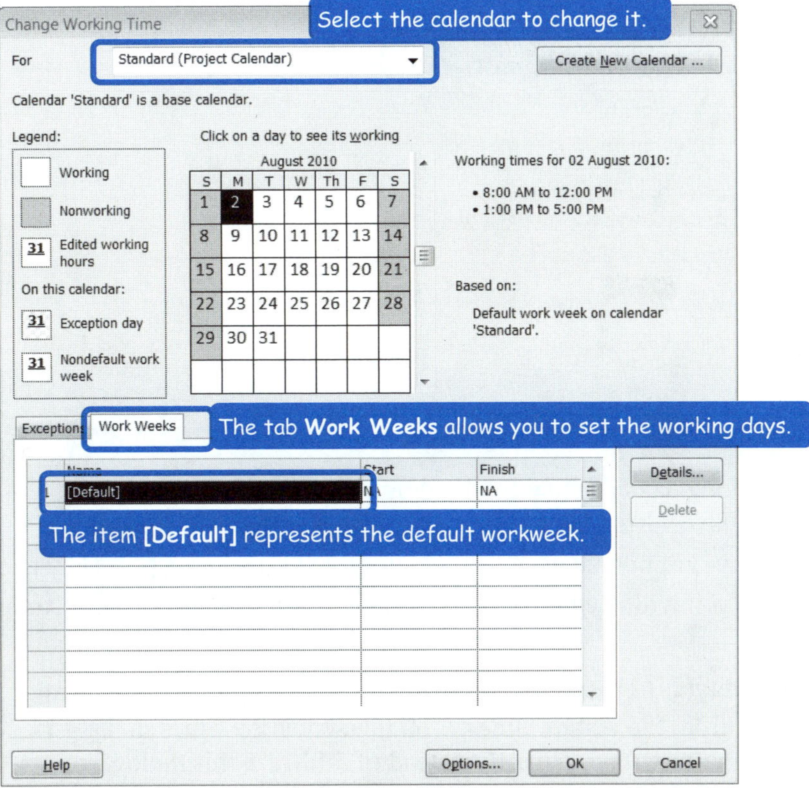

5. The item **[Default]** is the default workweek and you could add items in this list to create multiple workweeks: For example, you may want to schedule different working hours for summer and winter. If you have a single, common workweek, double-click the line item **[Default]** or select the item **[Default]** in the list and click [Details...]. If this button is grayed out, it is likely because you are connected to *Project Server* and are using one of the *Enterprise calendars*. Your Project Server administrators are responsible for maintaining the enterprise calendars; one less task for you!

6. The **Details for '[Default]'** dialog appears:

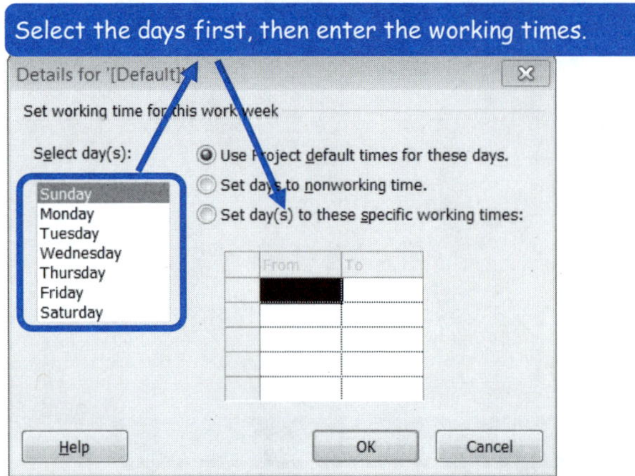

7. Select the working days of the week by dragging over the weekdays in the list **Select day(s)**. If you have a Monday to Friday workweek, drag over **Monday** to **Friday**. If the working days are not adjacent to each other, hold down the [Control] key and click on other days (you will need this to create calendars for Algeria, Saudi Arabia and Iran).

8. Select ◉ **Set day(s) to these specific working times** if you need to change the working hours from the default times. You then enter the times in the grid. Note that you can enter *military times* (like 17 instead of 5 PM) in this dialog.

9. Select the weekend days in the list **Select day(s)**. If the weekend days are Saturday and Sunday, select **Sunday** and hold down [Control] and click on **Saturday** and select the option◉ **Set days to nonworking time**. Note that in the Middle East the weekend days are different.

10. Click [OK] when done; you are now back in the **Change Working Time** dialog. Notice the gray shading for the **Nonworking** weekend days.

11. If you diverted from the default 8 working hours per day (**8:00 AM - 12:00 PM** and **1:00 PM - 5:00 PM**) on the **[Default]** workweek, make sure you also click the button [Options...] at the bottom of the dialog to adjust the *time unit conversion factors*: **Hours per day** and **Hours per week** accordingly. This will ensure that MS Project interprets your estimates correctly! You should also change the **Default start time** and **Default end time** to keep everything aligned. Lastly, you may have to change the **Week starts on** setting as well for Middle East workweeks.
    Click [OK] when done; you are now back in the **Change Working Time** dialog.

12. Click OK when done; you are now back in the main screen of the MS Project application.

Entering the Corporate and National Holidays

Mark the corporate and national holidays as nonworking time in the project calendar if they apply to (almost) everybody involved in the project. If you have team members in multiple countries, see page 311. On the *resource calendar* of an individual resource, the project calendar can still be overridden, and certain holidays can be changed back to working days. Therefore, the project calendar should merely be considered and used as a time saver for creating and maintaining shared holidays on the resource calendars.

1. Click ribbon **Project** and find its section **Properties**.
2. Click 

 – the **Change Working Time** dialog appears.
3. At the top of the dialog under **For** select the **Standard (Project Calendar)**, as this is the calendar that acts as the default project calendar.

4. Navigate to the month and select the days of the holiday in the calendar grid for which you would like to create an exception. In the original release of Project 2010, this dialog is quirky (dare I say there is a bug?) in that it will not allow you to change the selected dates once the exception is created. This step is therefore essential. If you ever need to change the dates, remove the entire exception first and recreate it.
5. Holidays need to be entered as exceptions to the default calendar; click tab **Exceptions**.
6. In the first available field under **Name** enter the name of the holiday (exception), for example *Labor Day: 1st Monday in September* (in North America)

7. While keeping the entered holiday selected, click Details... (If the button is grayed out, you are likely connected to *Project Server* and are using one of the *Enterprise calendars*. Your Project Server administrators are responsible for maintaining the enterprise calendars.) The **Details for <name of the exception>** dialog appears; for *Labor Day* in North America you would fill it in as shown:

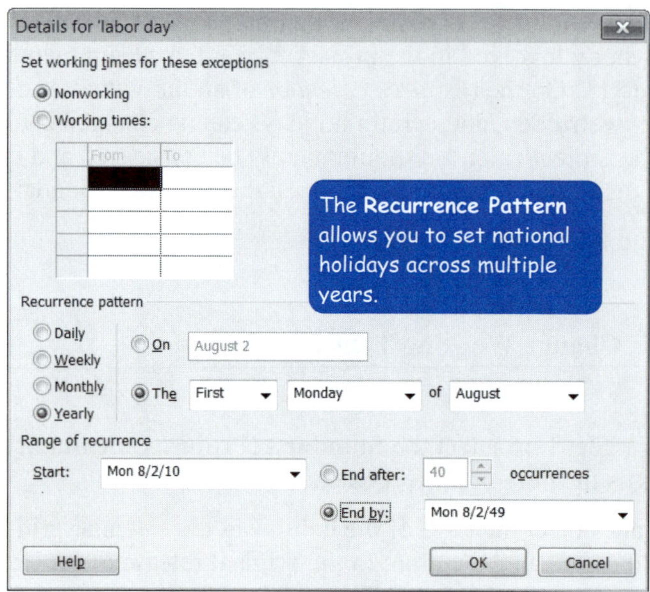

8. Enter the **Recurrence Pattern** and **Range of recurrence** in this dialog. For *Labor Day*, you would select ◉ **Yearly** and as the range we recommend **Start:** *Sun 1/1/10* and ◉ **End by**: *Fri 12/31/49*, which covers the entire timescale available in MS Project (runs until 2049).

9. Click OK when done; you are now back in the **Change Working Time** dialog. Notice the light blue shading for the exception you created.

10. Repeat steps 5 through 8 for other holidays and click OK when done.

The holidays set in the project calendar are carried over to the individual resource calendars. Even if the project calendar is changed after resource calendars are created, the changes will show up automatically in the resource calendars. The calendar information is saved in the project schedule. If you want to distribute a project calendar among colleagues in MS Project standalone, you have to transfer it to a blank project file via the ribbon **File**, tab **Info**, button **Organizer** (see page 197) and send them the file.
OR
In Project Server, your Project Server administrators can publish project calendars as enterprise standards that will apply to all projects.

Checks on Setting Up a Project

Here are some checks to verify if you used the best practices when setting up a new project. The numbering corresponds to the complete checklist in the summary chapter, see page 711.

2

1 Background Information

Certain background information is needed for an evaluation of a schedule: see the questions in the complete checklist starting on page 711.

2 Setup

2.1. Does your schedule contain a succinct description of the objective or final product of the project?
We recommend you use the field **Comments** (ribbon **File**, tab **Info**, button **Project Information** on the right side of screen**, Advanced Properties**, **Summary** tab) which makes it visible as a **Note** on the project summary task. It does not hurt to have a one-liner on your project ready for when you need to explain to an executive what your project is all about, for example, if you are only with this person in an elevator for one minute between the third and fifth floor. Also, if you submit your schedule for evaluation, the evaluator will need this description as project background to understand it and better assess the quality of the schedule.

2.2. Do the business days, the working hours and holidays (corporate and national) on the project calendar align with a typical, full-time resource on the project?

2.3. Do the working hours on the **Standard (Project Calendar)** (ribbon **Project**, button **Change Working Time**) correspond to the **Hours per day** option (ribbon **File**, [Options] **,** tab **Schedule)**?
For example, working times of 8:00 AM - 12:00 PM and 1:00 PM - 5:00 PM are consistent with 8 hours per day and 40 hours per week. If these settings are inconsistent, your forecasts are either too optimistic or too pessimistic. Also, you might see decimals in the durations of tasks.
The quickest way to check consistency is by clicking ribbon **Project**, button **Change Working Time**. If you click [Options...] the **Project Options** dialog will appear (ribbon **File,** [Options] **,** tab **Schedule**). If the hours-per-day setting is wrong, see page 95 for a trick to align these two settings. If the working hours on the calendar are wrong, you can correct them with the steps on page 102.

Exercises

Review

1. Does MS Project function more like MS Excel or MS Access? Why?
2. In which situations would you recommend the use of project templates?
3. What view would you use for:

	Recommended view
Entering tasks?	
Entering resources?	
Entering assignments?	
Checking the network logic?	

4. Why would you use a split screen (combination view) in MS Project?
5. What steps do you recommend for creating a new project schedule?
6. How do the settings **Hours per day** (ribbon **File,** Options **,** tab **Schedule**) and the working hours on the **Standard (Project Calendar)** (ribbon **Project**, button **Change Working Time**) relate to each other?
7. How can you edit the *Standard Project Calendar* object in the *Global.MPT?* This calendar acts as the default calendar.

Relocation Project — Scope Statement

The goal of this exercise is to be able to create a new project and enter project-level information.

You are put in charge of relocating your office. You have to find a new location and organize the move. The following is the *scope statement* created for the project. Your CEO has already signed the scope statement.

Scope Statement

Project: Relocation of DEVOM, Inc. to a new, 150-people location
Project accounting code: MOVE001

The Business Need

DEVOM, Inc. is growing and needs larger facilities to accommodate the expanding workforce.

The Project Objectives

- To be moved and operational in the new location by November 1, 2012
- To stay within the available budget of $100,000 for labor cost
- To have an 80% satisfaction rate from the personnel for the new work environment

The Project Deliverables and Requirements

- A project plan (including WBS, Network Diagram, Gantt Chart, budget, resource list and assignments)
- A new rented or leased location that has a maximum capacity of 150 work spaces
  - The location should be accessible to disabled people
  - The location should have parking facilities for at least 150 cars
  - The location should have modern work cubicles and an open workspace
- Contracts with the landlord, the general contractor and the moving company
- The physical move of people and equipment

The Project Constraints

- The work on the project is to be started no earlier than August 1, 2012
- The personnel have to be asked for input as to the location and facilities needed
- The disruption to the normal operations of DEVOM should be minimized and may

not exceed a loss of 500 person days caused by the project, including the packing and unpacking by staff.

- Clients will have to be able to contact DEVOM at any time by phone, fax and e-mail
- The purchase of new materials and equipment shall be budgeted and approved separately
- The new location will be within the boundaries of the city and its suburbs
- The need for expansion is so urgent that the project has priority over normal operations
- Any changes to the project objectives will require the approval of the CEO

The Project Assumptions

- The market will continue to grow at the same rate
- The current furniture can be reused
- The current workstations can be reused
- The current LAN and servers will be replaced

Date: ....

Your signature	Signature CEO:
....	*NR Salin*
Project Manager, Relocation Project	CEO, DEVOM, Inc.

You decide to take charge of this project and to create the schedule in Project 2010:

1. At the bottom of the scope statement, fill in the date and sign the charter.
2. Create a new MS Project file.
3. Click ribbon **Project**, button **Project Information**. In the **Project Information** dialog:
   - ◇ Set the start date for the project to *August 1, 2012*.
   - ◇ Make sure the **Calendar** is set to **Standard**.
4. Display the ribbon **File**, tab **Info**, list button **Project Information**, item **Advanced Properties** dialog, **Summary** tab.
   - ◇ Enter the **Title** of the project, it is *Relocation Devom Inc.*
   - ◇ You are the responsible project manager; enter your own name under **Manager**.
   - ◇ Enter *Devom Inc.* under **Company**.
   - ◇ Formulate one sentence that captures the essence of the relocation project and enter it in the field **Comments**.
5. Close the dialog and save the file as *Relocation.mpp*.

Relocation Project — File, Options

The goal of this exercise is to be able to set the options for a new schedule.

2

Continue to work in the file *Relocation.mpp* and enter only the following options in the ribbon **File,** [Options] dialog. Save the schedule when done.

Tab	**Set to**
Schedule	Hours per day: 7.5 [9]
	Hours per week: 37.5
	Days per month: 20
	☑ Show scheduling messages
	Show assignment units as a: Decimal [10]
	Duration is entered in: Days
	Work is entered in: Days
	Default task type: Fixed Duration
	☐ New tasks are effort driven
	Calculate project after each edit: ◉ **On**
General	Date Format: Jan 28 '09 [11]

[9] Enter this by typing instead of using the spin buttons.
[10] In this project we will use mostly individual and group resources and will therefore use decimals rather than percentages.
[11] If you do not see *mmddyy* here, you could go to the Control Panel to change the date order.

Relocation Project — The Project Calendar

The goal of this exercise is to be able to create a project calendar for a new schedule.

1. Continue to work with your file *Relocation.mpp*.
2. Display the following dialog: click ribbon **Project** and button **Change Working Time**. Set the working hours on the **Standard (Project Calendar)** to:
   8:00 to *12:00* and
   13:00 to *16:30*
3. Enter the following national holidays for the months August, September and October in the **Standard (Project Calendar)**. Since this project takes place in the USA, enter the following national holidays of the United States for 2012 into the project calendar. Make sure you first select the dates below and then :
   - ◇ *Labor Day*, the first Monday of September
   - ◇ *Columbus Day,* second Monday of October
   - ◇ *Veterans Day*, on November 11th, but if November 11 falls on a Saturday it is observed on the Friday before; if it falls on a Sunday, it is observed on the following Monday: Monday Nov. 12.
4. Compare your file with the solution file *03A WBS.mpp* available for download at www.ProjectProCorp.com (see page vi for the procedure to access these files).
5. Save your file.

Chapter 3 Entering the Work Breakdown Structure

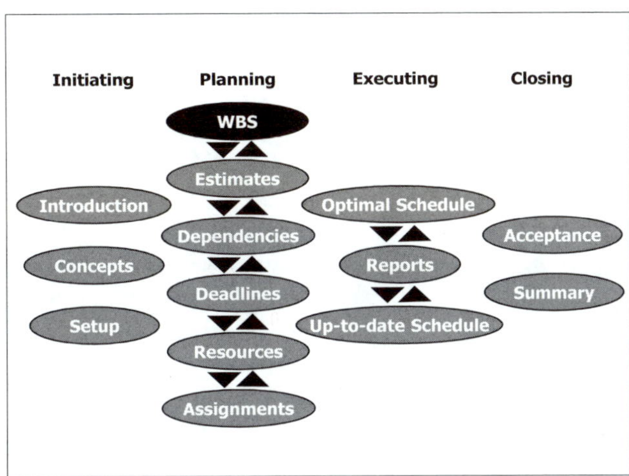

We have finished the *Initiating* column and will now begin with the *Planning* process group. The first step in Planning is entering the Work Breakdown Structure or WBS (see the black ellipse above). We recommend you enter all the schedule data in the order shown in this overview illustration: first WBS (deliverables and tasks), then estimates, dependencies, deadlines (as well as constraints and task calendars), resources and assignments as the last item.

After reading this chapter you will:

- understand what a Work Breakdown Structure (WBS) is
- understand the importance of the WBS as the foundation of the project schedule
- be able to create a WBS that is logical and hierarchical
- be able to enter and modify the WBS into MS Project
- be able to create summary tasks, detail tasks, milestones, recurring tasks and overhead tasks
- be able to apply guidelines for the formulation of the different types of tasks
- be able to establish the right level of detail in the WBS
- know how to edit, copy and move summary and detail tasks
- be able to check if a WBS reflects the best practices of scheduling

This is not What I Had in Mind…

Nob picks up the phone; it is Dan from ABC Corporation, a new client. The client says he needs a quote for "a system that handles customer inquiries". Since Nob's specialty is developing call center support databases, this looks like a request that is right up his alley. He puts a quote together for the development of a call center database and calls it "customer inquiry system". As a consultant, he knows that adopting the exact words from the client is always a smart thing to do.

Dan receives the quote from Nob and thinks it is quite reasonable. He expects a telephone answering system that will provide automated and prerecorded answers for frequently asked questions. Nob is quite pleased when Dan agrees to hire him on a fixed price basis. Nob engages system analysts and programmers to put it together. Bob asks Nob if he identified the deliverables and discussed these with the client. Nob dismisses the question with "I know what I am doing!" After working a few weeks, Nob is ready to present some first screens to the client. When the client sees the computer interface, astonishment sets in: "This is not what I had in mind…"

3

Work Breakdown Structure

The list of tasks in MS Project should contain a logical grouping. We recommend you group the activities by deliverable, because it allows you to keep a good overview of the entire project. A deliverable-oriented grouping also enables you to get good reports from MS Project, like the effort or cost by deliverable. This deliverable-oriented grouping is known as the *Work Breakdown Structure* (*WBS*). The WBS is defined in the PMBOK® Guide as *a deliverable-oriented, hierarchical decomposition of the work to be executed by the project team to accomplish the project objectives and create the required deliverables*.[12]

The WBS is very important for two main reasons:

- The WBS is the foundation of the schedule
- The WBS is an implicit contract

Time spent on your WBS is, generally, time well spent.

The WBS is the Foundation of the Schedule

The WBS is the most important component of a schedule, since all other scheduling activities need the WBS as input. In a sense, the WBS is the foundation of the schedule (see illustration); much like a building has a foundation. If the foundation is weak, the building (the schedule) will be weak; if the foundation is strong, the building (the schedule) can be strong. If the grouping in a WBS is oriented towards deliverables, the rest of the schedule can be created more easily.

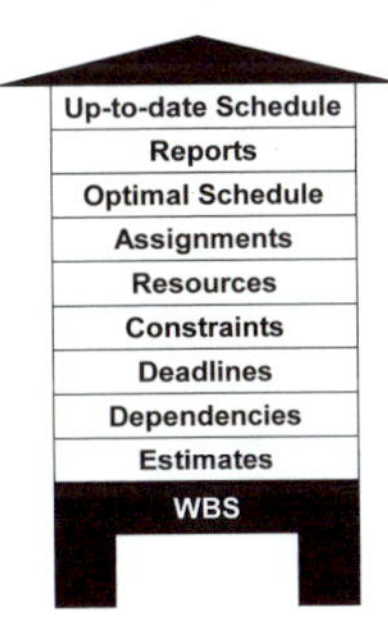

For example:

- Estimating is easier for tasks that create a well-defined deliverable.
- Dependencies are easier to find between deliverables.
- Deadlines and constraints are often agreed upon by deliverable.
- Resources are often made responsible for distinct deliverables.

---

12 See the *PMBOK® Guide*, Fourth Edition, published by the PMI.

- The optimal schedule can be found more easily. In a software development project, the client can easily find the features (deliverables) that are expensive and may have to be postponed.
- Large schedules can be kept up-to-date more easily by deliverable.

The WBS is an Implicit Contract

A second reason the WBS is the most important component of the project plan is that the WBS is a "*contract*" between:

- The project manager and the external customer, for example in consulting projects.
- The project manager and the internal executives (*project sponsor*), for example in system development projects for in-house systems.

The next illustration shows a WBS for an aircraft manufacturer:

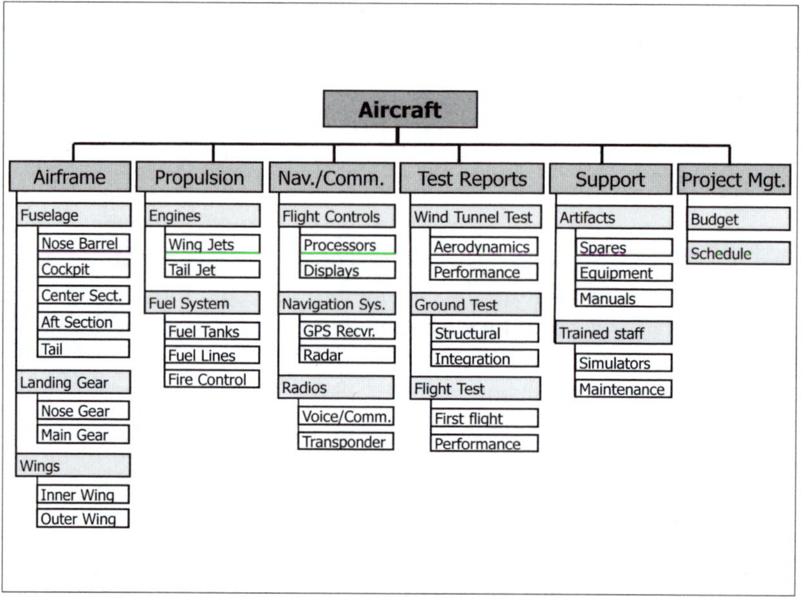

This illustration shows the *WBS* as a chart, the *WBS chart*. MS Project does not have such a view, but *WBS Chart Pro* [13] is an add-on tool you can buy that will allow you to lay out the WBS in such a graphic format. The graphic format is easy to read and

---

[13] WBS Chart Pro is available from Critical Tools, Inc. Please refer to www.CriticalTools.com.

understand for most people, because it resembles an organizational chart. Another tool called *MindManager* [14] creates a star-like chart or mind map of the WBS and also allows multiple levels of breakdown.

The *WBS* specifies explicitly what deliverables should be created. If the client requests output during project execution, the WBS should explicitly contain the output to be delivered. The *Practice Standard for Work Breakdown Structures* [15] frames this as the *100% rule*, which states that the WBS should cover 100% of the work of the scope of the project and include all interim and final deliverables to be completed, including project management deliverables. During project execution, the project team should create the deliverables as specified in the WBS.

The WBS also indicates implicitly what should NOT be done, since it will not be shown in the WBS. If it is not in the WBS, it is *out-of-scope* and you can then make a case to the client that the requested deliverable was not agreed upon. Therefore, if it is not explicitly in the WBS, it is implicitly out-of-scope. Or, as some people put it: *If it is not in the WBS, it is not in the project!*

In past projects your client may have forced you to deliver something that was never promised; this is commonly known as *scope creep*. From those projects you have probably learned to explicitly specify in the project plan which elements are out-of-scope. Otherwise you will continue to be burned by scope creep. If you expect any possible misunderstanding about the scope of the project, it is a good habit to also document the deliverables that you consider to be out-of-scope. Then you could ask the client to sign off on the WBS to make the WBS an explicit contract instead of leaving it an implicit agreement.

To capture *out-of-scope* elements use the **Notes** tool [Notes] on the **Task** ribbon or in the **Comments** field (ribbon **File**, tab **Info**, button **Project Information** on the right side of screen, item **Advanced Properties**, **Summary** tab). We recommend paying careful attention to clarifying what is in-scope and out-of-scope to manage the expectations of your client carefully and early in the life of the project. Creating a detailed WBS and out-of-scope list with your client ensures that you have had a veritable meeting of the minds with the client, the essence of a *contract*.

---

[14] MindManager is from MindJet, see www.mindjet.com.

[15] *Practice Standard for Work Breakdown Structures*, Second Edition, PMI, Newtown Square, PA, USA, 2006.

In large, expensive projects, the in-scope deliverables are often described in more detail, using several paragraphs per deliverable to convey specifications or acceptance criteria. The out-of-scope deliverables are also described in detail. Such a document is often called a *WBS-dictionary*.

In MS Project you can capture the scope of the project in the **Task Name** column by creating an indented list of deliverables and tasks, the WBS. As you can see the title of the column **Task Name** is quite misleading; it actually causes many MS Project users to enter activities only in this column, which does not make a WBS. The column should have the more appropriate title *WBS,* which will set MS Project users in the right direction. You can change the title by right-clicking on the column heading **Task Name** and clicking **Field Settings**. In the **Field Settings** dialog, you can change the **Title** of the column to **WBS**.

What Is a Deliverable?

Deliverables are the items that are handed over to internal or external clients during the project execution (*interim deliverables*) or at the end of the project (*final deliverables*). The deliverables are often broken down further into their components and eventually into tasks (activities). It is important to note that the PMBOK® Guide defines deliverables as: *Any unique and verifiable product, result, or capability to perform a service that must be produced to complete a process, phase or project.*[16]

Deliverables have three characteristics:

- **Deliverables must be verifiable.**
  A deliverable is not a deliverable if it is not verifiable or better yet, measurable. This means that by incorporating deliverables into the WBS and formulating them properly, you create verifiability in the project. You basically clarify what you are going to produce. When you ask your client to sign off on the WBS, you have established how both parties can verify if the contract has been completed. This will decrease misunderstandings early in the project that become fatal near the end. Misunderstandings typically result in nasty disputes near or after the end of the project, and, when you are a contractor they result in litigation.
- **Deliverables must have a client**
  Deliverables are always handed off to either internal clients within your organization or external clients outside your organization, hence the word deliver-able. For example, a company that designs and manufactures hard drives may produce design

[16] *PMBOK® Guide*, Fourth Edition, published by the PMI.

documents that need to be delivered and reviewed by engineers as the internal customers. There may be test reports that need to be delivered and reviewed by quality control as the internal client. The company may never share these interim deliverables with their external customers that buy the hard drives. However, because there is an internal client who demands that the interim deliverables be created, the design documents and test reports are essential deliverables in the new product development project. The resulting hard drive is a final deliverable that will be handed off to external customers.

- **Deliverables must be of value to the client.**
  If a deliverable does not have value for its client, it should not be created, or, if it is a waste product, the creation of this waste should be minimized. There are many other side-products that are not necessarily of value; they should not be deliverables in the WBS. For example, project team members may produce waste that is of no value to the customer and, therefore, not a deliverable.

According to its definition, a WBS is supposed to be deliverable-oriented. You may not be used to thinking in terms of *deliverables*, and sometimes it is difficult to identify the deliverables in a project. However, if you put some effort into finding the deliverables, you will be surprised how easy it is once you begin. For example, consider an office relocation project and ask yourself: *What are the deliverables in this project?* Better yet, ask yourself: *What will my customer or sponsor expect to receive?* You will find that the new location, the lease contract, the remodel contract, the remodeled location and the moved materials are deliverables in this project.

Deliverables versus Phases

When people have difficulty identifying deliverables, they often group the tasks in *phases*. Phases are distinct periods in the life of a project, a much vaguer concept than deliverables. Vagueness does not help us control projects. Phases are merely time-oriented groupings of tasks that do not necessarily provide verifiability as deliverables do. People may use phases either because they find phases easier or because phases provide chronology at the same time as grouping. Establishing chronology is a separate project management activity that comes later than creating the WBS. At this point, we are just breaking down the work logically. A WBS should be a *logical breakdown*, not a *chronological breakdown*. After the WBS is complete, the sequencing and scheduling of activities can start and then we will introduce the time dimension.

There is another reason to stay away from chronological breakdowns. There are many iterative processes in the practice of projects. Iterative processes repeat themselves with steps of progressive elaboration. For example, a requirements document is created during the requirements phase, refined to detailed requirements in the analysis phase, and finalized in the development phase. A chronological orientation in a WBS will tie your brain in a knot when you deal with iterative processes. In a deliverable-oriented breakdown you simply add one (interim) deliverable for each iteration, for example *summary requirements document*, *detail requirements document*, and *final requirements document*.

Small Projects: Phases or Deliverables?

In small projects we recommend creating a deliverable-oriented WBS rather than a phase-oriented WBS. Particularly in IT project schedules, we find too often only phases and no deliverables. As per the PMI definition, a WBS with only phases and activities without deliverables is not a WBS. A deliverable-oriented WBS is often clearer to all and establishes verifiability. A deliverable-oriented WBS has activities that are focused on producing interim deliverables or components of the final project product. Deliverables are often tangible and are easier to assign to teams than phases. An office relocation project could be broken down into phases or into deliverables, as shown in the illustration. In most projects you can do either, and we then recommend using the deliverable-oriented breakdown rather than the phase-oriented breakdown. You can convert a phase into a deliverable by asking: *What is the result of this phase?* or: *What do we expect to have in our hands at the end of this phase?* The answer to this question will lead you to the deliverable.

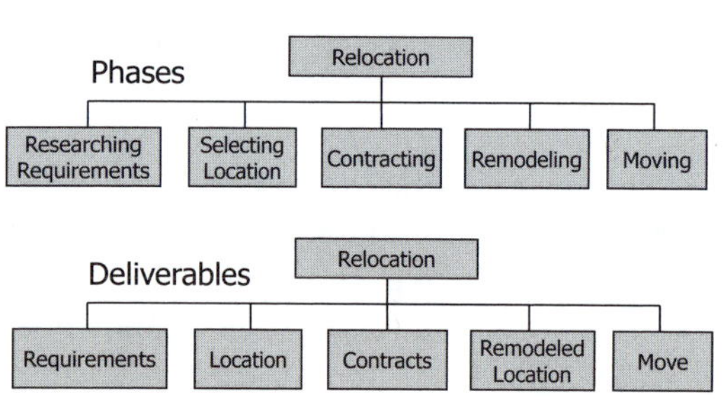

Deliverables provide more direction to the team; they help the team members focus on what to create. Imagine you were made responsible for either *researching requirements* or for delivering the *list of requirements* in the office relocation project. The latter is a concrete deliverable; it is verifiable and therefore creates a firmer commitment. Imagine you are subcontracting work; it is better to have a subcontractor commit to delivering a thing rather than doing something without a specific end result. Deliverables specify the end result better than phases. If you commit a subcontractor to a phase, you may end up with nothing, because you did not ask for a deliverable. If that is true for a subcontractor, it is true for your project team members as well.

Using a deliverable-oriented WBS also makes it easier to identify and formulate milestones. Deliverables typically have an event associated with them, such as when the deliverable is *completed*, *handed over*, *sent*, *published*, *received*, *signed off* or *approved*. You simply capture the (most important) event by inserting it as a milestone. Examples of milestones are *requirements summarized, report ready*, *preliminary design accepted* and *document delivered*. As you can see, they all refer to a deliverable. You typically create one milestone for each deliverable, which is a best practice.

Large Projects: Phases and Deliverables!

In large projects, you often see that the first breakdown level is phases, which are broken down into deliverables on the next level. The *WBS* then contains both phases and deliverables on level 1 and level 2 respectively. This is still a deliverable-oriented breakdown, because there are deliverables in the WBS. In a large project, you do not need to do away with the phases specified in your project life-cycle or methodology. You just have to add at least two deliverables subordinated to each phase to arrive at a "real" WBS, as shown in the next illustration (note: RTM means *release to manufacturing*):

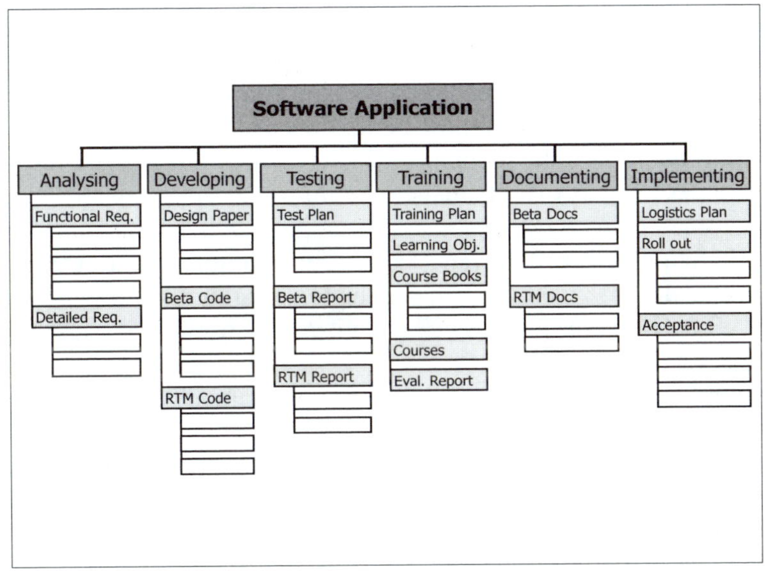

Mega projects can have the following levels and still be deliverable-oriented: phases (level 1), product components (level 2), subcomponents (level 3), interim and final deliverables (level 4) and activities (level 5). Some branches may have fewer levels, but they still need to contain deliverables!

We have often received schedules that use the *PMBOK® process groups* as the phases: initiating, planning, executing, monitoring & controlling and closing. These phases apply to any type of project and provide a good base structure for the phases as long as:

- At least two deliverables are added to each phase! If this is difficult, remove the phases and keep the deliverables.
- The orientation toward chronology does not make it difficult to find the deliverables on the next breakdown level. If it does, please remove the phases and keep the deliverables.

Benefits of a Deliverable-Oriented WBS

Summarizing the previous discussions, there are important benefits of a deliverable-oriented WBS:

- Deliverables are measurable and provide verifiability. They enhance your control of your project. The WBS is like a contract between you, as the project manager, and the sponsor that funds the project. It tells the sponsor explicitly what will be delivered, and implicitly what will not.
- Deliverables focus the project team members: they are directed toward producing things of value that will be delivered to real people as clients. These clients can be internal or external to the organization. If an activity is not contributing to an agreed upon deliverable, it should not be done. Those activities are hobby activities that should be kept out of the project.
- Deliverables provide extra management information that supports solid decision-making by the sponsor. For example, the deliverables in a software development project are the new features or functions of the software. In a feature-oriented WBS, management will see the total duration, effort and cost of each new feature. This helps executives make decisions as to which feature will go into the next release.
- Deliverables make it easier to assign responsibilities that are clear and verifiable. If you assign the responsibility for a deliverable to a person or department, you have a verifiable assignment, because the deliverable is verifiable.
- Deliverables make it easier to identify dependencies. The dependency between the deliverables *architectural drawing of the foundation* and creating the *foundation of the building* is clear. It is clearer than between the phases *designing* and *constructing* that may overlap and may even have circular dependencies.

Breaking Down the Work

In the top-down approach, you enter the deliverables first and then you determine all the tasks needed to accomplish the deliverables. In the bottom-up approach, you brainstorm the tasks together with your team and then you group them under their deliverables. Each deliverable becomes a summary task.

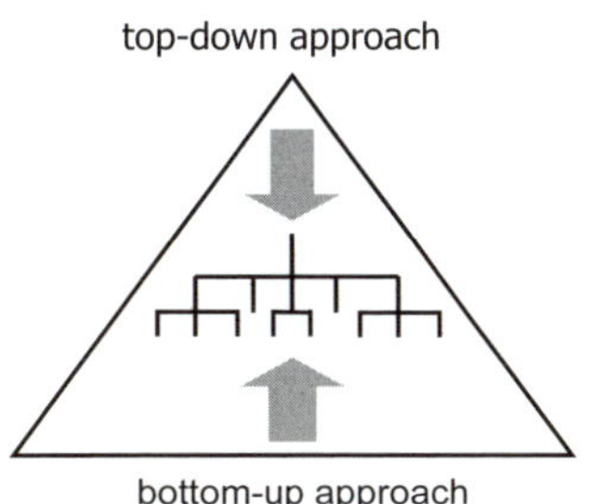

The two opposite approaches can lead to the same result. A person who is a novice at the type of project often prefers the bottom-up method. An experienced project manager usually takes the top-down approach. It requires experience to start from the top-down. Either approach can be successful; there is no one best way.

A WBS as a Logical Hierarchy

While breaking down the work, it is important to keep in mind that the *WBS* should be a *logical hierarchy*. You can check if a WBS is a true logical hierarchy with the following checks.[17] You can perform these checks by expanding the outline structure to the right level using the **Outline** button on the **View** ribbon. The checks are:

- There should be more than one level in the WBS.
  A hierarchy is only a hierarchy if it has multiple levels.
- The most important items are on the highest level.
  The importance of an item determines its level in the WBS. Generally speaking, the importance decreases from the project product to phases, to deliverables and finally, tasks. In an organizational chart, levels reflect importance: the higher the level, the greater the importance of the individual. Similarly in a WBS, the more important an item is, the higher its level should be in the WBS.
- Within each branch there should be at least two items on each level.
  If there is only one item on a level within a branch, it should be removed and merged with the higher level since it is not necessary. You may have to reword the item you keep and make sure you keep the deliverable rather than the phase.

---

[17] These checks have been adapted from the *Practice Standard for Work Breakdown Structures*, Second Edition, PMI, USA, 2006.

- There should be no duplication or logical overlap between items.
  If there are duplications or logical overlaps between phases, deliverables or activities, then the WBS does not have a logical breakdown. Simply put, there cannot be two items that are similar or the same or two deliverables that are essentially the same. You should remove the logical overlaps from the WBS. Of course, there can be a time overlap (*chronological* overlap) between phases in the schedule.
- Each group of sub items should capture all the work of its summary item (top-down check and *100% rule*).[18]
  The final project product breaks down into all its component and interim deliverables. The list of deliverables should be complete. Each deliverable breaks down into all the activities that create it. It should be as easy for project team members as: *If I do all the listed activities, I will have the deliverable in my hands as a result*. We recommend this top-down check particularly if you used the bottom-up approach to create the WBS. You can easily forget a deliverable or a detail task needed to create a deliverable. Use your project team effectively to catch those missing items; many pairs of eyes see more than just one pair. Check if you have listed all deliverables and if each deliverable will be completed when all its activities are done (top-down check).
- Each lowest-level item should have a logical relationship with its higher-level items on every higher level of the hierarchy (bottom-up check).
  For example, each activity needs to contribute to a deliverable, and each deliverable needs to contribute to the final project product in a logical relationship.
  We recommend bottom-up check particularly if you used the top-down approach to create the WBS. Sometimes engineers and programmers have great ideas and start to create wonderful little things that were not solicited by the sponsor or client. Check if all activities have a logical relationship with all their higher-level items (bottom-up check).

An *organizational chart* is a better known example of a logical hierarchy than a WBS. For an organizational chart, a logical hierarchy means that an organization should have multiple levels with the most important person at the top. Nobody should be left out of an organizational chart. You will not find one person in two different positions, and you will not find subordinates who do not report to anybody.

---

[18] *Practice Standard for Work Breakdown Structures*, Second Edition, PMI, Newtown Square, PA, USA, 2006.

However, a WBS should not follow the lines of an organization. Do not break down the project work by *functional group*.[19] Eventually, the *Responsibility Assignment Matrix* will assign deliverables to functional groups. Again, this is a different project management activity which is done later than creating the WBS.

From WBS Chart to WBS List

MS Project expects you to create an indented list in the *Task Name* column (Note that its underlying field name is *Name*). The *WBS chart* has to be converted to an indented list of tasks. The next illustration shows how the chart is converted to an indented list. The chart is rotated 90 degrees and the lower levels then become indentation levels. The add-on tool mentioned before, *WBS Chart Pro,* does this automatically for you.

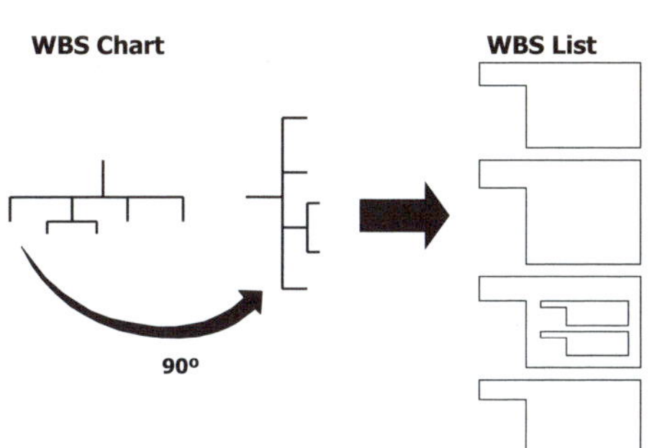

We recommend you use the Gantt Chart view for creating the WBS, because you can create and see the levels of the breakdown structure. The hierarchical levels are shown through indentation of the tasks in the list. The farther indented to the right, the lower the level of the task, and the less important the item is. To switch to the Gantt Chart click ribbon **View**, button **Gantt Chart**.

[19] This important point was made by Frank Walker, TWG Project Management, LLC.

Choosing the Options

To set the options that relate to the WBS and tasks, click ribbon **File**, Options and click on the tab of the dialog box indicated in the table below where to change settings:

Tab	Option
Schedule	Section **Scheduling options for this project:** **New tasks created: Manually Scheduled** or **Auto Scheduled**; see page 96. Use **Manually Scheduled** if you create a draft or high-level schedule. If you create a detailed schedule use **Auto Scheduled**. **Default task type** Many people enter the duration immediately. [20] If you do this, we recommend setting this option to **Fixed Duration**. If you normally enter **Work** estimates, we recommend **Fixed Work** as the default task type. In this way you protect the estimates you enter. It is the default task type for new tasks you create. On a task-by-task basis you can still decide what type serves you best and switch the task **Type** to it (see page 96 for the how-to) ☐ **New tasks are effort driven** This option changes the number of resources assigned (*assignment units*); we recommend you turn it off for **Fixed Duration** and **Fixed Units** tasks. It functions like **Fixed Work** tasks, and we recommend you use that task type instead. **Fixed Work** tasks are by definition effort-driven and have this option always on. See page 375 for a detailed discussion on task types and effort driven.
Advanced	Section **Edit**: ☑ **Allow cell drag and drop** This allows you to move or copy the selected cells by dragging the selected area by its border. With this option on, you can quickly re-arrange your WBS by dragging tasks (see page 149 for the how-to). This option is global across all your schedules.

[20] The *PMBOK® Guide*, Fourth Edition, published by the PMI has *Activity Duration Estimating* as one of the core planning processes after all.

Categories of Tasks

If you analyze an indented list of tasks, you will find that a standard building block or module recurs. The module consists of a summary task (the deliverable) with its detail tasks and a milestone indented. The summary task summarizes the cost, work and duration of all its sub-tasks. That is where the name *Summary task* originates. [21] These standard modules can even be nested inside one another, thus creating the next indentation level, as the illustration also shows. The indentation level is captured in the field *Outline Level*. The first level is called *outline level 1*; the next indentation is *outline level 2*, etcetera.

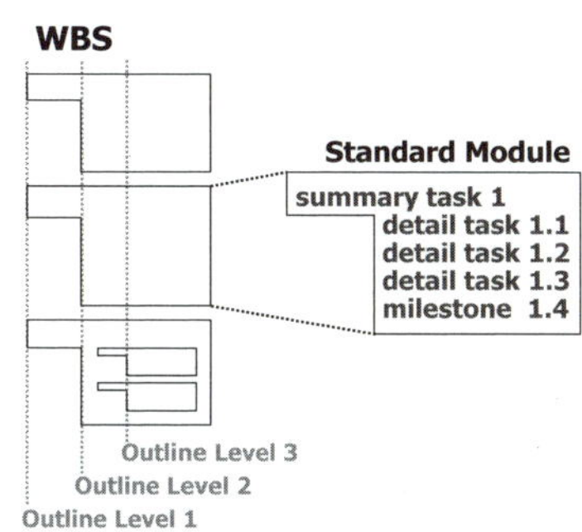

Build your plan in a modular way and use the following standard module of tasks. Your WBS will consist of several of these standard modules:

Standard Module	Example
Summary task 1	1. Report
Detail task 1.1	1.1 Gather data
Detail task 1.2	1.2 Categorize data
Detail task 1.3	1.3 Write report
Milestone 1.4	1.4 Report ready

Please note that most project managers indent the milestones on the same level as the detail tasks. The milestone relates to its deliverable, and should be subordinated just like other detail tasks.

[21] The term "*summary task*" is not a very fortunate choice of words, because a summary task is seldom a task (activity), but more likely a deliverable or phase. The term "*detail task*" is similarly flawed; detail tasks can also be milestones that are events instead of tasks.

We will now discuss the categories of tasks in more detail:

- **Project summary task**
  The project summary task is a special case of summary task, because it summarizes the entire project, displaying the project duration, total cost and total effort (**Work**). It can be toggled on and off in task views by clicking the **Format** ribbon and selecting [✓ Project Summary Task]. The project summary task will always have ID number 0 (zero), and its **Task Name** text is exactly the same as stored in the ribbon **File**, tab **Info**, list **Project Information**, item **Advanced Properties**, tab **Summary**, field **Title** and vice versa. The data are always the same in both places.
- **Summary task**
  Summary tasks are tasks with lower level subtasks. To make a plan better understood by stakeholders, it is recommended that you group detail tasks and give each group a label that summarizes it. Summary tasks are often deliverables that give the list a logical and hierarchical structure.

  MS Project will sum the cost and effort from the detail tasks up to their summary tasks. MS Project summarizes the duration of the detail tasks as well, but not through addition. For example, suppose a deliverable has two detail tasks that are scheduled in parallel. One task has a duration of 5 days, the other 8 days in parallel. The summary task of the deliverable would indicate a duration of 8 days. The summary task duration is the time span of its subordinate detail tasks. MS Project determines the summary duration and fills it in for each **Auto Scheduled** summary task. It is a *calculated field* that you cannot change. For **Manually Scheduled** summary tasks you can enter a duration.
- **Detail tasks**
  A detail task is the opposite of a summary task. A detail task is any task that does not have lower level subtasks indented beneath it. *Detail Tasks* or *Activities* are the items that you would typically assign to resources. Detail tasks are, by definition, on the lowest level of the *WBS*. We use the terms *detail task* and *activity* interchangeably in this book.
- **Milestones**
  A milestone is any important event in your schedule. Milestones are often evaluation points or critical points that executives and clients monitor closely. Often, a milestone is the event of handing off a deliverable. A milestone has a zero duration; it is an event at a point in time, not an activity. [22] As a general rule of thumb, we recommend you enter at least one *milestone* for each deliverable and one milestone

---

[22] You can mark tasks with non-zero durations as "*milestones*" also. This creates hard-to-explain gaps between task bars in the timescale. We recommend you use *lag* on dependencies instead (see page 240).

among the detail tasks of each deliverable summary task. Most people will indent the milestone on the same level as the detail tasks of the deliverable.

Even though as practitioners we make the distinction between *summary tasks*, *detail tasks* and *milestones*, MS Project simply expects that we enter all of these different items in the field called *Task Name*. This label misleads some people to think that you should only enter tasks in this field, and not phases, deliverables or milestones.

Styles of Task Bars

Each category of task has a distinctive shape and color in the timescale of the Gantt views. The illustration on the left shows the different task *bar styles*. You can change the shape and color of the task bars through ribbon **Format**, button **Format**, item **Bar Styles** or by right-clicking in the timescale pane of the Gantt Chart. This dialog shows the appearance of the bars in the current view. MS Project has other types of task bars: split task bars and recurring task bars. In a split task bar, the task has extra stop and resume dates connected with dots. Recurring task bars have many splits without the dots (see the illustration).

Some more remarks:

- *Summary task bar*
  A summary task bar indicates its start and end point with small, hanging triangles. Notice that the **Auto Scheduled** summary task bar starts when its first detail task starts, and it ends when its last detail task (or milestone) ends.
- *Detail task bar*

  Manually scheduled task bars have either washed out ends or square brackets: [to indicate the start date and] to indicate the end date. An **Auto Scheduled** detail task bar is shown as a simple bar with rounded ends. The length of a detail task bar represents its estimated duration.
- *Milestone diamond*
  Auto Scheduled milestones appear as black diamonds and figure prominently in the Gantt Chart. **Manually Scheduled** milestones are gray (without dates or *unscheduled*) or blue when they have dates (*scheduled*). Milestones have a zero duration.
- *Split task bars*
  A split task bar has multiple parts connected by dots. The work on a split task bar is

scheduled to be interrupted and resumed at a later date. For example, when electricians wire a building, they have to come back to install the switch plates after the inspection. Another example is when a resource has to interrupt work on a task to attend a one-day meeting. Splits are often not planned, but occur when you update your schedule during execution. In fact, we would like to discourage you from splitting task bars during *planning*, since splits typically need to be rescheduled constantly (the meeting does not move, but the rest of the tasks do). As a result, planned splits often require too much maintenance of your schedule.

- *Recurring task bars*
  Recurring task bars have multiple parts that occur at a regular interval. Recurring tasks are useful to model things you do regularly, such as *team status meetings*, *schedule updates*, *change request reviews* and *status reports*. Recurring tasks are in fact summary tasks with detail tasks indented beneath (see page 141). Recurring tasks are often used to capture overhead tasks (see page 143).

Formulation of the WBS Elements

Pay attention to the wording you choose for each *WBS element*:

- *Summary task*
  Summary tasks can be deliverables or phases:
  - Deliverables: We recommend you use *nouns* for *deliverables*, for example *location* or *design*. A noun is any word in the English language that you can put "*the*" in front of. You can also add a descriptive word (adjective) to improve the measurability of deliverables. This is desirable because it adds precision, such as the *signed contract* rather than *contract* or the *final design* rather than *design*.
  - Phases: We recommend you use a verb in the *present continuous tense* (*-ing*) for phases. This tense best indicates that something is ongoing for a period of time, which is typical of phases. Examples are *Researching* or *Remodeling*.
- *Detail tasks*
  We recommend you use verbs for detail tasks. The preferred tense for the verb is the *present tense*. The present tense indicates action, and that is exactly what you want, because you will delegate detail tasks to your team members. Examples are *discuss with publisher*, *code universal logon feature* or *purchase equipment*. As you can see a detail task is in fact an instruction, order or command. To some tasks you will not assign resources, like *drying of paint*, or you may assign groups of people, like *training*. These tasks are *fixed duration* tasks and often have the *–ing* ending
- *Milestones*
  Typically, the milestone is expressed as follows:
  < deliverable> <past perfect tense verb>
  where *< deliverable>* is a noun that describes the deliverable, and the *<past perfect tense verb>* describes what is supposed to happen to the deliverable at that

point in time. We recommend the *past perfect tense* for milestones that typically has an *-ed* ending in English, for example: *delivered, accepted, completed, done, sent, shipped* and *finished*. Alternatively, you could use the word *ready* to indicate completion, as in *report ready*. Or you could use the word *sign-off* as in *requirements sign-off*.
Examples of well-formulated milestones are *module completed, server installed, printer delivered* or *report accepted*.

3

- *Recurring tasks*
Recurring tasks will become summary tasks in MS Project. We recommend using plural *nouns* for recurring tasks when they reflect recurring deliverables, for example *schedule updates*, *change request reviews* and *status reports*. The plural indicates there is more than one. You could also use *present tense* verbs to capture recurring tasks when they are activities. Examples are: *review change requests, meet with team, meet with sponsor* or *meet with steering committee*.

A few more general guidelines:

- When you apply these guidelines, it is important that you apply them consistently throughout the entire WBS. We sometimes find that schedulers lose their consistency halfway through building their WBS.
- Avoid overusing acronyms.
If you do use an acronym, please spell it out the first time you use it, so the reader knows what the letters stand for as they are repeated throughout the schedule. Otherwise, the schedule can be too cryptic to understand. We also recommend use of uppercase for acronyms to make them stand out as acronyms, so there can be no confusion as to whether, for example, *prepare bad report* is an instruction to prepare a report of poor quality or a report for *Ballistic Aerodynamic Deflection*. Explanation of acronyms is particularly important if you work with subcontractors and consultants.
- Keep the task names concise.
2010 Task names can become very long when you try to incorporate instructions to team members. Instead, capture detailed instructions to team members using the **Notes** field. If one task name is much longer than other ones, Project 2010 will wrap the long task name onto two lines automatically by increasing the height of its row.

You may think to yourself, *Why should I follow these guidelines? Why can't I call the items whatever I want?* If you do follow the simple guidelines we explained, you will ensure that your WBS will be clear to your team members and any other stakeholders. Your team members may not have been schooled in our profession of project management and, therefore, need this simplicity. Furthermore, your WBS will be the part of the project plan that you share first and often with stakeholders. We recommend you make it is as clear as it can be for people who may not be subject matter experts.

Sharper Formulation of Deliverables

The deliverables are supposed to create *measurability* and *verifiability* in the project schedule. This is where project management becomes an art, because capturing deliverables in a few words and in such a way that they also reflect essential acceptance criteria is truly an art. We have found that most schedules can be greatly improved in this respect. It is challenging to align the expectations of all project stakeholders — sponsor, team members, final users of the project product, and so forth. A properly formulated WBS that is approved by all stakeholders is the best guarantee that alignment has been achieved. It can only be achieved when the deliverables are formulated as specifically as possible.

The following are examples of "deliverables" we found in real-life schedules (in the left column) and our suggestions for a tighter formulation (in the right column) of deliverables that are easier to verify on completion:

Ambiguously formulated deliverable	**Verifiable, measurable deliverable**
closing	customer approval of the project product
subcontracting	signed contract
moving to new location	operational new location
renovation	renovated facility
planning	approved project plan
material procurement	procured construction materials
prototype development	developed prototype
training	300 trained application users
staff	50 newly hired staff members
implementation	new workstations operational for entire team

The Right Level of Detail

One of the biggest challenges in breaking down the work is finding the appropriate level of detail. The WBS should have neither too little detail nor too much! In the illustration the right level is the bold lines on the middle levels. Notice that they are not necessarily on one particular level in the WBS. If one deliverable is bigger than others, this deliverable ends up with extra levels, as you can see in the middle of the illustration. Finding the right level of detail for each deliverable is an art for the project manager.

Adding levels generally improves the accuracy of the estimates; however, a larger WBS also requires more work from the project manager to update the schedule during project execution. If updating your schedule takes an hour every day, you will probably decide to go home instead of slaving on your schedule in the early evening after some weeks. Finding the right level of detail in your WBS and project schedule will help you keep your schedule alive during project execution when you are very busy. Only 30% of the over 1,000 schedules we evaluated were up-to-date, so this is a big issue.

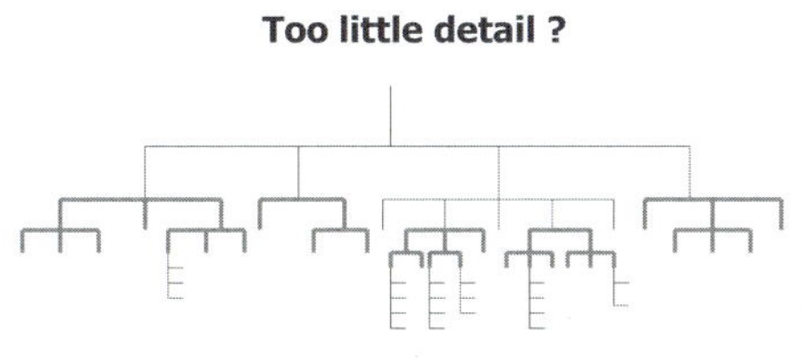

Here are some guidelines for determining if you have found the right level of detail.[23] Remember: the term *detail tasks* as we use it refers to the items on the lowest level in the WBS.

Too Little Detail?

If you think you have a schedule that does not have enough levels, ask yourself the following questions while you go through your *WBS*:

- Is it clear how the *deliverable* will be created and what the activities involved are?
  If you answer *no* to this question, you may need to add activities as detail tasks, especially if you plan on delegating to team members.
- Can I *estimate* the duration, effort and cost of the detail tasks?
  If you find estimating too hard without breaking the detail tasks down into smaller tasks, you should break them down.
- Can I find the *dependencies* between the detail tasks?
  Dependencies are links between tasks that capture how they affect each other. The concept of dependencies is abstract; however, finding the dependencies is easy once you have found the right level of detail. In order to set the dependencies, you may have to add another level of detail tasks. Each detail task will end up being a node in a network of dependencies.
- Can I *assign* the detail task to somebody?
  Eventually we will assign each detail task to a resource. If you cannot assign an activity to an individual, you may have too little detail in the WBS.

---

[23] For more guidelines, see the *Practice Standard for Work Breakdown Structures*, Second Edition, PMI, 2006.

Too Much Detail?

If you think you may have a WBS that is too detailed, ask yourself the following questions while you go through the list of tasks:

- Is this item contributing to a deliverable of value that someone will be looking for?
  If it is not, get rid of it while you can. If you do not eliminate it now, team members may be wasting their time on it. Worst of all, you will be updating it and waste your own time.
- Is this line item merely a *reminder* to myself?
  A WBS is not meant to be your external memory support. A WBS is supposed to capture tasks with significant effort involved. For example, a reminder that you need to refresh your password is not meant to become an item in the WBS. Reminders can be entered in the **Notes** field by selecting the task and clicking the button [Notes] on the **Task** ribbon.
- Is this line item a *to-do list item* or a real task that will take significant effort?
  If the items do not take much time or effort, you have not created a WBS, but a to-do list. To-do items are what you list on a sheet of paper at the start of the day to organize your work for that day, for example, call Fred at 3 o'clock. Some to-do items may only take 5 minutes. To-do items can best be managed by using the to-do list feature in *Outlook 2010*. In Outlook 2010, click ribbon **View**, button **To-Do Bar**, and item **Normal**. A sidebar appears on the right that allows you to create to-do list items. Outlook 2010 will allow you to:
  - Mark items completed and automatically move items you did not get done to tomorrow.
  - Attach other things: due dates, reminders, files or email messages.
  - Flag items and personalize the meaning of the flags.
  - Assign to-do items to other people and request a status report.
- Is this line item an *acceptance criterion*?
  We recommend you transfer acceptance criteria to the **Notes** field using [Notes] on the **Task** ribbon. *Acceptance criteria* are typically captured in a checklist format and belong in the notes. The task name could then be instead: *complete checklist*.
- Will I continue to update all these detail tasks even when I am busy during project execution?
  If you think you may not be able to update all the tasks during the busy executing of the project, this is the time to roll small ones up into higher level tasks, or remove them from the WBS.
- Do I have at least two subtasks for each summary task?
  If you have only one subtask under a summary task you can leave it out, since you are only restating what the summary task does. Each breakdown level within a branch should have at least two items. On average, each summary task should have

5 to 7 detail tasks. Psychologists have figured out that most people have difficulties processing lists that are longer than nine items.[24]

We recommend keeping your schedule lean and mean! Remember, scheduling is modeling, which deliberately simplifies the reality of the project. Only by doing so will you be able to keep the schedule alive as a forecasting model during the hectic *execution* of the project.

Not Longer Than a Reporting Period

Detail task durations should not be longer than one reporting period. [25] For example, if you report the status of your project every week, your reporting period is one week and detail task durations should have a maximum of one week. If detail tasks are no longer than a reporting period, you will quickly notice when a task is out-of-control because it will be reported as in-progress in two consecutive status meetings. As a project manager you know that, if a task is still in progress in the second status meeting, there is a problem that requires your immediate attention.

The 1%-10% Rule

We created another guideline that we call the *1%-10% rule*. The duration of any lowest-level task should be between a minimum and a maximum duration. The minimum duration is 1% of the project duration. The maximum is 10% of the project duration.

For example, if you have a project that you think will take 3 months, you can immediately calculate the right level of detail for all duration estimates. Three months is about 60 business days. The minimum duration is 1% of 60 days or 0.6 day, which we round off to 0.5 day. Detail tasks should not last less than half a day. If they are smaller, lump them together into larger tasks. The maximum is 10% of 60 or 6 days, which we round off to one week. Detail tasks have to be one week or less in duration. Thus, in a 3-month project, all detail tasks should have a duration between 0.5 day and 5 days.

You can easily find the project duration by:
Clicking ribbon **Project**, button **Project Information** and clicking Statistics...,

---

[24] Miller, G. A. (1956). "*The magical number seven, plus or minus two: Some limits on our capacity for processing information*". Psychological Review 63 (2): 81–97
[25] Contribution from Frank Walker, TWG Project Management, LLC.

OR
Viewing the **Duration** field of the project summary task. You can display the project summary task by clicking ribbon **Format** and selecting ☑ Project Summary Task. This task will appear at the top of the list as a task with ID number 0.

If you find tasks that are longer than 10% of the project, you can:

- Check if the resources are working part-time on it. If you can change their involvement into full-time, the duration will decrease. See page 514 for the how-to.
- Split the task into multiple subtasks. See page 446 for detailed steps.

The beauty of this 1%-10% rule is that it can be applied to projects of any size or duration, unlike other published guidelines for the size of *work packages*. Other authors suggest a maximum of 40 or 80 hours for each work package as a guideline. This is an absolute guideline that is not universally applicable, because a fast-track, one-week project would not be helped by this guideline. We believe the 1%-10% rule has a more universal applicability.

There are some exceptions to the 1%-10% rule. We recommend you do not apply it to the following items:

- *Summary tasks*
- *Overhead tasks* (*level of effort tasks*)
- *Recurring detail tasks*
- *Milestones*
- Tasks in high-level schedules that are only created to estimate duration and cost of the whole project in order to gain approval for the project.

Notice that the 1%-10% rule should only be applied to durations and not to work (effort) values. If there are many part-time assignments, the range for work estimates should be narrower. If there are many multiple assignments per task, the boundaries should be wider. The range for work values is harder to indicate, which is why we stayed away from that.

Why Is the Right Level of Detail Important?

The rationale behind finding the right level of detail is to create enough checkpoints for monitoring and controlling the progress of the project. *Systems theory* tells us that we need a certain number of feedback loops to control a process. As project managers, we need many feedback loops with our team to control a project. For the client or sponsor, we recommend a minimum of ten feedback loops.

3

In the ten-period project shown in the illustration, the first status report often becomes available halfway through the second status period. If the report shows a problem, the client would suggest that an action must be taken. You will take the action in the rest of the second period, and you will likely see the results of this corrective action appear in the third period. The report on the third period becomes available in the fourth period. Consequently, problems in the first period will be visibly corrected for the client or sponsor only in the fourth period. There is always a delay in determining the problem, taking action and seeing the result of the action. If you have ten *checkpoints,* clients really only have approximately six *manage-points* before the project is supposed to be finished. You need, therefore, a safe number of reporting periods. Creating at least ten formal feedback loops seems like a good norm when dealing with clients or sponsors.

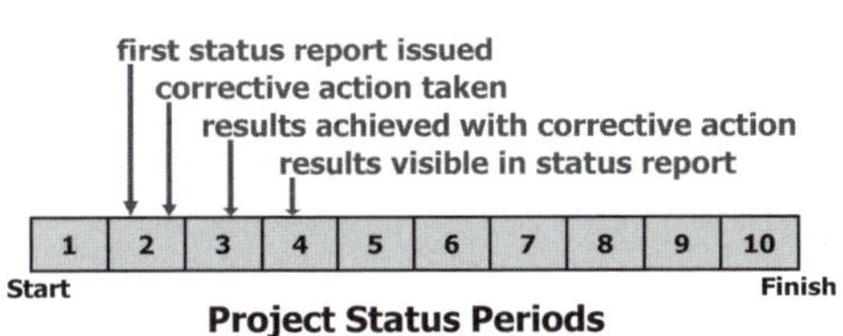

Executives and clients tend to get too nervous when you do not give them enough visibility on your project. You need to give them opportunities to make a difference. If executives or clients do not have enough visibility on your project, they will come and get the information they need. As a result they will start micro-managing you (as the project manager).

Of course, successful project managers make sure they have at least 1,000 manage-points with their team members, and they stay in touch with their team constantly. Good project managers know the status of their project at any time; you can ask them for it 24 hours a day, 7 days a week. (Do not call them at 3AM though!) Successful project managers continuously check up with their team and do much communication while walking around. This increases the number of feedback loops dramatically and thus the chance for successful completion of the project. Successful project managers do not use their own status reports to find out what is happening in their project. Those who do will not be successful.

Entering Tasks

We will discuss how to enter the different elements of a *WBS* into the Gantt Chart view on the pages indicated:

- Summary tasks (see below)
- Detail tasks (see page 139)
- Milestones (see page 140)
- Recurring tasks (see page 141)
- Overhead tasks (see page 143)

Notice that Project 2010 will automatically wrap the task name and increase the row height when the task name you enter or paste exceeds the width of the **Task Name** field; if you increase the column width, it will decrease the row height again. Great feature!

Entering Summary Tasks

For summary tasks enter only the name, since most other fields are calculated. Summary tasks summarize their subtasks in terms of duration, work and cost. By default, summary tasks are **Auto Scheduled** as shown by the icon in the **Task Mode** field.

1. Switch to **Gantt Chart:** click ribbon **View** and click the  portion of Gantt Chart.
2. Click on the cell in the **Task Name** column where you want to enter the name of the summary task.
3. Type the name of the summary task. If the summary task is a deliverable, it is preferably formulated with a *noun*. You can insert an adjective in front of it to reveal the most important acceptance criterion for the deliverable, for example *signed contract* instead of just *contract*. If the one adjective is not enough, use Notes on the **Task** ribbon (or double-click on the task) to add more explicit acceptance criteria.
4. Press Enter to go to the next summary task. The task will only become a real summary task when you indent detail tasks below it.

The name is normally the only thing you need to enter for summary tasks. A summary task will only start summarizing when a task is indented on the next row. At that time it will also get its characteristic task bar .

Inserting a Summary Task for a Set of Tasks

Project 2010 has a new feature that allows you to create a summary task for a set of tasks. This is helpful when you do bottom-up planning and you are ready to start entering deliverables for all activities you have brainstormed.

1. Select the set of contiguous tasks in the Gantt Chart for which you want to create a new summary task.
2. Click ribbon **Task** and find the section **Insert**.
3. Click 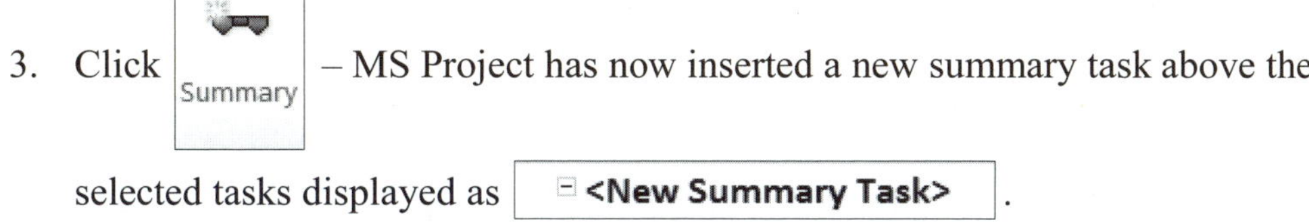 Summary – MS Project has now inserted a new summary task above the selected tasks displayed as <New Summary Task> .
4. Type the summary task name overriding **<New Summary Task>**.

Entering Detail Tasks

For detail tasks you typically enter the task name and the duration estimate. We will discuss estimating in more detail in the next chapter.

1. To insert a new row for a detail task in the Gantt Chart, click on any cell in the row before which you want to insert a new task (row).
2. Press Ins or click ribbon **Task** and find its section **Insert** and click .
3. Enter the **Task Name** – make sure you use a *present tense* verb for activities.
4. Decide in the **Task Mode** field if want to make the task **Auto Scheduled** or leave it to be **Manually Scheduled** , see page 96 for an explanation of both.
5. Press Tab to go to its **Duration** field and enter an estimate and press Tab. See the next chapter for more on estimating.
6. If necessary, indent it under its summary task by clicking (**Indent Task**) on the **Task** ribbon.

We recommend you list the tasks in their chronological order where possible; however, do not force this ranking because you will always have difficulties with tasks that are meant to be done in parallel, for example *train staff in software* and *install software*. In those cases we recommend you allow the *logical* structure of the breakdown to prevail over the chronology of the tasks. Most projects have tasks that run in parallel. The more tasks you can do in parallel, the faster you will finish the project!

Do not enter **Start** or **Finish** dates for detail tasks on **Auto Scheduled** tasks; this will automatically add *constraint dates* to those tasks, which will make the schedule rigid. Let the task bars move freely, based upon their dependencies. This will be elaborated on in chapter 5 on dependencies (see page 203) and chapter 6 on deadlines and constraints (see page 253).

Entering Milestones

For milestones, you enter the name of the milestone, then a zero in the duration field and perhaps a deadline date. You typically would create one milestone for each deliverable. The milestone should capture an important event for this deliverable, like being *sent, approved* or *delivered.*

1. In the **Gantt Chart**, click on the task before which you want to insert a milestone
2. Click ribbon **Task** and find its section **Insert**.
3. 

Milestone is set to **Yes**.
4. Enter the name of the milestone in the **Task Name** field overriding the **<New Milestone>** placeholder. Use the past perfect tense that typically has an –ed ending in English, as in *report delivered* or *software installed.*
5. If necessary, indent it under its summary task by clicking (**Indent Task**) on the **Task** ribbon.
6. Decide in the **Task Mode** field if want to make the task **Auto Scheduled** or leave it to be **Manually Scheduled** , see page 96 for an explanation of both.
7. To enter a deadline on the task, click the **Task** ribbon and click Information or hold down Shift and press F2 – the **Task Information** dialog appears. See page 256 for more on deadlines.

8. Click tab **Advanced**; the dialog should now look like:

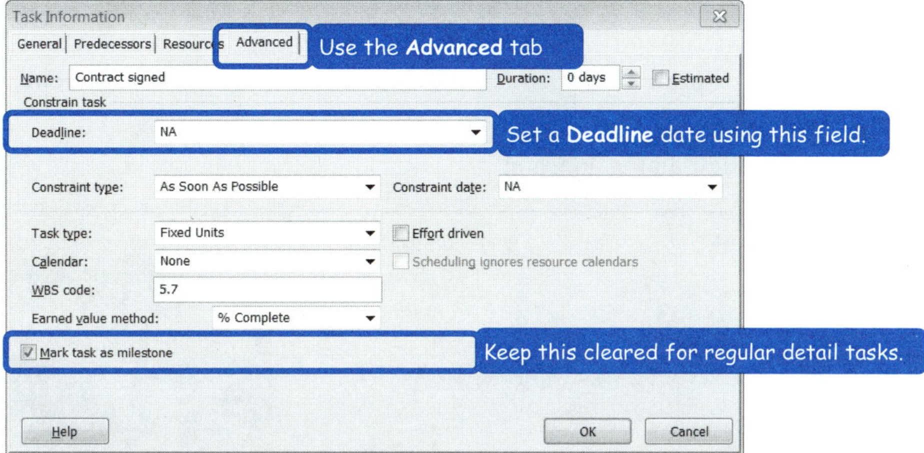

9. If you have a deadline, enter this target date in the field **Deadline** and press [Enter]. The deadline in the Gantt Chart timescale is shown as a green arrow ⇩. When the milestone is pushed past its deadline, a red exclamation icon ◆ will appear in the indicators ❶ column.

The ☐ **Mark task as milestone** feature in the **Task Information** dialog box can be selected for regular tasks as well. This will change a regular detail task bar into a diamond. It will shrink a 10-day task bar into a 0-day diamond in the timescale while keeping the 10-day duration in the spreadsheet. When dependencies stem from the task, it looks like there is a gap between the task and its linked task. We do not recommend you use this. Instead of using ☑ **Mark task as milestone**, we recommend you use the field *Marked* or one of the extra *Flag* fields to handpick tasks that are important for reports.

Entering Recurring Tasks

Recurring tasks are tasks that take place repeatedly and regularly, for example every other week (biweekly) or monthly. Typical examples of recurring tasks are *status meetings* or *progress meetings*.

1. Click ribbon **Task** and find its section **Insert**.

2. Click the Task portion of Task and then **Recurring task** – the **Recurring Task Information** dialog appears:

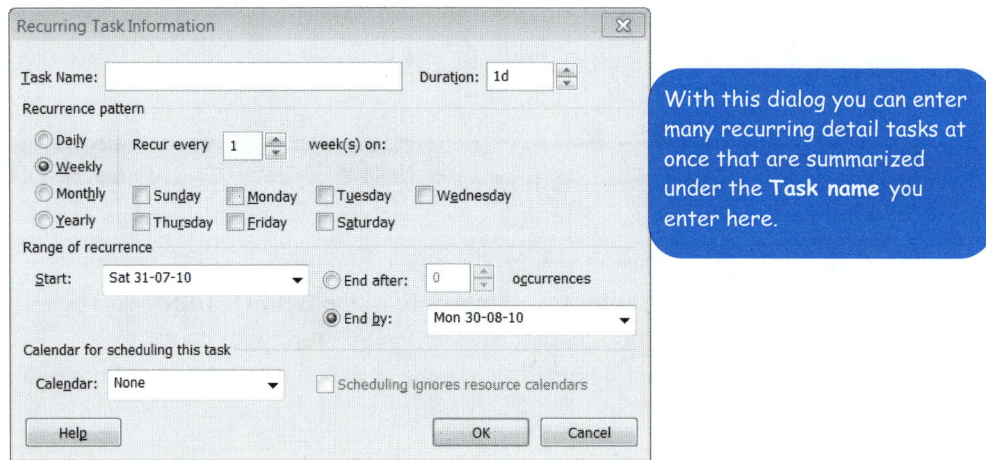

3. In the **Task Name** field, type the name.

4. In the **Duration** field, type the duration or use spin button to change the duration with pre-set increments.

5. Under **Recurrence Pattern** select the interval at which the task recurs — the dialog changes and presents appropriate choices for the selected interval.

6. Under **Range of recurrence** enter the period or the number of occurrences. Make sure that the *status meetings* or *meetings* with the client, sponsor or executive span the entire duration of the project and keep spanning it. We have found that this is often not the case in the schedules we evaluated for certification.

7. Click OK.

Some remarks about *recurring tasks*:

- Notice that recurring tasks are, in fact, a special kind of *summary task*, but have a different task bar than regular summary tasks. A recurring summary task bar only displays all the task bars of its detail tasks.
- Notice that the duration of the *recurring summary task* has no meaning; it encompasses the entire period of its detail tasks.

- MS Project sets constraints on each *recurring detail task* when they are **Auto Scheduled**. The constraints will keep them on their dates in the timescale. Although we recommend against using constraints in schedules, there is nothing wrong with constraints on recurring detail tasks. They are a legitimate exception. Recurring detail tasks are typically not hooked up into the network of dependencies and scheduling constraints will keep them on the proper dates.
- If one occurrence happens to fall on a national holiday (as entered in the project calendar), MS Project will ask you what to do with it. You can drop it or move it to the next business day.
- The number of recurrences for meetings may need to be adjusted when the project duration changes significantly.

- If you assign resources to the *recurring detail tasks*, you can level their workloads entirely. MS Project will not delay recurring detail tasks in the workload leveling process. This is because MS Project sets the field **Priority** to 1000 by default, which prevents MS Project from rescheduling the recurring tasks. The other tasks are scheduled in between or split by the recurring detail tasks, if you choose the option ☑ **Leveling can create splits in remaining work** in Leveling Options on the **Resource** ribbon. We will discuss workload leveling in more detail on page 468.

Entering Overhead Tasks

Where overhead tasks produce deliverables, we recommend you add these deliverables to the WBS. For example, the project manager creates the schedule and the budget – these can be added to the WBS as deliverables. If no distinct deliverables are created, you can add them as overhead tasks.

Overhead tasks are tasks that are often ongoing during the entire project. They are also called *hammock tasks*, because their start and end dates are really driven by or “hung up on” other tasks. Examples of overhead tasks are:

- *project management*
- *technical support*
- *quality control*
- *issue and risk tracking*

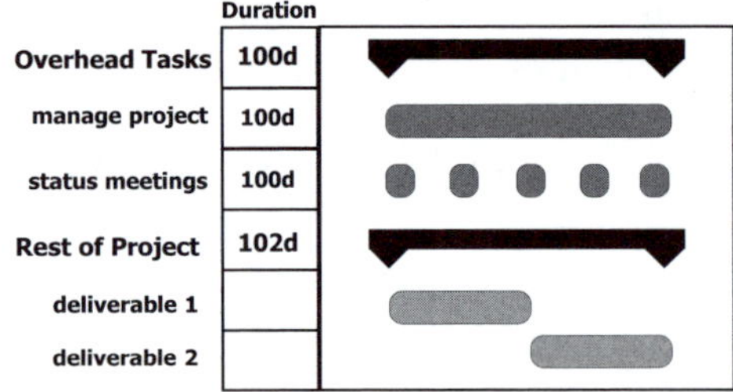

As the illustration shows, you can enter overhead tasks as:

- *Long-duration tasks*: tasks with a duration that extends over the entire project duration (long task bar), see *manage project*.
- *Recurring tasks*: many short tasks scheduled at fixed intervals, see *status meetings*.

The next table provides pros and cons for each approach:

Long task bar	**Recurring tasks**
You need to keep the workload leveled yourself. If you assigned the resource at 10% to the long, overhead task, you can assign the same resource at only 90% to other detail tasks.	MS Project can help with leveling the workloads around the recurring detail tasks. MS Project will split the detail task bars around the recurring tasks.
Every time the project duration changes significantly, its duration needs to be adjusted.	Every time the project duration changes significantly, recurring detail tasks need to be added or removed.
Easy to maintain; when you extend them, you do not need to assign resources again.	When you create new recurring detail tasks, you may have to assign resources to them again.
Models by averaging when overhead effort happens.	Models (too?) precisely on what dates overhead effort happens.
Creates just one line item in PWA for the resource.	Creates as many line items in PWA for the resource as there are recurring detail tasks.

We do not recommend one over the other; the best approach depends on your situation.

Creating an Outline

Outline Structure

You enter the WBS as an indented list of tasks into MS Project. The hierarchy of the WBS chart is preserved through indentation in the list of tasks (see the illustration). The more indented to the right, the less important the item is. The most important items are outdented to the left.

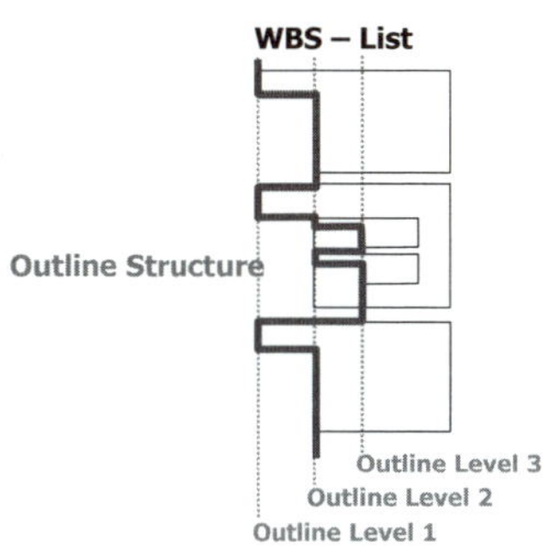

The tasks on the lowest level are called *detail tasks*. Detail tasks do not have subtasks. Elements that do have lower level tasks are called *summary tasks*. Tasks can be promoted to a higher level by outdenting them. They can be demoted by indenting them. Thus, an outline structure is created with multiple *outline levels*.

Purposes of the *outline structure*:

- Outlining makes the plan easier to read and understand. How can you eat a whole loaf of bread? Slice by slice! Similarly, people will digest a large WBS deliverable by deliverable.
- Outlining generates extra aggregate information on the summary tasks. MS Project automatically calculates the duration, cost and work fields on the summary tasks. You can immediately see what a deliverable costs. For example, if you are a programmer with a *software feature* as your deliverable, executives can now see how many person hours are spent on the feature and how much it costs. They will use this information when decisions have to be made about which feature will make it in this release of the *software*. With a *deliverable-oriented breakdown structure*, executives can easily make these *trade-off decisions* when you need them to.
- Outlining easily provides views of the schedule on different levels of detail. Summary tasks can be collapsed and expanded as needed. Collapse the summary tasks to show a *high-level schedule*. Most executives like a high-level overview of the phases, deliverables or milestones and prefer to leave the detail tasks for you as the project manager.

MS Project automatically keeps track of the level of indentation in the field **Outline Level**. You will find numbers in this field: Level 0 is the project-related level, level 1 is the highest level in the WBS of the project.

Indenting Tasks

1. Select the detail tasks by dragging anywhere over them in the spreadsheet.
2. Click ribbon **Task**, then click [icon].
   OR
   Hold down [Alt] + [Shift] and press [→].

After indenting tasks, their summary task shows a calculated duration that covers the time span of all its detail tasks.

MS Project does not allow you to use the [Tab] key to create indentation, unlike *MS Word* and *MS PowerPoint.*

Outdenting Tasks

1. Select the tasks by dragging in the spreadsheet.
2. Click ribbon **Task** and then click [icon].
   OR
   Hold down [Alt] + [Shift] and press [←].

Indenting and Outdenting by Dragging

1. Select the tasks by dragging over them in the spreadsheet.
2. In the **Task Name** column, point to the first characters of the task name; the mouse pointer changes to a two-headed arrow: ↔. Before proceeding, make sure you see this arrow (and not the mouse pointer ✛).
3. Hold down and drag to the right for indenting or to the left for outdenting. A vertical gray line indicates the resulting outline level when you release the mouse.
4. Release the mouse button when the gray line appears at the proper level of indentation.

To Hide and Reveal Detail Tasks

Click the minus button ⊟ in front of the summary task name to hide its detail tasks.
OR

Select the summary task and hold down [Alt] + [Shift] and press [-].

The detail tasks can be displayed again by clicking the plus button ⊞ in front of the summary task name.
OR
Select the summary task and hold down [Alt] + [Shift] and press [+].

To hide all detail tasks, you click ribbon **View**, 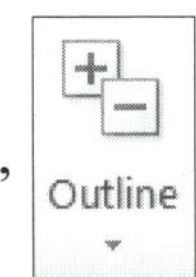 and select **Hide subtasks**. From this same drop-down menu, select **Show subtasks** to display subtasks on the next level for the selected task(s) only or **All Subtasks** to display all levels of the entire WBS.

To reveal a certain level, click  and select the level you want to see.

If you are not sure how MS Project counts the levels, please insert the column **Outline Level**, and study the numbers that MS Project displays. The left-most level is outline level 0 for the *project summary task*.

If you only want to see all summary tasks and no detail tasks, you can apply the out-of-the-box filter called **Summary Tasks** on the **View** ribbon, list **Filter**.

When you manipulate summary tasks, realize that what you do to a summary task affects all its subtasks as well. If you delete a summary task, you delete its subtasks as well. The same applies to cutting and copying (see page 150). If you indent a summary task, you indent its detail tasks as well.

Changing the WBS

Editing a Task Name

You can replace a task name by typing over it. If you need to make small editorial changes (correct a typo), it is better to edit the task name.

1. Click on the cell to edit and press [F2]. The cursor blinks as a vertical line in the cell, as in the following screenshot (sorry, I could not show the blinking on paper):
   write report|.

OR
Click once in the field and, after one second, click another time and a blinking insertion point will appear in the cell: [write report].

2. Move the cursor by clicking with the mouse or by using the arrow keys on the keyboard. Or use the [Home] to jump to the start of the cell and [End] to jump back to the end. Or hold down [Control] and press [←] to jump one word to the left, or [→] to jump to the right.
3. Make the changes.
4. Press [Enter ↵] to accept the changes and finish the editing.

If many ribbon buttons are grayed out and MS Project seems stuck, chances are you are in the middle of editing a cell. Look for an insertion point. Press [Enter ↵] or click on another cell to finish the editing or press [Esc] to cancel editing – the buttons are re-enabled. Now you can click on the ribbon buttons again.

Inserting Multiple Tasks

We have already discussed how to insert one task: press [Ins]. Here we will discuss how to insert multiple tasks at once:

1. Point to the row heading before which you wish to insert multiple tasks, click and drag down to highlight as many rows as you need inserted.
2. Press [Ins] and the number of rows you selected are inserted as blank rows
   OR

   Click the [button] top portion of [Task] and as many <**New Task**>s appear.

Deleting Multiple Tasks

Note that Project 2010 has a new feature called *inactive tasks*. When you make a task inactive, it will not disappear but it will not have any effect on the rest of the schedule and its cost and workload will not be aggregated on summary tasks. If this is what you need, set the field **Active** to **No** instead of deleting the tasks outright.

1. Select the tasks by dragging over their row headings (where you see their ID numbers).
2. Press Del.

Notice that if you do not select row headings first, the Del key deletes cells instead of entire rows – just like in *MS Excel*.

3

Copying or Moving Tasks

For copying or moving tasks, it is important to select the entire task including its fields that are hidden from view. You can select an entire task (row) by clicking either its row heading (the first column with the ID numbers and gray color) or its task bar. It will highlight all the visible data of the task and select all 300-some fields of a task, including the ones that are not visible.

The gray color of the first column tells you that the column is *locked*, which means:
- that it will not scroll off the screen,
- that its data cannot be edited, and
- that you can select the entire task by clicking on it.

Some people use this locked first column to display the *WBS-codes* (field **WBS)** instead of the *ID* field. Other people lock the *Task Name* column to prevent task names from scrolling off their screen. You can change which column is locked in the **Table Definition** dialog (ribbon **View**, button **Tables**, **More Tables**, button **Edit**, make the field you want locked the first field in the list and select ☑ **Lock first column**).

Copying Tasks

1. Select the tasks by dragging over the locked row headings by using the ➡ mouse pointer.
2. Release the mouse button when you have selected all tasks to copy; they are now highlighted.
3. Point to one of the selected row headings and the mouse pointer changes to . Hold down the Control key, and hold down the primary mouse button. The mouse pointer changes to . The small plus sign indicates that you are copying. Drag the copied tasks to their new place. The option ☑ **Allow Cell drag and drop** needs to be selected (ribbon **File,** Options, tab **Advanced**).

OR

Click ribbon **Task** and click Copy OR press Control + C; the task is now stored in the clipboard. Select the task before which you wish to insert. Click the top part of the 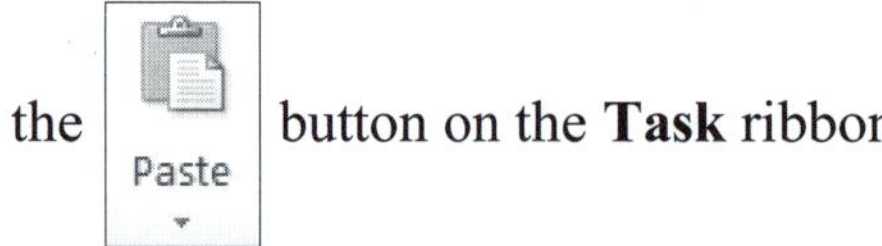 button on the **Task** ribbon.

4. Notice that MS Project puts the tasks on the same indentation level as the task directly above them. You may need to adjust the indentation level.

Moving Tasks

1. Select the tasks by dragging over locked row headings using the ➡ mouse pointer – the tasks should now be highlighted.
2. Point to one of the selected row headings; you should now see the mouse pointer. Click and hold the primary mouse button and start dragging; you should now see the mouse pointer. Drag the tasks to their new place; a horizontal gray line will indicate where the tasks will end up when you release the mouse. The option ☑ **Allow Cell drag and drop** needs to be selected (ribbon **File,** Options, tab **Advanced**).

   OR

   Click ribbon **Task** and click Cut OR press Control + X; the task is now stored in the clipboard. Select the task before which you wish to insert. Click the top part of the 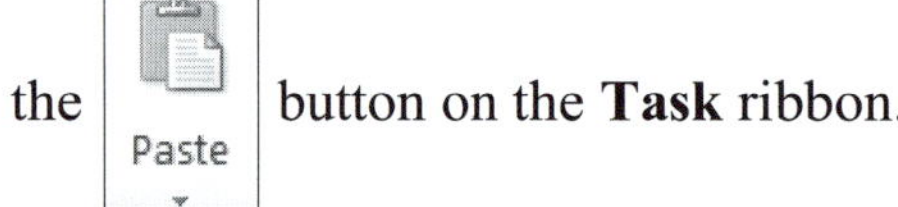 button on the **Task** ribbon.
3. Notice that MS Project creates new rows inserting the moved tasks.
4. Notice that MS Project puts the tasks on the same indentation level as the task right above them. You may need to adjust the indentation level.

To Copy or Move a Summary Task Family

Select the summary task by clicking on its row heading. (Hold the Control key down if you want to copy instead of move.) Hold down the primary mouse button and drag the summary task; MS Project will immediately highlight all of its detail tasks. Release the summary task where you want it.

If you use the clipboard instead, the detail tasks will also be copied or moved.

Checks on the WBS for Your Project

The *WBS* of the schedule is as important for the project as the foundation is for a house. The house is built on top of the foundation, and everything in the schedule is built on top of the WBS. Here is a way to remember this: *Everything goes wrong, if the WBS isn't strong!*

Here is a summary of the best practices for the WBS of your project. The numbering corresponds to the complete checklist in the summary chapter, see page 711. The filters mentioned in the checks can be found in the file *ProjectPro tools to check project schedules.MPP* available for download at www.ProjectProCorp.com (see page vi for the procedure to access these files).

3 WBS

3.1. Are there deliverables in the task list?
If there are not, the schedule does not have a WBS. Deliverables should be captured using nouns (perhaps with adjectives, but without verbs). Verbs change a deliverable into an activity. If there are no nouns (without verbs) in the task list, there are no deliverables and the list is not a *WBS*. See page 116 for a detailed discussion.

3.2. Is the list of deliverables *complete*, but *lean*? See page 116 for details.
- ◇ Are all expected deliverables explicitly included in the WBS? The WBS should also include significant reporting items, like monthly status reports and test reports.
- ◇ Are the project management deliverables, like schedule and budget included in the WBS (or modeled as overhead tasks)?
- ◇ Are there only deliverables in the WBS that were explicitly agreed upon with the *client* or *project sponsor*? There should not be extra deliverables in the WBS.
- ◇ Are *out-of-scope* deliverables that the client may expect explicitly excluded from the WBS? We recommend you capture exclusions in the **Notes** field on the project summary task (task 0) or the **Project Information** dialog (ribbon **File**, tab **Info**, button **Project Information**, list item **Advanced Properties,** tab **Summary, Comments** field).

3.3. Is the breakdown of the WBS *deliverable-oriented*?
The breakdown is deliverable-oriented if the deliverables are entered as summary tasks. Alternatives for a deliverable-oriented breakdown are a phase-oriented breakdown, a chronological breakdown or an organizational breakdown. From a project control perspective, these alternatives are less effective, see page 118 for a detailed discussion. Apply the filter **Summary Tasks** (**View** ribbon) to display all summary tasks. See also page 122.

3.4. Does the WBS have a *logical hierarchy*?
If you do not have a logical hierarchy, you may report the wrong cost or duration by phase or by deliverable. You can perform the next checks by expanding the outline structure to the right level using the **Outline** button on the **View** ribbon. See page 123 for a detailed discussion.
- ◇ Is the WBS an indented list with multiple hierarchical levels instead of one long list without structure?
- ◇ Are the most important items on the highest levels in the WBS?
  - Are the phases, if present, on a higher level than the deliverables?
  - Are the tasks, if present, on a lower level than the deliverables?
- ◇ Does each summary task have at least two subtasks?
- ◇ Is there no duplication or logical overlap between deliverables?
- ◇ Does each group of sub items capture all the work of its summary item (top-down check)? Check if the deliverable would be completed if all the activities are done.
- ◇ Does each lowest-level item logically relate to all of its higher-level items (bottom-up check)? Check if (a sample of) the detail tasks relate to all their summary tasks.
- ◇ Is the feature ☑ **Project Summary Task** on the **Format** ribbon of the Gantt chart used instead of a physical project summary task?
  MS Project's project summary task has ID number 0 (zero) in the first column.

3.5. Is there one *milestone* for each deliverable?
Milestones typically capture when the deliverable is completed, approved, sent, signed-off, published or shipped. Those events will have dependencies to other activities and allow you to keep the logic on the detail tasks (milestones) instead of on summary tasks (deliverables). You can check this by applying the filter **3.5 One Milestone per Deliverable** and verifying if most summary task deliverables have a corresponding milestone, see page 140 for more.

3.6. Are the WBS elements properly formulated?
If you use the following guidelines you will ensure that everybody can understand the WBS (see also page 130):
- ◇ Phases are formulated using the *present continuous tense* (-ing).

- ◇ Deliverables are formulated using a *noun* (perhaps with an adjective, but without a verb).
- ◇ Detail tasks are formulated using a *present tense* verb except for *fixed duration* tasks with no resource assigned (like *backing up server*) or a group of resources assigned (like *training*), which can have the *–ing* ending.
- ◇ Milestones are formulated using the noun of the deliverable and a verb in *past perfect tense* that typically has an *-ed* ending in English. Instead of a verb, the words *ready*, *complete* or *sign-off* can be used. You can apply our filter **3.6 Milestones Only** to display only milestones without summary tasks which allows you to copy the milestones into a schedule evaluation report.

3.7. Are the names of the deliverables, tasks and milestones used consistently in the WBS?

3.8. Does the WBS have enough *detail*?
Too little detail does not provide enough control on your project, see also page 133. There may be too few levels in the WBS:

- ◇ If you cannot estimate the duration or work on the detail tasks.
- ◇ If you have difficulties finding the dependencies between the detail tasks.
- ◇ If you often *assign* more than one resource per detail task or more than one department per deliverable.
- ◇ If there are detail tasks with a duration longer than a reporting period.
- ◇ If there are detail tasks with durations longer than 10% of the project duration (1%-10% rule). You can check this by applying the filter **3.8 Level of Detail > 10% of Proj Dur...** The filter prompts you to enter a duration equal to 10% of the project duration. You can find the project duration by looking at the **Duration** field of the project summary task (task 0). The filter will display all detail tasks that are longer than 10% of the project duration. We recommend you break down all these tasks into smaller ones.
  There are two exceptions to this 10% maximum:
  - *overhead tasks* (like *project management* or *technical support*), and
  - tasks in *high-level* schedules that are created only to estimate duration and cost of the entire project and to gain approval for the project.

3.9. Does the WBS have too many items, too much detail?
Too much detail will cause you to spend too much effort updating your schedule during project execution, see also page 134. There may be too many levels in the WBS:

- ◇ If you think there are too many levels or if you think the task list is too long.

- ◇ If you cannot guarantee you will be able to keep all detail tasks updated in the schedule during project execution.
- ◇ If there are items that do not contribute to deliverables of value that someone expects to receive.
- ◇ If you added reminders, to-do items or acceptance criteria into the task list. Transfer these to the **Notes** field.
- ◇ If there are tasks with durations shorter than 1% of the project duration (1%-10% rule). You can keep a few tasks that are shorter than 1%, but if you keep many, you will spend too much effort on updating your schedule during project execution. You then risk letting your schedule become obsolete at some point.
  You can check how many you have by applying the filter **3.9 Level of Detail < 1% of Proj Dur...** The filter prompts you to enter a duration that is equal to 1% of the project. You can find the project duration by looking at the **Duration** field of the project summary task. The filter will display all detail tasks that are shorter than 1% of the project duration while skipping milestones and recurring detail tasks.
  Two exceptions to the 1% minimum are:
  - *Milestones*
  - *Recurring detail tasks* are typically short and can be shorter than 1%.

3.10. Is the WBS clear to all project stakeholders?
All stakeholders — customers, suppliers, executives, team members and support staff — need to fully understand the WBS. If you do not understand it as a project manager, nobody will. If an outside reviewer does not understand it, chances are other stakeholders will not either. Ideally, a total stranger should be able to understand your WBS without further explanation.

3.11. Do project management overhead tasks (see page 143), if present, cover the entire duration of the project? It does not make sense to stop managing the project halfway.
- ◇ Do the long task bars representing overhead tasks (like *project management)* extend over the entire duration of the project?
- ◇ Do the *status meetings*, as recurring tasks, continue over the entire duration of the project?

3.12. Are task bar splits in the schedule kept to a minimum during the *planning* phase of the project?
Task bar splits often require extensive maintenance and should be applied with restraint (see page 129). During project *execution* you will see enough splits appear when updating your schedule with actuals.

Exercises

Review

1. What is the definition of a WBS as per the PMBOK® Guide by the PMI?
2. What are the differences between a to-do list and a WBS?
3. You ask a person to manage a project. The objective of the project is to write a document. An author, an editor and a graphic artist are on the team. After a while, the person presents four different first-level breakdowns to you and asks you to choose one. Which one will you choose and why?
   - ◇ First draft, final draft, final document
   - ◇ Writing, editing, formatting, printing
   - ◇ Draft text, edited text, final text, charts
   - ◇ Table of contents, body of text, summary
4. Which of the following are proper formulations for deliverables? If you find the wording can be sharpened to improve verifiability, please enter your formulation:

	Your formulation of the deliverable
Planning	
research phase	
approved project plan	
pilot	
Prototype	
deliver code to Harry	

5. Which of the following are proper formulations for detail tasks? If you find the wording can be improved, please enter your formulation:

	Your formulation of the detail task
program module XT607	
print	
design of house	
writing proposal	

6. Which of the following are proper formulations for milestones? If you find the wording can be improved, please enter your formulation:

	Your formulation of the milestone
report ready	
project close	
design approved	
contract sign-off	

7. How do you know you have found the appropriate level of detail in your WBS? Why is finding the right level of detail important?

Relocation Project — Entering the WBS

The goal of this exercise is to be able to enter the WBS of a project into an MS Project schedule.

1. Continue to work with your file *Relocation.mpp* or open the file *03A WBS.mpp* available for download at www.ProjectProCorp.com (see page vi for the procedure to access these files).

2. Check in ribbon **File,** Options, tab **Schedule**, section **Scheduling options for this project** if the following options are selected:
   - ◇ If the **New tasks created** is set to **Auto Scheduled**.
   - ◇ If the **Default task type** is set to **Fixed Duration**.
   - ◇ If the option ☐ **New tasks are effort-driven** is cleared.

3. Enter the WBS into MS Project as shown in the next table. [26] For detailed instructions on how to enter tasks, see page 138.
4. Indent the detail tasks under their summary tasks. The summary tasks are the tasks with names in capital letters (see page 145).
5. Compare your file with the solution file *04A Estimates.mpp* available for download at www.ProjectProCorp.com (see page vi for the procedure to access these files). See page 697 of this book for an automated way of comparing and reporting differences between two versions of one schedule.
6. Save your file when done.

Below you will find the WBS for the Relocation Project.

ID	Task Name
1.	REQUIREMENTS
2.	research staff requirements
3.	summarize requirements
4.	LOCATION
5.	select the realtor
6.	visit the sites
7.	evaluate the sites
8.	meet to select the location
9.	legal review
10.	location selected
11.	REMODELING CONTRACT
12.	select the contractor
13.	meet to discuss contract
14.	revise the schedule
15.	negotiate the contract
16.	contractor contracted
17.	REMODELED LOCATION

[26] Notice that the use of capital letters indicates which tasks will eventually become summary tasks. MS Project displays the summary tasks in bold type to make them stand out by default. This will happen upon indenting detail tasks.

ID	Task Name
18.	relocate walls
19.	install electric wiring
20.	paint
21.	drying of paint [27]
22.	install cabinetry
23.	install LAN
24.	lay carpet
25.	facility remodeled
26.	MOVE
27.	select mover
28.	pack
29.	move
30.	unpack
31.	new location opened

[27] You might wonder if *drying of paint* should be entered as a task, because it happens by itself. I merely use it here to illustrate the use of an elapsed duration. Alternatively, you could enter it as lag on the dependency between *paint* and its successor.

Chapter 4 Entering Estimates

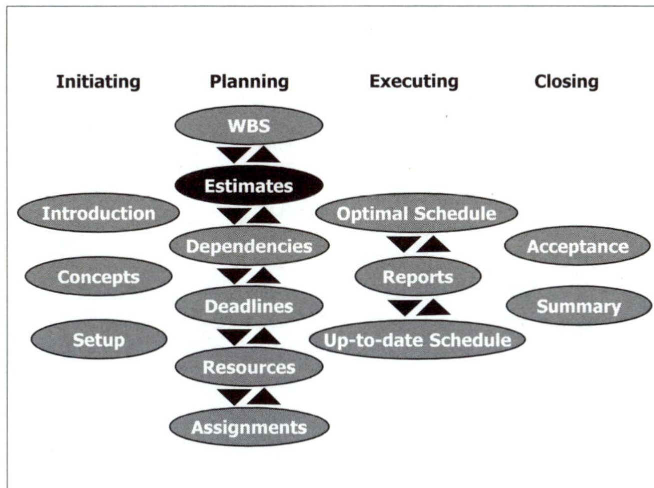

We have the WBS (Work Breakdown Structure) with *deliverables* and *tasks* entered into our project schedule. The next step is to enter the *estimates*, see the black ellipse above.

After reading this chapter you will:

- know a process for generating estimates
- understand the difference between duration and work (effort) estimates
- be able to enter duration and work estimates into MS Project
- understand how MS Project uses the formula **Duration** * **Peak Units** = **Work** when assignments are made or changed
- be aware of the human tendencies in estimating and know how to manage them
- be aware of difficulties in estimating and know how to address them
- understand and be able to apply the rolling wave approach to scheduling
- understand the difference between pure and gross work time estimates
- be able to check the estimates of the schedule against scheduling best practices
- know how to enter, move and copy data with the least amount of effort

Grand Guesstimates and Hairy Heuristics

Nob: "An executive asked me for a rough estimate on implementing this new Enterprise Resource Planning system and added that 'he won't hold me to it'! Of course, when I do give him a number, it is entered into the budget for next year and the number will be cast in concrete."

Bob: "Propose to form a team of analysts and technology experts and have them come up with the design document and a detailed estimate in a few months."

Nob: "He has no time or patience for that! They need the estimate within a few hours. So I am going to use a totally unscientific but quick method. I will estimate the weight of the specification documents that we will need, then multiply the weight by $200K and I will have the cost."

Bob: "I have another way of producing an estimate within the hour. I take the number of users times the number of stakeholders times the number of data entities times the number of generic skills needed and that is my estimate. So for the ERP system it could be 800 users * 10 stakeholders * 24 data entities * 25 skills is, let's see... 4.8 million."

Nob: "Should we create a range for it perhaps?"

Bob: "Yeah, let's apply the 'cone of uncertainty' approach. At this stage of estimating, the product is known and the error factor is 2, so the low estimate is 2.4 million with a 25% chance and the high estimate is 9.6 million with a 90% chance."

Nob: "That looks scientifically sound but is ... artfully vague!"

What Are Estimates?

Estimates are predictions of how much time a task will take. You can make predictions in terms of the duration of a task or in terms of the effort required to perform a task. The difference is evident in this example. If you have 3 carpenters working for 2 business days (duration), the effort is 3 * 2 = 6 person days of effort.

You express a duration estimate in *business days* (working days), which will be the weekdays in most cases. A business day has 8 hours in MS Project by default. Enter a duration estimate into the field **Duration;** the default time unit is **Days**. To enter a duration of five days (1 week), you could type:

- *5 days*
- *5d*
- *5* (since the default time unit for **Duration** is days; ribbon **File,** Options, tab **Schedule**)
- *1w*

Notice that MS Project displays it as *days* and not as *business days.* However, it will help you understand MS Project though, if you think of the **Duration** as the number of business days.

You express an effort estimate in *person hours* or *person days*. A person hour is one person working one hour. Enter the effort estimate into the task-related field **Work** in MS Project. The default time unit of the **Work** field is **Hours**. To enter effort of 16 hours on a task, type:

- *16 hours*
- *16h*
- *16* (since the default time unit for **Work** is hours; ribbon **File,** Options, tab **Schedule**)
- *2d* (notice that MS Project will convert this into the default time unit of hours)

Realize that MS Project displays the estimate as *hours* and not as *person hours.* To understand MS Project, think of the **Work** as the number of person hours (person days) needed for a task.

Choosing the Options

Before entering the estimates, it is important to understand how MS Project will function. Click ribbon **File**, Options and click on the tab indicated in the table below where you want to change settings:

Tab	Option
Schedule	Section **Scheduling options for this project**: **Duration is entered in:** MS Project will use the setting as the default time unit for the field *Duration*. With the default duration time unit set to days, you can type in 5 instead of 5d to get 5 days. You do not need to type a 'd' in the duration fields. Choose the unit that fits the majority of your inputs to save some keystrokes. The Duration field will display whatever time unit you entered.
	Work is entered in: Explanation is the same as for previous Duration field. Unlike the Duration field, the Work field will convert all entries to its default time unit. If you switch the time unit, MS Project will convert all values.
	Default task type: Most people enter the duration immediately, and MS Project should not change it, unless required. If you normally enter duration estimates rather than work (effort) estimates, we recommend setting it to **Fixed Duration**. [28] If you normally enter work estimates, we recommend setting it to **Fixed Work**.

[28] The *PMBOK® Guide*, Fourth Edition, published by the PMI, has *Estimate Activity Durations* as one of the planning processes.

Tab	Option
Schedule	☐ **New Tasks are effort driven** When turned on, this option can change *assignment units* (the number of resources assigned); we recommend you turn it off. This option works similarly to the task type **Fixed Work**. We recommend you use the task **Type** instead of **Effort Driven**. The option takes effect only when you create new tasks.
	☑ **Show that scheduled tasks have estimated durations** will add a question mark to the durations that you did not enter yourself.
	☑ **New scheduled tasks have estimated durations** will add a question mark to the durations of new tasks you may create.
Advanced	Section **Edit**: ☑ **Allow cell drag and drop** This allows you to move or copy the selected cells by dragging the selected area by its border. This option is global.
	Section **Display options for this project** **Minutes, Hours, Days, Weeks, Months** and **Years** This allows you to change the way time units are shown in your project. The shorter you make the time unit, the more space you save. (I set them habitually to the shortest label.) Select **All New Projects** first from the list if you want the short labels to be used from then on.

4

Difficult Situations

Estimating is one of the most difficult skills in project management. It is particularly difficult in the following situations:

- When the task is entirely new for the organization or done rarely, like *moving* or *implementing new hardware* and *software*. For these tasks you should contract outside expertise and have these consultants help you plan the project.
- When tasks have uncertain outcomes, like *R&D*-type tasks. How can you map out the remainder of the project if it entirely depends on the results of research you are currently conducting? As a result, scientists often hesitate to apply regular project management principles, but we think these principles are applicable to R&D-projects as well. Apart from applying the common principles, in these projects you need to apply special techniques for R&D projects like *stage-gate project management* (see page 232), *rolling wave* (see page 187) and *risk management*.

- When assigned team members have little or no experience with estimating the tasks in their areas of responsibility. We will discuss in more detail how to deal with inexperienced team members.

Estimating is difficult in all projects, because, by definition, projects are about creating new things or creating them in a new way. Estimating is a skill, and the only way to acquire a skill is by doing it. That is how we learned to drive a car.

The Human Tendencies in Estimating

We will discuss five common tendencies that people expose when estimating in projects, and we will provide ways to handle these situations. You will hear things like:

- "*Can you give me an estimate right now?*" from clients and executives
- "*Can't you do it?*" from executives and sales representatives
- "*I can't predict the future!*" from team members
- "*I am always off!*" from team members
- *"What is the date you'll be done?"* from project managers

"Can You Give Me an Estimate Right Now?"

Clients and executives have their way of asking for instant estimates or *ballpark estimates*, often adding that they will not hold you to it. As a project manager, it is very difficult to provide these on the spot without asking more questions to explore the scope, then breaking it further down, estimating the pieces and arriving at an overall estimate in a bottom-up fashion. We recommend you take the following approach:

- Clarify with the executive what type of estimate she wants: hard numbers she can bank on or a guess. Asking this question makes people realize that you need more information and time for a reliable estimate.
- Make sure you ask questions to be clear on the scope of the job at hand. It may be difficult to get more information from a rushed executive who is just looking for a rough number to enter into a draft budget.
- Ask for time to come up with a reliable estimate or to simply excuse yourself from the situation for a while to have private time to think about it.
- Make sure you always give a range estimate or give a single-point estimate in combination with a margin of error. An often-used margin of error for an *order of magnitude* estimate is -50% and +100%, in other words, between half and double the quoted estimate.
- Always provide your assumptions with the estimate even if the person did not ask for them or does not want them.

"Can't You Do It?"

I have seen organizations get stuck in scheduling a project when they use estimates produced by people other than the people who do the work. Examples of people who tend to produce unsolicited "estimates" are:

- **Executives and upper management**: "*Can't you do it in two weeks?*"
  Project managers all know the stress that occurs when executives impose their "estimates" on a project. Executives like to get the extra revenue from the project in the earliest possible fiscal quarter. Some executives will try to make you feel guilty to get you to commit to a crazy deadline. When executives make their guesstimates and impose them as committed dates, your unfortunate fate as a project manager is that they will also do your performance appraisal and you are put in a double-bind position. You are damned if you do commit to their estimate and damned if you do not. However, estimates from executives should really be treated as targets, not as estimates. Enter these as deadlines in MS Project (see the discussion of deadlines on page 256) and then create a detailed schedule to see how feasible they are. If you sincerely feel it cannot be done in the suggested timeframe, you should report this back to the executives. If you are a Project Management Professional (PMP) [29], you signed a code of ethics and you have to report back that it cannot be done in that timeframe.
- **Sales representatives**: "*The client wants it before their fiscal year-end.*"
  Project managers know the disastrous effects that occur when salespeople present their own "estimates" to the client without consulting you as the project manager. You cannot win in such a situation. These "estimates" are not estimates; they are commitments to please the client and win a sale, often at the project manager's expense. All too often salespeople are tempted to say what clients want to hear just to close the sale and receive their sales commission.

Estimates from executives or salespeople often suffer from wishful thinking. As a project manager you have to rely on the estimates of the resources on your team. If you feel the team estimate is high, you can explore with the team members whether there are better, smarter or more novel ways of working. In an open discussion it is often possible to decrease the project duration with new ideas. A brainstorming session can do miracles. Also, past projects can provide guidance on what is feasible.

In Project 2010, you can display both top-down estimates and bottom-up estimates next to each other to compare them and show to executives where there are huge

---

[29] A professional accreditation administered by PMI.

discrepancies. If you turn all Summary Tasks to **Manually Scheduled** tasks, you can enter their durations (top-down estimates). Then you enter all durations on the detail tasks (bottom-up estimates), and you easily see how far the top-down and the bottom-up estimating is apart. The resulting view could look like this:

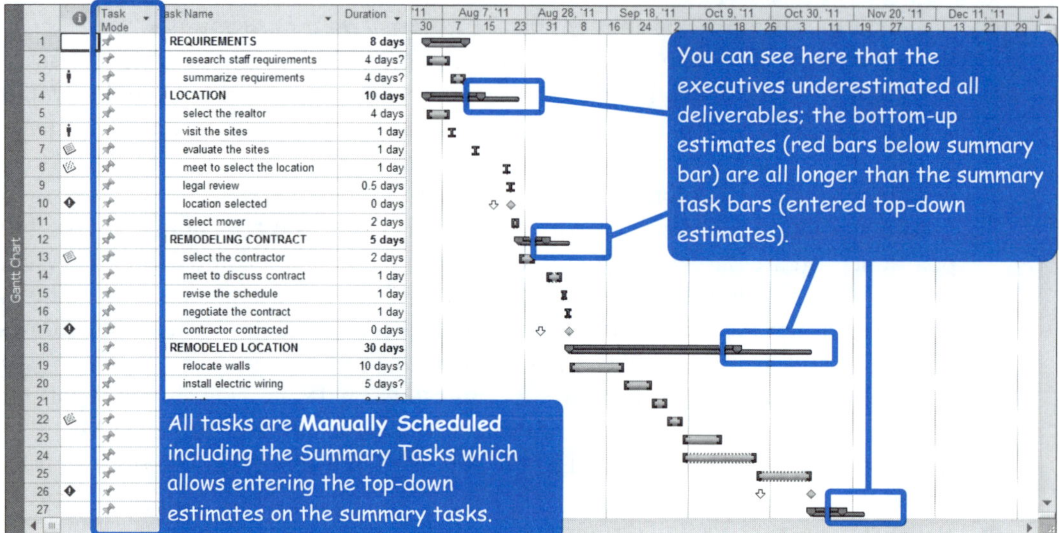

"I Can't Predict the Future!"

In MS Project you can capture that you are not sure of the estimate in the duration field. You can have the program treat an estimate like a "*guesstimate*" by adding a "?" to the entry. For example, you can enter "*3d?*" in the duration field if you are not entirely sure of the 3-day estimate. In its default settings, MS Project will add question marks to the durations that the software application entered itself. The durations MS Project enters can be default durations of "*1 day?*" or calculated durations. It can calculate a duration from the total effort required and the number of people assigned on **Auto Scheduled** tasks. Unfortunately, MS Project calls durations with a question mark '*estimated durations*'. They really are *default durations* (*1 day?*) or *calculated durations*. You can make the question marks disappear in ribbon **File,** Options, tab **Schedule** by clearing ☐ **Show that scheduled tasks have estimated durations** and ☐ **New scheduled tasks have estimated durations.**

Team members often have difficulty coming up with estimates. This is particularly true for team members who have never estimated the durations of their tasks or who are new to the type of task to which they are assigned. The latter is very common, because a fundamental characteristic of a project is that the final product is new and unique or produced in a new way. There is always improvisation and on-the-job learning in projects.

What happens if you are impatient and fill in an estimate when a team member states that he cannot produce one? This is not a good idea for several reasons:

- The people doing the work always know best how much time it will take, provided they have some experience with it.
- A team member who is late with a task during project execution may simply say: "*I never told you it would be done in only five days; you came up with that yourself!*" You have to get the estimates from team members themselves, so they own them, and then own up to them.
- If you allow team members to avoid estimating, they will never learn how to do it. The only way to develop estimating skills is by estimating.
- If you allow one team member to avoid estimating, it sets precedence for other team members. Soon you will get no estimates.

If a team member has difficulty producing estimates, try asking for two or three estimates instead of one. An interesting paradox: people who cannot give you one estimate may be able to give you more than one! It is usually easier to provide a *range estimate* than a *single-point estimate*. When you ask for a range estimate, you have an optimistic and a pessimistic estimate.

- You can solicit a pessimistic estimate with the question: *What if the things that typically go wrong, indeed go wrong; how long would it take then?* Notice that the question asks "*… things that typically go wrong…*", which is not the same as "*everything goes wrong*". When you ask for the worst case, the person will soon consider disasters like "*What if I get run over by a bus?*" or "*What if the whole world crashes down?*". You can tell the team member that if those things happen, neither of you will be around, the project will not be needed any longer and neither will the estimate! It is fine to think of those circumstances and have a good laugh about those extreme situations, but you should not consider them when estimating the job. Therefore, call it a *pessimistic* estimate rather than a *worst-case* estimate. Alternative questions to solicit for pessimistic estimates would be: "*What is a safe estimate?*" or "*In how many days do you feel very confident you can accomplish this?*"
- You could solicit for an optimistic estimate with the question: "*What if many things go smoothly; how long would it take you then?*" or "*What would be an aggressive estimate?*"

Asking for more than one estimate gives you a better idea of what to expect. It also helps you determine how much padding or buffer you need to apply to the duration estimate. Best of all, range estimates are much easier for people to make, particularly when you deal with people who want to get it right (such as engineers maybe?).

In summary, when a team member feels insecure about an estimate:

- You ask for a range estimate, for example:
    - Two estimates: an optimistic and a pessimistic estimate.
    - Three estimates: an optimistic (D_o), a realistic (D_r) and a pessimistic (D_p) estimate. Three-point duration estimates originate from *PERT* (Program Evaluation and Review Technique). PERT proposes a formula to convert the range into a single-point duration estimate MS Project can schedule: $D = (D_o + 4 \times D_r + D_p)/6$
- With the pessimistic estimates, you can display a pessimistic version of the schedule that has a higher probability to be met. Alternatively, you could use the realistic estimate but add a buffer to the schedule. See page 452 for how to calculate the size of the buffer with *Monte Carlo simulation* that uses the range estimates as input.
- When the target date is not met, you forgive the estimator. Use the buffer you applied as the project manager to swiftly forgive the team member. If you are not forgiving, the person may stop providing estimates altogether. If you cannot get estimates from your resources, it is worse than if you get estimates that are less reliable. You can always pad less reliable estimates to create a feasible schedule.
- At the end of the project, sit down with the team members who were insecure about their estimates and take a look at their original, aggregated estimate and compare it to the factual actual. Help them improve their estimates for the next time around. See the next section on how to do this. Evaluation provides a learning opportunity to become a skilled estimator. Making errors is human; not learning from them is stupid.

"I Am Always Off!"

People are optimistic or pessimistic by nature. Their personalities greatly affect their estimating. When you have worked with your team members on previous projects, it will be easy to determine their *personality factors*.

People are quite consistent in their tendency to err toward pessimism or toward optimism. Once you have found out the tendencies of your team members, you should be able to correct their estimates with a personality factor. You can determine someone's tendency by studying their track record of estimates and actuals from previous projects. You can get a quick impression if you look at a schedule of a finished project. Look at the resource-related *Actual Work* field and compare it to the *Baseline Work* field. These numbers are aggregates from all the estimates that the person provided in the project. The person's personality factor is the **Actual Work** divided by the resource's **Baseline Work**. For example, if you find that Rich had 420 hours of actual work and 300 hours in his baseline, his personality factor is 420 / 300 = 1.4. The next time you receive an estimate from him ask with a smile: *Does that take your 1.4 personality factor*

into account? The beauty of this calculation is that the *law of averages* takes effect, since the actual work and baseline work numbers are aggregated from all commitments the resource had in the past project. As long as the number of estimates of a person is more than twenty in the project, the personality factors are accurate through averaging.

If you get a date forecast from team members whom you know are very optimistic, you can ask certain questions to make them realize that the estimate may be unrealistic. Ask questions like:

- *What is the end result of this task? How do you plan to go about it?*
- *Is this estimate in terms of 100% fully focused work time or does it include the normal workday interruptions?*
- *Does it include continuing to answer your e-mail and voice mail as well?*
- *Do you have other ongoing responsibilities that will take time as well, like providing technical support, help-desk duties, troubleshooting, attending meetings or training?*
- *Do you have any personal commitments or other work commitments that will take time out of your workday?*
- *If you look at your schedule in Outlook, how many business days would it take to get this done?*

4

Together you may come to the conclusion that time needs to be added before entering the forecast into MS Project.

If the person tends to be pessimistic, you can ask questions that may lead to subtracting time. Questions you could ask are:

- *I would tackle this task like this …<explanation>… – how would you go about it?*
- *Do you realize that you do not need to meet this estimate 100% of the time?*
- *Is this a very safe estimate?*
- *Look at the assumptions for the task estimate: Are these assumptions real?*

In any case, you should leave the final decision with the estimator; otherwise you take the ownership and responsibility away from the team member. The team member will not learn from discrepancies and will say: "*It is not MY estimate!*" Also, the next time, the person may refuse to provide estimates to you, since "*You are going to change them anyway!*".

"What Is the Date You'll Be Done?"

Some project managers habitually ask for dates from their team members and then enter these into their schedule. Project managers tend to like dates because they are responsible for meeting the project finish date themselves. There are three things wrong with asking team members for dates:

- If you ask for dates you will likely enter them into the schedule. You should not enter start and finish dates into a schedule, as we discussed on page 53. If you do, you are still living in the age of paper instead of the electronic age. The result is that you will be spending more time on your schedule than you have to. If you do want to enter a few dates, enter them as deadline dates (see page 256) and still build up the schedule from duration (or work) estimates and dependencies.
- If you ask for *dates*, you ask for the most difficult estimate from your team members. You are expecting that people can quickly recall their other tasks, the dates promised to other project managers, the hours they will be working, availability of co-workers, personal commitments, personal vacations, and national holidays. Clearly, people cannot process this much information within one second. Project managers need to ask simpler questions if they want to get good estimates. Asking for a duration estimate or an effort estimate (work) is much easier than dates for team members.
- If you ask for dates, people will tend to give themselves a nice buffer and as the project manager you will lose ownership of the buffer in the project.

A Process for Estimating

The Difference Between Duration and Work

The *duration* of a task is the number of time units of working time the task will take. Duration is expressed in *business hours* or in *business days*, even though MS Project will just call it *hours* or *days*.

The *work* is the number of *person hours* or *person days* planned or spent on a task, even though MS Project will just call it *hours* or *days*. The term *work* in MS Project is synonymous with *effort* in daily life.

For example, one person who works for two business days (duration) delivers two person days of effort (work). Two painters who work for three business days (duration) to paint your house spend 2 * 3 = 6 person days of effort (work).

The business days are entered in the *Duration* field and the effort is entered in the *Work* field.

The Formula Behind the Screens

MS Project uses the *formula*: **Duration** * **Peak Units** = **Work** behind its screens:

- *Duration* is how many *business days* you have to finish the job.
- *Peak Units* are how many *resource units* are assigned to the task to do the work.
- *Work* is how many *person days* it will take.

The formula is meant to make your life easier, because you only have to provide two out of the three variables in the formula and MS Project will calculate the third one for you. However, if you are not aware of this formula, MS Project will start filling in fields for you that you did not expect it would. At that point, you are working in trial and error mode with the tool and your life will be more difficult.

Given the formula, we recommend you work as follows:

- Estimate the **Duration** or **Work** and enter it.
  The first variable in the formula is a given in most project situations. It is the estimate you first come up with. In most situations, you know the *duration* or *work* first.
- 2010 Protect this estimate by setting the task **Type** field accordingly
  MS Project has three task types: *Fixed Duration*, *Fixed Units* and *Fixed Work*.
  If you entered a **Duration** estimate, you set the task **Type** to **Fixed Duration**. If you entered a **Work** estimate, you set the task **Type** to **Fixed Work**. This will protect the number you entered from any calculating by MS Project with its **Duration** * **Peak Units** = **Work** formula. If MS Project has ever inadvertently changed numbers on you that you wanted to keep, this step is important for you.
  Manually Scheduled tasks do not allow you to change the task **Type**, so change the field **Task Mode** first to **Auto Scheduled**.

An Example of an Estimation

Let us assume you want to repaint the guest room in your house. You wonder when you could be done; you need to know the number of *calendar days* this task will take. You know that the guests will arrive on a certain date. In the illustration the calendar day estimate is on the far right. Estimating the number of calendar days, however, is very difficult and you have to step back in the process and try to estimate the number of *business days* or *workdays* the job will take. Once you know the

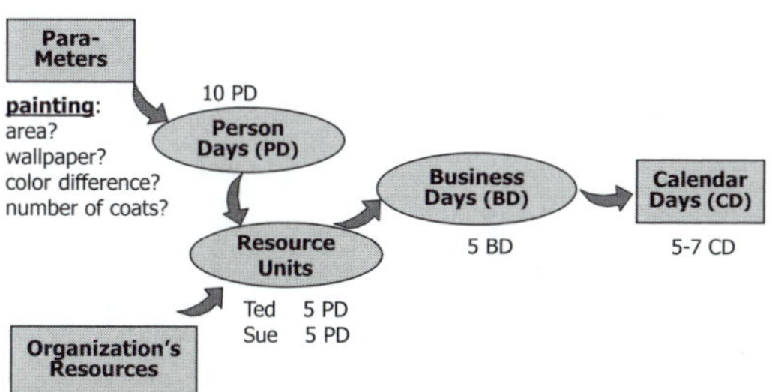

number of business days and the day of the week on which you will start the job, you can convert the business days into calendar days. In fact, MS Project can do this for you if you enter your weekend days and national holidays on the project calendar (see page 99).

Estimating in business days, however, may be difficult as well, because you may not know how many resources will be available. You take another step back in the process and decide to focus on a *person day* estimate that represents the effort of the task. To estimate the effort (work), you realize you only need to look at parameters for painting: what you will do with the wallpaper, area to be painted, the difference between the old and new color and the number of coats needed. After you have decided all of those factors, you figure it will take, say, 10 person days (see illustration).

You still cannot say how many business days this requires, because you have no firm commitments from family members or friends to help you. You ask around, and you find that your significant other is willing to help and that the two of you will share the workload equally. This means that each of you will take 5 person days of effort in the 10 person days total; 10 days of effort can be delivered by 2 people in 5 business days: *Ted 5 PD* (person days) and *Sue 5 PD*.

If you start on a Monday, you can have your house painted by Friday (5 business days and 5 calendar days). However, if you start on a Tuesday and you decide not to work on the weekend, you will be done on Monday of the next week (5 business days but 7 calendar days). You now know what you wanted to know: the project end date.

Please note this would be different in the Middle East, where the workweeks are: 5 days from Saturday through Wednesday (Algeria and Saudi Arabia), 5 days from Sunday through Thursday (Egypt and Israel), or 6 days from Saturday through Thursday (Iran).

MS Project elegantly takes care of the last conversion from business days to calendar days. Once you have filled in the project calendar, you can count on the eager and rapid cooperation of MS Project. The challenge in estimating with MS Project lies in solving the puzzle of *person days*, resource *units* and *business days*. We will present a process for solving this puzzle.

Estimating: Types of Tasks

Eventually MS Project needs to know the start date and the finish date of a task in order to create the schedule. To get to those dates it needs to find out the number of calendar days a job will take, as shown in the illustration. Normally you will find it too difficult to estimate the number of *calendar days*. You will immediately get bogged down with questions like: *When will we start this task? If we start it on a Monday, it will take 2 calendar days, but if we start on a Friday, it will take 4 calendar days!* Estimating would be easier if you did not need to deal with those issues while coming up with the estimates. You can have MS Project do the conversion from business days to calendar days for you, if you estimate the number of *business days* instead. The software does an excellent job here once you have filled in the project calendar, which you did when you set up the new project (see page 99).

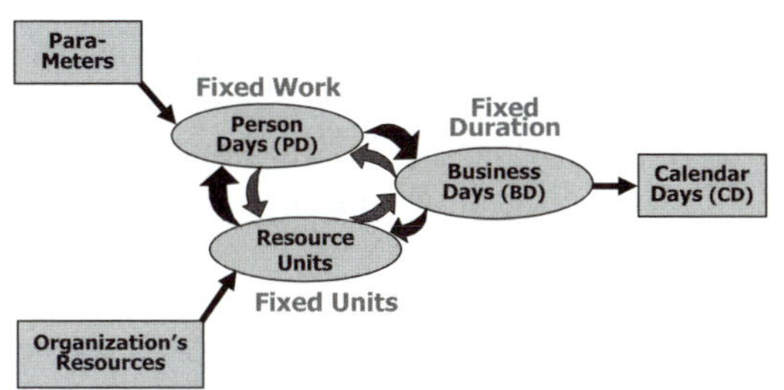

Sometimes it is possible to directly estimate or decide the number of business days (or business hours), for example, for tasks like *meeting, training* and *presentation.* If you want the meeting to last 2 business hours, you know the duration immediately. Meetings or courses do not shorten in duration when resources are added; these are tasks with a relatively *Fixed Duration*. You could even argue the contrary: meetings tend to take longer when more people attend.

For tasks with a relatively fixed amount of associated effort, it is impossible to estimate the number of business days right away. For these, it is important to estimate how much effort will be required and how many resources are available to do the work. You have to step back in the process and estimate the amount of effort first in *person days* (see the previous illustration). MS Project calls effort *Work*; you can treat these terms as synonymous when working with MS Project.

In order to estimate the work (effort), you may have to consider the relevant *parameters* of each job. For a programming job you might look at how many input screens and how many calculations the application will have. For a construction project you might look at how many cubic feet of concrete you will need to pour. You may have to ask clients or subject matter experts to provide some of these parameters.

Looking at the parameters of the job is important. Each industry has its own *metrics* to refine the estimates of a job; this is also known as *parametric estimating*:

- The construction industry has its *quantity surveyors*; they can tell exactly how much a brick wall will cost given the square footage and choice of brick. They can derive the footage from the architectural drawings.
- The software industry works with *function points*. Once software estimators know the number of function points of an application to be built, they can calculate their estimates. Dividing the function point total by 150 approximates the number of analysts, programmers and technicians they will need. Raising the function point total to the power of 0.4 gives a rough estimate of the time in months that the team will need.[30]

Once you have determined the amount of effort (**Work**), you have to decide how many resources will be assigned to the job and find out when they will be available. After that, you can usually determine how many business days the task will take (**Duration**). This task is a *Fixed Work* task, because you estimate the work first. Note that for these tasks, the Gantt Chart only starts to make sense after the durations have been calculated, since the task bars in the Gantt Chart depict durations. The durations will be calculated for **Auto Scheduled** tasks when you *assign* resources to the task by entering the resource *units* of the *formula* **Duration** * **Peak Units** = **Work**. Until you assign resources, the **Durations** will be the default *1 day* for **Auto Scheduled** tasks; **Manually Scheduled** tasks will have no duration displayed.

If you do not intend to enter resources and assignments, you will have to estimate the durations for all tasks, since MS Project needs durations to create the Gantt Chart! If you will assign resources eventually, you can enter work estimates for now. We will discuss assigning resources in chapter 8 (see page 351).

What you estimate first is entirely up to you, but it will typically depend on the situation. If you first estimate the **Duration**, we recommend you create a *Fixed Duration* task. If you estimate the **Work**, we recommend you create a *Fixed Work* task. In any situation you will have to estimate the first value, decide on the second and let MS Project calculate the third. The result is that you will know the finish date and cost of the task.

---

[30] These metrics were taken from "*Sizing Up Software*" by Capers Jones, *Scientific American*, December 1998.

Preparing the Gantt Spreadsheet

We recommend you prepare the Gantt spreadsheet so you have the right fields for entering estimates. The illustration on the left shows which fields to insert. We recommend you insert them in the spreadsheet of the Gantt Chart in the order shown. You typically have to insert the fields **Type, Effort Driven** and **Work** into the spreadsheet; **Duration** is already there in the default task **Entry** table. We have prepared this table for you, and it is available for download from our website in a file called *04 Entry Table - ProjectPro.mpp*. See page vi for the procedure to access these files. You will need to copy the table titled *Entry Table ProjectPro* to your file, see page 197 for the how-to steps.

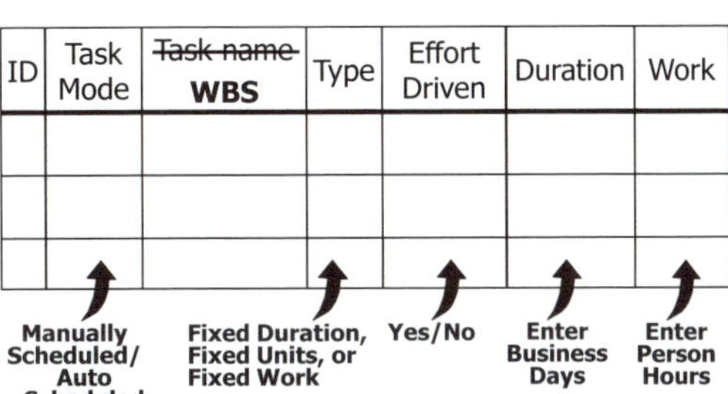

We need the following fields in the Gantt spreadsheet:

- **ID**
- **Task Mode**: You can change tasks from **Manually Scheduled** to **Auto Scheduled** in this field. Only Auto Scheduled tasks allow you to change the task **Type** to **Fixed Duration** or **Fixed Work**.
- **Task Name**: note that the database name of this field is simply **Name**. You can see this if you right-click on the column heading and click **Field Settings**. We suggest you change the **Title** of the column to **WBS**. We recommend this more appropriate title for this column, because you will also enter deliverables and milestones here apart from tasks, see page 115. Note that there is already a field called **WBS** in MS Project that should really have been called *WBS-codes*.
- **Type**: by setting the right task type, you tell MS Project to leave the entered estimate alone. For example, if you estimate that a task will take 10 person days, you enter 10 days in the *Work* field and you set the task type to *Fixed Work*. The tool may (re)calculate the duration or the *resource units* needed, but never the *Work* when the task type is *Fixed Work*.
- **Effort Driven**: MS Project always sets this field to **Yes** for **Fixed Work** tasks, which illustrates that *Effort Driven* and *Fixed Work* act similarly. To keep things simple, we recommend you keep **Effort Driven** to **No** for *Fixed Duration* and *Fixed Units* tasks. See page 378 for more detail on this.
- **Duration**: to enter the duration estimate for *Fixed Duration* tasks.
- **Work**: to enter the effort estimate for *Fixed Work* tasks.

If you have the default **Entry** table displayed, you need to insert the fields **Type, Effort Driven** and **Work**:

1. Click ribbon **View**, button **Gantt Chart**.
2. Right-click on the column heading **Task Name** and click **Field Settings.** Change the **Title** to **WBS** in the dialog. Click OK.
3. Click anywhere in the column **Duration** and click ribbon **Format,** 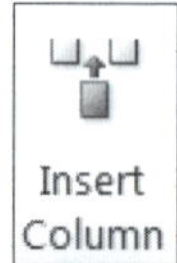

   OR
   Right-click on the **Duration** column heading and click **Insert Column**.
4. A list with available columns appears. Start typing the name of the field **Type** and the list narrows down. Select from the list the item **Type**.
5. Repeat the previous two steps to insert the columns **Effort Driven** and **Work**. We recommend you order the columns as shown in the previous illustration.

If you created tasks with the wrong default task type, you can change all tasks at once by clicking on a column heading to select all tasks and clicking ribbon **Task**, section **Properties**, button **Information**. Click tab **General** and select ◉ **Auto Scheduled**. Click the **Advanced** tab, select the type you want from the list **Task type**, and clear ☐ **Effort Driven** if needed (Make sure it is white, not gray. Click another time if it is gray; the check box has gray as a third state when multiple tasks are selected, for use when some tasks are on and others are off). Click OK.

Fixed Duration Tasks

A *fixed duration task* is a task that has a duration that does not fluctuate with the number of resources assigned to it, or with the working hours of those resources. Examples of tasks like these are *status meeting, training, backing up computer system* or *drying of paint.* Tasks tend to have a fixed duration when you assign many resources to them (meeting, training) or none (backing up computer system, drying of paint). Notice the tendency to use words ending in *-ing* for these task names, just like for phases.

For *Fixed Duration* tasks, enter the duration first. A task such as *meeting* is a prime example of a fixed duration task, because you decide the duration up front (it is more a matter of deciding than of estimating). Then you can decide who you will invite to the meeting and *assign* the number of units (clockwise arrows in illustration). Once you have assigned the number of *resource units*, MS Project will calculate the total amount of work.

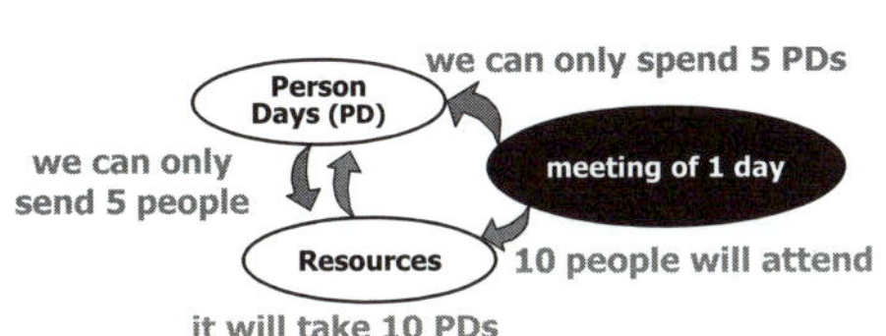

Sometimes you know the maximum number of person hours you are willing to spend in the meeting and you enter it as work (counter clockwise arrows in the illustration). In this case MS Project will calculate the number of resources needed.

To enter a Fixed Duration task:

1. Change field **Task Mode** to **Auto Scheduled**. This will allow you to change the task **Type** field.
2. Enter the name of the task in the field **Task Name**.
3. Change field **Type** to **Fixed Duration**. This will prevent MS Project from changing this estimate.
4. Change field **Effort Driven** to **No**.
5. In the **Duration** field enter the number of business days you estimate the task will take. This will override the default duration of **1 day?** that MS Project had entered. You need to enter only the number and MS Project will append *days*. [31] If you want to display a different time unit, for example hours, you have to type the time unit abbreviation as well; you would enter "2h".

Fixed Work Tasks

A *fixed work task* is a task with an amount of effort dependent only upon the technical specifications of the job. Unlike duration, the amount of effort is not dependent upon the

---

[31] *Days* is the default time unit for the *Duration* field as set in ribbon **File**, button **Options**, tab **Schedule**. The default 'abbreviation' for *days* is set in tab **Advanced** in this same dialog.

number of resources that will be assigned to the task or their working times (*resource calendars*).

Once you determine the amount of work, you will often find that your next step will be to establish how many resources will do the job (counter clockwise arrows in the illustration). When you know the work and the number of *resource units*, MS Project will derive the number of business days (duration).

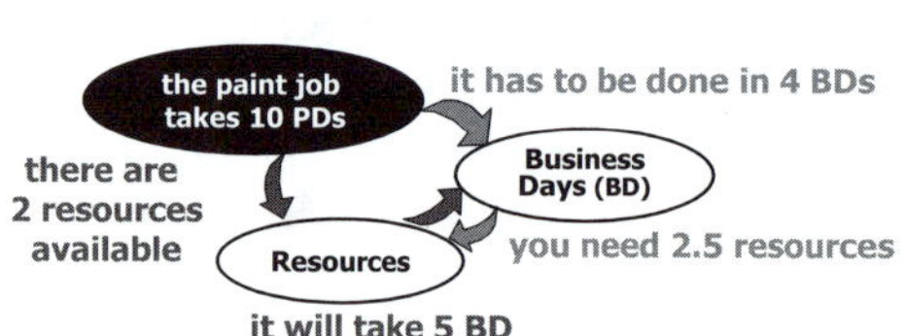

In this chapter we will only discuss the steps for entering **Work** estimates; in chapter 8 we will explain how to assign the resources (see page 351).

Once you know the amount of work (10 person days), you sometimes know the number of business days required to do the work (clockwise arrows in the illustration). Let us say you have only 4 business days for the task (duration). From this MS Project can derive for you the number of resources you need: 2.5.

To enter a Fixed Work task:

1. Change field **Task Mode** to **Auto Scheduled**. This will allow you to change the task **Type** field.
2. Enter the name of the task in the field **Task Name**. Notice that MS Project already entered a *default duration* of **1 day?** in the **Duration** field.
3. Change field **Type** to **Fixed Work**. This will prevent MS Project from changing the estimate you will enter.
4. The field **Effort Driven** is automatically set to **Yes**; it cannot be changed for **Fixed Work** tasks.
5. In the **Work** field enter the number of person hours you estimate the task will take. Review the parameters of the job, if needed. You only need to enter the number and MS Project will append "**hrs**". [32] If you want a different time unit, for example weeks, you have to type the "w" as well; for example, enter "3w".

---

[32] *Hours* is the default time unit for the *Work* field as set in ribbon **File**, button **Options**, tab **Schedule.** The default abbreviation for hours is set in the tab **Advanced** of this same dialog.

Estimating: Difficulties and Techniques

The following factors make estimating difficult, and we will discuss what options you have to make it easier:

- What time unit to use for estimating? See next.
- What to include? See page 181.
- Unknown events (see page 187)
- Unknown resources (see page 188)
- Unknown experience and skill level (see page 189)
- Unknown learning curve (see page 189)

We will discuss each of these difficulties in more detail.

What Time Unit to Use for Estimating?

Choose if you are going to express your estimate in person days, business days, or calendar days (elapsed durations):

- *Person days*
  One person day is one person working one full day. The number of person days is the amount of *work* or *effort* needed on the task. For example, if you have to write 20 pages of text and you know it takes you about 2 person hours per page, the total effort is 20 * 2 = 40 person hours. You enter the effort into the field **Work**.
  MS Project needs the effort estimate to calculate the cost of the project. Each person hour applied needs to be multiplied by the appropriate rate to arrive at the cost.
- *Business days*
  A business day is one working day. The number of working hours in a full working day is defined in ribbon **File**, Options, tab **Schedule, Hours per day**. You enter the number of full working days a task will take in the **Duration** field.
  MS Project needs to know the number of business days in order to calculate the calendar days needed and the start and finish dates, which are used to create the Gantt Chart. The length of the task bars in the Gantt Chart is driven by the duration of the task (in combination with the project calendar).
- *Calendar days*
  One calendar day is 24 hours; this is simply how everybody thinks of one day, whether educated in project management or not. For example, if paint dries in 2 days, the number of calendar days is 2. The number of calendar days needed is not dependent on the working times, since paint dries during the night and weekend as well. You need to know the number of calendar days if you are asked to commit to a date on which you will deliver the project product. Calendar days are also known in MS Project as *elapsed days*.

Elapsed durations are used for tasks that go through the night and weekend, rather than following working hours, as shown in the illustration. Examples of situations in which

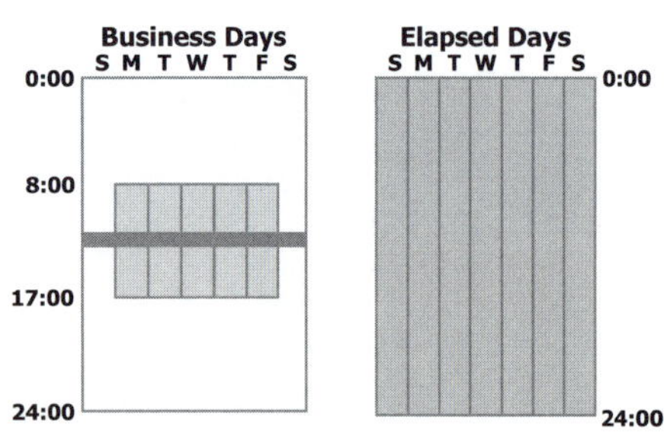

you will need elapsed durations are backing up a computer system or drying of paint. At food companies, new products are shelved for months in order to find out if the food preservation procedures are adequate. These months are elapsed months, because they continue over Christmas and through the summer holidays. Defense systems developers will keep a new monitor for a tank in a shake and bake oven for 2 days to test its ruggedness. The 2 days are elapsed days. Elapsed activities continue *24 * 7* (24 hours and 7 days a week). If you want to enter an elapsed duration in the *Duration* field, you have to specify the time unit as follows:

Time unit	Enter in business time as	Enter in elapsed time as
minutes	m	em
hours	h	eh
days	d	ed
weeks	w	ew
months	mo	emo

For example, to get 5 elapsed days you have to enter "5ed" instead of "5d".

What to Include? Pure Work Time versus Gross Work Time

What do your resources include in their estimates? Do they imagine being able to work full-time without interruptions on the task? Do they include personal time, like visits to the washroom and calls to their significant other? Do they include time spent in meetings to discuss or present deliverables?

Pure

Gross

The term *Pure Work Time* expresses an important concept very well. Pure work time is work time spent 100% productively (also known as *crunch time*)!

In contrast, *Gross Work Time* includes time spent on things other than project tasks. If you look at your time during a regular workday, you will find that a lot of it is lost on nonproject tasks. People spend their time at work in the following four categories:

1. **Project productive time**
   Time spent on project tasks which is pure work time (for project planning purposes).
2. **Administrative time**
   Time spent on nonproject but work-related tasks, for example:
   - ◇ Performing operational tasks
   - ◇ Answering e-mails that do not pertain to the project
   - ◇ Answering phone calls that do not pertain to the project
   - ◇ Walking to and from meetings, traveling between buildings
   - ◇ Attending company meetings (for example, employee benefits or recognition)
   - ◇ Participating in professional development, like training (not project-related)
   - ◇ Providing technical support to colleagues
   - ◇ Lobbying decision makers
   - ◇ Managing the politics or bureaucracy
   - ◇ Introducing and training new staff
   - ◇ Troubleshooting and answering support calls (help desk)
   - ◇ Debugging released versions of software applications (hot fixes, service packs)
   - ◇ Maintaining electrical, mechanical, chemical or nuclear systems.
   - ◇ Maintaining buildings and facilities.

3. **Personal time**
   Time spent that is nonproject and non work-related time; in other words, time spent on yourself to maintain your personal hygiene, sanity and health, for example:
   - ◇ Changing into the company uniform
   - ◇ Making private telephone calls (with your significant other, for example)
   - ◇ Browsing the Internet and text chatting
   - ◇ Chatting with colleagues and other passers-by
   - ◇ Providing emotional support to colleagues
   - ◇ Daydreaming
   - ◇ Taking coffee breaks
   - ◇ Visiting the restroom, water fountain, and fridge
   - ◇ Participating in TGIF,[33] anniversary and farewell lunches with colleagues
   - ◇ Taking sick leave

4. **Time-off**
   This is a special case of personal time that is future-oriented and, therefore, will affect the scheduling of project tasks. We have separated it from other personal time because it needs to be treated differently and entered on the resource calendar:
   - ◇ Vacation days
   - ◇ Civic duty
   - ◇ Jury duty
   - ◇ Planned medical procedures
   - ◇ Maternity/paternity leave
   - ◇ Bereavement
   - ◇ Time-off without pay

Since time-off is future-oriented and resource-specific, time-off should be captured in MS Project on the *resource calendar*; MS Project will then schedule project tasks around the off–time, not during. See page 314 for the steps how to capture time-off on the resource calendar in MS Project.

In Project Server, you can use the *administrative time* feature to capture time-off that transfers the time-off onto the resource calendars. If resources enter vacations or medical leaves into their timesheet in the future, Project 2010 will automatically create a nonworking exception on the resource calendar of the resource as soon as their resource managers approved those entries. You can display these exceptions on the resource

---

[33] TGIF stands for *Thank Goodness It's Friday*.

calendar by double-clicking on the resource name in the Resource Sheet view and clicking [Change Working Time ...]. They are listed on the tab **Exceptions**.

It should be clear if the estimates you received from your team members are expressed in pure work time or in gross work time. We have asked many course participants what percentage of their gross work time on project tasks is purely productive, and we have heard the average is only 70%, even though it differs from industry to industry. As you can see, the gross time estimate is almost 1.5 times the pure estimate! Your projects will always be late if you treat pure work time estimates as if they were gross.

A separate issue is whether the estimates should include *waiting time*. Waiting time is, for example, the time you have to wait to receive an approval or input from others. Many people include these waiting times in their duration estimates. We recommend entering them as lags on dependencies instead. For a discussion on *waiting time dependencies* (see page 235).

Considerations When Deciding To Estimate Pure or Gross

When you decide whether to go with pure or gross estimates, it is important to consider:

- All team members in your project should estimate consistently in either pure work time or gross work time; a project manager cannot use a mix of the two. If one team member estimates in pure work time and another in gross work time, it will lead to misunderstandings that can make the difference between meeting a deadline and missing it. Mixing pure and gross estimates can even lead to painful questions like: *Why is Joe getting more time for this same task?* On an enterprise level, an organization also needs to clarify if its employees need to make pure or gross work time estimates. This is one of the issues that need to be addressed during *Project Server implementation*, the configuration and the training.
- Every estimator needs to have the same understanding of what a "*gross working time estimate*" or "*pure working time estimate*" includes. This has to be clarified with every person who estimates or interprets estimates, which is just about every stakeholder in a project. You can use the previous lists of *administrative time, personal time* and *time-off* to clarify the terms to estimators.
- Timesheets should be filled in consistently with the type of estimates you collected. Otherwise, you cannot compare actual hours with estimated hours! In practice, it is horrendously difficult to get team members to enter pure actual hours. Pure actual hours have a maximum of 28 pure hours per week (70% of 40 hours). Of course, employees with a 40 hour per week labor contract want to show 40 hours on their timesheets. Pure work time estimating will not allow them to fill in 40 hours. As a result, almost all organizations with timesheets use gross work time estimates.

Many organizations create extra administrative line items on their timesheets to capture certain items separately to approach pure estimates.

- You need to resolve whether you want the costs in your project to be calculated based on pure work estimates or gross work estimates. The cost of pure work estimates will be lower than what you want to report to clients, since administrative and personal time is typically included in their cost estimates, but not in pure work estimates. If your organization needs to bill clients on a time and material basis, you will need to get gross hours.

What Many Organizations Decide To Do In Practice

The percentage of gross time that is purely productive can vary significantly from industry to industry. Your organization can decide what items in the lists (see page 181) should be included in the estimates and what items should be excluded. Many organizations have resolved this issue in the following way:

- All items in the *time-off* category are typically captured on the individual resource calendars. This removes the availability of the resource for project tasks during those times off. MS Project will schedule around them, and forecasts will be accurate.
- If your team members spend a large portion of their working hours on technical support or maintenance tasks, gross estimates are too rough from a cost perspective. In that case, you may want to exclude these tasks from the gross estimates. Many organizations do this by creating *technical support* or *maintenance projects*, which are MS Project schedules with many small tasks (*support tickets)*.

  In Project Server you can assign resources to these tasks and publish them to the timesheets. This allows you to capture separately time spent on support and maintenance tasks, and takes care of several items in the *administrative time* category that are potentially large.
- Project Server provides an easy way to capture the remaining items in the *administrative time* category by letting you create administrative time line items in the timesheets of resources. This allows resources to enter administrative time in the timesheets separately from time spent on project tasks (the *project productive time*). Typical administrative line items are *admin tasks* (voicemail/e-mail), *meetings*, and *professional development*.

The last two bullets address all items in the administrative time category. The issue that remains is what to do with the *personal time* category. Items like *sickness* and *vacation* are also suitable to be added to the timesheets as administrative line items, but I have yet to see a timesheet that has *coffee breaks* or *visits to the washroom* as a line item.
So, several items from the personal time category need to be included in the estimates. It is important that, as an organization, you clarify which items you expect to be buried in the estimates. The estimates will then no longer be entirely pure but your best approximation of it.

We think that about 15% of employees' time is spent on personal items that you do not want to add as separate line items to the timesheet. You may think that 15% is very high, but realize that almost half of this is used for coffee breaks (most people in the Western world are allowed to take two 15 minute breaks, which are half an hour out of 8 hours or 6.25%).

How To Set Up MS Project with Pure or Gross Estimates

The type of estimate (pure/gross) that you collect needs to be consistent with the working times you set on the project calendar. Only when the collected data are consistent with the project calendar can you produce accurate schedules that produce *valid* forecasts of finish dates and times.

MS Project is set up by default to receive gross work time estimates based on 8 hours for a full workday, because the default working times are 8:00 AM - 12:00 PM and 1:00 PM - 5:00 PM. If everybody estimates in gross work time based on 8 hours per day, you do not have to change the default settings in MS Project; in any other case, you do have to make an adjustment.

If you want to work with pure work time estimates, you have to do the following:

- Establish what you want and can capture separately in the timesheets and what *personal time* items you want to include in the estimates, as we discussed in the previous section. Estimate the percentage of time that will be spent on those personal time items. Better yet, measure and calculate it for a sample of your project employees for some time.
- You can then adjust the working times for everybody in the *project calendar* by clicking ribbon **Project**, button **Change Working Time**. In Project Server, the administrator needs to do this. You can simply shorten the working times. For example, if you found that the resources are 85% productive, you could change the working times to reflect 85% * 8 hour = 6.8 hours, then round it to 7 hours. You could enter this on the project calendar as: 8AM - 12PM and 1PM - 4PM. See page 99 for the detailed steps. As soon as you do this, all start and finish dates for Auto Scheduled tasks will be recalculated. We recommend you also adjust the **Hours per Day** setting accordingly (ribbon **File**, Options, tab **Schedule**), but when you do this be prepared to have all your durations recalculated while the start and finish dates stay the same.
  OR
  You could decrease everybody's availability from 100% to less than 100%. If you find that people are purely productive 85% of their work time, you have to enter this as their availability in the **Max Units** field in the Resource Sheet. Max Units applies this percentage to the work times on the calendar to calculate the number of hours

that a person is available per day (see page 322 under Part-Time Availability). Max Units has, therefore, an effect similar to changing the working times on the calendar. The difference is that the Max Units number is also used as the default for the assignments units when you assign resources to tasks. Consequently, the person will only work up to 85% on each assigned task from then on. This may not be desirable on all tasks; for example, 85% presence in a meeting is not appreciated.

We recommend you capture pure working times on the calendars (ribbon **Project**, button **Change Working Time**), because this affects existing tasks immediately. Start and Finish dates will be recalculated when you make the change, and the forecasts that your schedule produces will be more accurate. If you capture pure working times in the **Max Units** instead, the only result is that MS Project will flag the resource earlier as overallocated in existing schedules and the forecasted dates may still not be accurate. Only when you resolve the overallocations will you see the impact on the schedule.

Project Managers Need To Clarify Estimates: Pure or Gross?

For your current project you have to find out if your resources provided you with pure work time or gross work time estimates. If your resources provided you with pure work time estimates, whereas you thought they were gross estimates when you created your schedule, your resources will never meet their deadlines! On the other hand, if you received gross estimates that you scheduled using pure working hours on the calendar, your project schedule will be unnecessarily long, perhaps as much as 50% longer than it needs to be.

As project manager of a new project, you have to decide how you want your team members to estimate work time. When you ask a team member for an estimate, you should ask explicitly for *pure work time* or *gross work time.* If you suspect that the team member is not clear on exactly what gross work time includes, explain it briefly and give examples from our lists to illustrate the difference between pure and gross. You can also use these clarifying questions to get from pure to gross work time estimates:

- *You have given me an estimate of 3 days of effort; if you look at your calendar in Outlook, how many days will it take to schedule these 3 days of effort?*
- *How much time would you actually bill me if you were a consultant?*

The following clarifying questions will get you from gross to pure work time estimates:

- For programmers and writers: *How many hours will you actually have your hands on the keyboard to accomplish this task?*
- *If you only needed to focus on this task, how long would it take you?*

Unknown Events: The Rolling Wave Approach

Any project has many unknown events. For example, with an office relocation it is hard to estimate how long it will take to remodel the new location that is yet unseen. Perhaps only minor remodeling will be necessary if you find a location in good shape, or maybe you will spend a long time getting an old building up to par.

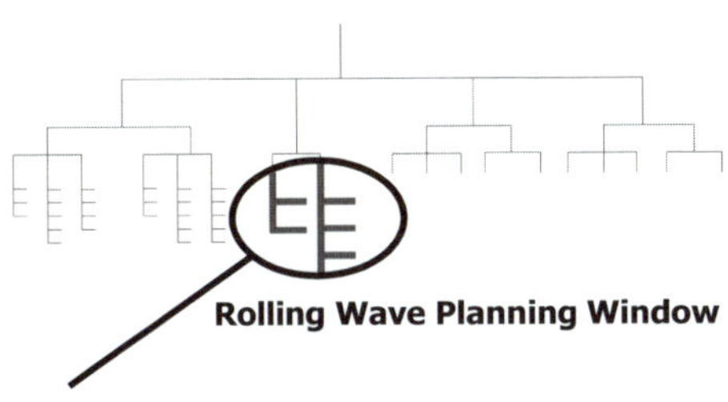

Some project managers would keep the estimate on the safe side for this part of the project by assuming they have to remodel the new location drastically. They enter just one deliverable, the *remodeled location*, in the *Work Breakdown Structure* (*WBS*) and the safe estimate. Once they have an idea which remodeling activities the new location needs, they start listing the detail activities as detail tasks for the deliverable and create the appropriate level of detail in the WBS. Notice in the illustration that the first 6 deliverables were already detailed to the task level, the next 2 deliverables just came within the *rolling wave planning window* and are currently broken down into tasks, whereas the last 10 deliverables are high level and still far in the future.

This is called the *Rolling Wave* approach; you do not detail the activities of the deliverables until you know well enough what they are. The project manager will use a planning window when applying the rolling wave technique. A *planning window* is a look-ahead window of a certain number of months. For example, in a project of one year, you could use a planning window of three months. As time goes by, the planning window moves ahead; as soon as a deliverable falls within it, you break it down to the level of detail tasks. In this one-year project, you would typically monitor this every month, and add detail to the WBS at the start of every month.

The rolling wave technique is useful to handle the unknown events that are far into the future and avoids having to redo large portions of the WBS that were uncertain. Often, the planning window is either a three or six month look-ahead window.

You can even apply the *1%-10% rule* (see page 135) when working with rolling wave planning to find the right level of detail for both the detail schedule and the high-level schedule. You take 1% and 10% of the planning window period to find the right level of detail for the detailed schedule. You take 1% and 10% of the total project duration to find the right level of detail for the high-level schedule of deliverables.

Unknown Resources

During the *planning* of the project it is often unclear whether enough resources will be available, who will be available and if they will be available at the time they are needed. Consulting companies often start the search for resources immediately after the ink has dried on a new contract.

If you do not know which actual resources you will get, you have to make assumptions just for planning purposes. If you do not make assumptions, you cannot finalize your detailed schedule. One common assumption project managers make is that the resources will be available when their project needs them. Of course, it is a good idea to discuss your resource needs with the resource manager, HR or executives as a reality check on this assumption. Make the assumption clear and explicit in the project plan, so no one's lack of memory will come back to haunt you.

"C++ Programmer"

"Winston"

If you do not know the names of the individuals you will have on your team, enter them as *generic resources* in terms of roles, functions or positions. The illustration shows that you do not know for sure who you will get on your team, and you therefore enter *C++ Programmer* instead. This simple technique will allow you to do your estimates and enter (generic) resources and assignments as well. You can now produce a detailed schedule. Once you know the names of the individuals, there are simple techniques to update your schedule to reflect this (see page 389) and replace the generic resource with *Winston*.

In *Project Server*, your Project Server administrators will define *generic resources* in the enterprise resource pool. As a project manager you can then assign the generic resources to tasks and accumulate workloads for them, and resource managers can do resource capacity planning with them. Generic resources are resources that have the field **Generic** set to **Yes** and the indicator . Generic resources allow you to finalize a detail schedule even when you do not know yet who you will get on your team. See page 297 for more detail.

You may have to formulate certain assumptions about the experience and skill levels of the actual resources that will eventually replace the generic resources.

Unknown Experience and Skill Level

If you create just one generic resource per skill you need (e.g., *C++ Programmer*), you assume that every *C++ Programmer* is equally productive. Programmers and their managers know that this is not true. If you think this will affect your first estimates, you can create several generic resource categories such as *Junior C++ Programmer* and *Senior C++ Programmer*. Assign the junior resource to the easy tasks and the senior resource to the tasks that require experience or skill. Once again, you need to substitute the generic junior and senior resource with the names of the actual individuals. We will discuss these techniques on page 389.

Junior

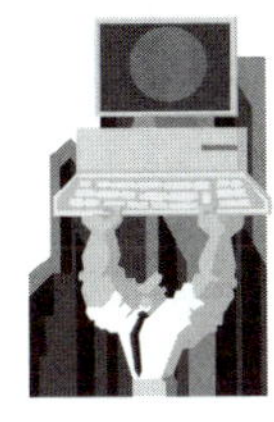

Senior

4

Unknown Learning Curve

Learning curve theory states that the time needed for similar and repeated deliverables will decrease with each repetition. Therefore, repetitions will affect estimates.

Projects create products that are unique. Some say that, because of the lack of repetition, the effect of the learning curve is limited in projects. The number of repetitions in projects is considerably lower than in manufacturing operations. However, in some projects, there is a lot of repetition. In implementation projects the same system is installed in many different locations. The learning curve theory is therefore applicable particularly to implementation projects and their duration estimates.

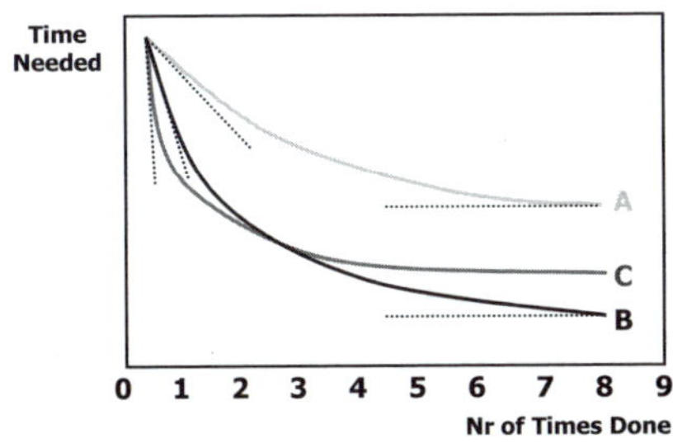

The amount of learning and the lack of repetition in projects combined imply that resources hired on projects have to be very fast learners. The ability to learn quickly is perhaps even the most important characteristic of good project resources.

Fast learners (B and C in the illustration on the left) have a *learning curve* that has a steep slope down. The next time they repeat something, the time needed goes down fast. Fast learners can also end up with a faster time per deliverable after many repetitions than slow learners (compare the horizontal dotted lines for A and B). However, it is not a given that the fastest time possible per deliverable is eventually lower for fast learners. To see this, compare the horizontal lines for B and C: C is faster initially, but B catches up:

- If you have little repetition in projects, the initial learning rate seems to be more important than the eventual fastest time per unit for most projects. We recommend you hire people with a C learning curve for your projects.
- In implementation projects, there can be many repetitions of installing the same hardware and/or software in many locations. Learning curves are important in this type of project. Here you probably want the resources that have learning curve B instead of C, because B-resources will eventually be fastest wherever they go.

The learning curve poses difficulties in terms of estimating. In order to produce the right estimate the estimator should not only look at the job, but also at who will do the job. How much repetition does the job have? Is the resource a slow or a fast learner? How can I maximize the learning by mixing fast and slow learners on an implementation team? These factors complicate estimating and, again, you may have to make some assumptions as to the rate of learning of the resources. Do not forget to make these assumptions explicit in your project plan, otherwise you may end up with a slow learner (and be blamed for late delivery). In addition, if you do not document how you arrived at your estimates, you will not be able to learn from the discrepancies between original plan and actual execution.

Living Document Approach

As we just saw, there are many unknowns in projects: unknown events, unknown resources, unknown experience, unknown skill levels and unknown learning curves. A common way to deal with all unknowns is to make assumptions and treat the project plan as a living document that is subject to *progressive elaboration*.

When dealing with the unknowns, you can always estimate by making *assumptions*. An assumption is something you treat to be true just for the purpose of being able to do your estimating. We recommend you document the assumptions on which you based your estimates. If any of the assumptions change, you have a more supportable position for revising your estimate.

The *living document approach* basically says that your detailed project plan is not finished and final until the project is closed. You keep reviewing your assumptions, revising and refining the plan during the entire project life; you progressively elaborate it. The project plan "lives" in a sense. You will continue to refine the task list, the estimates and assignments during project execution. *Rolling Wave* is one example of how the living document approach can be implemented.

Note that the high-level project plan does not change in a living document approach; the *scope* and *quality* requirements, the major *deadlines* and the *budget* may not change at all. The *baseline* may not change. Changes in the high-level project plan only happen through a formal approval process that typically involves your executives and clients. In the living document approach, changes happen at the lower levels of detail.

Checks on the Estimates

Here is a summary of the best practices for the estimates of your project. The numbering corresponds to the complete checklist in the summary chapter, see page 711. The filters mentioned in the checks can be found in the file *ProjectPro tools to check project schedules.MPP* available for download at www.ProjectProCorp.com (see page vi for the procedure to access these files).

4 Estimates

4.1. Do all detail tasks have an estimate?
When the **Task Mode** is **Manually Scheduled**, one of the essential pieces of schedule data may be missing: duration, start or finish. If one piece is missing, the task is called *unscheduled* and is just a placeholder with its field **Placeholder** set to **Yes**. By filtering on this field you can easily check if you have entered all estimates. **Auto Scheduled** tasks always have all three pieces of information, because MS Project will enter default durations of 1 day, if needed, and dates (the project start date as the default start date). You can perform this check by applying the filter
4.1 All Estimates Entered?

4.2. Are the estimates that you collected consistent with the working hours entered in the **Standard (Project Calendar)**?
If they are not consistent the schedule will be too long or too short.
- ◇ Gross working time estimates should be entered in a schedule with gross working hours on the project calendar (typically 8:00 AM - 5:00 PM). This is what most organizations use, see page 183 for the reason why.
- ◇ Pure working time estimates should be entered in a schedule with pure working hours on the project calendar – a shorter working day. If you estimate that the productive hours are 70% of the time spent at work, the working hours should be 70% * 8h = 5.6 hours, rounded to 5.5 hours. Working hours that correspond to this are, for example, 9:00 AM - 12:00 PM and 1:00 PM - 3:30 PM.
We recommend that you set working hours like these on the project calendar if you want to work with pure work time estimates.
See page 185 for more details. For the steps to enter working hours,

see page 102. If you adjust the working times, you also need to adjust the conversion factors, see page 95.

4.3. Are the *estimates* reasonable given the work that needs to be performed?

- ◇ Some types of tasks are easily underestimated; for example, writing documents takes a lot of time (I sigh deeply while writing this), at least 2 hours per page. For other tasks, you will need some technical expertise to verify if the estimates are reasonable. If you do not have this technical expertise, you could review the schedules of similar, completed projects. You can ask your team members who have the technical knowledge to review each other's estimates (peer review) or you can ask a *subject matter expert* (*SME*) to review the estimates.
- ◇ Sometimes tasks are overestimated. Some project managers incorporate waiting time into the duration estimates, such as when they have to wait two weeks for approvals or one week for a review by the end user. Waiting time is more appropriately modeled as a lag on the dependency; see page 214 for how to enter lags. Any review or approval cycle includes waiting time.

4.4. Is the amount of effort on overhead tasks reasonable compared to the total amount of effort (Work)?
The percent of overhead effort needs to be between 10% (construction projects) and 30% (research projects) of the total effort in the project.

Copying and Moving Data

Entering estimates can be a tedious job. We will discuss some quick ways to enter data into MS Project.

Editing Fields of Multiple Tasks at Once

1. Select the tasks by clicking on the first task, then hold down Control while clicking on the next ones until they are all selected.

2. Click ribbon **Task** and find its section **Properties**. Click 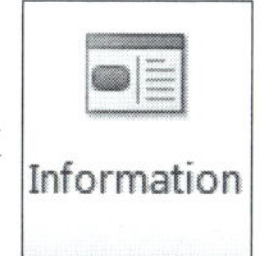

   OR

   hold down Shift and press F2 – the **Multiple Task Information** dialog appears:

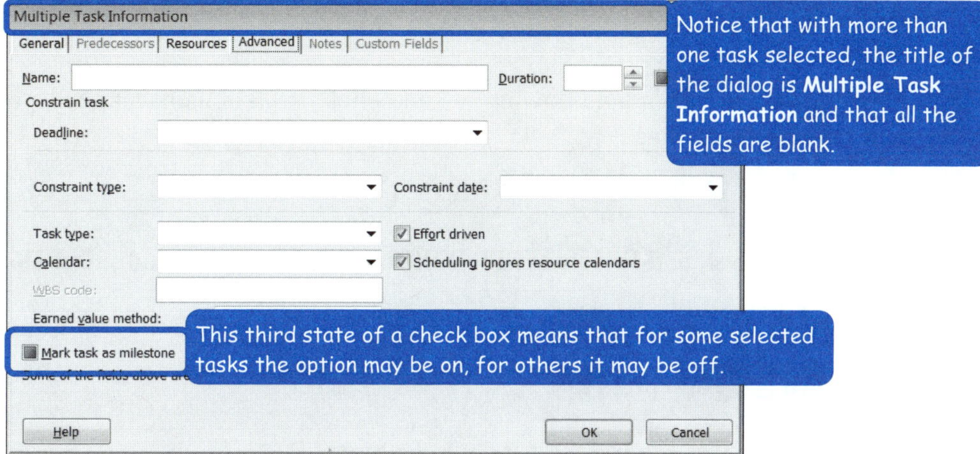

3. Make the changes needed on each tab.
4. Click OK.

The **Multiple Task Information** dialog can be used as a time saver for many purposes, for example:

- Setting the duration of all the milestones to 0 (zero) and clearing ☐ **Estimated** to make the question marks disappear.
- Changing the task type on the **Advanced** tab in the field **Task type**. For example, you can change the type of task from **Fixed Duration** to **Fixed Work** for a series of tasks. This shows up in the field **Type** in the spreadsheet.
- Assigning a resource to many tasks at once on the tab **Resources**.

4

Copying with Fill Down

1. Enter the value that you want to copy down in the top cell.
2. Click and hold down on the top cell and drag down over all adjacent cells you want to fill.
   OR

   Hold down Shift and press ↓ until you have selected the top cell and all cells you wish to fill.
   OR

   Select the top cell, then hold down Control and click on all nonadjacent cells to fill with the value.
3. Right-click within the selected area and select **Fill Down**.
   OR

   Click ribbon **Task** and find its section **Editing**. Click Fill and select **Down** in the drop-down menu.
   OR

   Hold down Control and press D.

Examples in which you can use the fill down feature:

- Changing the constraint types for many tasks. To get rid of constraints, fill *As Soon As Possible* in the field *Constraint Type*.
- Enter a certain **Task Mode** or task **Type** for many tasks at once.

Fill Up or Fill Down Using the Fill Handle

1. Enter the value you wish to fill in the top or the bottom cell of the area to be filled.
2. Make sure you have the cell selected and at the bottom right of the cell you will see a fill handle 1 day? Fill handle
3. Point to the fill handle; watch the mouse pointer : 1 day? Crosshair mouse pointer
4. When you see a crosshair mouse pointer, click and hold down and drag over the cells to be filled. Note that you can only fill adjacent cells in this way.

Copying, Moving or Clearing Cells

Some remarks upfront:

- When copying or moving cells, you have to make sure that the receiving cells can accommodate the type of data you paste in. MS Project will warn you if the cells cannot receive the data and will refuse the data if it does not make sense. For example, you cannot copy dates into the duration field.
- You have to be careful to paste the data into blank cells; otherwise existing cell entries may be overridden. Click **Undo** on the **Quick Access Toolbar** when an accident occurs.
- You cannot copy one cell and paste it into many other cells, like you can in *MS Excel*. MS Project will only paste the value into the first cell of all paste cells you selected.
- If you would classify yourself as "mouse-challenged" or a "careless clicker", you should consider turning the *cell drag and drop* option off to prevent accidental moving or overriding of data. You can do so by clicking ribbon **File**, Options, tab **Advanced**, section **Edit** and clearing ☐ **Allow Cell Drag and Drop**.

Copying Cells

Select the cells and click Copy on the **Task** ribbon, then select the cells to paste into and click the part of Paste.

OR

Select the cells and point to the border of the selected area. Make sure the mouse pointer changes from a plus sign to a . Hold down Control while dragging the cells to their new place.

Moving Cells

Select the cells and click Cut on the **Task** ribbon, then select the cells to paste into and click the top part of Paste.

OR

Select the cells and point to the border of the selected area. Make sure the mouse pointer changes from a plus sign ✚ to ✥. Drag the cells to their new place.

Clearing Cells

The Delete key clears the content of the selected cells.
OR
Select the cells (not the row heading — the locked first column) and click ribbon **Task**, and find its section **Editing** on the far right end of the ribbon, click button Clear.

The drop-down menu of this button can be used to selectively clear only the hyperlinks, only the notes or only the formatting of a task.

Clearing Rows

You can delete entire rows with the Delete key. First select the entire row by clicking on its ID number and then pressing Delete. You can select multiple adjacent rows by dragging over their row headings. To select non-adjacent rows, select one row first, then hold down Control while selecting the other rows.

Copying or Moving the Data in an Entire Column

1. Select the whole column by clicking on its column heading.
2. Select the cells, click ribbon **Task** and click Copy.
3. Click the column heading of the column into which you want to paste the data.
4. Click the top part of Paste (**Task** ribbon).

Make sure the receiving column can handle the type of data being added; for example, only dates can be copied into date columns, text into text columns and numbers into number columns. The *Duration* column is a text column in Project 2010. The *Scheduled Duration* column looks like a text column, because of the time unit, like *5 days,* but it is a number column. You will receive an error message from MS Project if it cannot paste the data.

4

Copying Tasks or Resources between Projects

1. Open the project you wish to copy from.
2. Select the tasks or resources by dragging over their ID numbers (the first column with the gray color) to select entire tasks or resources.
   OR
   Select non-adjacent tasks or resources by clicking one ID-number first, holding down Control and clicking other tasks or resources.
3. Select the cells, click ribbon **Task** and click Copy. The data are now temporarily stored in the clipboard.
4. Open the project to be copied to.
5. Select the row before which to insert the data and click the top part of .

Note that copying between earlier versions of MS Project and the 2010 version is not supported, because Microsoft changed the Duration, Start and Finish fields to text fields in Project 2010.

Copying Objects between Projects

Objects are views, reports, calendars and other things that change the appearance of the data or affect the scheduling (see also page 59). Copy objects between projects using the *Organizer*.

1. Click ribbon **File**, tab **Info**, button **Organizer** – the **Organizer** dialog appears:

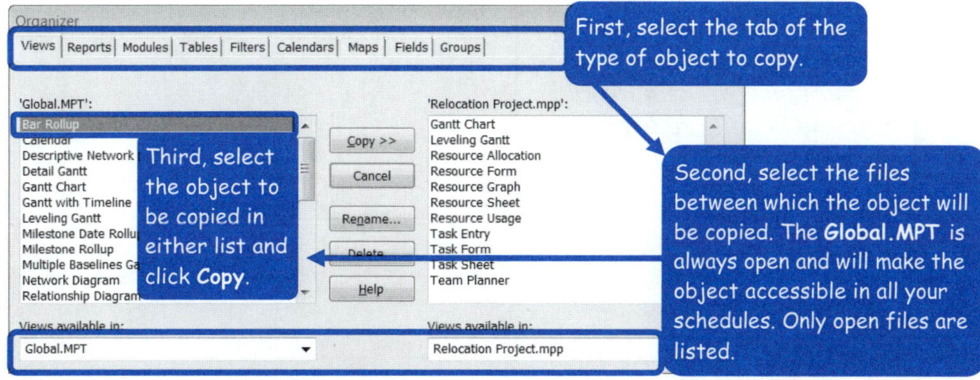

2. Click on the tab of the type of objects to transfer.

3. From the lists at the bottom of the dialog select the schedule from which to copy the object; in the other list, select the schedule to copy to. Only the files currently open will be in the list.

4. Select the object and click [Copy >>] to copy from the left list to the right or [<< Copy] to copy from right to left.

5. Click [Close] when done.

The organizer allows you to copy objects to other project schedules or to the *Global.MPT* – the global template. Any objects you put into this *global template* are visible in all your projects, unless they have the same name as other objects that are already in the project schedule.

With the organizer you can, for example:

- Create a standard report and make it available to colleagues.
- Share views, tables and filters with other people who would like to present their project in a format similar to yours.

Exercises

Review Questions

1. Why is estimating the duration of project activities difficult?

2. You are the project manager. When you are working with your team members on estimating the tasks, somebody makes one of the following statements to you. What would you say?

Somebody's statement	**Your response**
Your team member says: *"I can't give you an estimate, because I can't predict the future! I don't possess higher powers."*	

Your team member says: "*Listen, we went over this already. I am not going to give you any more estimates, because my estimates are always off! My estimates don't help you anyway!*"	
Your executive says: "*You are one of our most experienced and best project managers. Can't you do this project in three weeks?*"	

3. In your own words, what is the difference between *Duration* and *Work*?
4. What formula is working behind the screens of MS Project that relates *Duration* to *Work*?
5. Rank the following time units on difficulty to express estimates in (for most detail tasks in a typical project) and then for your own projects:

Time unit	Difficulty for most projects	Difficulty for your own projects
Business days		
Calendar days		
Person days		

6. What is the difference between a pure work time estimate and a gross work time estimate?
7. Somebody gives you an estimate of 100 person hours of effort for a task and says that the estimate assumes uninterrupted and fully focused work time. You just created a new project schedule that has all options set to the default settings in MS Project.
   a. What other fields or dialog boxes would you have to change in order to get a valid finish date forecast for this task from MS Project standalone?
   b. In which field would you enter this estimate in MS Project?
8. What are two easy ways to change the task type to *Fixed Work* for multiple tasks in the task list?

9. One of your fellow project managers has created a project calendar that has all the national holidays and the company holidays filled in for the next five years. You would like to use that same project calendar for your projects. Explain in detailed steps how you would go about that in MS Project standalone.

Relocation Project — Entering Estimates

The goal of this exercise is to be able to enter duration and work estimates and protect them by setting the task type accordingly.

Continue to work with your file *Relocation.mpp* or open the file *04A Estimates.mpp* available for download at www.ProjectProCorp.com (see page vi for the procedure to access these files).

1. Insert the fields *Type*, *Effort Driven, Duration* and *Work* in the Gantt spreadsheet in the order they appear in the column headings of the next table (see page 175 for how-to steps).
2. Check in ribbon **File,** [Options], tab **Schedule** if the time unit for **Work is entered in** is set to **Days**.
3. Check if the default **Task Mode** is set to **Auto Scheduled**. In the bottom left of the screen, click [New Tasks :] and select **Auto Scheduled** OR click ribbon **File**, [Options], tab **Schedule** and switch **New tasks created** to **Auto Scheduled**.
4. Enter the data from the next table into the Relocation project file. Please note:
   - ◇ The tasks with zero duration will become milestones.
   - ◇ Where no data are provided (blank cell), do not enter anything; MS Project will fill in the default duration of *1 day?* and the default work of *0 days*. Leave these as they are; you cannot blank them out.
   - ◇ You can enter the data very fast by using the methods explained, see page 192 and 194.
5. Compare your file with the solution file *05A Dependencies.mpp* available for download at www.ProjectProCorp.com (see page vi for the procedure to access these files). See page 697 of this book for an automated method of comparing and reporting differences between two versions of one schedule.
6. Save your file.

ID	Task Name	Type	Effort Driven	Duration	Work
1.	REQUIREMENTS	Fixed Duration [34]	No		
2.	research staff requirements	Fixed Work	Yes		2 d
3.	summarize requirements	Fixed Work	Yes		2 d
4.	LOCATION	Fixed Duration	No		
5.	select the realtor	Fixed Duration	No	4 d	
6.	visit the sites	Fixed Duration	No	1 d	
7.	evaluate the sites	Fixed Duration	No	1 d	
8.	meet to select the location	Fixed Duration	No	1 d	
9.	legal review	Fixed Duration	No	0.5 d	
10.	location selected	Fixed Duration	No	0 d	
11.	REMODELING CONTRACT	Fixed Duration	No		
12.	select the contractor	Fixed Duration	No	2 d	
13.	meet to discuss contract	Fixed Duration	No	1 d	
14.	revise the schedule	Fixed Duration	No	1 d	
15.	negotiate the contract	Fixed Duration	No	1 d	
16.	contractor contracted	Fixed Duration	No	0 d	
17.	REMODELED LOCATION	Fixed Duration	No		
18.	relocate walls	Fixed Work	Yes		100 d
19.	install electric wiring	Fixed Work	Yes		25 d
20.	Paint	Fixed Work	Yes		8 d

---

[34] Notice that you cannot change the **Type** of a summary task; it is set by MS Project to **Fixed Duration**. Also notice that **Durations** or **Work** numbers are not provided for summary tasks, because they are calculated by MS Project for **Auto Scheduled** tasks.

ID	Task Name	Type	Effort Driven	Duration	Work
21.	drying of paint	Fixed Duration	No	4 ed [35]	
22.	install cabinetry	Fixed Work	Yes		40 d
23.	install LAN	Fixed Work	Yes		60 d
24.	lay carpet	Fixed Work	Yes		60 d
25.	facility remodelled	Fixed Duration	No	0 d	
26.	MOVE	Fixed Duration	No		
27.	select mover	Fixed Duration	No	2 d	
28.	pack	Fixed Duration	No	2 d	
29.	move	Fixed Work	Yes		20 d
30.	unpack	Fixed Duration	No	2 d	
31.	new location opened	Fixed Duration	No	0 d	

[35] Notice the "*e*" in "*4ed*"; this is an elapsed duration that continues through the night and weekend.

Chapter 5 Entering Dependencies

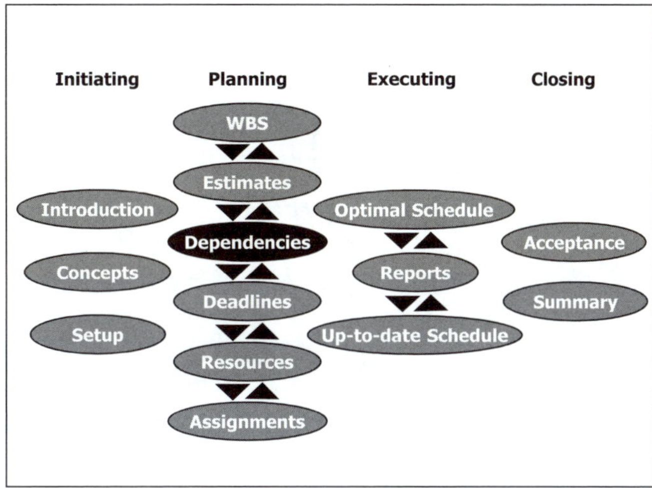

We have the WBS and the estimates entered into our project schedule at this point and are ready to enter the dependencies, as the black ellipse above shows. *Dependencies* are relationships between tasks.

After reading this chapter you will:

- know what dependencies are and think of them in terms of cause-and-effect relationships
- realize how important dependencies are for dynamic scheduling
- be able to choose the right type of dependencies
- be able to enter all types of dependencies into an MS Project schedule
- be able to determine if you need a lead or lag on a dependency, expressed in absolute or relative terms
- be able to give a task multiple predecessors or successors
- know the best practices for the network logic in project schedules
- be able to check if the network logic of a schedule follows the best practices
- be able to format the Network Diagram view in a useful or attractive way

Go Slow To Go Fast

Nob: "Hey Bob, are you still working on your schedule? I kept my schedule simple: just activities and dates. I am done already and have started the work in my project." Bob: "Yeah, I'm still firming up the activities and working out the dependencies between them; it does take some time to figure them out." Nob responds: "I didn't bother with dependencies. Bob, you waste too much time on your schedule!"

A few months later our friends meet again when their projects are well under way. "Nob, you look stressed. What's up?" Nob replies: "My schedule is taking a lot of time; every Friday I need to go through all the dates with my team and adjust them in the schedule. It's a lot of work adjusting all those dates."

Bob's face can't hide a smile: "My schedule updates most of its dates by itself, thanks to the dependencies I set. Now I just need to enter revisions to the durations, and the rest of the schedule is forecasted automatically."

Nob concludes: "I guess you went slowly in the planning phase in order to go fast in the execution phase."

Dependencies

The Principle of Dynamic Scheduling

Too often we hear: *I do not have time to plan my project*! As outside observers, we find it odd that these people find themselves too busy to get organized. A *dynamic schedule* is not just a fashionable term – it can help you. We would like you to think of a schedule as a forecast model that reflects your real-life project all the time and allows for easy updating when you are busy during project execution. You will only come close to this dynamic ideal if your schedule meets the following *requirements*:

- You find and enter all the *relationships* between the tasks that may impact your forecasts. These relationships are called "*dependencies*" and are discussed in this chapter.
- You minimize the number of *hard dates* in your schedule. Hard dates or *fixed dates* are called *constraints* in MS Project. We will discuss constraints in the next chapter.

Finding the dependencies between the tasks and entering them into your schedule takes considerable effort. A legitimate question therefore is: *Why is it important to strive towards this principle of dynamic scheduling in your schedules?*

Many changes occur in every project. Every time a change happens, you need to change your schedule to reflect the new reality. If you have a static model, you need to review the dates of all future tasks every time and adjust many of them. If you have a dynamic model, when one thing changes in your real-life project, ideally you would have to change only one field in your MS Project model to have accurate forecasts again. If you did an excellent job on dependencies, you probably do not even need to review all dates of future tasks and you can rely almost blindly on the dependencies to adjust their dates appropriately. Network logic tends to stay the same during the entire project.

If you do not use dependencies, you have to review and redo the future portion of the schedule by hand. This may seem acceptable during the *planning*, when you still have the time, but it becomes impossible during the execution of the project, when too many things change and they change continuously. I have seen too often that early in the *execution* of a project, the Gantt Chart ended up in a drawer and was never looked at again. Some companies have never been able to keep any of their schedules alive during project execution. It is during project execution that you reap the greatest benefits from your forecast model: the continuous forecasts of project end date and final cost. The schedule has to be a dynamic model of your project to gain those benefits, and it is only a dynamic model if it has all the dependencies set and few constraints. A schedule without all dependencies is just a one-time snapshot of your project; it is a nice chart to look at and often used as wallpaper at the office. In order to manage your project and address all things that happen, you need a forecast model inside a computer.

Expected Gains from Dynamic Scheduling

Let us see if we can approximately quantify how much time you may gain by applying the principle of dynamic scheduling. Imagine a 3-month schedule with 100 tasks. It will take approximately 8 hours of effort to discuss, identify and set all the dependencies and make the model dynamic.

How many changes occur? This is the hard question. We do know for sure that each task needs to be updated at least once, and about 30% of them twice. This already results in 130 changes to the schedule, if you enter them all individually.

Other changes that typically happen in projects are:

- Clients change their mind on requirements
- Deliverables are dropped, others are added
- Activities that were overlooked are inserted
- Activities that cannot be done are dropped
- Resources get sick or need leaves of absence
- Resources are kept longer in prior projects or need to start earlier on new projects
- Resources are interrupted with higher priorities

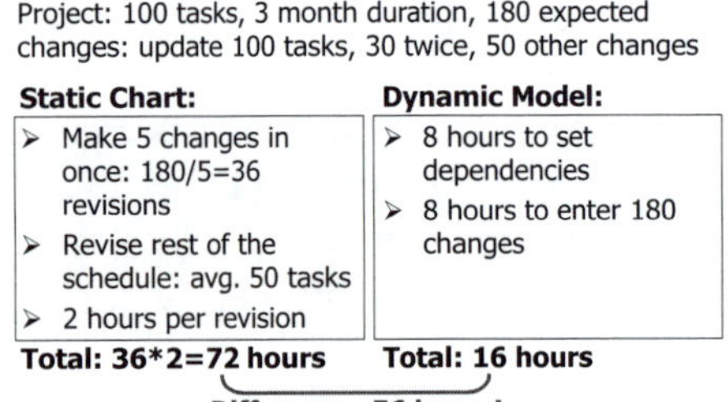

Let us be conservative and say that these things cause 50 more changes, for a total of 180 changes for a 100-task schedule. Entering 180 changes in a dynamic model would take you about 8 hours, since you typically only need to revise one (or two) fields for each change. Identifying and entering all the dependencies in a 100-task schedule takes about 8 hours: Total 16 hours.

With every change in a static version of this schedule, you have to review and adjust the start and finish dates of 50 tasks on average. If adjusting 50 tasks takes you about 2 hours for each change, the total time spent to keep the schedule alive will be 180 * 2 = 360 hours. Working with a static schedule becomes a full-time job and does not allow project managers to manage the project.

What you will see in practice is that people who work with static schedules get smart and enter 5 changes at a time and only then review the rest of their schedule. In other words, they update their schedule only 180 / 5 = 36 times instead of 180 times. Notice that now the schedule is no longer up-to-date all the time, another disadvantage of static schedules. Even in this case they will spend at least 36 * 2 = 72 hours on their schedule. The difference in effort spent on a static schedule versus a dynamic schedule is: 72 - 16 = 56 hours for a 100 task schedule, which is approximately the gain you can expect from applying the *principle* of *dynamic scheduling*. This is time you can spend with your family or friends instead of with MS Project.

The expected gains from applying the principle of dynamic scheduling are:

- Save about 50 hours of scheduling time on a 100-task project
  If you adjust the averages and calculation for the typical project in your organization and multiply the saved hours by the number of projects your organization has, you will get an idea of the potential savings when the principles of this book are implemented.
- These 50 hours saved in a 100-task schedule do not include how much time you will save when developing what-if scenarios with a dynamic model instead of a static model. Every time the project slips, you will have to develop what-if scenarios to find solutions for the slippage; the dynamic model will be much more helpful than a static model, providing additional time savings.
- Another advantage of working with dependencies instead of with dates is that you set dependencies during the *planning* of the project when you have time; you reap the benefits of them during the *execution* of the project when you do not have time. If you hard code all dates, you save time during the planning, but you waste much more time during execution.
- A dynamic model can be up-to-date all the time. If you use Project Server as a communication platform, executives can see *real time status* in the project schedules online.

Organizations may need to invest in training to ensure that their project managers apply the principle of dynamic scheduling properly and that people, indeed, adjust their behavior and habits. If you ask your project managers to get their schedules checked on quality, it is even more likely that the schedules will be better.

Hopefully, we have convinced you that finding the dependencies is the way to go. They make the schedule come alive. In other words, *do the logic well, and your life will be swell.*

What Are Dependencies?

A *dependency* is a relationship between the (start or) finish of one task and the start (or finish) of another task. The dependency reflects the cause-and-effect, or logical *relationship* between the two tasks. The dependency shown in the illustration causes the finish of the independent task *write* (predecessor) to drive the start of the dependent task *print* (successor); when the finish date of *write* changes the start date of *print* will move with it. If *write* extends or slips, *print* will slip.

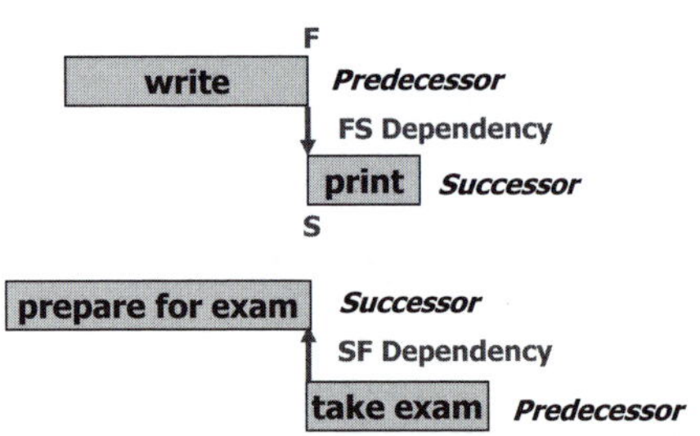

Many people think of dependencies as the *chronological* sequencing of tasks. If you belong to that category of project manager, you may get stuck on the concept of dependencies. I once met a project manager with 15 years of experience who was still struggling with the difference between a predecessor and a successor. He thought that the predecessor task is always identified by its earlier occurrence in time and by its chronology in the schedule. In fact, it is not identified by the occurrence in time (chronology). He became confused when he saw that a successor task might occur in the schedule before a predecessor task like in the second example in the illustration: *prepare for exam* and *take exam* where the date of the university exam drives when the preparation is scheduled. As a result, he never truly understood the difference between a predecessor and a successor; he took the terms literally.

The words *predecessor* and *successor* are in fact misleading, because they imply chronology: the predecessor precedes and the successor succeeds. Dependencies are not a matter of chronology, but about cause-and-effect! Cause-and-effect dependencies can come from:

- *Practical necessities*: for example, the book needs to be written before it can be printed. If you ever succeed in printing a book before writing it, please let me know.
- *Mandatory processes*: for example, if your organization requires a quality review before releasing a report, this would also create a dependency.

Think of the predecessor as the *independent* or driving task (*driver*) and of the successor as the *dependent* or *driven* task. In order to find the predecessor, the right question to ask is *"Which task drives the other task?"* When you try to identify dependencies with your team members, we suggest you use the terms *driver* and *driven* task, instead of *predecessor* and *successor*. For example, ask the question: Of the tasks *"prepare for university exam"* and *"take exam,"* which drives the other? This question produces the right dependency (Start-to-Finish from exam to prepare). Instead, if you ask the question: *Which of the tasks precedes the other?,* you produce the wrong dependency (Finish-to-Start from prepare to exam). A *Finish-to-Start* dependency from *prepare for exam* to *take exam* is wrong for most exams because it will move the exam date when preparing takes longer. If the exam date is changed, the preparation should be rescheduled, because the exam date has an impact on the timing of preparation, not vice versa. Therefore the *Start-to-Finish* dependency is better. The arrow of the dependency always points in the direction the impact goes. No matter what, the dependencies will be stored in MS Project in the fields called **Predecessors** and **Successors**.

The whole network of dependencies is also called the *network logic*. The word "*logic*" provides a much better reference to the cause-and-effect character of dependencies.

5

Why Should I Use Dependencies?

Most people think of a schedule as a list of deliverables and dates. Therefore, many people tend to enter start and finish dates into scheduling software. This is not necessary. We even strongly recommend not entering start and finish dates, because this creates rigid schedules. Instead, MS Project only needs to know the durations and dependencies.

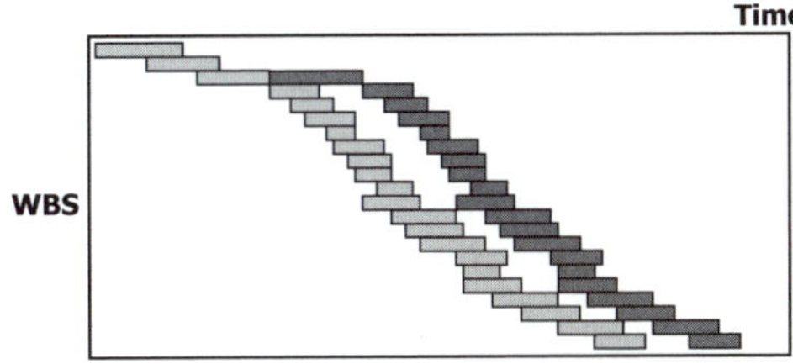

Automatic updates !

The main benefits of making all the dependencies between the tasks explicit in MS Project are:

- When one task slips or extends, MS Project knows how to recalculate the entire schedule for you. You can start relying blindly on the network of dependencies to do this. I often do not check the dates of the rest of the schedule but directly look at the impact of the slip on the project finish date. In the illustration, the duration of the third task was extended and all the dependent tasks were immediately rescheduled as a result.
- If you enter all the logical relationships as dependencies, MS Project will determine the correct *Critical Path* in your schedule. The Critical Path is that subset of tasks in your schedule that drives the project finish date. See page 418 for more on the Critical Path. You can now focus on a subset of tasks, the Critical Path, to bring your project in on time. This will make you more efficient and effective as a project manager.

Why Should I Treat Dependencies as Cause-and-Effect?

There are several reasons for treating dependencies as logical relationships (cause-and-effect) rather than as chronological relationships (precede and succeed):

- **Logical relationships stay the same**
  Logical relationships do not change over time, whereas chronological relationships may need to be revised when a task slips or extends. This means that if you enter logical relationships, you need to enter them only once and you do not need to maintain them. If you enter chronological relationships, you will be twisting and tweaking them repeatedly. For example, you are creating a new software application and you need to train people in its use. At first glance, you would finish the application and then train the users (after). However, we observed in many situations that the training takes place while the application is debugged (during). Sometimes, the training is done before the programming was finished (before), but after the screens of the application had been decided upon. If you were to look for the logical instead of the chronological relationship, you would realize that the finalization of the screens drives the training no matter what; you cannot do computer application training without having the final screens. This relationship is a practical necessity and will not change.
- **You will spend less time maintaining the network logic**
  Logical relationships will bring you closer to implementing the *principle of dynamic scheduling*; if one thing changes, you need to change only one thing in the schedule. Chronological relationships will move you away from the principle of dynamic scheduling, because when you make a change, you often have to change other chronological dependencies as well. Ask yourself: *Do I often change dependencies during project execution?* If the answer is *yes*, you have been creating chronological dependencies rather than logical dependencies.
- **Logical dependencies provide more reliable automatic updates**
  Logical relationships withstand the changes you throw at them better than chronological relationships. Unforeseen events often force you to revisit the chronology of events, whereas logical relationships are necessary relationships that will stay true under a wider variety of circumstances. Almost all projects have unforeseen events. By implementing the *principle of dynamic scheduling*, you can start to blindly rely on your network logic to always produce a feasible version of the schedule. See page 216 for an example.
- **Logical dependencies make always-up-to-date schedules possible**
  Because logical dependencies withstand more changes and update schedules more reliably, it may be possible to realize the ideal of always-up-to-date schedules. Just imagine that your schedule is up-to-date all the time with minimal effort. Executives can check the status and forecasts of your project 24 * 7 hours per week. This will remove the delay in the management feedback loop for executives and clients, reduce the need for many formal status cycles, and perhaps eliminate status meetings

entirely. If executives do not like what they see, they will talk to you as the project manager.

- **Logical relationships produce the tightest possible schedules**
  Logical relationships will provide the true range of possible project finish times. These cause-and-effect relationships will tell you the absolute minimum duration of the project and protect the sanity of the schedule. Because logical relationships model what is necessary to proceed from a practical viewpoint, they automatically lead you to create a schedule with a maximum of overlap and concurrence between activities. In the first bullet of this list, we gave the example of software training after the software has finalized screens instead of after final software release. Logical relationships will tell you the minimum duration, whereas chronological relationships often tell you the nice-to-have duration of the project.

Choosing the Options

Click ribbon **File**, Options and click on the tab indicated in the table below where you want to change settings:

Tab	Option
Schedule	☑ **Autolink inserted or moved tasks** With *Autolink* on, MS Project itself will set or break dependencies inside a waterfall chain of Finish-to-Start dependencies. It assumes that you want sequential dependencies for the tasks you inserted or moved inside a waterfall chain. If you want to switch this option in all your projects, first select **All new projects** from the list **Scheduling options for this project**.

Autolink works inside a chain of tasks with Finish-To-Start dependencies. If you insert a task inside the chain as shown in the illustration, MS Project will immediately incorporate it into the chain of dependencies. It breaks one dependency (the one crossed out) and sets two new ones (the thick black arrows).

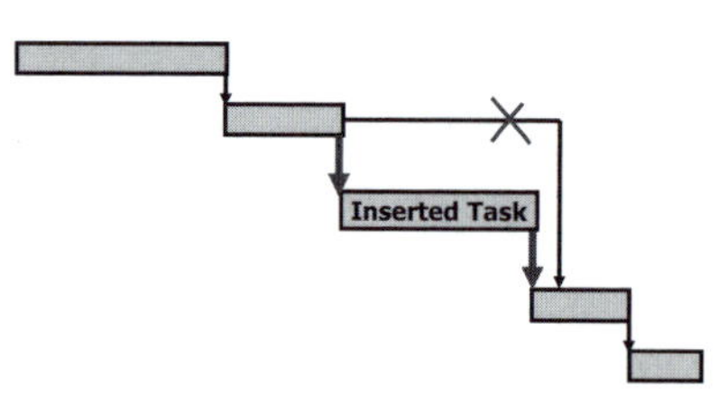

If you move a task, it closes the chain by cutting two dependencies and creating one new one. At the location where you insert the task, Autolink incorporates the task in the chain of dependencies (cutting one dependency and creating two new ones).

This feature can be helpful during the *planning* of the project. However, after you have checked the network logic carefully, we recommend you turn it off. MS Project's Autolink makes its own decisions on which dependencies to set or break. To the uninformed scheduler, they may seem arbitrary.

Types of Dependencies

You will be using mostly FS-dependencies that run from the finish (F) of the driver to the start (S) of the driven task.

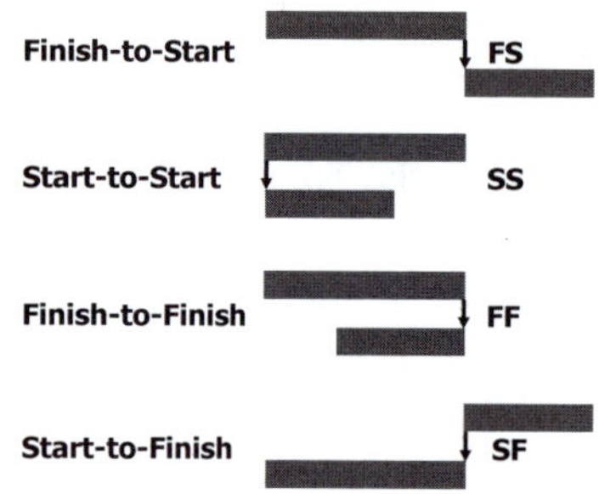

The driver task (predecessor) can be linked from its start or from its finish. The driven task can be linked to its start or to its finish. This gives a total of four different possibilities and four types of dependencies. The dependencies are characterized by the following abbreviations: FS, SS, FF and SF as shown in the illustration. Examples for each type of dependency:

- *Finish-to-Start* (*FS*):
  A Finish-to-Start dependency (without lag) causes the driven task to start when or after the driver finishes.
  - ◇ The foundation has to be poured before erecting the walls. The finish of the foundation drives the start of the walls. Similarly, the walls need to be up before the roofing can begin.
  - ◇ A report has to be written before it can be printed. If the finish date of the writing slips, the start date of the printing should slip with it.

- *Start-to-Start* (*SS*):
  A Start-to-Start dependency (without lag) causes the driven task to start when or after the driver task starts.
  - ◇ When you pour a concrete floor, you want it to be leveled and finished right away before it cures. There is an SS link between the tasks *pour concrete* and *level concrete*.
  - ◇ The start of launching the rocket should cause the start of monitoring the orbit of the rocket.
  - ◇ Two days after the carpenters start to break out old drywall and put up new, the electricians can start (SS + 2 days).
- *Finish-to-Finish* (*FF*):
  A Finish-to-Finish dependency (without lag) causes the driven task to finish when or after the driver task finishes.
  - ◇ If you train people in how to use a new software application, you would like to have the software installation finished just as they return to their workstations. There is an FF link between *train users* and *install application*.
  - ◇ Researchers conduct their research and write the report as they go along, but only when the research is finished can they finish the report. After the writing is finished, the editing will be ready in 2 days. (FF + 2 days).
  - ◇ You conduct a series of workshops and only need 1 day after the end of the last workshop to complete the evaluation report for all courses (FF + 1 day).
- *Start-to-Finish (SF)*:
  A Start-to-Finish dependency causes the driven task to finish when or after the driver task starts.
  - ◇ When the new ecommerce website comes online, the old one will stop.
  - ◇ The fixed start date of a university exam schedules the preparation to finish when the exam starts (SF).

Note that all these dependencies schedule the driven tasks *when or after* the driver task and, therefore, all dependencies can be characterized as *later-than dependencies*.

Absolute Lead or Lag Time in Business Days

When you want the driven task (successor) to wait some time before it starts, you can add a *lag* to a dependency. The lag is expressed in *business days* or *elapsed days* just like the duration. Lag time acts as if the dependency has a duration, and it always keeps the two task bars apart by the amount of lag time. For example, if you apply for a building permit, you often have to wait 6 weeks before you can start construction. This would be an FS dependency with a lag of 6 weeks between the tasks *apply for permit* and *dig the foundation,* as shown in the second example in the illustration.

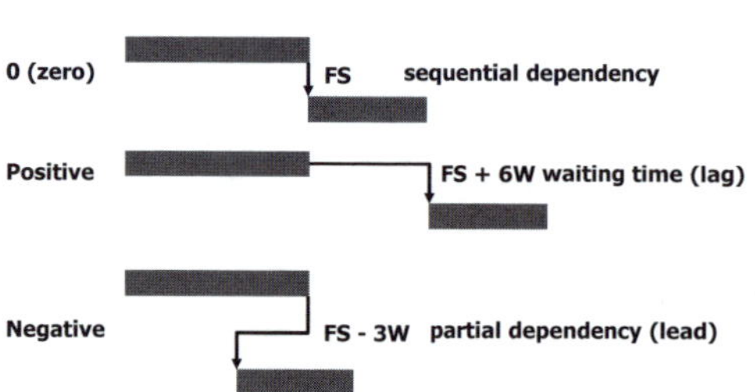

A lag can also be negative. A negative lag is called a *lead*, since the start of the successor will be earlier than the finish of the predecessor. In such a *partial dependency*, the driven task (successor) is dependent upon the partial completion of its predecessor. As a result, the task bars overlap each other in time. For example, if you write a report, you could finish the entire report before you send it to the editor. You could also send the first half of the report and then write and edit concurrently. This would be an FS dependency between *write report* and *edit report* with a lead of, say, 3 weeks. MS Project only has one field called *Lag*, and you will enter leads as negative lags, so in this case you would enter *FS-3W*, see the third example in the illustration.

Note that in the previous illustration lag and lead are shown only on the Finish-to-Start (FS) dependency; they can be applied to all other types of dependencies as well.

Absolute Lead or Lag Time in Elapsed Days

You can even enter the lag as an elapsed time, and MS Project will schedule the driven task accordingly. *Elapsed days* are calendar days and are scheduled *24 * 7*, ignoring the nonworking hours of evenings and weekends. You can enter an *elapsed lag* by entering in the **Lag** field, for example, *2ed* instead of *2d*. If the driver finishes at the end of Friday, a lag of *2ed* will cause the FS driven task to start on Monday (weekend days count as elapsed days), whereas a lag of *2d* will make it start on Wednesday (weekend is skipped and Monday and Tuesday count as the 2 business day lag). Elapsed lags are useful when modeling legal waiting periods; for example, when the justice system treats a court case as a project, there are prescribed periods for responses, interrogation and counter claims in lawsuits, and these are expressed in calendar days. For more details on elapsed durations (see page 179).

Relative Lead or Lag Time

You can also express the amount of *lead* or *lag* as a *percentage* of the duration of the driver task (predecessor), as you can see in the illustration. The driven task bar (successor) takes a relative position to the driver task bar (predecessor). With this feature it is possible to have a successor start halfway through the duration of the predecessor and to keep it at the halfway mark. It will stay at the halfway point even if the duration of the driver task is changed later on!

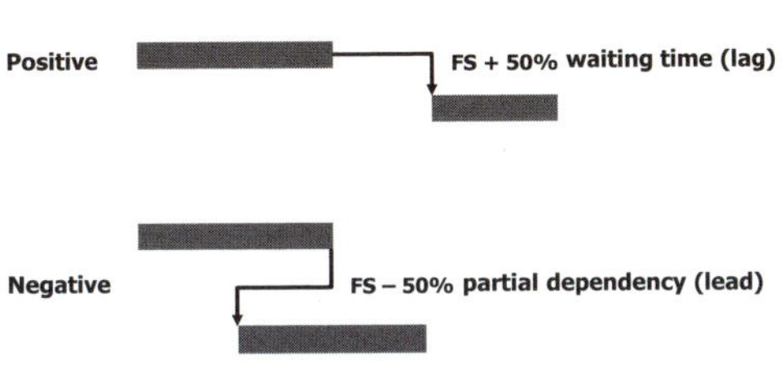

Examples:

- There are two tasks *write report* and *edit report*. After writing the first half of the report, we want to send it to the editor. We need an FS-50% dependency between *write report* and *edit report* in this case (the second example in the illustration).
- In the food sector, the shelf-life of new food products has to be tested, but these tests are long. Driven tasks, like the marketing of the food product, are often started at 50% of the duration of these shelf-life tests when it starts to look like the shelf-life will be good. If the test turns unfavorable later, marketing is stopped before big expenses are incurred.
- In construction projects, the electrical engineering design often starts when the civil engineering design is 60% complete: SS+60% or FS-40%. The lag is relative to the duration of its driver task.

Multiple Predecessors and Successors

Each task can have more than one predecessor and successor as the illustration shows. This will allow you to schedule several activities concurrently. Tasks that do not have a logical relationship should not have a dependency between them but may have the same driver task (predecessor). These tasks are then scheduled in parallel. This creates a network of dependencies where some parallel (chains of) tasks will take longer than other

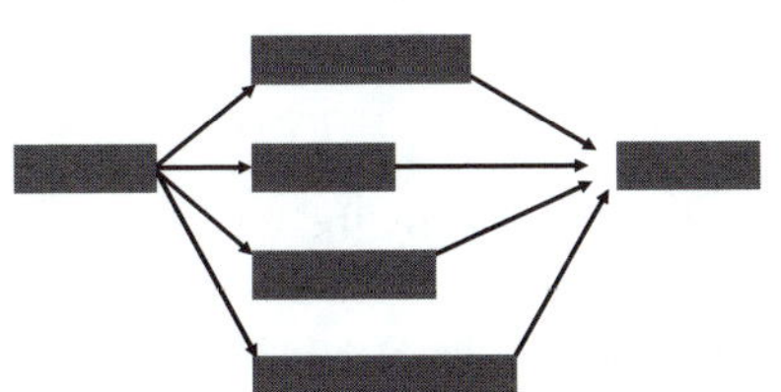

shorter ones. An example of activities that can take place in parallel is installing systems at several different sites.

Choosing the Right Type of Dependency

Sometimes when you are creating your project model, you may not be certain about the type of dependency to use. Of the two types used in the illustration, the appropriate one depends on the situation that is modeled. If the situation allows you to postpone the exam when you are not done preparing for it, the FS dependency is the best (top one in the illustration). The FS dependency will move the exam to a later date when preparation takes longer. An example is the PMP® exam [36] that can be postponed if you are not ready to take it.

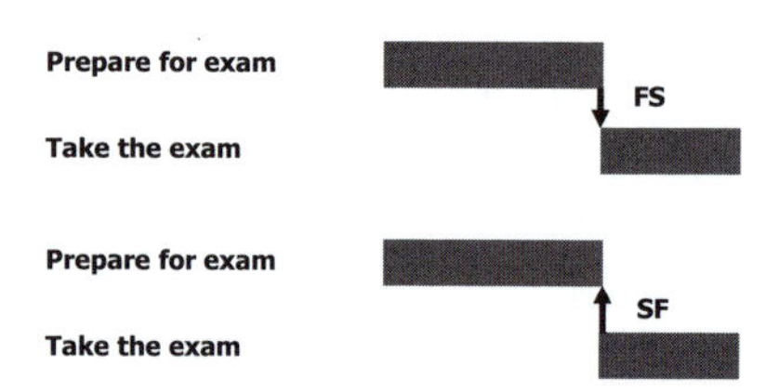

If you cannot postpone taking the exam, as is the case for a university exam, the Start-to-Finish is best (bottom one in the illustration). The moment an exam starts, the preparation will stop. I tended to *schedule backwards* in preparing for an exam: *What is the latest date I have to start preparing for the exam so that everything will be fresh in my memory?* Of course, there were always unforeseen events that haunted me.

Note that the Start-to-Finish dependency does not force the preparation to finish. This is because all dependencies, including the Start-to-Finish dependency, are when-or-after dependencies (a.k.a. *later-than dependencies*). To *schedule backward* properly and really force the *prepare exam* task to finish when the exam starts, we need a new class of dependencies, *earlier-than dependencies* – not yet available in scheduling software. [37]

---

[36] PMP® stands for Project Management Professional, an accreditation by the Project Management Institute (PMI). See www.pmi.org for more information.

[37] For more discussion on earlier-than dependencies, please retrieve the article *Scheduling is not about chronology; it is about logic!* From our website www.projectprocorp.com: click *Articles* in the side bar.

Steps for Choosing the Right Type of Dependency

The following six questions will assist you in identifying the right dependency:

1. *Which task drives the other?* or *What do you need in order to do this task?* Use these questions to determine which task is the predecessor. Too often, people ask themselves: *What should be scheduled first or earliest?* This question asks for the chronology of tasks. Remember, dependencies are not about chronology, but about cause–and-effect. Another good question to ask is: *What do you need in order to do this task?* People may find it easy to come up with things they need as input before they can start. Often dependencies follow the flow of data, hand-offs and deliverables (documents) that are passed on among team members. For example, the detailed design document is passed from the software architect to the software programmer. Ask your team members to identify what they need from other people to do the task. You will slowly but surely identify all dependencies from the end of the network to the beginning of it. Both questions focus on practically necessary, logical relationships.

2. Does the start or the finish of the predecessor drive the other task? This question helps to find the type of dependency you need, an S (Start) or an F (Finish) dependency.

3. Does the predecessor drive the start or the finish of the successor? Once you know the answer to this question, you know the type of dependency you need: SS, FS, SF or FF.

4. Do you need a gap (positive lag), or an overlap (negative lag or lead)? If your answer is *no*, you are ready with this dependency. A positive lag delays the successor in time (farther to the right in the timescale) and creates a gap in an FS-dependency. A negative lag (lead) schedules the successor earlier in time (farther to the left in the timescale) and creates an overlap in an FS-dependency. If negative, you will need to type a "–" (minus) and a number in the **Lag** field, for example, *-3d*, which means a negative lag of 3 days.

5. Is the lag an absolute number of days or weeks, or is the lag relative to the duration of the predecessor (driver)?
   - ◇ If absolute, you have an additional question: *Should it be in business days or in elapsed days (calendar days)?* Enter the number of business days (or weeks) while including the time unit, for example *5d* (*business days*) or *5ed* (*elapsed days*).
   - ◇ If relative, enter a percentage in the **Lag** field, like *+50%* or *-30%* (including the percentage sign).

6. How much should the lag or lead be? After you answered this last question, you should know the complete dependency

definition, for example *FS+50%*, *SS+3d*, or *FF+2ed*. MS Project displays codes like these in the *Predecessors* and *Successors* fields and prefixes them with the ID number of the linked task. When you see only an ID number in this field, the dependency type is *FS*.

Switching Tasks to Auto Schedule

We discussed **Manually Scheduled** tasks first on page 96. Manually scheduled tasks can have dependencies. When you first create the dependencies, Project 2010 reschedules the manually scheduled tasks if the option ☑ **Update Manually Scheduled tasks when editing links** is kept selected (ribbon **File**, Options, tab **Schedule**, section **Scheduling options for this project**).

However, there are several reasons why linking **Manually Scheduled** tasks makes little sense:

- As soon as you link **Manually Scheduled** tasks, MS Project will enter the default duration of *1day?* on tasks that did not have a duration yet, just like it does on all Auto Scheduled tasks. This removes some of the flexibility of **Manually Scheduled** tasks.

- Links between **Manually Scheduled** tasks are *static dependencies*; they work only once when you create them and then they stop working when other changes happen, like revisions of estimates or tasks that slip during updating. You may want to start relying on the dependencies to reschedule the tasks continuously (*dynamic dependencies*) and make the schedule come alive. Otherwise, why did you enter the dependencies?

- If you do not switch the linked tasks to Auto Scheduled tasks, you should be prepared for an avalanche of warnings and indicators that beg for attention. When **Manually Scheduled** tasks violate a dependency, you will see red wavy underlines in the **Finish** date field and dotted outlines on task bars. When you resolve one issue, the issue moves to its successor and cascades through the schedule dependency-by-dependency as the next screenshots will show.

In the first screenshot, the dependency between task 1 and 2 is violated (after the estimate of task 1 was increased) creating a *schedule conflict*:

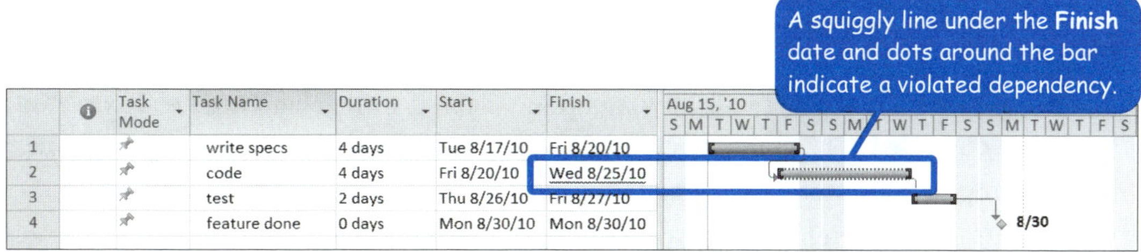

The user solves the issue by clicking the **Respect Links** button on the **Task** ribbon and the issue moves to its successor task 3:

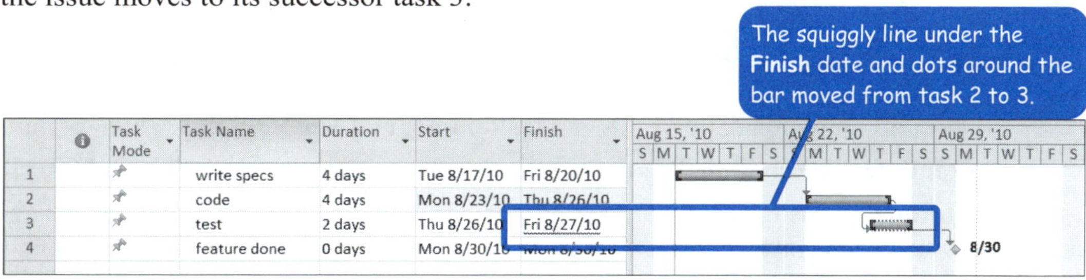

Of course, you can select multiple tasks before clicking **Respect Links**, but you will inevitably omit some links at times. MS Project always and automatically respects all links on Auto Scheduled tasks.

If tasks are finished earlier than originally planned, Manually Scheduled successors will not be rescheduled earlier and you will not take advantage of the *schedule gain* of tasks finishing early.

In summary, manually scheduled tasks prohibit dependencies from doing their work. You may want to switch the **Task Mode** from **Manually Scheduled** to **Auto Scheduled** for all tasks (except perhaps overhead tasks). Project 2010 will then:

- Calculate the **Start** and **Finish** date of the tasks.
- Wipe out any reminders you had left in the fields **Duration, Start** and **Finish**.
- Make summary tasks summarize their detail tasks.
- Allow you to create date constraints, like Start-No-Earlier-Than.
- Start respecting the dependencies continuously (unless overridden by date constraints) – dynamic dependencies.
- Allow you to change the task **Type** to control the calculations MS Project makes with the *formula* **Duration** * **Peak Units** = **Work**. This field is disabled for **Manually Scheduled** tasks.

In other words, Project 2010 will start forecasting your project accurately and you will realize the principle of *forecast scheduling*: making your schedule forecast your project by itself.

We recommend you switch all tasks that you will link to auto scheduled before entering the network logic. Keep the following option cleared while changing the **Task Mode** to **Auto Scheduled**. The option is called ☐ **Keep task on nearest working day when changing to Automatically Scheduled mode** (ribbon **File,** Options, tab **Schedule**, section **Scheduling options for this project)**. With this option on, the tasks you change to auto scheduled will also get a Start-No-Earlier-Than constraint which makes the model less dynamic.

To Switch Tasks to Auto Scheduled

First, turn off an option called ☐ **Keep task on nearest working day when changing to Automatically Scheduled mode** (ribbon **File,** Options, tab **Schedule**, section **Scheduling options for this project)**. When selected, this option will create constraint dates on all tasks you switch from **Manually** to **Auto Scheduled**. You do not want those!

You can switch tasks from **Manually Scheduled** to **Auto Scheduled** for all tasks in your schedule or for multiple, selected tasks. For all tasks:

1. To select all tasks, click on any column heading.
2. Click ribbon **Task** and click 

.

OR for multiple, selected tasks, do this:

1. To select adjacent tasks, drag over them. To select multiple, non-adjacent tasks, click on the first task and hold down the Control key while you click on or drag over the other tasks.
2. Right-click in the selected area and select **Auto Schedule**.

It may make sense to switch the default **Task Mode** to **Auto Schedule** as well for when you create new tasks. In the bottom left of the screen, click New Tasks : and select

Auto Scheduled OR click ribbon **File**, Options, tab **Schedule** and switch **New tasks created** to **Auto Scheduled**.

Entering Logic

Project 2010 offers a variety of ways to enter dependencies into the schedule. Dependencies can be entered either in the Gantt Chart or in the Network Diagram. In both views, the tools and forms work very similarly. We will discuss:

- Using the *Link tool* (see page 221)
- Using the mouse (see page 222)
- Using the *Task Information* dialog (see page 224)
- Using the *Task Form* (see page 225)

5

We will now discuss these different ways in more detail starting with the Gantt Chart view.

Entering Dependencies in the Gantt Chart

Using the Link Tool

With the link tool you can create a chain of Finish-to-Start dependencies between many tasks with one click.

To Set a Chain of Dependencies

1. Select adjacent tasks by dragging over their task names starting with the driver task (predecessor). You can select more than just two tasks.
   OR

   If the tasks are not adjacent, select the driver (predecessor) first, hold down Control and click on the driven task (successor). You can click on the task name in the spreadsheet or on its task bar in the timescale. You can click on as many tasks as you want to link. The only thing to remember is to select the tasks in the order in which you want the tasks to be linked (from driver to driven task), even if the driven task is higher in the list.

2. Let go of the Control key when you selected them all.

3. Click ribbon **Task** and find its section **Schedule** and click [link icon]
   OR
   hold down [Control] and press [F2]
4. The tasks are now Finish-to-Start dependent.

This method allows you to set *Finish-to-Start* dependencies only.

To Delete a Chain of Dependencies between Tasks

1. If the tasks are adjacent, select all predecessors and successors by dragging over their task names.
   OR
   If the tasks are not adjacent, select one task first and then hold down [Control] and click on the other task involved in the link. You can click on the task name or on the task bar, and you can click on more than two tasks that you want unlinked.
2. Click ribbon **Task**, then find its section **Schedule** and click [unlink icon]
   OR
   hold down [Control] + [Shift] and press [F2].
3. Only the dependencies that ran between the selected tasks are now removed.

To Delete All Dependencies on one Task or all Tasks

Select the task and click [unlink icon] on the **Task** ribbon.

You can easily delete all dependencies in the entire schedule if you select all tasks first by clicking on any column heading and then click [unlink icon] on the **Task** ribbon. Be careful with this, because it can wreck many hours of work in a large schedule faster than you can blink your eye.

Using the Mouse

This method is useful if you want to create parallel paths.

To Draw Dependencies

1. Point to the center of the driver task bar (predecessor); make sure you see a four-headed arrow mouse pointer like [four-headed arrow]. (Near the front of the task bar you will

see another mouse pointer: and near the back: .) If necessary, click zoom in on the zoom slider in the bottom right of your screen to make the task bars wider/longer.

2. Click and hold down the primary mouse button and drag vertically toward the successor task bar making sure the mouse pointer now looks like . If you drag horizontally, you are rescheduling the task bar and setting a schedule constraint that will make your schedule static instead of dynamic! Notice the feedback popup window that tells you what the result will be:

Finish-to-Start Link	
From Finish Of:	Task 5
To Start Of:	Task 6

2007 If the task bar of the successor is not visible on the screen, you can bump into the edge of the screen and the screen will start to scroll slowly.

3. Release the mouse button inside the task bar of the successor. A dependency is set and shows up as an arrow. The task bar of the successor moves out to just after the finish date of the predecessor's task bar. A *Finish-to-Start* dependency is set and visible as an arrow between the task bars:

This method of setting dependencies allows you to set FS dependencies only, but you can change to another type of dependency with the next steps.

5

To Edit or Delete the Dependency

1. Point the tip of the arrow mouse pointer precisely to the dependency arrow you want to change, as in the next screenshot:

2. Dependency arrows can overlap each other, so wait one second until the feedback window pops up to confirm which dependency you are on.

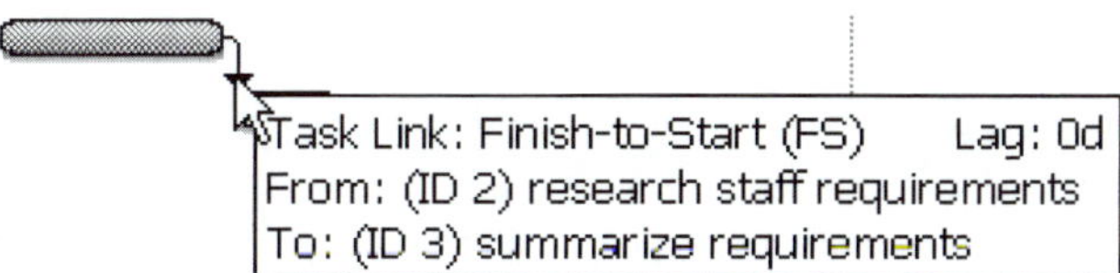

3. If you have the proper dependency arrow selected, double-click and the **Task Dependency** dialog appears:

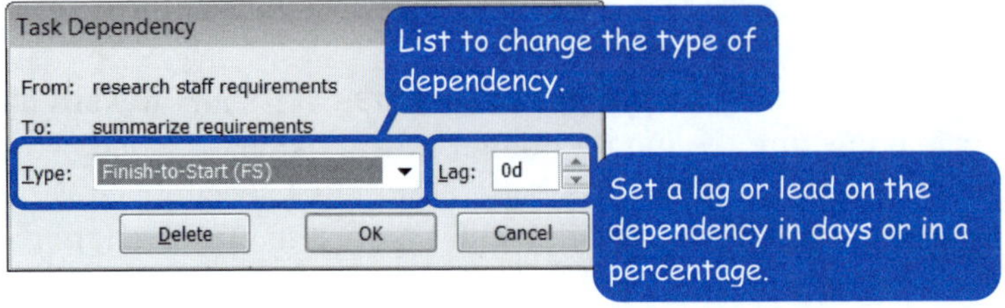

4. Select the type of dependency using the list **Type** and enter a positive *lag* or a negative lag (*lead*) time, if needed. You can also enter a percentage in the **Lag** field. The percentage will be taken from the duration of the predecessor task and treated as lag time. Click [OK].
   OR
   You can also click [Delete] to get rid of the dependency.

Using the Task Information Dialog

This method may be best if the predecessor and successor are listed far apart.

1. Double-click on the successor task OR

   Select the successor task and click [Information] on the **Task** ribbon, or hold down

   [Shift] and press [F2] – the **Task Information** dialog appears.

2. Click the **Predecessors** tab; the dialog should now look like:

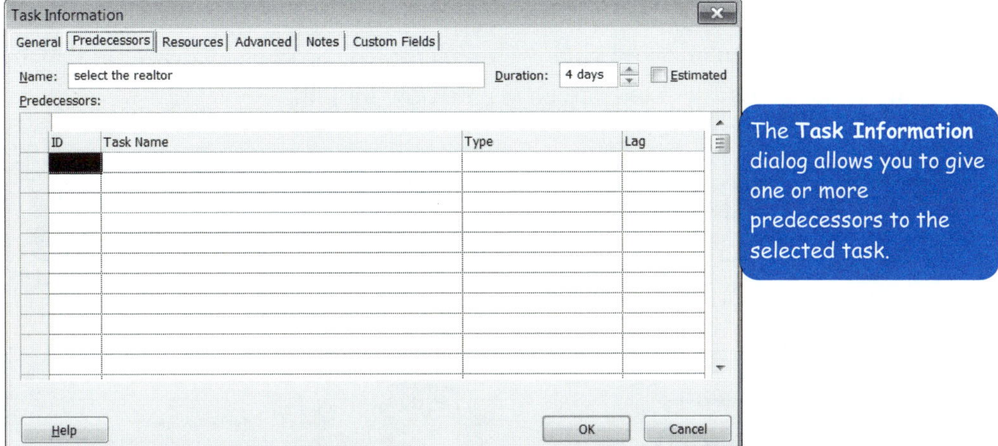

The **Task Information** dialog allows you to give one or more predecessors to the selected task.

5

3. Click in the **Task Name** field in an empty row and select the predecessor task name from the list that appears.
   OR
   Enter the ID number of the predecessor in the **ID** field.
4. Select the type of dependency from the list in the **Type** field.
5. Enter a (negative or positive) lag in the **Lag** field. Instead of days, you can enter a percentage in the **Lag** field. The percentage will be taken from the duration of the predecessor task and then treated as the lag time.
6. Click OK and the dependencies are entered into the schedule.

Unfortunately, the dialog does not have a successors tab to set successors on it at the same time.

Using the Task Form

This method allows you to set multiple predecessors and successors on one task and to set dependencies when tasks are listed far apart.

1. In the Gantt Chart, display the Task Form:
   Right-click in the timescale (not on a task bar) and select **Show Split** from the popup menu
   OR
   Click ribbon **View** and select Details.

2. The **Task Form** appears by default in the bottom of the screen. Click on the **Task Form** to make this view active.

3. Click ribbon **Format** and click [Predecessors & Successors] to view all dependencies of the selected task. Your screen should now look like:

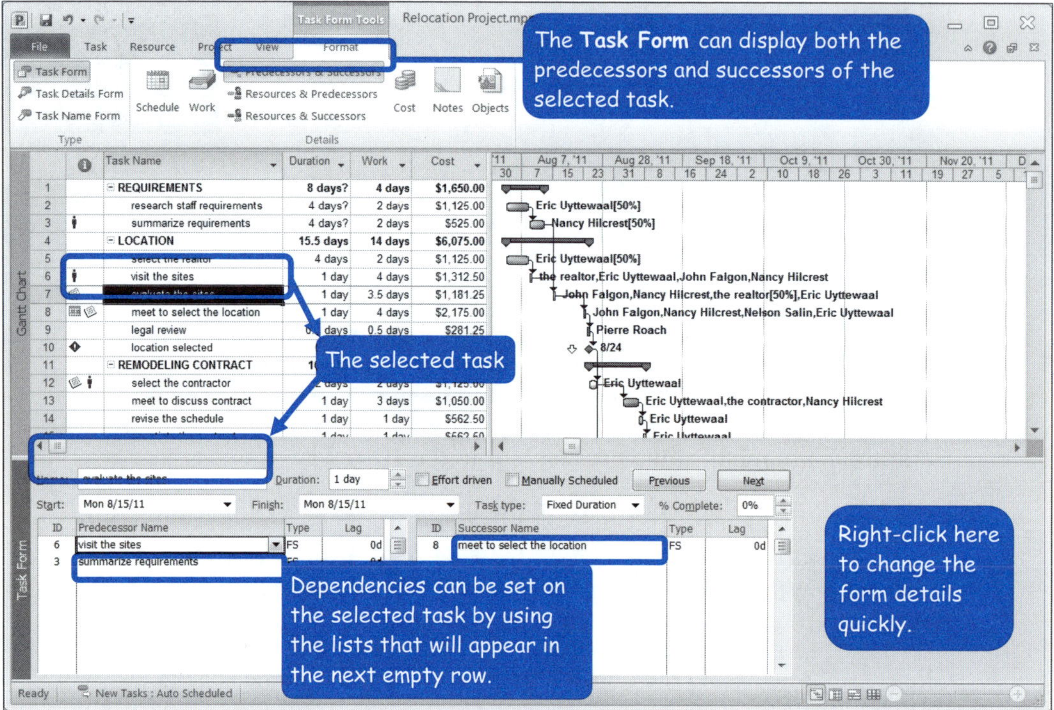

4. Select the task to link in the top Gantt Chart view.

5. On the bottom Task Form view, click in the field **Predecessor Name** or **Successor Name** in an empty row and use the list [▼] that appears to create the dependency.
   OR
   Type the ID number of the predecessor or successor task in the **ID** field.

6. Set the type of dependency in the **Type** field and add a positive *lag* or negative lag (*lead*) in the **Lag** field, if necessary. Instead of days, you can also enter a percentage in the **Lag** field. The percentage will be taken from the duration of the predecessor and treated as lag time.

7. Click [OK] on the Task Form – the data are entered into the schedule only after this button is clicked.

The **Task Form** allows you to set many dependencies on a task at the same time. You can set predecessors and successors on it all at once. The Task Form allows you to see exactly how dependencies run in the Gantt timescale where the arrows can run on top of one another. The Task Form shows you exactly how they run.

To delete a dependency on the Task Form, select the task name, and when it is highlighted press the [Delete] key on your keyboard. Then click [OK] to enter this into the schedule.

Entering Dependencies in the Network Diagram

The Network Diagram

To apply the view, click ribbon **View**, button **Network Diagram**. The Network Diagram can display an overview of all the dependencies you have set; the dependencies are depicted as arrows in this view.

By default, the **Network Diagram** displays the types of tasks in differently shaped nodes:

- Summary tasks in a parallelogram
- Detail tasks in a rectangle
- Milestones in a hexagon

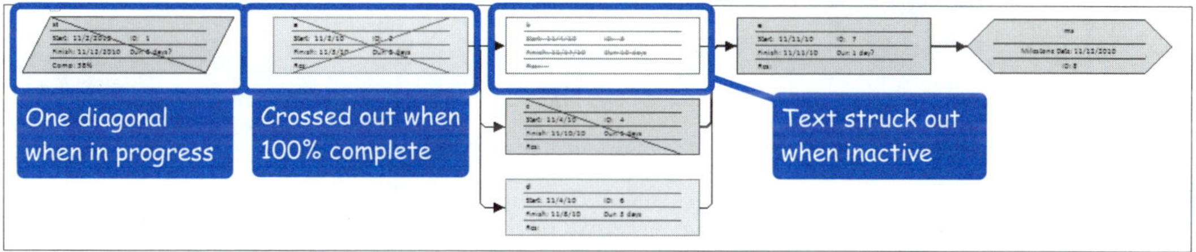

The default formatting in the Network Diagram is as follows in Project 2010:

- *Critical tasks* have a red fill and red border.
- Noncritical *Auto Scheduled* tasks have a white fill and blue border.
- Noncritical *Manually Scheduled* tasks have a light blue fill and dark blue border.

The color and the shape of the nodes can be changed by clicking ribbon **Format,** button **Box Styles**.

Gaining an Overview of the Network

The challenge with the Network Diagram is that even large screens cannot display large networks in their entirety. In the past large networks were printed on plotters and hung in rooms like wallpaper. However, the point of this book is to transcend the paper age to the electronic age. We have to find a way to see the entire network while keeping the task details legible. Here is the screen we propose:

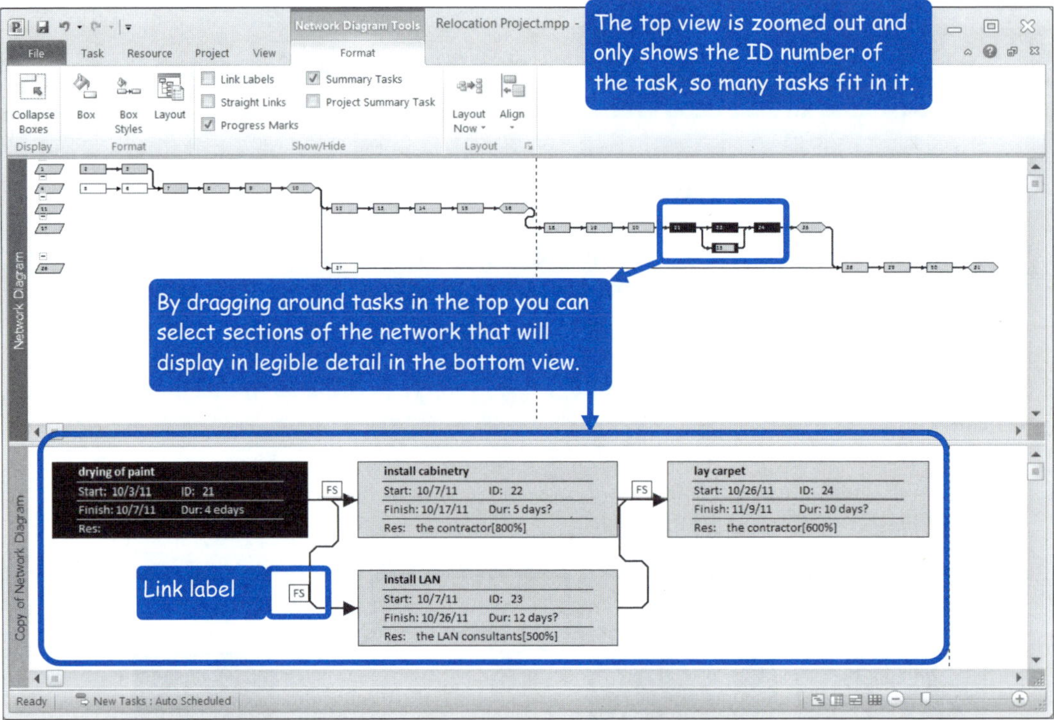

This view allows you to keep the overview and analyze the details. Seeing the overview is useful to spot if the network has loose ends and see the entire *Critical Path* (red), see page 418. Analyzing the details is important when making corrections to the network.

In order to create this view, follow this procedure:

1. Click ribbon **View,** find its section **Task Views** and click Network Diagram (or on a low resolution screen).

2. Click [Other Views ▾] (or [▾] on a low resolution screen) and select **More Views** from the drop-down menu – the **More Views** dialog appears:

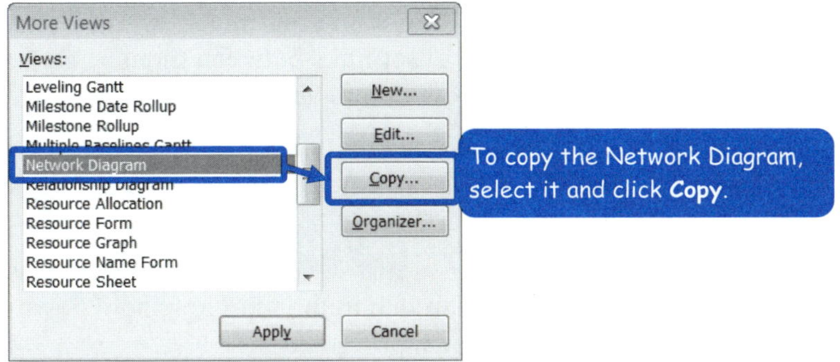

3. Make sure the item **Network Diagram** is selected in the list and click [Copy...] – the dialog **View Definition** appears.

4. Leave the **Name** to **Copy of Network Diagram** and click [OK] – you are back in the **More Views** dialog.

5. Click [Close] in the **More Views** dialog.

6. On the **View** ribbon in the section **Split View**, select [Details] and from its list select the newly created view **Copy of Network Diagram**. You should now see a combination view with the **Network Diagram** view in the top and the **Copy of Network Diagram** view in the bottom.

7. Click in the top view, click ribbon **Format** and click [Collapse Boxes].

   OR
   Right-click and select **Collapse Boxes** from the popup menu.

8. The boxes in the top are now tiny and only display their ID number. Use the zoom slider [slider] in the bottom right of your screen to zoom out so you can see the whole network (or most of it) in the top view.

9. Click in the bottom view, click ribbon **Format** and select [Link Labels] – the type of dependency and leads or lags are now shown in a small box in the bottom view. You should now see a screen similar to the screenshot before this procedure.

5

The split view acts like a master and slave, where those items that are selected in the top view determine what is displayed in the bottom pane.

To read and analyze a section of the network, drag with your mouse around those boxes in the top view and you will be able to see the exact links between them in the bottom view. This is a great way to verify if the links are complete and correct. You can also randomly select multiple tasks by holding down the Control key while clicking on the second task, third task, and so forth. This is a great way to prepare for creating new dependencies.

To quickly find all the successors of a particular task in the top view, hold down Shift and click a task node – all its successors will be highlighted.

Using the Mouse to Set Dependencies

Once you gain the overview and start to identify places where you are missing important links, you can create them right here in the Network Diagram.

1. Point to the center of the driver (predecessor) node and make sure the mouse pointer is a plus sign: ✣.
2. Click and hold down the primary mouse button, and drag towards the node of the successor; the mouse pointer should change into a ⚭. Even if the node is not visible, you can drag against the side of the screen, which will then start scrolling slowly.
3. Release the mouse button in the center of the driven (successor) node; an arrow appears and the dependency is now set.

This method allows you to set FS dependencies only, but you can easily change the type by double-clicking on a dependency arrow, see page 231 for the steps.

If you release the mouse button outside of the successor node, a new task is created accidentally! For those who like to build the task list and the network at the same time, this is a great feature. If this happens inadvertently, click undo on the Quick Access Toolbar in the top left of the screen.

Using the Link Tool to Set Dependencies

When you use the **Link** tool, you have to select the tasks in the order in which you want to link them. In other words, you select the predecessor first, then its successor, then the successor of the successor, etc.

1. Click on the driver task (predecessor) and then hold down Control while clicking on the rest of the tasks to link Finish-to-Start.
   OR
   You can select multiple tasks quickly by dragging a box around them. As soon as you hold down the mouse, the mouse pointer will change to a **+** . When you drag, you are drawing a box with a gray border. Any tasks that you partially enclose in the box will be selected upon releasing the mouse button. You can even select another set of tasks by holding down Control before you drag again.
2. Click on the **Task** ribbon to link the tasks.

As in the Gantt Chart, you can also set dependencies in the Network Diagram using the **Task Information** dialog or the **Task Form**. The steps are the same as for the Gantt Chart (please refer to page 224 and 225, respectively).

To Edit or Delete a Dependency in the Network Diagram

Point with the tip of the mouse pointer to the dependency arrow you want to delete, which should look like this:

1. Double-click and the **Task Dependency** dialog appears:

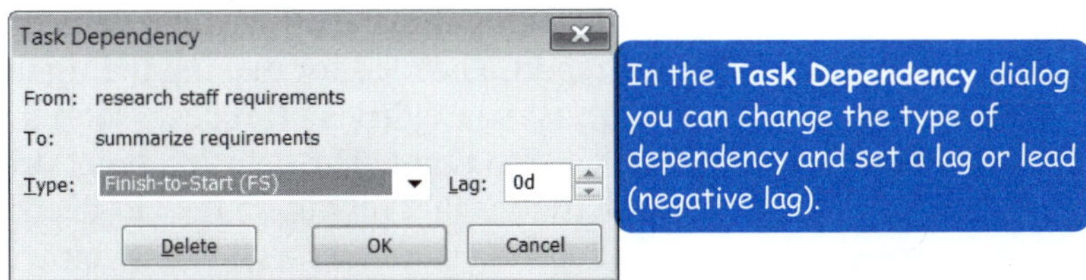

2. Change the **Type** of the dependency using the list **Type** and set a **Lag** time, if needed. The *Lag* can be positive, which creates a gap, or negative, which creates an overlap (*lead*). You can also enter a negative or positive percentage in the **Lag** field instead of days. The percentage will be taken from the duration of the predecessor task and then treated as the lag time.
   OR
   Remove the dependency, by clicking 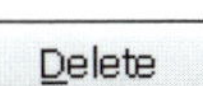. When you delete a dependency

arrow, all successor nodes move to the left. They may disappear from your screen. We recommend you create new dependencies first and then delete the old dependency to prevent nodes from disappearing from your screen.

Special Situations

Certain situations need more discussion:

- *Decision point dependencies* (see next section)
- *Hard and soft dependencies* (see page 233)
- *External dependencies* (see page 234)
- *Cross-project dependencies* (see page 235)
- *Waiting time dependencies* (see page 235)
- *Resource dependencies* (see page 236)
- *Summary Tasks dependencies* (see page 236)

We will discuss each of these in more detail.

Decision Point Dependencies

Decision points are important nodes in the network of dependencies. Decision points are also called "*gates*". If your schedule has decision points, you are using *stage-gate project management*. [38] Often these decisions are *Go/No-Go* decisions: continue or abort the initiative.

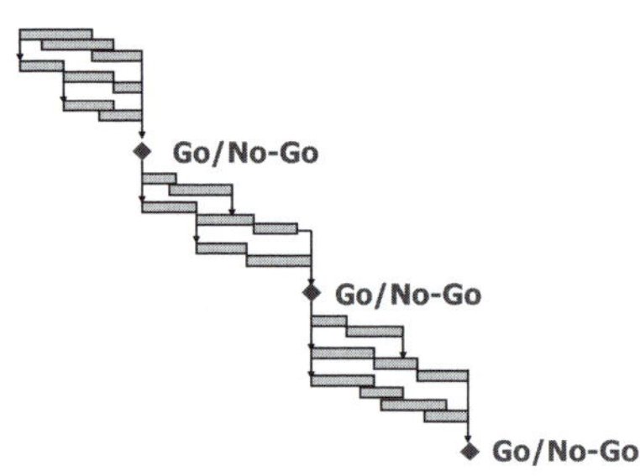

What central stations are to railroads, gates are to networks; many tracks are coming together and springing from them, as you can see in the illustration. All the deliverables (reports) needed for making the right decision are drivers (predecessors) for the decision point. The decision point drives all activities that rely upon the Go-decision (dependent successors). What you will see in a schedule with decision points is that several sub networks of dependencies are linked together at the decision points.

[38] See the books by Dr. Robert G. Cooper and Dr. Scott J. Edgett on www.stage-gate.com.

Hard and Soft Dependencies

Some tasks have to be done in an absolute sequence, while others have a preferred sequence. *Hard* or *mandatory* dependencies are dependencies that have an absolute sequence. Common sense dictates creating these hard dependencies. For example, the two activities *write* the report and *print* it, require a hard dependency. It does not make sense to schedule the printing in any other way than driven by the finish date of the writing. (If you do find another way to do this, let me know; you can make authors really happy.)

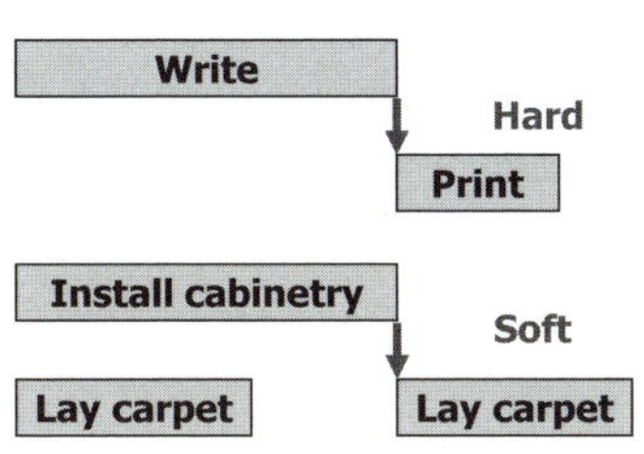

Soft or *discretionary* dependencies are a matter of preference from a practical or personal point of view. For example, the two tasks *installing cabinetry* and *laying the carpet* are not necessarily dependent on each other. The project manager may prefer to set a dependency to make sure that the cabinetmakers do not spill glue that damages the new carpet. However, if you are in a time crunch, you could do both tasks in parallel. You could ask the cabinetmakers to cover the new carpet with plastic and still gain time in your project.

MS Project does not have a special feature for creating soft dependencies. If you remember where you created the soft dependencies, it will be easier to optimize the schedule later on. We recommend you document the soft, discretionary dependencies by flagging the predecessor and successor in one of the extra flag fields, Flag1-Flag20. This will allow you to find the soft dependencies that are on the Critical Path by using a filter, so you can quickly shorten the Critical Path. (It would eventually be better if Microsoft allowed us to set an attribute on the dependency itself that indicates it is a soft dependency and allow us to see a version of the schedule with only hard dependencies.)

External Dependencies

In general, when you are dependent on an event that is outside of your control, you are dealing with an external dependency or a cross-project dependency (see next section). If you cannot create a cross-project dependency with another schedule, you can create an *external dependency*. You need one when you:

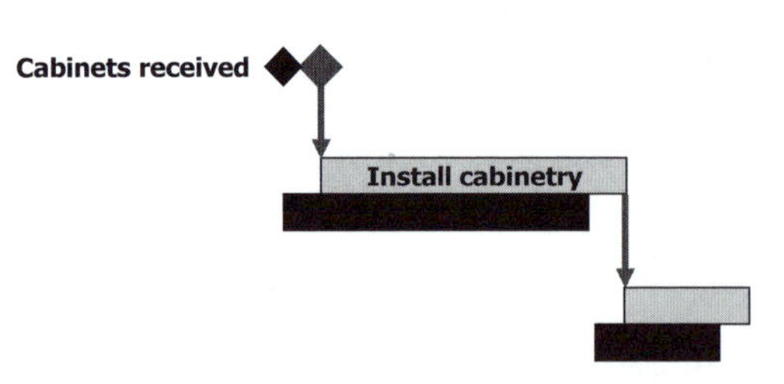

- Need to receive goods or materials from a supplier
- Require input from another department or project

In the illustrated example, you could leave the milestone, *cabinets received*, out of the schedule. If you do this and the cabinets arrive late, it would just show as a slipped start date on the task *install cabinetry*. Who will get blamed for the slip in the schedule? The installers would receive the blame. In the case of external dependencies, we recommend you insert an extra milestone for the event in your schedule that is outside your control. You can set a *Start No Earlier Than* schedule constraint on the extra milestone. The constraint will keep the milestone diamond on the date you have agreed to. Then you create dependencies from the external event milestone into your activities. We will discuss constraints in the next chapter (see page 253). We even recommend flagging these external milestones in one of the extra flag fields, Flag1-Flag20, so you can give them a different color in the **Bar Styles** dialog (in the Gantt Chart view, click ribbon **Format**, button **Format**, select **Bar Styles**). See page 557 for more on customizing fields.

The advantage of the extra milestone is that if the shipment of cabinets arrives late, it is immediately clear that this was because the supplier messed up, which was beyond your control as the project manager. If the milestone were omitted, it would look like the installers started working late on their task, which would reflect badly on your performance as a project manager. These external event milestones build *traceability* into your schedule.

Adding extra, external event milestones is a simple technique that keeps the fingers pointed at the right people in the case of a slippage or, worse, a contract dispute.

Cross-Project Dependencies

We are venturing into the area of *program management* here, [39] but will briefly address this type of dependencies. If the external dependency is from a project schedule to which you have access, you can model this situation by creating a *cross-project dependency* instead of an external dependency. Essentially, a cross-project dependency is a dependency that runs between two schedules, as opposed to between two tasks within a single schedule.

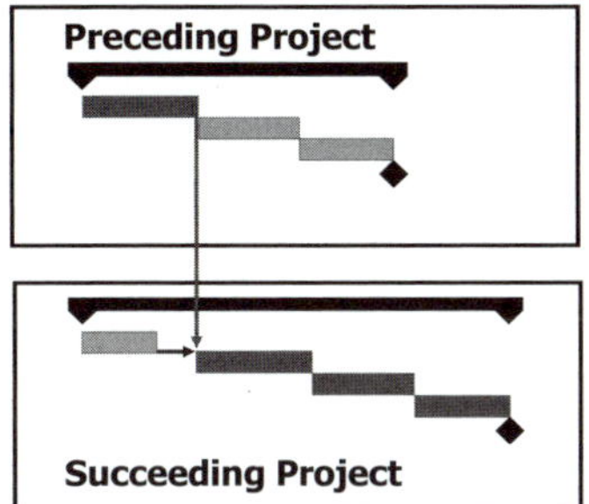

5

MS Project allows you to create cross-project dependencies. We recommend you create cross-project dependencies in a *master project* with the *subprojects* inserted inside it; you can create a master project by deciding where you want to insert a subproject and clicking the **Subproject** button on the **Project** ribbon. After inserting both subprojects between which you want to create a cross-project link, you can create the cross-project links in much the same way as you do in a single schedule, see page 221 for the how-to steps using the link tasks buttons.

Waiting Time Dependencies

On a software development project, you may work closely together with your client. Every time an important interim deliverable is ready (like *functional design, detailed design, data model*), the client may need some time to review it. If the client needs, say, one week for review every time, these waiting times need to be incorporated into the model. Do this by creating a dependency with a lag of one week — this is a *waiting time dependency*, see page 223 for the how-to.

---

[39] See the separate courses *Forecasting Programs* and *Managing Programs* on our website *www.ProjectProCorp.com*. Click *Courses 2010* in the sidebar to access them.

Resource Dependencies

A *resource dependency* occurs when two tasks compete for the same resource. If you cannot find another solution for the overallocation, one task has to be delayed in order to keep the workload reasonable for the resource. Of course, you could force the sequence by setting an extra *logical dependency* as shown in the illustration, but the two tasks are really independent and could be done in any order. Harry could either read report X or Y first. We do not think you should model resource dependencies by setting extra logical dependencies, because you use a static solution for a dynamic problem. What happens if you reassign one of Harry's tasks to Sam? Will you remember to take the logical dependency out again? We added question marks to the illustration for this reason. You should at least write yourself a reminder in the **Note** field if you hard-code resource dependencies by creating extra logical dependencies.

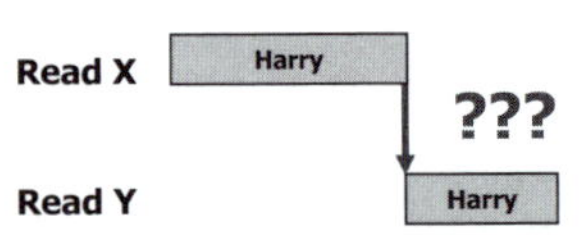

Also, MS Project has special features to keep the workloads leveled and we would invite you to use those features instead. We will discuss them on page 468. In the same chapter we will also explain how to optimize a schedule with many resource dependencies (see page 499).

Summary Tasks Dependencies

What are the advantages and disadvantages of setting dependencies on summary tasks?

Advantages of summary dependencies

- Summary logic is high-level logic that executives sometimes like to see.
- Setting dependencies on summary tasks seems easier and quicker. In certain situations, you can make do with one summary dependency instead of several dependencies on detail tasks. When detail tasks all need to start at the same time independently of each other, one dependency on their summary task will do the trick.

In the next screenshot, tasks 19 to 21 are all driven by the dependency on their summary task, 18:

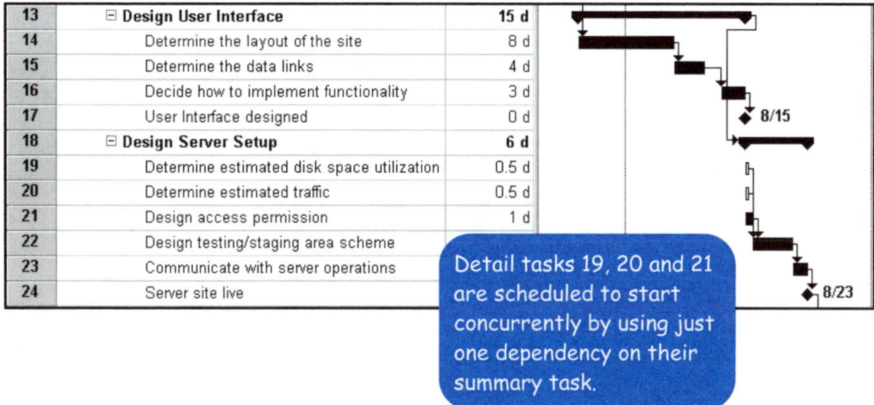

Disadvantages of summary dependencies

- It is too difficult to check if the network of dependencies is complete if you use a mix of dependencies on summary tasks and detail tasks. The check is simple if you have dependencies between detail tasks only; you just have to find the detail tasks and milestones that do not have an entry in the predecessor or successor field. If you have logic both on summary tasks and some detail tasks, you can no longer perform this simple check. Checking the logic then becomes a very painstaking process that will waste many hours of your precious time. I have been there, done that and will not likely do it again!
- The Critical Path is more difficult to follow when some dependencies run over summary tasks. The *Critical Path* is the subset of tasks that drives your project finish date (see page 417 for more on Critical Path). When you follow the Critical Path, a critical detail task may not have any successor, and it looks like the Critical Path stops. You may not realize that the Critical Path continues through a dependency on the summary task.

For example, in the next screenshot, task 17 appears to be the end of the Critical Path (black task bars), but really continues via the summary task 13 to summary task 18, and then continues with the detail task 21:

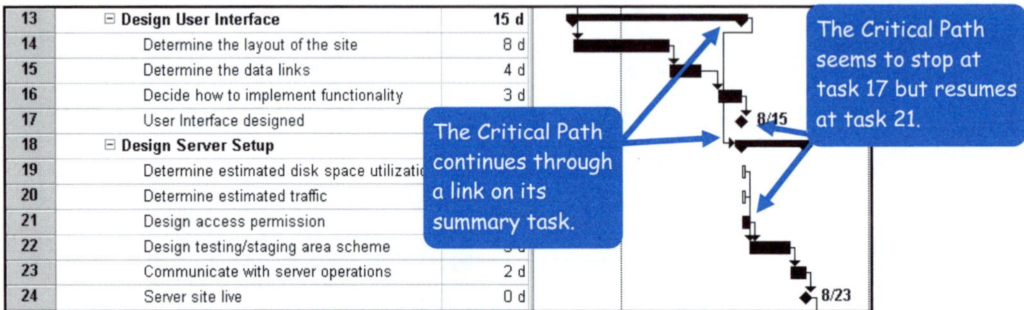

If you had kept the logic on detail tasks only, you would see a dependency arrow from task 17 to task 21 and your Critical Path would be easy to follow.

- On summary tasks, you can only set rough, high-level logic. High-level logic often does not allow you to create the tightest schedule possible.
- Not all types of dependencies can be used on summary tasks; you cannot link to the end of a summary task; you cannot use the dependencies *Finish-To-Finish* (FF) or *Start-To-Finish* (SF) to summary tasks.

Even though there seem to be some advantages to setting dependencies on summary tasks, they do not measure up against the disadvantages. Time gained with setting fewer dependencies is lost threefold when checking the logic and analyzing the Critical Path. We therefore recommend that you keep the logic on detail tasks and milestones only, and that you do not set any dependencies on summary tasks.

Checks on Dependencies

All the dependencies together are called the *network*, the *logic* or the *network logic.* At this point, you check the network to determine if it will, indeed, produce the desired benefit: namely, if you change one field in the schedule, the rest of the schedule is updated automatically in such a way that you immediately have a *valid* and accurate schedule of your project again. We called this the *principle of dynamic scheduling.* Dependencies should ensure that when we start entering changes, the resulting schedule makes sense. With dependencies we can protect the sanity of the schedule.

We recommend you apply the following checks to verify if your schedule is a dynamic schedule:

- Have you turned the **Task Mode** of all tasks to Auto Scheduled (see page 240)?
- Is the network of dependencies complete (see page 240)?
- Is the network of dependencies correct (see page 243)?
- Is the network logic simple enough (see page 245)?
- Does the resulting high-level schedule make sense (see page 246)?
- Have you turned off **Autolink** after checking the network (see page 246)?

The schedule will update itself properly only if the answers to the first two questions are yes.

Why a Complete and Correct Network Is Important

There are three reasons why you should aim for complete and correct network logic in your schedule:

- The schedule will, for the most part, maintain itself and take less effort
  If you forget to set dependencies, the schedule will not update itself properly when you make a change to it. The schedule is not a *dynamic schedule*. Having a dynamic schedule is very important during project *execution*. Every time you enter actual progress, you want the rest of the schedule to update itself automatically so that you immediately have a *valid* model of the project again. Project managers who do not carefully check the logic of their schedule have to check the start and finish dates of all future tasks every time they enter actual progress. They soon find that they do not have enough time to do this at every status cycle, and they typically abandon their schedule sometime during project execution. See page 206 for how much time you might save with complete and correct logic in your schedule.
- You will have a reliable Critical Path
  Only with a complete and correct network will you have a meaningful *Critical Path*

in your schedule. If the logic is incomplete or incorrect, MS Project might lead you to think that tasks are critical when they really are not critical at all, which will cause you to focus on the wrong tasks. To be in control of their projects, project managers need to see a Critical Path that is correct. The true Critical Path harbors possibilities for shortening the project and bringing it in on time. For more on the *Critical Path Method*, see page 418.

- You can easily develop what-if scenarios
  Only with complete and correct logic can you easily develop several scenarios of your schedule to address problems and resolve schedule conflicts. You often have to change just one cell of the model to see the result of a what-if analysis in a dynamic model.

Is the Network of Dependencies Complete?

The network is complete if the task bars of all detail tasks and the diamonds of all milestones are tied up at both ends. The network can have multiple starting points, but only one ending point, otherwise the Critical Path calculation in the network cannot be correct. The Critical Path is the most widely used technique to manage the time dimension of a project (see page 418 for a detailed explanation of the technique).

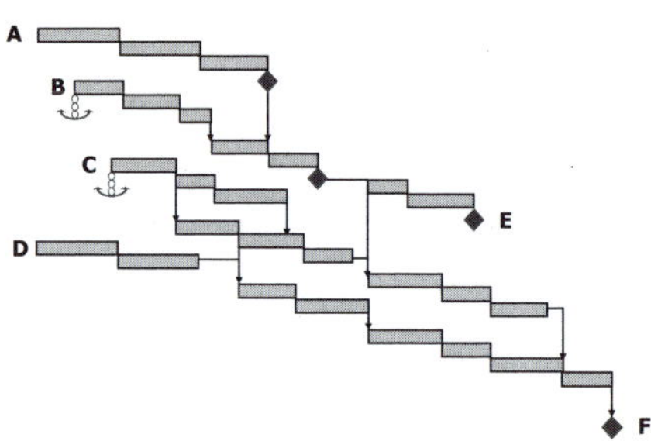

A typical network will look like the illustration (where boxes touch each other, there is a link as well). Unlike other authors, we do not require the network to start with just one starting point. We find that this makes the network unnecessarily complex and does not provide additional benefits. However, when you have multiple starting points, you need to check the task list to see if these detail tasks (A, B, C and D in the illustration) are perhaps missing a predecessor. If they are not, ask yourself if they have an *external dependency*. If task B and C can only start when certain supplies arrive, they have an external dependency and are legitimate starting points in the network. They will need a Start No Earlier Than constraint (under *forward scheduling*, see page 259 and 261) and perhaps no predecessor. You can see that B and C have a constraint (depicted by the anchor), since they start later. We have often found that schedulers used Start-No-Earlier-Than constraints to make the schedule look good and compensate for missing predecessors. If B and C are not dependent on external events, they will need a predecessor. You always have to check the starting points carefully.

Even more important are the ending points of the network. There can only be one ending point (ignoring overhead tasks and recurring tasks). In the illustration, there are two ending points: E and F. Task F is likely the legitimate ending point, while E may be missing a successor. Missing successors make the Critical Path calculation incorrect, which is a serious issue. Without a reliable Critical Path, it is hard to manage a project to a timely completion.

These are the checks to perform. The numbering of each check corresponds to the complete checklist in the summary chapter, see page 711. The filters mentioned in the checks can be found in the file *ProjectPro tools to check project schedules.MPP* available for download at www.ProjectProCorp.com (see page vi for the procedure to access these files).

5

5 Dependencies

5.1. Have you turned the **Task Mode** of all linked tasks to **Auto Scheduled**?
What is the use of dependencies if you do not take advantage of them?
See page 218 for the detailed discussion on why switching tasks to Auto Scheduled is important at this point.
You can perform this check by applying the out-of-the-box filter **Manually Scheduled Tasks** (ribbon **View**, list button **Filter**, item **More Filters**, item in list **Manually Scheduled Tasks**). If you find any, please refer to page 220 for the steps to switch them to **Auto Scheduled**.

5.2. Is the logic set only on detail tasks and milestones (not on summary tasks)?
If some dependencies run through summary tasks and others through detail tasks, it is too hard to check if the network is complete. It is also too hard to trace the Critical Path and understand it. Only with a complete network can the schedule be a fully dynamic model of the project. Therefore, we recommend that you keep the logic on the detail tasks and milestones only. We discussed this point in more detail on page 236. You can check if there are dependencies on summary tasks by applying the filter
5.2 Summary Tasks with Dependencies.

5.3. Are all the starts of the detail tasks and milestones linked to at least one other detail task or milestone?
You can verify if all starts are linked by applying the filter
5.3 Detail Tasks without Predecessors. Note that if the project manager used SS or FF dependencies, the filter is not conclusive. There will be another check we need to do on those dependencies.
Exceptions for having a predecessor are:
◇ *Summary tasks* (see page 232).

◇ All tasks that can start independently from each other when the project starts.
◇ All tasks or milestones driven by deliveries from suppliers outside the project team (*external dependency*) rather than by hand-offs within the project. We recommend you create extra milestones for delivery events. You can put a **Start No Earlier Than** constraint date on these delivery milestones (see page 234).
◇ *Recurring tasks* (see page 141).
◇ *Overhead tasks* (see page 143).

5.4. Are all the ends of the detail tasks and milestones linked to at least one other detail task or milestone?
A detail task that does not have its end tied to another task is a *loose end*, *hanger* or *dangling task*. In any project there should only be one loose end: the project finish milestone (ignoring the summary, recurring and overhead tasks). You can verify whether all ends are linked up by applying the filter **5.4 Detail Tasks without Successors**. Note that if the project manager used SS or FF dependencies, the filter is not conclusive. There will be another check that we need to apply on those.
Exceptions are:
◇ The project end milestone
◇ *Summary tasks* (see page 232)
◇ *Recurring tasks* (see page 141)
◇ *Overhead tasks* (see page 143)

5.5. Do you have SS dependencies properly linked up?
Project managers often forget to link a task bar on both ends when they use SS or FF dependencies. People often forget to set a dependency on the finish of the predecessor involved in an SS dependency (see the question marks in the illustration at the left). The finish of the predecessor task must also be linked; otherwise, it could still continue even though the project is already finished. If you just check that each detail task has a successor, you will not find these loose ends. In the illustration, *pour concrete* has an SS successor, but its finish is not tied to any other task.

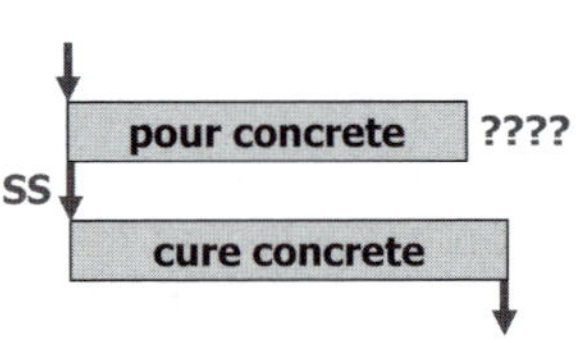

You can display the tasks with an SS dependency by applying the filter **5.5 Detail Tasks with SS in Successors**. Then insert the column **Successors**. Does a task with SS in the **Successor** field also have, in the same cell, an FS or FF entry that ties up its end? Note that MS Project does not display the label *FS* since it is the default type of dependency; it will only display the ID-number. For example, if you see "*33*", you know this

is an FS dependency with task 33.
Many people have asked Microsoft to allow setting an SS- and an FF-dependency between two tasks; we will explain a workaround to accomplish this on page 248.

5.6. Do you have FF dependencies properly linked up?

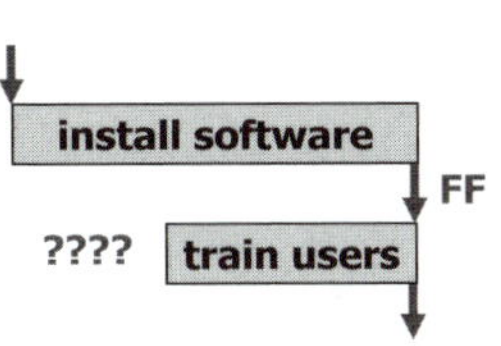

Also, project managers often forget to set a dependency on the start of the driven task in an FF dependency (see the question marks in the illustration at the left).
The task *train users* has an FF predecessor that links its finish, but its start is not linked to any other task. This means that it could extend backwards to before the project start date. In other words, MS Project thinks that you do not need to find a trainer or create course material for the task trainees, which is hard to believe. You are probably missing a link that becomes important when you start developing what-if scenarios with the schedule or run simulation software.
You can display the tasks with an FF dependency by applying the filter **5.6 Detail Tasks with FF in Predecessors**. Then insert the column **Predecessors** and check if the task with *FF* in the predecessor cell also has an SS or FS entry that ties up its start in the same cell. Again, MS Project does not display the label FS. If you cannot create a link to other detail tasks in your schedule, you should create a link to the project end milestone. If you do not have a project end milestone, you should create one even if this only serves the purpose of hooking up all your loose ends. Certain tasks can be linked only to the project end milestone. For example: Tasks to inform other organizations or tasks that create entirely independent parts of a system, which can be assembled with very little effort.

Is the Network of Dependencies Correct?

Once you have ensured that all detail tasks and milestones are linked up on both ends, you still need to check if you set the right dependencies. There can be so many dependencies that you will inevitably make some mistakes, as I always do until I check the network.

These are the checks to perform on the accuracy of the network. We recommend the first check in particular, since it is very effective:

5.7. Do all tasks have a reasonable amount of *Total Slack*?
For now, you can treat the Total Slack on a task as the *time buffer* on that task. For an explanation of total slack, please refer to page 421. Insert the **Total Slack** field by right-clicking on a column heading and selecting **Insert Column**. You can check if the total slack is reasonable by doing a sort on **Total Slack**. Click ribbon **View**, button **Sort**, item **Sort by...** and select **Total Slack** from the **Sort by** list. Select ◉ **Descending** to display the tasks with the most Total Slack at the top of the list. Also, clear ☐ **Keep outline structure** because this sorts only the summary task families instead of all detail tasks.
Check whether you expected that much slack on the tasks listed at the top comparing their slack amount to the project duration. If not, you have found missing or incorrect logic. [40] In a healthy project, most tasks should have slack that is less than 25% of the project duration. This check is very effective in catching missing or incorrect logic even in large schedules. Remember that if you miss just one essential dependency, your Critical Path is wrong, your forecasts are not *valid* and your model is not *dynamic*.

5.8. Are there no circular dependencies?
There should be no *circular dependencies*, because a schedule with circular dependencies will not be dynamic, but entirely static. As soon as a circular dependency is created, MS Project can no longer recalculate and maintain a schedule. How could it schedule two tasks over time where A drives B, but B also drives A? The application will warn you if you try to create circularity in the logic within a single schedule. When you set dependencies across multiple schedules (*cross-project dependencies*), circular dependencies can still easily occur. They will manifest themselves in the *master schedule* that contains all *subschedules*. This topic ventures into *program management*, which is the subject of another course.[41]

5.9. When a change is entered into the schedule, does it update the rest of the schedule automatically and appropriately through dependencies?
This check is a matter of trial and error, but we recommend you try some likely what-if scenarios. Is the entire schedule still *valid* after you made a change? Where the schedule is not valid, an essential dependency might be missing. If you always have to check the entire schedule after each change, you do not have a dynamic model. You should be able to rely on the logic

[40] This check was contributed by Frank Walker, TWG Project Management, LLC.

[41] Visit www.ProjectProCorp.com for more information on the courses *Forecasting Programs* or *Managing Programs*.

to always produce valid scenarios of the schedule, whatever change you throw at it, see page 210 for a detailed discussion. Remember, the logic should be helpful, especially during project execution when you update your schedule regularly.

Is the Network Logic Simple Enough?

A network that is too complex to understand and maintain is not helpful in managing the project. Redundant dependencies clutter the view unnecessarily and make the network overly complex. If the network is complex, team members will not try to understand it or use it. Thus, the value of the network decreases.

Many project managers fall prey to the following fallacy: *All tasks are related to each other, and I have to set dependencies everywhere I notice any relationship*. Yes, indeed all tasks relate to each other (that is how you arrive at a complete network of dependencies eventually). Most tasks, however, are only related indirectly to each other (i.e., via other tasks) instead of directly. You only have to link the tasks that have a *direct relationship* and not the ones that have *indirect relationships*.

The following questions will help you to determine if the network is simple enough:

5.10. Are there dependencies that leapfrog each other?
Dependencies that skip over the back of other dependencies within a chain are indirect relationships that you can remove.

5.11. Are there dependencies that run in parallel on detail tasks and their summary tasks? If that is the case, keep the detail task dependency and remove the dependency on the summary task. See page 236 for why logic should be kept to the detail level.

5.12. Can you, as the project manager, explain the network to your project team? If you cannot explain it, the network is too complex. If you can explain the network, you can immediately show team members who else will be affected if their tasks slip. In this way the network diagram becomes a powerful tool for team members to coordinate their activities and act as a team.
A clear network also allows you to do a quick *impact analysis* of

suggestions made by team members or executives. Imagine that the project sponsor of your software development project comes to you during the *execution* of the project and asks: *What if we wait for the new release of this operating system?* or *What if we use this new line of more powerful computers?* With a simple network, you will be able to easily indicate the impacts by following the dependency arrows from the components that will be affected by such a change in direction. You may be able to stem unwanted turbulence, or immediately negotiate for more time or money when superiors throw *what-if scenarios* at you.

Other Checks on the Network

5.13. Does the Resulting High-Level Schedule Make Sense?

If you followed our recommendations, the start and finish dates of all tasks are entirely driven by the network of dependencies. If the network is complete and correct, the high-level schedule should make sense. You can check the high-level schedule by showing only the first few outline levels of the Work Breakdown Structure. You will then check if the dates of the deliverables (or phases) make sense relative to one another. You can use the **Outline** button on the **View** ribbon to display **Outline level 1, Outline level** 2 or **Outline Level 3**, depending on the size of your project. Even though you may not be an expert in the field of this project, with your common sense you will check if the *walls* are scheduled before the *roof*, *writing* before *publishing*, and so forth. If the schedule does not make sense on its higher levels, you probably overlooked an essential dependency.

This check is important because your executives will look at the high-level schedule. We recommend that you catch any anomalies before sharp executive eyes pry into it. For example, in the next screenshot it looks like the *move* starts too early; perhaps an essential dependency is *missing*. In a schedule where all tasks are scheduled *As Soon As Possible* (*ASAP*), missing dependencies will be visible in a high-level view of the schedule, and will appear as too much overlap or concurrence.

If you expanded the *move* summary task in this next example, it would become clear that the task *select mover* is scheduled for August but the actual move takes place in November after the new location is remodeled. In this schedule all the essential logic was in place:

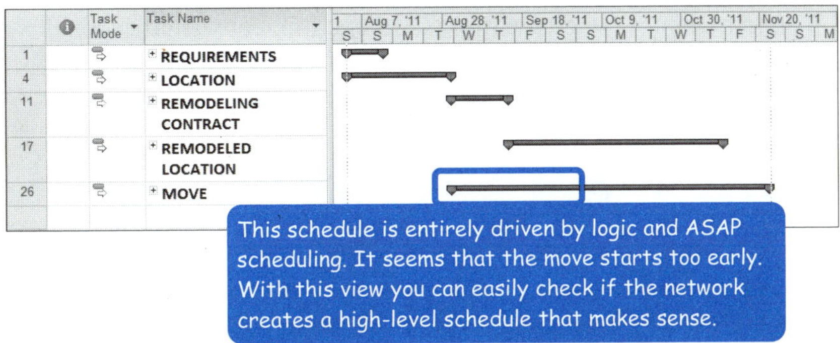

Perhaps the task *select mover* should be moved up in the list to the *Remodeling Contract* deliverable, which then should be renamed *Remodeling and Move Contract*. The result looks easier to explain:

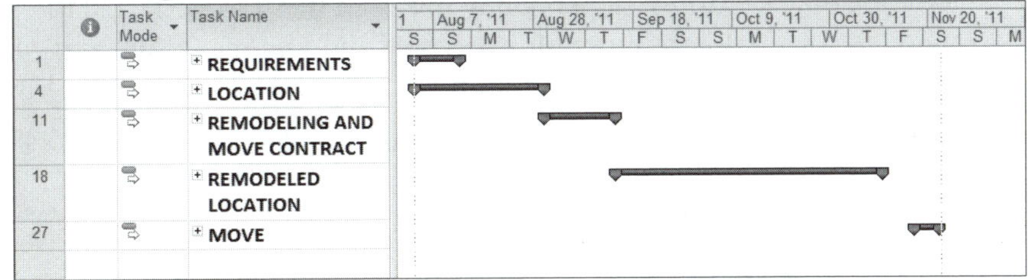

5.14. Have you turned off *Autolink* after checking the network?
After you have done all the previous checks and have ensured that you now have a complete network of logical dependencies between all detail tasks and milestones, it is time to turn this option back to off: click ribbon **File**, Options, tab **Schedule**, section **Scheduling options for this project**, ☐ **Autolink Inserted or Moved Tasks**. You have just crafted your network very carefully, and you do not want MS Project to change any dependencies you deliberately created. See page 211 for a discussion on what this option does.

Limitations of Dependencies

There are some technical limitations when creating dependencies:

- **You can set only one link between two tasks**
  It is impossible to create more than one link between the same two tasks. You will receive the following error message:

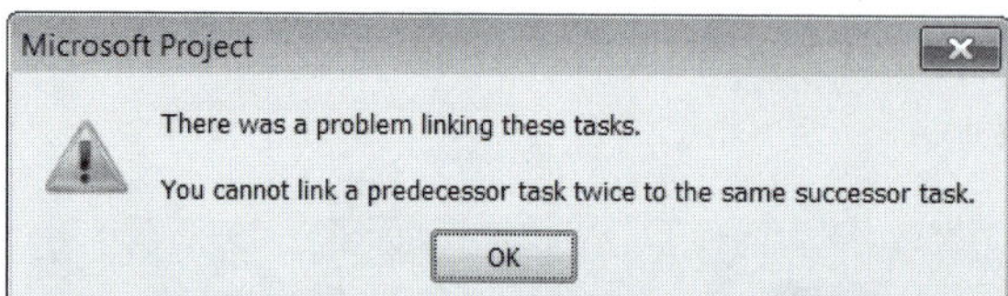

Therefore, you cannot hook up both the start and the finish of two tasks using an SS as well as an FF dependency. For example, you may have created an SS dependency between *relocate the drywall* and *wire the electricity*. If relocating the walls takes longer than planned, your model may show that the electricians finish earlier than the carpenters, which is unreasonable.

If you could set an FF dependency between these same tasks, the problem would be solved. As a workaround, you can insert an extra milestone and run two FF dependencies to and from that milestone, as shown in the following screenshot:

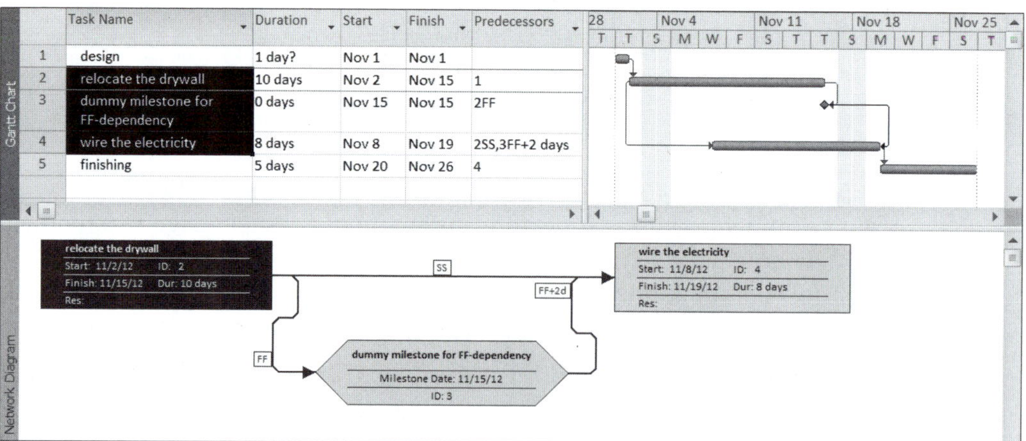

- **You cannot set links on all parts of a split task bar**
  We discussed split bars first on page 129. You can only link the start of the first part and the finish of the last part. Therefore, you cannot create very dynamic models with split task bars. This is why we do not recommend the use of split task bars when you are planning the project; you will see enough splits appear when you update your schedule during project execution.

- **You cannot link to the finish of a summary task**
  You cannot set an FF or SF dependency to a summary task as the successor, because the finish date of a summary task is always calculated. However, you can link from the finish of the summary task. Remember that we do not recommend logic on summary tasks (see page 236), so this limitation should not bother you at all.
- **Percentage lags only apply to the duration of the predecessor task**
  You cannot set a *lag* that takes a percentage of the duration of the successor task; the percentages are always taken from the duration of the predecessor. So you cannot create a dependency that drives, for example, the halfway point of a successor.
- **All dependencies are later-than dependencies**
  All four types of dependencies (FS, SS, FF, SF) make the driven task (successor) start or finish at or later than the start or finish of the predecessor. If you want to schedule some (or all) of your tasks *backward* from a hard finish date, you will need *earlier-than dependencies* that force the driven task to start or finish before the start or finish of the driving task. No scheduling software has earlier-than dependencies. We, therefore, do not recommend backward scheduling.

5

Exercises

Review

1. Why should project managers set all the dependencies in their schedules?
2. What are the criteria for a good, solid network of dependencies that creates an entirely dynamic schedule?
3. If you are dependent upon supplies to arrive from outside for one deliverable in your project, how would you recommend scheduling that situation?
4. This book discusses many different ways to set dependencies. Provide at least 3 ways.
5. Are the following valid entries in the lag field? Yes or no? Why?
   - ◇ 5d
   - ◇ –3d
   - ◇ +30%
   - ◇ +5ed
6. Does it make sense to create a schedule with only manually scheduled tasks and set all the dependencies between them?
7. Should you allow logic on summary tasks? If yes, why? If no, why not?

8. For each of the situations in the next table determine:
   - ◇ Which task is the predecessor and successor: A or B?
   - ◇ What type of dependency do you need: FS, SS, FF or SF?
   - ◇ Would you advise to add a lead or a lag to the dependency? If so, as a relative lag or absolute lag? And how much?

	Predecessor (A or B)	**Type of Dependency**	**Add Lag? Relative/absolute? How much?**
You *gather requirements* (A) and then you *analyze requirements* (B).			
After you *apply for a permit* (A), you have to wait 3 weeks for *permit received* (B).			
Halfway through *perform system analysis* (A) we typically start *programming code* (B).			
You have to *pour foundation* (A) and let the concrete dry before you *lay bricks* (B) to erect the walls.			
One day after the finish of *conduct courses* (A), you must finish *write evaluation report* (B).			
Prepare for PMP exam (A) and *take PMP exam* (B).			

9. You have a task, *test unit*, with a 10-day duration, and you hesitate between using a FS-5d or a SS+5d dependency with this task as the predecessor. The FS-5d dependency will give the successor a different start date than the SS+5d when:
   a. The start date of *test unit* changes
   b. The finish date of *test unit* changes (while its start date stays the same)
   c. The duration of *test unit* changes
   d. b and c

10. You have two tasks, *survey clients* and *summarize survey results*, and you hesitate between using a FS-30% or a SS+70% dependency between the two tasks. The FS-30% dependency will cause a different start date of the successor than the SS+70% dependency when:
   a. The start date of *survey clients* changes
   b. The finish date of *survey clients* changes (while its start date stays the same)
   c. The duration of *survey clients* changes
   d. None of the above gives a difference in impact between FS-30% and SS+70%

5

Relocation Project — Dependencies

The goal of this exercise is to be able to enter a complete network of cause-and-effect dependencies into the schedule.

Continue to work with your file *Relocation.mpp* or open the file *05A Dependencies.mpp* available for download at www.ProjectProCorp.com (see page vi for the procedure to access these files).

Enter the following dependencies (see page 221, 222, 224, 225 or 227 for steps):

1. Finishing the task *research staff requirements* allows the task *summarize requirements* to start.
2. Finishing the task *summarize requirements* allows the task *evaluate the sites* to start.
3. The detail tasks of the deliverable *LOCATION* are all Finish-to-Start dependent upon each other.
4. Accomplishing the milestone *location selected*, allows you to start the task *select the contractor* and the task *select mover*.
5. The detail tasks of the deliverable *REMODELING CONTRACT* are all Finish-to-Start dependent upon each other. The dependency between *select contractor* and *meet to discuss contract* has a lag of 5 days; it will take a time frame of 5 days to get the participants together to meet.

6. Accomplishing the milestone *contractor contracted* allows the task *relocate walls* to start.
7. The tasks *relocate walls* through *install cabinetry* of the deliverable *REMODELED LOCATION* are all Finish-to-Start dependent upon each other.
8. In the deliverable *REMODELED LOCATION* the tasks *install cabinetry* and *install LAN* can take place concurrently after the paint dries. *Drying of paint* is the predecessor for both tasks.
9. Accomplishing both tasks *install cabinetry* and *install LAN* can start the task *lay carpet*.
10. Completing the task *lay carpet* achieves the milestone *facility remodeled.*
11. Accomplishing the milestone *facility remodeled* allows the task *pack* to start.
12. The detail tasks of the deliverable *MOVE* are all Finish-to-Start dependent upon each other.
13. Compare your file with the solution file *06A Deadlines.mpp* available for download at www.ProjectProCorp.com (see page vi for the procedure to access these files). See page 697 of this book for an automated way of comparing and reporting differences between two versions of one schedule.
14. Save your file.

Chapter 6 Entering Deadlines, Constraint Dates and Task Calendars

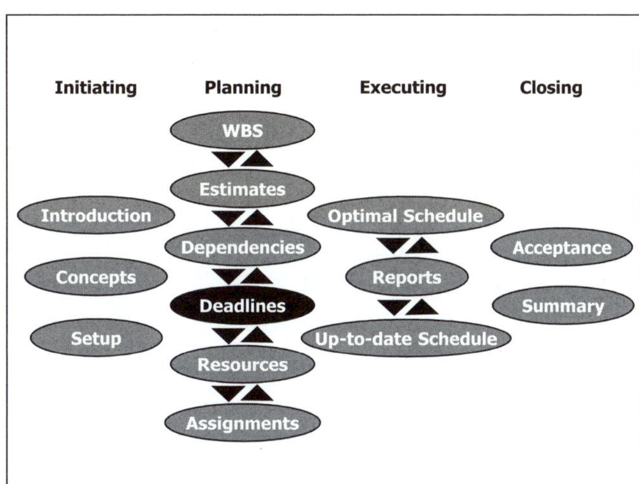

6

The Gantt Chart of the schedule is starting to take shape. We may want to capture the dates that we promised as deadlines (see black ellipse above). Furthermore, we may need some hard dates as constraints and add some task calendars to make our schedule more realistic. Deadlines, constraints and task calendars are all features that capture specific dates.

After reading this chapter you will:

- know the difference between deadlines and constraints
- know the advantages and disadvantages of constraint dates
- realize that deadlines are preferable to constraints
- know in which situations to use deadlines, constraints or task calendars
- know the different types of date constraints
- be able to choose the right type of constraint
- be able to enter constraint and deadline dates into the project model
- be able to create a task calendar and restrict the scheduling of a task with it
- be able to check if you used scheduling best practices with regards to deadlines, constraints and task calendars
- know how to format and print the Gantt Chart view

Show Restraint with Constraints!

"Nob, how did you end up with all those constraint dates in your schedule?" "What do you mean constraints? Where do you see those, Bob?" "Do you see all these calendar-like icons in this i-column? Those are constraint dates; if you point to one with your mouse, the screen tip will tell you what type of constraint it is." Nob points to an icon and exclaims: "I'll be darned! I did not realize I had them in my schedule. I never entered them; how did they get there?"

Bob: "Well, did you enter Start or Finish dates?" "I didn't enter dates!" "Did you drag task bars to where you wanted them scheduled?" "No" "Did you assign resources using the Team Planner view?" Nob's voice now sounds surprised "Does that create constraints?" "Yes, it does, unfortunately!"

Nob asks: "Should I spend the time to remove them?" Bob: "If you don't, you will need to review and revise all future dates every week when you update your schedule. If you remove them now, the dependencies will do a lot of the updating for you later!"

What Are Deadlines and Date Constraints?

A deadline is a date you commit to that does not restrict the scheduling of a task. A constraint is a date that restricts when MS Project can schedule a task.

It is possible to force tasks to be scheduled on certain dates, which is necessary for certain tasks like *attend meeting, attend conference* and *audit seminar*. The dates for tasks like these have to be agreed upon beforehand and do not change often. Fixing dates is a matter of putting a schedule *constraint* on the task. You could consider a Must Start On constraint for the aforementioned tasks. A *Must Start On* is a hard constraint, and MS Project cannot reschedule tasks with hard date constraints. Date constraints affect the network of dependencies. The more constraints you create, the less freely your network will flow back and forth when you enter changes. Therefore, the more constraints you have in your schedule, the more effort you will spend revising (constraint) dates to keep your schedule *valid*.

6

Deadlines, on the other hand, do not restrict the scheduling of tasks. Deadline dates stay visible in the timescale as down-facing green arrows ⇩ . When you miss a deadline date, MS Project displays a red indicator ◆ in the indicators ❶ column.

We recommend, therefore, that you enter dates that you commit to as deadline dates rather than as constraint dates. When you want to track a target date for a specific task, you can set a deadline date for that task. Since deadlines do not restrict the scheduling, they do not require immediate attention, like constraints do when they cause scheduling conflicts.

In this chapter, we will discuss:

- Deadlines, see next section
- Constraints (see page 258).
- Task calendars (see page 273).

Deadlines

Deadlines are essential for implementing *Forecast Scheduling*. In the **Deadline** field, you can capture the dates you promised – long before you are ready to create the *baseline schedule*, see page 604. Too many project managers use the schedule itself (**Start** and **Finish** date fields) as the repository for promised dates and do not want the schedule to change, thus killing the live schedule. We recommend you use the **Deadline** field instead to capture promised dates, which also keeps them static and ready for comparison against the live schedule. This will allow you to keep your schedule dynamic, alive and up-to-date.

For example, we recommend you enter deadlines:

- On the project finish milestone, the most important forecasted date to monitor.
- When you promise a date to a stakeholder, it is important not to lose that date. The **Deadline** field will hold it even when you are not ready to set a *baseline* yet. The deadlines will help you check if the baseline will be acceptable when you are ready to set the baseline. See page 604 for more on baselines.
- We also recommend you enter several deadline dates on the milestones for the *interim deliverables* with your team (*interim deadlines*). You need to discuss and agree on what are reasonable dates. Interim deadlines will help teams spring into action early and keep their focus.

Entering Deadlines

1. Click ribbon **View** and find its section **Task Views**, click the top part of [Gantt Chart].

2. Double-click on the task to set a deadline on.
   OR

   Click on the task, click ribbon **Task** and click [Information].

   OR
   Select the task and hold down [Shift] while pressing [F2] – the **Task Information** dialog appears.

3. Click the **Advanced** tab; the dialog should now look like:

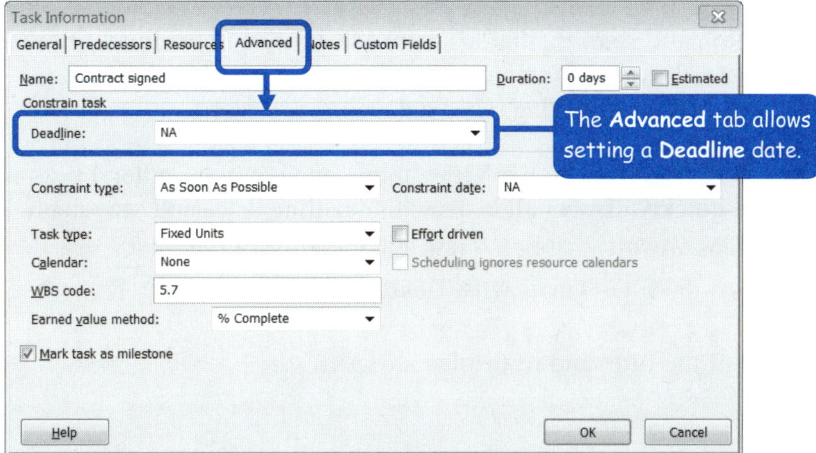

4. Enter the deadline date in the **Deadline** field or use the pull-down calendar to click on a date.
5. Click OK and you will now see an arrow ⇩ in the timescale that represents the deadline date you entered. If you rest your mouse pointer on it, you will see its screen tip that reveals the deadline date. You can move deadline dates by simply dragging the ⇩ in the timescale to a new date. You can start dragging as soon as you see the four-arrow mouse pointer ✥.

If you have to be done before November 1, you have to enter October 31 as the deadline date. The deadline time will be at the end of the day by default unless you enter a time as well. If you enter *November 1* as the deadline date, the task will be done by 5:00 PM on November 1. You could add the time to the deadline date by entering *November 1, 8 AM*, for example.

The symbol for a deadline ⇩ does not stand out in the timescale, particularly when there are many dependency arrows. We suggest you change it to a more striking color by clicking ribbon **Format**, section **Bar Styles**, button **Format**, item **Bar Styles** – the **Bar Styles** dialog appears. Scroll to the bottom of the list and select **Deadline** in the **From** list; on the tab **Bars** you can now select a more striking shape and color for deadlines.

To remove a deadline, simply delete the date from the **Deadline** field on the **Advanced** tab of the **Task Information** dialog.

Managing Deadlines

You will not get automatic warning dialogs from MS Project if deadlines are not met. What you do get is a red exclamation icon ◆ in the indicators ❶ column, MS Project's way of raising a red flag when a deadline is missed.

Also, if you use the list of filters on the **View** ribbon and apply the filter **Tasks with Deadlines**, you can quickly display all tasks with deadline dates and see which deadlines are slipping. The steps are: click ribbon **View**, click the list button of Filter: and select **More Filters** – the filter **Tasks with Deadlines** will be listed.

Press F3 to get rid of the filter and re-display all tasks.

Constraints

Choosing the Options

Click ribbon **File**, Options and click on the tab indicated in the table below where you want to change settings:

Tab	Option
Schedule	In the **Scheduling Options for this project** section: ☑ **Tasks will always honor their constraint dates** This option makes tasks obey their constraint dates. We recommend you keep this option on to make sure your schedule observes the few real and hard constraint dates that you may have in it. If you turn this option off, you allow the dependencies to do their work and forecast a project with many constraints properly. This may be useful to see accurate forecasts in a schedule with many constraints (created against our recommendation to minimize the use of constraints).

Forward Scheduling or Backward Scheduling

Before discussing the types of constraints, we need to discuss the basic scheduling regime you choose. The two choices are:

- *Forward Scheduling* from the project start date. You do forward scheduling if you enter the project start date in the ribbon **Project**, button **Project Information** dialog and want the schedule to tell you what the expected finish date is for the project. Under forward scheduling, tasks are scheduled *As Soon As Possible* (*ASAP*) by default. Some people call this therefore *ASAP scheduling*.
- *Backward Scheduling* from the project finish date. You schedule backward if you enter the project finish date in the ribbon **Project**, button **Project Information** dialog and want to find out when to start the project to meet this date. Under backward scheduling tasks are scheduled *As Late As Possible* (*ALAP*) by default. Some people call this therefore *ALAP scheduling*.

You can see whether you are scheduling forward or backward by checking the **Project, Project Information** dialog in the pull-down list **Schedule from**. It shows there that you schedule from either the **Project Start Date** (forward scheduling) or the **Project Finish Date** (backward scheduling). MS Project calculates the resulting finish or start date, respectively, and its field is grayed out; it cannot be set. If you change from forward to backward scheduling after you have entered some tasks, the constraint for these tasks will stay ASAP; new tasks will be ALAP.

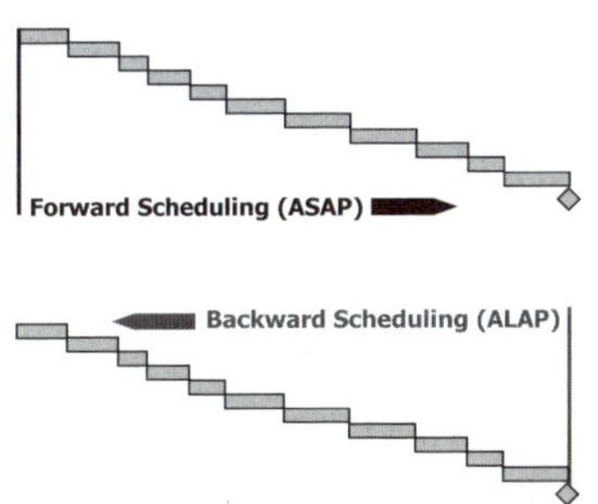

We think that for backward scheduling, we need an entirely new class of *earlier-than dependencies* that drive impacts backward into the schedule. Since there are only *later-than dependencies* (see page 212), we recommend you stick with forward scheduling. Or, you can use backward scheduling to just find the project start date and then you switch to forward scheduling to manage the project.

Types of Constraints

The eight types of *constraints* can be categorized as tendencies, one-sided constraints or rigid constraints:

Tendencies: for more detail see next section.

- *As Soon As Possible* (*ASAP*; the default under forward scheduling)
- *As Late As Possible* (*ALAP*; the default under backward scheduling)

One-sided constraints; [42] see page 261 for more detail.

- *Start No Earlier Than (SNET)*
- *Finish No Earlier Than (FNET)*
- *Start No Later Than (SNLT)*
- *Finish No Later Than (FNLT)*

Rigid constraints, see page 262 for more detail.

- *Must Start On (MSO)*
- *Must Finish On (MFO)*

Tendencies

Even though ALAP and ASAP do not have a *Constraint Date***,** they have a tremendous impact on the schedule and are in that sense "constraining". In terms of their impact on the schedule, we recommend you think of them as schedule *tendencies*.

MS Project has forward scheduling as its default regime. Under *forward scheduling* MS Project automatically puts the **As Soon As Possible** (ASAP) tendency on all tasks. This means that MS Project will pull task bars in the timescale as far to the left as the project start date and the network of predecessors will allow. Even when the regime is ASAP, you can still schedule certain tasks **As Late As Possible** (ALAP). For example, in a move project you should schedule, *packing equipment* ALAP just before the move. *Training* is another example of a task that should take place as late as possible; otherwise people have forgotten it when they need it.

Under backward scheduling, tasks are ALAP by default. ALAP task bars will tend to go to the right in the timescale as much as the project finish date and the network of successors allow. Again, you can still change some tasks to ASAP scheduling in an ALAP schedule. For example, tasks like *reserve training room* are perhaps better scheduled ASAP, because if you do them ALAP, you might be too late to get the facility.

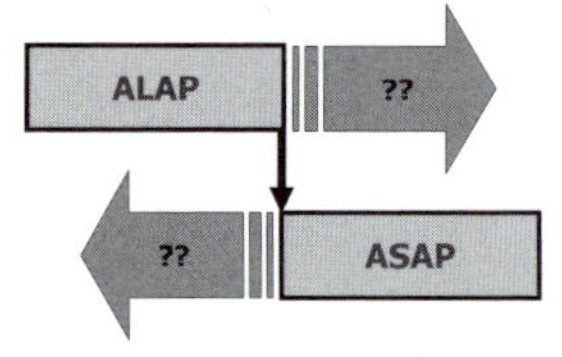

Combining ASAP tasks with ALAP tasks within one schedule creates tension between these tasks. It raises an interesting question: which is stronger when they push against each other, ASAP or

---

[42] Why they formulated these constraint names in the negative (no earlier than, no later than) instead of in the positive (later than, earlier than) is beyond me. Negatives are more difficult to understand.

ALAP (see the illustration)? When you try this, you will see that an ALAP task wins in an ASAP schedule (forward), and an ASAP task wins in an ALAP schedule (backward). In other words, the odd one wins.

However, one ALAP task in an ASAP schedule will not push the project finish to eternity; it stays within its available time buffer or *Total Slack*. For more info on Total Slack (see page 421).

One-Sided Constraints

This group of one-sided constraints limits the movement of task bars to only one direction, either to the left (no earlier than) or to the right (no later than):

- Start No Earlier Than (SNET) and Finish No Earlier Than (FNET) limit free movement of the task bars towards the left in the timescale; the start date (SNET) or finish date (FNET) cannot go to the left of the No Earlier Than date.
- Start No Later Than (SNLT) and Finish No Later Than (FNLT) limit free movement of the task bars towards the right in the timescale; the start date (SNLT) or finish date (FNLT) cannot go to the right of the No Later Than date.

6

No Earlier Than Constraints

An example of a *Start No Earlier Than* (*SNET*) constraint is when supplies will not be delivered until a certain date (*external dependency*). You can start the activity for which you need the supplies no earlier than the delivery date.

An example of a *Finish No Earlier Than* (*FNET*) is when you need an approval for the deliverable. You know the approval can take place during the next board meeting planned for March 13th. You enter an FNET constraint on that date.

The *No Earlier Than* tasks cannot move earlier in time (to the left in the timescale). They can be pushed to the right by the network without a limit. Under *forward scheduling* or *As Soon As Possible* (*ASAP*) scheduling, they will not be able to cause a schedule conflict. In other words, they are *soft constraints* under *forward scheduling*.

Under *backward scheduling* or *As Late As Possible* (*ALAP*) scheduling, the project finish date is hard. As you enter dependencies you will see that the *ALAP* task bars will be pushed out earlier in time (moving to the left in the timescale). They can be pushed to the left as far as the *No Earlier Than* date allows. If pushed any further, a *schedule conflict* will occur. *No Earlier Than* constraints are therefore said to be *hard date constraints* under backward scheduling.

A tiny little red dot in the constraint icon in the indicators column will tell you that a constraint is hard. If the dot is blue, it is a soft constraint. The icons are only displayed for **Auto Scheduled** tasks.

No Later Than Constraints

An example of a *Start No Later Than* (*SNLT*) constraint might be that in most of Canada you do not want to start asphalting a road later than November 1st because of cold, inclement weather. An example of a *Finish No Later Than* (*FNLT*) constraint is when you commit to deliver a report no later than March 13, and this date is a do-or-die date.

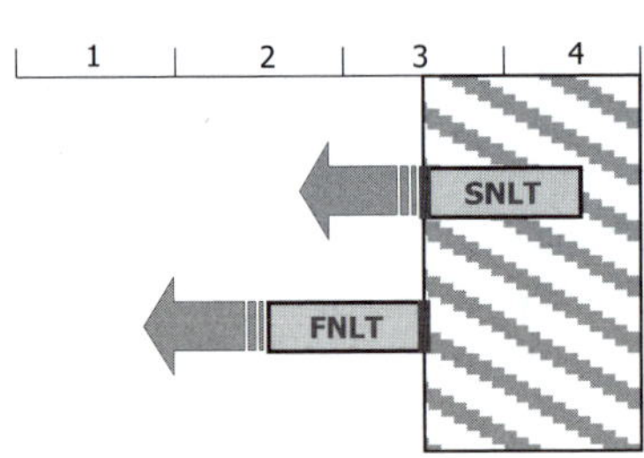

The *No Later Than* constraints are restricted from moving later than the date specified (moving to the right in a timescale view). They can be allowed earlier by the network all the way up to the start date of the project. Under backward scheduling, with all tasks *As Late As Possible* (*ALAP*), these constraints will not be able to cause a schedule conflict. In other words, they are soft under backward scheduling.

Under *forward scheduling* with all tasks *As Soon as Possible*, when you enter dependencies, you will see that MS Project pushes the *As Soon As Possible* (*ASAP*) task bars out to the right in the timescale (to later in time). They can be pushed out as far as the No Later Than constraint date allows. If pushed any further, a *schedule conflict* will occur. Therefore, No Later Than constraints are said to be *hard date constraints* under forward scheduling.

A tiny little red dot in the constraint icon in the indicators column will tell you that a constraint is hard. If the dot is blue, it is a soft constraint. The icons are only displayed for **Auto Scheduled** tasks.

Rigid Constraints

The last group of rigid constraints, Must Start On (MSO) and Must Finish On (MFO), lock the task bar entirely to the date indicated and deny any free movement. These rigid constraints severely affect the schedule.

An example of a *Must Start On* (MSO) constraint is holding an important meeting that must start on January 9 at 9:00 AM.

An example of a *Must Finish On* (MFO) constraint is when you have a contractual date by which you must move out of an office space or pay a steep penalty.

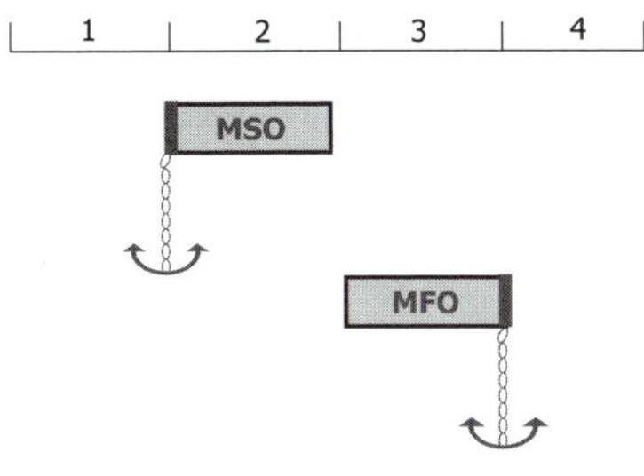

Where you use an MSO constraint, the start will always be on the date indicated. With an MFO constraint, the finish will always be on the date specified. MSO and MFO constraints can easily cause *schedule conflicts*. These constraints are always *hard date constraints* under both forward and backward scheduling. You should use them only when you absolutely need them to keep the schedule *valid*.

Note that the task bar can still grow or shrink in size when you revise the estimate of a MSO or MFO task. This will make the other, unconstrained end of the task bar move.

6

Schedule Conflict

A *schedule conflict* is when MS Project cannot find an acceptable and feasible schedule for your project based on the input you provided. For example, your schedule is currently 12 weeks long, but now you try to force a Finish No Later Than week 11 constraint onto the project. Typically, a schedule conflict occurs when a constraint date cannot be met.

MS Project will immediately tell you when there is a schedule conflict with a message similar to the following:

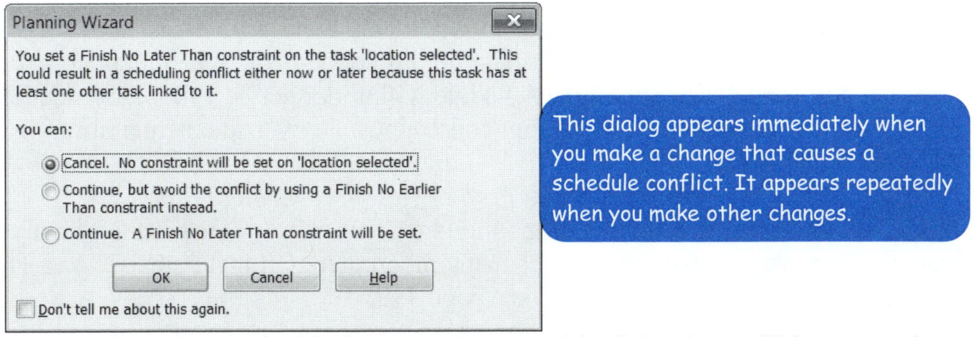

You are forced to deal with the issue, because this dialog box will keep popping up (unless you check ☑ **Don't tell me about this again;** if you change your mind and want to see this dialog again, click ribbon **File**, Options, tab **Schedule**, section **Schedule Alerts Options** and select ☑ **Show task schedule warnings**).

If you do not understand why your schedule has a conflict, please:

- Click Help or
- Select the third option ◉ **Continue** and click OK. Then analyze why there is a conflict: Select the task to analyze. Click the top part of 

on the **Task** ribbon to get an explanation of what factors drive it out to the date it is scheduled on, or
- Use the checklist with schedule troubleshooting questions in the Summary chapter (see page 701).

Disadvantages of Constraints

In schedules with **Auto Scheduled** tasks, we think that you should minimize the use of constraints. Here are the reasons:

- Constraints are maintenance hungry
  Constraints override the dependencies. If you have many unnecessary constraints in your schedule, you will find yourself constantly revising those constraint dates. Constraints can cause schedule conflicts, which make dialogs pop up. If you do not solve the conflicts right away, MS Project will keep nagging you with messages until you do. Constraints require immediate attention when you may not have time to deal with them. If a task does not have any constraints, its dependencies push it into place in the timescale.
- Constraints make forecasts invalid if you have scheduling conflicts
  Constraints are stronger than dependencies and may bend dependencies out of whack in case of a schedule conflict that you did not resolve. When that happens, the forecasts further downstream in the schedule will no longer be valid. Dependencies protect the validity of the forecasts, but constraints can override them and can make the forecasts look rosy.
- Constraints can fragment the *Critical Path* or *Resource-Critical Path*
  If you end up with a fragmented or incomplete Critical Path, it is hard to effectively manage your project. For more on repairing incomplete Critical Paths see page 425; for more on Resource-Critical Paths see page 499.
- Constraints make it difficult to develop what-if scenarios
  Schedules with unnecessary constraints are hard to change, and it is difficult to develop what-if scenarios with them.

We recommend, therefore, that you enter only the constraints that are absolutely necessary. This is when the constraint actually increases the validity of the forecasts in your schedule instead of just increasing the rigidity of the schedule. If you know that an event like *opening of the new location* has to happen on November 23rd come hell or high water, it is a good idea to set a **Must Start On** constraint on that event; it makes the schedule more valid.

We recommend that you explain in the **Notes** field why you set each constraint. You click [Notes] on the **Task** ribbon and document your reason. This will cause you to use constraints thoughtfully, as we suggest. Use constraints with restraint!

You can enter many deadlines in your schedule without disadvantages. Deadlines do not have any of the listed disadvantages of constraints, whereas they will tell you if you miss a promised date.

6

In Which Situations Do You Need Constraints?

Constraints should not be used for:

- Modeling *temporary availability* of resources.
  A better place to capture temporary availability is through resource *availability profiles*. We will discuss them on page 321.
- Modeling *windows of opportunity* for certain tasks
  For example, to force an *office move* task to the weekend. Instead of constraints, we recommend using a *Task Calendar*, which we will discuss on page 273. Task calendars create a more *dynamic model* than constraints, because you can mark every weekend as a target for the move task, whereas with constraints you would be restricted to one particular weekend. If one weekend cannot be met the Task Calendar will force it to the next weekend and will update all dependent forecasts. Task calendars keep the schedule more dynamic.

In schedules with only **Manually Scheduled** tasks, each task is constrained and does not flow with the network logic. You cannot create constraints on Manually Scheduled Tasks, and you will not need them either. For **Auto Scheduled** tasks, we do recommend *constraints* for the following situations:

- *External dependencies*
  On page 234, we recommended that an external dependency be entered as an extra milestone and that the milestone be held in place by a Start No Earlier Than (SNET) constraint.
- *Group activities*
  Meetings, presentations, training or, in general, tasks that involve a group of people may require constraints. In order to get a group together, you have to set a date;

otherwise the event will not happen. When the date is agreed upon, you should set a constraint on that date so MS Project does not move it off its date. For group activities, you will often use Must Start On or Must Finish On constraints.

- *Weather restrictions*
  For example, if you have to get road construction done before the rainy or winter season starts, constraints can help. They can also help for outdoor construction activities that can start only after the winter is over. However, MS Project has another feature, called *Task Calendars*, with which you could create windows of opportunity across multiple years (see page 273).
- *Public events*
  Examples of public events are seminars, conferences, performances and other events to which the public is invited. They can be one or more days in duration. Their dates are fixed and do not change under normal circumstances.
- Certain milestones (see next section).

Types of Milestones

Use milestones in a schedule to indicate events like decisions, approvals, sign-offs, target dates and ceremonies. The type of constraint needed will depend on the "*hardness*" of the milestone date. The hardness of a milestone date is the resistance you will experience in practice when you try to reschedule it. For *soft dates*, use the *deadline* feature instead of constraints. For *hard dates*, use the *constraint dates* feature. The harder the date, the harder the constraint should be. The hardest date constraints are *Must Start On* (*MSO*) and *Must Finish On* (*MFO*).

The different types of milestones used in schedules are (listed from soft to hard):

- *Decision points* or *gates*
  These are important events on which decisions about the remainder of the project are made. The decision can be:
  - Go/No-go: a no-go decision will end the project. A go decision will authorize spending for the next phase.
  - Go-left/Go-right: the how-to or direction is determined for the rest of the project. You will often find this type of milestone in R&D projects where the research findings determine the direction (what activities will be done) for the rest of the project.

If there is a target date for the decision point, we recommend using the deadline feature to capture this target date; we discussed the deadline feature on page 256. The decision makers will typically postpone their decision until the required information is available. That is why these dates are often *soft* dates.

- *Target dates*
  These are soft deadlines that are inserted to break up a long series of tasks. They focus the efforts on finishing a component of a deliverable. The project manager agrees with the team what dates to target. The project manager then inserts these target dates in the schedule. Teams need target dates on all the components of their deliverable in order to meet the deadline of the overall deliverable. It is like driving from Ontario in Canada to Florida in the USA, which takes 2 to 3 days, and checking to see if you are still on schedule at the end of every day. Target dates are interim evaluation points that keep everyone focused and on track. For target dates we recommend the use of deadline dates and not constraint dates.
- *Do-or-die dates*
  These are *hard* dates, often contractual dates by which you are committed to hand over a deliverable. There may even be a penalty clause in the contract if the date is not met. These dates should be clear in the schedule at all times. We recommend that you enter these into the schedule as deadlines as much as possible in order to keep the schedule dynamic; you will get accurate feedback on all deadlines. However, if you have just one very hard contractual date (with a huge penalty associated), you could consider a Finish No Later Than (FNLT) constraint, because you will want to be notified immediately with a message when that date is not met.
- *Deliveries*
  We recommend you enter the delivery dates of raw materials, supplies or vendor deliverables as separate milestones in the *Work Breakdown Structure*. We discussed these *external dependencies* on page 234. You can enter the delivery date you agreed upon with the vendor or supplier as an event milestone with a Start No Earlier Than (SNET) constraint; this allows tracking of late delivery.
- *Ceremonies*
  Ceremonies are short official events to which many people are invited. If the duration of the ceremony is negligible, it can be entered as a milestone with zero duration. An example might be the official ribbon cutting to open a new plant. The date of a ceremony is often hard, because ceremonies are public events. The schedule needs a Must Start On (MSO) constraint for these events. If the ceremony has a duration, it is no longer a milestone, but a task and will also need a constraint.
- *Project end date*
  This is the delivery date for the project product. Meeting the promised project end date is always a challenge in project management. All the chains of dependencies come together in the project end milestone. A Must Finish On (MFO) or a Finish No Later Than (FNLT) constraint is often set on the project end milestone. You will immediately see a schedule conflict dialog pop up when this date is in jeopardy. In many projects, a deadline date could do the trick as well. You will then only see the red exclamation icon ◆ appear in the indicators ❶ column if the deadline is missed.

The **Deadlines** feature reminds you of a date promised without constraining the schedule. It is a feature we strongly recommend in most examples above rather than constraint dates. The more constraints you have, the more time you will spend on maintaining your schedule. And you will have to do this during project execution, when you do not have much time. The fewer constraints you have, the more dynamic your schedule will be. Here is a way to remember it: *Show restraint with constraints!*

Entering Constraints

If you have to be done before November 1, you have to enter October 31 as the constraint date in MS Project. By default the constraint time will be at the end of the day on the date you enter. If you enter November 1 as the date, the task will be done by 5:00 PM on November 1. You could enter a time with the date if you have a specific time during the day as the cut off time.

You cannot set constraints on **Manually Scheduled** tasks. On **Auto Scheduled** tasks, you can set constraint dates in a variety of ways:

- Dragging task bars:
  This method will allow you to set only *Start No Earlier Than* (SNET) constraints under forward scheduling or only *Finish No Later Than* (FNLT) constraints under backward scheduling.
- Entering dates:
  Under forward scheduling you can enter a start date that will set an SNET constraint, or you can enter a finish date that will set a *Finish No Earlier Than* (FNET) constraint. Under backward scheduling, entering a start date will create a *Start No Later Than* (SNLT) constraint; a finish date creates an FNLT constraint. This is probably too much to remember.
-  Using the new move feature in Project 2010: ribbon **Task**, section **Tasks**, button **Move**.
- Using the task fields *Constraint Type* and *Constraint Date*:
  This is where you can select the type of constraint from a list and the date from a pull-down calendar.
- Using the **Advanced** tab on the **Task Information** dialog (ribbon **Task**, section **Properties**, button **Information**).

As is often the case in MS Project, you can enter constraints in several different ways. The first two ways are easy and quick, but do require you to know and predict which constraints MS Project will set. Therefore, we recommend using the last two ways, but will discuss all in more detail so you become aware of how you could inadvertently end up with many constraints and a rigid schedule.

Setting Constraints by Dragging Task Bars Horizontally

Point to the middle of the task bar; make sure you see a four-headed arrow: ✥.

1. Click and hold down to drag the bar to the right *horizontally* to where you want it scheduled. Make sure you see a horizontal two-headed arrow as a mouse pointer at this point: . If you dragged *vertically*, you will see the mouse pointer instead – you are creating dependencies instead of constraints!
2. Look at the popup window to see what the new dates will be:

Start:	Wed 8/5/09
Finish:	Fri 8/14/09

3. Release the mouse when the task bar is scheduled on the date you want. The Planning Wizard dialog may appear and prompt you:
   - ◇ if you want to set a constraint and remove or keep the link when you moved the bar away from its predecessor, or
   - ◇ if you want to create a link instead of a constraint when you moved the bar just behind another bar.

   Answer the prompt of the Planning Wizard and click OK.
4. The bar you dragged has a **Start No Earlier Than** constraint on it to keep it in its new place. (Under backward scheduling it will be a **Finish No Later Than** constraint.)

6

Setting Constraints by Entering Dates

In the field **Start** you can pick a date from the drop-down calendar. By default, this creates a *Start No Earlier Than* (*SNET*) constraint on the task under *forward scheduling*, and it creates a *Start No Later Than* (*SNLT*) constraint under *backward scheduling.*

In the field **Finish**, you can pick a date from the drop-down calendar. By default, this creates a *Finish No Earlier Than* (*FNET*) constraint on the task under *forward scheduling*, but it creates a *Finish No Later Than* (*FNLT*) constraint under *backward scheduling*.

Many people use the **Start** and **Finish** fields to schedule all their tasks. Most do not intend to create constraints, but are unaware that MS Project does so. Their schedules become rigid and require a lot of work to maintain. If you use dependencies instead of constraints, your schedules need much less maintenance. We do not recommend using the **Start** and **Finish** fields at all for data entry. We would even go as far as recommending that you eliminate those fields from the entry table. You can do this by clicking on their column heading and pressing [Delete].

Setting Constraints with the Task Move Feature

This feature is new in Project 2010. It is useful for updating schedules during project execution, but less so during the planning phase, as it creates constraints on **Auto Scheduled** tasks.

1. Select the task to reschedule forward or back
2. Click ribbon **Task** and find its section **Tasks**. (Make sure you are not on the **Project** ribbon since it has a **Move Project** feature.)
3. Click [Move] – a drop-down menu appears with several choices.
4. Click the choice you want.

Notice that often a Start-No-Earlier-Than constraint is set on Auto Scheduled tasks under forward scheduling; you will see an icon in the indicators column.

Setting Constraints Using the Constraint Fields

We recommend this method to set constraints.

1. Insert the field *Constraint Type* by right-clicking on the column heading before which you wish to insert it – a popup menu appears.
2. Click **Insert Column** – a new column is inserted with **[Type Column]** as it heading and a long list of fields.
3. Start typing the name of the field you need, *Constraint Type,* and the list will shorten to display only some items.
4. Click **Constraint Type** – the column will now be inserted.
5. Repeat these steps to insert the field **Constraint Date** as well.
6. You can now enter any type of constraint in the Gantt spreadsheet by selecting the type from the list in the field **Constraint type** and picking the date from the drop-down calendar in **Constraint date**. Note that these fields are disabled for **Manually Scheduled** tasks.

Setting Constraints Using the Task Information Dialog

We recommend this method to set constraints.

1. Double-click on the task in the spreadsheet pane
   OR

   Select the task. Click  on the **Task** ribbon in the **Properties** section.

   OR

   Select the task, hold down Shift and press F2.

2. The **Task Information** dialog appears. Click the **Advanced** tab; the dialog should now look like:

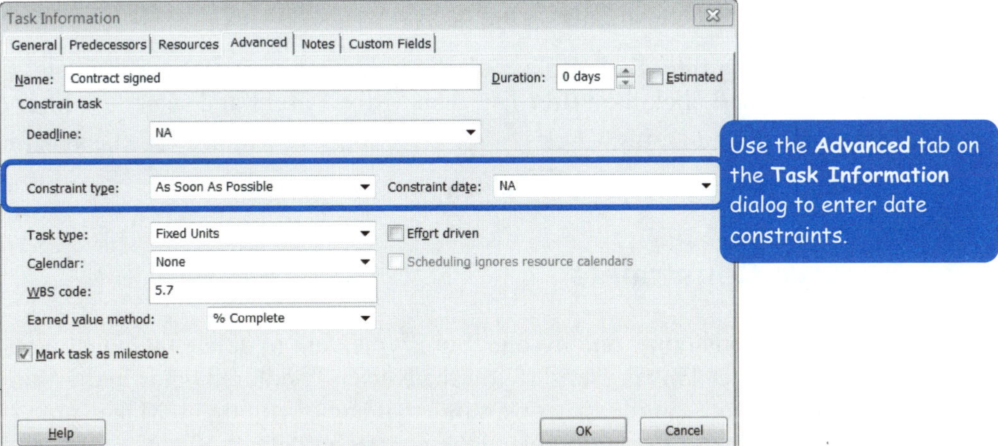

3. Select the type from the **Constraint type** pull-down list and select a date from the **Constraint date** drop-down calendar. Note that these fields are disabled for **Manually Scheduled** tasks and disallow data entry.

4. Click OK – the constraint is now entered into the schedule.

To Check All the Scheduling Constraints

1. In the Gantt Chart click ribbon **View** and find its section **Data.**

2. Click  and select from the drop-down menu **More Tables.**

3. The **More Tables** dialog appears:

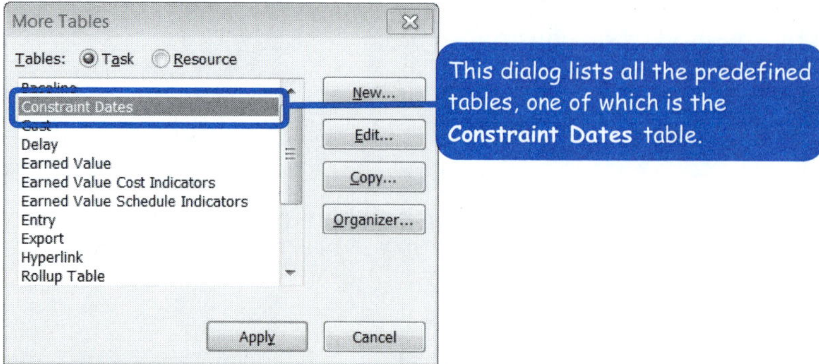

4. Select the **Constraint Dates** table in the list.
5. Click Apply. You can now see the fields **Constraint Type** and **Constraint Dates** to check all constraints on the tasks.
6. You can apply a filter that displays all the tasks that have a constraint date. Click the **View** ribbon and click the **Filter** list, then **More Filters** and select the filter called **Tasks with Fixed Dates**. Click Apply and you will only see tasks with a constraint. When done, press F3 to remove the filtering.

To Remove Constraints

You can remove constraints one-by-one, but if you want to delete them fast, you can use the fill-down feature. This is useful if you inadvertently entered dates in the **Start** and **Finish** fields without wanting the constraints that came with them. Make sure you first create the dependencies that will replace the constraint dates!

1. To remove all constraints, click on a column heading in the Gantt chart
   OR

   To remove constraints on certain tasks, select the first one and hold down Control while clicking on the rest of them.
2. Click Information on the **Task** ribbon – the **Multiple Task Information** dialog appears.

3. Click tab **Advanced** and in the list **Constraint type,** select the right constraint type:
   As Soon As Possible under forward scheduling or
   As Late As Possible under backward scheduling.
4. Click OK.

Make sure you do not remove real *constraint dates* that are necessary to keep your project schedule *valid*. Constraints you may need to keep are constraints on group activities, public events, ceremonies and external deliveries that are Auto Scheduled, see page 265.

Limitations of Constraints

- You can only set *FNLT* and *SNET* constraints on summary tasks.
  MS Project does not allow other types of constraints on summary tasks, because summary tasks would not be summarizing their detail tasks any longer. Personally, I use constraints sparingly and I have not missed the other types for summary tasks.
- You can set a *maximum of one constraint* per task. Sometimes it would be nice to set two constraints on a task when the task has to be done in a *window of opportunity*. For example, you can only do a test when a specialized lab is available. You cannot model this availability window with constraints, because you can only set one constraint on a task. Instead, we recommend you use the feature of *Task Calendar* that allows you to create a calendar for the task that reflects all the windows of opportunity. Task calendars essentially allow you to set multiple constraints per task.

Task Calendars

MS Project allows you to schedule tasks using *Task Calendars*. You can apply a task calendar to the task using the field *Task Calendar*. Examples of situations in which you may need task calendars are:

- You want to make sure that the backing-up of a computer system happens during the night.
- You want to make sure that office demolition activities take place in evening hours or during the weekend and not during business hours!
- You want to make sure that an office move takes place in evening hours or during a weekend. During weekdays employees would not be able to work when their things are packed up for the move.
- You want to adhere to regular meeting dates. For example, if the steering committee meets every first Monday of the month, you can make sure that the task *present at the steering committee meeting* will be scheduled only on the first Monday of any month.

- In a multi-year construction project, you want to create a winter weather task calendar to schedule all outdoor construction activities affected by winter weather.
- In R&D projects, you can schedule testing in an expensive lab with a task calendar when you are only given certain *windows of opportunity* to use the lab. You assign the task calendar to the test activity.

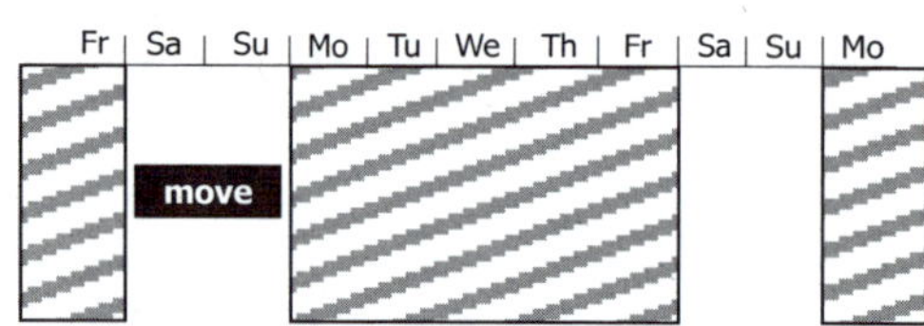

Task calendars are particularly useful when you have regular intervals when tasks can take place. Task calendars create a list of opportunities for MS Project to schedule the task, the windows of opportunity. If you do not have hard dates, but regular intervals, task calendars should be used. For example, if you use a task calendar on a *move* task, and you make sure that only the weekends are workdays on this calendar, MS Project will schedule the move in the earliest weekend possible, and when a slip occurs, the network of dependencies may push the move to the next weekend (see the illustration). The model predicts the best weekend to schedule the move; somewhere along the line you will lock-in the date with a constraint date.

Task calendars are good for tasks with or without resources assigned. If resources are assigned, the resource calendars and the task calendar may fight with each other, and if there are conflicts between these calendars, the following message will appear:

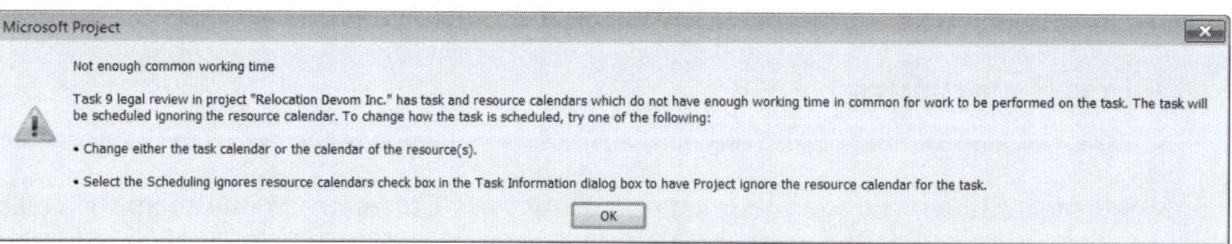

Also, the indicators column will display the icon when there is an unresolved conflict between calendars. You cannot leave these conflicts unresolved.

When calendars fight with one another and do not have any hours in common, the order of precedence between the calendars is from high to low:

1. *Task calendar*
2. *Resource calendar*
3. *Project calendar*

In other words, task calendars override resource calendars, which override the project calendar. There is a task field **Ignore resource calendar**; if you set this to **Yes**, you will make the calendar conflict icon disappear.

If the Task Calendar and Resource Calendar do have hours in common, MS Project will only schedule work during those hours. For example, if the resource calendar has seven mornings per week as work time and the task calendar has weekend days only as workdays, MS Project will only schedule work on Saturday and Sunday mornings. If you then turn **Ignore resource calendar** to **Yes**, MS Project will only schedule according to the Task Calendar and schedule work on Saturday and Sunday mornings and afternoons. The result may be that task durations become very long.

Unlike resource calendars, task calendars are not changed when you make further changes to the *project calendar*. The project calendar keeps updating the resource calendars, but not the task calendars!

6

Applying a task calendar to each individual task, as some people do, is not recommended; it would guarantee hardship when troubleshooting and changing the schedule. Task calendars generally make the schedule more rigid and they can fragment the Critical Path (see page 425).

Creating a New Task Calendar in MS Project Standalone

When you work with Project Professional in a Project Server environment, all calendars are typically created and owned by the Project Server administrator. As a project manager, you typically do not have the rights to create new calendars in Project Server. However, it is reasonable to request the administrator to create task calendars like: weekend only, evenings and weekends, and 24*7. You may need these to force the scheduling of certain tasks; for example, with a weekend-only task calendar you can force a *Move* task to a weekend, as moves typically happen on weekends.

Since project managers in a Project Server environment do not have the privilege to execute the following steps, these steps are only meant for people who use MS Project as a standalone tool:

1. Click ribbon **Project** and click 
.

2. The **Change Working Time** dialog appears:

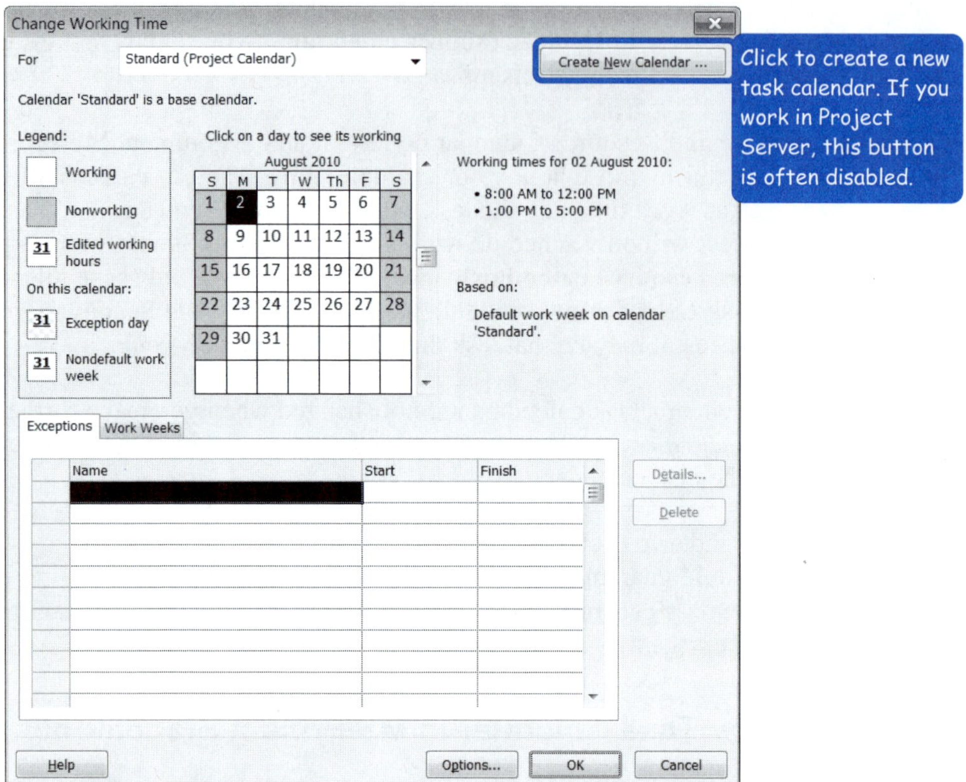

3. Click Create New Calendar ... – the **Create New Base Calendar** dialog appears:

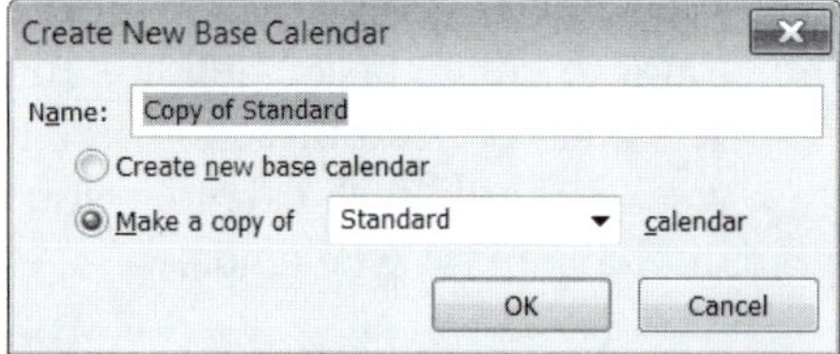

4. Enter a descriptive name for the task calendar and select either:
   ◉ **Create new base calendar,** or
   ◉ **Make a copy of** a calendar that is close to what you need.

5. Click OK – you have now created a new task calendar and you are back in the **Change Working Time** dialog where the new calendar is active.

6. Enter the working days, working times or holidays on the new task calendar and click OK when done.

Using a Task Calendar

Double-click on a task; the **Task Information** dialog appears. Click the **Advanced** tab, and select the task calendar in the **Calendar** list. You can also select the option ☑ **Scheduling ignores resource calendars** if that is your decision in case of conflicts.

OR

1. Right-click on the column heading before which you wish to insert the column **Task Calendar** – a popup menu appears.
2. Click **Insert Column** – a new column is inserted with **[Type Column]** as it heading and a long list of fields.
3. Start typing the name of the field you need, *Task Calendar,* and the list will shorten to display only some items.
4. Click **Task Calendar** – the column will now be inserted.
5. Click in the **Task Calendar** field of a task and select a task calendar from the list provided.
6. The task will now display a task calendar icon in the indicators column.

6

Deleting a Task Calendar

1. You need to go to the *organizer* – click ribbon **File**, tab **Info** and then button **Organizer**.
2. On the **Calendars** tab look in the list on the right (listing the objects in your schedule) for the calendar you need to delete.
3. Select it and then click Delete... in the middle of the dialog box.

Formatting the Gantt Chart View and Printing

For those who are ready to present their Gantt Chart at this point, we will discuss preparing the Gantt Chart view for printing here. MS Project operates on the principle of what-you-see-is-what-you-get (*WYSIWYG*); therefore, if you adjust the screen you will see it on paper. Notice that this section is specific to the Gantt Chart view; for other views there are different format options. The options you select will be stored in the Gantt Chart view.

To Adjust the Text Styles

Text styles can be applied to certain task types. The dialog is similar to the **Format, Font** dialog except that the font dialog is used for formatting only those tasks that are selected, whereas the **Text Styles** dialog allows you to format types of tasks.

1. In the Gantt Chart, click ribbon **Format**, 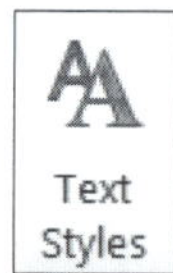 – the **Text Styles** dialog appears:

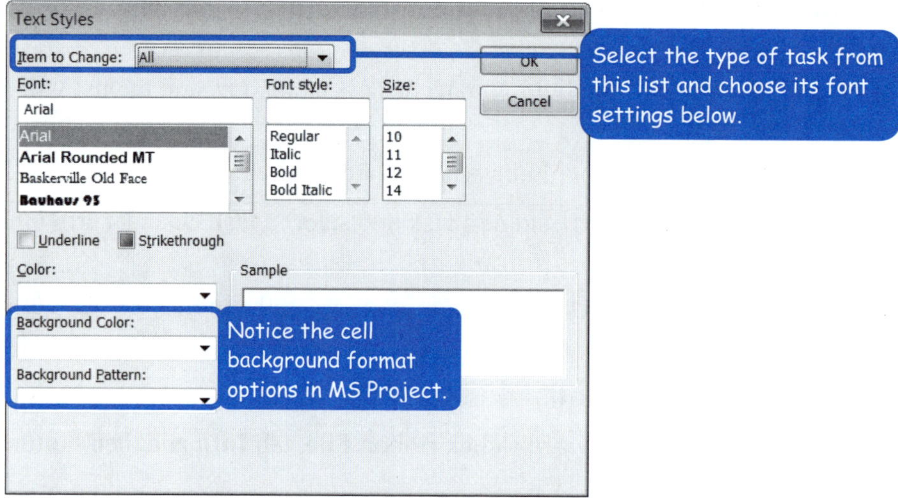

2. From the list **Item to Change** at the top, select the type of task to change. Then select the format using **Font, Font style, Size** and **Color**. MS Project provides cell format options: **Background Color** and **Background Pattern**. Notice that there is also an item in the list called **Changed Cells** that allows you to adjust the coloring for the change highlighting feature.
3. Click OK.

If you select the item **All**, all the text will be affected, even the text styles you set previously.

In Project 2010, we have access to the full color palette instead of a limited list.

You can color the text (or the background color) of the critical task names red to make them look uniform, whether you look in the spreadsheet or in the timescale.

To Adjust the Column Width

The text in the **Task Name** column will wrap or unwrap automatically in Project 2010 when the column width is changed.

Point to the divider in the column heading; make sure you see a double-headed mouse pointer as shown in the next screenshot; then drag to adjust or double-click to best fit the width:

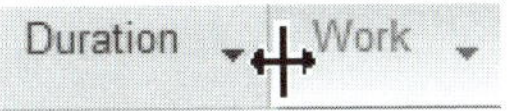

OR

Right-click on the column heading and click **Field Settings**; the dialog shows up. Click Best Fit – the width of the column is now wide enough to accommodate the widest entry in the field for all tasks in the project, even the ones not currently visible on the screen.

6

The text in the column headings will wrap automatically if the option ☑ **Header Text Wrapping** is left checked in the **Field Settings** dialog.

To Position the Pane Divider on a Column Split

You can put the vertical divider between the spreadsheet and the Gantt Chart exactly on the border of a column.

1. With the mouse pointer, point anywhere on the vertical divider that separates the spreadsheet from the timescale; you should now see the mouse pointer ◂||▸.
2. Drag it close to the column split where you want it; release the mouse.
3. While you continue to see the mouse pointer ◂||▸ double-click; the divider now jumps to the column split that is closest to it.

To View all Task Bars in the Timescale

MS Project can zoom the project such that you always see task bars in the timescale:

In the Gantt Chart, click ribbon **View,** Entire Project (or Entire Project on low-resolution screens)

To View Selected Tasks in the Timescale

If you want to see just a subset of tasks and see their task bars zoomed into in the timescale:

1. Select the tasks
2. On the **View** ribbon, click Selected Tasks (or Selected Tasks on low-resolution screens)

This is a great way to explore a schedule.

To Get the Timescale You Want

Use the Timescale: Weeks list on the **View** ribbon to zoom the bottom tier of the timescale to a particular time unit.
OR
If you want to customize the middle tier (or other tiers) of the timescale also to your exact preference:

1. Double-click on the timescale itself: July 7/3 7/10 7/17 7/24.

   OR

   Click ribbon **View** and click the list button of Timescale: Weeks and click on **Timescale** at the bottom of the list.

2. The **Timescale** dialog appears:

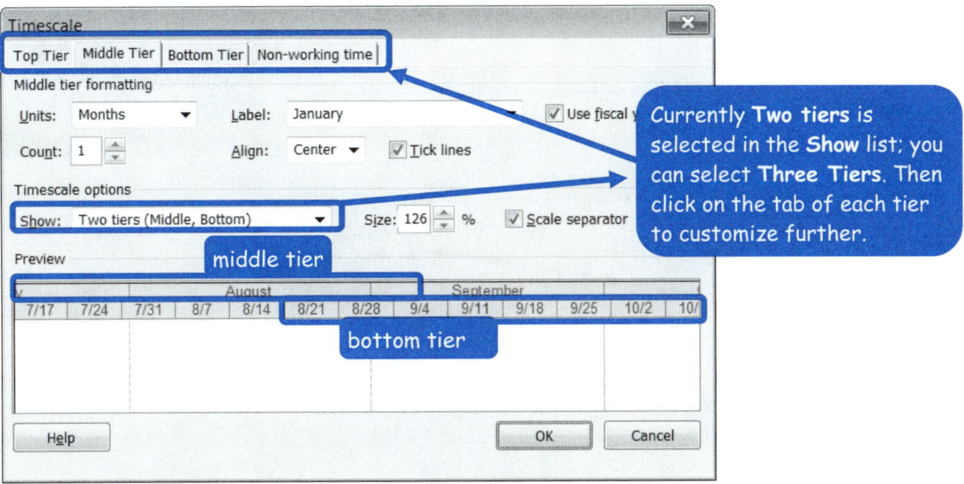

3. If you want to display the third tier as well, you need to first select **Three tiers (Top, Middle, Bottom)** in the **Show** list.

4. Click one of the tabs **Top Tier** (top of the timescale), **Middle Tier** (middle) or **Bottom Tier** (bottom) and select the settings you want. The **Count** is like an increment or skip factor. If it is set to "2" in a day-by-day timescale, the timescale will display day 1, 3, 5 and so forth; only every other day will be displayed.

5. Click OK.

6

Having three tiers in the timescale allows you to show the *fiscal year* and *calendar year* timescales next to each other so that there can be no misunderstanding about the exact dates. You need to select ☑ **Use fiscal year** for one of the tiers. You can set the start month of the fiscal year in ribbon **File**, Options, tab **Schedule**, section **Calendar options for this project** under **Fiscal year starts in**. You can toggle the starting year with the option below it.

To Format the Task Bars

1. Double-click anywhere in the background white of the timescale pane.
   OR

   Click ribbon **Format**, then  and select **Bar Styles**

2. The **Bar Styles** dialog appears:

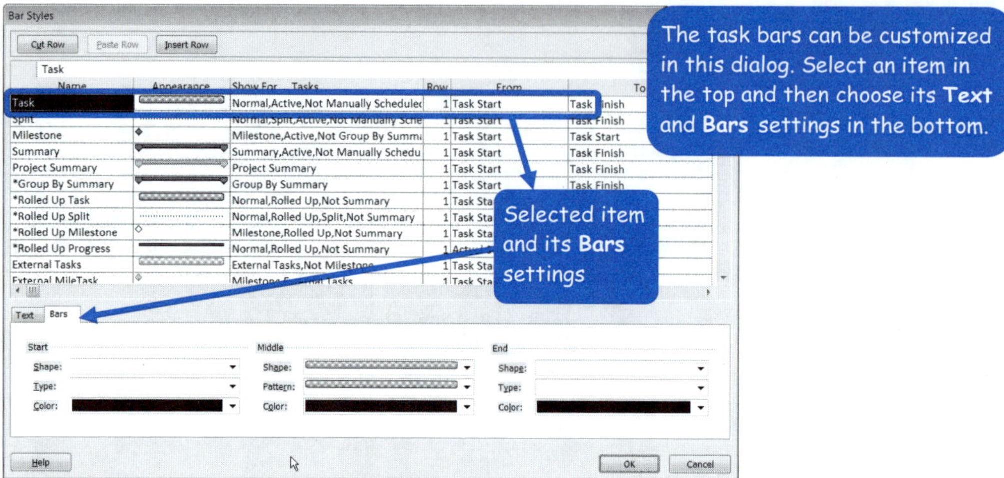

3. In the grid in the top half, select the type of task for which you want to change the appearance.

4. Choose your settings for the selected task type on the **Text** and **Bars** tabs at the bottom of the dialog. Click OK.

Some remarks about this powerful, but not so intuitive, dialog box:

- In the Gantt Chart, MS Project first creates, the task bar listed at the top in the dialog, and then draws the second task bar. If they overlap, only the second bar can be seen fully. Therefore, the order in which the items are listed is important. Lower ones can cover and even hide higher ones in the list.
- Under **Show For … Tasks**

  - You will have to key in multiple items separated by a comma; the list only allows you to pick one item, which is not enough in most cases if you have many new task types: **Active** (task that affects the schedule and is aggregated in the totals), **Manually Scheduled** (not Auto Scheduled), **Placeholder** (task without a duration, start or finish), **Warning** (manually scheduled task with a schedule conflict), **Deliverable** (hand-off posted on a SharePoint site). You can use the list to find the exact word you need to type.
  - The word **Normal** is used for a rest category, the default type of task. It means a task that is not any of the other task types shown in the drop-down list.
  - You can also type in the word **Not** in front of each item to create an exception for that type of task. "**Not Summary**" means format the task bars as specified for any task type except for summary tasks.
  - You can specify multiple criteria separated by a comma. The comma functions as a *logical and* — in other words when it says **Normal, Critical**, it means that

it will apply this bar style only to normal tasks that are critical as well. Any other tasks are not affected.

- The lists you can display in the fields **From** and **To** have all the regular task fields in them, but also some additional ones specifically for the timescale, like the **CompleteThrough** date and **Negative Slack**. Neither one is a regular task field which you can display in the spreadsheet. The **CompleteThrough** is used in the Tracking Gantt to display progress bars. For an explanation of **Negative Slack** (see page 423).
- On the **Text** tab (in the bottom half of the dialog) you can add text to the left of, right of, or even inside the task bars. You will find the following default settings in the Gantt Chart:
  - **Resource Names** are put to the right of the detail task bars.
  - The **Start** dates are shown to the right of the milestone diamonds.

To Adjust the Page Setup for Printing

Notice that the page setup settings are view specific. For each view listed on the **View** ribbon, you can select different settings that are stored in the view object itself.

To Fit to One Page

1. Click ribbon **File**, tab **Print** – the print backstage screen appears.
2. Click hyperlink **Page Setup** (below all options, left of preview pane) – the **Page Setup** dialog appears:

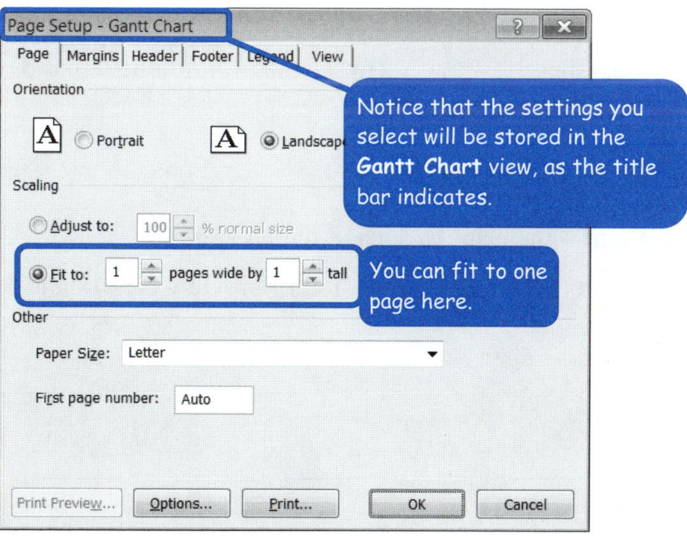

3. Select ◉ **Fit to 1 pages wide by 1 tall**. Click [OK] and the resulting print preview is shown in the backstage screen.

Setting the Margins

1. Click ribbon **File**, tab **Print** – the print backstage screen appears.
2. Click hyperlink **Page Setup** (below all options, left of preview pane) – the **Page Setup** dialog appears.
3. Click the tab **Margins** – the dialog should now look like:

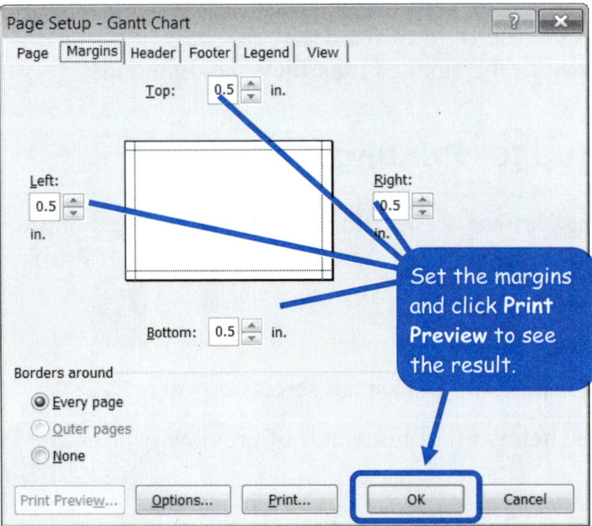

4. Set the margins you need. Click [OK] to see the print preview in the backstage screen.

Creating a Header, Footer or Legend

1. Click ribbon **File**, tab **Print** – the print backstage screen appears.
2. Click hyperlink **Page Setup** (below all options, left of preview pane) – the **Page Setup** dialog appears.

3. Click tab **Header, Footer** or **Legend**:

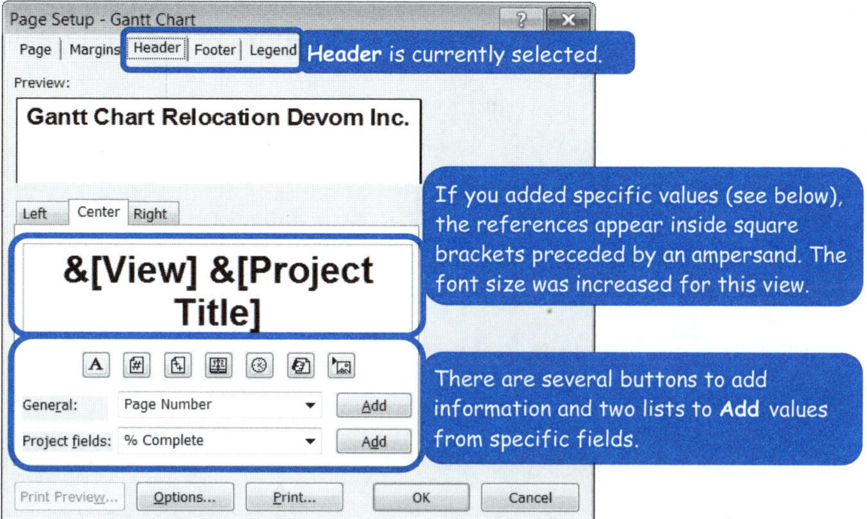

4. Click tab **Left**, **Center** or **Right** and position the cursor in the text box where you want to add a reference to project data. You can press Enter ↵ to create extra lines.

5. Click one of the buttons to add information quickly:

Button	For
A	Font, size and style: In order to format the text in the header, select the text (or references) first, then click this button.
#	Page number
	Total number of pages
	Date: the system date
	Time: the system time
	The schedule name (this comes from the ribbon **File**, tab **Info**, list **Project Information**, item **Advanced Properties**, and field **Title**)
	Takes you into a dialog for inserting a picture into the header, footer or legend; often used to insert the *project logo* or *company logo*.

6. Select a reference from the **General** list at the bottom and click [Add]. The reference is inserted at your cursor position. Add as many text references as needed; most people refer to data entered in the ribbon **File, Info, Project Information** (on the right of the screen), **Advanced Properties**. All references start with an ampersand (&). You can also key in literal text between the references, like: *Page &[Page] of &[Pages]*, which will print as *Page 1 of 9*.
7. Select a reference from the list **Project fields** at the bottom and click [Add] to add project-level information, like the **Baseline Finish** and forecast **Finish** date, or the **Baseline Cost** and forecast **Cost,** or calculated values, like the **% Complete** and **Remaining Duration** for the project.
8. Select a reference and format its font by clicking the [A] button. You often need to increase the font size of headers. Click [OK].
9. Click [OK] – and you will see the print preview in the backstage screen.

Checks on Deadlines, Constraints and Task Calendars

Next you will find some checks to verify if you have applied best practices in the use of deadlines, constraints and task calendars in your forecast model of the project. The numbering corresponds to the complete checklist in the summary chapter, see page 711. The filters mentioned in the checks can be found in the file *ProjectPro tools to check project schedules.MPP* available for download at www.ProjectProCorp.com (see page vi for the procedure to access these files).

6 Deadlines

6.1. Is the project deadline date captured in the schedule?
It can be set using the **Deadline** feature date or using the **Constraint** feature in MS Project. The deadline or constraint date needs to be set on the project finish milestone. Only use a constraint if the project target finish date is a very hard date, see page 266.

6.2. Are deadlines used to capture target dates on milestones that are promised to clients? Are deadlines used to capture agreed-upon dates?
If you promised a date to a client, we recommend you capture it in the schedule using the **Deadline** date feature. If you agree with your team on certain target dates, we recommend you capture these as deadlines as well. Interim deadline dates help you meet the project deadline, see page 256.
You can check this by applying the filter **6.2 All Milestones and Deadlines**.

6.3. When task calendars are used, are they used to create *windows of opportunity* to schedule certain tasks?
Task Calendars are useful when you want to create recurring periods when certain tasks can happen (see page 273). Examples are: evening tasks (office demolition), night tasks (back up computers), weekend tasks (move), seasonal tasks (road construction in Russia).

6.4. Does the schedule have as few *constraint dates* as possible?
Constraints should be used only when they increase the validity of the schedule apart from increasing the rigidity of the schedule, see page 263 for detailed discussion. Constraint dates are maintenance-hungry. Constraints can fragment the *Critical Path.* Constraints are stronger than dependencies and will bend dependencies out of whack, thus jeopardizing the forecasts downstream. However, constraints are useful when they improve the schedule's ability to forecast. When you enter a constraint, we recommend explaining why you use it in the task's **Notes** field. You can display all tasks that have constraints by applying the filter **6.4 Constraints other than ASAP**. The filter will not display recurring detail tasks; they should have constraints.
Exceptions to this rule are:

- ◇ *Recurring detail tasks*, like *status meeting 1, status meeting 2, etc.*
- ◇ External dependencies, such as *delivery of supplies* or *arrival of materials*.
- ◇ Group activities that have to take place on a hard, agreed-upon date, like *deliver presentation* and *conduct training*. These are activities for which a group of people needs to get together.
- ◇ Do-or-die-by dates: e.g., when you represent your company at a conference, you need to have the booth, marketing materials and demonstrations ready; the conference date will not move.
- ◇ Activities affected by (winter) weather conditions; i.e., in most of Canada asphalting streets can only start in April, because of the cold. Alternatively, you can use **Task Calendars** for these situations in MS Project (see page 273). Task Calendars are better for creating *windows of opportunity* in a multi-year planning.

6

Exercises

Review Questions

1. What is the difference between constraint dates and deadline dates in the way MS Project treats these dates?

2. What is the main output from a project model that is scheduled forward? And from a project model that is scheduled backward?

3. Which of the following constraints can cause a scheduling conflict? In the next table, add a check mark in the cells where scheduling conflicts could occur:

	In forward scheduled project	In backward scheduled project
ASAP		
ALAP		
FNET		
FNLT		
MFO		
MSO		
SNET		
SNLT		

4. Would you set a constraint in the following situations? If so, which type of constraint? In the next table, if you recommend using a constraint, indicate the type.

Situation	Type of constraint
You have a board meeting coming up on January 16 in which a go/no-go decision will be taken on the next stage of your project. The board expects certain reports to be ready.	
A vendor needs to deliver custom-made computers to you that you need for testing activities in your project (computers delivered).	
You have planned a "project closing" ceremony. You have invited senior executives and dignitaries for this special occasion.	
A testing lab is only available from March 1 to March 15.	

5. Why would you want to minimize the number of constraint dates in your project model? Name at least two reasons.

6. As a car manufacturer, you would like to use an outdoor test lab that consists of a 10 km stretch of highway on which different weather conditions can be simulated. The lab is fully booked except for two opportunities for your project from Nov. 10-17 this year or after Apr. 1st next year. How would you model this in MS Project?

7. Is there a way in which you can easily display the entire project duration in the timescale on your screen? If so, what are the steps in MS Project to accomplish this?

Relocation Project — Constraints and Deadlines

The goal of this exercise is to be able to enter deadlines and constraints in MS Project.

1. Continue to work with your file *Relocation.mpp* or open the file *06A Deadlines.mpp* available for download at www.ProjectProCorp.com (see page vi for the procedure to access these files).
2. Set deadlines on the following milestones by double-clicking on the task to display the **Task Information** dialog and clicking the tab **Advanced**. Note that these deadlines will be missed and that the warning icon ◆ appears in the ❶ column. When we optimize the schedule in chapter 9, the icons will go away again.

ID	Milestone	Deadline Date
10	location selected	August 20, 2012
16	contractor contracted	August 31, 2012
25	facility remodelled	October 26, 2012
31	new location opened	November 1, 2012

3. The CEO, *Mr. Salin,* is out of the country until *August 23*, 2012; we will need a *Start No Earlier Than* constraint on task *8 meet to select the location*.
The task *pack* should be scheduled *As Late As Possible*, otherwise the equipment may be packed days before the actual move takes place over the weekend. You want the employees to be packed as late as possible on the Friday before the weekend. Enter the following constraints by double-clicking on the task to display the **Task Information** dialog and clicking the tab **Advanced**:

ID	Task	Constraint
8	meet to select the location	Start No Earlier Than August 23, 2012
28	pack	As Late As Possible

4. Notice that the As Late As Possible constraint does not display an icon in the indicators ❶ column. Compare your file with the solution file *07A Resources.mpp* available for download at www.ProjectProCorp.com (see page vi for the procedure to access these files). See page 697 of this book for an automated way of comparing and reporting differences between two versions of one schedule.
5. Save your file for the next exercise.

Relocation Project — Printing the Gantt Chart

The goal of this exercise is to be able to print the Gantt Chart with a custom timescale, header, footer and legend.

With the tasks, estimates, dependencies, deadlines and constraints completed, we now have entered all the data needed to print a draft Gantt Chart. Note that some durations are still default durations of *1 day?*; they will be adjusted when assigning resources.

1. Continue to work with the file from the previous exercise.
2. Format the timescale of the Gantt Chart: Click ribbon **View** and click the list button of [Timescale: Weeks] and click on **Timescale** at the bottom of the list:

	Middle Tier	Bottom Tier
Units	Months	Days
Label	Jan '09	1, 2,...
Count	1	7
Align	Center	Center
Size	100 %	100 %

3. Format the header, footer and legend of the Gantt Chart. Click ribbon **File**, tab **Print** – the print backstage screen appears. Click hyperlink **Page Setup** (below all options, left of preview pane):

		Section	Set to	Font
Tab	**Header**	Center	&[View] &[Project Title]	Arial, Bold, 20
	Footer	Left	&[Manager] &[Company]	Arial, Regular, 8
		Right	&[Date]	Arial, Regular, 8
	Legend	Legend on	⦿ None	

4. Compare your file with (a printout of) the solution file *07A Resources.mpp* available for download at www.ProjectProCorp.com (see page vi for the procedure to access these files).
5. Save your file.

Chapter 7 Entering Resources

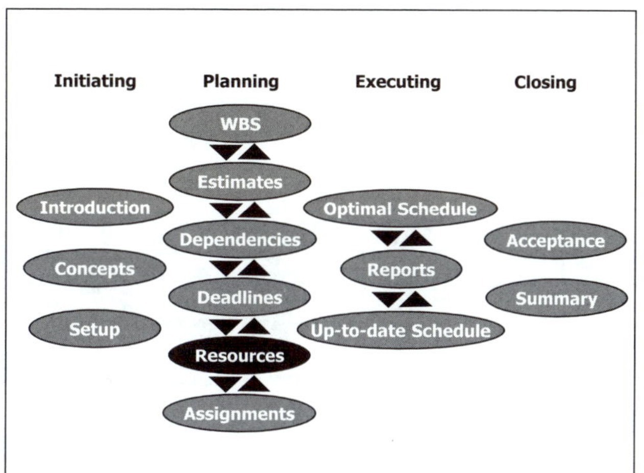

7

With the WBS, duration estimates, dependencies and deadlines entered, we now have a Gantt Chart that is a *forecast model* of the project. You can stop adding more detail to the schedule at this point if resources, their workloads and costs are of little concern to you. If they are important, you will have to add resources to the model and *assign* them to tasks. We will discuss defining the resources in this chapter (see black ellipse above), and assigning them in the next chapter.

After reading this chapter you will:

- know what resources are and when to add a resource to the project model
- know the different types of resources: human, facilities, machines and materials
- know the difference between actual and generic resources
- be aware of important resource-related fields and what they mean
- be able to efficiently enter resources into the schedule by using the enterprise resource pool, downloading resources from your address book, or keying them in
- know to use generic resources if you do not know who will be on your team
- know how to review or enter the different types of resource availability
- be able to review or create resource calendars
- know how to create a budget in MS Project
- know the cost management features of MS Project
- be able to check the list of resources against scheduling best practices
- know how to create a resource report

Is When-You-Are-In-Need a Blessing Indeed?

Nob is driving to work and realizes that he can't wait to get there because he finds his current project very interesting. His boss tells him that he is doing a great job and even captured that in writing in his last performance evaluation. His boss is now asking him if he can take on a second, similar project simultaneously. His boss really compels Nob by saying: "Nob, you are one of the very few who can do this!" Nob feels great that he is really needed at work and tends to say yes.

Several weeks later, he finds himself with the second project on his plate and now Nob needs to juggle his time trying to move two projects forward. Because each project really requires his full-time attention, Nob feels squashed by the weight of his workload. He finds that he can't do either job well enough which makes him feel bad.

One day, Nob shares this with Bob as they walk across the parking lot to their workplace. Bob listens carefully to Nob's lamenting and stops walking, turns to Nob and slowly says: "Nob, the cemetery is full of people who also thought they were indispensable!" That sealed the coffin on Nob's naïve belief that it is always great to be much needed.

What Is a Resource?

Resources are *people*, *facilities*, *machines*, *materials* or *money* necessary to create the project deliverables.

If you add resources and *assign* them to the tasks, you have created a *resource-loaded schedule*. Each activity typically needs one or more resources. If you find that an activity does not need resources, we recommend you remove the task and model the time lapse as a *lag* on a dependency instead. For example, the task *drying of paint* does not need resources and would perhaps be better modeled as a lag (see page 214 for the how-to steps). If you capture only discrete effort through tasks, each task bar actually represents effort by team members and would need a human resource assigned.

Resource or Responsible?

Apart from resources, there are also *responsible* people. A *resource* and a *responsible person* differ in that:

- The responsible person does not necessarily spend time and effort on project activities. People are only resources to a project if they spend effort on that project.
- Resources also include facility, machine and material resources that cannot have responsibility.
- Resources are normally assigned to activities on the lowest level in the *Work Breakdown Structure* (WBS), whereas responsibilities are normally assigned on a higher level, often the level of deliverables.

Project managers typically capture responsibilities for deliverables in a *Responsibility Assignment Matrix* [43] also called *RAM* or *Responsibility Chart*. MS Project does not have special features to create a chart like that, but responsibilities can be captured in other ways.

Each deliverable needs a responsible person or team. We recommended capturing deliverables as summary tasks, and if you *assign* a person to a summary task, the assignment will create effort (work) for the responsible person during the entire duration of the summary task, which you probably do not want.

---

[43] See the *PMBOK® Guide*, Fourth Edition, Project Management Institute.

If you want to indicate responsibilities in your schedule without adding effort, you can accomplish this in one of two ways; the first way is our recommended way:

- Assign responsibilities using an extra text field
  MS Project has enough extra, task-related text fields to capture responsibilities. For example, use the extra **Text1** field (right-click on a column heading and select **Insert Column**), and rename it *Responsible Person* (right-click on the column heading and click **Custom Fields** and click [Rename...]. If you click [Lookup...] you can even create a *pick list* for this field in a *lookup table*, see page 557 for more). You can also display the names of the responsible people next to the task bars in the timescale (ribbon **Format**, button **Format**, item **Bar Styles**, see page 281 for more. We recommend displaying the names to the left of the task bars, since MS Project displays the names of resources to the right by default). In this way, it is clear who is responsible and who is a resource. This method has the fewest complications and may therefore be the best method.
- Assign responsibilities by assigning to milestones
  We recommended you create one milestone for each deliverable in your WBS. You can assign the responsible people to the milestone of the deliverable. Since milestones have a duration of zero and therefore no effort, there is no disadvantage to capturing responsibilities by assigning resources to milestones. For how to assign resources (see page 361).

When to Add a Resource

You should only enter a resource in the model of the project if you expect that the resource may significantly affect the quality, duration or cost of the project. If the resource will not have an impact on quality, duration or cost, you can keep your model leaner by leaving the resource out.

A resource that is *easy to replace* will not likely affect the schedule. In fact, in construction, contractors rarely allow their schedule to be driven by a lack of resources. Generally, it is relatively easy to find bricklayers, carpenters and electricians. Resources that are scarce could increase the duration of the project. Resources will increase the duration of your project:

- If they are not available when you need them. For example, you need a sign-off and the busy executives are out of the country, which may affect the duration of your project. Materials that have to come from afar can also affect the schedule. Generally speaking, the more borders that need to be crossed, the more time risk there is.
- If you assign human resources to many tasks and the resources become overallocated, their workloads need to be leveled. *Experts* are an example of

resources that are often overallocated. Leveling their workload often leads to longer projects.

If you overallocate resources, they may affect the duration of the project. Sometimes you can solve overallocations within the project duration, and sometimes they will extend the project duration. If you find that limited resource availability affects the scheduled dates of tasks, you have a *resource-constrained schedule.*

Choosing the Options

Click ribbon **File**, Options and click on the tab indicated in the table below where you want to change settings:

Tab	Option
Advanced	Section **General Options for this Project**: **Default standard rate** By entering a rate you can reduce the amount of typing you have to do. If the standard rate is set to $50/hr, you do not need to enter a rate for any resource that is $50/hr.
	Default overtime rate By entering a rate you can reduce the amount of typing you have to do.
Schedule	Section **Schedule**: **Show assignment units as a: Percentage** or **Decimal** Units of resources can be expressed as a *percentage* or in *decimals* in the resource-related **Max Units** field (availability) and in the assignment-related **Units** field *(*workload). This option is a global option and applies to all your projects, existing or new. For example, you have a resource that is available half-time to your project. This option gives you the choice of entering this as *50%* (percentage) or as *0.5* (decimal) in the **Max Units** field. For part-time resources, **Percentages** seem to make the most sense. It is different for team resources. If you have 3 carpenters available to your project, you could enter them as one *team resource* called *carpenters* and enter *300%* (percentage) or *3* (decimal) in **Max Units**. For team resources the **Decimal** seems easier to understand. You can switch this option at any time; it is entirely your preference.

7

Types of Resources

MS Project has three types of resources: **Work, Material** and **Cost** resources. These are the three choices given in the resource field **Type**. In practice, you will come across five different kinds of resources: *human*, *facility*, *machine*, *material* and *monetary*.

Important questions for each of these kinds of resources are:

- Should the resource add to the total amount of effort in the project?
- Should the resource be included in workload leveling?
- Does the resource have a time-related or a unit-related cost?
- Should **Work, Material** or **Cost** be chosen in the resource-related field **Type?**

We will discuss these questions for all five kinds of resources and recommend a setting for the resource field **Type**:

- *Human resources* are people whose efforts should add up in the *Work* field. The total amount of work per week should be reasonable, which means it is within, or close, to their weekly availability. If there are overallocations, their workloads should be leveled. Human effort costs money, and human resources should be given a standard rate, an overtime rate and a cost-per-use rate, if applicable. They typically have a time-related cost. Human resources need to be entered as **Work** resources.
- *Facilities* are capital resources and should not add to the total amount of effort of the project (**Work**). We, therefore, have to make them **Material** resources. The cost of facilities is typically time-related, like monthly rent, for example. Material resources cannot have a time-related rate, unfortunately, but you could use a workaround, which we will discuss on page 338.

  If you enter facilities as material resources, MS Project cannot prevent double reservations by leveling "workload of the facilities"; you would not want two different meetings held in one room at the same time. You have to keep an eye on the reservation of the facility yourself. We recommend you create a reservation system for facilities using the appropriate features in *MS Outlook*.
- *Machines* are similar to facilities in terms of the points just made.
- *Material* resources are *consumable* resources. They should not add to the amount of effort (**Work**) of the project. Materials do not have a capacity like humans or facilities, and therefore do not need to be leveled. Materials can affect the schedule when they are low in supply or delayed in delivery. Materials do cost money and typically have a unit-related cost only. Materials should always be entered as a **Material** resource. The cost per unit should be entered in the **Std. Rate** column (**Standard Rate** field) without a time unit.

- *Monetary* resources are financial resources with which human, facility, machine, material resources and services can be bought and are therefore the most flexible resource. The new **Type** of resource called **Cost** is useful for modeling other expenses that happen in projects, like travel (airfares, cabs, car rental, hotel and food), licenses, bonuses and others. The best way to look upon a cost resource is as an expense category. Cost resources do not add to the **Work** (effort) of the project. Leveling is relevant for money resources to manage the cash flow.

As you can see, Project 2010 only has three types of resources that can be found in the field *Type*: *Work*, *Material* and *Cost* resources. However, we found five types of resources in practice that are fundamentally different from each other. As a result, we had to shoehorn facility and machine resources into the mold of **Material** resources; hopefully Microsoft will add these two as separate resource types in future releases.

What If You Do Not Know Who You Will Get?

During the *planning* of the project, you often do not know exactly who is going to do a given task. However, if you know you are going to need a programmer, you can enter this resource in the resource sheet under the generic name *programmer*. A *generic resource* is a resource with the field **Generic** set to **Yes** and with the icon in the indicators column. If you need more precision in your model, you could consider creating *junior* and *senior* generic resources, such as *junior programmer* and *senior programmer*. Generic resources are useful as placeholders on which to accumulate workloads and to indicate resource needs to resource managers. If all project managers use them in the Project Server environment, the resource managers will see the total resource needs across all projects, and they can then perform *resource capacity planning*.

7

In Project Professional with *Project Server*, actual and generic resources in the *enterprise resource pool* will be set up by the Project Server administrators. The administrators will have added the generic resources that you may need. If you cannot find the resource you need, you would ask your administrators to add the generic resource. You need the proper access right to edit the enterprise resource pool. If you are blessed with the rights to maintain the enterprise resource pool, you can open it in PWA by navigating to the *Resource Center*.

Not knowing the exact names of the individuals should not stop you from creating a *resource-loaded* schedule. You can always assign to tasks to generic resources. Once you know the names of the people whom you will have on your team, you can reassign the tasks from the *generic resources* to the real people. There are several easy ways to accomplish this; we will discuss these ways on page 389.

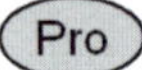

In Project Server, you can also:

- Create one generic resource for each role, skill or position you need on your projects in order to do long-term resource planning. As project managers assign generic resources to future tasks, Project Server will accumulate their workloads far into the future. In this way, you can find out what the future demand will be for each skill.
- Create *team resources*; they have the resource field **Team Assignment Pool** set to **Yes**. Project managers can assign the tasks to the team resource instead of to a generic resource or to an individual. Any individual member of the team resource can take on tasks assigned to the team (in *PWA* (not in MS Project!) ribbon **Timesheet**, button **Insert Row**, item **Insert Team Task**, see page 664 for more on the PWA interface for team members). After the project manager approves this self-assignment and publishes it, the team member can report time against it. This allows individuals to take on tasks that they really feel up to and ensures that they have enough work. The downside is that some individuals may be a bit too happy to let others take on many or difficult tasks.

Change the View to Enter Resources

1. Click ribbon **View**, Resource Sheet – the Resource Sheet view appears.
2. Check if the table **Entry** is active:
   - ◇ Click ribbon **View** and find its section **Data**.
   - ◇ Click  and click **Entry**.

Resource Fields in the Entry Table

You will find the following fields in the Resource Sheet. If the field is *required* (as opposed to *optional*), an entry is expected. If a field is *enumerated*, a pick list will be presented once you cursor into the field. The fields discussed below are in the order in which you will find them in the default resource **Entry** table:

Indicators

This indicators field will display for a variety of situations. If a resource is overallocated, this column will show an icon. Generic resources will have the icon. *Local resources* have the icon in Project Server. Local resources are resources that are private to the project; they are not in the Project Server resource pool.

Resource Name — required field
Note that the actual name of the field in the database is *Name*; *Resource Name* is just a custom title for the field. This is where you enter the name of the resource. We recommend using a standard naming convention to prevent duplicating resources inadvertently. The convention should allow you to sort the resource names. We recommend the convention *FirstName LastName* if you have fewer than 50 resources and *LastName - FirstName* if you have more than 50, because last names are more likely to be unique than first names. What you type in this field will show up in the lists used for assigning resources, like in the **Assign Resources** dialog. Only the names entered in this field will show in lists like that. It is therefore imperative that you:

- Make the resource names easy to recognize.
- Make each resource name unique in this field. If you have more than one *John Smith*, you can look at other fields in the Resource Sheet like **Group** to find out who is who, but in the Gantt Chart you cannot distinguish between one *John Smith* and the other. Therefore you have to make the names unique in the **Resource Name** column.

Type — required, enumerated field

The type of resource can be **Work** (default), **Material** or **Cost**. Work resources are human resources or people. Material resources are facilities, equipment or materials. Examples of material resources are *desktop computers*, *electric cable*, *meeting room* or *concrete*. The **Cost** resources are for capturing any other costs in your project, like hotel or car rental costs. For each type of resource certain fields will be editable, others not. For example, for **Cost** resources you cannot enter **Max Units**, any rates or **Base Calendar**.

7

Material Label — optional field, only for **Material** resources
The label you enter will show up in several other views and reports. For example, the label *desktop computers* will show on the y-axis in the Resource Graph view to indicate the number of units needed over time. In the timescale of the Gantt Chart, it will show up to the right of the task bars. The label is particularly important for bulk resources to indicate the unit of measurement. For example:

- Concrete is measured in *cubic feet (USA), cubic meters (Europe)*
- Cable in *yards* (USA) or *meters* (Europe)

When *500* units of the bulk resource *concrete* are assigned, the material label will show up in the Gantt timescale as *500 cubic feet*. The material label defines what one unit is for the bulk resource.

Initials — optional field
Initials may be of use for abbreviating resource names in reports; the full names would be too long in the timescale of the Gantt Chart when more than one resource is assigned.

Group — optional field
This field can be used for a variety of purposes, for example to capture the name of the department to which the resource belongs. If you enter department names as the group, you can filter all the tasks for a department. Better still, with the group feature, you can group resources together in their respective departments and see department totals for work and cost.

Max Units (*Maximum Units*) — required field, only for **Work** resources
This is the maximum availability of the resource to your project. A resource who is available full-time to your project needs 100% in the **Max Units** field, 50% for half-time availability. The percentage is taken from the working hours on the resource calendar. For a *consolidated resource* the **Max Units** is the total number of team members on the team. You do not need to enter **Max Units** availability for material resources.
If you entered an availability profile (see page 321) where the availability varies over time, the **Max Units** field will display the Max Units value as per the *current date* (*system date*).

Std. Rate (*Standard Rate*) — optional field
Enter the standard rate for regular work in this field. For example, if you enter *10.50/h*, it means the person earns $10.50 per hour. For material resources, you do not need a time unit; MS Project will multiply the rate you enter with the number of units (**Material Label**) that you assign to the task. We will discuss assigning in the next chapter.
You can use the following time units:

If you type	You will see	Which means
m	min or mins	minutes
h	hr or hrs	hours
d	day or days	days
w	wk or wks	weeks
mo	mon or mons	months
y	yr or yrs	years

Ovt. Rate (*Overtime Rate*) — optional field, only for **Work** resources
Enter the rate for overtime work in this field. Do this only:
- if you will pay for overtime instead of compensating with extra time off, and
- if you will pay a higher rate than the standard rate.

MS Project expects you to indicate separately how many overtime hours are worked on each assignment; only those hours will be charged against the overtime rate. MS Project will charge overallocated hours (not marked as overtime) at the standard rate. Material resources cannot have an overtime rate.

Cost/Use (*Cost per Use* field) (*per-use-cost*) — optional field
Enter in this field the rate that has to be paid every time the resource is used, which means on each task it is assigned. It can be an *up-front fee*. For example, if you need a bulldozer transported to your site, this may cost $200 up front before it does any work. The cost per use will be incurred on every task assigned to the resource. MS Project calculates the cost as the Cost/Use rate times the number of units assigned.

Accrue At — optional, enumerated field
Select **Start**, **Prorated** or **End** to indicate when the costs are incurred. Tab to the **Accrue at** field and a pull-down button ▾ appears. Select one of the following options from the list:

Accrue at	Incurs the Cost	Example
Start	As soon as the task starts.	*actors*
Prorated	The cost is incurred as the task progresses; the cost goes up with the **% Complete**.	*employees*
End	As soon as the task finishes.	*consultants*

Base Calendar — optional, enumerated field
Select a calendar from the list. The *base calendar* specifies the general working hours and working days for the resource. You can create new base calendars. Base calendars are useful in international projects; you can base the resources working in the UK on the *UK base calendar* and the resources in the USA on the *USA base calendar*. These base calendars would have to be created first, which is typically done by your project management office or by the Project Server administrators. Material resources cannot have a base calendar.

Code — optional field
Type an alphanumeric code, such as an accounting code. This is used to charge the expenses for the resource to a particular cost account. It can be useful for the finance department, but often the tasks or assignments, instead of the resources, are charged to cost accounts.

Enterprise Resource Fields

In addition to the fields in the default resource **Entry** table, you will find more fields that are worthwhile to know about when working in Project Server. You can insert them as columns: click ribbon **Format**, button **Insert Column**. Many of these fields are read-only fields for the project manager; only the Project Server administrator can change them. However, the project manager can use the field:

2010 *Department* — read-write
The department field allows you to indicate to which organizational unit (department) each resource belongs or reports. The field is also a project –related field in which you can indicate to which department owns the project.

Pro *Enterprise* — read-only
If this field indicates **Yes** the resource is an *enterprise resource* that is present in the enterprise resource pool. It is meant to be shared across projects. If it is *no*, the resource is only available in the current project; it is a *local resource* that is private to the project.

Pro *Enterprise Team Member* — optional, enumerated field
When you have multiple enterprise projects open in MS Project, each Resource Sheet will display the resources from all open projects. If you want to focus on the resources of just the active project, you need to filter on where *Enterprise Team Member equals Yes*.

Pro *Generic* — read-only
The yes/no field *generic*, which can be inserted in the resource sheet, allows you to mark a resource as a generic resource. This is usually done by the *Project Server* resource pool administrator. Generic resources are roles, positions or function labels (like *carpenter* or *system analyst*); they are not names of individuals (like *Mary Cameron* or *Ben Yong*). See page 297 for more.

Pro *Team Assignment Pool* — read-only
This field indicates if a resource is a *team resource* or an individual. The project manager can assign tasks to teams versus individuals. See page 297 for more.

Pro *Inactive* — read-only
The yes/no field *inactive* indicates whether the resource is still active in the enterprise resource pool (current employee) or is inactive (left the company) but kept to preserve any actual hours of the resource in the project archive.

Pro *Default Assignment Owner* — read-only
The assignment owner is the person who will update the assigned tasks in the **Tasks**

screen in PWA (Project Web App). You can enter any enterprise resource or user in this field if somebody else will update the assignments. A substitute updater may be needed if:

- The assigned resource is unavailable, for example: business trip, sick, vacation or jury duty.
- The team leader enters all hours worked (e.g., in automotive plant only some people will have access to a computer).

For project managers, there is a corresponding, assignment-related field called *Assignment Owner*. The project manager can enter here who will update the assignment in either the Task Usage or the Resource usage view.

Entering Resources

You can enter the resources into the resource sheet in four ways:

- Use the *enterprise resource pool*. The resources in this pool can be shared by all projects saved in the enterprise database of Project Server (see next).
- Download the resources from *Active Directory* (see page 305)
- Download the resources from your *address book* (see page 307).
- Key in (the rest of) the resources manually (see page 308).
  In a Project Server environment, the resources to key in are only the *local resources*, which are resources specific to the project; they are not shared with any other project.

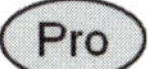

You may think that if you use Project Server, you need only know how to use the enterprise resource pool. This overlooks that projects often need extra resources that are unique to the project and that are not in the enterprise resource pool. They are called *local resources*. You have to enter them yourself. But let us start with the easy way.

7

Using the Enterprise Resource Pool

The enterprise resource pool can be used only if *Project Server* has been implemented. Project managers can then easily retrieve the resources they need from the enterprise resource pool. Project managers first need to connect to Project Server while starting MS Project (see page 66); the feature of **Build Team from Enterprise…** will then become available for accessing the enterprise resource pool:

1. Switch to the Resource sheet: click ribbon **View** and Resource Sheet.

2. Start the team builder (requires Project Professional): click ribbon **Resource**,

, **Build Team from Enterprise**; the **Build Team for <project title>** dialog appears.

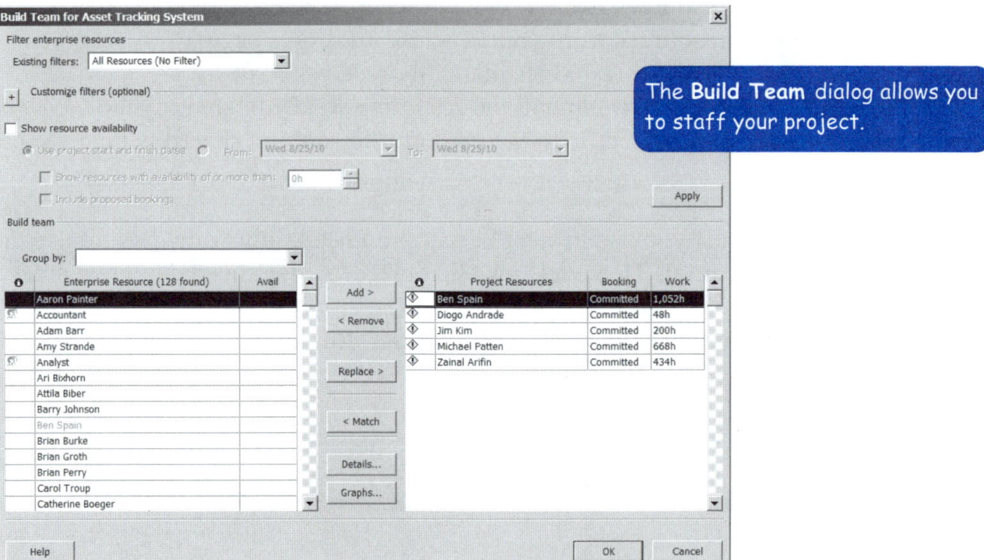

3. In the list **Enterprise Resource** on the left, all enterprise resources are listed to which you have access. In the list **Project Resources** on the right, your current project team members are listed.
   - ◇ As a project manager you can build your team from generic resources or actual resources (named individuals). You can build your team from actual resources right away if you have the authority to do so. You would use generic resources if you want to show a resource manager how many resources of each skill you

need. You can filter generic resources by clicking the button + **Customize filters**, entering: **Generic equals Yes** and clicking Apply – you should now only see generic resources listed on the left.

◇ The list **Enterprise resources** can be very long. It will make your life easier if you + **Customize filters** on the field **RBS** (in which you will likely find your organizational chart) or by categorizing the list using **Group by** on the field **RBS**.

◇ If you want to see the entire list again, remove the filter condition by selecting it in the + **Customize filters** list, clicking and clicking Apply.

4. In the **Project Resources** list on the right in the column **Booking**, you need to indicate for each **Project resource** if the resource is **Proposed** or **Committed** to the project, which communicates the status of the resource commitment. A *proposed resource* is a request for a resource, whereas a *committed resource* is an approved resource allocation. Clicking in a cell in the column **Booking** makes a list button appear that allows toggling the status.

5. If skills are entered by the Project Server administrators, you can ask for matches on skills. Select the generic resource with the skill you need on the left and click Add >. Then select that same generic resource on the right and click < Match to see the list on the left narrowed-down to those who have that particular skill. The match feature automatically creates a filter condition under + **Customize filters**.

6. You can check availability by selecting an actual resource and clicking the Graphs... button.

7. When done, click OK.

7

Download the Resources from Active Directory

Active Directory is the list created by your IT department of Windows User accounts that typically has all employees in it. This list can be accessed to quickly populate the project with resources.

1. Switch to the Resource sheet: click ribbon **View** and Resource Sheet.

2. Access Active Directory: click ribbon **Resource**, 

, **Active Directory** – the **Select Users or Groups** dialog appears. If you know the name, you can key it here

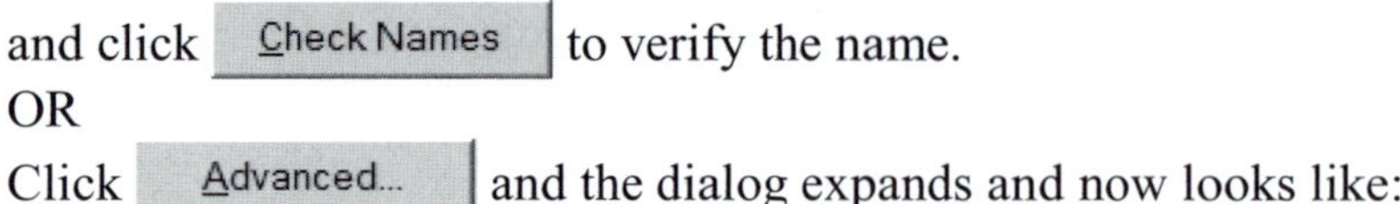

and click Check Names to verify the name.
OR
Click Advanced... and the dialog expands and now looks like:

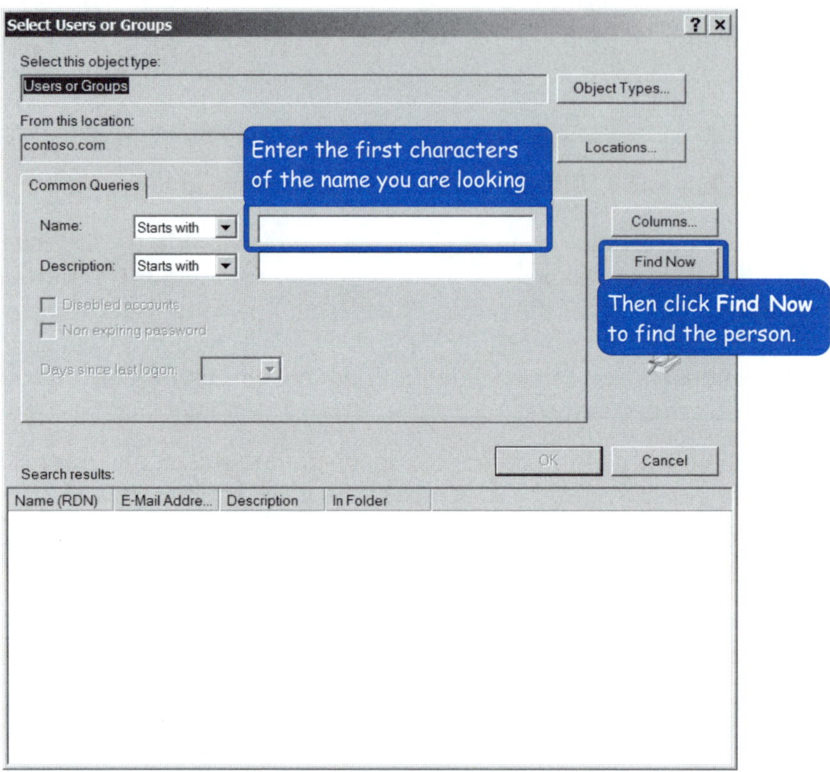

Select the name in the list and click OK – you are back in the small **Select Users and Groups** dialog.

3. Click OK – the resource is now added to the Resource Sheet.

4. You may want to sort the list alphabetically again to make it easy to find one. Use ribbon **View**, Sort, **Sort by…** and select ☑ **Permanently renumber resources**.

Downloading the Resources from Your Address Book

If you are using *Outlook 2010* for your contact information and address list, you may be able to download the resource names easily from that list. This means you do not have to retype all of them. You can import them into MS Project using the following steps:

1. Switch to the Resource sheet: click ribbon **View** and .

2. Click ribbon **Resource**, , **Address Book** – the next dialog appears:

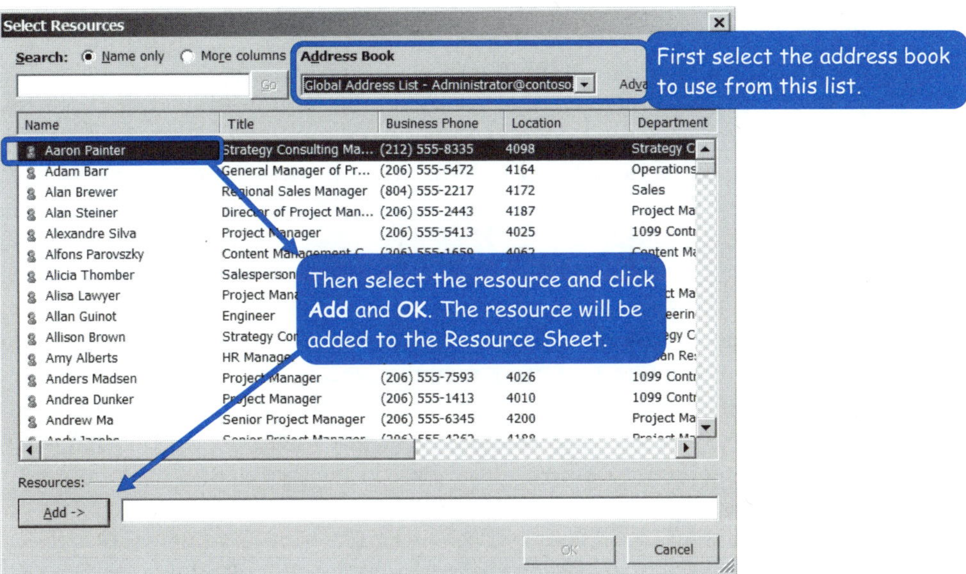

3. Select the address list from the **Address Book** list; the names of the resources are now shown in the big list.

4. Select **Search** on ◉ **Name only**.

5. In the field **Search,** key in first characters of the name of the person whom you wish to find – the list should now be narrowed down to match your search criterion.

6. Select the right resource from the list and press Enter or click Add ->.
   OR
   Double-click on the resource name; the resource is now added to the **Resources** list at the bottom that will be transferred into the resource sheet in MS Project.

7. Repeat the previous two steps for all resources you would like to add.

8. Click OK – the resources are now added to the end of the resource list. You can always go back into the address list to pick up more resource names.
9. You may want to sort the list alphabetically again to make it easy to find one. Use

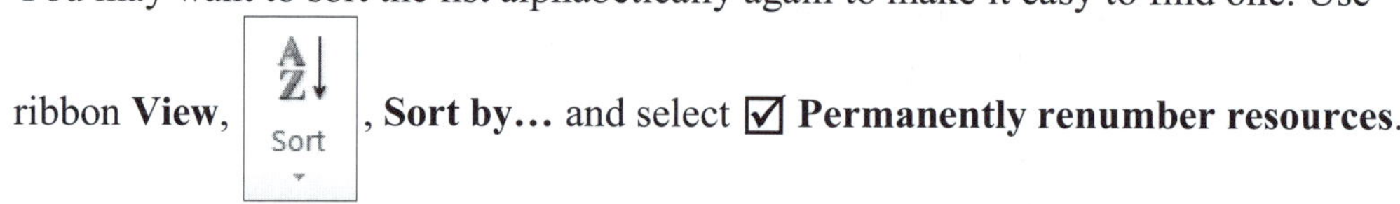

Keying in the Resources Manually

After using the enterprise resource pool, Active Directory or your address book, you may still have to:

- Enter people that were not in these lists.
- Add consultants or companies that are used only in your project; they are also known as *local resources*. Local resources have the field *Enterprise* set to *No* (and the icon in the indicators column when connected to Project Server).
- Enter the **Material** and **Cost** resources you need for facilities, machines, materials and expense categories.

Depending on which **Type** of resource you create, certain fields will be editable. We will therefore discuss in separate procedures how to enter each type of resource (**Work, Material** and **Cost**). Note that if you change the type of the resource afterward, you will lose some entries in the resource fields. For example, if you change a **Work** resource to a **Material** resource, you will lose any rates you may have entered for the resource. This is because **Work** resources require a time-related rate, like *$50/h*, whereas **Material** resources need a per-unit cost, like *$150 per door*.

The following table provides an overview of editable fields displayed in the columns — for each **Type** of resource: **Work, Material** and **Cost** that are displayed in the rows. (X = field is not editable):

	Editable fields				
	Material Label	**Max Units**	**Std. Rate Ovt. Rate Cost/Use**	**Accrue at**	**Base Calendar**
Work	X	availability	all rates	select	select
Material	unit of measure	X	**Std. Rate Cost/Use**	select	X
Cost	X	X	X	select	X

Before keying in resource names, we recommend you customize the table first so that it has the right columns in the right order for entering data. Please consult the previous table to identify the columns you will need for your resources:

1. Delete all columns you will not need by clicking on their column headings and pressing [Del] on your keyboard.
2. Insert new fields by right-clicking on the column heading before which you want to insert a new column. Select **Insert Column** from the popup menu and key in the first characters of the field name to narrow down the list. Click on the field name you need. Repeat this step for all the fields you need.
3. You can drag a column around by its heading if you want to move it. First click the column heading and when you see the mouse pointer drag the column to its desired place (☑ **Allow cell drag and drop** must be selected in ribbon **File**, Options, tab **Advanced**, section **Edit**).
4. Now you are ready to manually enter the resources.

Entering a Human Resource (Work)

1. Enter the name of the resource in the column **Resource Name (**field **Name**) and press [Tab] to go to the cell to the right.
2. In the field **Type** enter **Work** for human resources.
3. Enter the availability in the column **Max Units**, in the **Resource Availability** profile (see page 321) or on the resource calendar (see page 314).
4. Enter the cost rates in the **Std. Rate** column (**Standard Rate** field)**, Ovt. Rate** column (**Overtime Rate** field) and **Cost/Use** column (**Cost per Use** field). If there

is sensitivity in your organization about actual rates, then use a *blended rate* or *average rate* to arrive at an approximate cost for the resources being expended.

5. In the field **Accrue at** determine when the cost will be incurred by selecting **Start**, **Prorated** or **End**.

6. Enter the **Base Calendar** field and a list button will appear. Select the appropriate base calendar for the resource from this list. Normally this would be *Standard* unless more *base calendars* were created for countries in international projects (see page 312 for more).

7. When you assign **Work** resources to tasks, the finish dates of the tasks will be driven by the availability of the resource. MS Project calculates the cost of using the human resource on the task using the following *formula*:
Cost=Std.Rate x Regular Work+Ovt. Rate x Ovt. Work+Cost/Use x Assigment Units
where *Regular Work* is the number of hours designated as regular work (normally scheduled during regular working times as entered on the *Project Calendar*, see page 98) and *Overtime (Ovt.)Work* is the number of hours designated as overtime work (see page 516). MS Project displays this cost in the **Assign Resources** dialog for each assignment.

Entering a Material Resource

1. Enter the name of the resource in the column **Resource Name (**field **Name**); press [Tab] to go to the cell to the right.

2. In the field **Type** enter **Material** for facility, machine or consumable materials.

3. Enter the unit of measure for the material resource in the column **Material Label**, for example *cubic yard* for the resource *concrete*.

4. MS Project assumes that material resources are available in unlimited quantities (i.e., that we live in a rich country); you do not need to fill in the field **Max Units**.

5. Enter the per-unit cost rate in the **Std. Rate** column (**Standard Rate** field) and/or **Cost/Use** column (**Cost per Use** field). Make sure the rate per unit you enter corresponds to the unit of measure you entered in the **Material Label** field. Note that you cannot enter an **Ovt. Rate** (**Overtime Rate** field) for **Material** resources (have you ever seen materials charging more for overtime?).

6. In the field **Accrue at** determine when the cost will be incurred by choosing **Start**, **Prorated** or **End**.

7. MS Project calculates the cost of using the material resource on the task using the following *formula*:
Cost = Std. Rate x Assignment Units + Cost/Use x Assignment Units,

where *Assignment Units* is the number of units of the material resource needed as input for the task. MS Project displays this cost in the **Assign Resources** dialog for each assignment.

Entering a Cost Resource

1. Enter the name of the resource in the column **Resource Name (**field **Name**) and press Tab to go to the cell to the right.
2. In the field **Type** enter **Cost** for money resources or expenses.
3. In the field **Accrue at** determine when the cost will be incurred by choosing **Start**, **Prorated** or **End**.
4. You cannot enter rates; you can indicate the cost amount in the **Cost** field in the **Assign Resources** dialog when you assign the cost resource to tasks, see page 340.
5. MS Project calculates the cost of using the material resource on the task using the following *formula*:
   Cost = Std. Rate x Assignment Units + Cost/Use x Assignment Units,
   where *Assignment Units* is the number of units of the material resource needed as input for the task. MS Project displays this cost in the **Assign Resources** dialog for each assignment.

Base Calendars and Resource Calendars

A *resource calendar* is a calendar that is specific for an individual (a **Work** resource). The resource calendar is automatically created when the resource is created. You can enter individual working times and vacations in a resource calendar. All resource calendars will have the settings that you entered in the project calendar (see page 99). Apart from the project calendar, there can be one or more *base calendars* on which individual resource calendars can be based. For example, you will need base calendars:

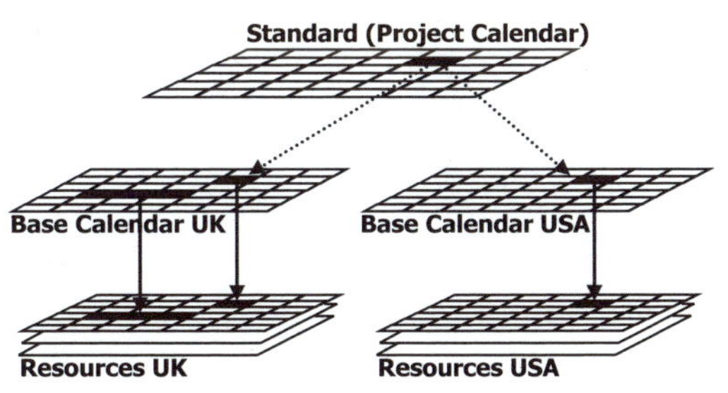

- If your team members are in other countries. You would create a base calendar for each country and then base each resource on his country calendar (see the illustration).

- If resources belong to different companies, you may also need multiple base calendars, but only if the calendars are significantly different between the companies.
- If some resources work regular workweeks and others *compressed workweeks*, see page 323.
- To model working in *shifts*

In the illustration, you may have noticed a dotted arrow between the *Standard (Project Calendar)* and the *Base Calendars* that reflects a one-time copying of holidays and working times if you choose that when creating the Base Calendar. The solid arrow between the Base Calendar and the Resource Calendars depicts that there is continuous one-way communication from the Base Calendar to the Resource Calendars. If you change the Base Calendar, all resource calendars based on it will be updated. On the Resource Calendars, however, you can overwrite the holidays and working times from the Base Calendar at any time.

Creating a Base Calendar

In Project Server, all calendars are maintained centrally by the Project Server administrators. Individual project managers typically do not have the rights to create or change calendars – project, task, resource and base calendars.

The calendar you have chosen as the *project calendar* will be the default base calendar for all resources. You can create new *base calendars* (and new *task calendars*) in the following way:

1. Click ribbon **Project** and 

– the **Change Working Time** dialog appears:

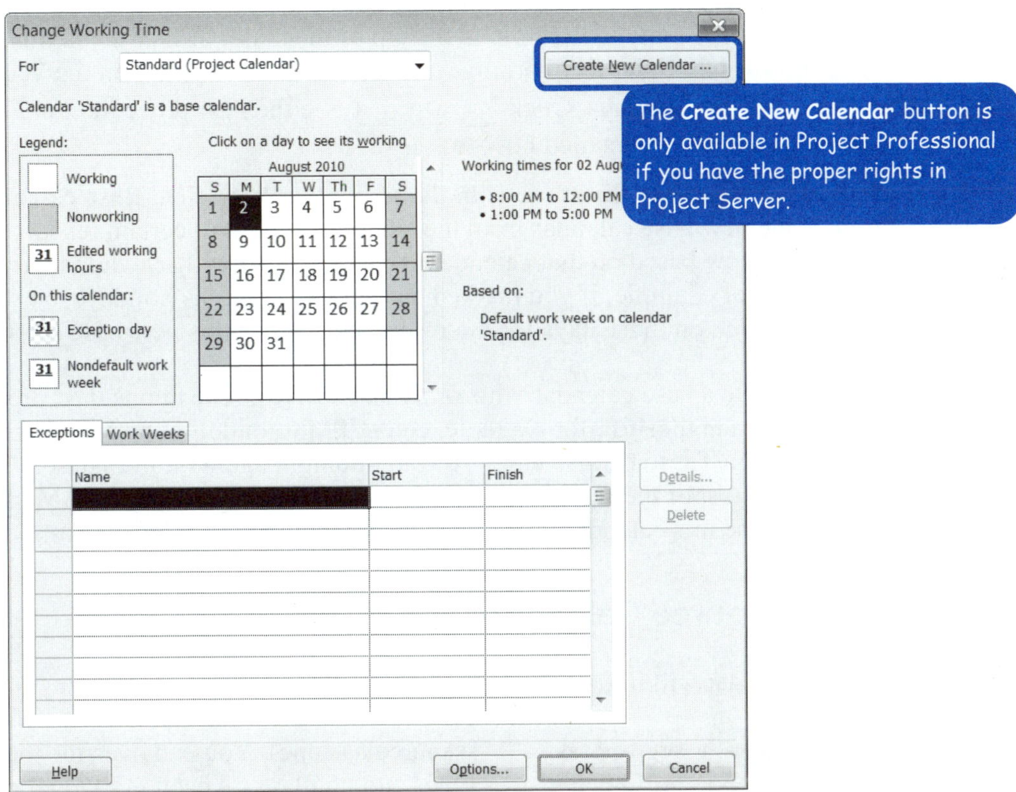

2. Click Create New Calendar ... . This button is not available in *Project Professional 2010*, since base calendars are often created centrally by your Project Server administrators; they own and maintain the base calendars. The **Create New Base Calendar** dialog appears:

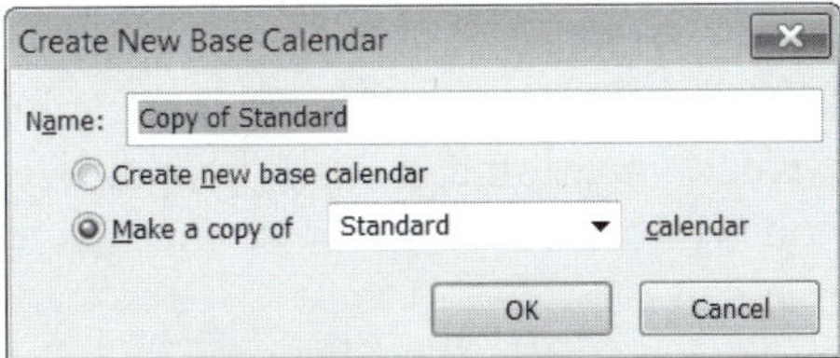

3. Enter a **Name** for the base calendar. You can choose to copy the *Standard (Project calendar)* as a starting point for the new base calendar. This is a one-time affair; the *Standard* calendar will not continue to be synchronized with the base calendar. The

base calendars, on the other hand, will continue to update all the resource calendars. Enter a name and select either ⦿ **Create new base calendar** or ⦿ **Make copy of Standard** and click OK.

4. You are now back in the **Change Working Time** dialog, but with the newly created base calendar shown in the list **For:** at the top of the dialog. Enter the holidays on the **Exceptions** tab. Enter the working times for the base calendar on the **Work Weeks** tab and the holidays. Click OK. See the next procedure on *Editing a Resource Calendar* for detailed how-to steps.

5. Switch to the **Resource Sheet** view. In the resource-related field **Base calendar** you can select the new base calendar from the list and assign it to certain resources. The resources are now based on that calendar and MS Project will schedule their work accordingly. For example, if you marked days at Christmas as holidays, no work will be scheduled on those days for the resources that use this new base calendar.

If you want to create a base calendar with *shifts* that span more than one day, proceed as follows. To create a night shift, for example, enter 7PM to midnight on Monday and midnight to 7AM on Tuesday; also enter 7PM to midnight again on the Tuesday. Repeat this pattern for the rest of the weekdays. The Saturday needs midnight to 7AM as working time. Name this calendar *Graveyard Shift* or something more elegant.

Editing a Resource Calendar

The resource calendar will initially have the same holidays and working times as the project calendar (or its base calendar if the resource has one). You can override these times and holidays on each individual resource calendar and capture when a person goes on vacation. If someone takes a vacation, the task assignments will be delayed until the resource returns. The duration of the project increases, and the resource has an impact on the schedule. It is important to model vacations in MS Project, because they can have a huge impact on the schedule. A poorly timed two-week vacation can easily jeopardize precious deadlines. Entering resource vacations is not a lot of work, so there is no good reason not to.

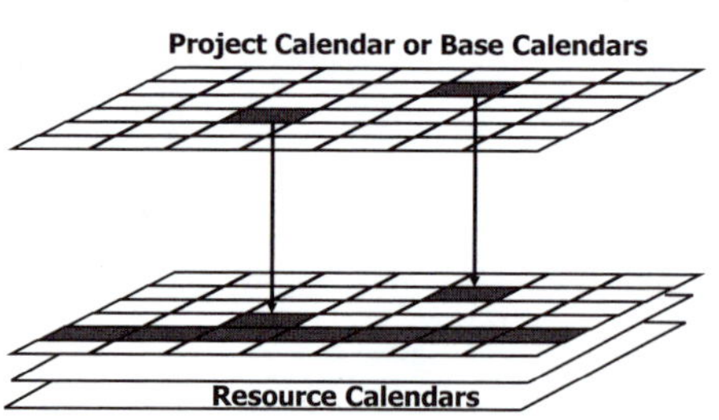

To edit a resource calendar you can:

Double-click on a resource and in the **Resource Information** dialog, click on tab **General** and then click Change Working Time ... . This will allow you to do one resource at a time.
OR
If you want to edit several resource calendars in a row:

1. Click ribbon **Project** and  – the **Change Working Time** dialog appears:

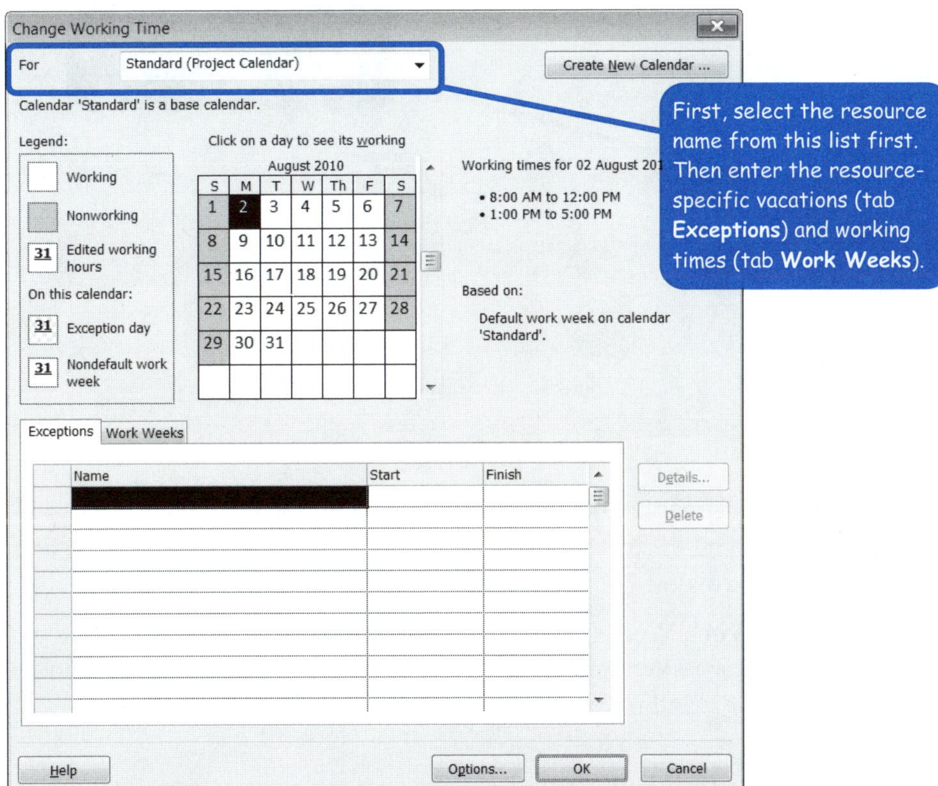

2. In the list **For** select the resource whose resource calendar needs to be changed. If you do not find any resource names in this list, you have not entered the resources yet into your schedule.

3. Click the tab **Exceptions** where you can enter the vacation days of the individual. We strongly recommend you enter the vacation days of your team member because

they can throw off forecast dates annually by at least 10 vacation days (USA) or 20 vacation days (Europe) out of approximately 260 working days.

4. Either select the vacation days in the calendar grid and then type the name of the vacation in the field **Name** at the bottom and press [Enter ↵],
OR
you enter a **Name** first and click [Details...] – the **Details for <name of the vacation>** appears:

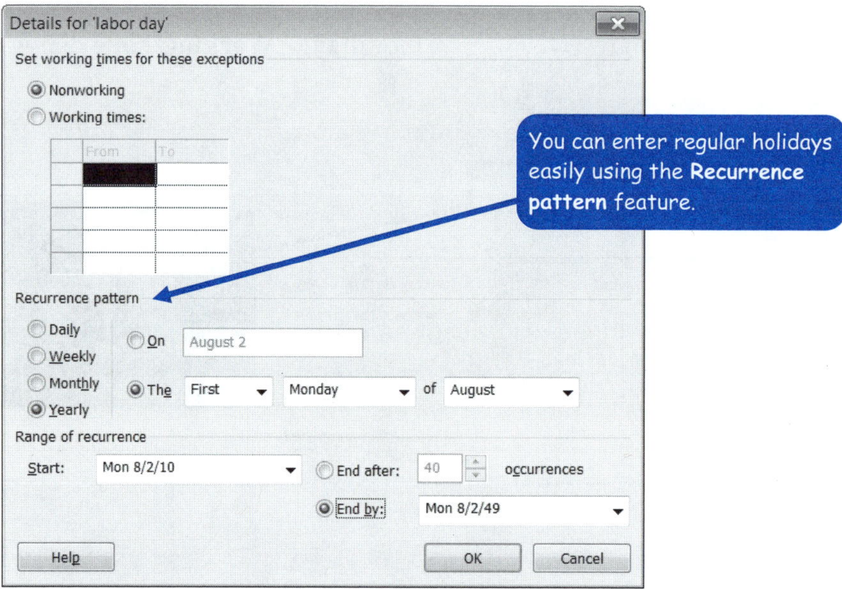

5. Select ⦿ **Nonworking** and under **Range of recurrence** enter the **Start** and **End by** dates for the vacation days. Click [OK] and you are back in the **Change Working Time** dialog.

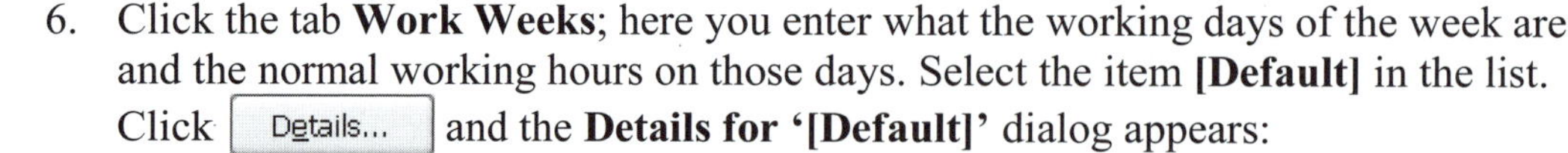

6. Click the tab **Work Weeks**; here you enter what the working days of the week are and the normal working hours on those days. Select the item **[Default]** in the list. Click [Details...] and the **Details for '[Default]'** dialog appears:

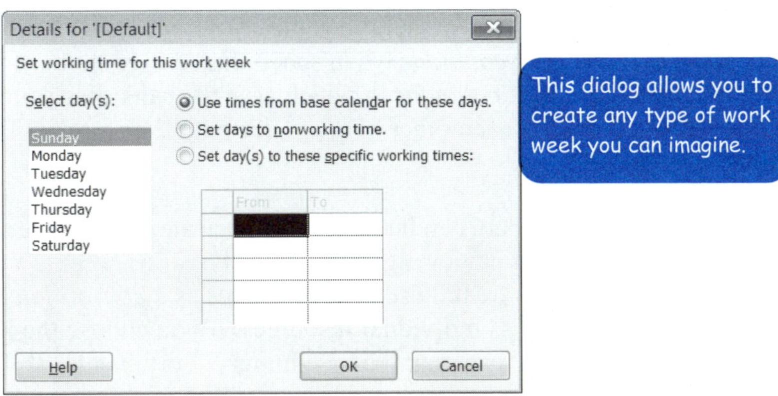

7. Select the workdays of the week by dragging over the weekdays in the list **Select Day(s)**. If you have a Monday to Friday workweek, drag over **Monday** to **Friday**. If the days that you select are not consecutive, select one and then hold down the Control key to select the other days.

8. Select one of three options:
   ⦿ **Use times from base calendar for these days**
   (note this option appears as ⦿ **Use Project default times for these days** when editing the project calendar or a base calendar). This option sets the times back to the times of the calendar which is the basis of this resource calendar (the project calendar by default or a **Base Calendar** you chose for the resource), or
   ⦿ **Set days to nonworking time** for indicating what days weekend days are
   ⦿ **Set day(s) to these specific working times:** for changing the working hours; then enter the times in the grid. Note that you can enter *military times* (like 17 instead of 5 PM) in this dialog.

9. Select the weekend days in the list **Select Day(s)**. If the weekend days are Saturday and Sunday, select **Sunday**; hold down Control and click on **Saturday**. Select the option ⦿ **Set days to nonworking time**.

10. Click OK when done; you are now back in the **Change Working Time** dialog. Notice the gray shading for the **Nonworking** weekend days in the calendar grid.

11. To enter another resource calendar select the next resource from the list **For** at the top and enter the workweek or click OK when you are done with all resources.

7

The task-related field **Ignore Resource Calendar** (shown as **Scheduling Ignores Resource Calendar** in the **Task Information** dialog, tab **Advanced** that you can display by double-clicking on the task) is by default set to *No* for all tasks. This means that MS Project will use the *resource calendar* when scheduling assignments. The field is useful when the task also has a *task calendar* in which case the calendars could have some hours in common or contradict each other entirely, see page 273 for details on what happens in these situations.

The working hours in resource calendars can become very intricate and require a lot of data entry, such as resources working day or night shifts in alternating weeks. You have to ask yourself if you would prefer to treat these shift resources as a *consolidated resource* or *team resource* instead of as individual resources. If you choose the latter option, your schedule might become very maintenance-hungry. Fortunately, shift work is less prevalent in projects than in the ongoing operations of manufacturing. Generally speaking, we do not recommend you model the exact working hours of individual resources, which would require a lot of effort. You gain an hour here, lose an hour there; overall it averages out. We do not think modeling the exact working hours of individuals pays off.

Fixed Duration tasks will keep their duration when you assign a resource that is not available and simply not schedule any work for the resource during days off. Essentially, Fixed Duration tasks decrease the work when the *resource calendar* has nonworking time. *Fixed Units* and *Fixed Work* durations and task bars tend to extend when a resource has days off during the task. When the resource is not available at the start of the task, it reschedules the task.

The Max Units of a Resource

The maximum units (**Max Units**) of resources determine what percentage of one's work hours is available to the project. The maximum units set the threshold with which MS Project will find overallocations. In the illustration you can see that Tom's working hours are 8 hours per day in his *resource calendar*, but all the tasks he is assigned to amount to 10 hours of work per day (125%).

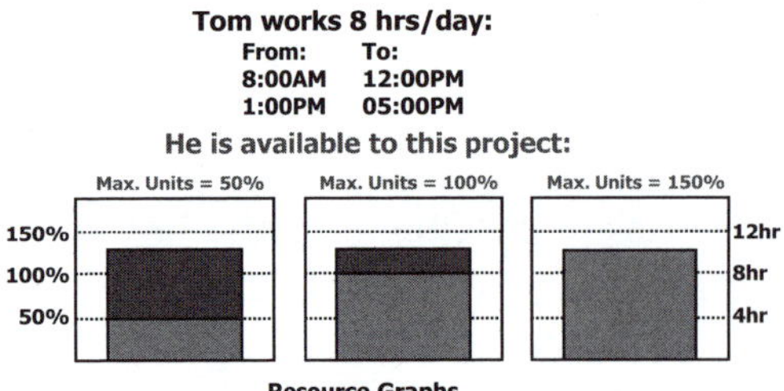

If the **Max Units** is set to 50%, he would be available 4 hours per day and he would have a steep overallocation (dark gray). If the **Max Units** is set to 100%, he would be available 8 hours per day and he would have a small overallocation. If it is 150% there is remaining availability. You can see that the percentage entered in the **Max Units** field determines what will constitute an overallocation for the resource.

The **Max. Units** percentage can vary from week to week. Enter this by double-clicking on the resource; enter it on the **General** tab in the grid under **Resource Availability**. For example, if the maximum units in one week are 50%, the person would be available 4 hours per day during an 8-hour working day. If the maximum units are 75% in another week, the availability would be 6 hours per day. This is an efficient way of creating an *availability profile*. Please note that availability profiles are very useful in a non-enterprise environment; in the Project Server enterprise environment you will be able to see the total workload of a resource across projects and compare it to the total availability of the resource (see page 585 for an example). As a result, you will not need availability profiles as much.

We think that the **Max Units** field should never be set to a value over 120% for individuals. Labor productivity research makes it very clear that when employees exceed a certain amount of overtime on a sustained basis, the extra hours spent physically present at work do not generate any added productivity. If pushed to a high level of sustained overtime, people will apply *systematic production limitation* to protect their own health or jobs. [44] If pushed to the extreme, overtime will even bring productivity down because people will start to resist and obstruct. If pushed over the limit, resources will burn out and their productivity will fall to zero. On a sustained basis, each resource can reach only a certain plateau of productivity even at very high levels of motivation as depicted in the illustration. This plateau differs for each resource; I depict in this chart my own personal productivity plateau based on detailed timekeeping while writing this book. As a self-employed and self-publishing individual, I assumed unlimited motivation. If you set the **Max Units** field to 120%, you are basically telling MS Project that you will work 48 hours every week from now until eternity; since none of us has eternal life, this will, in reality, be until your retirement.

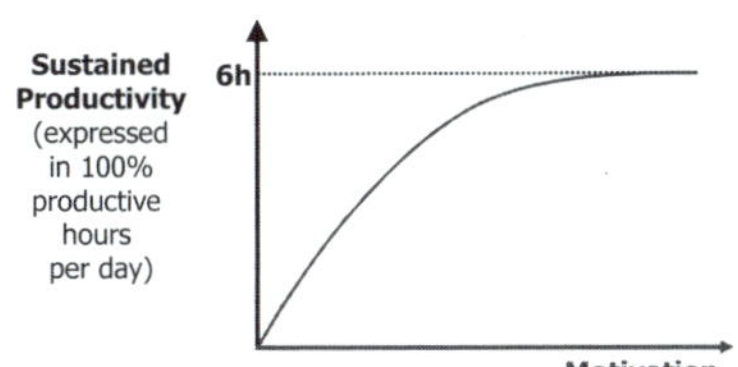

From personal observation, I have found that I can only work 16 hour days for one day, perhaps two, and then I need a day and a half of nothing, which means that this peak of 16 +16 + 0 + 0 = 32 hours averaged out to only 32/3.5 = 9.14 hours per day of gross work time multiplied by 70% (see page 181) = 6.4 hours of pure work time per day.

[44] *Principles of Scientific Management*, Taylor, Frederic W., 1911

Pure work time per day is 100% productive work time during physical presence at work, which is what I charted in the illustration.

Resource Availability

The availability of resources varies from one resource to another and can vary from week to week. The different types of availability are:

- *Temporary* or *varying availability* (see page 321)
  A temporary resource is a person who is available from a certain date or until a certain date. A resource with varying availability is, for example, available full-time one month, but only half-time the next month.
- *Part-time* (see page 322)
  This is a person who works fewer hours a day or fewer days a week than a *full-time-equivalent* resource (defined in the ribbon **File**, [Options], tab **Schedule,** setting **Hours per day**).
- *Full-time* (see page 323)
  MS Project considers a full-time person to be someone who works 40 hours in 5 days a week from Monday to Friday. That is also known as the *default workweek*. You can define what a full-time resource is on the **Standard (Project Calendar)** in combination with the conversion factors in ribbon **File**, [Options], tab **Schedule, Hours per day**.
- *Compressed workweeks* (see page 323):
  - *4-40 workweek* or *every Friday off*
    A person works only 4 days per week, but 10 hours per day.
  - *9-80 workweek* or *alternating Fridays off*
    This type of workweek means that a person works for 9 days a total of 80 hours and then takes 1 day off, normally a Friday.
- *Overtime* (see page 325)
  If the deadline is in jeopardy, you can ask resources to start working overtime to compensate for the lack of progress. You typically do not enter overtime during the *planning* of the project, but rather during the *execution*.
- *Team resources* or *consolidated resources* (see page 328)
  Team or consolidated resources are resources that are entered into the schedule as a group of interchangeable resources instead of as separate individuals. For example, you can enter a group of 5 Visual Basic programmers as 5 separate individuals, but you can also enter them as one team of 5, a consolidated resource.

  In Project Professional, team resources allow the project manager to assign to the team instead of to the individual. The team members can then assign themselves to the team tasks that they would like to take-on in *Project Web App*. Team resources have the field **Team Assignment Pool** set to **Yes**.

- *Generic resources* (see page 329)
  Generic resources represent a particular skill, for example *C++ programmer*. Generic resources have unlimited availability, unlike team resources. Project managers can always assign generic resources when they do not know what named resources (individuals) they will get. Generic resources have the field **Generic** set to **Yes**.

  Generic resources act as placeholders for accumulating workload. In Project Server, they can also be used to do *resource capacity planning*.

On the next pages, we will discuss how to enter all resource availabilities. In many cases, you will have to edit the resource calendar. As a project manager in the *Project Server* environment, you may not have the proper access rights to add or change resource availability in the enterprise resource pool, but you always have the right to view resource availability. You need to be able to check if resource availability is entered correctly for enterprise resources. You also need to know how to enter the availability of the *local resources* (that are present only in your project).

Temporary or Varying Availability

In MS Project you can easily model *temporary* or *varying availability*. You can set up an entire profile of availability, such as 80% in April, 50% in May, 100% in June, and so forth. To enter the *availability profile*:

1. Double-click a resource in the Resource Sheet
   OR

   Select the resource, click 

   on the **Resource** ribbon

2. Click the tab **General**; the dialog should now look like:

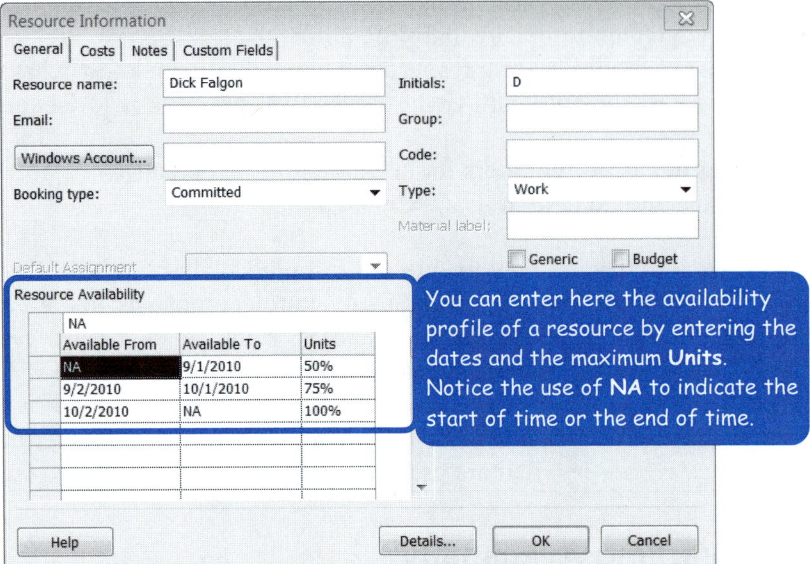

3. In the fields **Available from** and **Available to** enter the dates when the resource is available; in the field **Units** enter the maximum availability. If you leave one date set to *NA*, it means *the-start-of-time* in the **Available from** field and *the-end-of-time* in the **Available to** field. If you set the **Units** to 0 it means unavailable. For example, **Available From** set to *NA* and **Available To** set to *Sep. 1, 2010* and units set to *100%* means temporarily full-time available until Sep. 1, 2010 inclusive, after that not available.

In an availability profile, you only need to enter the **Available to** dates and MS Project will automatically enter the corresponding **Available from** dates; it takes the next day.

MS Project stores the **Units** numbers you entered in the **Max Units** field. The **Max Units** field in the Resource Sheet can only display one percentage of all percentages entered in the availability profile. The one number displayed in the **Max Units** field will be the **Units** availability percentage as per the current date (system date). As time goes by, the field **Max Units** will display all the different values from the availability profile.

Part-Time Availability

Part-time resources can be:

- People who work, for example, 4 hours each workday.
  You can set the working-time hours in the resource calendar to only 4 hours per day. For example, the working hours could be set to 1:00 PM - 5:00 PM for an afternoon

job. We recommend this method.
OR
They can be entered in the resource sheet with the **Max Units** set to 50% = 4h/8h * 100%. A problem with this method is that all assignments will be at 50% involvement, and the person assigned to a meeting of 2 hours will only spend 2h * 50% = 1 hour of effort in that meeting, which may be unintended.

- 2007 People who work 4 out of 5 weekdays; enter this into the schedule by changing a weekday to a nonworking day in their resource calendar. Double-click on the resource, click on the tab **General** and click [Change Working Time ...]. Click tab **Work Weeks**; click [Details...] then edit the workweek.
- Someone who is working on multiple projects and only available part-time to your project. We recommend you use a *shared resource pool* in this situation, so you can track someone's total workload. The *Project Server* enterprise resource pool automatically calculates and displays the remaining availability in all projects that utilize the resource.

A resource can also be assigned to work part-time on one task, which we will discuss in the next chapter on page 356.

7

Full-Time Availability

People who work *full-time* need to have their **Max Units** set to 100% (or 1 if you work in decimals) and they need to show full-time working hours on their resource calendar.

Their working hours as set in the resource calendar should correspond with the number of **Hours per Day** and **Hours per Week** settings in the ribbon **File**, [Options], tab **Schedule**. For example, if the hours per day in ribbon **File,** [Options] is set to 7.5 hours/day, the calendar should show, for example, 8:00 AM - 12:00 PM and 1:00 PM - 4:30 PM (double-click on the resource and click on the tab **General** and click [Change Working Time ...] to check this). If these two settings are out of sync, you will typically see decimals appear in durations, like 1.07 day (calendar has 8 hour working days but **Hours per Day** is set to 7.5).

Compressed Workweeks

4-40 Workweek or Every Friday Off

One example of a *compressed workweek* is when a person works 10 hours per day, but only 4 days per week; this is known as a *4-40 workweek*. This is often the case for people who commute a long distance to work; they may travel on Sunday evening and return home late on Thursday evening for a three-day weekend.

Since more than one resource may work a 4-40 workweek, we recommend you create a *base calendar* first (see page 312). You can then base all 4-40 resources on this base calendar. We will explain how to create a base calendar for 4-40 resources:

1. Click ribbon **Project**, 

; the **Change Working Time** dialog appears.

2. Click [Create New Calendar ...] to create a new base calendar. This button may not be available if you are using *Project Professional* with *Project Server;* only the person with administrative access privileges can create new base calendars. In that case, you have to request that the 4-40 calendar be created for you. In MS Project standalone, you can create your own base calendars.

3. The **Create New Base Calendar** dialog appears. Enter a **Name** for the calendar; we recommend you enter a descriptive name, like 4-40 *workweek*. Select ⦿ **Create new base calendar** and click [OK]. You are now back in the **Change Working Time** dialog, but with the new calendar active.

4. Click tab **Work Weeks**, select **[Default]** and click [Details...] – the dialog should now look like:

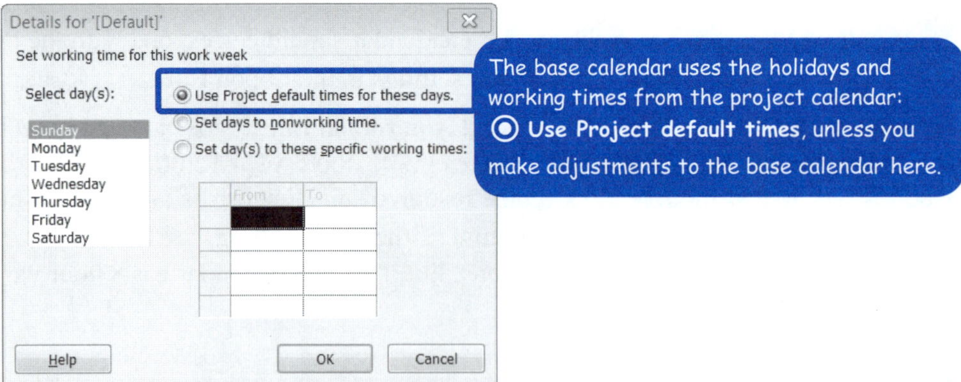

5. Select the working days **Monday** through **Thursday** for this resource by dragging over them.

6. Select ⦿ **Set day(s) to these specific times**.

7. Enter the longer working hours that correspond to a 10 hour workday in the **From** and **To** fields. For example, the workday could be from 7AM-12PM and 12:30PM-17:30PM.
8. Select the Friday by clicking on the **Friday** and select the option ◉ **Set days to Nonworking time**.
9. When done, click [OK] – the 4-40 resource calendar is now created.
10. To use the 4-40 workweek for a resource, switch to the **Resource Sheet** view.
11. Click in the field **Base Calendar**, which is one of the last columns in the resource **Entry** table; a list button [▼] appears. Click [▼] and select **4-40** from the list.

9-80 Workweek or Alternating Fridays Off

Another example of a compressed workweek is if a person works a total of 80 hours over 9 consecutive business days and then takes 1 day off, often a Friday.

Because multiple resources may also work this type of week, we recommend you create a *base calendar* first, and then base those resources on the 9-80 calendar.

The steps are very similar as for the 4-40 workweek, except for in the **Change Working Time** dialog:

- Tab **Work Weeks**; select item **[Default]**; click [Details...]. In the **Details for '[Default]'** dialog, increase the working hours on workdays to almost 9 hours per day. Click [OK].
- Tab **Exceptions** and enter a descriptive name like *Every other Friday off;* click [Details...] – the **Details for** dialog appears. Select ◉ **Nonworking**, ◉ **Weekly,** enter 2 in **Recur every 2 weeks on**, select ☑ **Friday**; enter the range of dates. Click [OK]. Every other Friday is now marked as nonworking.

Overtime Availability

Overtime work is work done outside the regular work hours as indicated in the *resource calendar* (or *project calendar*).

During the *planning* of the project, you would normally not schedule overtime already, unless the project is extremely time-constrained right off the bat. Typically the overtime feature is used only during project *execution*, when you may need it to compensate for slippages. It seems fair to ask the people who are slipping their tasks to work overtime to catch up. That is better than asking other resources to solve problems they did not cause.

Of course, this is only necessary when the tasks that slip are (*resource*) *critical tasks*, see page 516 for how overtime is used to shrink a project.

Overtime is entered in several different ways depending on whether you pay and what rate you pay for it:

- If the resource is not paid for overtime, but instead is compensated with extra time off, there are several ways to model this using one of the following methods:
  - Enter the overtime by increasing the **Max Units** in the resource sheet to greater than 100%. This is the quick and easy way to enter overtime. The resource will be working overtime during the entire project.
  - To be more precise, create an *availability profile*. Double-click the resource and in the **Resource Information** dialog, tab **General**; in **Resource Availability** grid you can specify overtime just for the period in which the resource works more than 100%.
  - Increase the working time in the resource calendar. For example, somebody works 10 hours overtime in one week, and in the second week time-off is compensation for the overtime.
  - Enter the overtime by changing holidays or weekend days in the resource calendar to working days. Later on, weekdays are set to nonworking days to compensate in time.
- If the resource is paid for overtime hours at the regular rate, you only need to check whether you kept the overallocations reasonable. All regular and overallocated hours worked are charged at the same standard rate.
- If the resource is paid for overtime hours at a higher rate, you must separately enter all hours worked in overtime. You enter them on the *Task Form* in the Gantt Chart or in the *Resource Usage* view. We will explain this in more detail next.

Entering Overtime Hours at the Overtime Rate

1. Click ribbon **View,** [Resource Sheet] and enter the overtime rate in the field **Ovt. Rate**.
2. Click the top part of [Gantt Chart] on the **View** ribbon – the Gantt Chart view appears.

3. Set the **Task Mode** field to **Auto Scheduled** – the **Ovt. Work** field will now be enabled.
4. Select [Details] on the **View** ribbon to display the **Task Form** view in the bottom.

5. Right-click almost anywhere on the Task Form and select **Work** from the popup menu, OR

   click on the Task Form to make it active and click ribbon **Format**,  to

   display the field **Ovt. Work**.

6. The view should now look like:

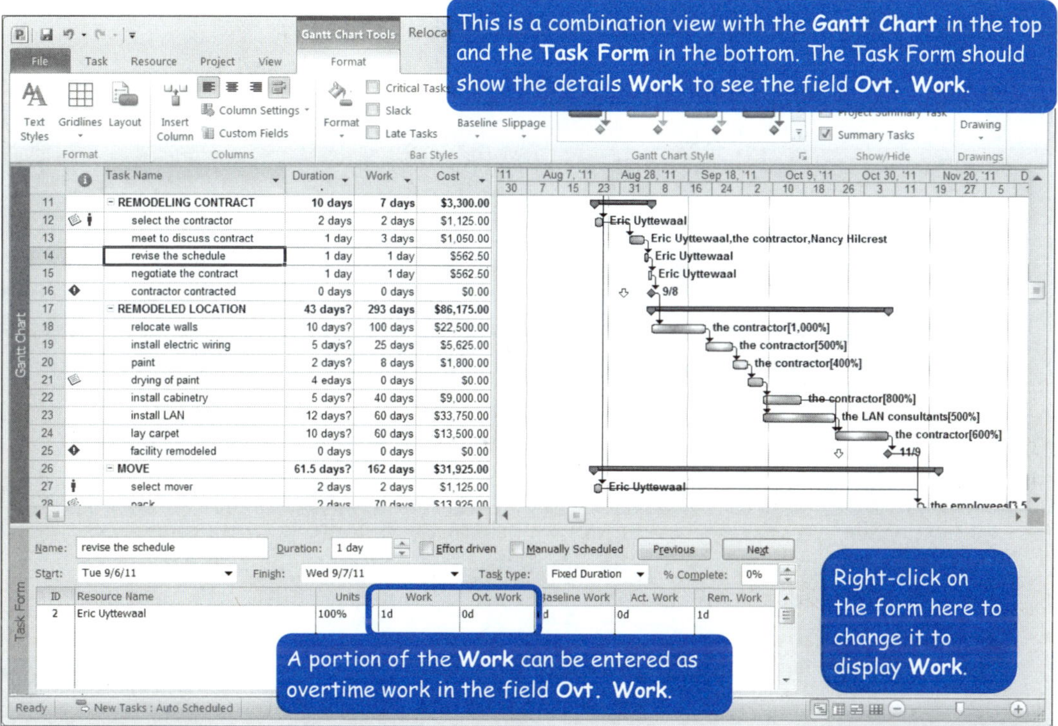

7. Select the task first in the top view, the Gantt Chart, then indicate in the bottom view Task Form in the field **Ovt. Work** how many of the hours shown in the field **Work** will (or should) be worked in overtime.

8. Upon making changes in the Task Form, the Previous button transforms to OK and when you click it, the data are entered into the schedule. The overtime hours will be charged at the overtime rate.

The number of overtime hours must be reasonable relative to the total number of **Work** hours. If an assignment is 10 hours, you could ask for, at most, 2 hours in overtime on a weekday and finish the task in 1 business day. If the assignment is 20 hours, you cannot expect a resource to work 8 hours and then 12 hours in overtime to finish within the same day. MS Project would schedule this as one 20-hour workday, which is asking a little too much … for most of us. On the other hand, if the assignment happens to fall on a Friday, you could ask the resource to work on the weekend, and the percentage of overtime could be higher.

If you forgot to enter the overtime rate, you may actually see the cost of the project go down when you assign overtime.

Team Resources (Consolidated Resources)

A *Team resource* or *consolidated resource* is a group of individuals that can replace each other. You enter the group of people as one resource on one line item in the resource sheet instead of as separate individuals.

Consolidating resources to team resources is a beautiful way to keep the devilish details out of your schedule. You basically make an agreement with the team of 3 resources that you will not give them more work than up to 3 full-time equivalent resources. They will have to determine among themselves who will do which task, and because they know each other's expertise best, teams can be very good at that. As a project manager, you will spend a lot less time maintaining detailed resource data and keeping the individual workloads leveled. It requires that the team be mature and that there be no strife among the members.

To ensure that you do not assign more workload than there is availability, we recommend that you set the maximum units (*Max Units*) to the number of *full-time equivalent* individuals who are part of the team resource. Full-time equivalency is defined in the**, Hours per day** setting (ribbon **File,** [Options], tab **Schedule**). For example, if you have 2 full-timers and 2 half-timers on a team, the maximum units for that team resource should be set to (2 * 1) + (2 * 0.5) = 3 or 300%. MS Project will mark any workload that exceeds the availability red and overallocations will be easy to find.

In Project Professional, the project manager will assign tasks to the team resource instead of to the individual. The team members can then assign themselves to team tasks that they would like to take on in *Project Web App*, the web-based interface for team member to access project server. Team resources have the field **Team Assignment Pool** set to **Yes**.

Creating team resources makes sense only if the resources can substitute for each other. If you have novice and experienced resources, you could create two team resources: *junior* and *senior*. If that does not provide enough precision, you have to revert to modeling resources individually. MS Project is a modeling tool in which you should capture only significant parameters of the reality of your project that affect the forecasts.

Generic Resources

1. To create a generic resource, enter the name in the column **Resource name** (field **Name**). The name should reflect a skill or role.
2. Insert the column **Generic** and enter **Yes** for the generic resource – the icon will appear in the indicators column.
   OR
   Double-click on the resource – the **Resource Information** dialog appears, click the tab **General** and select ☑ **Generic**.

Cost Management

To manage the cost of the project you have to define, in the resource sheet, all the *people*, *facilities*, *machines* and *materials* that have a significant cost associated with them. For example, if you need outside legal advice, you will pay high hourly rates that you need to capture for your project budget; a corporate lawyer in New York may set you back $450 per hour. You do not have to enter small expenses into your MS Project model. MS Project is not meant to be accounting software. There are several reasons for this:

- MS Project is a modeling tool with which you should deliberately simplify the reality. *Accountants* cannot permit themselves to simplify; they need to reflect the reality as precisely as they (humanly) can. *Project managers*, on the other hand, should focus on the big picture from a 10,000-foot distance. Project managers have to stay away from the details to keep their sanity, or they risk overloading their schedule with so much information that it becomes too large and too time-consuming to keep up-to-date.
- Project managers can use averaging when they model their project, for example, by averaging levels of effort. Averaging makes accountants cringe because they want facts — like bills — and nothing else.
- In a sense, accountants are the "*historians*" of the company, whereas the project managers are the "*futurologists*" of the company. Accountants are obsessed with the past, whereas project managers are obsessed with the future. The future has no facts, only the past has facts.
- Project managers need be concerned only with expenses that have to be paid from the project budget. Accountants have to be concerned about any expenses within the company. Resources you will not pay for from your project budget can have a zero rate or can be left out of the model. For example, if you use a boardroom that is paid

for by the corporation, you would not add it as a resource to the resource sheet from a cost perspective. On the other hand, if you will be paying the rent for a training room from your project budget, you should add the training room as a resource to the resource sheet in MS Project.

As you can see, accountants have an entirely different orientation than project managers and MS Project is meant only for project managers.

Creating a Project Budget in MS Project

Budget resources can be used to create a budget for the entire project. There is a resource field called **Budget**, which is an optional field enumerated with **Yes/No**. This field allows you to indicate if you have added the resource just for budgeting purposes. If you set it to **Yes**, you also need to indicate in the resource-related field **Type** if you want to budget **Cost** (monetary budget), **Work** (effort or units budget) or **Material** (units of material resources). The table below shows which resource fields can be entered (X = field is not editable):

	Editable fields				
	Material Label	**Max Units**	**Std. Rate Ovt. Rate Cost/Use**	**Accrue at**	**Base Calendar**
Work (Budget)	X	X	X	X	Select
Material (Budget)	unit of measure	X	X	X	X
Cost (Budget)	X	X	X	X	X

You must assign budget resources to the project summary task (ID=0); budget resources can only be assigned to the project summary task, not to regular detail tasks.

Then you enter budget values in the assignment-related or time-phased **Budget Cost** or **Budget Work** fields (depending on whether you choose **Cost** or **Work** for the type of resource). These fields are accessible in the Resource Usage or Task Usage view only. We will discuss this in more detail next.

Cost Budgeting

This feature allows you to create a budget and to compare its amounts with cost forecasts during the *project execution* phase or actual costs after completion. The feature is not intuitively understood, so carefully follow these steps:

1. In the Resource Sheet, create budget resources and give them distinct names with *Budget* as their prefix, for example *Budget Labor, Budget Travel* etcetera. Monetary budget resources have the field **Type** set to **Cost** and the field **Budget** set to **Yes**.
2. Switch to the Gantt Chart. Display the project summary task: Click the **Format** ribbon in a task view and select [✓ Project Summary Task].
3. Assign the budget resources to the *project summary task* (ID=0); see page 361 for the how-to on assigning.
4. Click ribbon **View** and click the top part of 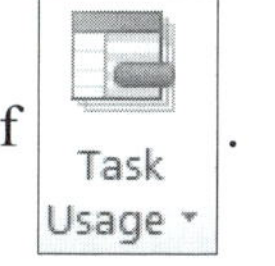.
5. Zoom the timescale to display months using the **View** ribbon by selecting **Months** from the list [Timescale: Weeks] that may currently display a different time unit.
6. Prepare the view for entering monetary values into the timescale: Insert the editable fields in the timescale by right-clicking in the timescale pane and selecting **Detail Styles** and selecting the field **Budget Cost** from the list **Available Fields** on the left and clicking [Show >>]. Click [OK].
7. You can now enter values in each month in the timescale in this **Budget Cost** field for the assignments of the project summary task. Notice that you can use the fill feature to quickly enter the same number in adjacent cells. Like Excel, you can enter the first number and then drag the fill handle:

The result could look like this for the first half of the budget year:

	Task Name	Details	2012 Jan	Feb	Mar	Apr	May	Jun
0	Project XYZ	Budget Cost	$4,004,000	$4,006,000	$4,002,000	$4,004,000	$4,005,000	$4,006,000
		Budget Work						
	Budget travel	Budget Cost	$4,000	$6,000	$2,000	$4,000	$5,000	$6,000
		Budget Work						
	Budget Labor	Budget Cost	$4,000,000	$4,000,000	$4,000,000	$4,000,000	$4,000,000	$4,000,000
		Budget Work						

Notice this is task 0, the project summary task. The items below it are indented and in italics; they are assignments of a budgetary resource.

Cost Situations

We will explore the kinds of costs you will encounter in practice and how to enter them into MS Project.

Economists distinguish between variable cost and fixed cost:

- Variable costs can vary with the amount of time needed, units consumed or number of times used. *Labor cost* is a variable, time-related human resource cost. *Facilities* can also have time-related costs, like rent or lease expenses. *Machines* can have:
  - time-related cost such as rent,
  - unit-related cost such as for paper used in a newspaper printing press, or
  - use-related cost such as the setup cost of the printing press. This can be entered in the **Cost/Use** field if the cost is incurred on every use of the resource. Another example is the up-front cost to transport a bulldozer to the construction site.
- Fixed costs do not vary with anything (that you can enter into MS Project) unlike the variable costs. Fixed costs can be associated with:
  - Resources: for example, expenses for travel.
  - Tasks: for example, expenses for any fixed price contracts given to subcontractors.

The following table provides an overview and examples of the different types of costs as well as the way we recommend you enter these costs into MS Project:

Cost Type	Example	Type	Rate Column	Accrue at
Time related	3 days of work @ 300/d	Work	Std. Rate	Prorated
	2 months' rent @ 400/mo	Material [45]	Std. Rate	Prorated
Unit related	3 doors @ 150/door	Material	Std. Rate	Start
Use related	$200 up front for bulldozer transport	Material	Cost/Use	Start
Varying rate	Work @ $300/d, after January 1st $350/d	Work	Cost Rate Table	Prorated
Fixed Cost for resources	Airfare of $450 up front	Cost	Assign Resources dialog: Cost	Start
Fixed cost for tasks	Fixed price contract painting the house: $8,500	—	Gantt Chart: Fixed Cost	Gantt Chart: Fixed Cost Accrual [46]

The first question we have to answer for the expense is: what **Type** of resource should we make it: *Work, Material* or *Cost*? Then the rate needs to be entered in the appropriate rate field; MS Project has many resource-related rate columns: **Std. Rate** (*Standard Rate* field)**, Ovt. Rate** (*Overtime Rate* field)**, Cost/Use** (*Cost per Use* field), see page 298 for a description.

---

[45] If you make the facility a **Material** resource, you have to enter the *consumption rate* in the assignment **Units** field (see page 378) in order to get a time-related cost. The consumption rate is the number of "*units*" used per time unit.

[46] The task-related field **Fixed Cost Accrual** has the same options as its resource-related sister field: **Accrue At: Start, Prorated** or **End**.

7

In the field *Accrue At*, you determine when the cost will take place:

- If you select **Start**, the cost will be scheduled on the start date of the assignment. Actual costs will be incurred on the **Actual Start** date.
- If you select **Prorated** the cost is spread across the task duration proportional to the number of hours that are scheduled to be worked on each day. This will only be in effect during the *planning* of the project; during project *execution*, the *actual costs* accrue on the dates on which the *actual hours* were worked times the standard rate of the resource.
- If you select **End** the cost accrues on the finish date of the task. Actual costs will be incurred on the **Actual Finish** date.

Material costs often accrue at the start since you need to buy them before use, whereas facility and machine costs often accrue as prorated. For human resource costs, employees are typically prorated, whereas cost for consultants is often incurred at the end. The **Cost/Use** (**Cost per Use** field) can be incurred at the start or the end of the task. Even if you select prorated, it will be incurred at the start.

MS Project has **Cost** resources (as set in the resource-related field **Type**) and a corresponding field **Cost** (assignment-related) in the **Assign Resources** dialog that can be edited for **Cost** resources only. You can also access this field in either the Task Usage or Resource Usage views. This field allows you to:

- Capture expenses like airfare, hotel and food, or license expenses for software, trademarks or patents
- Separate capital expenses from operating expenses. You can do this by creating separate **Cost** resources for capital expenses, like *capital real estate* or *capital equipment*. Even labor can sometimes be capitalized, often when it is related to R&D.

MS Project also has task-related cost fields: *Fixed Cost* and *Fixed Cost Accrual*. These fields are accessible in the task views and are useful for entering fixed price contracts. Fixed price contracts often relate directly to a deliverable. It makes sense to enter them into the task-related field **Fixed Cost**.

In practice, you will find more variations:

- A resource can have more than one type of cost associated with it. For example, a maintenance man can have a per-use fee of $50 for travel in addition to an hourly rate of $100. In this case, you would enter the per-use fee in the **Cost/Use** column (**Cost per Use** field) and the hourly rate in the **Std. Rate** column (**Standard Rate** field).
- The cost rates themselves can change over time; this is known as *varying cost rates* or *rate profile*. In MS Project you can capture a rate profile in the feature *Cost Rate Table* by double-clicking on the resource and clicking the tab **Costs**.

Depending on when the effort is scheduled, MS Project will automatically take the appropriate rate to calculate the cost (see page 339 for more).

- You can have multiple *cost rate tables* per resource. MS Project provides up to five tables for each resource (A through E), so you can create five *rate profiles* per resource (see page 339). If you have a *jack-of-all-trades* resource that does systems analysis, programming and occasionally some testing as well, you could specify different rate profiles (**A, B** and **C**) for each of these three different activities. This is important if the effort is billed to clients with rates that are different for each type of work. When you *assign* the resource, you have to indicate per assignment which rate profile you would like to use. We will discuss this on page 388.
- Materials may have a *consumption rate*. The consumption rate of materials is how many units of the material are used per time unit. For example, you pour concrete that costs $1 per cubic foot and you know that you typically pour 2000 cubic feet a day with your crew of five. This consumption rate can be entered into the assignment-related **Units** field when you assign the resource to the task. In the **Assign Resources** dialog you would enter *2000/day* in the field **Units**. If the duration of the task is 3 days, the cost will be:
  3 days * 2000/day * $1/cubic foot = $6000.
  The duration of the task will determine the total cost for the task, and if the duration expands, more units of material will be consumed, which will increase the cost of the task. Essentially you have modeled a *time-related cost* for material resources. See page 338 for more details.
- You may need to attribute a portion of a large *capital cost* expenditure to a project. For example, you may need to buy expensive test equipment that will be used in future projects as well. You only want part of this capital expense charged to your project (i.e., the part that your project uses and should carry as an expense). If you know the amount you can enter it into the task field **Fixed Cost**, or you can create a separate **Cost** resource, called *Capital Equipment* for it. MS Project does not have features to calculate the amount to charge to one project (also known as *depreciation cost)*. You will have to revert to *MS Excel* to calculate the contribution of the project to the capital expense.
- You may encounter volume discounts when purchasing large amounts of supplies or raw materials; you would need a lookup table with all rate segments. This is something MS Project cannot easily handle. Again, you need to revert to *MS Excel.*
- You may need to charge taxes or subtract refundable taxes to the cost amounts. Again, MS Project does not have features for this and *MS Excel* or your accounting system might help.

Pro

We will now discuss how to enter the different cost situations. As a project manager in a *Project Server* environment, you may not have the proper access privileges to add or change resource rates in the enterprise resource pool. However, you will still need to know how to review the rates and enter the rates for the *local resources* (the resources that are in your project only).

Entering Human Resource Costs

For example, if you temporarily hire a programmer at $600/day, you can enter this in the resource sheet with the following steps:

1. Click ribbon **View** and click Resource Sheet.
2. Enter the name of the resource in the field **Resource Name**.
3. Leave the **Type** of the resource set to the default setting of **Work**.
4. Enter the rate in the column **Std. Rate (Standard Rate** field**)**; for the programmer you would enter *$600/d*.
5. Enter the other cost rates in the **Ovt. Rate** column (**Overtime Rate** field) and **Cost/Use** (**Cost per Use** field), if applicable.
6. Select an **Accrue At** option; select **Start**, **Prorated** or **End**. The accrual determines when the cost will be incurred in the schedule and is important for cash-flow reports.
7. Assign the human resources to the tasks, which we will discuss in the next chapter.

Entering Material Costs for Consumable Materials

You should incorporate the cost of material into the project model only:

- if it will be paid from your project budget, and
- if it is significant enough to track.
  Please do not work with MS Project as if it were your accounting system by tracking each small expense separately. We recommend you create a petty cash **Cost** resource and manage it as a separate budget line item.

If a material expense meets these two criteria, you can enter it in this way:

1. Click ribbon **View** and click Resource Sheet.
2. Enter the name of the resource in the field **Resource Name**.
3. Click in the field **Type** for the resource and a list button appears Work – select **Material** from this list.

4. Enter a **Material Label**, which will show up in other views to remind users that this resource is a material resource.
   - For *unit resources*, enter the label in plural, for example *bricks* instead of *brick*, because you typically *assign* more than one unit. You can even enter *thousand bricks* if you will enter the cost of 1000 bricks in the **Std. Rate** column (**Standard Rate** field) instead of the cost of one brick.
   - For *bulk resources*, you have to enter the *unit of measurement*; for example, for concrete this would be *cubic yards* or *cubic meters*, and for cables it would be *feet* or *meters*.
5. In the **Std. Rate** column (**Standard Rate** field), enter the cost per unit (or unit of measurement) for this resource. For the bricks you could enter *$2.00,* for example. Notice that you cannot enter the time unit (*/h* or */d*) for material resources; you need to use *consumption rates* to model time-related cost for material resources (see page 338).
6. You can fill in the **Cost/Use** column (**Cost per Use** field) as well; for the bricks this could be the cost of transportation to the site, let's say *$400.00*.
7. The overtime rate field is neither available nor needed for material resources.
8. Select the **Accrue At** method to determine the date on which the cost will be scheduled in a time-phased view. You can select **Start**, **Prorated** or **End.** Materials often accrue at the start. Prorated means that the cost is spread evenly with the number of hours that resources work on each day of the task duration. The **Cost/Use** is always incurred at the start of the task and cannot be changed.

The next screenshot of the **Resource Usage** view shows how the accrual for material costs works. The 1,000 bricks cost $2 each and accrue at the start of the task: 1,000 * 2 = $2,000. The mortar costs $5 per cubic foot and accrues evenly with the hours worked on the task. The 4 trowels at $20 each accrue at the end of the task:

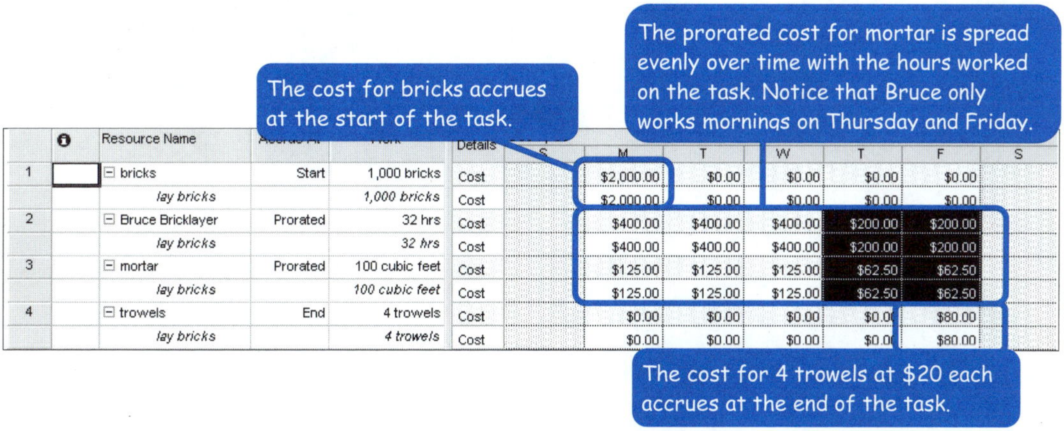

The cost for bricks accrues at the start of the task.

The prorated cost for mortar is spread evenly over time with the hours worked on the task. Notice that Bruce only works mornings on Thursday and Friday.

	❶	Resource Name			Details	S	M	T	W	T	F	S
1		⊟ bricks	Start	1,000 bricks	Cost		$2,000.00	$0.00	$0.00	$0.00	$0.00	
		lay bricks		*1,000 bricks*	Cost		$2,000.00	$0.00	$0.00	$0.00	$0.00	
2		⊟ Bruce Bricklayer	Prorated	32 hrs	Cost		$400.00	$400.00	$400.00	$200.00	$200.00	
		lay bricks		*32 hrs*	Cost		$400.00	$400.00	$400.00	$200.00	$200.00	
3		⊟ mortar	Prorated	100 cubic feet	Cost		$125.00	$125.00	$125.00	$62.50	$62.50	
		lay bricks		*100 cubic feet*	Cost		$125.00	$125.00	$125.00	$62.50	$62.50	
4		⊟ trowels	End	4 trowels	Cost		$0.00	$0.00	$0.00	$0.0	$80.00	
		lay bricks		*4 trowels*	Cost		$0.00	$0.00	$0.00	$0.0	$80.00	

The cost for 4 trowels at $20 each accrues at the end of the task.

We still need to learn how to assign the number of material resources to the tasks. We will discuss assigning on page 361.

Entering Material Costs for Facilities and Machines

The time-related cost for facilities, like rental and lease, can be entered as material costs. This is the most difficult cost situation to enter into MS Project. The use of facilities and machines should not add to the **Work** (effort) of the project, which means that they have to be entered as **Material** resources. However, material resources cannot have a time-related rate, like *$400/day*, into the *Standard Rate*, which is quite common for facilities and equipment rental. You can enter only unit- or use-related cost. If you pay a fixed amount for every use of a training room, you can enter that cost in the **Cost/Use** field.

The best way to model time-related cost for facility and machine resources is to enter the resource as a *Material* resource and use the *consumption rate* feature as a workaround to model its time-related cost for the task. The consumption rate is entered into the assignment-related *Units* field, which is found in the *Assign Resources* dialog or the *Task Form*. For example, you organize training and the training room costs your project $600/day. Enter the resource *training room* as a **Material** resource in the Resource Sheet and enter *$600* as the **Standard Rate**. Then, create the *train employees* task and assign the training room as the resource. Enter the consumption rate of *1/d* as the **Units** for the assignment to indicate that you will use one room per day.

This will appear in the Gantt Chart as follows:

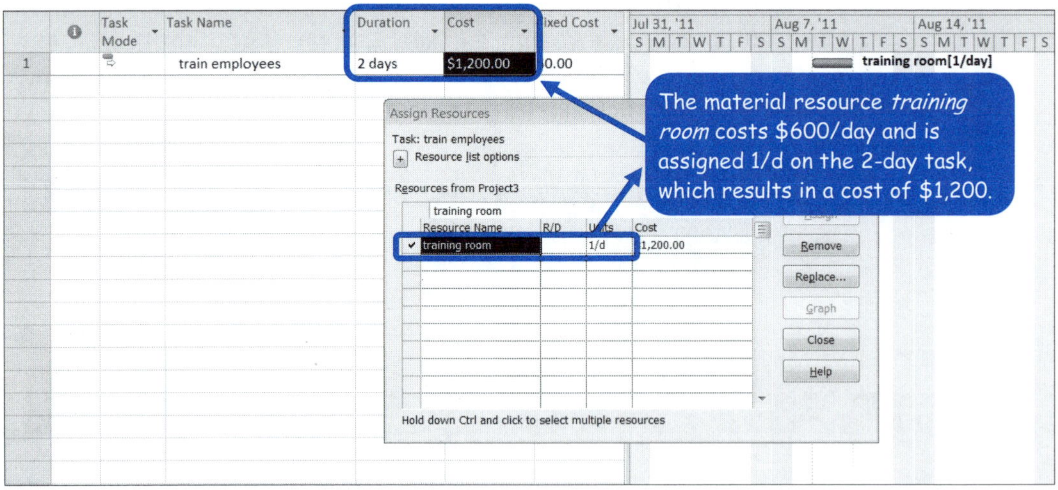

As you can see, we have used the consumption rate feature in MS Project to work around the lack of a specific resource type for facilities. We can use this same workaround model to time-related cost for renting equipment, for example. Facility and machine costs are often accrued as prorated or at the end of a task.

Entering Varying Cost Rates for Labor or Materials

Cost rates can vary over time which creates a *rate profile*. You can enter varying cost rates in the cost rate table in the **Resource Information** dialog:

1. Click ribbon **View** and click Resource Sheet.
2. Double-click a resource and the **Resource Information** dialog appears. Click the tab **Costs** and the dialog will look like:

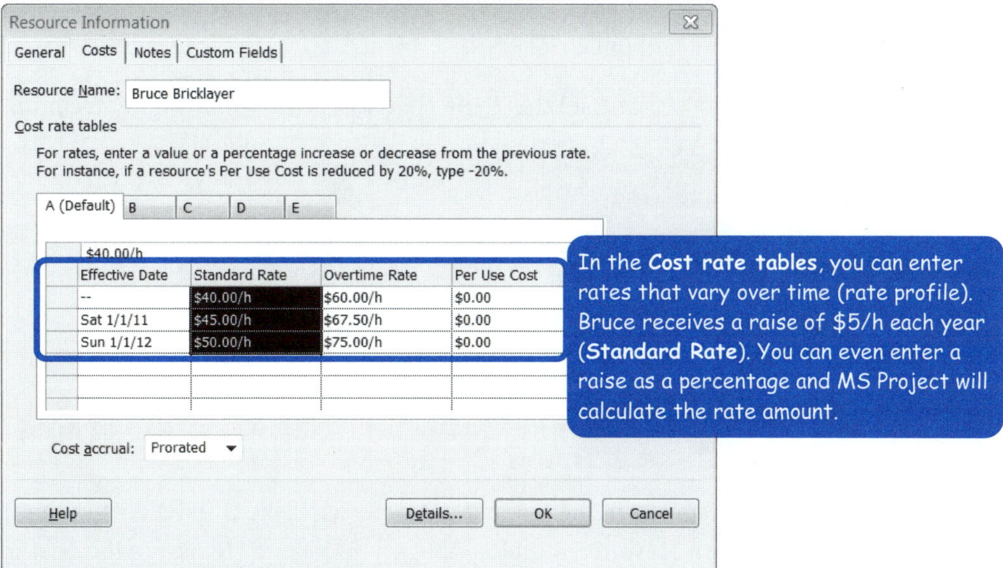

3. Enter the **Effective Date.**
4. Enter the rates that will apply after that date.
   OR
   Enter the percentage change that you want to apply to the previous rate. MS Project will calculate the new rate for you. For example, if there is an increase of 10%, you enter +10%; for a decrease, -10%.
5. Repeat the previous steps as many times as the rate will change over time.
6. Click OK. MS Project will calculate cost using the applicable rate. The rate MS Project uses depends on when the task is scheduled over time.

Multiple rates per resource are used in:

- Consulting firms: IT resources have multiple rates depending on the type of work they are hired to do: analysis, programming or testing.
- Oil industry: an oilrig worker gets higher pay for offshore work as opposed to onshore work.
- Defense contracting: In MS Project, you can create rate profiles for all the different types of costs: **Standard Rate**, **Overtime Rate** and **Per Use Cost** (same as **Cost/Use**). This *rate escalation* feature is of particular benefit in multi-year defense contracts in which new military equipment is envisioned and developed by the government.

Entering Fixed Costs for Resources

The **Cost** resources are useful for capturing travel expenses like airfare, hotel and food.

1. Click ribbon **View** and click Resource Sheet.
2. Create a new resource and set the **Type** field to **Cost**. Notice that you cannot enter **Max Units** or rates.
3. Click ribbon **View** and click the top part of Gantt Chart.
4. To display the **Assign Resources** dialog, click ribbon **Resource** and  

.
5. Select the cost resource in the list and enter the associated fixed cost in the field **Cost** in the **Assign Resources** dialog. Click Assign to assign the cost resource to the task. You should now see that the cost is added to the total **Cost** of the task.

Let us say a programmer *Ted Bitmaker* (rate $800/day) needs to travel for training (cost resource named *Travel*): Airfare, hotel and food will cost $1,200. This would look like:

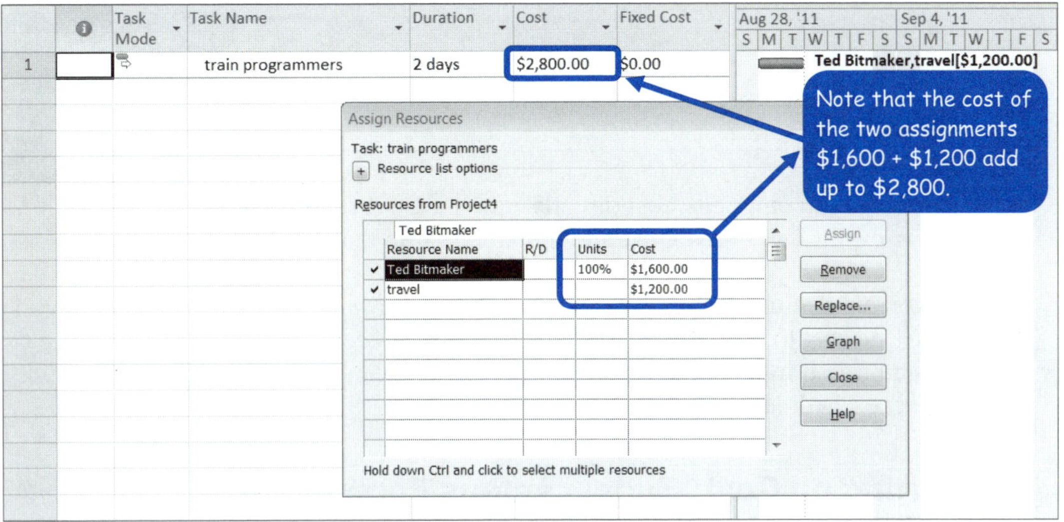

7

Entering Fixed Cost Contracts for Tasks

You can enter fixed cost contracts as a task-related cost in the Gantt Chart in the column **Fixed Cost.**

1. Click ribbon **View** and click 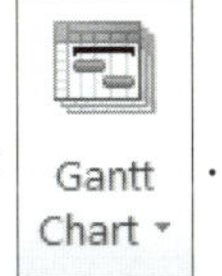

.

2. Insert the column **Fixed Cost** and **Fixed Cost Accrual** or apply the table **Cost**.

3. Enter the fixed cost value in the field **Fixed Cost**. Also indicate when to accrue the fixed cost in the field **Fixed Cost Accrual.** Your choices are at the **Start** of the task, **Prorated** or at the **End** (finish date). Notice that *Prorated* fixed cost will be spread evenly over the entire duration of the task, regardless of the spread of the effort. All resource-related costs, on the other hand, are spread similarly to the spread of the effort.

4. MS Project will then calculate the *total cost* for the task in the field **Cost** as: *Cost = Fixed Cost (task) + (fixed cost resources) + (material costs) + (labor costs).* The next screenshot shows the **Task Usage** view to illustrate this formula. The total

cost of $3,800 for the task *lay bricks* consists of *$600 fixed cost*, *$2,000* material cost for the bricks and *$1,200* labor cost for the bricklayers:

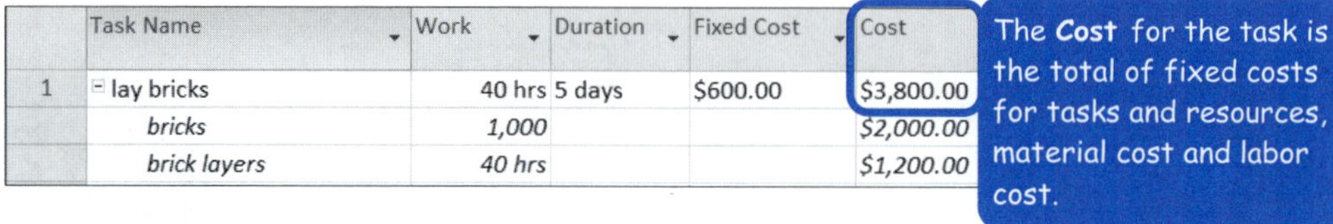

	Task Name	Work	Duration	Fixed Cost	Cost
1	lay bricks	40 hrs	5 days	$600.00	$3,800.00
	bricks	*1,000*			*$2,000.00*
	brick layers	*40 hrs*			*$1,200.00*

Notice that if you enter any cost directly into the **Cost** field for a task, MS Project interprets the cost as **Fixed Cost** and transfers it into that field.

When you are dealing with *capital costs*, *volume discounts* or *taxes,* we recommend you calculate the cost to attribute to your project in *MS Excel*. Then copy the resulting cost value and paste it into the task-related *Fixed Cost* field or other appropriate field in your MS Project schedule.

Reporting on Cost: Budget versus Forecast Cost

1. Add a pull-down list to a resource-related **Text** field that lists the different types of budget *expense categories*, like *labor (external/internal), facilities, machines, material, capital and travel*. Name the field *Expense Categories* or something descriptive (see page 557 for how-to steps on customizing fields).
2. Code all resources (including the budget resources) using the new, custom field *Expense Categories*. This tells MS Project under what expense category their cost should be aggregated in the field **Budget Cost**. MS Project aggregates the cost in a time-phased manner.
3. Group the resources on the new field *Expense Categories* to view how they compare against the budget. Create a new grouping by clicking **Project, Group by <name of current group>, More groups**. In order to compare budget with latest forecasts, insert the columns **Budget Cost** and **Cost**. The field **Cost** contains the latest forecast of the total cost for the resource.
4. Set the decimals for cost to zero decimals; click ribbon **File**, Options, tab **Display**, set field **Decimal Digits** to 0.

The final result of this complex procedure will be a view in which you can track the budget expense categories and compare them to the currently forecasted cost for each category at each status date during the execution of the project. This allows you to get a handle on the cost side of the project as well:

	Resource Name	Budget Cost	Cost
	⊟ **facilities**	**$108,000.00**	**$130,350.00**
5	budget cost facilities	$108,000.00	
19	meeting facilities		$1,200.00
20	work facilities		$129,150.00
	⊟ **labor (external)**	**$143,000.00**	**$90,543.75**
6	budget cost labor (external)	$143,000.00	
9	the contractor		$52,650.00
10	the LAN consultants		$33,750.00
11	the movers		$3,750.00
12	the realtor		$393.75
	⊟ **labor (internal)**	**$43,500.00**	**$37,781.25**
7	budget cost labor (internal)	$43,500.00	
13	John Falgon		$675.00
14	Nancy Hilcrest		$1,575.00
16	Nelson Salin		$1,125.00
15	Pierre Roach		$281.25
17	the employees		$26,250.00
18	you		$7,875.00
	⊟ **material**	**$8,000.00**	**$800.00**
21	boxes		$800.00
8	budget cost materials	$8,000.00	

This budget shows that the project manager budgeted spending of *$143,000* (**Budget Cost**) on *labor (external)* (subcontractors) and is currently forecasting that only *$90,543* will be spent (**Cost**).

The **Budget Cost** is created top-down on the project summary task, whereas the **Cost** is aggregated bottom-up from the detail tasks. You can see that this budgeting feature can be a tremendous help to keep the project on track financially.

Checks on the Resources

The following checks need to be performed to verify whether the resources have been modeled well. The numbering corresponds to the complete checklist in the summary chapter, see page 711:

7 Resources

7.1. Are all resources identified in the Resource Sheet?
This is the case if all resources that could have a potential impact on the project schedule are entered into the Resource Sheet. Resources can have an impact on *scope*, *quality*, *duration* or *cost* of the project. If you expect an impact, you should enter those resources and assign them to the tasks in the project to create a *resource-loaded schedule*:

- ◇ Where you expect that limited resource availability or huge workloads will affect the forecasted end date of the project, see page 294.
- ◇ Where you expect that significant differences in the productivity of resources will affect the forecasts. In programming computer applications, for example, it is well known that one programmer can finish a module in hours, whereas another needs days.
- ◇ If you have a *cost budget* for the project and you are responsible for staying within that budget.
- ◇ If you have an *effort budget* expressed in *person months* or *person days* and you have to stay within this effort budget. This is quite common in government IT projects.
- ◇ If you foresee a *quality* or *scope* impact on the project depending on which resources you will get.

7.2. Are all resources named consistently using a naming convention like *<first name> <last name>* or *<last name>-<first name>*?
Note that a comma as a separator between last name and first name is not allowed because MS Project uses this as its default *list separator* for when there are multiple values shown in one cell. We do not recommend changing this list separator in the Control Panel because the setting is machine-dependent and will not allow you to give your schedule to someone else.

7.3. Are there no overlaps between the resources or duplication of resources?
If there are overlaps or duplications of resources, the workload and availability numbers will be useless when you start checking on overallocations. For example, if *Bill Tan* is listed twice as a resource (*Bill Tan* and *William Tan*), you would have to sum all time-phased workloads of *Bill Tan* and *William Tan* in order to determine if he is overallocated.

There is also duplication if *Bill Tan* is listed individually and also as part of a *consolidated resource*. When there are overlaps or duplications, the workloads appear to be smaller and the availability greater than they really are. This may affect the validity of the forecasts in the schedule; it can make the forecasts too optimistic.

7.4. Is the availability of the resources appropriately modeled?
The limited availability of expert resources often affects forecast dates. Check if the availability is modeled properly by asking yourself the following questions:

- ◇ Does the availability of individuals not exceed 48 hours per week in the working times on the resource calendar, or 120% in the resource field **Max Units** (or in the **Resource Availability** profile in the **Resource Information** dialog, tab **General**)? See page 318 for the reason why.
- ◇ If the **Max Units** are less than 100%, is there a valid reason for this? The only valid reason is if the resource has other work or other projects. In any other case including part-time resources, we recommended adjusting the working times on the resource calendar instead, see page 322 for why.
- ◇ Are the working times on the resource calendar appropriate?
The working times need to be adjusted, if the project manager collects *pure work time* estimates from the team members (see page 181) instead of *gross work time* estimates, or if the resource is a part-time resource instead of a full-time resource, see page 322.
- ◇ Are the vacations of individual resources captured in their resource calendar?
Vacations need to be entered, particularly when there are important deadlines close to the vacations. To check whether they are entered, click ribbon **Project**, button **Change Working Time**; select the resource name from the list labeled **For**. Click the tab **Exceptions** and you will see individual vacations listed that are departures from the **Base calendar** for the resource. The bias in the forecasts can be as much as10% if you do not capture individual vacations, since resources in Europe typically have 5 weeks of vacation in 52 weeks per year.
- ◇ If the project resources are located and working in multiple countries, are base calendars created for each country? Do all resources have the proper country calendar entered in their field **Base Calendar** (see page 311)?

7.5. Do all resources have their **Type** field set right?

- ◇ Are human resources entered as **Work** resources in the resource field **Type**?

7

- ◇ Are resource-related fixed costs captured using the type of **Cost** resources?
- ◇ Are facilities, machines and materials entered as **Material** resources, see our discussion on page 338?
- ◇ Do *consumable* or *bulk resources* have an appropriate **Material Label** to indicate their unit of measure? The *material label* should reflect the unit of measure, for example, the material label for cables could be *feet, yards* or *meters*.

7.6. Are the rates entered in the appropriate fields?

- ◇ Time-related costs for **Work** resources in the **Std. Rate** column **(Standard Rate** field)
- ◇ Unit-related cost for **Material** resources in the **Std. Rate** column **(Standard Rate** field)
- ◇ Time-related cost for facilities and machines as **Material** resources using two fields: in the **Std. Rate** column **(Standard Rate** field) you enter the per-unit cost, and in the assignment-related **Units** field you enter the number of units used per time unit (as the *consumption rate),* see page 338.
- ◇ Use-related costs in the column **Cost/Use** (field **Cost per Use**).
- ◇ Overtime costs in the **Ovt. Rate** column (**Overtime Rate** field), but only if the overtime is paid and also paid at a higher rate than the standard rate (see page 326 for more detail).
- ◇ Rates that vary over time in the **Cost Rate Tables** (see page 339).
- ◇ Multiple rates per resource in the five **Cost Rate Tables** and the appropriate cost rate table (A, B, C, D or E) selected for each assignment, see page 339.
- ◇ Resource-related fixed costs in the assignment-related **Cost** field that is visible in the **Assign Resources** dialog (see page 340)?
- ◇ Task- or deliverable-related fixed costs in the task-related **Fixed Cost** field in the Gantt Chart view (see page 341 for more).

7.7. Is the cost scheduled when it will occur?
This is important for managing the cash-flow of the project: Can bills be paid when they are supposed to be paid?

- ◇ Does the resource-related field **Accrue At** reflect when the cost occurs: at the **Start** or at the **End**, or **Prorated** with the time-phased amount of work?
- ◇ Does the task-related **Fixed Cost Accrual** field reflect when the fixed cost will be incurred?

Exercises

Review A

Is it possible to model the following availability situations in MS Project? If so, how?

1. Movers who only work during the weekends
2. A free-lancer who typically works on the weekend and delivers the work on Monday
3. Somebody who works a compressed workweek of 10 hours per day and 4 days per week
4. An expert resource that will be available to your project for 10% in March, 20% in April and 50% in May; after that, she is unavailable
5. A part-time resource that only works mornings on Tuesdays and Thursdays

Review B

Which of the following resources should have its workload leveled in MS Project? Enter **Yes** or **No** in the column *Level Workloads* and explain your answer.

Resource	Level Workloads?
1. expert	
2. computer	
3. mortar	
4. boardroom	

Review C

Is it possible to model the following cost situations in MS Project? If so, how? If not, what would be a possible workaround?

1. Up-front fee of $500 for a bulldozer at a rate of $1,000/d for onsite work
2. A consultant who charges $400/d until January 1, then $450/d
3. Car rental with free mileage for the first 100 miles, then a fee of $0.45/mile
4. Penalty of $1,000/d for delivering late
5. Harry, who works as a business analyst at $500/d and as a systems analyst for $400/d
6. Volume discount for materials (for example, if you buy one door, it costs $150; if you buy 10 doors or more, they cost $90 each)
7. Pay an invoice within 30 days or pay an additional late charge of 10% of the invoice amount
8. Overtime hours accumulated throughout the year and paid at the end of the year
9. Courier costs for packages
10. Low and high season rates for hotel rooms (for example, in New York the hotel rates double in December)
11. Travel costs like $440 for an airfare and $300 for the hotel

Relocation Project — Entering Resources

The goal of this exercise is to be able to enter resources into a new schedule.

Continue to work with your file *Relocation.mpp* or open the file *07A Resources.mpp* available for download at www.ProjectProCorp.com (see page vi for the procedure to access these files).

1. See table below: The fields *Position* and *Function* are not standard fields in MS Project; you will have to create them. Click ribbon **Project**, button **Custom Fields**; select ◉ **Resource** and select from the list **Type**, the item **Text** to display extra text fields. Click Rename... and rename field **Text1** to *Position* and **Text2** to *Function.*
2. Customize the table for the Resource Sheet view as shown in the table below. You will need to insert the fields *Position* and *Function* and remove some other fields (see page 308 for detailed steps).
3. Notice that in the table below we present the **Max Units** in decimals, whereas MS Project shows percentages by default. Click ribbon **File**, Options, tab **Schedule** and, in the section **Schedule**, change **Show Assignment units as a** to **Decimal**.
4. Enter the resources from the table below into the Resource Sheet. Use the **Fill Down** feature (see page 194 for steps) for the columns *Function* and *Accrue at*. Notice that there are generic resources in the table, like *movers*. There is no **Cost/Use** for these resources.
5. Sort the list of resources on resource *Name* as the first sorting key (ribbon **View**, button **Sort**, item **Sort By**). Select the option to permanently renumber the resources.
6. *Nancy Hilcrest* will go on a 1-week vacation in the third full week of August 2012, see page 314 for steps. Create an **Exception** called *Vacation Nancy*.
7. You realize that due to the project requirement of minimal disruption to normal operations, the move will have to take place over the weekend. Set the weekend days to working days and all the weekdays to nonworking days for the resource *movers,* see page 314 for steps. The result should be that the move task takes place over a weekend once the *movers* are assigned to the task. The *movers* will work 8 hours per weekend day.
8. Compare your file with the solution file *08A Assignments.mpp* available for download at www.ProjectProCorp.com (see page vi for the procedure to access

7

these files). See page 697 of this book for an automated way of comparing and reporting differences between two versions of one schedule. Make sure you select to compare the resource information by selecting the **Resource Table** named **Entry**.

Resource Name	**Type**	**Material Label**	**Position**	**Function**	Max Units	**Std. Rate**	**Accrue at**
<enter your own name here>	Work		project manager	manager	1	$75/h	Pro-rated
Nelson Salin	Work		CEO	manager	1	$150/h	Pro-rated
John Falgon	Work		employee represen-tative	employee	1	$30/h	Pro-rated
Nancy Hilcrest	Work		planner	employee	1	$35/h	Pro-rated
Pierre Roach	Work		Lawyer	external	1	$75/h	Pro-rated
the employees	Work		employees	employee	75	$25/h	Pro-rated
the contractor	Work		contractor	external	50	$30/h	End
the realtor	Work		Realtor	external	1	$35/h	End
the movers	Work		movers	external	40	$25/h	End
the LAN consultants	Work		LAN consul-tants	external	20	$75/h	End
Boxes	Mat-erial	boxes		material		$2	Start

Chapter 8 Entering Assignments

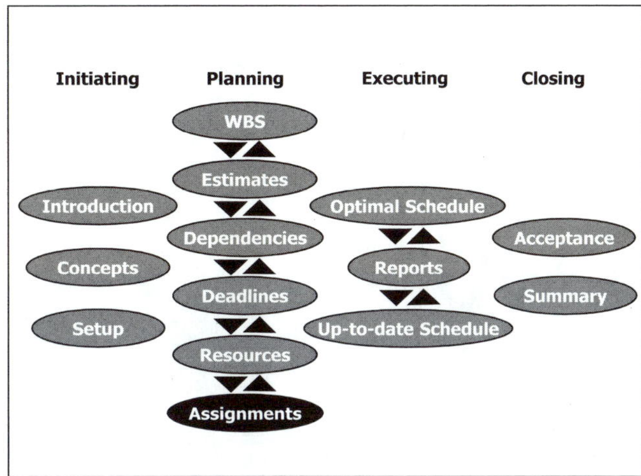

The assignments are the last type of data to enter into our project schedule (see the black ellipse in the illustration above). After completing this chapter, we will have a draft schedule of our project that contains the workloads of the resources: a *resource-loaded schedule.*

8

After reading this chapter you will:

- know what an assignment is as well as what part-time and full-time assignments are
- know the difference between Fixed Duration, Fixed Units and Fixed Work tasks
- be able to enter each type of task into MS Project
- know how to assign resources using the Team Planner view, Assign Resources dialog or the Task Form view
- be able to enter part-time, full-time and team resource assignments
- be able to assign efficiently: assign multiple resources to multiple tasks
- know how to make changes to assignments while controlling the resulting calculations by MS Project
- be able to check if the assignments reflect the best practices of scheduling
- know how to create a report of the assignments

The Tug of War for Expert Resources

"Hey Nob, can I borrow Mary from you for a while? I heard she is not doing much on your project right now."

"No, you can't have her; she is committed to my project", Nob exclaims in horror.
The thought occurs to Nob that if he lends Mary out, his project may fall apart. Mary is his top system analyst, and Bob knows this all too well!

Bob insists: "But Nob ... Mary is expensive and our bosses want us to use her time as efficiently as we can! A friend of Mary told me she has to wait two weeks for input from the client." As he speaks these words, Bob is thinking that if he can get Mary started on his project, he might reel her into tackling some of the tough challenges. After all, she is his best bet to finish his project on time.

Nob is surprised by the intelligence Bob has gathered about Mary's workload: "Bob, I have plenty of work for her!" But Nob also realizes that this might be a bit of an overstatement.

Bob hopes that an exact commitment might convince Nob: "Can I have her for just one week? I guarantee you will have her back after that."

What Is an Assignment?

An *assignment* is a combination of one task and one resource. Assignments reflect who works on a task. In the next screenshot you can see the assignments; *Nancy* is assigned to *summarize requirements* and *visit the sites* among other tasks. Assigning resources to tasks is also called *loading resources*, and the result is a *resource-loaded schedule*.

You can view assignments in either the **Task Usage** view, where they show up as resource names indented below the task name, or in the **Resource Usage** view, where they show up as task names indented below the resource name. You can easily recognize the assignment records, because they have no ID number, their text is in italics and their timescale cells have a lighter background; see the next screenshot:

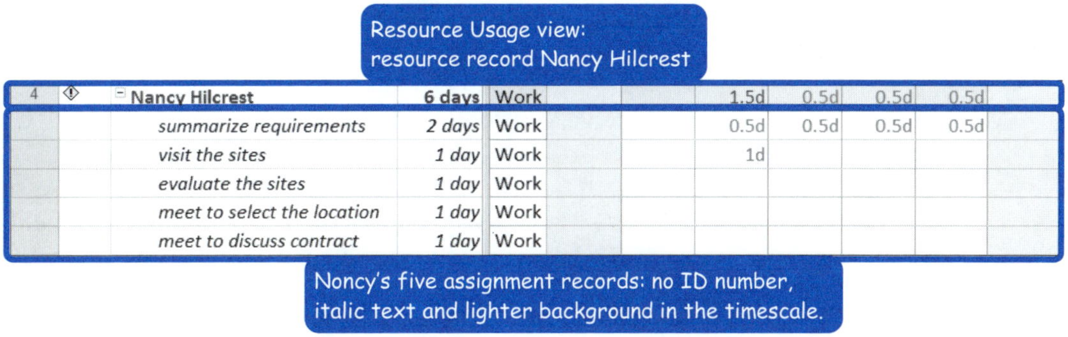

Resource Usage view:
resource record Nancy Hilcrest

4		Nancy Hilcrest	6 days	Work			1.5d	0.5d	0.5d	0.5d	
		summarize requirements	*2 days*	Work			0.5d	0.5d	0.5d	0.5d	
		visit the sites	*1 day*	Work			1d				
		evaluate the sites	*1 day*	Work							
		meet to select the location	*1 day*	Work							
		meet to discuss contract	*1 day*	Work							

Noncy's five assignment records: no ID number,
italic text and lighter background in the timescale.

Double-click on an assignment and the **Assignment Information** dialog will appear with only assignment-specific fields. If you double-click on the resource record, you get the **Resource Information** dialog.

Assignment-Specific Fields

All three data-entities, *tasks*, *resources* and *assignments*, have their own specific fields. Some fields may have the same name, but contain different information. This depends on whether they belong to the task, resource or assignment. We will discuss three examples in more detail:

- *Start* and *Finish* dates (task, resource and assignment-related)
- *Max Units* (resource-related), *Units* (assignment-related) and *Peak* units (resource- and assignment-related)
- *Work* (task, resource and assignment-related)

8

Start, Start and Start

Tasks, resources and assignments all have **Start** and **Finish** dates, so there is a task-related **Start** field, a resource-related **Start** field and an assignment-related **Start** field. The start date of a task is not necessarily the same as the start date of its assignments. The start date of a task is when any one of the resources starts working on the task. The start date of a resource is her earliest assignment in the entire project. For example, if Mary only works the last 2 days of the 5-day task, the start date of her assignment is different from the start date of the task.

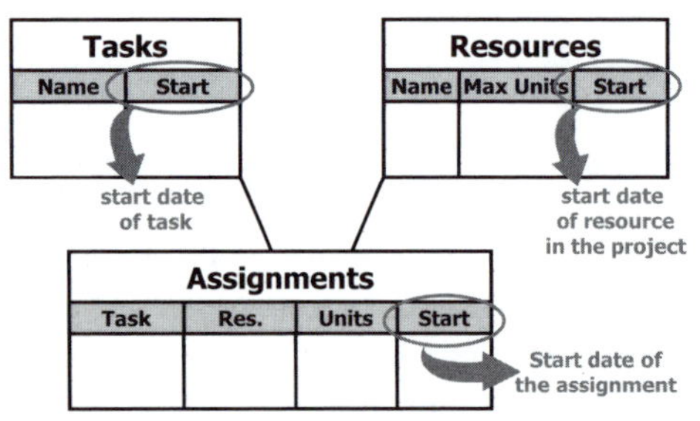

Max Units and Units (Assignment Units) and Peak (Peak Units)

More fields that look alike, but are very different, are:

- resource-related field **Max Units**,
- assignment-related field **Units** that also appears as the **Assignment Units** field in the usage views
- resource- and assignment-related field **Peak** that appears as a resource field as **Peak** but in the usage views it appears in the timescale pane as the *Peak Units* field.

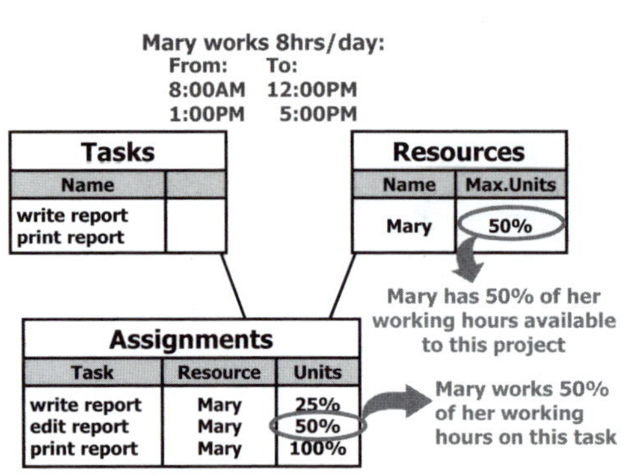

As you can see, Microsoft has not made our life simple here with its naming convention. The **Max Units** field of a resource reflects the maximum availability of the resource to the project. For example, the **Max Units** would be 100% for a person who is available to the project during all of his working hours. **Max Units** would be 50% for a resource who is available half of her working hours. In the illustration, *Mary* has **Max Units** of 50%; she has only *50%* of her working hours available to this project. We discussed resource availability on page 320.

The assignment-related field **Units** on the Assign Resources dialog (which is the same as the **Assignment Units** field) is the percentage of her working hours that the resource is working on the task. In the illustration, Mary works a regular workweek of 8 hours per day, and 50% assignment units means for her 50% * 8 hours = 4 hours of effort per day on the task *edit report* (not 50% * 50% = 25%). Four hours per day equals her maximum availability. If Burke works a compressed workweek of 4 days a week and 10 hours per day, 50% assignment units means 5 hours of effort per working day on his task. MS Project always takes the percentage from the working hours on the resource calendar.

The assignment-related field **Units** (**Assignment Units**) reflects:

- whether a person works all or part of available hours on a task, or
- how many individuals of a *team resource* the task needs (see page 328 for a definition of a team resource).

If you want a resource to work all of her available working hours on the task, simply enter 100% in the field **Units** on the **Assign Resources** dialog. If you enter less than 100%, you are asking the resource to work part of the available time on the task; you have created a *part-time* assignment for a *full-time* employee. In the previous illustration, *Mary* will work *25%* of her working hours on the task *write report*. The assignment units can be changed quickly in the **Assign Resources** dialog (**Resource** ribbon).

In Project 2010, the **Units** field (**Assignment Units**) is no longer a calculated field. You can now only enter values in this field, and it always displays the last value entered; the formula does not affect it any longer. Instead, Microsoft added a new field called **Peak** (called **Peak Units** in the timescale) in which the results of the calculation by the formula are displayed. You enter values in the **Units** field on the Assign Resource dialog or the Task Form, and you monitor the **Peak** units field to see the outcome of the calculation.

The **Peak** field (**Peak Units**) is predominantly assignment-related, but it also displays resource-related values. As a resource-related field, it shows the highest percentage across all the assignments of the resource, an indication of overallocation. As an assignment-related field, it shows the highest percentage across all days of the assignment (all time-phased **Peak Units** values). Most assignments are flat and have just one time-phased percentage. The **Peak** field is calculated by MS Project and is, therefore, an important field to monitor.

In summary:

- The resource field **Max Units** represents entered *availability*.
- The assignment field **Units** (**Assignments Units**) represents entered *usage*.
- The assignment field **Peak** (**Peak Units**) represents calculated *usage*.

Work, Work and Work

The third and last example of how a field is different for tasks, resources and assignments, is the field **Work**. Although they all bear the same name, the field **Work** for tasks in the Gantt spreadsheet is not the same as the field **Work** in the Resource Sheet, nor is it the same as the assignment-related field **Work** on the Task Form. In the Gantt Chart, **Work** is the total effort of all resources working on the task. In the Resource Sheet, **Work** is the total effort for the resource in the entire project. (For material resources, it is the total number of units used in the project.)

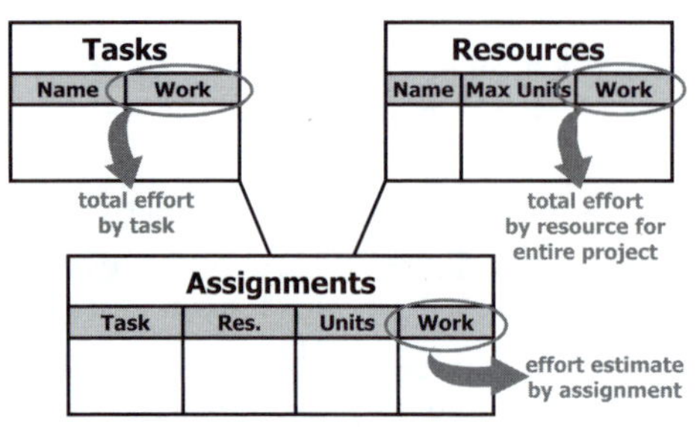

On the Task Form, you see the assignment-related **Work** field, which displays the effort of one resource on one particular task. This is a very low-level estimate and not a total like the other two.

Full-Time or Part-Time Assignment

You can see three different *assignments* in the illustration. In the 100% and the 60% assignment, the work of the resource will be spread evenly across the duration of the task; the work (effort) is spread in a flat *pattern.* You can spread the work over the task duration in eight predefined patterns, and MS Project calls these *work contours*. Alternatively, you can spread the work over the task duration yourself by entering the spread in the time-phased **Work** field in the timescale.

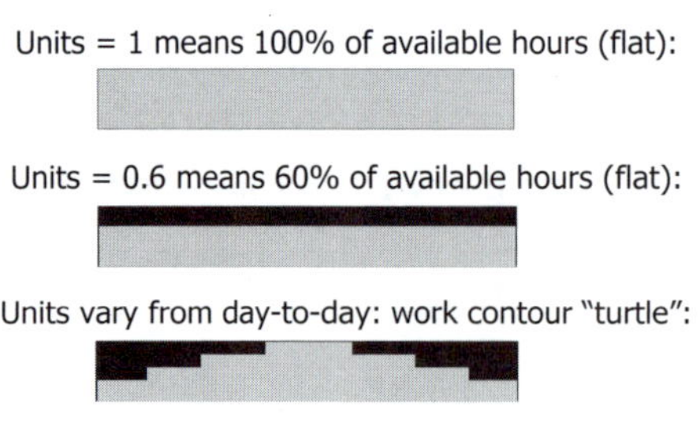

Some remarks about work contours:

- You can apply one of the predefined work contours using the **Assignment Information** dialog. To display the **Assignment Information** dialog, double-click on an assignment (a row without ID number) in either the **Task Usage** or the **Resource Usage** view. You can then select a predefined contour from the list

Work contour. MS Project will maintain the selected pattern of the contour when the duration or the work is changed. Even when the task is in progress, it will maintain the pattern on the remaining duration of the task.

- You can even enter the number of hours that you need from the resource over the duration of the task on a day-by-day basis. You can enter the needed hours directly into the **Work** field of the assignments in the timescale of the **Task Usage** or **Resource Usage** view. This level of detail is seldom needed in the planning of projects.

- If you do decide to enter numbers in the timescale yourself, you will spend a lot of time maintaining your schedule, since MS Project has no clue about your rationale for the spread. This is especially true if you enter the required hours on a day-by-day basis. We do not recommend this, because of the real danger that you will abandon your schedule during project execution when you are simply too busy to maintain that amount of data.

Choosing the Options

The following table shows the assignment-related options. Click ribbon **File**, Options and click on the tab indicated in the table below where you want to change settings:

8

Tab	Option
Schedule	In the **Schedule** section: **Show assignment units as a:** Percentage **Percentage** is the best choice when you have part-time resources. If there are mostly *team resources* (consolidated), **Decimal** is better, since "5 carpenters" is easier to understand than "500% carpenters". This option is a global option; if you change it to **Decimal** in one project, all your projects will use decimal numbers.
	In the **Scheduling options for this project** section: **Default task type:** Fixed Units Choose the type of task for any new tasks you create. See the next section for more explanation.

Tab	Option
Schedule	☐ **New Tasks are effort driven** Using this option may result in MS Project changing assignment units. For now, we recommend you turn it off. See the next section for more explanation.

Types of Detail Tasks

There are three types of detail tasks: *Fixed Duration*, *Fixed Units* and *Fixed Work*. Each task has three variables:

- **Duration** is the amount of time a task takes, expressed in *business days* or *business hours*.
- **Units** (also displayed as field **Assignment Units**) reflects:
  - The percentage of the available working hours from an individual resource. For a resource working half of his available hours on the task, it would be 50%; for a resource working all of her available hours: 100%; and for two resources working all of their available hours: 200%.
  - The number of people assigned from a *team resource* (consolidated resource). You can change the percentages to **Decimal** numbers via ribbon **File,** Options, tab **Schedule** in the field **Show assignments as a**. The **Units** field would then display 0.5, 1 and 2 respectively for the previous example. For team resources, decimals make more sense; "2 programmers" is easier to understand than "200% programmers".
- **Work** is the amount of effort a task takes expressed in person hours or person days. A *person day* is one person working full-time for one business day.

We already discussed the process of estimating (see page 170), which is shown in the illustration. We recommended using Fixed Duration or Fixed Work tasks when first entering estimates. It is important to be aware of the task type when you assign resources, because each type of task makes MS Project calculate differently. For example, MS Project will never recalculate the duration of a fixed duration task, and if you add a second resource, it will double the work for the task following the formula **Duration** * **Peak Units** = **Work,** where **Peak Units** is the number of resources assigned.

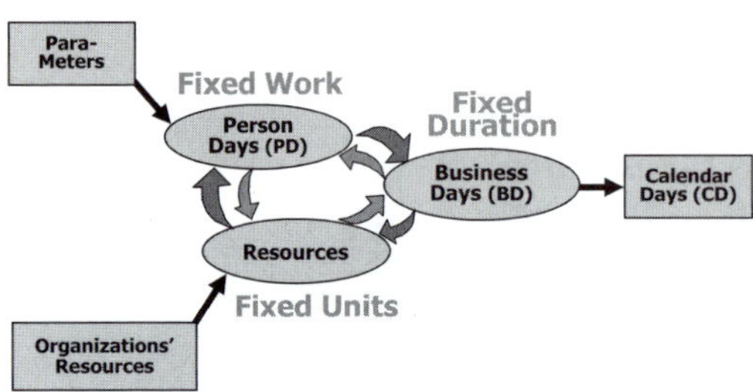

The new field **Peak** (or **Peak Units** in the usage views) is a calculated field, but its value can be changed by entering a number into the field **Units** in the **Assign Resources** dialog.

In order to manipulate the way the formula calculates, we will insert the column **Type**, so we can always see the type of task. You may also want to insert the field **Effort Driven**, because MS Project changes **Effort Driven** to **Yes** when you set the task **Type** to **Fixed Work**. When you then change the task type again, the **Yes** will stay in **Effort Driven**; it is sticky. The Effort Driven attribute works in a way that is similar to the Fixed Work task type, as indicated by the fact that Fixed Work tasks are always effort driven.

To keep things simple, we recommend having **Effort Driven** turned off; this reduces the total number of combinations of three task types and two options for **Effort Driven** (on or off) from six to three.

Project 2010 has the two fields *Assignment Units* (same as **Units** field in **Assign Resources** dialog) and **Peak** units. In **Assignment Units**, you enter a value; **Peak** displays the result of the calculation. We recommend you display at least the **Peak** field. Since both of these fields are assignment-related, you also need to switch to the Task Usage view where you can see assignments. The Gantt Chart displays only task-related data.

If you insert the field **Work** as well, the resulting layout of columns we recommend is as follows when working with assignments:

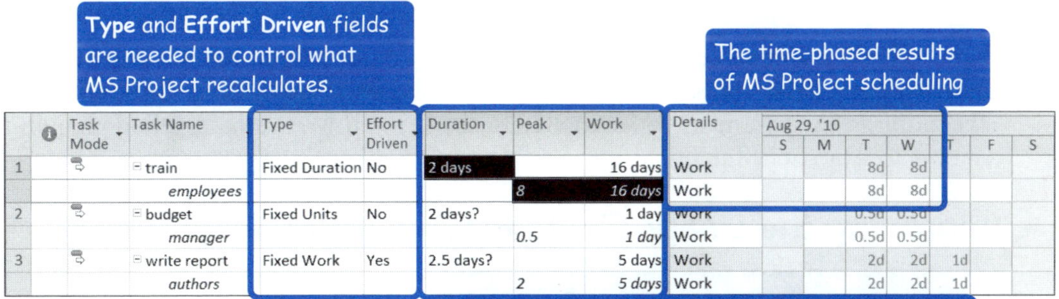

	Task Mode	Task Name	Type	Effort Driven	Duration	Peak	Work	Details	S	M	T	W	T	F	S
									Aug 29, '10						
1		train	Fixed Duration	No	2 days		16 days	Work			8d	8d			
		employees				8	*16 days*	Work			8d	8d			
2		budget	Fixed Units	No	2 days?		1 day	Work			0.5d	0.5d			
		manager				0.5	*1 day*	Work			0.5d	0.5d			
3		write report	Fixed Work	Yes	2.5 days?		5 days	Work			2d	2d	1d		
		authors				2	*5 days*	Work			2d	2d	1d		

We can now see all three variables of the formula **Duration** * **Peak Units** = **Work**
If there are multiple resources assigned to a task, you have to add their **Peak units** to arrive at the total number of units used in the formula.

Switching to Auto Scheduled Tasks

If you have not already switched your tasks from **Manually Scheduled** to **Auto Scheduled** when setting dependencies (see page 218), we recommend you do so at this time for the following reasons:

- The fields **Type** and **Effort-Driven** are disabled for Manually Scheduled tasks. You will not be able to control the calculations MS Project makes using the **Type** field if you continue to work with Manually Scheduled tasks.
- Manually Scheduled tasks always behave as **Fixed Duration** tasks in Project 2010 (regardless of what their field **Type** displays as their task type). Why limit yourself to only one task type when you can have three?
- If you started with **Work** estimates (*effort-based scheduling*), MS Project will not calculate the **Duration** on Manually Scheduled tasks but only the *Scheduled Duration* (the sister field of Duration for Auto Scheduled tasks), and you will still not have a schedule to publish; Duration values are needed for a Gantt Chart as illustrated in this screenshot:

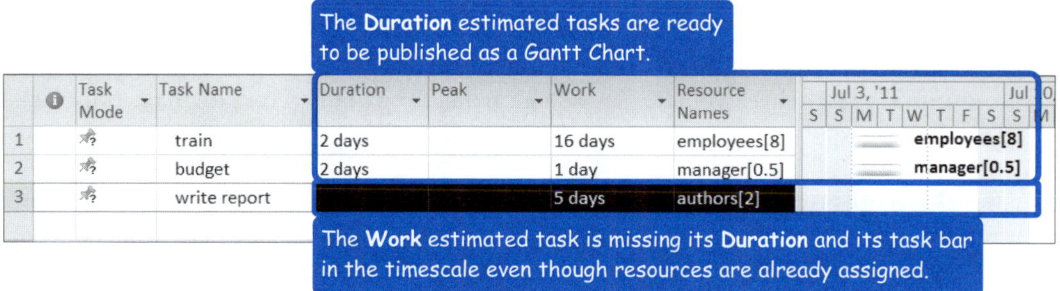

We recommend you make all tasks to which you will assign resources **Auto Scheduled** using the field **Task Mode**. See page 220 for the how-to steps. If you apply *rolling wave* scheduling, we recommend you switch all tasks that fall within the detailed planning window to Auto Scheduled.

Improving the Usage Table for Assigning Resources

This is how you can create the recommended layout of columns:

1. Click ribbon **View**, button **Task Usage**; the **Usage** table is applied and by default it has the columns: **🛈 , Task Mode, Task Name, Work, Duration, Start** and **Finish** respectively.

2. We will insert the column **Type** before the column **Duration**. Right-click on the column heading **Duration** and select **Insert Column** from the popup menu. Start typing the name of the field, *Type*, and the list narrows. Click on **Type** – this column is now inserted.

3. Repeat step 2 for the fields **Effort Driven** and **Peak**; we recommend you insert them in the order indicated in the next screenshot or drag them around afterwards:

	ℹ	Task Mode	Task Name	Type	Effort Driven	Duration	Peak	Work	Details	Aug 29, '10 S	M	T	W	T	F	S
1			- train	Fixed Duration	No	2 days		16 days	Work			8d	8d			
			employees				*8*	*16 days*	Work			8d	8d			
2			- budget	Fixed Units	No	2 days?		1 day	Work			0.5d	0.5d			
			manager				*0.5*	*1 day*	Work			0.5d	0.5d			
3			- write report	Fixed Work	Yes	2.5 days?		5 days	Work			2d	2d	1d		
			authors				*2*	*5 days*	Work			2d	2d	1d		

Copy this improved **Usage** table into your Global.MPT, so that you will have it in all new projects. Click ribbon **File**, tab **Info**, button **Organizer** and click tab **Tables** and select ⦿ **Task** related tables. Make sure that at the bottom left in the pull-down list **Tables available in**, you select **Global.MPT (**or **Global)**. In the pull-down list **Tables available in** on the right, select the current project, if needed. From the list on the right select the item **Usage**. Click [<< Copy] and answer [Yes] to the prompt, if you would like to replace the **Usage** table. From now on, you will see this table when you switch to the Task Usage view.

8

Overview of Assigning

The following are the many different ways you can *assign* resources to tasks. We listed the methods from simple (and quick) to sophisticated (and cumbersome) starting with the simple methods. The more sophisticated the method, the lower it appears on the list and the more detail you can enter about the *assignment*:

- Team Planner View (see next section)
  - It is not easy to assign multiple resources.
  - It is not easy to adjust the Units of resources.
  - You create constraints by assigning.
- Task Sheet view (see page 366)
  - It is not easy to adjust the Units of resources.
- Assign Resources dialog box (see page 367)
  - You can assign or replace resources.
  - You can specify units or work by assignment.
  - The dialog box floats and does not need to be closed every time.
- Task Information dialog box
  - You can assign units or work.

  - ◇ You can enter multiple assignments simultaneously.
  - ◇ You have to display and close the dialog for every task.
- ◆ Task Form view (see page 374)
  - ◇ You can assign units or work.
  - ◇ You can enter multiple assignments simultaneously.
  - ◇ The form stays on the screen all the time.
- ◆ Task Usage or Resource Usage view
  - ◇ You can assign work "day-by-day" and create workloads on each task that vary over time in the timescale.

In all ways of assigning except the last one, MS Project creates a *flat workload.* Generally, a flat workload is an adequate approximation of the true workload. If it is not, you should consider breaking up the tasks into smaller tasks or using the work contour feature. Predefined *work contours* allow you to spread the work across the task duration in a certain pattern, see page 356 for more. We do not recommend the last way of assigning resources, because it requires entering too much data, and all data need to be maintained for the life of the project. During project execution you will have little time to maintain the schedule.

We will discuss some methods that will give you the speed and the flexibility you may need.

Team Planner View

Only the professional version of Project 2010 has this new *Team Planner* view. This view is designed specifically for the following user scenario: A manager of a small team wants to delegate tasks to team members, monitor their vacations and workloads and solve overallocations quickly by dragging workload bars. This view works well with other features of using manually scheduled tasks (see page 96) and updating tasks through SharePoint task list (see page 628).

The main goal of scheduling with this view is delegating as opposed to forecasting (see page 49 on reasons why we schedule). The view does not support forecasting well because when you assign a task in this view, it always creates a Start-No-Earlier-Than constraint. We, therefore, do not recommend this view for *forecast scheduling*.

To display the Team Planner view, click ribbon **View** and button **Team Planner**. The view consists of four panes as shown in the screenshot below:

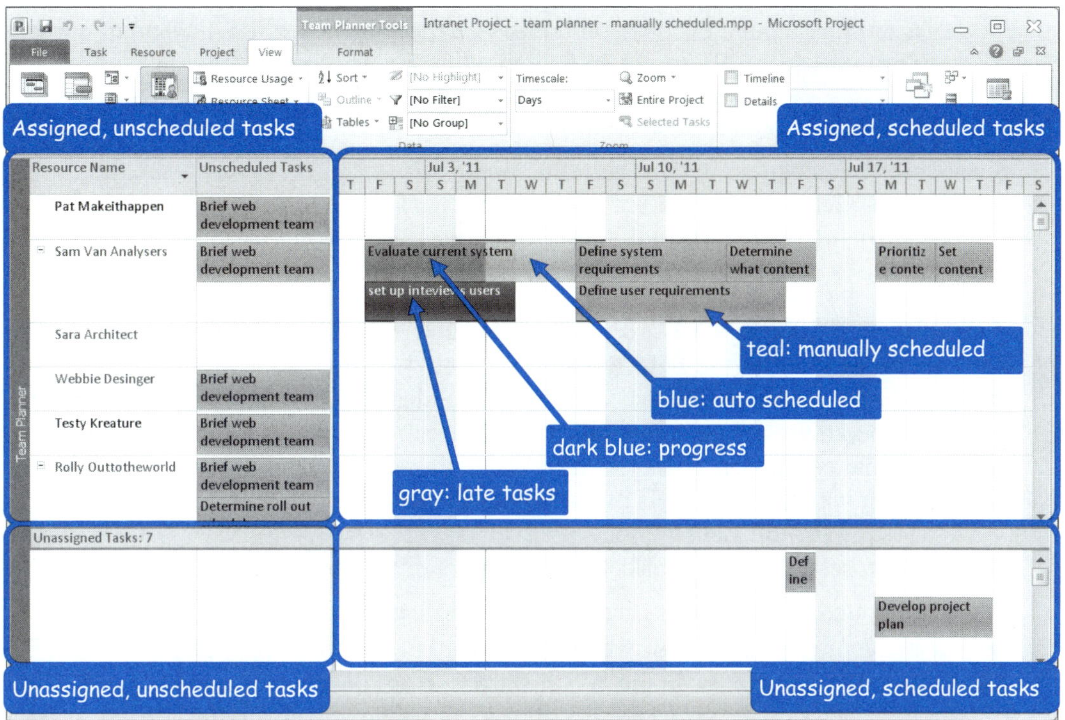

Unscheduled tasks are tasks without a Start or Finish date (*manually scheduled*); they have the field **Placeholder** set to **Yes**. Assigned tasks are assigned to a resource. You can see that the *Status Date* has a dotted gridline on Monday, July 4. The late task bar has no progress but should have been in progress as per the status date and is therefore colored gray.

Things you should know about the Team Planner view:

- If you cannot see the task bars, click ribbon **Task** and button **Scroll to Task** or press Control + Shift + F5.
- The top left pane consists of the list of resources. The timescale displays a task bar for each assignment that each resource has. These bars can be displayed on one row by clicking the resource's collapse ⊟ button. When collapsed, you will see more resources but the bars will overlay each other. To collapse all resources quickly: click the **Format** ribbon and clear ☐ **Expand Resource Rows**. When the resource is expanded, no bars overlay each other, as shown in the previous screenshot.

8

- **Unscheduled tasks** can be hidden by clicking the **Format** ribbon and clearing ☐ **Unscheduled Tasks**.
- The bottom pane displays all **Unassigned Tasks**. The counter tells you how many tasks are unassigned even if you do not see their task bars. To display all unassigned task bars, click the **View** ribbon and click the **Entire Project** button. To hide the bottom pane, click the **Format** ribbon and clear ☐ **Unassigned Tasks**.

Some things you can do in the Team Planner view:

- Double-clicking on a task bar displays the **Task Information** dialog (not the **Assignment Information** dialog), which will allow you to assign the task to other resource as well on the tab **Resources**.
- You can easily filter or group resources using the Autofilter button [▾] in the column heading of the field **Resource Name**.
- *Nonworking time* (individual *vacations*) are clearly indicated for each resource with the same gray used for weekends. Double-click on it to get the **Change Working Time** dialog with detail information about the nonworking time exception.
- You can view higher levels of the schedule by clicking ribbon **Format**, button **Roll-Up, Outline Level 1** or **2**.
- You can select multiple tasks by dragging over task bars or by clicking on the first task bar and holding down the [Control] key while clicking on the rest of the task bars.
- Hover your mouse pointer over a bar to display a screen tip, which shows the **Task Path** to that detail task in the WBS, starting from the project summary task via its summary tasks to the selected detail task. This lets you check the context of the task in the WBS, which is useful when you have tasks with similar names.
- Right-clicking on a bar allows updating the % Complete on the task.

Scheduling and (Re)Assigning Tasks in the Team Planner View

The Team Planner view makes it very easy to drag task bars into the timescale to schedule them, to drag task bars to resources to assign them, and to drag task bars between resources to resolve overallocations. This view also makes it very easy to see when a resource is on vacation:

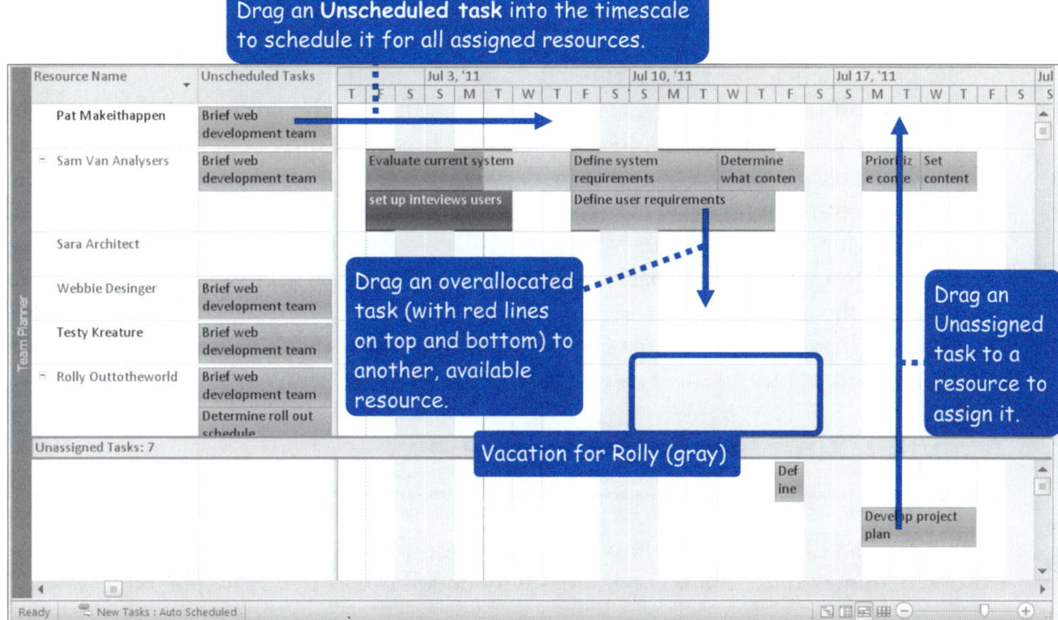

The results of all the dragging of task bars would be:

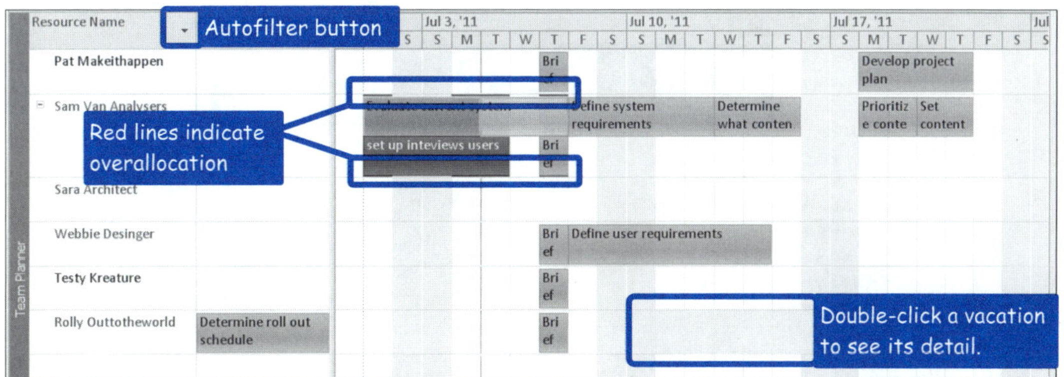

This shows how easily you can schedule and assign tasks and level the workloads.

Weaknesses of the view:

- Dragging task bars creates Start-No-Earlier-Than (SNET) constraints:
    - ◇ Dragging unassigned tasks to resources creates SNET-constraints.
    - ◇ Dragging task bars to resolve overallocations creates SNET constraints.

  We recommend minimizing the number of constraints to keep the schedule dynamic (see page 286). When you hover your mouse pointer on a bar, the screen tip reveals the constraint.
- You cannot easily assign one task to more than one person by dragging. You can only do that with the Task Information dialog (double-click on the task bar or select the bar and click the **Task** ribbon, button **Information**).
- In large projects, the screen is simply too small … or the amount of data is too large to handle in this view – another reason why this view only supports delegation to small teams.
- If you unassign a task (by dragging it to the unassigned pane) that does not have predecessors, it may suddenly disappear from view. This happens because the task is not constrained and falls back to the start date of the project, which may be out of range of the current view.
- When using a *shared resource pool*, it is hard to see which tasks belong to which project, except for in the **Task Path** when resting the mouse pointer over a task bar.

Assign Using the Task Sheet View

New in Project 2010, you can now easily assign multiple resources to a task in the Resource Names field, thanks to the list with check boxes that is displayed:

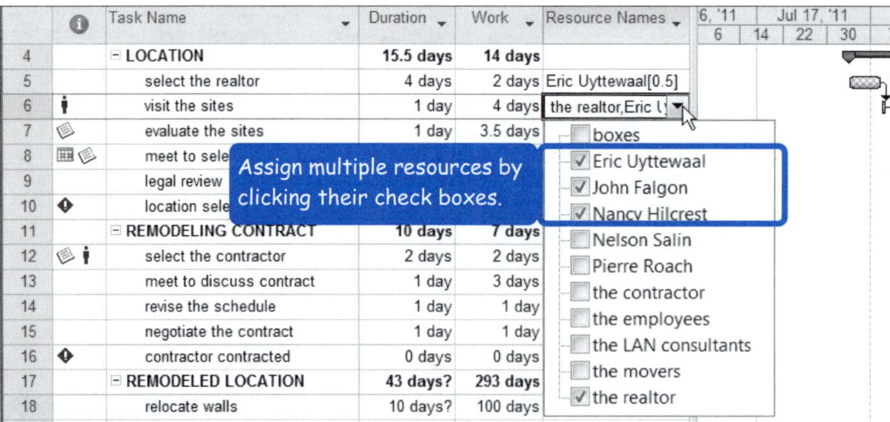

If you assign in this way, Project 2010 will assign the maximum availability of an individual resource (*Max Units*) and only one unit of *team resources*.

Assign Using the Assign Resources Dialog Box

The **Assign Resources** dialog has the following features:

- It is only enabled in a task view, not in resource views.
- It is a floating dialog that allows you to click on tasks while it remains displayed.
- It puts all the resources that are assigned to the selected task at the top of the list. Every time you click on a task, you can immediately see which resources are assigned instead of scrolling up and down the list.
- It always sorts the rest of the resources alphabetically so that you can easily find another resource to assign. It sorts alphabetically regardless of what the sort order is in the resource sheet.
- It provides filtering options to determine which resources are available.

Assigning Resources by Dragging

Click ribbon **Resource**, 

– the **Assign Resources** floating dialog appears:

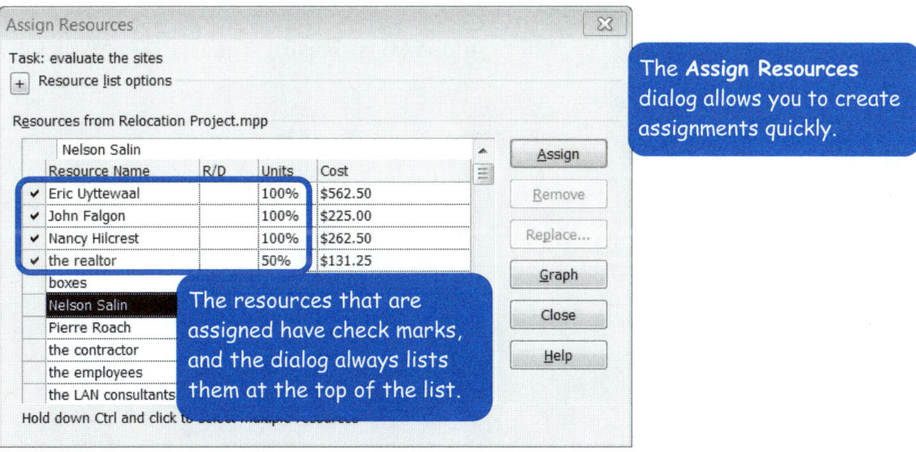

1. Click on the resource to be assigned.

2. Point to the resource selector ☐ in front of the resource name; the mouse pointer now has a person's (decapitated!?) head attached:

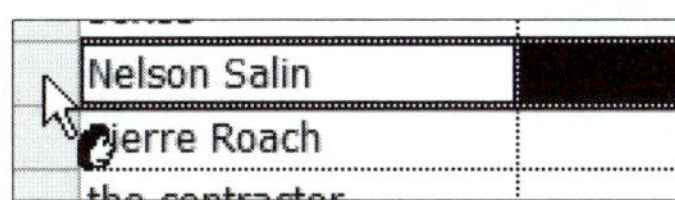

3. Holding down the primary mouse button, drag and drop the resource onto the task you want to assign. The resource is now assigned; it has a check mark in front of its name. The name of the resource appears in the field **Resource Names** and to the right of the task bar in the timescale.

When you drag resources onto tasks, MS Project assigns:

- The maximum availability (*Max Units*) of individual resources
- Only one unit of *team resources*
- You may need to edit the number of units which will trigger a recalculation by MS Project, so check the task **Type** first (see page 375).

To Enter the Units on an Assignment

You can enter the resource units as a percentage or as decimals, see page 357 for details.

Select the task and check what task **Type** it has. It should not be **Fixed Units**, because we are about to change the **Units**; you are not controlling what MS Project recalculates. Set it to **Fixed Duration** or **Fixed Work** depending on which value you would like to protect.

1. Click ribbon **Resource**, 

– the **Assign Resources** dialog appears.

2. In the field **Units**, enter the percentage of the resource's available working hours. (You can quickly check the working hours of a resource by double-clicking on its resource name in this list, selecting tab **General** and clicking Change Working Time ... Cancel out of the two dialogs before continuing).

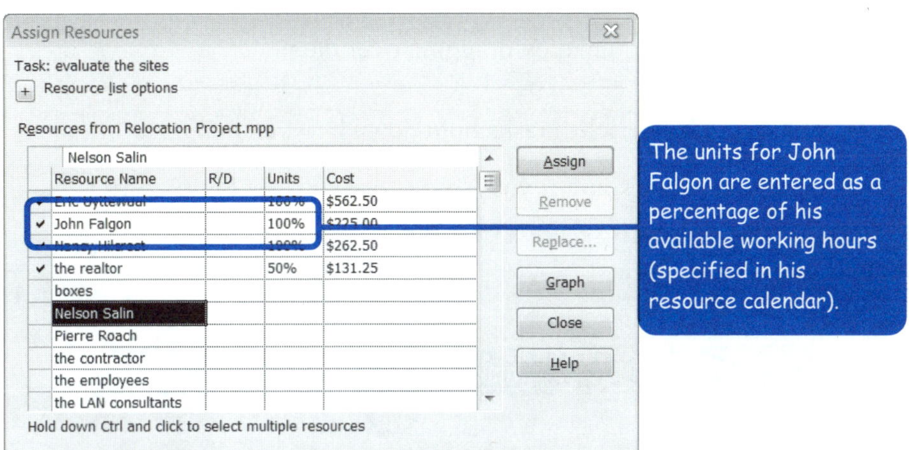

3. Click Assign – MS Project recalculated the work of a **Fixed Duration** task, or recalculated the duration of a **Fixed Work** task.

4. In the field *R/D* you can indicate whether the assignment is a **Request** or a **Demand,** (i.e., if the resource is requested to work on the task or must work on the task to complete it successfully). More precisely, the Request setting indicates that the specified resource should be used unless the resource is overallocated. The *Demand* setting indicates that the specified resource must be used and cannot be substituted. Entering this is only important if the *Project Server* feature *Resource Substitution Wizard* is used to increase resource usage across the projects. [47] You do not need to click Assign again; just click elsewhere to enter the R/D attribute.

Although the field **Units** requests that you enter units, you can even enter *work* in this field and MS Project will calculate the units required. If you do want to enter work, you have to ensure that you include the time unit (the *d* in *5d*) to make it clear to MS Project that it should interpret your entry as person days of work instead of as units.

---

[47] This is discussed in our courses *Managing Resources* and *Managing Portfolios*, see our website www.ProjectProCorp.com and click *Courses 2010* in the side pane.

Assigning Multiple Resources to Multiple Tasks

1. Click ribbon **Resource**, 

– the **Assign Resources** floating dialog appears.

2. Select the tasks to be assigned by dragging over them.
   OR
   If you want to randomly select tasks hold down Control and click.

3. Select the resource or resources you want to assign by holding down Control – click on their names in the **Assign Resources** dialog:

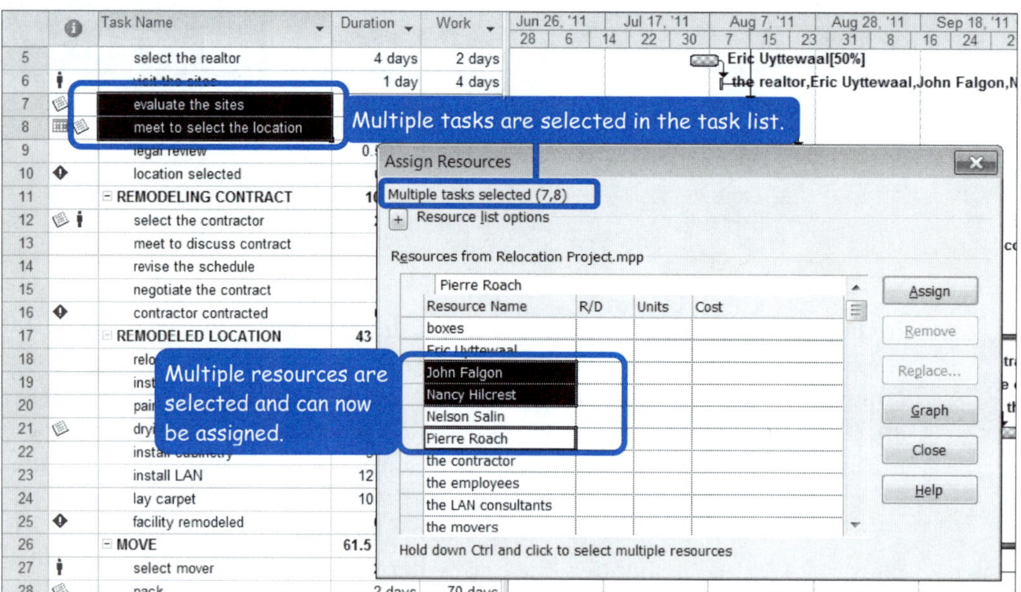

4. Click Assign – a check mark appears in front of the name in the resource selector: ✓ and the resources are now listed at the top.

Checking Availability before Assigning

We recommend you check if the resources are available before you assign them. If you have Project Server you can even *check availability* across all enterprise projects. This feature helps you *prevent overallocations* from occurring in the first place, and spares you from having to sort them out later. Resolving overallocations is a nasty job that necessitates awkward meetings, because all project managers will try to get the resources when they need them. After all, project managers only need to meet their own deadlines. As a team of project managers, you can prevent overallocations:

1. Insert the column **Work** by right-clicking on a column heading and clicking **Insert column**. From the list **Field name**, start typing the name of the field you need, *Work*, the list narrows down, and then select **Work**. In this field, you can see the total effort required on the task.
2. Select the task to which you are about to assign resources. This is an important step, because MS Project checks the availability of resources between the start and finish dates of the task that is currently selected.
3. Click ribbon **Resource**,  – the **Assign Resources** dialog appears.

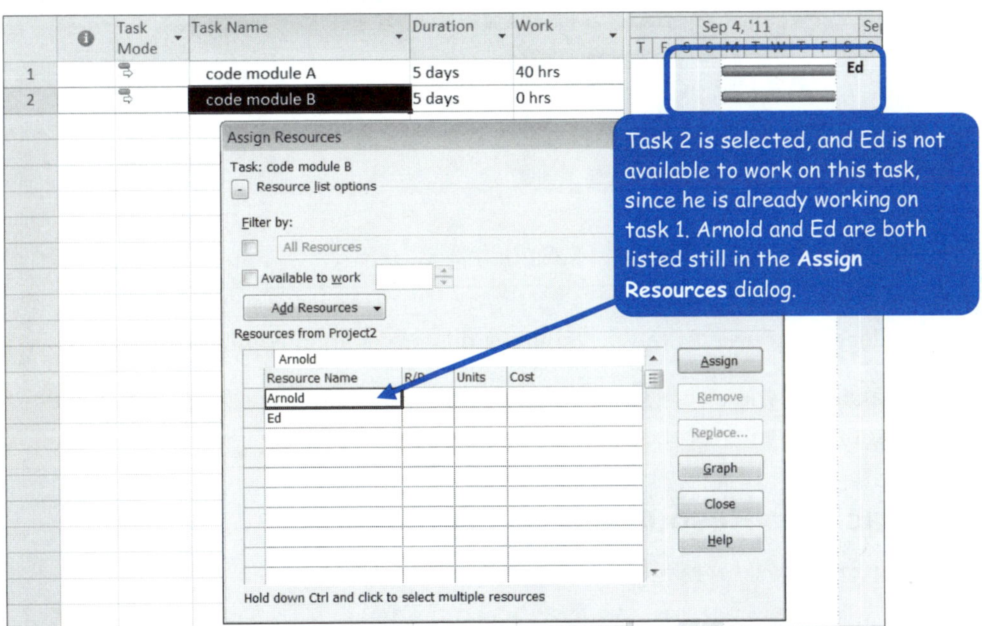

4. Select the resource(s) in the list and click [Graphs...] – the **Resource Graph** view will appear as the bottom view, which can only display one resource at a time. Select the resource in the dialog for which you want to see the workload and availability in the **Resource Graph** view.
   OR
   Select ☑ **Available to work** and enter the amount of effort that you need from the resource in the field to the right of it. MS Project will immediately list only the

8

resources with enough availability (between the start and finish dates of the selected task). This feature prevents you from having to switch to the Resource Usage view and back before you can make one assignment.

5. The screenshot would look like:

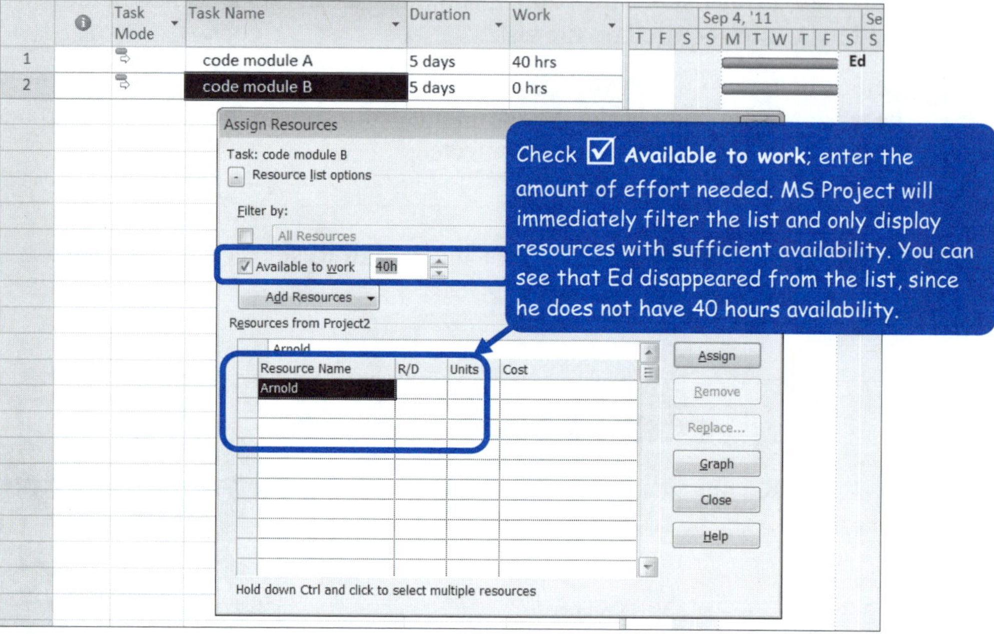

6. Select a resource from the resources that are available and click Assign.

7. Make sure you clear ☐ **Available to work** so that you see the entire list of resources again for the next task.

Replacing a Resource on Assignments

1. Select the task(s) requiring *resource replacement.*

2. Click ribbon **Resource**, Assign Resources – the **Assign Resources** dialog appears.

3. Select one assigned resource (with a check mark at the top of the list) requiring replacement.

4. Click Replace... – the **Replace Resource** dialog appears.

5. Select the substitute resource and click OK – the resource will now be replaced (without a recalculation, if the resource calendars are similar).

If a task is in progress, only the remaining duration of the assignment will be reassigned to the new resource; all *actual hours* worked remain with the original resource. Assignments that are 100% complete will trigger an appropriate prompt:

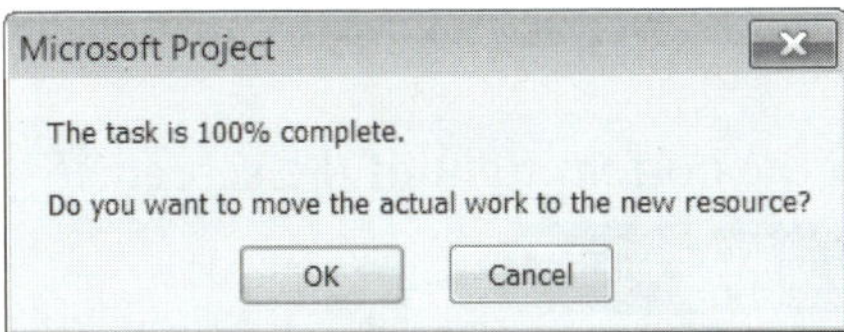

If you get this prompt, you may need to cancel and select the tasks more carefully. The filter **Using Resource in Date Range…** (ribbon **View**, list Filter:, **More Filters**) is very useful for selecting only tasks that are in the future for a resource. This filter will help you replace a resource on a project that is in progress.

To Remove an Assignment in the Assign Resources Dialog

1. Click ribbon **Resource**, 

– the **Assign Resources** dialog appears:

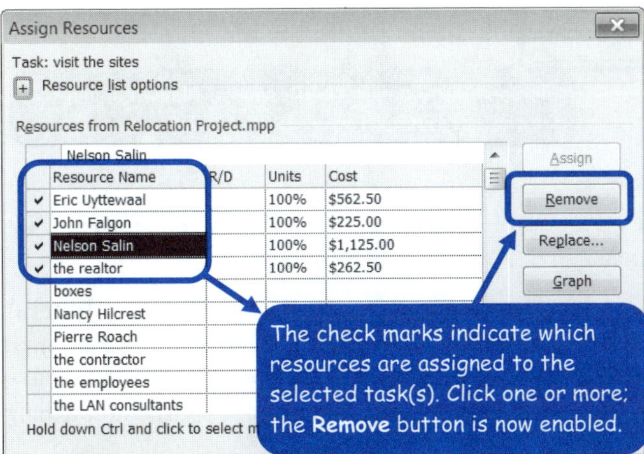

2. Look at the check marks ✓ in front of the resource names that indicate which resources are assigned to the task(s) selected in the spreadsheet. Select the resource to be removed.

3. Click Remove – the resource is unassigned and the associated work is removed.

Assign Using the Task Form

To Assign with the Task Form

1. In the Gantt Chart, click ribbon **View,** Details to display the Task Form,
   OR
   Double-click on the sliding window handle at the bottom right of the screen:

2. On the Task Form, we need to see at least the fields **Resource Name**, **Units** and **Work**. You can display more fields that may be useful:

   Click ribbon **Format** and click Work, OR

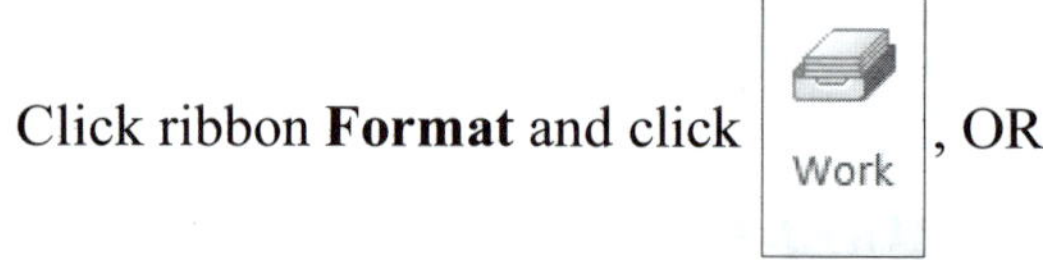

   Right-click anywhere in the gray on the Task Form and select **Work** from the popup menu. The Task Form should now look like:

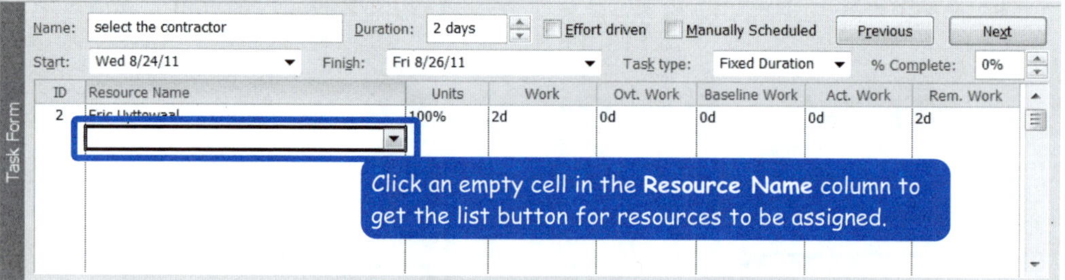

3. On the Task Form, click on an empty cell in the field **Resource Name**; a list button, as shown above will appear.

4. Click the list button, then select a resource from the list that appears. Enter the **Units** (the percentage of the available working hours) or the **Work** (person hours of effort needed). We recommend you enter only one of the two and let the third be calculated by MS Project. You can assign more than one resource at a time.

5. Once all resources are assigned, click OK. Upon clicking this button all new assignments are entered into the schedule simultaneously. This click triggers only one recalculation by MS Project, which makes it a better method for assigning

multiple resources with specific **Units** or **Work** values than the **Assign Resources** dialog box.

To Remove an Assignment in the Task Form

Display the **Task Form**, select an assigned resource, press Delete and click OK.

Changing Tasks and Assignments

Assigning and the Types of Tasks

MS Project uses the following *formula* behind its screens:
Duration * Peak Units = Work for both **Auto Scheduled** and **Manually Scheduled** tasks. Notice that the field **Peak** units, new in Project 2010, is an assignment field. It is only visible in the Task Usage or Resource Usage view. You cannot enter units in the **Peak** field because it is a calculated field. Instead, you can enter the units in the **Units** field in the Assign Resources dialog or Task Form view in Project 2010.

The **Units** value in the Assign Resources dialog or Task Form view only changes in Project 2010 if you change it yourself, which is a strong departure from all previous releases of MS Project.

It is not a coincidence that each **Type** of task relates to one of the variables in the formula: **Fixed Duration**, **Fixed Units** and **Fixed Work**. As their names indicate, each of the three types protects one of the three variables in the formula. If you set a task to be **Fixed Duration**, MS Project will never change this duration. That is a comforting thought, particularly if you have been haunted in the past by having numbers that you did not want changed, be changed by MS Project in the middle of the night …

	Duration * Peak Units = Work		
Fixed Duration training	2 d	8	.....
Fixed Units budget	2 d	0.5	.....
Fixed Work write report	.....	2	5 d

When you enter the second value, MS Project will calculate the third one for you. For example, if you have a task *training* with a **Fixed Duration** of 2 business days, and you invite 8 people to the training, MS Project will calculate 2 * 8 = 16 person days of **Work**. Another example: the task *write report* with 5 person days of **Fixed Work** could be worked on by two people, and MS Project will calculate a **Duration** of 2.5 business days.

When entering the data for the first time, most of your tasks will be either **Fixed Duration** or **Fixed Work**. The **Fixed Units** task type becomes useful when you start making changes to the task and you want to keep the number of resources that are working on it the same. For example, if you want to change the amount of **Work** on the 2 day **Fixed Duration** task *training* to 12 person days to save money, MS Project will change the number of **Units** from 8 to 6 people, thus uninviting 2 people from the training. Alternatively, it will reduce the **Units** for all assigned individuals from 100% to 75% (some people say 75% mental presence is an accurate model for training …). Since the duration is fixed, changing the *peak units* is the only thing MS Project can do. This is not the correct approach if you want to train the same number of people and have the duration recalculated. In order to accomplish that, you have to first change the (**Task Mode** to **Auto Scheduled** so you can change the) task type to **Fixed Units** to tell MS Project that it should not change the resource **Peak Units** on the assignment. Then you can proceed to change the **Work**.

Of course, you could ask yourself at this point: *Why is MS Project constantly recalculating all these values? It makes my life miserable*! If MS Project did not calculate the values, you would need to make many calculations yourself, enter the results, and constantly recalculate. MS Project tries to help you, and it uses the broad assumption that every resource is equally effective and efficient. In 90% of the cases, this assumption is accurate enough for modeling purposes. Remember that we are deliberately simplifying the reality when we model projects (see page 52). We try to approach reality as closely as possible, but with as little effort as possible. Many project managers seem to forget they should not be trying to recreate reality in all its complexity when they use MS Project.

The following table suggests the best use of each task **Type**. Note that you can only change the task **Type** on tasks with the **Task Mode** set to **Auto Scheduled**. **Manually Scheduled** tasks always work like **Fixed Duration** tasks (regardless of what their **Type** field displays).

Type of task	Use in situations like:
Fixed Duration	When the task is *schedule driven*: ◆ When the duration is the first thing you estimate. ◆ If the duration does not decrease when human resources are added, such as when backing up a computer system. ◆ Tasks that always have a group of resources assigned, such as *meeting* or *training*. ◆ When the deadline is so tight that it drives the duration of the task; you have to make it work within the time frame. ◆ When workload is not your problem (e.g., tasks for external resources, such as subcontractors and consultants).
Fixed Units (default)	When the task is *resource driven*: ◆ When the number of resources you have for the task is the first thing you know. ◆ When you cannot get more resources to do the work, for example, you only have two internal resources. ◆ When you want MS Project to recalculate the duration or the work on a task while keeping the same number of people working on the task (*peak units*). ◆ When you want to keep the resource working on a task at a certain percentage of his available hours.
Fixed Work	When the task is *effort driven*: ◆ When the effort required is the first thing you estimate. ◆ When the effort required is the easiest thing to estimate, which is often the case. For example, you estimate that painting a home takes 12 person days of effort; or a software developer may estimate that coding a module in an application will take 20 person hours. Estimating effort is often easier and more accurate than estimating duration. After all, you do not need to take resource availability and vacations into account.

The *formula* **Duration** * **Peak Units** = **Work** does not apply to:

- Tasks that have *assignments* with a *work contour* (see page 356). The work contour spreads the effort in a certain pattern over the duration of the task.
- Tasks with multiple assignments where one assignment is longer than the others or starts later (*multiple, uneven assignments*, see page 386). In this situation you would find that the formula still applies on the level of each individual assignment: **Duration** of assignment * **Units** of the resource = **Work** of assignment.

8

Three Rules to Make MS Project an Easy Tool for You

Now that you know about the formula in MS Project, you have four options:

- You do not want to use the formula: we recommend you either use MS Excel instead of MS Project to manage your project, or use Project 2010 in **Manually Scheduled** mode as set in the **Task Mode** field.
- Call Bill Gates and get the formula ripped out of MS Project. Even if you are successful at this, you will have to start using your calculator to make this simple calculation over and over.
- Ignore the formula: You will end up with unpleasant surprises. The tool will keep recalculating the numbers you entered, which will, eventually, drive you crazy.
- Adopt the formula and work with it to make MS Project do what you want it to. We think this is the way to go.

We would like to suggest three rules to memorize and follow when you enter or change assignments. If you do so, MS Project will become your obedient servant instead of *"an obnoxious piece of software with a bad attitude"* as somebody once put it. If you do not look at the task **Type** when working with MS Project, it will inevitably recalculate values that you did not want changed. You can even find yourself trapped in an endless loop if you keep changing the value back that MS Project just recalculated.

If you want to work pleasantly with MS Project, simply follow these three rules:

1. Enter the duration estimate and/or work estimate and protect that number by setting the task **Type** accordingly (as mentioned in the Estimates chapter, see page 170; you may need to first change the **Task Mode** to **Auto Scheduled** so you can set the task **Type**):
   - ◇ If you enter a **Duration** estimate, you need to set the task **Type** to **Fixed Duration** and set **Effort Driven** to **No**.
   - ◇ If you enter a **Work** estimate, you need to set the task **Type** to **Fixed Work.**
   - ◇ If you enter both **Duration** and **Work**, you protect one of them.

   This rule will ensure that MS Project does not change estimates that you determined and entered.
2. Provide the second value in the formula **Duration** * **Peak Units** = **Work** and always let MS Project calculate the third value.
   For example, if you created a fixed duration, non-effort-driven task, you *assign* the units of resources and let MS Project calculate the work. Enter the units into the **Units** field in the Assign Resource dialog or the Task Form view, or into the **Assignment Units** field in one of the **Usage** views. If you created a fixed work task, assign the resources and let MS Project calculate the duration. If you entered the duration and the work, MS Project only needs to know who will do the task and it

will calculate the number of resources (units) needed (up to their **Max. Units** value). You always provide only two of the three values.

3. Before making a change to any of the three values in the formula, reconsider the task **Type** by asking yourself: *What type of task do I need for this particular change?* More on this next.

Changing Duration, Units or Work

To make MS Project do what you want it to do, you may need to switch the task type between **Fixed Duration**, **Fixed Units** and **Fixed Work**. In Project 2010 you can only do this for **Auto Scheduled** tasks. You will have to switch the **Task Mode** field from **Manually Scheduled** to **Auto Scheduled** first, see page 218 and 360 for other reasons to switch.

Before you manipulate values in the *formula* **Duration** * **Peak Units** = **Work**, you should always think first about the task type you need for that change. With every change, MS Project will surely recalculate one other value, and it may recalculate the one you did not want changed, if you do not think about it first and tell MS Project specifically what value to protect.

8

Changes that will trigger a recalculation in the formula **Duration** * **Peak Units** = **Work** are, for example:

- Changing the **Duration** of a task by editing the value or by stretching the task bar with the mouse.
- Changing the **Peak Units** through the **Units** field in the Assign Resources dialog box or Task Form view, or the **Assignment Units** field in the Task Usage or Resource Usage view. You will change it when you add a resource to a task, remove a resource from a task or change the 100% units to a different percentage.
- Changing the **Work** (W) of a task or an assignment.

The **Type** of the task and the **Effort Driven** attribute determine what value MS Project will recalculate. We suggest these steps when changing an *assignment*:

1. Protect one of the three values first by setting the task **Type** and turning off **Effort Driven**. You can determine the appropriate task **Type** by asking yourself: *If I change this value in the formula; which of the other two values do I want to keep the same?* The answer to this question will tell you which task type you need to protect. For example, if you want to change the units and protect the duration value, you should set the **Type** to **Fixed Duration** and set **Effort Driven** to **No**. Fixed Work tasks are effort driven by definition; you cannot turn it off. **Fixed Duration** and **Fixed Units** should not be effort driven. You may need to change the **Task Mode** to **Auto Scheduled** before you can make changes to the task **Type** field.

2. Change the value that you wanted to change.
3. Let MS Project recalculate the third value.
   For example, if you change the **Units** on a **Fixed Duration** task, MS Project will recalculate the **Work**.

Note that you should never change the value that is protected with the task type (i.e., do not change the **Duration** when the task type is **Fixed Duration**. If you do this, you are basically telling the tool: *I am giving you unclear instructions, but I want you to recalculate one of the other two values.* MS Project could adjust the **Units** or the **Work** and you do not control what it changes. You have to change the task type first to keep one of the other two variables the same. Then you will master MS Project!

The task **Type** is not something you set once and never look at again. You continue to monitor and adjust this field to control what MS Project calculates. If you reconsider the type of task first before every change, you will always control what MS Project will do and you can even predict it easily.

Here is an example of how this works. Assume you have created a **Fixed Duration** task *write* of *4 days* with one resource assigned. This will appear in MS Project as:

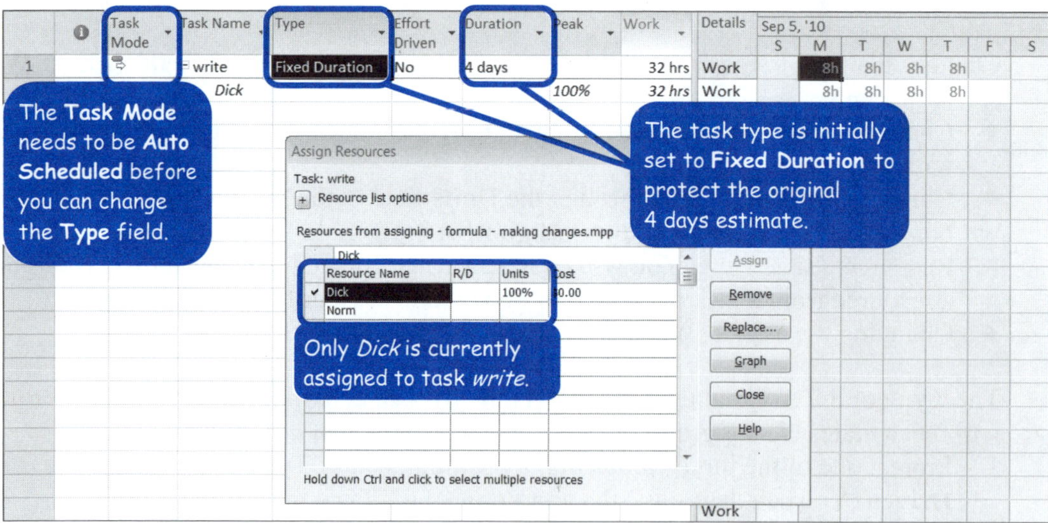

You want to add a second resource, but you want MS Project to keep the **Work** (effort) the same when you add the resource. You need the task type **Fixed Work** (which is automatically **Effort Driven**):

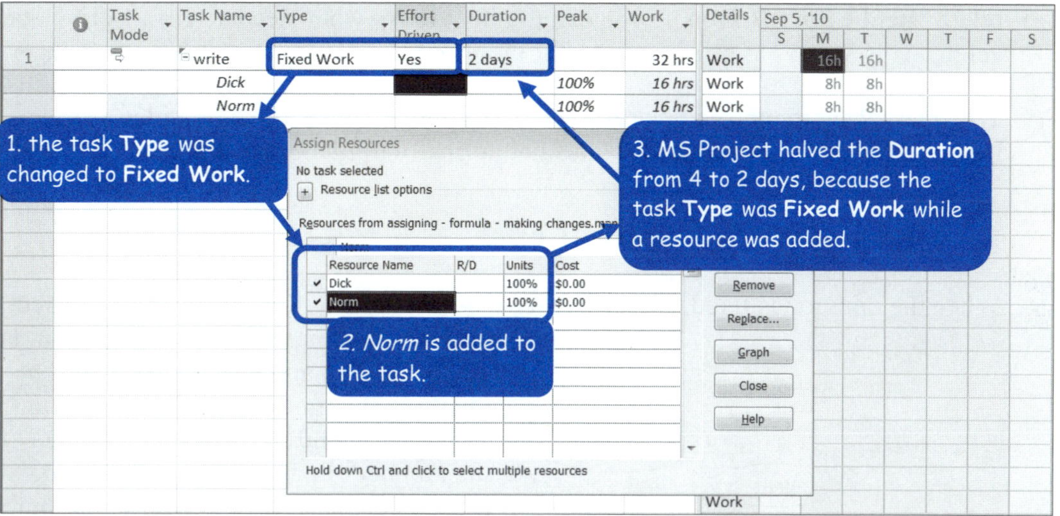

In this example, you should ask the question: *If I change the units, do I want to keep the Duration or the Work the same?* You want to keep the **Work** the same, and therefore, you need the task type **Fixed Work**. First change the task **Type** to **Fixed Work** (which also sets **Effort Driven** automatically to **Yes**), then add the second resource, which cuts the **Duration** in half from *4 days* to *2 days*. If you add a resource to a **Fixed Work** task, the duration will go down.

You will find that you often want to lock in the assigned units on a task while changing the duration or the work. In this case you will need the **Fixed Units** task type. This task type is commonly used when making changes. For example, if you change the work on a **Fixed Units** task, MS Project will recalculate the duration on an Auto Scheduled task. If the Duration = 10 days, Units = 1 (fixed), Work = 10 days and you change the work to 5 days, MS Project will decrease the duration from 10 to 5 days; one person can deliver 5 person days of effort (work) within 5 business days (duration). You will also use the **Fixed Units** task type when you update our schedule (see page 636).

When there are multiple, uneven *assignments*, one (or more) of the assignments can drive the duration of the task. Before you make a change, you should find out which assignment drives the duration of the task. Consider changing values on the level of assignments instead of on the level of the task level.

Notice that when you apply the task type **Fixed Work** the attribute **Effort Driven** is automatically turned on by MS Project. When you change to a different task type again, the **Effort Driven** attribute stays on and sticks. If you leave it set to **Yes**, it may create unexpected recalculations. That is why we recommend you always display the task-related field **Effort Driven** so you can toggle it to *No* when needed. Effort-driven tasks act in a way similar to fixed work tasks; therefore it seems to be a redundant field.

When you want to replace one resource with another, MS Project provides a shortcut in the Assign Resources dialog that does not normally trigger recalculations, see page 372.

Changing a Fixed Duration Task

When the duration is fixed, changes in assignment units or total work will not affect the duration. Examples of **Fixed Duration** tasks are *train users* and *meet with client*. The duration of a training session or meeting is typically set and will not vary (much) with the number of participants, which makes it a perfect candidate for fixed duration. In the illustration we see a meeting with a 1 day fixed duration. If the number of attending resources is changed to 10, MS Project will recalculate the total work to 10 person days.

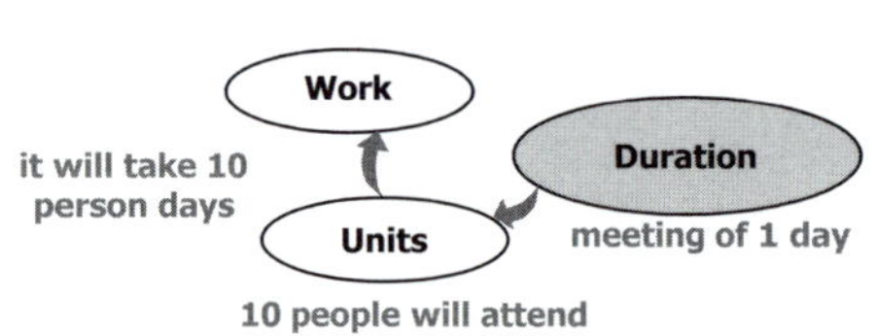

1. In the Gantt Chart spreadsheet pane, set the task *Type* to **Fixed Duration**. Set **Effort Driven** to *No* if needed.
2. Change the number of resources assigned (see page 368 for steps) – MS Project will have recalculated the **Work** value.
   or
   Change the work estimate in the field **Work** – MS Project will have recalculated the **Peak** units value.

Changing a Fixed Work Task

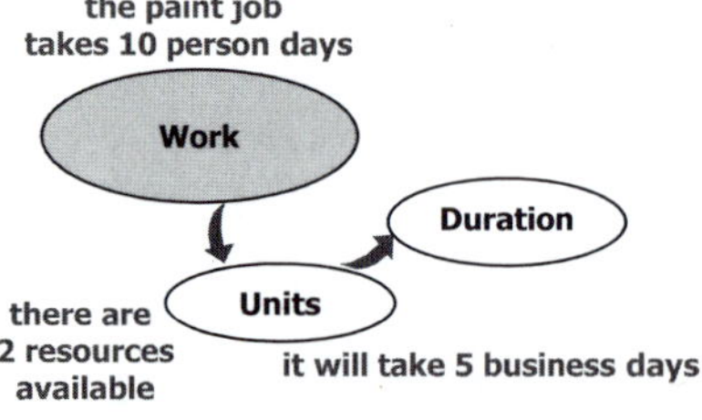

When the work is fixed, changes in assignment units or duration will not affect the work (effort). Examples of *fixed work* tasks are *program feature*, *write report, research* and *paint*. In the illustration, the estimate on the paint job is 10 person days of work. When the number of assigned resources is changed to 2 people, MS Project will determine that it will take 5 business days of duration.

1. In the Gantt Chart spreadsheet pane, set the task **Type** to **Fixed Work**. MS Project changes **Effort Driven** to **Yes**.
2. Change the number of resources required (see page 368) – MS Project will have recalculated the **Duration**.
   or
   Change the duration – MS Project will have recalculated the **Peak** units.

Changing a Fixed Units Task

With *Fixed Units*, changes in the duration or work will not affect the units, the number of resources assigned to the task. The illustration on the left shows an example in which there are 2 resources available for the job (*Units*). You want to change the estimate to 10 person days of *Work*. MS Project will recalculate the *Duration* to 5 business days. Again, you protect one value, change the second and MS Project will recalculate the third.

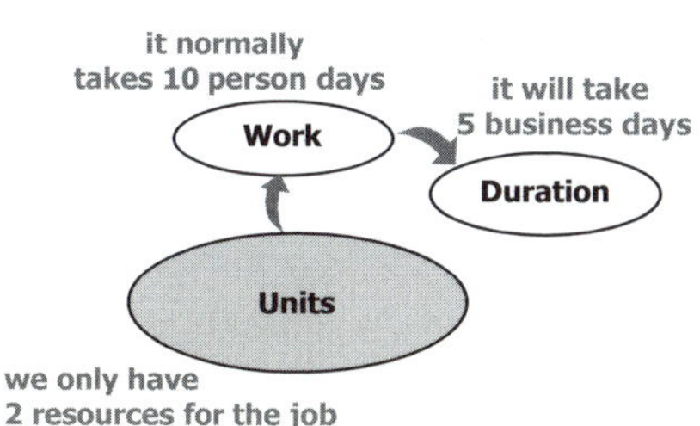

The **Fixed Units** task type is mostly used when updating the schedule. The Fixed Units task type allows you to protect the number of assigned units when you change the work or the duration.

1. In the Gantt Chart spreadsheet pane, set the task **Type** to **Fixed Units**. Set **Effort Driven** to *No* if needed.
2. Change the **Work** value – MS Project will have recalculated the **Duration**.
   or
   Change the **Duration** value – MS Project will have recalculated the **Work**.

Changing the Task Type for All Tasks in a Schedule

At this point, you may have become interested in using the **Type** task field. If you are currently not using this field, you can easily switch your schedule to a task type that is most appropriate for your schedule. For example, if you know you estimated the duration most often, you could switch the task **Type** for all tasks to **Fixed Duration**. In this way you protect most of your estimates from being recalculated by MS Project. To change all tasks to a useful task **Type**:

1. Click on any column heading to select all tasks, then click ribbon **Task**, 

   and the **Multiple Task Information** dialog appears.
2. Click tab **Advanced**. In the field **Task type** change the type for all tasks selected, then clear ☐ **Effort driven** if you select **Fixed Duration** or **Fixed Units**. Click OK.
3. You may also want to set the default task type: Click ribbon **File**, Options, tab **Schedule**, section **Scheduling options for this project** and set the field **Default task type** to the same task type and clear ☐ **Effort driven**, if needed. This will take care of any new tasks that you might create. Click OK.
4. You are now set to start working with the field **Type** to control the calculations of MS Project.

Assigning Resources to Summary Tasks?

MS Project happily allows you to *assign* resources to *summary tasks*, but we would like to discourage this. Assigning resources to summary tasks eventually results in overallocations. The only resolution is to then reverse the original assignment by removing the resource from the summary task. Let us explain.

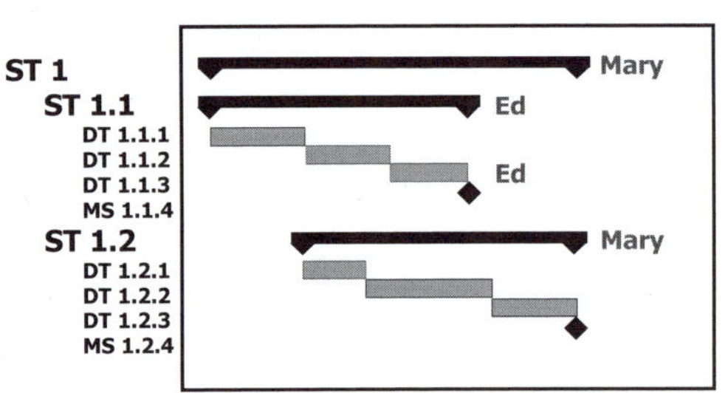

If you assign a resource full-time to a summary task and also to one of its detail tasks, the workload of the resource will be twice its availability during that detail task. In the illustration, you can see that Ed is assigned to the summary task *ST 1.1* and its detail task *DT 1.1.3*. You may think that you would never create a situation like this, but realize that you cannot easily see *assignments* on summary tasks, because they are not displayed in the default timescale in MS Project as they do in the illustration; only assignments on detail tasks are displayed. Note that you can change this in a Gantt Chart view: ribbon **Format**, button **Format**, item **Bar Styles** dialog, select item **Summary**, click tab **Text**; in the field **Right**, select **Resource Name**. Do the same for item **Manual Summary**.

An assignment on both the summary task and its own detail task causes an overallocation that MS Project cannot solve. After all, if MS Project moves the detail task to a later date, the summary task will automatically extend as well and continue the overallocation. Nor can you resolve the overallocation manually, other than by removing the resource from the summary task (or from its detail task). So why bother assigning to summary tasks in the first place?

There is another way in which a similar overallocation can happen between the different levels of summary tasks. In the previous illustration you can see that Mary is assigned only to summary tasks *ST 1* and *ST 1.2*. Because *ST 1.2* is subordinate to *ST 1*, the overallocation cannot be solved unless you remove the resource from one of the summary tasks. This situation could easily occur if you have several indentation levels.

There are three disadvantages of assigning resources to summary tasks:

- You will inevitably create overallocations that cannot be solved by MS Project, see our previous discussion.
- If you assign resources to summary tasks, the fields **Work** and **Cost** will no longer simply total the detail tasks on the summary task; because, upon assignment of resources, the summary task itself also contains work and cost.
- Finally, assignments on summary tasks make updating schedules more cumbersome than when all assignments are on the detail tasks. This is especially true in the *Project Server* environment.

You may be tempted to assign to a summary task because you might think you will be quicker by assigning to the summary task. However, you will not save many mouse clicks, since you can select all detail tasks and assign the resource(s) to all of them with one click as well. Therefore, we do not recommend it even for that reason.

In short, in our view, there are no situations in which you are better off assigning to summary tasks rather than to detail tasks. We recommend keeping the assignments on the lowest level only, the detail tasks.

There is one exception to this rule: you can assign resources to a *recurring summary task* with the **Assign Resources** dialog (ribbon **Resource**), because MS Project will automatically transfer these to its detail tasks and the assignment on the recurring summary task is actually no longer there.

However, you can use one of the extra text fields to capture who is responsible for a deliverable, see page 293 for detailed steps.

Assigning Resources to Recurring Summary Tasks

3 Status Meeting Mark, Brad
3.1 Status meeting 1 Mark, Brad
3.2 Status meeting 2 Mark, Brad
3.3 Status meeting 3 Mark, Brad

If you *assign* a resource to the *recurring summary task* with the **Assign Resources** dialog (ribbon **Resource**), the *assignments* are immediately transferred to the detail tasks. You can see this clearly if you check the task-related field **Resource names**. MS Project does this automatically. In the illustration on the left, the resources *Mark* and *Brad* are assigned to the recurring summary task *3 Status Meeting* and are automatically transferred by MS Project to the *recurring detail tasks*. That is where we want the assignments anyway.

Note that MS Project does not transfer the assignments to the recurring detail tasks if you assign with the **Task Form** view or with the field **Resource Names** instead of with the **Assign Resources** dialog.

If you assign resources to the *recurring detail tasks*, you can level the workloads entirely, see page 141 and 468.

Entering Multiple, Uneven Assignments

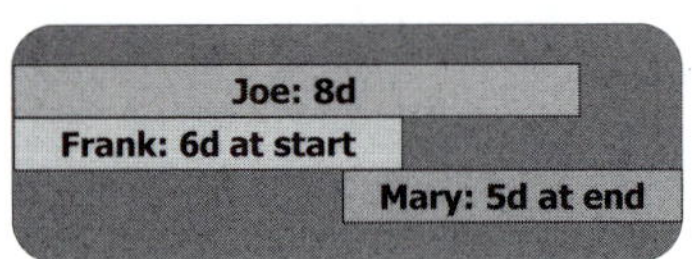

If there are multiple *assignments* on a task, often one of the assignments drives the duration of the task. The assignment that takes the longest or finishes the latest will drive the duration of the task. The illustration shows a 10-day task with three engineers assigned: *Joe*, *Frank* and *Mary*. *Joe* will work 8 days, *Frank* only the first 6 days and *Mary* only the last 5 days. *Mary* determines or "drives" the duration of the job; the assignments are uneven.

To create *multiple, uneven assignments* on a task:

1. Display the Task Form in the Gantt Chart by clicking the **View** ribbon and selecting ☑ Details.

2. Change the details in the Task Form to show assignment start dates by:

Right-clicking in the gray on the Task Form and clicking **Schedule**
OR

Click on the Task Form and click ribbon **Format,** .

3. To enter multiple uneven assignments, in the Task Form set the **Task Type** to **Fixed Units**. Click OK.
4. In the field **Resource Name** click in an empty cell and select a resource to assign from the list that appears. Repeat this for all resources to be assigned. Click OK.
5. Enter different amounts of **Work** for each assigned resource. Click OK.
6. Enter a specific **Scheduled Start** date, a **Leveling Delay** or **Delay** for the assignments you want to start later than the task start date. Click OK.
7. You can see the result of the uneven assignments by clicking ribbon **View, Task Usage**. The result of the previous example would look like:

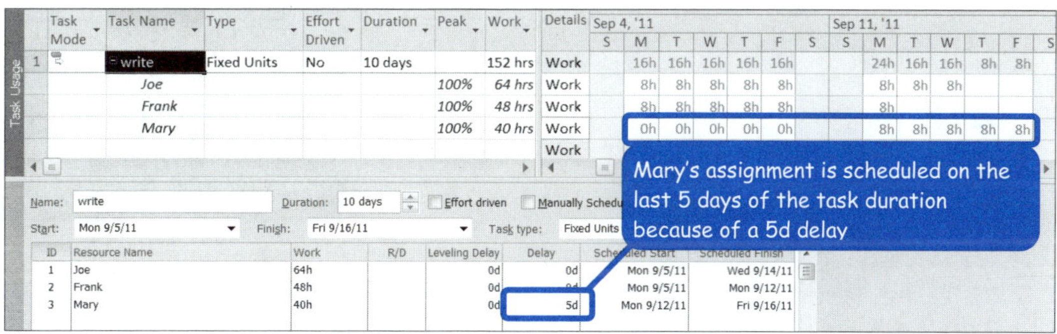

In our example, *Mary* drives the task finish date because of the 5 day delay.

We recommend splitting one task with multiple, uneven assignments into multiple tasks with a single assignment wherever you can. The task *write* could have been split into *write text* for *Joe*, *create tables* for *Frank* and *create graphics* for *Mary*. There are several reasons for this recommendation:

- The *formula D * PU = W* does not apply to a task with multiple, uneven assignments (it does apply to single assignments).

- The project schedule will remain simpler if you split the one task into multiple tasks, creating one task for each resource assignment. Of course, you cannot do this when people need to collaborate as a group. For groups you can create a short meeting task. In the example shown in the screenshot, the meeting would take place on Monday, September 12, 2011.

- Leveling workloads is simpler when there is only one resource assigned per task.
- Optimizing schedules with multiple, uneven assignments is more difficult. This is because you have to first find the driving assignment on every critical task before you can find a way to shorten the task.
- When multiple people are assigned to a task, it is not clear who needs to take the lead. People can start pointing fingers at each other when nobody took the lead.

Changing Assignment Attributes

1. Switch to a usage view, either the **Task Usage** or **Resource Usage**.
2. Double-click on an assignment. *Assignments* do not have a number, but do have italic text and a light background in the timescale. The **Assignment Information** dialog box appears:

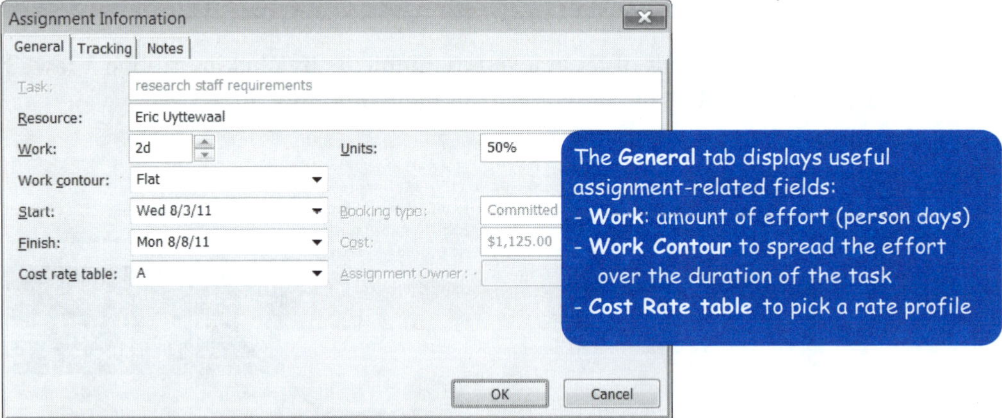

3. Make the changes to the assignment. Note that you can edit the **Cost** field only when you assigned a **Cost** resource (as set in the resource-related field **Type**).
   Click OK.

You can change many assignment-specific attributes. Assignments have about 50 purely *assignment-related fields*. Some useful examples are:

- **Work**: work is the amount of planned effort from the resource on this task.
- **Work contour**: this allows spreading the effort on a task in a pattern you choose.
- **Start** and **Finish**: these fields allow one or more resources to start later on a task or to finish earlier than the other resources.

- **Cost rate table**: this allows you to select a specific rate profile for each assignment. This is useful for jacks-of-all-trades in small consulting firms who are cost rated differently for each skill they use in the different jobs.
- **Units**: this field reflects the percentage of available hours of the individual assigned to the task (or the number of individuals of a *team resource* assigned to the task).
- **Notes**: you can document actual findings and lessons learned by assignment.

Replacing Generic Resources with Individuals

We have mentioned before that if you do not know who you will get on your team, you should simply assign *generic resources* (see page 297). I like to call generic resources *clones*, because they seem unlimited in number, or *zombies*, because they are lifeless. It will be really eerie if you ever get to shake hands with a generic resource. There are several ways to replace generic resources with individuals of flesh and blood who rent about 40 hours of their 168-hour week to your organization:

- In the Resource Sheet, type over the generic resource name with the name of the individual. This will replace the generic resource on all of its assignments.

- In Project Professional with Project Server, you can use the *Team Builder* to replace generic resources if the skills are captured for all resources (generic and actual resources). Click ribbon **Resource**, **Add Resources**, **Build Team from Enterprise** and select the generic resource in the list **Project Resources** on the right and click [< Match] to see who has the right skills. Then click the substitute resource in the list **Enterprise Resource** on the left and click [Replace >] which will replace the generic resource on all of its assignments.
  OR
  Click [Add >] to only add the resource to the project. Then replace the generic resource: Either drag all assignments from the generic resource to one or more real people in the Resource Usage view, or use the [Replace...] button in the **Assign Resources** dialog to transfer all assignments of the generic resource, see page 372.

Pro

- In Project Professional with *Project Server*, you can use the *Resource Substitution Wizard* to quickly replace all generic resources with real people after a certain date. This method assumes that you have coded the skills of all resources (including the generic resources) in such a way that the wizard can determine which person has the right skills for the job. The Resource Substitution Wizard looks at availability as the second most important factor. So, the result can be that a person is overallocated by the wizard and you would still have to apply workload leveling after running the wizard.

8

Using the Resource Substitution Wizard

This wizard has two functions:

- Replace the generic resources with actual resources.
  This is typically done in a project template. The generic resources should have codes that reflect their *skills*. If all the actual resources in the resource pool also have their skills coded, then the substitution wizard can figure out what individual has a matching set of skills.
- Optimize the resource allocation across a portfolio of projects.
  The substitution wizard can also reallocate resources across any number of projects, optimizing the utilization of your resources across the project portfolio. We will not discuss this function here. [48] However, it is good to be aware of this alternative use, because the options in the dialog boxes of the wizard might otherwise be confusing.

Steps to replace generic resources with actual resources in a template (prepare yourself for the longest procedure in this entire book!):

1. Click ribbon **Resource**,  – the **Resource Substitution Wizard** appears.

2. In the **Welcome** screen click Next > – the **Step 1** dialog appears:

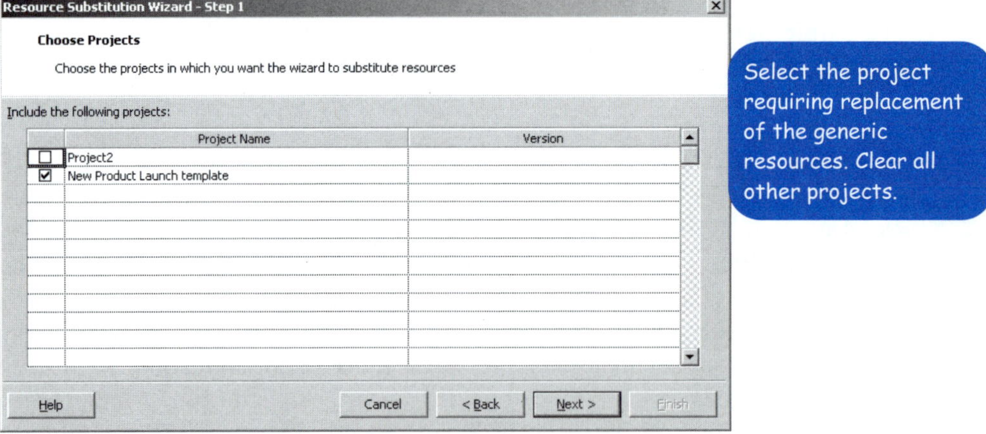

[48] We discuss it in other courses, see www.ProjectProCorp.com and click *Managing Resources* or *Managing Portfolios*.

3. It lists all open projects. Check the project that requires substitution of generic resources for real ones. Clear any other projects listed. Selecting other projects is necessary when you want to reallocate resources across multiple projects.

4. Click Next > – the **Step 2** dialog appears:

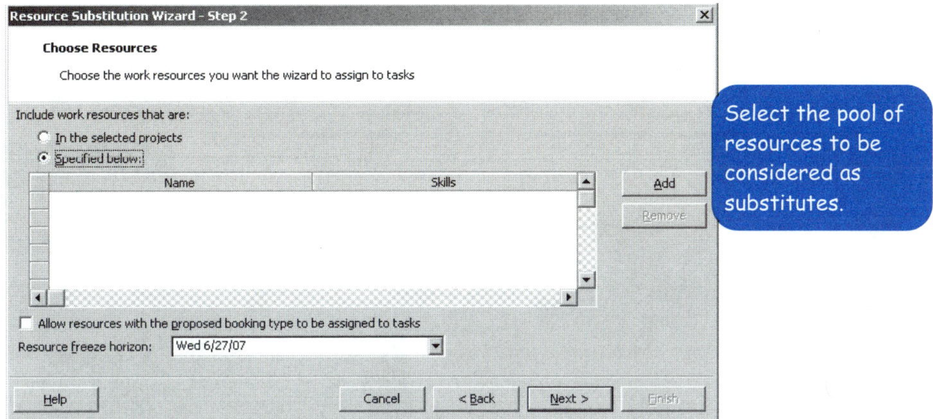

5. Choose the resources that you want the wizard to consider as substitutes. Select:
   - ⦿ **In the selected projects** for reallocating resources across multiple projects, or
   - ⦿ **Specified below** for indicating exactly who possible substitutes are.

6. You have to click the [Add] button – the **Build Pool for Resource Substitution** dialog box appears:

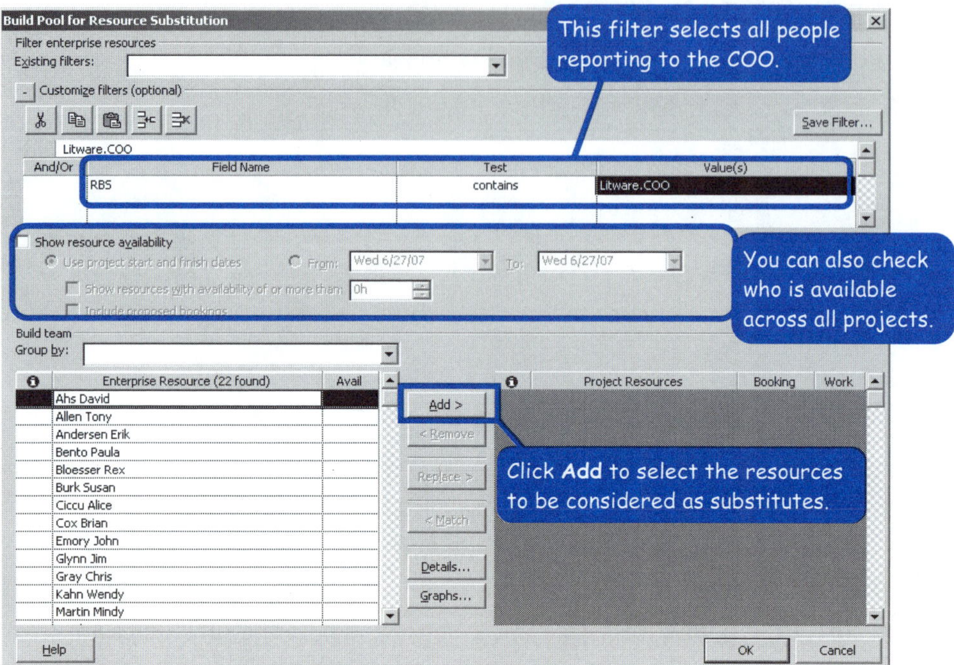

7. The **Build Pool for Resource Substitution** dialog allows you to quickly select resources by availability, skill or department. For the latter you can use the *resource breakdown structure* (*RBS)* field as shown in the screenshot; the RBS is usually based on the organizational chart. From the list **Enterprise Resource** on the left, select the resources to be added as possible substitutes. Click [Add ->] to add them to the list **Project Resources** on the right.

8. Click [OK] – you are back in the **Step 2** dialog. The list **Specified below** should list the candidate resources at this point. MS Project may not be able to find substitutes for the generic resources if you keep the list too short.

9. Enter the **Resource Freeze horizon**; before this date, no resource will be substituted. The later the date you enter, the fewer substitutions you will see.

10. Click Next > – the **Step 3** dialog appears:

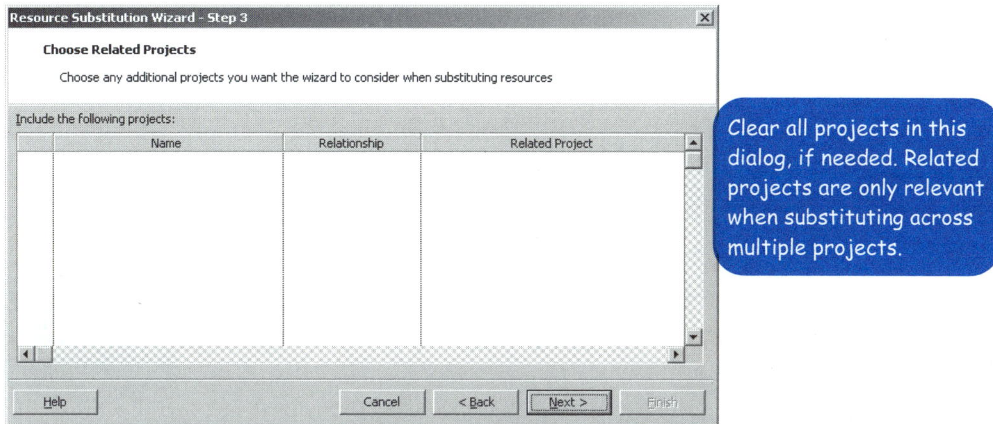

11. Related projects are projects that have cross-project links with this project, or, projects that share one or more of the same resources. Since the template will not have cross-project links and will only have generic resources, you will typically find that there are no or very few related projects. Clear any projects listed.

12. Click Next > – the **Step 4** dialog appears:

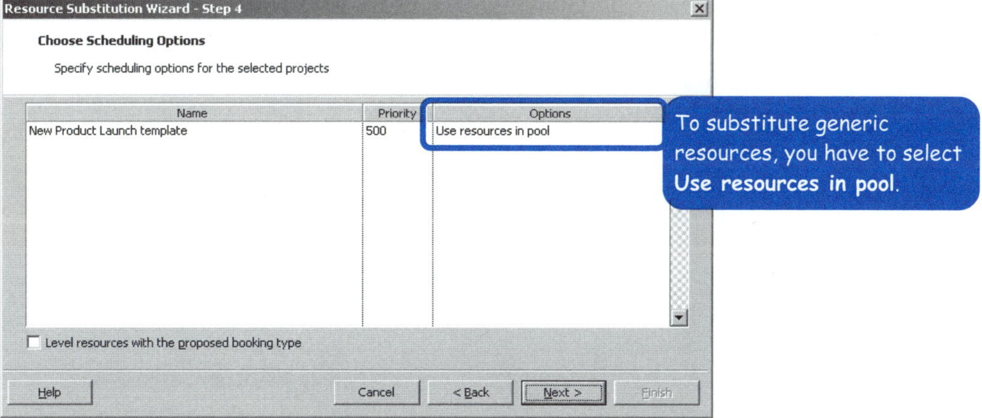

13. In the **Choose Scheduling Options** dialog, your options are:
    - ◇ The **Priority** level is relevant only when you substitute across multiple projects. You can enter a number from 0 to 1000. The higher the number, the higher priority the project will have when it competes for resources with other projects. MS Project will load resources into the highest priority projects first.
    - ◇ Under **Options,** you can specify for each project whether MS Project should keep the same resources in the project and only reassign within that project (**Use resources in project**) or should consider all resources that we selected in

the **Step 2** dialog (**Use resources in pool**). To replace generic resources, you would typically select **Use resources in pool** at this point. If you select **Use resources in project**, MS Project will not propose any substitutes, because it is only allowed to consider the generic resources that are already in the project.

14. Click [Next >] – the **Step 5** dialog appears:

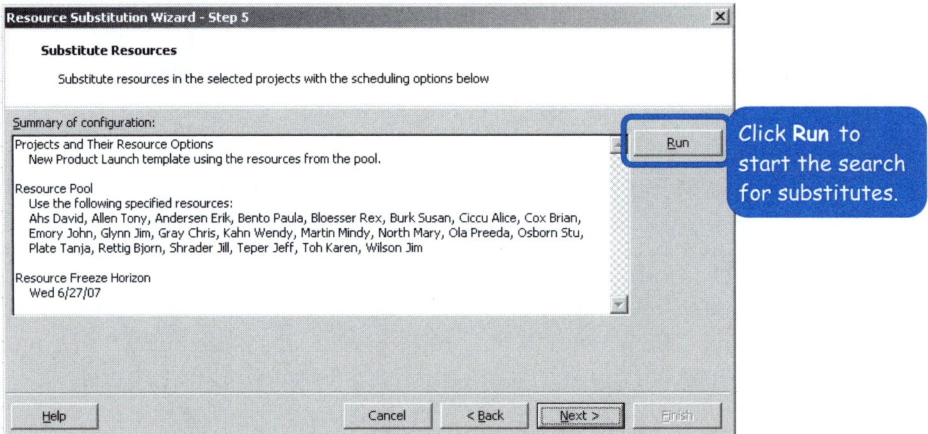

15. This dialog summarizes the settings you chose in the previous steps.
    Click [Run] to initiate the process of finding suitable substitutes. This process uses a complex algorithm that looks at project priorities, one or more skill fields, availability of the resources and other factors.
    Watch the buttons; once they are re-enabled, the substitution is done.

16. Click [Next >] – the **Step 6** dialog appears, showing the results of the resource substitution.

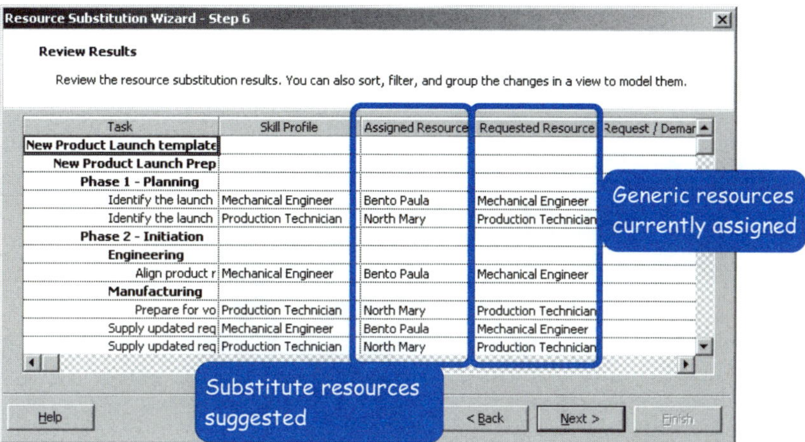

17. You can review the substitutions that Project Server proposes. The fields are as follows:
    - ◇ **Task** contains the task names.
    - ◇ **Skill profile** contains the skill profile required for the task. When generic resources are assigned, it is the skill set of that generic resource.
    - ◇ **Assigned Resource** is the actual resource the wizard recommends as a substitute for the generic resource.
    - ◇ **Requested Resource** is the generic resource originally assigned.
    - ◇ **Request/Demand** indicates whether the resource was just requested or was demanded for the task. The *Request* setting indicates that the specified resource should be used unless the resource is overallocated. The *Demand* setting indicates that the specified resource must be used and cannot be substituted.
    - ◇ This option is, again, only for substituting across multiple projects. The generic resources typically should not have this field filled in for their assignments.

18. Click [Next >] – the **Step 7** dialog appears:

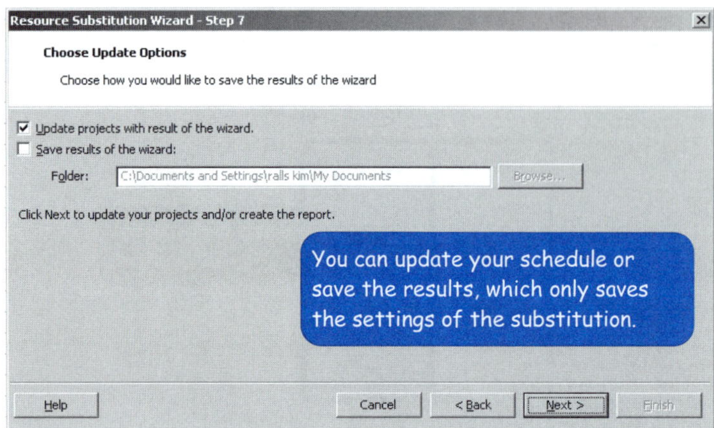

19. Check one or both options:

☑ **Update project with results of wizard**

When replacing generic resources, you would normally select this option. (However be careful because you cannot undo this action in Project 2010; it is one of the few things you cannot undo!)

☑ **Save results of the wizard** in a separate report file. Click [Browse...] to indicate the subdirectory.

When reallocating resources across projects, you would typically use this second option to store the settings in a report. Unfortunately, the report does not contain the detailed substitution suggestions by task as shown in the **Step 6** dialog of the wizard. The report does contain the date of creation, the settings you chose (so that you can reproduce the suggested substitutions) and the suggested team members for the project (the highest level result of the wizard). If the report did contain all suggested details, the report could also be used to discuss proposed substitutions with your team before updating the projects. Selecting both options would be useful for creating a change log. The report would then register what changes were made at what time (Hoping that Microsoft picks up on these hints).

20. Click [Next >] – the **Step 8** dialog appears; this is the last dialog.
Click [Finish] – the substitutions of the generic resources will appear in the project schedule.

Checks on Assignments

Next you will find checks to verify if you have applied best practices to the *assignments* in your schedule. The numbering corresponds to the complete checklist in the summary chapter, see page 711. The filters mentioned in the checks can be found in the file *ProjectPro tools to check project schedules.MPP* available for download at www.ProjectProCorp.com (see page vi for the procedure to access these files).

8 Assignments

8.1. Are you using the task-related field **Type** for **Auto Scheduled** detail tasks?
Your choices in the field **Type** are: **Fixed Duration, Fixed Units** or **Fixed Work**. With this field, you can control what MS Project recalculates on **Auto Scheduled** tasks: duration, units or work. If you do not monitor the field **Type**, you are not controlling what MS Project changes in the schedule. You are using a software tool, but you are using it in a trial-and-error fashion. This is similar to having a carpenter's stud finder, but not knowing how to use it. Instead you start drilling many holes in the drywall to find the studs by trial and error. This can result in the wall looking like it was hit by a machine gun. If you do not use the field **Type**, you are not controlling MS Project. We expect that people learn to use the field **Type** in MS Project. Only then will they master the tool. If we see the default task type **Fixed Units** and **Effort Driven** set to *No* (default setting) for all tasks in the schedule, we know people are not using this powerful feature in MS Project that makes it a pleasant tool to work with. You can check if the user has changed the **Type** of some **Auto Scheduled** detail tasks by applying the filter **8.1 Non default task Type**.

8.2. Is **Effort Driven** off for **Fixed Duration** and **Fixed Units** tasks (**Auto Scheduled**)?
Effort Driven tries to keep the work value constant. **Fixed Duration** and **Fixed Units** tasks that have **Effort Driven** on as well, have two out of the three variables fixed in the formula **Duration** * **Peak Units** = **Work**. It is then very hard to predict what MS Project will do when you change one variable. You can check this easily by applying the filter **8.2 Effort Driven tasks**.

8.3. Are there no assignments on the summary tasks?
As discussed on page 384, there are several reasons not to have assignments on summary tasks and to strictly keep assignments on detail tasks only. You can check if there are resources assigned to summary tasks by applying the filter **8.3 Summary Tasks with Resources Assigned**.

8.4. Do all detail tasks have a human resource assigned?
If there are activities without human resources assigned, you have not yet captured all the workloads in your project and not assigned responsibility. If workloads are missing, the schedule may be too optimistic, since leveling workloads often leads to longer schedules and later forecasts. An exception to this rule is that *recurring detail tasks* do not require that

8

resources be assigned to them.

You can check if all detail tasks have a human resource assigned in one of two ways:

- ◇ In the **Resource Usage** view, there should be no detail tasks with effort listed under the first category **Unassigned**.
- ◇ In the **Gantt Chart** view, you can also apply filter **8.4 Detail tasks without Resources Assigned**. The filter allows you to easily copy the tasks, including their ID number, into a schedule evaluation report to send back to the project manager.

Note that there may still be detail tasks with only material resources assigned, if you check the **Unassigned** category or apply the filter, so neither check is bullet proof.

8.5. Do detail tasks have just one human resource assigned?

As a guideline (not a hard check), we recommend that you formulate the tasks in the WBS in such a way that each task will have one resource assigned. This makes very clear who is responsible for the work and will avoid confusion and finger-pointing. There are exceptions to this guideline:

- ◇ Where people are supposed to meet to make decisions, or collaborate on tasks or work together as a group, there should obviously be more than one person assigned to the task.
- ◇ When you have a high-level schedule, you will often have multiple resources per detail task.

8.6. Are the workloads on long, elapsed duration tasks reasonable?

Elapsed duration tasks continue 24 hours a day, 7 days per week and could easily create unreasonable workloads for human resources. The elapsed durations should be less than one day when there are human resources assigned. You can apply the filter **8.6 Tasks with Elapsed Durations** to display all tasks with an elapsed duration.

Printing the Assignments

If you want to produce to-do lists across multiple projects, we recommend you use Project Professional 2010 with *Project Server*. Team members will see their entire task list from multiple projects brought together on one web page, called **Tasks,** in Project Web App.

If you only have MS Project, you can still do it, but it requires more work.

Alternatively, you can display the assignments below each resource, click ribbon **View**, **Resource Usage**. Assignments appear in this view as task names indented in between resource names:

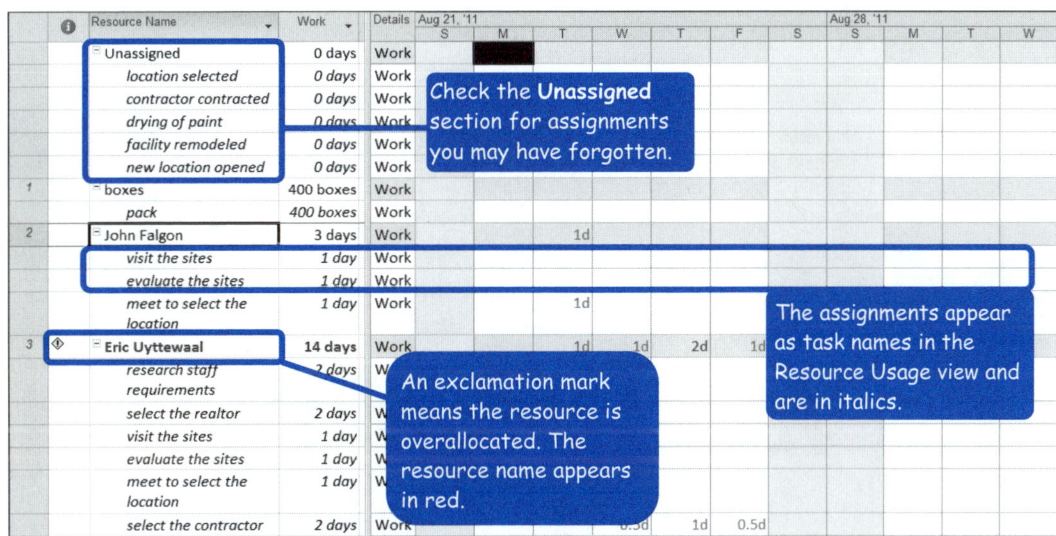

If you do not see the numbers in the timescale, select a resource and click ribbon **Task** and **Scroll to task** (in the **Editing** section). To switch the time unit in the timescale between months, weeks and days, use the **Zoom In** or the **Zoom Out** tool in the bottom right of your screen, or click ribbon **View** and use the **Timescale** list to get it exactly right.

If you want to create a to-do list for one resource, you can apply the filter **Resource Range…** and enter the ID number of the resource (twice).
OR
You can insert page breaks between all resources by adding the button **Insert Page**

8

Break to the Quick Access Toolbar (see page 74), positioning the cursor on each resource and clicking this **Insert Page Break** button.

You can print row totals and column totals in the timescale of the usage views. In the Task Usage or Resource Usage view, you can select these totals in this way: click the **File** ribbon, click Print, click hyperlink **Page Setup**, tab **View** and checking ☑ **Print row totals for values within print date range** and ☑ **Print column totals.**

In Project 2010, you can now Save to PDF (ribbon **File**, item **Save As**, under **Save as type** select **PDF-files** from the list) then email the PDF-file instead, and save our beautiful trees here in Canada!

Alternatively, you can display the to-do list for one resource in a WBS-oriented view. Click ribbon **View**, button **Task Usage** to apply the **Task Usage** view, which shows all *assignments* in detail. The assignments appear in this view as resource names, since they are in between the tasks:

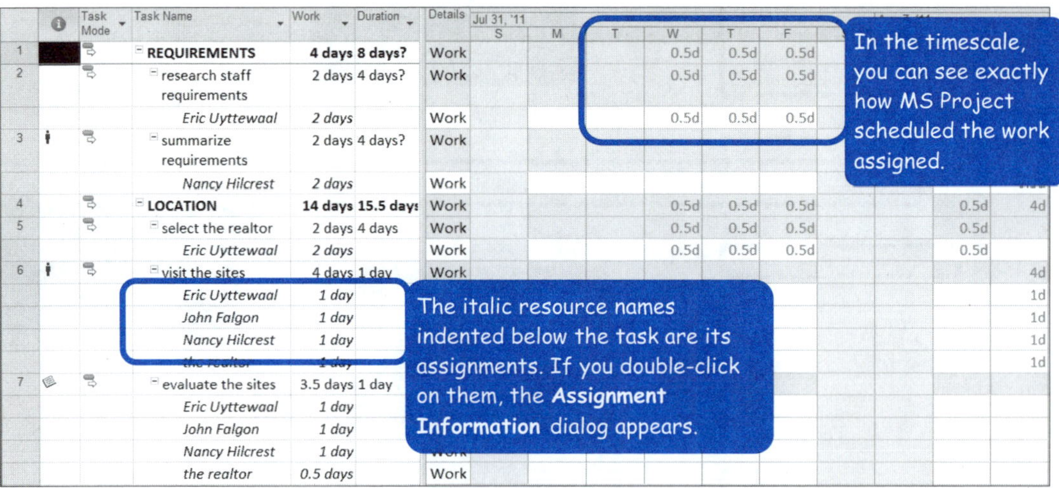

If you would like to print a to-do list of assignments for one resource you can apply the filter **Using Resource...** which will prompt you for the name of the resource.

Exercises

Review A

1. What is the definition of an *assignment*?
2. In your own words, describe what the following fields represent:
   a. **Units** field in the Task Form view
   b. **Units** field in the **Resource Information** dialog, tab **General**
   c. **Max Units** field in the Resource Sheet view
   d. **Work** field in the Gantt Chart view
   e. **Work** field in the Task Form view
   f. **Work** field in the Resource Sheet view
   g. Task-related **Work** field in the Task Usage view
   h. Assignment-related **Work** field in the Task Usage view
3. In your own words, what is a *Work Contour*?
4. A project manager realizes that she wants to model her project on a high level. She will enter only team resources (consolidated or pooled resources) in her Resource Sheet. What setting would you recommend to her for ribbon **File**, Options, tab **Schedule**, field **Show assignment units as a**?
5. What are the three task types (field **Type**)? How does each task type function? How would you use this feature of MS Project?
6. In your own words, what are the three rules that will help you control what MS Project calculates when creating and changing assignments?
7. Before you make a change on an assignment, what question should you ask yourself and what field(s) should you check?
8. Describe two different ways of assigning resources to tasks in MS Project. Describe them in detail in terms of mouse clicks or ribbon buttons. What are the differences between these two methods in terms of options you have?
9. Would you recommend making multiple, uneven assignments to many tasks in your schedule? Justify your answer in terms of pros and cons.
10. Would you recommend assigning resources to summary tasks? Justify your answer in terms of pros and cons.
11. A resource is writing two different documents concurrently and you cannot plan or predict when he will be working on one or the other. How would you model this situation in MS Project? In particular, what tasks and assignments would you create and what number of resource units would you assign?

Review B

Read the following situations; determine if you expect to make your first estimate in *person days* work (PD), in *business days* duration (BD) or in *elapsed days* duration (ED). Explain why. Indicate which type of task you recommend: Fixed Duration (FD), Fixed Units (FU) or Fixed Work (FW), and explain why.

	PD, BD or ED? Why?	**FD, FU or FW? Why?**
1. A 10-page report that normally takes a person 4 hours per page to produce		
2. One load to be transported over a distance of 4,000 miles with one driver		
3. One package that has to be flown a distance of over 4,000 miles and has to arrive in 2 working days		
4. A house painter who is asked for a fixed price quote and the earliest end date for painting a family home		
5. A contractor gives a painter a maximum of 2 weeks to finish painting a building		
6. Backup of a computer system before the conversion to a new operating system, where the backing up requires little supervision once started		
7. A meeting, with a presentation to all team members		

Relocation Project — Entering Assignments

The goal of this exercise is to be able to assign resources to all detail tasks.

1. Continue to work with your file *Relocation.mpp* or open *08A Assignments.mpp* available for download at www.ProjectProCorp.com (see page vi for the procedure to access these files).
2. Add the fields **Type, Duration** and **Work** to the Gantt Chart view in such a way that the view matches the column headings of the *task fields* in the next table (see page 175 for how-to steps). Note that you cannot add the column *Units* shown in the next table as a column to the Gantt Chart.
3. The units are presented in decimals in the table below, whereas MS Project will show percentages by default. Click ribbon **File**, Options, tab **Schedule** and change **Show Assignment units as a** to **Decimal** in order to enter the numbers as shown.
4. The next table provides all assignment information for the Relocation project. Enter all assignments including their units by using the **Assign Resources** dialog (ribbon **Resource**, button **Assign Resources**) or the **Task Form** (click ribbon **View**, Details). The **Task Form** is best when you want to assign multiple resources and enter specific numbers for units and/or work. Please note the following:
   - ◇ MS Project uses the formula **Duration** * **Peak Units** = **Work** and will calculate the third value not provided in the next table for each detail task.
   - ◇ No data are provided for summary tasks (blank cells), because assignments are not recommended on summary tasks.
   - ◇ Only the **Fixed Work** tasks are **Effort Driven**.
   - ◇ Schedule conflict messages will appear, because some deadlines are missed. Select ⦿ **Continue** on these messages.
5. Compare your file with the solution file *09A Optimal Schedule — Time.mpp* available for download at *www.ProjectProCorp.com* (see page vi for the procedure to access these files). See page 697 of this book for an automated way of comparing and reporting differences between two versions of one schedule. Notice that the project is missing its November 1 deadline. We will need to optimize the schedule.
6. Save the file when done.

8

TASK FIELDS				ASSIGNMENT FIELDS	
Task Name	**Type**	**Dur.**	**Work**	**Resource Names**	**Units**
REQUIREMENTS	Fixed Duration				
research staff requirements	Fixed Work		2d	you	0.5
summarize requirements	Fixed Work		2d	Hilcrest	0.5
LOCATION	Fixed Duration				
select the realtor	Fixed Duration	4 d		you	0.5
visit the sites	Fixed Duration	1 d		Falgon Hilcrest the realtor you	1 1 1 1
evaluate the sites	Fixed Duration	1 d		Falgon Hilcrest the realtor you	1 1 0.5 1
meet to select the location	Fixed Duration	1 d		Falgon Hilcrest Salin you	1 1 1 1
legal review	Fixed Duration	0.5 d		Roach	1
REMODELING CONTRACT	Fixed Duration				
select the contractor	Fixed Duration	2 d		you	1
meet to discuss contract	Fixed Duration	1 d		you the contractor Hilcrest	1 1 1
revise the schedule	Fixed Duration	1 d		you	1
negotiate the contract	Fixed Duration	1 d		you	1
REMODELED LOCATION	Fixed Duration				
relocate walls	Fixed Work		100 d	the contractor	10
install electric wiring	Fixed Work		25 d	the contractor	5

TASK FIELDS				ASSIGNMENT FIELDS	
Task Name	**Type**	**Dur.**	**Work**	**Resource Names**	**Units**
paint	Fixed Work		8 d	the contractor	4
drying of paint	Fixed Duration	4 ed			
install cabinetry	Fixed Work		40 d	the contractor	8
install LAN	Fixed Work		60 d	the LAN consultants	5
lay carpet	Fixed Work		60 d	the contractor	6
MOVE	Fixed Duration				
select mover	Fixed Duration	2 d		you	1
pack	Fixed Duration	2 d		the employees boxes	35 400
move	Fixed Work		20 d	the movers	10
unpack	Fixed Duration	2 d		the employees	35

Relocation Project — Changing Assignments

The goal of this exercise is to be able to control the calculations that MS Project makes when changing values of the assignments. Continue to work with your file *Relocation.mpp* or open the file *09A Optimal Schedule — Time.mpp* available for download at www.ProjectProCorp.com (see page vi for the procedure to access these files). Notice that the units are presented in decimals below, whereas MS Project may show percentages. Click ribbon **File**, Options, tab **Schedule** and change **Show Assignment units as a** to **Decimal**. You can now use the number of units as indicated below. You may need to change the **Type** and **Effort Driven** of the task first before changing an assignment. Please use the process as explained on page 379 and the **Task Usage** view (with columns **Type**, **Effort Driven, Duration, Peak** and **Work** inserted). The task *install LAN* currently has a duration of 12 days, 5 consultants working on it and 60 days of work. Enter the following what-if scenarios:

1. You would like to know how much work the task *install LAN* would take if there were 6 *LAN consultants* instead of 5 while keeping the duration the same. What task type do you need before you make this change?
   I used the task **Type**: …………………….. **Effort Driven**: ……….
   You should get a Work value of 72 days; continue with this number for the next scenario.

2. You want to know how many consultants are needed if you want the task *install LAN* done in 3 days while keeping the work the same. What task type do you need before you make this change?
   I used the task **Type**: …………………….. **Effort Driven**: ……….
   You should find that 24 *LAN consultants* are needed in the **Peak** field on the assignment; continue with this number of consultants for the next scenario.

3. You think you overestimated the work; you will need only 30 days instead of 72 days and you want to keep the duration to 3 days. What task type do you need before you make this change?
   I used the task **Type**: …………………….. **Effort Driven**: ……….
   You should find that 10 consultants are needed now in the **Peak** field on the assignment; continue with this number of consultants for the next scenario.

4. You want to keep the number of consultants to 10, but you want to change the duration from 3 to 12 days. How much work is now on the task? What task type do you need before you make this change?
   I used the task **Type**: …………………….. **Effort Driven**: ……….
   You should end up with 72 days of work; continue with this duration for the next scenario.

5. You want to bring the number of consultants down to 5 while keeping the 12-day duration. How much work is now on the task? What task type do you need before you make this change?
   I used the task **Type**: …………………….. **Effort Driven**: ……….
   The work should now be 60 days, which brings us back to where we were at the start of this exercise. You can see how quickly you can develop scenarios with a dynamic model of your project.

6. Close the file without saving!

Chapter 9 Finding the Optimal Schedule

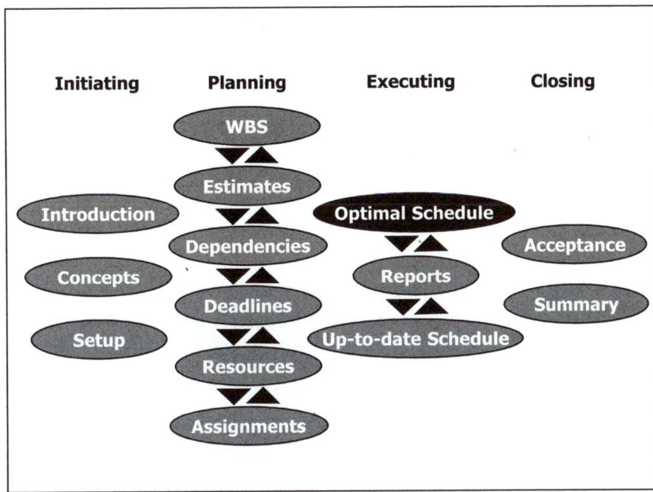

After entering all schedule data, we now have a draft schedule. In most situations, the draft schedule will show that the duration is too long, the cost is too high, the workloads are unreasonable (*overallocations*) or any combination of these. We need to work on the *draft schedule* to convert it into an *optimal schedule* (see the black ellipse above). An optimal schedule is a version of the schedule that, as much as possible, meets the requirements brought forward by project stakeholders.

In all previous chapters, we made sure that you created a dynamic, robust model of the project. With such a model, you can easily develop what-if scenarios of the schedule to explore what the optimal schedule could look like.

9

After reading this chapter you will:

- be aware of three approaches for optimizing schedules:
  - optimizing for time
  - optimizing for time and cost
  - optimizing for time, cost and resources
- be able to choose the approach that is appropriate for your own project
- be able to optimize the project for time (including scope and quality)
  - be able to display the Critical Path
  - be able to repair an incomplete Critical Path
  - understand the difference between Free Slack and Total Slack
  - be able to apply several techniques to shorten the project duration
  - be aware of the assumptions/shortcomings of the Critical Path Method (CPM)
  - know what Monte Carlo simulation is and why you would use it
- be able to optimize the project for time and cost
  - be able to reduce the cost of a project
- be able to optimize the project for time, cost and resource availability
  - be able to make workloads visible in MS Project and find overallocations
  - know how to level the workloads of the resources yourself
  - know how to make MS Project level the workloads
  - know what the Resource-Critical Path is and why it is important
  - be able to find and shorten the Resource-Critical Path
- be able to evaluate the impacts of a change to the schedule (scenario analysis)
- be able to check if the schedule is properly optimized using scheduling best practices

"Never, Ever Let MS Project Level the Workloads!"

Nob comes running around the corner and almost bumps into Bob. Nob exclaims: "I need your help, please come with me!" "What's the rush?" "My whole schedule is in shambles since I had MS Project level the workloads!"

They arrive at Nob's cubicle and sit down in front of his computer. "Look. The testing is now scheduled first when no code is ready. The implementation is done before the system was designed. MS Project made a mess of my schedule!"

Bob tries to calm Nob: "I can see that; it's not pretty!" Nob: "MS Project is a pretty dumb tool if it can't figure that out!" Bob: "Yes, it has no clue about the logical order in which things must be done unless you tell it. Let's see if you made the logic clear to MS Project. Did you set a dependency from the coding to the testing section? I can't find any." Nob: "Well, isn't it obvious that it should not schedule testing before the code is written?" Bob: "Obvious to me, but for the tool it is just another piece to put into the puzzle. You forgot to set a dependency from coding to testing ... that's why the tool thinks it can schedule testing first!" Nob: "Jeez, forgot one dependency and I end up in a mess!" Bob: "Yes, every task needs to be hooked up so the tool becomes aware of the practical necessities. You have to check the network logic carefully before you can allow MS Project to level the workloads and even before you can find a reliable Critical Path! Now that we've set these dependencies, you will see a leveled schedule that makes sense."

The Pulling Forces

Optimizing a schedule is the true art of scheduling. When optimizing, you have to consider the project in all its aspects. The Project Management Institute has identified the dimensions by which projects need to be optimized in its Guide to the Project Management Body of Knowledge (PMBOK® Guide). [49] These knowledge areas are shown with arrows in the illustration. A change in one area often impacts another. Eight forces are at work on each project, and project managers have to consider all of them in an integrated fashion. The PMBOK® Guide calls this *Project Integration Management*, the ninth knowledge area. MS Project provides sufficient features to manage the following four out of eight dimensions:

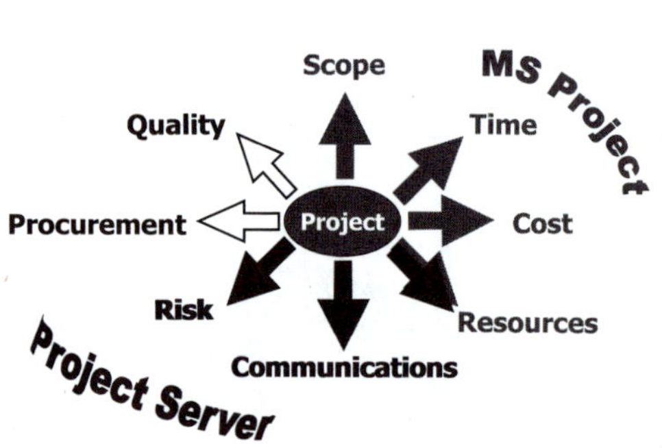

- **Scope**
  The scope of a project can be captured using the *Work Breakdown Structure* (WBS). The WBS contains the deliverables and may contain the activities to produce those deliverables. MS Project is an excellent tool for managing scope. Scope should always be considered when optimizing schedules. The scope of a project is the reason for its existence.
- **Time**
  You can schedule *deadlines* very well in MS Project and track meeting them. Since a project is a temporary endeavor, by definition all project managers will monitor and manage the duration of their project.
- **Cost**
  You can manage the expenses for labor, facilities, machines and material with MS Project so they stay within your budget. Not all project managers are given a monetary budget; therefore, not all project managers will monitor the cost of their project.
- **Resources**
  The *workloads* have to stay within the availability of the resources. You can do workload leveling by hand or have MS Project help you. When you ask MS Project to level workloads, the Critical Path can become incomplete and we will deal with

---

[49] See the *PMBOK® Guide*, Fourth Edition, published by the PMI.

this issue. A new concept, the *Resource-Critical Path*, is needed to optimize resource-constrained schedules. Project 2010 does not have features to identify the Resource-Critical Path, and we will refer to an add-in.

In MS Project as a standalone tool, we would not recommend building shared resource pools of more than 50 resources. In Project Professional with *Project Server*, you can have thousands of resources in the shared resource pool and also model the resource needs in the longer term, also known as *resource demand management* or *resource capacity planning*. Project Server allows capturing the availability of resources and keeping the workloads leveled on the shorter term. Project Server even allows you to perform skill-based scheduling and answer questions like: *What if we added another project to the portfolio and reallocated the resources; how would this impact the finish dates of our current projects?* As you can see, Project Server significantly enhances MS Project's capabilities in the resource dimension.

Project Server provides additional features to manage the following dimensions:

- **Risk**
  Risk is about adverse events that may happen in or to the project, risk is also about opportunities that may become apparent. Risk management activities can be scheduled and monitored in the schedule, but MS Project does not have adequate features for the risk processes: Plan Risk Management, Identify Risks, Perform Qualitative Risk Analysis, Perform Quantitative Risk Analysis, Plan Risk Responses and Monitor and Control Risk. [50] *Project Server* has a risk management interface that facilitates identifying risks and quantifying them using the simple probability-impact technique. In Project Server, you can also collect and manage issues. Team members can easily raise issues as they become aware of them. Managers will see an overview list of raised issues and will be able to respond to them.
  None of the Microsoft tools provides *Monte Carlo simulation*, but there are affordable add-ons that can do it. Monte Carlo simulation allows you to quantify the *time risk* in a schedule and the *monetary risk* in a budget. We will explain this technique on page 452.
- **Communications**

  You can create a variety of paper or online reports with MS Project standalone. *Project Server* enhances the communication features of MS Project tremendously, because it allows you to interact with all project stakeholders wherever they may be, as long as they can connect to the Internet or to your Intranet. If project managers

---

[50] These are the processes of the Project Risk Management knowledge area in the *PMBOK® Guide*, Fourth Edition.

keep their schedules up-to-date at all times, then executives can immediately see the latest status and forecasts at any time. With Project Server, Project managers can store documents centrally and protect their latest version by check out procedures. When checking the document back in, you are prompted to add comments on the changes you made, thus creating a change log for the document. As you can see, Project Server provides robust configuration management capabilities for project documents when you assess it using the *Practice Standard for Project Configuration Management* from PMI.[51] Furthermore, you can have up to three versions of a schedule inside the Project Server database: the initial *draft* version (called **Working** in MS Project), the *published* version, and the *archive* version you create when the project is done. You can even archive one schedule multiple times and create multiple versions in the archive.

Neither MS Project as a standalone tool or in combination with Project Server provides features for the following dimensions:

- **Procurement**
  You can schedule procurement activities in MS Project, but neither MS Project nor Project Server is a *contract management* system out-of-the-box. A separate system may be needed for managing the procurement in projects. Large projects in particular often have many contracts associated with them. You can store the contract documents in the online project workspace in Project Server and apply configuration management to them. You can also quantify the demand for resource to contract. However, even Project Server is not a contract management system. If you need that, you could custom develop it in SharePoint (custom lists wrapped into a workflow) or use an off-the-shelf ERP-system that integrates well with Project Server, like Microsoft *Dynamics AX* (was *Axapta*).
- **Quality**
  The quality of deliverables must correspond to the specifications and expectations of the client. You can schedule activities to ensure the quality in MS Project, but neither MS Project nor Project Server provides a full-fledged quality management system. Such a system typically contains the specifications, requirements, or acceptance criteria for the deliverables. For software development projects, we recommend you complement MS Project with a requirements tracking system, like Microsoft *Team Foundation Server* (*TFS*), for example, which integrates now really well with Project Server 2010. For *new product development* projects, you could use *Rational DOORS* (IBM). However, quality impacts can and should always be considered while optimizing, even without a quality tracking system. As a project

[51] *Practice Standard for Project Configuration Management*, PMI, Newtown Square, PA, 2007

manager you must ask yourself if a change to the schedule or budget will also have impact on quality, and you must keep your eye on quality at all the times. Always keeping your eye on quality is what we will do in this chapter on optimizing the schedule.

Improving one dimension of the project often impacts the others. When the impact is negative, you are *trading off* among the dimensions. For example, if you hire more resources to meet a tight deadline, this may reduce the time as desired, but increase the cost as well. Some methods are positive in one or more respect and neutral in others. These are the methods to find and apply first. We will suggest several such methods.

Three Approaches for Optimizing Schedules

We will present to you three different approaches for optimizing schedules. In all three, we include consideration of both quality and scope. Because these dimensions do not differentiate the approaches, we have not included the words *scope* or *quality* in their names. The different approaches are:

- *Optimizing for Time* (see page 417)
  When you optimize for time, you consider only the forces scope, quality and time. In fact, you try to find the scenario of the schedule in which you maximize scope and quality and achieve them in the least time possible. The common technique used in this situation is the *Critical Path Method* (*CPM*). Many industries have been using CPM for decades. Typically, the construction and consulting industries apply CPM. These industries tend to hire and release resources on an as-need basis, often working with *temporary* resources. Other industries find this optimization too narrow, particularly when cost is a concern or resources are not readily available. When you apply CPM, you optimize under the assumption of having access to *unlimited resources* – you can hire any resources when you need them or fire them when you do not need them. Being able to release your resources to other projects within the company, rather than firing them, also meets this criterion. Assuming unlimited resources also implies that cost is not of primary concern to you.
- *Optimizing for Time and Cost* (see page 459)
  If you have a limited financial budget and cost is your concern, you should apply this approach. It is also applicable if you can get more money to solve scope, quality or time problems. Money can be used to buy better raw materials, rent better equipment or pay penalties for late delivery. However, if you use the extra money to increase resource availability, you should use the next approach instead of just focusing on time and cost, since you are now manipulating the resource dimension.
- *Optimizing for Time, Cost and Resources* (see page 467)
  If you are in a *resource-constrained* situation where you must consider the availability and capacity of the resources in order to derive a feasible schedule for

9

your project, we recommend using this approach. You increase resource availability when you hire more people, subcontract to free-lancers or rent more facilities or equipment, but you also make trade-off decisions among scope, quality, time, cost and *resource availability*. An example of optimizing for time, cost and resources is when you consider paying extra to get more overtime from your team. If your resources are scarce, you will have to look at their availability and their workload. You will have to level the resource workloads. Leveling often breaks the Critical Path in MS Project and CPM does not help us any longer. Instead we will use a technique that is called the *Resource-Critical Path.*

As you can see, we are adding one dimension to the optimization with each approach. Most resource decisions impact the cost side of our model, and the logical progression in our opinion is optimizing for time, then time and cost, then time, cost and resources. The optimizations become more complex as we add more dimensions to consider. With Scope and Quality, we include five out of the eight dimensions. This is the most complex optimization we will discuss in this book. It also is the most complex one that MS Project can assist you with as a standalone application.

Do I Have a Resource-Constrained Project?

This is an important question to answer first. If you do not know the answer, you cannot decide which approach is best for your schedule. If you have easy access to resources, optimizing for time may be appropriate. If resource availability impacts your schedule, optimizing for time, cost and resources is the way to go. If you are not sure if resource availability impacts the forecasts in your schedule, you will get some indication by asking yourself the following questions:

- Are you using any *experts*?
  Experts are by definition rare and hard to get at the exact time you need them. If you use expert resources on your project team, you are likely in a resource-constrained situation. From a scheduling point of view the definition of an expert would be *any person who is not always available when needed.*
- Are resources shared across multiple projects and will your resources be affected when other projects slip? If this is the case, you are likely in a resource-constrained situation.
- Did you find in previous projects that your organization often changed its commitments of resources to your project? If this is the case, you are likely in a resource-constrained situation.

If you have built your detailed schedule already, including resources and assignments, and have not yet leveled the workloads, you can find out with certainty if you are in a resource-constrained project by performing the following test:

1. Save your schedule; you may have to return to this saved version.
2. Check what your current finish date is. Click ribbon **Project**, then [Project Information] – the **Finish date** field displays the date. Write it down.
3. Do a complete leveling of workloads; click ribbon **Resource** and [Leveling Options]:
   Clear ☐ **Clear leveling values before leveling**
   Select ◉ **Level entire project**
   Clear ☐ **Level only within available slack**
   Select ☑ **Level resources with the proposed booking type**
   Select ☑ **Level Manually scheduled tasks**

4. Click [Level All] – the workloads are leveled automatically. If you get a prompt to skip overallocations, you have used too many *constraint dates* in your schedule and this test will not be conclusive.
5. Check if the project finish date is later now?
   ◇ If yes, you have a *resource-constrained* schedule; you need to optimize for time, cost and resources (see page 467) and find the Resource-Critical Path (see page 499).
   ◇ If no, you have a schedule that is not resource-constrained; you can optimize for time only and you can apply CPM as your optimization technique (see page 417).

6. Click ribbon **File** and [Close] and do not save the schedule. Re-open the version of the schedule you saved before this procedure or use **Undo** [↶ ▾] to revert to it.

9

Choosing the Options

The following options are relevant for all optimizing approaches. Click ribbon **File**, [Options] and click on the tab indicated in the table below where you want to change settings:

Tab	Option
Advanced	In section **Display options for this project:** ☑ **Show project summary task** The project summary task is inserted at the top of the task list and summarizes the entire project. It has ID number 0 (zero) and everything indented beneath it. The project summary task displays the total duration, effort and cost of the project. Other schedules are not affected when you (un)check this option, because they are stored in the project schedule; see the label of this section **Display Options for this project <name of the project>**. You can turn it on for all new projects if you select **All New Projects** first from that list.
	In section **Calculation options for this project** at the bottom: ☐ **Calculate multiple critical paths** We recommend you keep this option off in a single project schedule. One schedule should have only one ending point in its network logic, and that is the end of the critical path. If there are multiple ending points, there are always multiple critical paths and this option can display them all. This may be useful if you have inserted multiple projects into one portfolio schedule. This option is also stored in the project schedule.
	Tasks are critical if slack is less than or equal to [0] **days** This field creates a threshold for marking tasks that are critical. MS Project calculates if a task is critical. By default, this option is set to zero, which means that MS Project displays tasks with zero or negative slack as critical and shows them in red. MS Project stores this option in the project schedule.

Instead of using the options above, there is an easier way of displaying the project summary task in a Gantt Chart. Click the **Format** ribbon and select

☑ Project Summary Task – the project summary task is displayed and shows the duration, total cost and work for the project. The task name of the project summary task is the **Title** of the project that can be found in ribbon **File**, tab **Info**, **Project Information** (on the right-hand side of screen)**, Advanced Properties**, and tab **Summary**. If no title is filled in, the file name (or schedule name from Project Server) will stand in for it. However, we recommend using the project **Title** field; it makes a better name for the project.

Switching to Auto Scheduled Tasks

You will not see the gains of your optimizing efforts immediately if you continue to work with *manually scheduled* tasks, since they are not rescheduled by the *network logic*. We want to make the schedule of the project dynamic at this point to see the gains of our optimizing efforts right away. We recommend you switch all tasks in your schedule over to **Auto Scheduled** (field **Task Mode**) at this point. See page 220 for the how-to steps. If you apply *rolling wave* scheduling, we recommend you switch all tasks in the detailed planning window over to auto scheduled.

Optimizing for Time

The three dimensions that we will consider in this type of optimization are *quality*, *scope* and *time* (see the solid black arrows in the illustration). When you try to decrease the duration of the project and trade off with quality or scope, you are essentially doing an optimization on the dimension of time. The technique for this type of optimization is the Critical Path Method (CPM). Many experienced project managers are used to keeping their eye on the cost and resources while crashing the Critical Path, but we will not do that. Here, we will discuss the CPM in its original form. Later, we will discuss including cost (see page 457) and resources (see page 467).

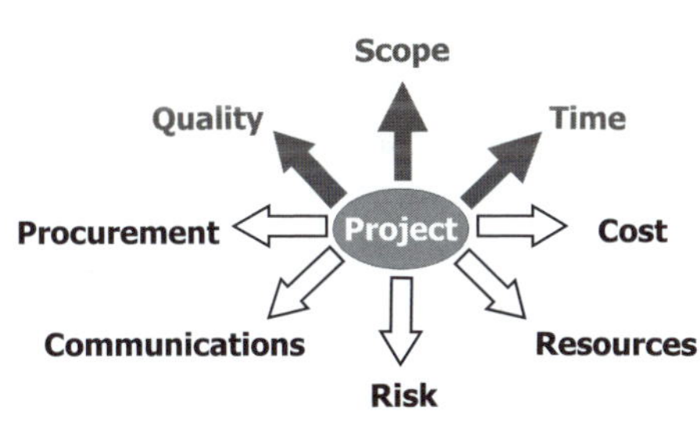

Techniques

- **The Critical Path Method (CPM)**
  CPM is a beautiful product of human logic. The beauty lies in helping project managers meet their deadlines by focusing their attention on the subset of tasks that

are most likely to affect the project finish date. Critical tasks have the least amount of buffer time (*slack*), and delays experienced on critical tasks often translate into slipping the project end date. Critical tasks have more time risk than noncritical tasks. CPM uses a single duration estimate for each task.

- **Simulation of the Schedule**
  Estimates are often more realistic when using *range estimates* instead of *single-point estimates*. The compounded effect of all these ranges can be quantified using *Monte Carlo simulation*. This type of simulation creates many versions of the schedule, while picking single points within the range estimates for each version. The simulation software then averages all the versions of the schedule to arrive at the probability for each possible finish date. For more on Monte Carlo simulation (see page 452).

The Critical Path Method (CPM)

The *Critical Path* is the longest path through the network of logical dependencies of the project. [52] The Critical Path in your schedule determines how long your project will take. The illustration depicts a simple authoring project: *outline* the document, *write* the text, *edit* the text, while somebody else *makes graphics*. When the text is edited and the graphics are ready, the *format* document task can commence. When done, the project is finished. All arrows are finish-to-start dependencies, and all durations are below the task names. Before we explain the Critical Path theory, you should ask yourself: *What is the longest path through this network?*

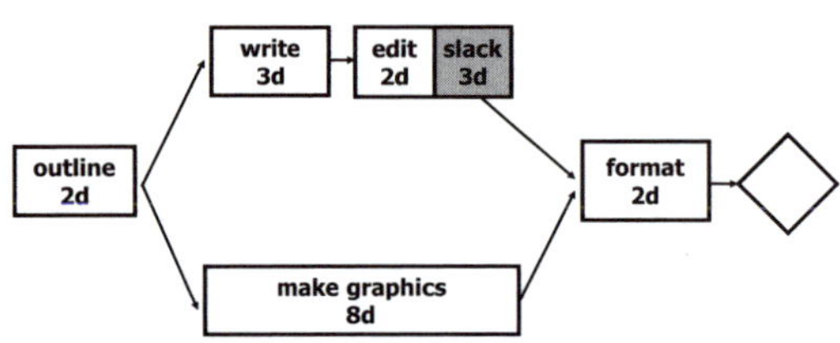

It does not take a rocket scientist to find that the longest path for this project is 12 days running through *outline*, *make graphics* and *format*. If you came up with the correct answer, you understand the Critical Path concept intuitively. To find the Critical Path, compare the parallel paths. Determine the duration of each path (taking leads and lags into account) and compare the totals. The longest one is the Critical Path that drives

[52] Adapted from the *PMBOK® Guide*, Fourth Edition, published by the PMI

when *format* can start. In the illustration, you can see that the two parallel alternatives for the Critical Path are the path *write (3d)* and *edit (2d)* which is 5 days long in total versus the path *make graphics (8d)*. It is clear that the *make graphics* path is the longest and determines the project end date. You need to continue comparing parallel paths in your schedule until you have checked them all and found the longest path in the whole network; the longest path is the Critical Path. In this simple example, there are no further parallel paths and we have found the entire Critical Path of 12 days consisting of: *outline*, *make graphics*, and *format*.

The Critical Path determines the minimum duration of the project. We call it the *minimum duration* of the project, because the real duration may be longer when some resources are overallocated. Overallocations may force tasks to be delayed past the minimum duration. Finding the Critical Path is challenging:

- When there are many *parallel paths*
- When different types of *dependencies* are used: Finish-to-Start, Start-to-Start, Finish-to-Finish, Start-to-Finish
- When there are *lags* or *leads* on the dependencies, especially when relative lags are used.
- When there are many challenging deadline dates which can make all tasks critical.

Given cases such as these and a large amount of data to digest, it is nice to have the help of a tool like MS Project that will identify the Critical Path automatically and quickly for you.

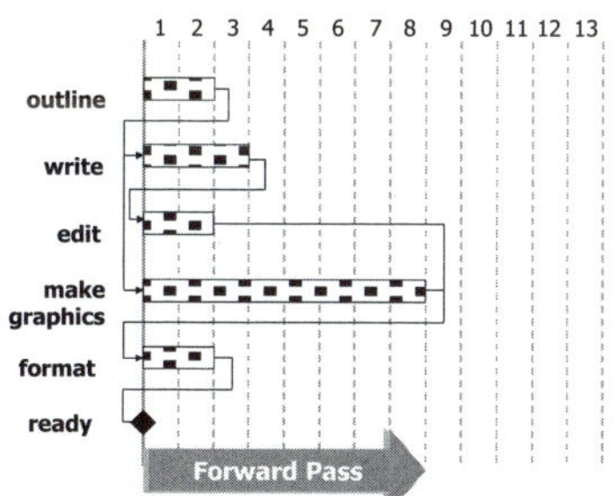

Let us look at how MS Project goes about finding the Critical Path. MS Project starts with all tasks cuddled up to the project start date, as shown in the illustration. Then it schedules them to their earliest possible dates; *as soon as possible* scheduling. MS Project then performs the forward pass calculation to determine the *earliest possible dates* (*early dates*). Then it schedules all tasks *As Late As Possible* in the backward pass and calculates the *latest allowable dates* (*late dates*) to meet the project finish date found in the forward pass.

Forward Pass

On the *forward pass*, MS Project calculates two dates for each task: the early start (ES) and the early finish (EF) date while ignoring any deadlines or date constraints. The result of this forward pass is shown in the illustration. MS Project starts with the first task (*outline*), looks at its duration (*2 days*) and calculates the earliest date it can be ready. This is the **Early Finish** (EF) date. The task *outline* will be ready at the end of day 2. MS Project will then continue determining the **Early Start** (ES) date of the successor(s). *Write* and *make graphics* are the successors; they can start on day 3. The early start of the successors will be the same as the early finish of *outline*, unless other dependencies on the successors cause them to start later. MS Project continues to calculate the early finish for *write*, *edit* and *make graphics*.

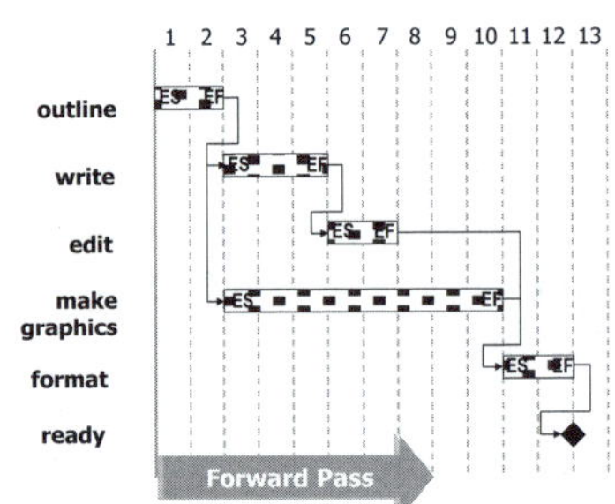

Format cannot start until both *edit* and *make graphics* are finished; if a task has more than one predecessor, it has to take both predecessors into account. The earliest start date for *format* is therefore day 11 even though *format* could start on day 8, if it depended solely on *edit*. MS Project continues through the last task in the chain. The software now knows what the earliest finish date for the project is day 12 in our example.

Backward Pass

MS Project then performs a *backward pass* through the network starting at the project end date, the end of day 12. It calculates the late finish (LF) dates for the tasks, as shown in the illustration. The **Late Finish** date is the latest date a task should be finished in order to meet the project end date. By subtracting the duration of the task from the finish date, MS Project then calculates the late start date. The **Late Start** (LS) date is the latest date you can start working on the task to finish by its late finish date. For *format,* this is day 11, the same as its early start date. We then continue with the late

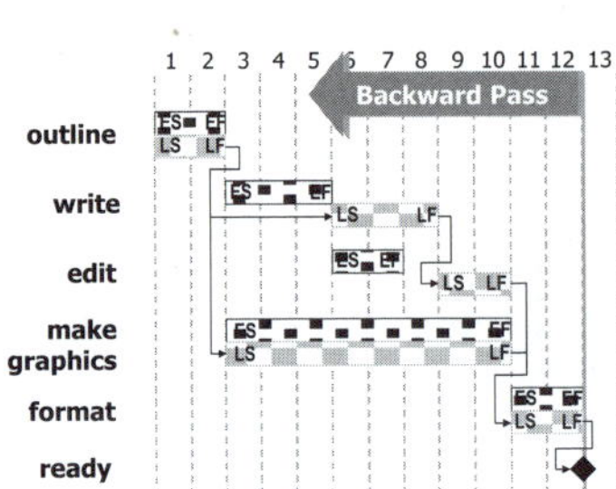

finish dates of the predecessors. *Edit* can finish on day 10 at the latest and the project will still end on day 12. *Edit* has a late finish date (day 10) that is 3 days later than its early finish date (day 7); therefore, *edit* has a time buffer called *slack*.

If a task has more than one successor, like *outline*, MS Project has to take all successors into consideration to determine the late date. The earliest of the late start dates of its successors determines the late finish date of the task, in this case start of day 3 (*make graphics*), not start of day 6 (*write*). So, the latest finish for creating the *outline* is determined by the late start date of *make graphics*, and not the late start date of *write*. As a result, the early and the late dates for *outline* are the same; *outline* does not have slack.

There are two kinds of slack in MS Project: Total Slack and Free Slack. The PMBOK® Guide uses the word *Float* rather than *Slack*; they are synonyms.

Calculating Total Slack

Total slack (*Total Float*) is the amount of time you can delay a task without affecting the project end date. The total slack (TS) is the *late finish* (LF) date minus the *early finish* (EF) date of a task:[53] TS = LF – EF

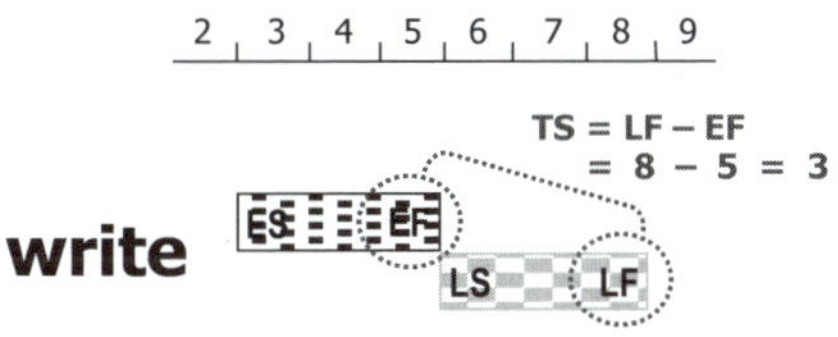

2 3 4 5 6 7 8 9
TS = LF – EF
= 8 – 5 = 3
write
ES EF
LS LF

Total slack tells you how much a task can slip before delaying the whole project, *hard constraint* dates or *deadline* dates in the schedule. For example, the illustration shows that the task *Write* has 3 days of total slack (*TS = 8 – 5 = 3*). If the author calls you and tells you he fell ill, you would ask, "*When do you think you might be better?*" If the answer is more than 3 days, you know you should find somebody else if you cannot permit the project to slip. If the answer is less than 3 days, you may still have a problem, because the editor will now receive the text later, which might cause conflicts in her schedule. You need to communicate!

The *total slack* of tasks can be:

- Greater than zero: *positive slack*
  These tasks have a buffer and can be delayed for as much total slack as they have. A lengthier delay will slip either the whole project, a hard constraint date or a

---

[53] In fact, MS Project also calculates total slack on the start dates: TS = LS – ES; the lesser of the two total slacks will be the total slack displayed on the task.

deadline date. You can often resolve some overallocations by using the total slack of a task.

- Equal to zero: *zero slack*
  Where the *late finish* date is equal to the *early finish* date, there is no slack. Tasks without slack are on the *Critical Path*; MS Project sees critical tasks as tasks with total slack that is less than or equal to zero.
- Less than zero: *negative slack*
  Tasks with a negative slack are tasks that do not meet hard constraint dates or deadline dates set in the schedule. Slack can only be negative if there are constraints or deadlines in the schedule that inhibit MS Project from finding and displaying a schedule that meets all those restrictions.

Calculating Free Slack

The *free slack* (FS) or *Free Float* of a task is the **Early Start** date of the task's successor minus the **Early Finish** date of the task itself. If there is more than one successor, you should take the earliest **Early Start** date of all its successors:
FS = ES $_{\text{earliest successor}}$ – EF.

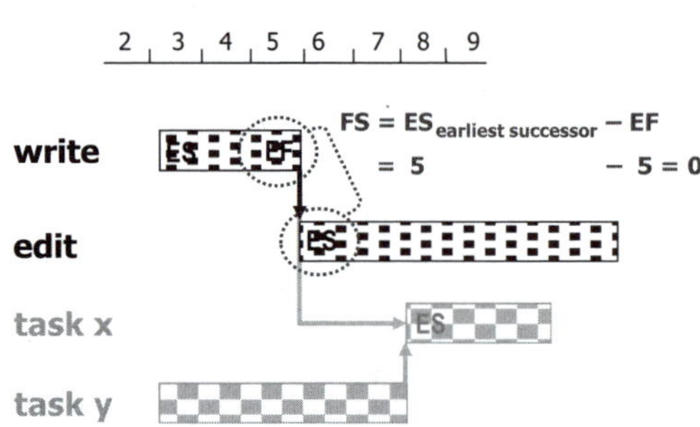

In the illustration, the earliest successor of task *Write* is *Edit* instead of *task x*. The free slack tells you how much you can let the task slip before it affects any of its immediate successors. *Write* does not have free slack, since the successor *Edit* starts immediately after *write* finishes. The free slack of a task is always less than or equal to its total slack.

The difference between total slack and free slack manifests itself in the task *Write*; it has no *free slack* but 3 days of *total slack*. It can use the free slack of its successor *Edit* and slip without delaying the project end date. That is the beauty of the concept of total slack; it tells for each task immediately when the project finish date, hard constraint dates or deadline dates are in jeopardy.

MS Project calculates all the dates we discussed; you can find these dates in the task fields **Early Start**, **Early Finish**, **Late Start** and **Late Finish**. The two slack fields are **Total Slack** and **Free Slack**.

The Critical Path

MS Project will then find the *Critical Path* by identifying the tasks that have the lowest number of total slack days. In our example, the tasks *Outline*, *Make Graphics* and *Format* have 0 days of total slack compared to 3 days total slack on *Write* and *Edit*. The tasks *Outline*, *Make Graphics* and *Format* are on the Critical Path. In the illustration, they are the dark task bars. MS Project can easily highlight the Critical Path by coloring it red. In any **Gantt Chart** view, you can click the **Format** ribbon and select

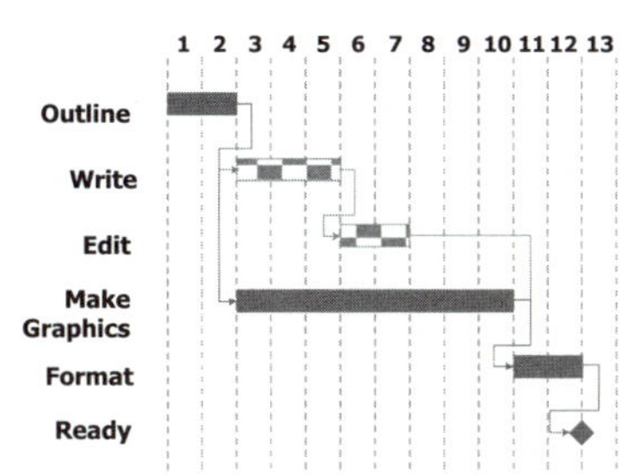

Critical Tasks to display the Critical Path as a red highlight. If the schedule currently shows that you miss the project deadline, you can display the Critical Path and optimize it to shorten your schedule and finish on time.

Every time you change the schedule, MS Project will quickly recalculate the Critical Path (if the ribbon **File**, Options, tab **Schedule**, section **Calculation**, **Calculate project after each edit** is set to ⦿ **On**, which is on by default). You can force a recalculation at any time by pressing F9.

Date Constraints, Deadlines and Negative Slack

Hard *date constraints* or *deadline* dates in the schedule may create more pressure on the network than the project finish date found in the forward pass. If this is the case, MS Project does the backward pass from that constraint or deadline date instead. The constraint or deadline date that presses hardest against the network of dependencies will determine the slack numbers on the Critical Path. Hard date constraints and deadline dates affect the late start and finish dates only, not the early dates. The forward pass determines the early dates, ignoring the constraint dates and deadlines dates.

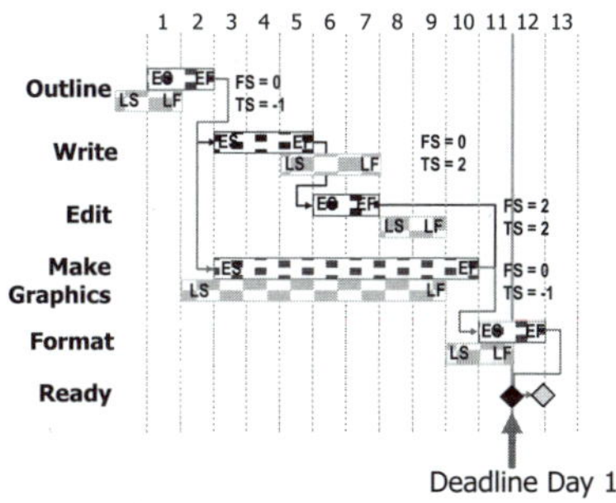

The backward pass takes deadline and hard constraint dates into account.

In our sample project, we will introduce a deadline that is one day before the earliest possible finish date of the project. The illustration shows how this changes the total slack numbers of all tasks. The backward pass is calculated from the deadline date, end of day 11, instead of the earliest possible project finish date, end of day 12. As a result, all late dates and total slack numbers change.

You can see that the slack turns negative when the latest allowable dates (LF) are before the earliest possible dates (EF). The critical tasks now have –1 day (minus one day) total slack. When slack is negative, project managers speak of *negative slack*. MS Project identifies this as a *scheduling conflict* and warns you with prompts.

Deadlines and certain constraints can cause scheduling conflicts, or negative slack. The following date constraints are the *hard date constraints* that can cause schedule conflicts under *forward scheduling*:

- *Must Start On*
- *Must Finish On*
- *Start No Later Than*
- *Finish No Later Than*

You should use these constraints as sparingly as possible without compromising the quality of the model of the project. We recommend entering constraints for very hard dates only, the do-or-die dates. If the dates are soft *target dates*, we recommend you use the deadline feature instead. Constraints have many disadvantages we discussed on page 263. If you have hard date constraints in the middle of your schedule, you will not see by how much the project end date is missed overall. This is because the hard dates are stronger than dependencies and prevent them from doing their work.

Deadline dates also affect the calculation of *Total Slack*. Notice that if you do use the deadline feature, you will not get warning dialogs that alert you to *scheduling conflicts*. Instead, a red flag will be raised in the indicators column; deadlines give silent alerts. Unlike constraints, deadlines do not violate dependencies; therefore they allow you to see what the total slippage is on the project end date. Therefore, we recommend deadlines over date constraints.

You can display a line in the timescale for the amount of negative slack a task has. The **Bar Styles** dialog (ribbon **Format**, button **Format**, item **Bar Styles)** has an item called **Negative Slack** in the list under **From**. This allows you to display a red line to the left of the task bar that represents the amount of time a task slipped past its latest allowable finish date (**Late Finish**) and by how much you need to optimize your schedule.

You can also display a green line for the amount of **Total Slack** to the right of the task bar. Then you will have a visual indicator where you have buffers in your schedule. To implement this, set the following:

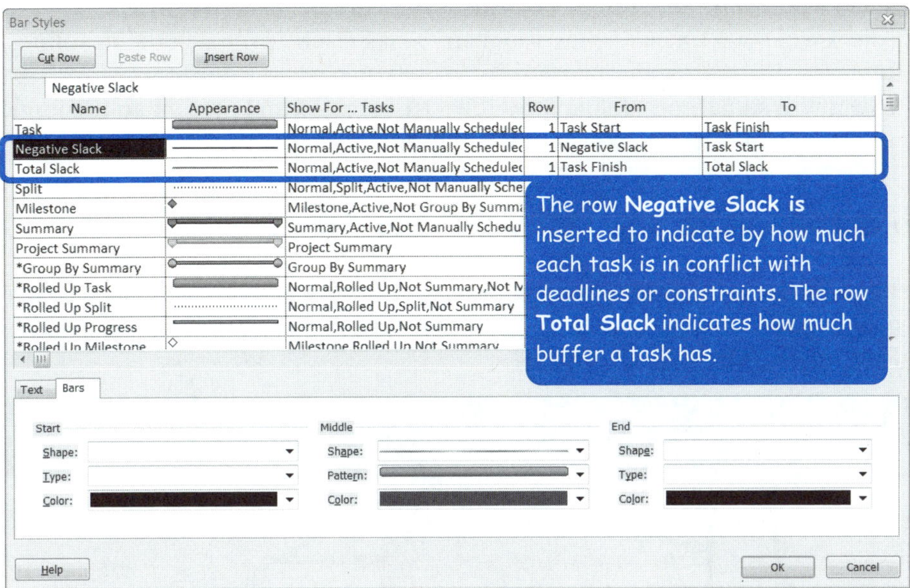

The result would look like the next screenshot; note the deadline at end of day 11:

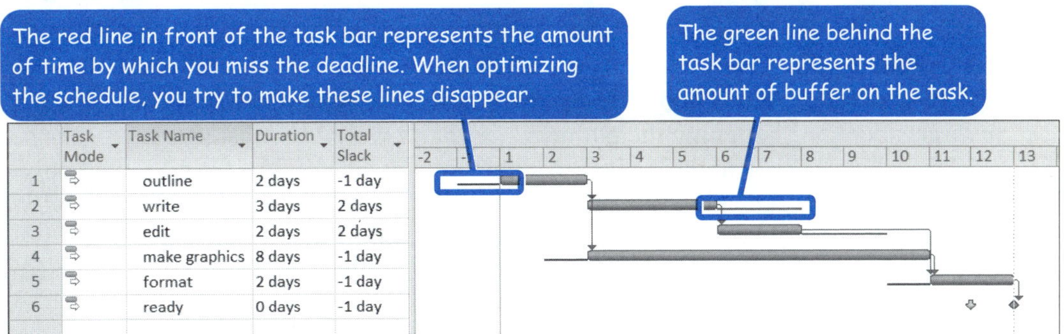

Microsoft Project's Critical Path Definition

The latest edition of the PMBOK, the fourth, defines the Critical Path as the longest path in the network. According to MS Project's definition of the Critical Path, a task is critical when it has zero or negative Total Slack. You can see this in the following dialog: click ribbon **File**, Options, tab **Advanced**, section **Calculations options for this project** and view option **Tasks are critical if slack is less than or equal to** (scroll to the bottom). This option is set to zero by default. The difference between PMBOK's and Microsoft's definition of Critical Path affects us in two ways:

- MS Project will sometimes display too many tasks as critical when the deadlines are very tight.
- MS Project will sometimes display too few critical tasks and present an incomplete Critical Path when schedule constraints are used.

MS Project Displays Too Many Critical Tasks

Consider the following example in the screenshot. It is the same example we saw before but with an even more challenging deadline at the end of day 9. This change causes MS Project to display all tasks as critical:

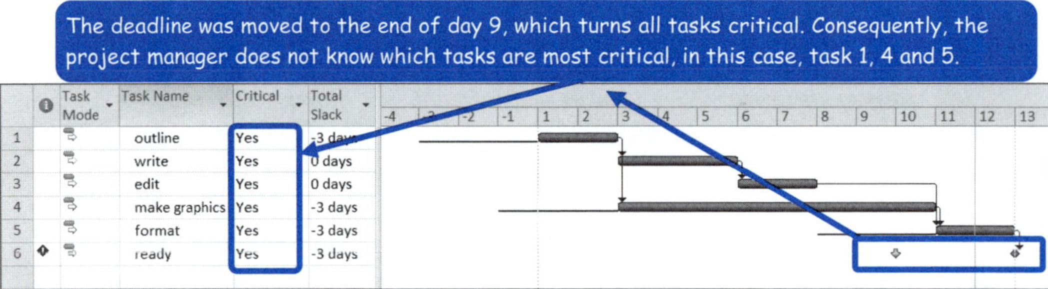

The project manager has no idea that it is better to try and shorten the most critical path of *outline*, *make graphics* and *format*, which is still the longest path; without doing this, any time spent on shortening the path *write* and *edit* would be wasted. As you can see, MS Project does not help the project manager the way it should. If it displayed only the longest path as its Critical Path (following the PMBOK definition), only tasks *outline*, *make graphics* and *format* would be red, which would be helpful, because that is where the project manager should start to optimize. If you look at the Total Slack numbers you can see that these tasks have the lowest numbers (*-3 days* as opposed to *0 days*). This shows you the most critical tasks when MS Project displays too many tasks as critical. The tasks with the lowest Total Slack numbers on the longest path in the network are where you should focus your optimizing first.

You can use our automated tool, *Complete Critical Paths* (see page 434) to display the most critical tasks in your schedule.

MS Project Displays Too Few Critical Tasks

When you display the *Critical Path* for the first time in MS Project, you will often see that it is incomplete. Project managers expect to see and definitely need a Critical Path that explains the entire project duration, a chain of tasks that stretches from the project start date to the project end date. Instead, you will often see an incomplete Critical Path that only explains part of the project duration, as shown in the illustration.

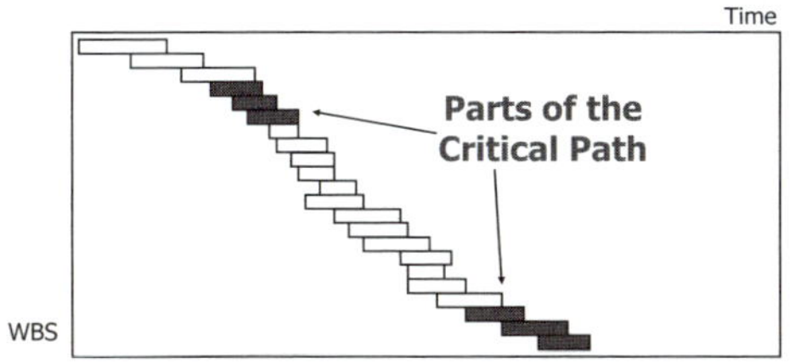

If you cannot see the complete Critical Path, optimizing becomes a painful process of trial and error. After all, only if you shorten the duration of a truly *critical task* will the project duration shorten. Therefore, we recommend you first find all the critical tasks. A complete path runs from the start date to the finish date of the project and explains the entire project duration. If you see gaps in the Critical Path, it can mean one of two things: the gap is legitimate or critical tasks are missing.

The Critical Path can have legitimate gaps if they are caused by:

- Actual progress: Completed tasks always have zero Total Slack. MS Project will not highlight any completed tasks in red; the Critical Path does not explain the completed portion of the project duration.
- Lags on dependencies between critical tasks
- Nonworking time on the calendars between critical tasks

Analyzing if a gap is legitimate requires some effort. Alternatively, you can use our automated tool, *Complete Critical Paths* (see page 434), which will explain these situations to you.

The following factors cause critical tasks to be missing:

- *Incomplete network logic*: if you have not checked the dependencies to see if you set them all, you may see a fragmented Critical Path. See page 239 for how to check the dependencies.
- *Constraint dates* (see next).
- *Elapsed durations* and *elapsed lags* (see page 429).
- *Resource calendars*: Unavailability of resources (see page 430).
- *Task calendars* (see page 430).
- *External predecessors* (see page 431).
- *Workload leveling* (see page 432).

9

We will discuss these factors in more detail and provide a manual way to complete your Critical Path. You can also use our automated tool, *Complete Critical Paths* (see page 434), which will do this for you.

Constraint Dates

We have already seen that constraints can cause negative slack when they are tight, but they can also cause positive slack when they are far out. The *Must Start On* and *Must Finish On* constraints can cause positive slack. Furthermore, the *No Earlier Than* constraints in forward scheduling and the *No Later Than* constraints in backward scheduling can also do this. Positive slack is essentially a time *buffer*.

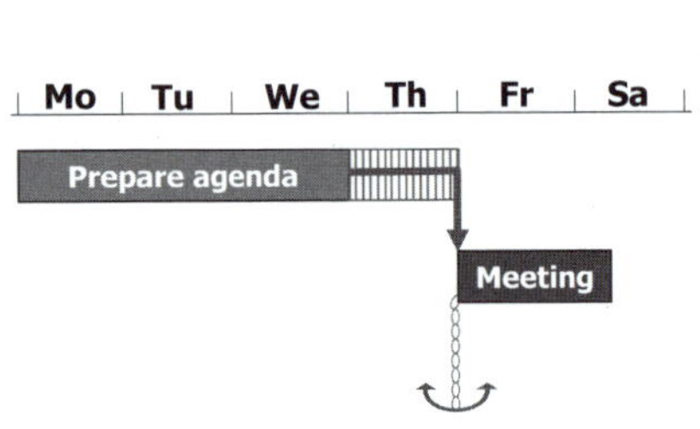

The illustration displays two tasks, *Prepare agenda* and *Meeting*. Typically, official meetings, presentations and gatherings occur on a specific date and should be entered with a *Must Start On* constraint (depicted by the anchor). As soon as you enter these fixed dates, slack can be created on the predecessors of that task, and the Critical Path starts to look disjointed. Only the task *Meeting* will be indicated as critical, because *Prepare agenda* now has slack.

This is another reason why we recommend using as few date constraints as possible (without compromising the *validity* of the model of your project, of course). In this situation, constraints make it more difficult to find the Critical Path, because they tend to break it in MS Project. The *constraints* that can break the Critical Path in *forward scheduling* are:

- *Must Start On*
- *Must Finish On*
- *Start No Earlier Than*
- *Finish No Earlier Than*

The indicators column will indicate if a task has a constraint depicted by the icon. The other types of constraints will not fragment a Critical Path in forward scheduling. We have to ask ourselves: *Is this real slack?* In this case, the slack is real, because slippage on the predecessor *Prepare agenda* does not impact the end date, unless it slips more than a day. We have to solve this by raising the threshold for critical tasks (see page 429). Notice that the most critical tasks actually have slack, and this is where Microsoft's definition of the Critical Path falls apart. MS Project will not see all tasks upstream from the meeting tasks as critical, only the downstream tasks. PMI's PMBOK longest path definition still applies in this situation because both tasks are on the longest path in the schedule.

Deadlines will not fragment the Critical Path in a forward schedule. However, deadlines can fragment the Critical Path in a backward schedule, just like *No Later Than* constraints. This is another reason why we recommend *forward scheduling*!

To repair the Critical Path manually and make it complete, we will have to raise the threshold for criticality. Slack may exist on tasks that are still the most critical tasks. We have to raise the threshold for critical tasks in order to highlight those most critical tasks – the question is by how much.

Raising the Threshold for Critical Tasks

1. Click ribbon **View** and click the bottom part of 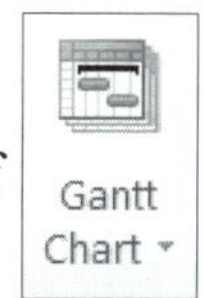 and select **Gantt Chart**.
2. Highlight the Critical Path: click ribbon **Format** and select Critical Tasks.
3. Insert the column **Total Slack**: right-click on a column heading and select **Insert Column**. Start typing the name of the field, *Total Slack*, and the list narrows down. Click on **Total Slack** – this column is now inserted.
4. Working backwards through the schedule, find the task where the Critical Path stops. Check if the task has a constraint date (similar to the task *Meeting* from our example). If not, check the other causes of an incomplete Critical Path (see next sections). Look at what the total slack is on its predecessor. If there is more than one predecessor, take the lowest number of total slack (Note that if you see negative numbers, -5d is lower than -4d). In our previous example *Meeting*, there is only one predecessor that has 1 day of slack, and we would raise the threshold for critical tasks to 1 day in that case.
5. Click ribbon **File**, Options, tab **Advanced** and scroll to the bottom of the dialog. Increase the field **Tasks are Critical if Slack is less than or equal to:** 0 to the value you established in the previous step.
6. Click OK – the Critical Path has now extended to a more complete Critical Path. It still may not explain the entire project duration, and you may have to check more tasks to find possible causes for an incomplete Critical Path. You may have to raise the threshold more often.

If this is too much work, we have an automated solution for you, see page 434.

9

Elapsed Durations and Elapsed Lags

An elapsed duration is expressed in calendar days, as opposed to business days for a regular duration. A task or a lag with an elapsed duration can end during nonworking time, whereas its successor with a regular duration cannot start right away during the nonworking time; it can only start on the next business day. This creates positive slack on the elapsed duration task. In the illustration, the task *Lay Carpet* is scheduled to start on Monday, because it has a regular duration. *Drying of Paint* can slip until 8:00 AM Monday morning without affecting *Lay Carpet*. This creates 1 day of slack on *Drying of Paint*, which has a duration of 3 *elapsed days* (*3ed*). The Critical Path is broken in MS Project, but both tasks may still be on the longest path in the network (PMBOK) and be most critical.

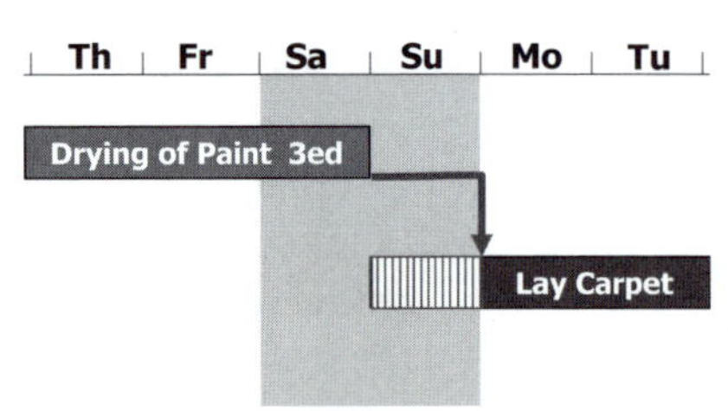

Once more we have to ask ourselves: *Is this real slack?* Yes, the slack is real here, because the *Drying of Paint* could continue for another day without impacting the project. We can resolve this by raising the threshold for critical tasks by another day (see page 429).

Resource Calendar: Unavailability of Resources

In the illustration, the move has to take place on a weekend, and the workweek of the movers is set so that only Saturday and Sunday are working days. The result is that MS Project will always schedule the *Move* on the weekend, as shown in the illustration. The predecessor of the move is done on Wednesday and causes 2 days of slack to appear. MS Project will only highlight the task *Move* and its successors as critical, an incomplete Critical Path. The Critical Path appears broken in MS Project, but both tasks may still be on the longest path in the network (PMBOK) and be most critical.

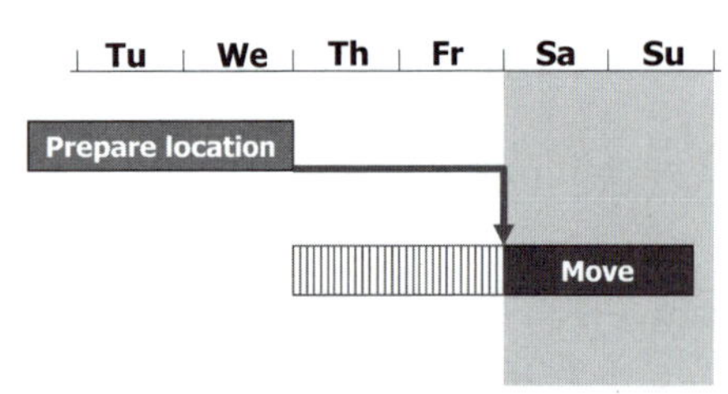

Is the slack *real slack*? Yes, the slack is real, because if the task *prepare location* slips or extends to Friday, this will not impact the project end date.

Task Calendars

Task calendars can fragment the Critical Path. If the task *Design* can be ready long before the weather is good enough to start construction, it will have slack, and therefore will not be seen as critical. The task *Construct* and its successors will be critical, as shown in the illustration. The Critical Path is broken in MS Project, but both tasks may still be on the longest path in the network (PMBOK). Just as in the previous examples, the slack is real, and the only way to complete the Critical Path is by raising the threshold for criticality (see page 429). If you do this, the Critical Path extends and will explain more of the project duration.

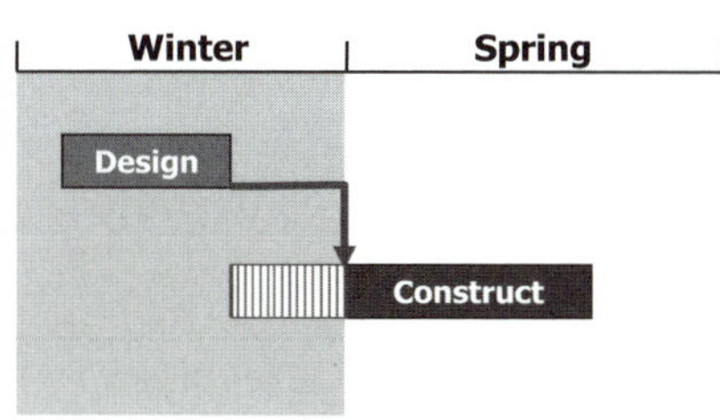

The indicators field will indicate with the icon if the selected task is scheduled by a task calendar.

External Predecessors

An external predecessor is a task from another project schedule that drives a task in your schedule (see the illustration). If a task has an *external predecessor*, this predecessor could very well drive the task farther out than the other *internal predecessors* that are inside your schedule. If it does, it creates slack on these predecessors and breaks the Critical Path in MS Project. The predecessors may still be on the longest path in the network (PMBOK). This slack is real slack, because it can be used to compensate for slippages in your schedule. Again, it can be taken care of by raising the threshold for criticality (see page 429).

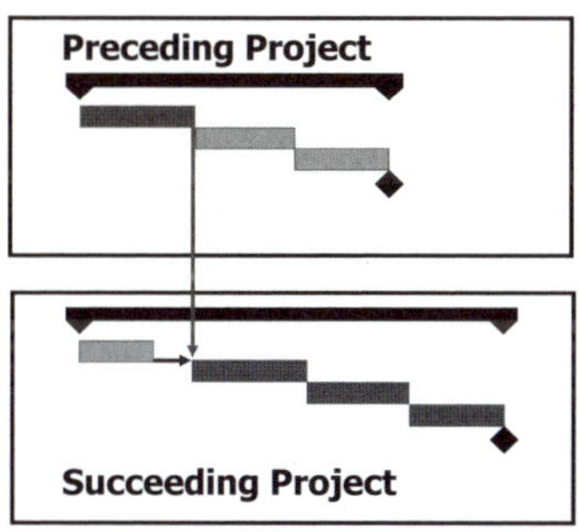

2010 The task inspector (ribbon **Task**, section **Tasks**, button **Inspect**, item **Inspect Task**) will tell you in its side pane if the selected task is driven out by a predecessor, but it will not tell you that the predecessor task is external to the schedule. You can recognize external tasks by their gray appearance and by their field **External Task** set to **Yes**.

Workload Leveling

The illustration shows two tasks, *write X* and *write Y*. Document Y is another, unrelated document. The tasks can be done independently of each other and in any order; there is no logical dependency between the two tasks. You have assigned Harry to both tasks; you overallocated him and decide to level his workload to make the schedule more realistic. In some instances, you cannot solve the overallocation in any other way than by delaying a task. In this instance, you could delay either task. As you delay *Write Y*, you create slack on *Write X* that competes for the same resource. It is weird that the Critical Path algorithm sees this as a real time buffer on task *write X*. As a result, the slack makes critical tasks noncritical, and the Critical Path turns into an incomplete Critical Path in MS Project. Even the longest path definition from the PMBOK does not mend this situation. Since there is no dependency between the two tasks, there is no path.

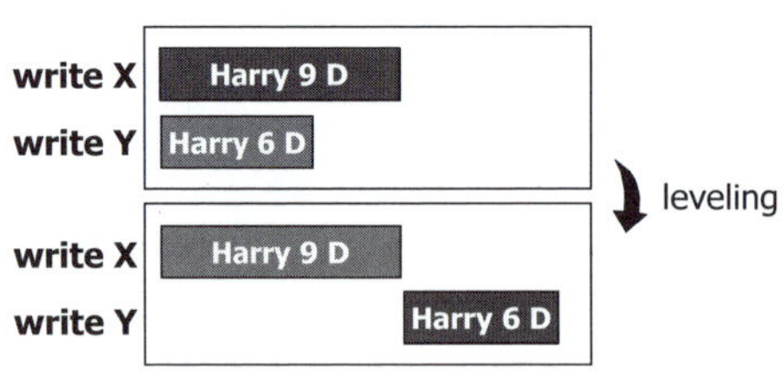

The task inspector (ribbon **Task**, section **Tasks**, button **Inspect**, item **Inspect Task**) will tell you in its side pane if the selected task is driven out by **Leveling Delay** and by how much.

One last time, we have to ask ourselves: *Is this slack real?* In this case, the answer is *no*, unlike in all previous situations. The slack is <u>not</u> real slack, because any delay in either task <u>will</u> impact the project end date. If Harry needs more time for *write X*, his other task, *Write Y*, will slip, because he will have to do that task too. You can see that the Total Slack numbers are no longer reliable when you are in a *resource-constrained* situation. How are we going to solve this?

Harry is assigned full-time to both tasks. Clearly, he cannot do both at the same time. (Cloning Harry is not an accepted project management practice yet, and hopefully, it never will be, even though instant cloning would make our profession of project management much easier.) Reassigning one of the tasks to other resources is not an option either when there are no other resources. Therefore, we often have to delay one of the two tasks, but when we delay one, we create slack on the other task. This slack is not real, because if you use it, the project end date will slip. If the task *write X* slips or extends, it will drive the task *write Y* farther out, because the same resource does both, and there is a *resource dependency* between the two tasks. Normally, you can use slack to compensate for slippages, but not in this case. Even though the current Critical Path algorithm suggests that only the task *write Y* is critical, both tasks are resource-critical. The CPM algorithm in MS Project (and any other scheduling software, for that matter) only looks at logical dependencies, not at resource dependencies, when it calculates the early and late dates. CPM does not take resource workloads into account when determining the Critical Path.

We may have forgotten that CPM assumes that resources are available in unlimited quantities, and here we can see the disastrous effect of this assumption. Only certain organizations can quickly hire (and release) extra resources in any quantity or of any quality they need, making them *unlimited resources*. For example, construction companies can generally find any number of resources when they need them. Some consulting companies consider the entire world as their resource pool and may also consider their resources to be unlimited.

Should We Add Logical Dependencies to Level Workloads?

Some people suggest that you should add logical dependencies to level out the workloads of the resources. Of course, you could model *resource dependencies* as *logical dependencies*. This works well until you start changing the *assignments*. In the illustration, if you substitute for Harry on one of his two tasks, your schedule could be shorter than it is, because of a dependency that has now become obsolete! Adding logic to level workloads and keep your Critical Path intact is a static solution for a dynamic problem. That is why we added question marks to the dependency in the illustration. We recommend keeping your schedule dynamic, because MS Project has different features to resolve overallocations (see page 468).

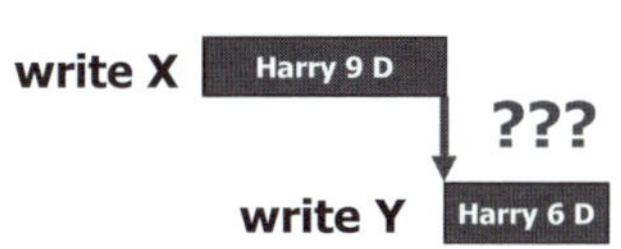

The extra dependencies to level the workloads do not reflect logical cause-and-effect relationships, like between *build wall* and *add roof*. More importantly, MS Project has features for leveling workloads; using dependencies to level workloads is an inappropriate use of the dependencies feature. If you tend to add dependencies to level workloads, we invite you to consider a new method instead: the *Resource-Critical Path* method (see page 499).

9

How to Get a Complete Critical Path?

Below you will see an example of a schedule that has an incomplete Critical Path because of several of the factors that we discussed previously. MS Project will only highlight in red as critical the solidly colored task bars 29, 30 and 31:

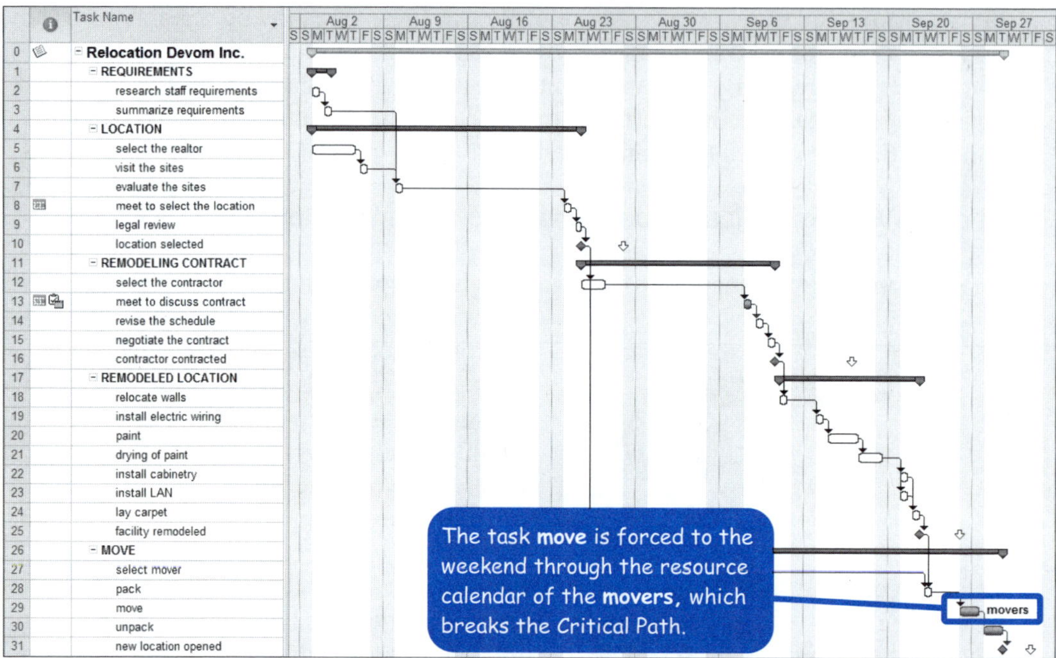

At ProjectPro, we developed an add-in to MS Project, called *Complete Critical Paths* [54] that finds the longest path in the network as per the PMBOK definition. It can even handle schedules in which the workloads are leveled and address all the factors that break the Critical Path as discussed.

[54] See www.projectprocorp.com: click **Products** in the sidebar.

The output of this tool looks like this for the previous schedule:

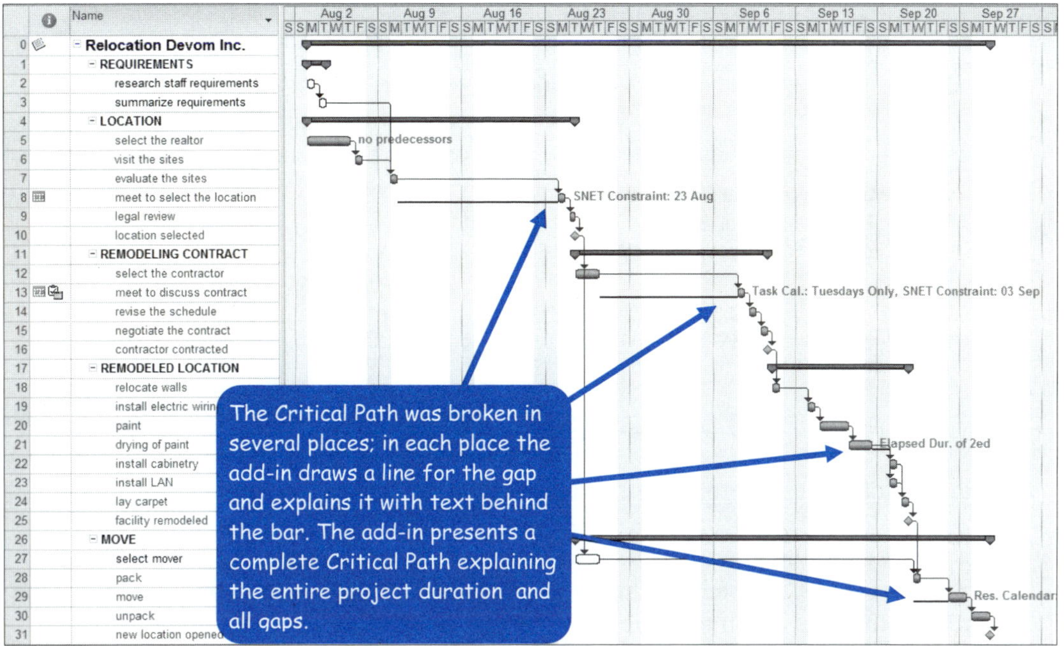

You can see that the add-in not only displays the complete Critical Path but it also explains any legitimate gaps between the most critical tasks. With this tool you will always know on which tasks to focus when optimizing your schedule. The explanations given will also lead you to ideas on how you can shorten your Critical Path quickly.

Our add-in will not display too many critical tasks (see page 426), since it uses the longest path definition of the Critical Path from the PMBOK® Guide. So, you can also use it to identify the most critical tasks when MS Project seems to show all tasks in red.

9

Steps to Optimize for Time

As shown in the process chart, to find the complete *Critical Path* you first must determine which tasks really drive the project duration and end date (step 1). If you have MS Project highlight the Critical Path in red and it shows a complete path, you can easily see whether a task is critical or not. While you are optimizing, another parallel path may become critical and MS Project will immediately highlight the new Critical Path in red. MS Project continues to show you which tasks are critical as long as it does not encounter one of the factors that can break the Critical Path as discussed (see page 427).

1. **Identify the complete Critical Path**
2. Find the longest critical tasks
3. Record the current project duration
4. Shorten the Critical Path
5. Consider impacts on quality, scope and time
6. Decide whether to keep the change
7. Repeat steps 1 to 7

The next step in the process is to determine which critical tasks have the longest durations (step 2). These hold the greatest opportunity for saving time. Focus on the long durations that allow you to achieve the largest gains first. In step 3 you record the current project duration.

After that, you have to come up with a way to do the work faster (step 4). We will suggest methods and explain them. Then you have to establish whether the change helped you enough, or if the trade-offs on *quality* or *scope* were too high a price to pay (step 5 and 6).

The explanation of all these steps will take quite a few pages. To keep the overview and indicate where we are in the process, we will repeat the chart shown above and indicate the current step in bold type.

Identify the Complete Critical Path

Switch to the Tracking Gantt view that colors the critical tasks in red by default. Click ribbon **View**, click the bottom of 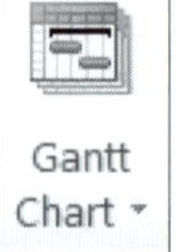

and select **Tracking Gantt**. Do not clear Critical Tasks (ribbon **Format**) in this view since it will make all your critical task bars disappear in the timescale! Microsoft has acknowledged this as a bug in the original release of Project 2010 and this may be resolved in later service packs.

OR

1. Display the Critical Path in the Gantt chart itself: Click ribbon **View,** click the  bottom of [Gantt Chart] and select **Gantt Chart**.
2. Click ribbon **Format** and select [Critical Tasks].
3. Check if MS project has marked too few tasks as critical. The Critical Path needs to explain the entire project duration. Check if the Critical Path shown by MS Project is complete. If there are any gaps, check each gap to determine whether critical tasks are missing or the gap is legitimate. If there are critical tasks missing, find them by using the manual procedure (see page 429) or with our automated tool, *Complete Critical Paths* (see page 434). The gap is legitimate if it can be explained by actual progress, lags on dependencies between critical tasks or nonworking time on the calendars between critical tasks. This requires some effort. Alternatively, you can use our automated tool, *Complete Critical Paths* (see page 434), which explains all gaps and repairs the Critical Path.
4. Check if MS project has marked too many tasks as critical; only the tasks on the longest path through the network of dependencies should be marked as critical. You can identify these by finding the critical tasks with the lowest *Total Slack* numbers (see page 426 for an example) and testing if they explain the entire project duration. Alternatively, our automated tool, *Complete Critical Paths* (see page 434) can do this for you.

You can color the text of the critical task names in the table red, or you can color the background of their cells:

1. Click ribbon **Format** and  [Text Styles].
2. From the list **Item to Change** select the item **Critical Tasks**.
3. From either list **Color** or **Background color** select red.
4. Click [OK] – notice that all critical tasks (except the critical milestones) are colored red.

Find the Longest Critical Task

Now that we have highlighted the complete Critical Path, next we must identify those tasks where we can gain the most time. Sort on duration to find the critical tasks with a long duration. When you optimize your schedule, it is smart to focus on long tasks because they harbor the most opportunity for gaining time in your schedule. On a 10-day task you could theoretically gain 10 days, but on a 1-day task, only 1 day.

1. Identify the complete Critical Path
2. **Find the longest critical tasks**
3. Record the current project duration
4. Shorten the Critical Path
5. Consider impacts on quality, scope and time
6. Decide whether to keep the change
7. Repeat steps 1 to 7

We will sort on criticality and on duration to find the longest critical tasks. We will reset the sort order as soon as we have found them:

1. In the Gantt Chart, click **View** ribbon and find its section **Data**, click 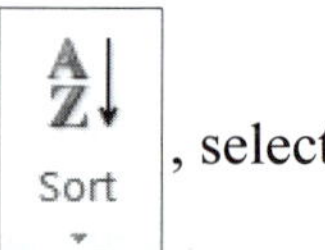

, select **Sort by…** – the **Sort** dialog appears:

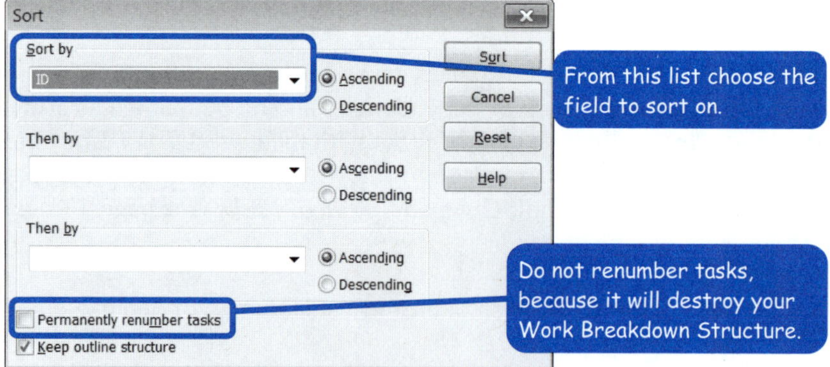

2. From the list **Sort by** select the item **Critical**.
   Set the sort order to ⦿ **Descending**.

3. From the list **Then by** select the item **Duration**.
   Set the sort order to ⦿ **Descending**.

4. Do not renumber the tasks! So, be sure to clear ☐ **Permanently renumber tasks**. If you were to renumber, you would likely have a catastrophe on your hands, because you would have lost the structure of your Work Breakdown Structure. Undo would be your last resort!

5. Make sure you sort the detail tasks and not the summary task families by clearing ☐ **Keep outline structure**.

6. Click [Sort]. The longest critical tasks are now at the top of the screen. Please ignore any summary tasks; we will focus on detail tasks only when optimizing. If you want to hide the summary tasks, please click ribbon **Format** and clear [☐ Summary Tasks]. Summary tasks should not have dependencies and should not be on the Critical Path. The longest critical detail tasks are the prime candidates for optimization; you can realize the biggest gains with the least effort by shortening them.

7. At this point we recommend that you write down the ID numbers of these longest, critical detail tasks.

After you have identified the tasks on which to focus your optimizing, you can restore the sort order to its original. Click the **View** ribbon and find its section **Data**, click the **Sort** button and select **by ID**. This should restore your *WBS*. If needed, re-display the summary tasks by clicking the **Format** ribbon and selecting [☑ Summary Tasks].

You may have to do this sort again after you have made several changes and want to find the next longest critical tasks.

Record the Current Project Duration

1. Identify the complete Critical Path
2. Find the longest critical tasks
3. **Record the current project duration**
4. Shorten the Critical Path
5. Consider impacts on quality, scope and time
6. Decide whether to keep the change
7. Repeat steps 1 to 7

We already discussed the *project summary task* feature as a way to check the total duration of the project, see page 416. This method forces you to jump to the top of the schedule every time you want to check on the project indicators. We need to see quickly what the project duration is without jumping to the top of the project every time.

You can monitor the duration of the project alternatively by:

- Using the **Project Information** dialog (ribbon **Project**) for the project **Finish date** only. This is the quickest way to find the current project duration; it is just two clicks away.
- Using the **Project Statistics** dialog that provides the duration and finish date but also cost and work totals.

To View the Project Statistics Dialog

1. Click ribbon **Project**, button **Project Information** and button Statistics... .
   OR
   Click ribbon **File**, tab **Info**, list **Project Information** (on right-hand side of the screen) item **Project Statistics**.

2. The **Project Statistics** dialog looks like:

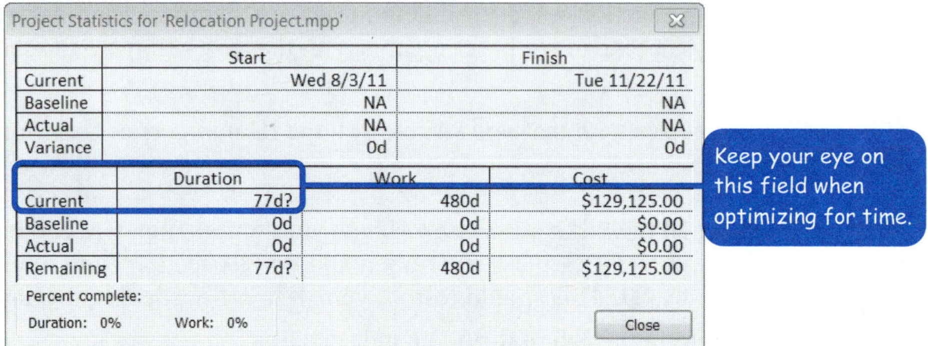

Project Statistics for 'Relocation Project.mpp'

	Start	Finish
Current	Wed 8/3/11	Tue 11/22/11
Baseline	NA	NA
Actual	NA	NA
Variance	0d	0d

	Duration	Work	Cost
Current	77d?	480d	$129,125.00
Baseline	0d	0d	$0.00
Actual	0d	0d	$0.00
Remaining	77d?	480d	$129,125.00

Percent complete:
Duration: 0% Work: 0%

Close

3. In the intersection of the **Current** row and the **Duration** column, you can see the current duration of the project.

4. Click Close when done.

Adding Project Statistics to the Quick Access Toolbar

Since Microsoft buried this dialog so deep into its application that accessing it regularly becomes cumbersome, we need to add it to the *Quick Access Toolbar* (QAT) at the top left of the screen. This makes it always accessible with one click:

1. Make sure the **File** ribbon is not active; it displays the backstage screen and disables the QAT.

2. Click ▾ of the QAT in the top left of the screen and select **More Commands** – the **Project Options** dialog opens.

3. In the list **Choose command from** select the item **Commands Not in the ribbon** and then select the item **Project Statistics** in its list, as shown in the following screenshot:

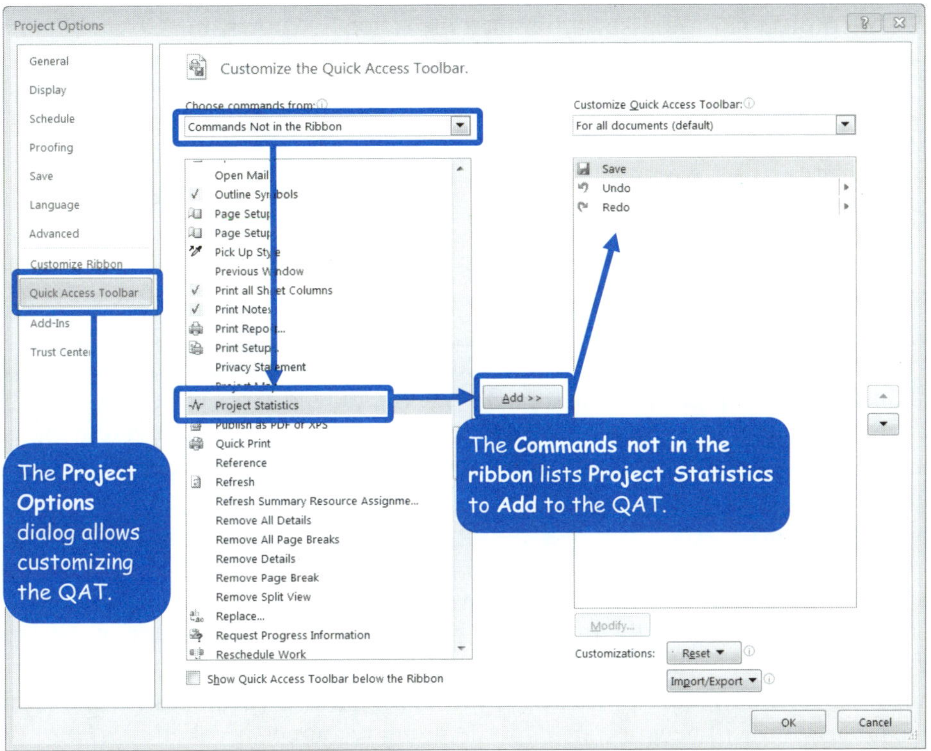

4. Click Add >> and the item **Project Statistics** is now shown in the list on the right.

5. Click OK when done – you can now always access the **Project Statistics** dialog with one click on [icon], which can be found at the top left on your screen on the Quick Access Toolbar.

Shorten the Critical Path

When the project has to finish earlier than the schedule shows, the Critical Path has to be shortened. At this point in the process we will make a change to the schedule. You need to evaluate each change in terms of the impact on at least three driving forces: *quality*, *scope* and *duration* of the project.

1. Identify the complete Critical Path
2. Find the longest critical tasks
3. Record the current project duration
4. **Shorten the Critical Path**
5. Consider impacts on quality, scope and time
6. Decide whether to keep the change
7. Repeat steps 1 to 7

The best methods are those that make the quality (Q) go up (↑), the scope (S) go up (↑) and the time (T) go down (↓). Unfortunately, there are no such ideal methods; all methods cause trade-offs. The next table indicates the effect of each method in a typical project; you will always have to determine the effects in your own project. If a question mark (?) is shown, you definitely have to look at your specific situation to determine the effect of the method. A zero (0) means that there is no expected impact in the typical project.

The table provides ideas on how to improve the schedule. We ranked the methods by overall effectiveness, with the most effective ones first. The first two methods are called *fast-tracking*, which will cause activities to overlap. Fast-tracking follows the principle of working smarter instead of harder. If you choose to add resources instead (listed last in the table), you will be working harder. Adding resources is called *crashing*. We recommend you start at the top of the table and apply the first method to the longest critical tasks that are the best candidates to cut time. Then work your way to the bottom of the table. That is the quickest way to find the most time in your project schedule. (Q=Quality, S=Scope and T=Time)

	Method	For	Q	S	T
1	Change sequential dependencies into partial dependencies (fast-tracking)	critical tasks	0	0	↓
2	Create parallel paths from a sequential path (fast-tracking)	critical tasks	?	0	↓
3	Split tasks with long durations	critical tasks	0	0	↓
4	Change constraint dates	critical tasks	0	0	↓

	Method	For	Q	S	T
5	Shorten *lags* (waiting periods)	critical tasks	0	0	↓
6	Split task bars around Must Start On tasks	critical tasks	0	0	↓
7	Decrease estimates	critical tasks	↓	?	↓
8	Reduce the scope or delete tasks	critical tasks	↓	↓	↓
9	Add resources (*crashing*)	critical tasks	?	0	?

The reason we ranked *add resources* as the least preferred method may not be evident, since most project managers immediately ask for more resources when they get into a time crunch. When you try to find extra resources at the last minute, you will get resources that are readily available and may be second best. They may not do as good a job as the original resources, and quality (Q) may suffer. Also, the new resources need to be trained, and you would typically take your best resources off their task crunching to train the new ones, because you want to set the right example for them. As a consequence, your progress will slow down (T) in the hope that it will pick up again later. Overall, it is not even clear if you will gain time. This is also known as *Brooke's Law*: *If you add resources to a project that is late, you make the project later*. Generally, the later you look for more resources, the less effective it is to add resources.

9

If you were confronted with an *incomplete Critical Path* (see page 427) and had to repair it, certain critical tasks will have some slack and other ones will not. In that case, we recommend you focus on the tasks that have the lowest slack numbers first when optimizing; they are typically in the back-end of your schedule.

Change Sequential into Partial Dependencies

All four types of dependencies can be combined with a positive *lag* time (waiting time/gap) or negative lag time (overlap/*lead*).

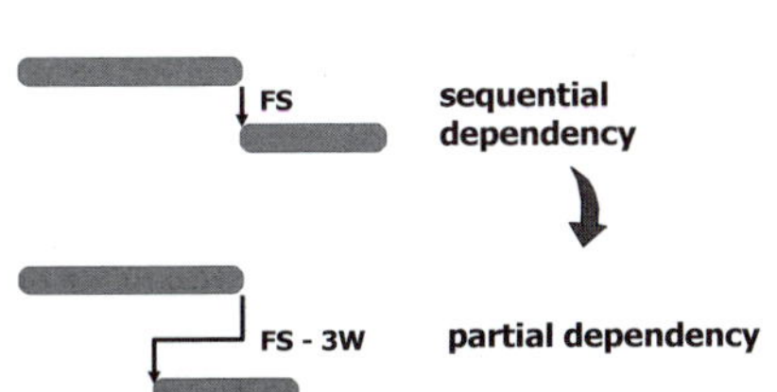

The illustration on the left shows a Finish-to-Start dependency that is changed into an overlap of 3 weeks (*lead* or *negative lag* of - 3w): FS - 3w. The overlap can be entered as an *absolute lag* in a number of days or weeks, like - 3w. It can also be entered as a percentage of the duration of the predecessor (*relative lag*), like - 40%. Since the start of the successor is dependent upon the partial completion of the predecessor, one could also speak of a *partial dependency*.

1. In the timescale of the Gantt Chart, point with the tip of the mouse pointer to the arrow of the dependency.
2. Wait for one second until the screen tip appears. Check to see if you are pointing to the right dependency, because the dependency arrows can overlap one another in the Gantt Chart.
3. Double-click if you have the right one; the **Task Dependency** box appears:

4. You can keep the **Finish-to-Start** and make the lag negative (lead). Enter a negative **Lag**, like *-2d*, or enter a percentage of the duration of the predecessor, like *-30%.* If you type a negative number, the task bar will move to the left in the timescale of the Gantt Chart and create an overlap.
   OR
   You can select from the list **Type** the **Start-to-Start** or **Finish-to-Finish** to overlap tasks and perhaps enter zero or a positive lag to create partial dependencies. A positive lag moves the task bar to the right.
5. Click OK – you should now see the overlap you wanted between the two task bars in the timescale.

If it is difficult to select the right dependency with the mouse, you can use the Task Form to create the overlap. Click ribbon **View** and select Details to display the Task Form. Click on the successor task in the Gantt spreadsheet and you can then change the dependency in the **Type** and **Lag** fields.

Create Parallel Paths

You can cut *soft dependencies*. Hard, mandatory dependencies should not be cut. If the tasks are critical, the time gain can be large when cutting the soft dependencies. In the top scenario in the illustration, there is no risk of damaging the new carpet, because it is laid after the cabinets have been installed (*sequential dependency*). In the bottom scenario, the two tasks are now scheduled concurrently (*parallel path*). The cabinet makers will have to work neatly and put plastic over the new carpet that has been laid so if they spill glue or paint, it will drop on the plastic sheet.

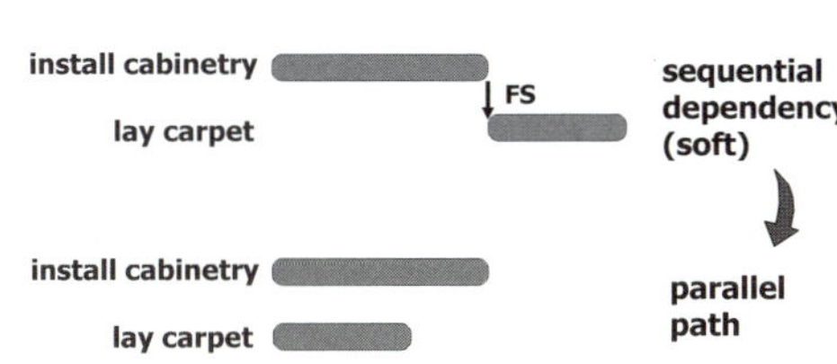

1. We recommend you create a new dependency into the soft successor first before cutting the soft dependency; otherwise, the successor task bar might disappear off the screen (to the start date of the project).
2. In the Gantt Chart, point with the tip of the mouse pointer to the arrow of the dependency and double-click on it; the **Task Dependency** dialog appears:

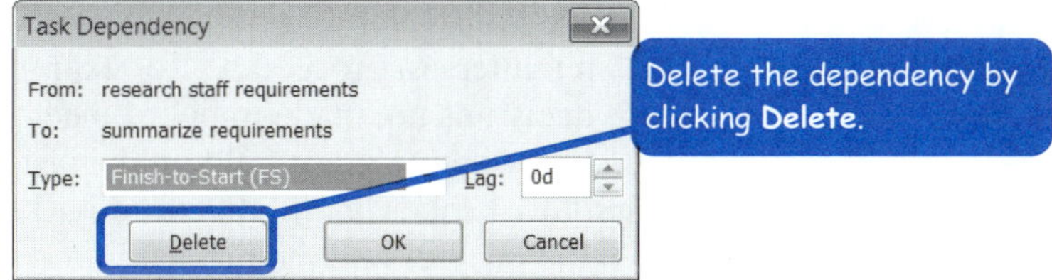

3. Verify whether the right dependency is shown and click Delete
4. Click OK – the dependency is now removed and the schedule recalculated.
5. You will likely need a new successor for the soft predecessor, because it is now a loose end in the network, unless it still has other successors.

Split Tasks with Long Durations

Breaking a long task into smaller tasks gives MS Project more possibilities to optimize, as depicted in the illustration. The benefit is immediate if you can:

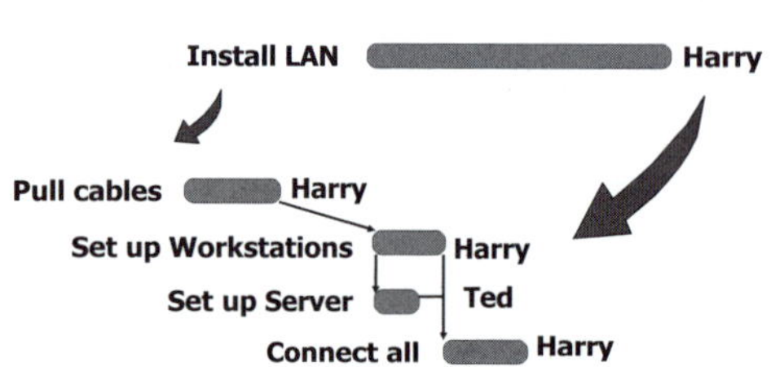

- Weave portions of the task into earlier parts of the network logic (see illustration: *Pull cables*).
- Assign portions of the task to other noncritical, and perhaps even cheaper, resources (see illustration: *Set up server* was re-assigned to *Ted*) and then schedule them in parallel.

The easiest way to break up a long task is by inserting detail tasks below it and changing it into a summary task. You will have to take the assignments and dependencies off the summary task. This offers the advantage that only the lower level of detail of your schedule has changed, which is not very visible in reports.

Change Constraint Dates

Your project may need authorization for certain matters to proceed. If, for example, these decisions are made in board meetings or steering group meetings held on the last Thursday of each month, this need will slow down the progress on the project immensely. If you lobby hard, you might get more expedient authorization through executive decisions, which will take some constraint dates out of your schedule. The anchor in the illustration represents a constraint date on the last Thursday of the month.

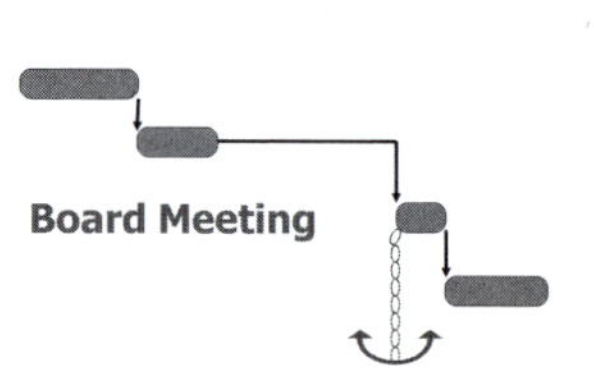

To remove or modify a constraint date:

1. Double-click the task
   OR

   Select the task with the constraint, click ribbon **Task**. Click .

2. The **Task Information** dialog appears. Click the **Advanced** tab, and the dialog should now look like:

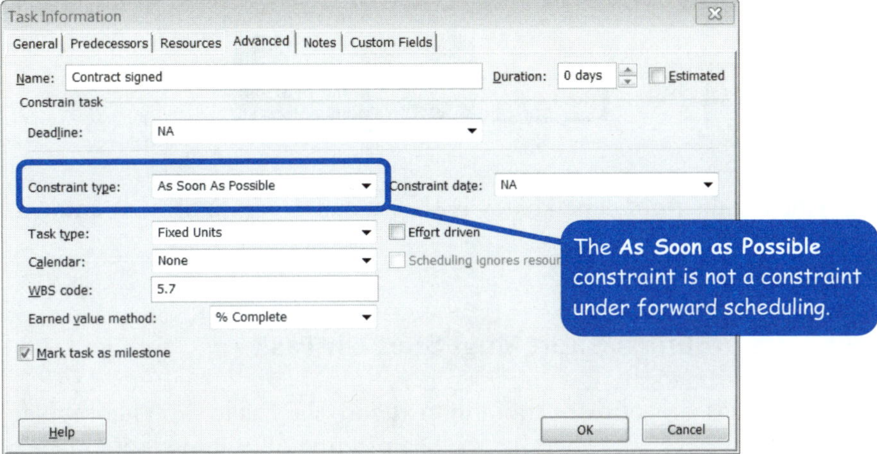

3. Change the **Constraint type** to **As Soon As Possible**.
   OR
   Change the **Constraint date** to an earlier date.

4. Click OK.

Shorten Lag

If you find any *lag* between critical tasks, you might be able to reduce it now that you are armed with the argument that the lag is on the Critical Path. In the example in the illustration, you need the board's decision, and you typically have to wait 3 weeks for the board to convene. You might be able to lobby for an executive decision instead of a full board decision, which would save a few weeks and be a significant gain.

If the wait is to receive supplies from a vendor, you can often work miracles by offering your supplier extra money for faster delivery.

The steps to decrease lag are:

1. In the Gantt Chart, point with the tip of the mouse pointer to the arrow of the dependency.
2. Double-click on the arrow. The **Task Dependency** dialog appears:

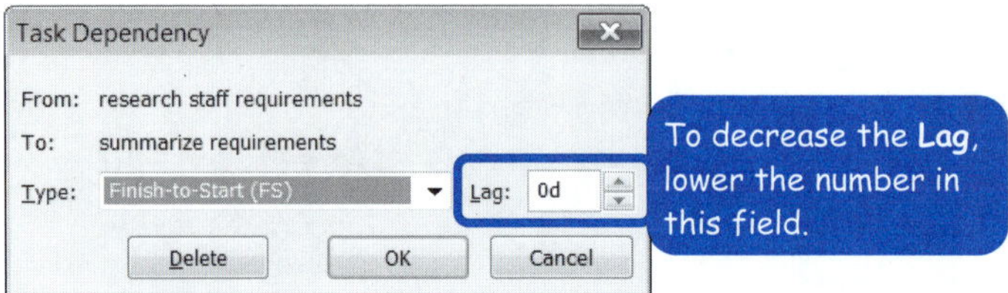

3. Verify whether the right dependency is shown and decrease the amount of **Lag**.
4. Click OK.

Split Task Bars around a Short Must Start On Task

If a team member has a meeting or training to attend, she has to drop her regular work. The meeting or training takes place on an agreed upon, fixed date. You can model this by using hard constraint dates, like Must Start On (depicted by the anchor in the illustration on the left). Your ongoing task cannot be completed before the meeting, and could be scheduled entirely after the meeting, but splitting it around the meeting gives the tightest schedule.

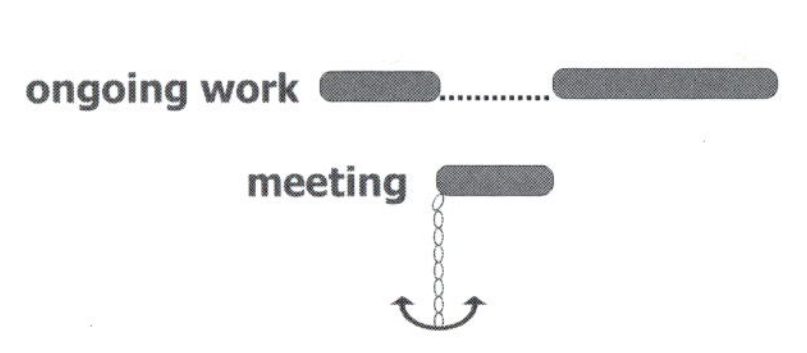

To split a task bar:

1. On the **Task** ribbon, click – the mouse pointer now looks like: and a popup window appears:

2. Point to where you want to split the task bar, click and drag the split to where you want it to be scheduled. In the popup, MS Project displays what the new start and finish dates of the split part will be when you release the mouse:

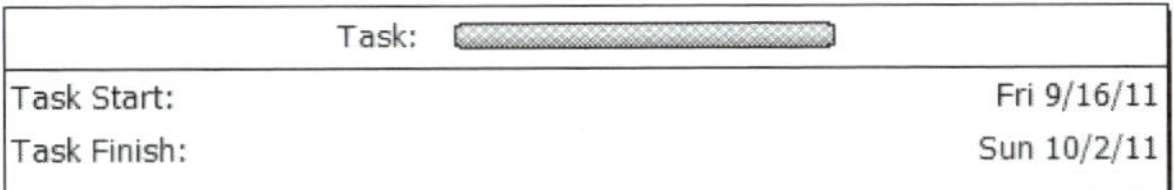

3. Release the mouse button; the task bar is now split into two parts. Notice that the two parts are connected by dots:

To remove the split, drag the second bar part back to its first part. You can also adjust the split by dragging the second bar part to new dates.

Even though this feature works well at first glance, we do not recommend using it during the planning of the project. The predecessors may reschedule the ongoing task, in which case its split should be moved accordingly to keep it scheduled around the short task with a fixed date. Since the split does not move automatically, you may have to regularly adjust your schedule manually. Thus, we do not recommend using this feature.

There are better approaches:

- You can split the task into multiple subtasks. For example, electricians wire a building, but after the inspection, they have to come back to install the switch plates. You could show this as one task with a split task bar, but it would be better to split it into two tasks: *pull cables* and *install switch plates*. Now you can set dependencies between these tasks and keep your model entirely dynamic. If you have a choice between task splitting and bar splitting, we recommend you split the task rather than its bar.
- You could allow the overallocation of the resource to occur and then level the workloads using the **Resource** ribbon, button **Leveling Options,** option ☑ **Leveling can create splits in remaining work**. In this case, the leveling will create a split, and when you level again, it will move the split as needed.
- Lastly, you could ignore the overallocation, assuming that the resources will work overtime, which is not uncommon in corporate America.

9

Decrease Estimates

Often when you get closer to the tasks at hand you can provide a more precise estimate.

Sometimes you will find that the team member can do a task faster than his original estimate. Sometimes, he finds a better and quicker way to do it. In both cases, you can sharpen the estimate and cut off some of the duration. In many cases, however, decreasing the estimate goes at the expense of the *quality* or the *scope* of the project, and the trade-off will have to be closely examined.

Reduce the Scope or Delete Tasks

Reducing the scope is a matter of deleting deliverables. If you delete deliverables that are on the Critical Path, you will reduce the duration of the project. Perhaps you are thinking at this point that you cannot delete deliverables that are *critical*. However, if a deliverable is critical, it does not necessarily mean it is important; in project management, the word *critical* simply means that it is driving the project end date.
If there are critical deliverables that qualify as nice-to-have, these are good candidates to cut. For example, in a course manual the deliverables *index* and *glossary* are often left out. However, not delivering on what you promised may be dangerous from a contractual point of view, not to mention the damage to your reputation.

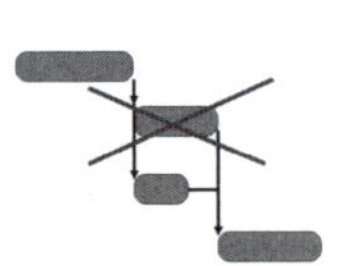

Alternatively, you could focus on the level below deliverables and find critical tasks to delete, as shown in the illustration. Again, *critical tasks* are not necessarily important tasks. Sometimes you can find activities in the realm of nice-if-we-get-around-to-it. These are the candidates to cut. This may happen at the expense of the *quality* of the deliverables. If the quality requirement is a nice-to-have, you could cut the task.

You can get rid of tasks in one of two ways:

- Deleting: Deleting tasks is as easy as clicking on their row heading (ID number) and pressing [Delete]. You may need to recreate some dependencies.

- Making them inactive: If you have set the *baseline* already, we recommend you make the task *inactive* (new feature in Project Professional 2010) instead of deleting it. Just select the task and click [Inactivate] on the **Tasks** ribbon (which sets the **Active** field to **No**). Once you get a formal approval to change the baseline, you can remove the task in its entirety. If you make a task inactive, you may need to reroute some dependencies.

Tasks with actual progress should not be deleted and cannot be made inactive.

Add Resources

Often, managers ask for more resources when they start to feel the heat of their deadlines. In the illustrated example, the project manager asked for and got Ed to help out. We have often observed that when new resources arrive, the best resources are taken off their jobs to train the new ones. This causes the slippage to increase at first instead of decrease.

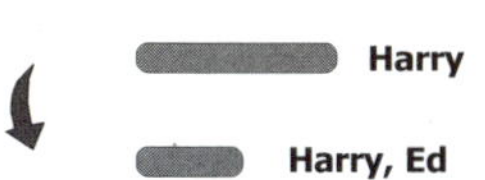

How many people can you add to tasks? When optimizing for time only, we could in theory add an unlimited number, but in practice, there are limits. If you add too many people, eventually nothing will get done. People will be in each other's way and keep each other from being productive. The *law of diminishing returns* is applicable when adding resources. How many carpenters can work in one 10-by-15-foot room? The classic example: adding another mother to carry the child does not shorten the pregnancy. There are simple practical limits. Even though we have assumed that we have access to unlimited resources, it definitely does not seem reasonable to add more than the maximum units available as entered in the resource sheet.

Make sure you change (the **Task Mode** to an **Auto Scheduled** task and) the task **Type** to **Fixed Work** before adding resources. This will ensure that the duration decreases when you add them.

Consider Impacts on Quality, Scope and Time and then Decide

1. Identify the complete Critical Path
2. Find the longest critical tasks
3. Record the current project duration
4. Shorten the Critical Path
5. **Consider impacts on quality, scope and time**
6. **Decide whether to keep the change**
7. Repeat steps 1 to 7

As the next step, you have to evaluate the impact on *quality*, *scope* and *time* of the change you made. We recommend you use the *project statistics* dialog to check the progress in optimizing the schedule, see page 439 for steps to display it. From the new project duration or finish date, you can see how much time you have gained, and whether it is worth the sacrifices you made on the scope of the project or the quality of the deliverables.

Realize that if you have used, for example, a **Must Finish On** constraint on the project end milestone, the project end date will be held captive by it. Constraint dates and odd resource or task calendars in the back end of your schedule can cause the project end date to stay where it is. If you have a Must Finish On constraint on the project end milestone, it is better to look at the **Total Slack** number of that milestone; if it increases, you are doing the right thing.

Only if you have minimized the use of constraints and calendars, as we recommended, will you see that changes immediately pull the project end date back. If you find that the change did not yield the anticipated result, simply display the undo list by clicking the triangle on and get rid of all the changes that you made for this what-if scenario.

MS Project has multiple levels of undo; this is very helpful for optimizing. Change highlighting is also very useful; it helps to analyze the impacts of a change. As soon as you enter the change, all affected cells will be colored light blue.

Continue to repeat steps 2 to 7 in the process of optimizing until you have at least solved the scheduling conflict. If you shorten your project further you can create a comfortable project buffer.

Monte Carlo Simulation

One thing is certain: unforeseen events will happen and you will need a time buffer to compensate for those events. This is generally accepted project management.

Once you have optimized the Critical Path, you should ask yourself: *How much buffer should I reserve in my schedule in order to protect the project deadline?* A *time buffer* is also known as *time contingency*. The harder your project deadline is, the more carefully you need to assess how much buffer you need. *Monte Carlo simulation* can help you determine that. Without simulation, you will have to guess what the size of the buffer should be.

What Is Monte Carlo Simulation?

The best-known simulation technique is *Monte Carlo simulation*. For tasks that are hard to predict, you specify the lower and upper limits of an estimate and choose a probability curve between those limits. Some tasks are renowned for their wide range between the lower and upper limit, for example *debug code* in a *software development* project. We do not recommend you enter range estimates for every task (even if you have enough time to do that).

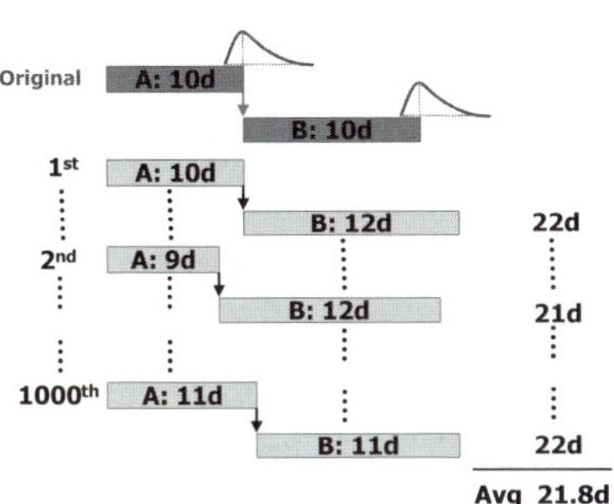

The simulating software generates estimates for all the tasks using these parameters. It uses number generators that produce estimates that comply with the range and the distribution curve you have chosen for the estimate. It creates the first version of the entire schedule and calculates the Critical Path. In the illustration on the left, the *original* schedule is shown as well as the *1st*, the *2nd* and the *1000th* version created by the simulation software.

Simulation will create as many *versions* as you want, but after many versions, every subsequent one has less and less added value. Simulations often create up to a thousand versions of the schedule. In each version, the Critical Path of the schedule is calculated. The simulation software will then calculate average project duration and probabilities for a range of finish dates.

Output of Monte Carlo Simulation

Simulation software creates an s-curve from the many versions of the schedule. An *s-curve* shows projected finish dates charted against the probability of meeting those dates. The illustration shows such an s-curve. The benefit of the s-curve is that you can see the chance of completing your project (*current probability* in the illustration) by the date that MS Project indicates as the project finish date in your schedule (*current finish date* in the illustration).

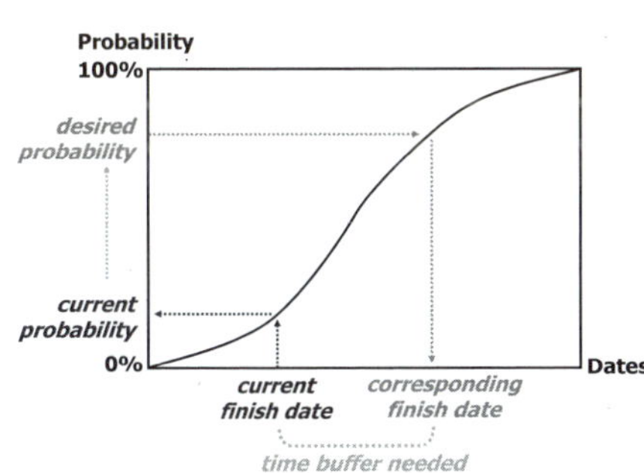

Alternatively, you can choose the level of probability you feel comfortable with and derive the project finish date, or you can let executives determine it (*desired probability* in the illustration). With the desired probability, you can find the *corresponding finish date*. You can quote this date to the client while knowing the degree of confidence that it can be met. There may still be other risks that you do not know about (*unknown unknowns*), but at least you have quantified *known unknowns* that we will discuss in the next section on why we need simulation.

You can also calculate the size of the time buffer you need in your project. If you read from the s-curve that you need to add 3 weeks as a buffer to your current MS Project schedule to have 90% probability, you should insert this as a *buffer "task"* just before the *project finish milestone* and have it push out the milestone. For more on that, see page 544.

MS Project does not have simulation capabilities, but there are good *add-ins* on the market with which you can simulate MS Project schedules. One add-in is *Risk+* [55] and another is *@Risk* for MS Project.[56]

Why Do We Need Simulation?

Why is *Monte Carlo simulation* necessary in schedules?

- Forecasts from one-point estimates tend to be too optimistic.
- Converging paths compound the time risk.

We will discuss both in more detail.

Optimistic One-Point Estimates

If you ask many different people for an estimate on one task, you can plot the estimated durations on the x-axis against the number of times you hear each estimate on the y-axis. The result will be a distribution curve that depicts the probability of a range of finish dates according to those estimators. It will look like the curve in the illustration. The estimate that you hear most often is the mode, which is why the mode is shown under the top of the curve. The median divides the surface under the curve into two equal parts; there are as many estimates to the left of it as there are to the right. The mean is the mathematical average of all estimates you collect.

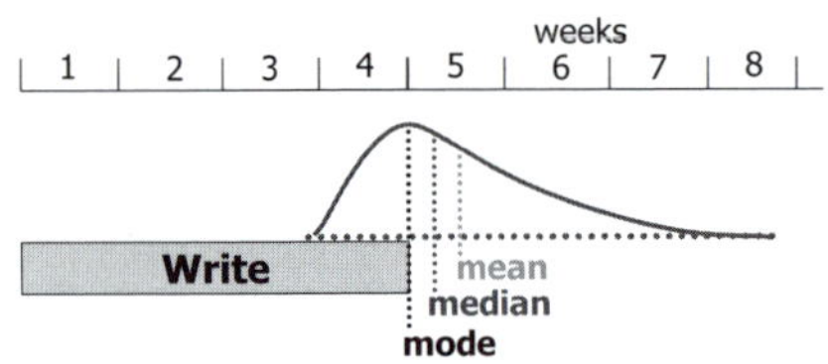

If you do this a few times, you will typically find that the resulting curve is skewed to the right. In other words, durations tend to stretch, rather than shrink. You probably

[55] Deltek (www.deltek.com)

[56] Palisade Corporation (www.palisade.com)

knew that already if you have been a project manager for some time. The skewed curve means that the duration of the task is more likely to increase 1 week than decrease 1 week. In other words, tasks will more likely take more time than less.

However, the Critical Path consists of many tasks. It could be that a task early in the schedule ran late. This overrun can be compensated for by later under runs. The overall effect of the skewing of estimates is, therefore, not that dramatic. Nevertheless, you can safely state that schedules made with single estimates per task are optimistic in nature.

Converging Paths Compound the Time Risk

Converging paths decrease the probability of meeting a milestone date. The chance that the milestone will be accomplished on time decreases with every path that is added leading into the milestone. In the illustration below, each path has an admirable chance for on-time delivery of 90%, but the chance of delivering the milestone on time is exactly 81%. If one path is early, the other may be late and vice versa. When two independent paths of equal duration both have to be finished for a milestone, you can multiply their chances: 90% * 90% = 81%. If one path is a bit shorter, only simulation can tell you what the percentage is.

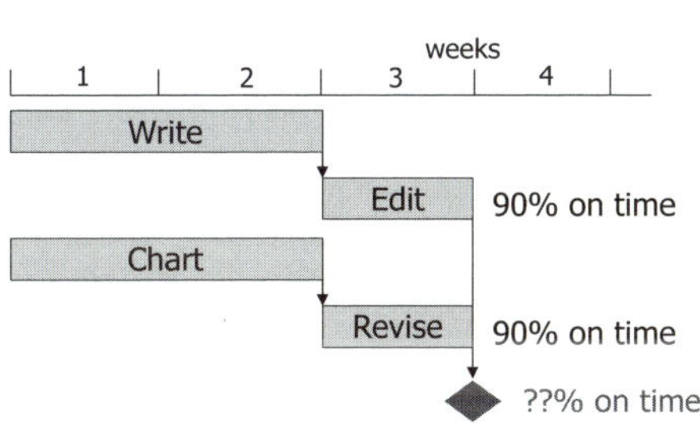

The more parallel paths you have in your schedule, the greater the *time risk*. The more equal the durations of the paths are, the greater the time risk. This phenomenon is known as *path convergence* or *merge bias*. The aggregated effect of many merging paths of different lengths is very difficult to predict; simulation is the only way to find out. The more parallel paths you see in your schedule, the more you will need to simulate the schedule. This need is even greater if those paths have similar durations.

The paths make it unlikely that your end date, as shown by your MS Project schedule, will be met. That is why project managers developed the habit of padding their schedules. You need to do simulation in order to find the compounded effect of the parallel paths. You can use simulation to quantify how much padding you will need in your schedule. We do recommend using simulation in combination with the *Critical Path Method.*

Assumptions of the Critical Path Method

In summary, the Critical Path theory is based on three assumptions:
- Assumption 1: Task *estimates* are *normally distributed.*
- Assumption 2: There is no *merge bias* or *path convergence*.
- Assumption 3: You have *unlimited resources* available.

We saw on page 454 that assumption 1 does not hold true, but we can determine the magnitude of its effect by applying *Monte Carlo simulation*.

As for assumption 2, we proved before that merge bias (path convergence) does exist. This effect often causes the largest slippages in projects. Simulation is the only technique that can make the compounded effect of converging paths visible. Applying the Critical Path Method (CPM) is good, as long as you simulate it as well. You can actually foresee and quantify many overruns before they happen when you apply simulation to schedules.

Assumption 3 is more difficult to deal with. CPM assumes that resources are available in unlimited quantities. This assumption holds true, if workload is not your problem. For example:
- If resources are readily available, workload is not an issue.
- If you intend to subcontract the work, workload is not your issue. Resource allocation is the contractor's problem.
- For a consulting firm that can hire free-lance resources easily in the quantity and with the expertise needed, workload is not a problem.

In these cases, the assumption can stand and the Critical Path Method is the technique to use.

However, many project managers do not have access to unlimited resources. In this era of global competition, many organizations cannot afford to supply unlimited resources to projects, nor can they afford to omit tracking the usage of their resources. Today in the global market, a 1% change in *return on investment* (*ROI)* can be the difference between a viable and a nonviable company.

If you are managing the workload of your own scarce, internal resources, workload is your concern. In that case, CPM is of limited value. For example, if you are managing IT resources, you probably are in a *resource-constrained* situation. You need a new technique to optimize such schedules.

Extra resources can be bought with money. We will, therefore, first introduce cost into the optimization (optimizing for time and cost, see next page), and then we will add the limited availability of resources (optimizing for time, cost and resources, see page 467).

The Future of the Critical Path Technique

As you may have noticed, the Critical Path technique has started to crumble under the weight of its own success. Software manufacturers have developed very sophisticated software that now allows the detailed modeling of projects with richness in features never seen before. The advent of project, task and resource calendars, date constraint, elapsed duration and lags, cross-project dependencies and workload leveling has exposed the weaknesses of the Critical Path technique as it was originally designed by Morgan R. Walker of DuPont and James E. Kelley, Jr. of Remington Rand. Particularly when you have a resource-constrained project, the first edition of the Critical Path technique, *Critical Path 1.0*, falls short; in fact, it falls on its face.

I started a working group in 2010 to work on the next version of the Critical Path technique, which we call *Critical Path 2.0*. The working group consists of some of the brightest scheduling minds from around the world. I firmly believe that we can address most, if not all, issues with the technique and that the technique can survive the next decades as long as we redefine it every now and then so it can withstand the test of time. I will share here the definition of *Critical Path 2.0* as we formulated it at the time of sending this book to the press:[57]

The Critical Path 2.0 is the subset of activities that determines the duration of the schedule when all schedule data entered into the scheduling application are taken into account. Schedule data typically includes WBS, estimates, dependencies, resources, assignments, priorities and schedule constraints. Schedule constraints can include among others:

- *Logical constraints: relationships between tasks that are necessary from a practical point of view: for example, complete concrete footing of an office building is needed before you can install its steel columns.*
- *Physical constraints: How many trades can work side-by-side on one location in a construction project?*
- *Resource availability constraints: There are different types of resources and they can be:*
  - *Materials: What inputs do we need in order to start our project tasks?*

---

[57] From: *Proceedings of the Critical Path 2.0 Working Group*, 2010, *www.CP2dot0.org*.

- ◇ *Machines: What equipment do we need to perform our project tasks?*
- ◇ *Labor: How many team members do we have and of what work experience and skill level?*
- ◇ *Facilities: What buildings and rooms do we need to accommodate our team members? What accommodations do we need to rent for our project events?*
- ◇ *Land: How much land (two-dimensional space) do we need to execute our project?*
- ◇ *Space: How much cubic yards (or meters) of three-dimensional space do we need to execute our project.*

- *Financial constraints: How much money do we have available in our project budget? When will the budget be available for us to spend? When can we make commitments with our suppliers?*
- *Date constraints: When will the contract be awarded? When does the client need the deliverables? When must the project be completed?*
- *Calendar constraints:*
  - ◇ *Project calendar: When are the statutory holidays? What are the common working times?*
  - ◇ *Resource calendars: When are the vacations of the individual team members?*
  - ◇ *Task calendars: When can roadwork happen in countries with a cold climate? When will this highly-specialized lab be available for our tests?*
- *Policy constraints: Can we release this product without a detailed quality review? Is a legal review of every contract required?*
- *Legal constraints: How many overtime hours are allowed in this country? Is an environmental assessment required by law?*
- *Ecological constraints: What is the effect of the project activity on the environment?*
- *Political constraints: Can we transport this radio-active material via these roads and rivers?*

Some remarks about the Critical Path 2.0:

- *Typically there is only one Critical Path in a schedule, but there can be multiple Critical Paths in parallel that are of equal length and that determine the duration of the project.*
- *Each scheduling application can highlight a different path as the Critical Path. For example, if a scheduling application contains a feature for Monte Carlo simulation, it can highlight a different path than another scheduling application without that feature. If the feature is not used, the application itself may highlight a different Critical Path. What the scheduling application highlights as the Critical Path in a schedule is dependent upon:*
  - ◇ *The features available in the scheduling application.*
  - ◇ *The (set of) algorithm(s) chosen by the software manufacturer to support the feature. For example, there are many different workload leveling algorithms. Each algorithm produces a different schedule with the same set of schedule data. Most scheduling applications use a single algorithm, but some*

applications allow you to choose multiple algorithms and present the shortest possible schedule to you.

- ◇ *The way the feature was implemented in the scheduling application. For example, if the application supports multiple leveling algorithms, does it allow you to indicate if you want to find the shortest or cheapest scenario of the schedule, or the one with the least risk?*
- ◇ *The existence of bugs in the code of the feature in the scheduling application.*
- ◇ *The options currently chosen in the scheduling application. For example, if the application supports multiple leveling algorithms, did you choose to find the shortest or the cheapest scenario of the schedule?*

The work on Critical Path 2.0 is constantly evolving. If you would like to monitor the progress, participate or contribute, please visit its website: www.CP2dot0.com.

Optimizing for Time and Cost

When you optimize for *time* and *cost*, you should consider the dimensions *scope* and *quality* as well. In the illustration, we are adding cost as the fourth dimension in our quest for the optimal schedule. Any project manager who has a budget in dollars (or in person hours) should apply this type of optimization.

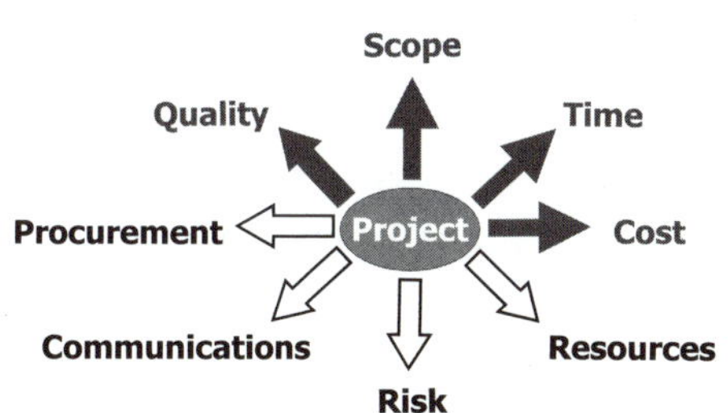

With money you could also buy more resources, but including resources in the optimization will be discussed later (see page 467).

Steps to Optimize for Time and Cost

The steps to optimize for time and cost are very similar to the steps when optimizing for time. The differences are highlighted in bold in the illustration. Because you should not lose sight of the time dimension of the project, you still have to find the complete Critical Path (step 1). If you want to shorten the duration of the project as well, you should also apply the optimizing for time methods discussed in the previous section (see page 442). Since we explained

1. Identify the complete Critical Path
2. Find the **most expensive** tasks
3. Record the current project **duration** and **cost**
4. Lower the cost of the project
5. Consider impacts on quality, scope, time and **cost**
6. Decide whether to keep the change
7. Repeat steps 1 to 7

those methods already, we can simplify the discussion here by focusing mainly on cost.

If you find that the restricted availability of resources is driving out your finish date, you will need to optimize for time, cost and resources (see page 467). In that case, you should read this section as well, because in the time, cost and resources approach we will not repeat any methods to reduce cost again.

An important step is to find the most expensive tasks (step 2). After recording the current situation (step 3), you can develop ideas for how you might bring down their costs with minimal or no compromise on time, scope or quality. Enter an idea (step 4) and check the results to see whether you want to keep it (step 5 and 6).

We will discuss how to accomplish some of these steps in MS Project.

Find the Most Expensive Task

To find the tasks on which we can make significant savings, we should sort the tasks on cost:

1. Insert the **Cost** column; right click on any column heading and select Insert Column from the popup menu. Select **Cost** from the list.

2. In the Gantt Chart, click ribbon **View**, Sort, **Sort by…** – the **Sort** dialog appears:

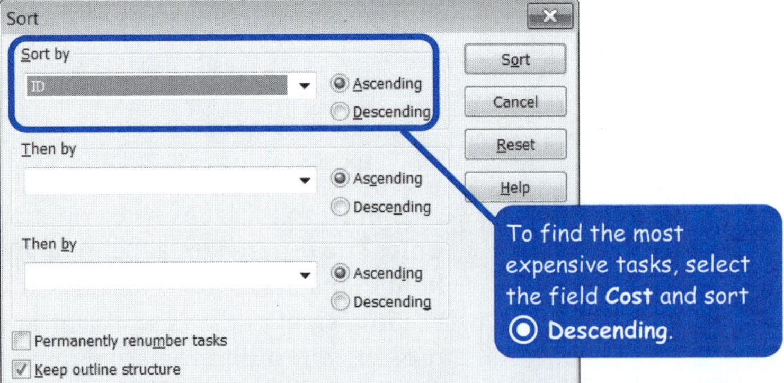

3. In the **Sort by** list, select **Cost** and set the sort order to ⦿ **Descending**.

4. Do not renumber the tasks; clear ☐ **Permanently renumber tasks**

5. Sort each line item by clearing ☐ **Keep outline structure** instead of sorting the families of summary task.
6. Click [Sort] – the tasks are now fully sorted, and you can easily find the ones where you can make significant savings.
7. If you want to hide the summary tasks, please click ribbon **Format** and clear [☐ Summary Tasks].
8. At this point we recommend that you write down the ID numbers of these most expensive detail tasks.
9. To restore the sort order to its original, click the **View** ribbon and find its section **Data**, click the **Sort** button and select **by ID**. This should restore your *WBS*.
   If needed, re-display the summary tasks by clicking the **Format** ribbon and selecting [☑ Summary Tasks].

Lower the Cost of the Project

To find the current cost and duration of the project, use the **Project Statistics** dialog (see page 439 for steps).

The best methods to lower the cost are those that make the *quality* (Q) go up (↑), the *scope* (S) go up (↑), the *time* (T) go down (↓) and the *cost* (C) go down (↓). Unfortunately, there are no such ideal methods. However, we will offer suggestions. The following table shows methods to lower the cost (C) and their likely impact on quality (Q), scope (S) and time (T) in a typical project. A question mark (?) indicates that you need to look at your specific project to determine the effect of the method. A zero (0) means that there is no expected impact.

	Method	**For**	Q	S	T	C
1	Find cheaper contracts	External contractors, consultants	?	?	?	↓
2	Reassign to cheaper resources	Expensive resources	?	?	?	↓
3	Break up a long task and reassign portions to cheaper resources	Long (critical) tasks	0	0	↓	↓

9

	Method	For	Q	S	T	C
4	Shorten the project duration to decrease overhead cost and generate revenue earlier	Critical tasks	?	?	↓	↓
5	Prevent overtime work	Resources with a higher overtime rate	0	0	↑	↓
6	Smooth the workloads	Resources with erratic workloads	?	?	?	↓
7	Decrease the effort estimate	Any tasks with labor costs	↓	0	↓	↓
8	Reduce the scope or delete tasks	Any tasks with costs involved	↓	↓	↓	↓

The actions are listed in order of overall perceived effectiveness. You should start at the top of the table and work your way down. If you need to bring down the duration of your project as well, use the optimizing for time methods as discussed on page 442. Make sure you select those methods that do not increase the cost again. If you shorten the project duration, the overhead costs will also decrease (see method 4) because you will save on expenses for project management, facilities, support staff and other overhead costs.

If you manage the cash flow of your project as well, another method might be to renegotiate when the costs accrue and change the resource field **Accrue at** accordingly. Delaying the accrual of expenses will improve your cash flow.

Find Cheaper Contracts

The question you should ask yourself is: *Do I always solicit more than one bid or proposal?* If the answer is *no*, then this method may create significant savings for you. After all, contractors and consultants are quick to find out whether or not they are in a competitive situation and will quote accordingly. Another option is to research whether there are specialized firms that are quicker or better at their trade than other

suppliers. If a specialized firm is using better technology, techniques, equipment or resources, it may be cheaper, even at a higher hourly rate.

1. If needed, create the new vendor resource in the resource sheet (for the how-to, see page 303).
2. Click ribbon **View** and click the top part of Gantt Chart to switch to the Gantt Chart where we will move the *assignments* to the new resource.
3. Select the task, and click ribbon **Resource** and Assign Resources – the **Assign Resources** dialog appears. The dialog displays the cost of each assignment; if you note the cost before replacing, you know immediately how much you saved:

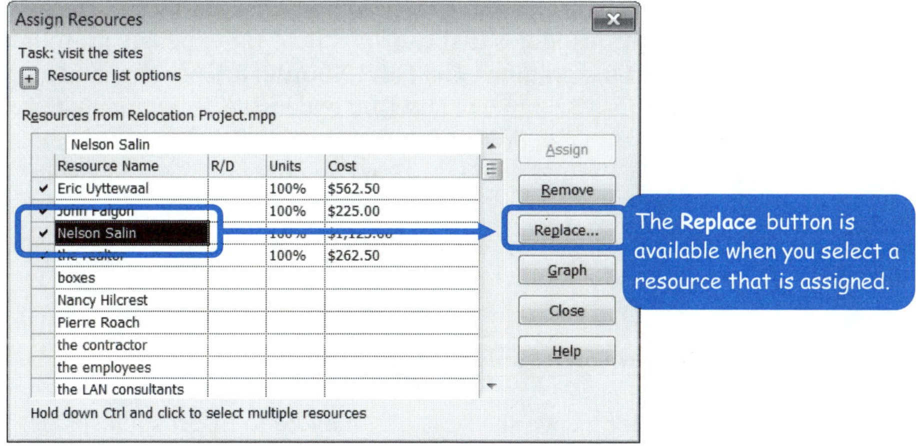

4. Resources that are assigned have a check mark in front of their name in the list and always appear at the top of the list. Click on the assigned resource to be replaced – the Replace... button is now enabled.

5. Click Replace... – the **Replace Resource** dialog appears on top of the **Assign Resources** dialog:

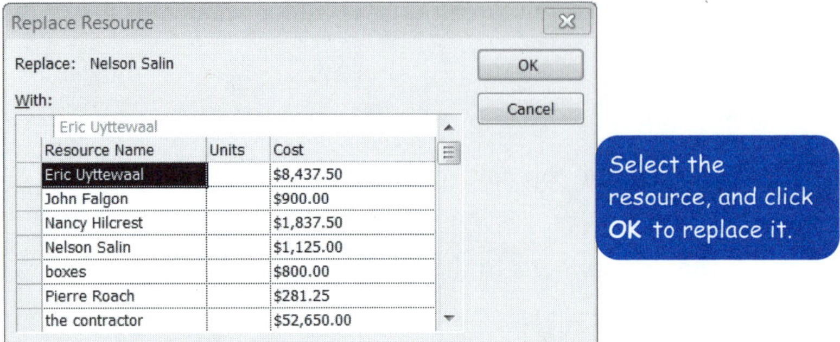

6. Click on the cheaper substitute resource you created in step 1, and click OK – the resource is now replaced on the task.

Reassign to Cheaper Resources

The best view to find cheaper resources that can substitute for expensive resources is the Resource Usage view. Insert the columns **Cost** and **Standard Rate**. Expand an expensive resource to view its assignments and find expensive assignments that you can move to cheaper resources. You can do this by simply dragging assignments to another resource: Select the assignment (has no ID number) by clicking on its row selector (make sure you see the mouse pointer at this point), click again and hold down, and then drag the assignment to another resource.

Break Up a Long Task and Reassigning Portions

If you decide to break up a long task, the best way may be to insert subtasks below it, thereby promoting it to become a summary task. Then you *assign* the cheaper resources to these subtasks and remove the expensive resource from the summary task. The cost should decrease as a result. Do not forget to set appropriate dependencies, so as not to leave any *loose ends* in the network logic. If you can hook up some portions to much earlier tasks, you will be saving time as well.

Shorten the Project Duration

If you decrease the project duration, two financial benefits are realized:

- *Overhead* costs will decrease. The longer a project takes, the longer the project manager, team leaders and support staff need to stick around, and the longer support, facilities and equipment have to stay available.
- *Revenues* are generated earlier. For example, if you develop a new product, you can release and sell the product earlier. Because of the time value of money (a dollar today is more valuable than a dollar next year), you will increase the return on investment. If you are in a time-to-market situation, you will get a larger market share and increase your revenues, thereby also increasing the return on investment.

We discussed the methods to shorten the project duration on page 442. This method brings down the time and cost of the project together.

Prevent Overtime Work

Preventing overtime work will only bring down the cost if you are actually paying a higher rate for overtime. For the how-to steps for decreasing overtime, refer to the section on how to create it in the first place (see page 516). Of course, if you reduce overtime, you may be extending your project duration, which is a trade-off with the time dimension. You can only do that if saving cost is more important than finishing as early as possible.

Smooth the Workloads

In the illustration, the total workload before and after smoothing is the same 100 person days, which would cost the same.

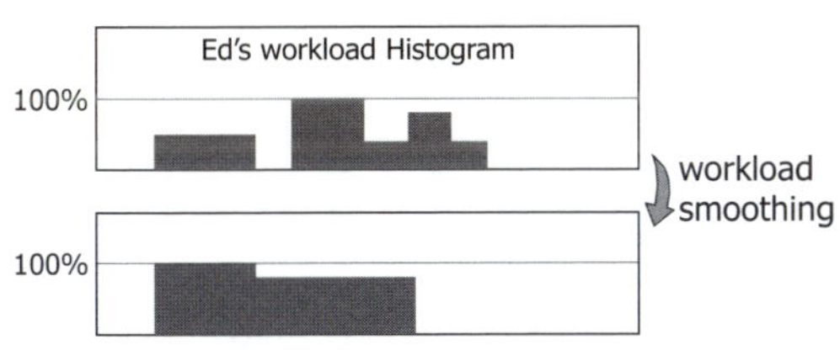

However, you should raise the question: *Would the eventual cost for an erratic workload be more or less than the eventual cost for a smooth workload?* If a resource has an erratic workload, there may be days or weeks when the resource is not needed. The resource may have other employment during those valleys, for which he is paid from funds other than the project budget. If this is not the case, the project manager will likely keep the resource around, particularly if his skill set is scarce. The project manager then assumes extra actual cost for the idle time, and the *actual cost* will be higher than planned. The project budget in MS Project does not show this extra cost, because it only shows the cost of the planned assignments. The extra cost of an erratic workload is hidden cost in the schedule. If you smooth the workload, you will decrease this hidden cost of the project and, therefore, not see the cost of the project decrease. This hidden cost is difficult to quantify during project planning, but in general, you can say that the more erratic the workload, the higher the hidden cost in the project plan. See page 468 for workload leveling.

An intriguing paradox: the scarcer a resource is, the more the resource should be shared between projects from the organization's point of view, but it is less likely that project managers actually will share this scarce resource, particularly if they do not have cost responsibility.

Decrease the Effort Estimate

If you decrease the effort estimate in the **Work** field for a task or an assignment, the cost will decrease as well. Of course, there is a trade-off with quality here. Use **Auto Scheduled** tasks and think about the task **Type** before changing **Work** estimates; use **Fixed Units** or **Fixed Duration**.

Reduce the Scope or Delete Tasks

We discussed this method on page 450. This concludes the second approach of optimizing for time and cost.

Optimizing for Time, Cost and Resources

We will now add the next dimension of resources to our optimizing; the next black arrow in the illustration is the *resources* dimension. The ones we already monitor are: *quality*, *scope*, *time* and *cost*. Adding resources means that we will need to monitor the workload of the resources relative to their availability. If you find that the limited availability of resources affects the forecast dates in your schedule, you are in a *resource-constrained* situation. On page 414 we explained how you can find out if you are in this situation. In resource-constrained projects, you need to include resources in your optimization. If you do not, your schedule will forecast too optimistically.

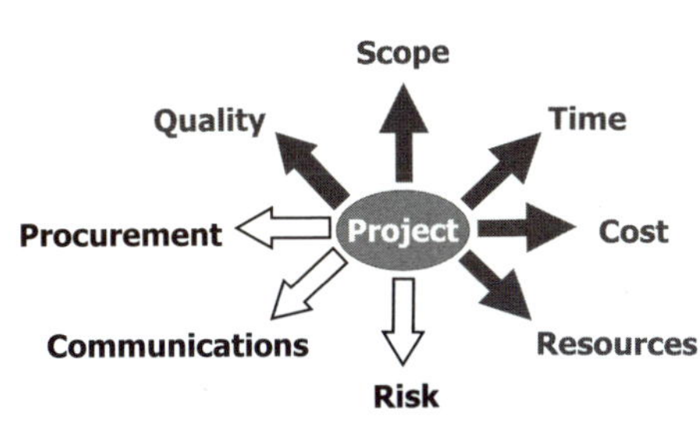

The resource dimension may make trade-offs with:

- Cost, when you have to pay for extra resources or pay more for overtime
- Time, when you cannot solve overallocations in any other way than by delaying tasks

9

To keep the discussion simple, in this section, we will only discuss how to trade off between time and resources. If you also need to bring down the cost of your project at the same time, you should consider the methods discussed in optimizing for time and cost (see page 461).

The optimization becomes more complex, but if we manage to handle this complexity, we will have confidence that the project is feasible as far as the resources are concerned. This will increase the *validity* of our forecasts.

Steps to Optimize for Time, Cost and Resources

1. **Check the workloads and level them**
2. Identify the **Resource-Critical Path (RCP)**
3. Find the **most critical resources**
4. Record the current project **duration** and **cost**
5. Optimize the RCP
6. Consider impacts on quality, scope, time, cost and **resources**
7. Decide whether to keep the change
8. Repeat steps 1 – 8

As the steps in the process chart below show, the first thing we have to do is *resource workload leveling* or *workload leveling.* (MS Project refers to it as *resource leveling*, but personally I find that term too macabre.) We have to check:

- Are the workloads within the availability of the human resources?
- Is the demand for facilities within the availability of the facilities?
- Is the workload within the capacity of the equipment?

When resources are scarce, you will often find that the schedule extends when you level the workloads. This renders the *Critical Path* incomplete, and you will need to find the *Resource-Critical Path* (*RCP*) as discussed on page 432. The differences between this process and the process of optimizing for time (see page 417) appear in bold type in the previous process chart. This approach to optimizing spans quite a few pages, so we will show our progress regularly using this process chart. Once you have found the RCP, optimization is very similar to the methods you used with the *Critical Path Method.*

Workload Leveling

Step 1, Workload *leveling* means changing the schedule in such a way that the workloads of the resources are within their availability at any given time. In the illustration, you can see that, on the left, Harry has to work double time on two tasks that are scheduled in parallel. This creates a workload that exceeds his availability of 100%, which is called an *overallocation*, as charted in the Resource Graph. The overallocation was solved on the right by delaying the task *Read y* until after *Read x*.

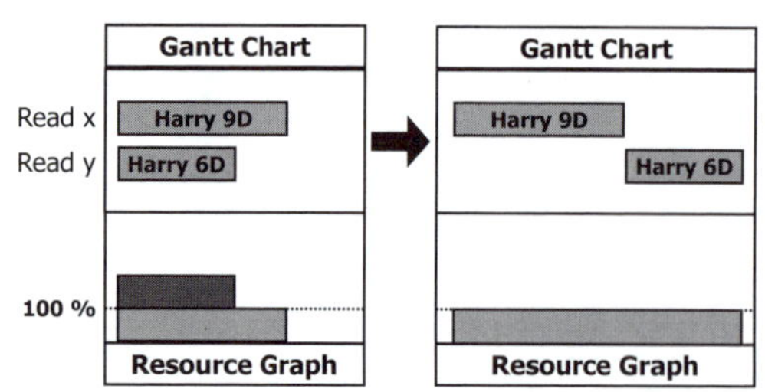

When the workloads from all the tasks in a project or across projects are aggregated, the total workload could exceed the availability of the resource. If you do find overallocations, they need to be resolved because they may affect the forecasted project finish date. *Workload leveling* is the process of resolving the overallocations to make the forecasts realistic.

Ideally, you will have prevented overallocations when you assigned resources to tasks, since they are always painful to solve, particularly when you are sharing resources with other project managers. We explained on page 370, how you can prevent overallocations when you use the **Assign Resources** dialog. If you have *Project Server*, you can even prevent overallocations across all enterprise projects. Organizations without infrastructure and business processes to prevent overallocations can end up with towering workloads across projects.[58]

Within a single project, each project manager has the responsibility to make sure that the workloads are reasonable. Of the 1,000 schedules we evaluated and certified, we found that this responsibility is often neglected; about 50% of the schedules we evaluated had overallocations.

If a task causes an overallocation, Project 2010 alerts you in the Gantt Chart by displaying an icon in the indicators column. Whenever you see the icon, it means that the task is fighting with another task for a resource. Whether Project 2010 alerts you to harmless overallocations of just one minute or serious overallocations of 35 hours of work in one day for one person depends on the following setting: ribbon **Resource**, Leveling Options, **Look for overallocations on a ... basis**. We recommend you carefully consider for what the time unit Project 2010 will alert you to overallocations. Typically, you need to relate this setting to your overall project duration; for example, if you are in a 6-month project, we recommend a **Day by Day** setting.

We will discuss how to level workloads in two different ways:

- Leveling the workloads yourself manually (see page 473) , or
- Have MS Project level the workloads automatically (see page 482).

Leveling Option: Automatic or Manual?

In the **Resource Leveling** dialog, you can select important options for workload leveling.

---

58 We teach how to deal with this in our *Managing Projects*, *Managing Resources* and *Managing Portfolios* courses. For more details visit www.ProjectProCorp.com.

9

1. Click ribbon **Resource** and Leveling Options – the **Resource Leveling** dialog appears:

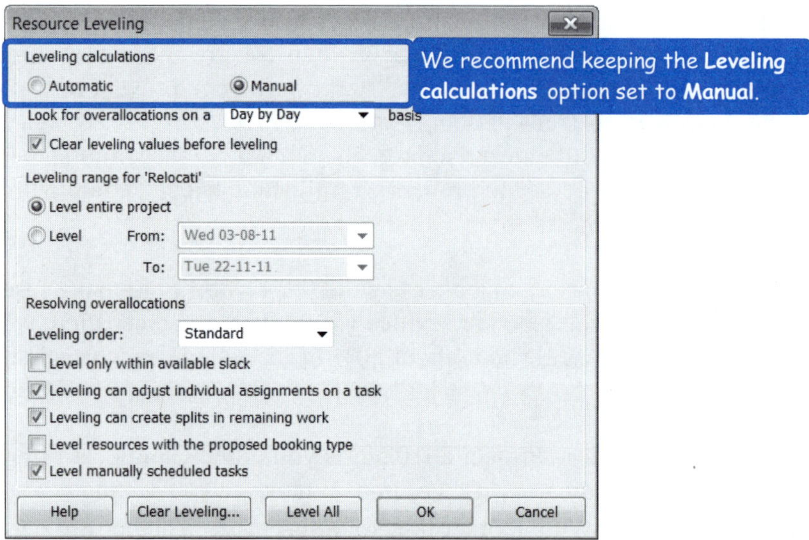

2. At the top in **Leveling calculations**, we recommend you select ⦿ **Manual**. This will still allow you to trigger a one-time automatic leveling of the workloads by clicking Level All. You can do this later again, whenever you are ready for it. We think that this is the way to go.

If you select ⦿ **Automatic** leveling, MS Project will constantly make changes to your schedule as it tries to keep the workloads leveled all the time; your task bars will start dancing across the screen at every change you enter. Also, the option is global, and leveling will take place automatically in each file you open from there forward as soon as you make one little change in them! Be careful!

3. Click OK when done.

Later we will generate some scenarios using the leveling features in MS Project (see page 484) and discuss the dialog box in more detail.

2010 Project 2010 has another feature that works similarly to the ⦿ **Automatic** leveling option in the **Resource leveling** dialog. It is in the Team Planner view: click ribbon **View**, button **Team Planner** and then click ribbon **Format**, button 

.

We recommend you keep it off as well, for the same reason: MS Project will constantly make changes if you leave it on.

The button is a toggle button; when selected, it is highlighted in orange. If it is gray currently, do not click it unless you want all workloads in your schedule to be leveled by Project 2010! This feature is not global, but rather project-specific. To remove leveling delay, see page 487.

Should I Level Workloads Myself or Ask MS Project?

You need to decide if you will resolve the overallocations yourself (*manual leveling*), or if you are going to invite MS Project to help you (*automatic leveling)* using the Level All button. Here is what we recommend:

- If you have not checked the completeness and correctness of the network logic, you should not ask MS Project to level the workloads, because it will produce very comical schedules. MS Project may schedule the task *print the document* before *write the document*, because it does not know that this is impossible if you forgot to tell the tool that. The network of cause-and-effect dependencies will protect the sanity of the schedule. We recommend you first improve the network logic (see page 239).
- If you have few overallocations in your schedule, you could probably resolve them all yourself fairly quickly. We recommend you do it by hand and do not use MS Project's leveling features.
- If there are many overallocations in your schedule, resolving them all by hand is too much work; you may be puzzling for hours. In that case, it may be easier to ask MS Project to perform a complete leveling. This will likely push your project end date out. You can then improve that date by finding the Resource-Critical Path in your schedule and optimizing it, which will bring the project end date back in. We will explain the concept of the Resource-Critical Path later (see page 499) as well as optimizing it (see page 511).

If you need the tightest possible schedule, you will need to invest some time in leveling the workload yourself or on shortening the Resource-Critical Path. MS Project's leveling algorithm is pretty good, but it does not consider things that you would when you level the workloads. For example, MS Project cannot re-allocating workloads from busy team members to less-busy team members. MS Project does not have a clue who could do what task, whereas you do.

9

Check the Workloads: Resource Graph

1. Click ribbon **View** and [Other Views]. Select item **More Views** from the pull-down menu, if needed, and then [Resource Graph] – the **Resource Graph** view appears. The *Resource Graph* is also known as the *resource histogram.* [59] This view displays the total workload for one resource from all its tasks. In Project Server it can even display the total workload across all projects.

2. Click the **View** ribbon, in the section **Zoom,** click [Entire Project]. This will display the workloads across the entire project, which makes it easy to spot any overallocations.

3. Press [Page Dn] to go to the next resource OR press [Page Up] to go to a previous resource or use the **Format** ribbon. You should now see a chart similar to:

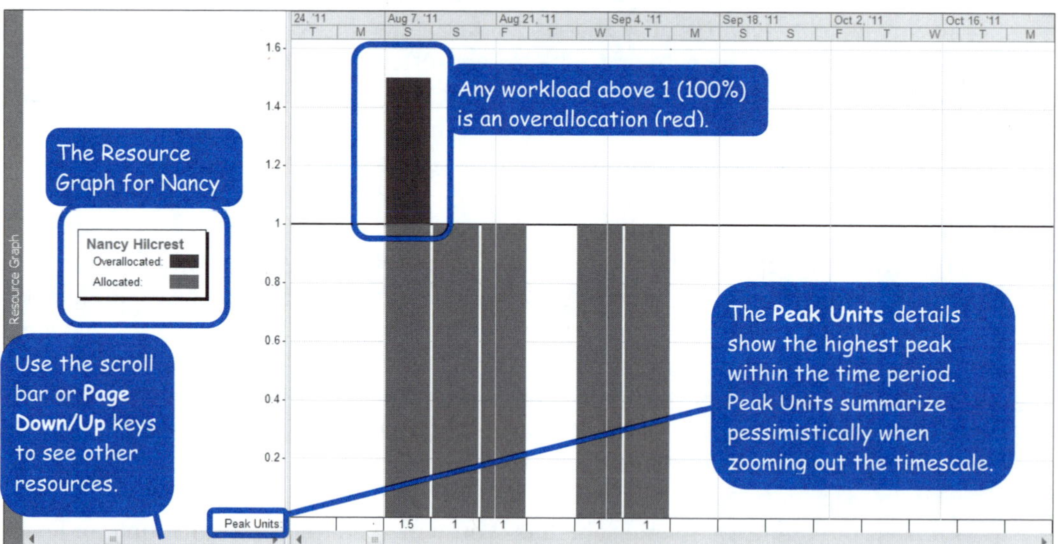

The Resource Graph shows, by default, the **Peak Units**. **Peak Units** allow you to find overallocations very easily; if you see a red bar, you have found an overallocation. Peak Units show the highest bar of minute-by-minute workload during the time unit shown on

---

[59] See the *PMBOK® Guide*, Fourth Edition, published by the PMI.

the timescale. If two tasks of the resource overlap just one minute, the allocation will be 200% (even if the **Leveling Options** on the **Resource** ribbon is set to look for overallocations on a day-by-day basis). Peak Units tend to overstate the real amount of work for the resource. To get a more realistic view of the workloads suited for submitting to your human resources department, click ribbon **Format** and use the **Graph** list to chart the **Work**. The **Work** chart is useful for *resource capacity planning* by HR.

Level the Workloads Yourself

There are many ways in which you can level the workloads by hand without using the automatic leveling (Level All) features of MS Project. The methods are listed in order of effectiveness; the first ones are most effective in our view. The term critical resource is used in this table. A *critical resource* is a resource that drives the project duration or drives the finish date of a *resource-critical task* in a schedule in which the workloads are completely leveled.

1.	Reassign the best resources to the most critical tasks and only to the most critical tasks. You can take noncritical tasks away from the best resources and thus reduce their workloads. Matching people to the tasks so that the best person does the most critical task also results in time gained, and is one of the rare methods for improving both time and workloads.
2.	Reassign tasks from critical resources to noncritical resources. Critical resources extend the project duration and if you take some of their tasks away, you level their workloads and perhaps shorten the project duration at the same time. You can reassign quickly in MS Project by switching to the Resource Usage view, where you can simply drag *assignments* (without ID number, italic text) from one resource to another. You may need to expand a resource by clicking its + button to see its assignments.
3.	Take the critical resource off a task. Sometimes you can do this when more than one person is working on the task, or as soon as you know who will be able to handle the task other than the critical resource. Remember that the word *critical* does not mean the resource is an important resource on the task. Therefore, it may be possible to simply remove critical resources from their task to bring their workload down, so they can focus on and restrict themselves to only the most critical tasks. Some critical resources simply want to be involved in all tasks, hence pulling too much work towards themselves.

9

4.	Hire extra resources. If you hire extra resources, you can reassign the tasks from your critical resources to the new resources. This works well if the new resources have skills similar to or better than your existing resources.
5.	Contract work out to subcontractors. One definition of a subcontractor is someone who solves your workload problems in exchange for money.
6.	Negotiate more resources from subcontractors. If you can get more resources from subcontractors, the workload of existing resources can be reduced.
7.	Fine-tune the number of units assigned to the tasks involved in the overallocation. For example, you could keep two tasks scheduled in parallel if you decrease the involvement of the resource to 50% on both tasks. Make sure, though, that you keep resources working at 100% on critical tasks.
8.	Split long tasks into many shorter ones and reassign the short tasks to noncritical resources. Splitting tasks dramatically increases the number of scheduling possibilities.
9.	Delay vacations until after the deadline. This is where you start to trade off with resources. You will require a lot of goodwill from your resources; be careful not to put unreasonable demands on them, because they will either burn out or leave.
10.	Work during the weekend. If an overallocation occurs on a Friday, you can easily solve such a situation by asking the resource to work some hours over the weekend. Again, you are trading off with resources.
11.	Assign overtime. Even though this does not solve the overallocation, it shows that it has been dealt with. Again you are trading off with the resource dimension.
12.	Change dependencies. Decrease overlaps between tasks that are done by the same resource. Or, in the special case in which you have a team of people going from city to city to install a system, consider setting extra, *soft dependencies* to prevent the team from being in two spots at the same time. This solidifies the order in which locations are rolled out and keeps the workloads of the teams reasonable.
13.	Lower quality standards and lower work estimates, which will decrease the workload. You can often cut corners in the category of nice-to-have requirements without jeopardizing the project product too much.

14.	Schedule assignments on a task individually instead of as a group. When multiple resources are assigned to a task, you can move the workloads of the individual resources to where the workloads fit in their availability. This often causes the task bar to split and people to work independently.
15.	Delay tasks. Slip one of the tasks that compete for the same resource. If you decide to delay one task, choose the task that has the most slack and the least number of resources assigned. If you delay a task with multiple resources assigned, you may cause several new overallocations. The fewer resources assigned, the less checking on workloads you need to do. Through dependencies, successors may cause new overallocations; you can never really tell what will happen when you start delaying tasks.

MS Project will never be able to replace you as the manager to make these decisions, because it cannot:

- Adjust the units on assignments; how can software determine what a reasonable level of involvement is for all assigned resources?
- Find out if more external resources can be found and if they are qualified substitutes.
- Talk to resources and find out what nonworking time they are willing to sacrifice for the betterment of the project.
- Determine which quality standards can be lowered without jeopardizing commitments or contracts.
- Determine who the best resource is.
- Determine who the most critical resource is. In the future, software could possibly figure this out and even suggest who to substitute to improve the schedule, but at this time MS Project cannot.

Using its automatic leveling features, MS Project can only do these things for you:

- Schedule assignments on a task individually instead of as a group (method 14), or
- Delay task bars (method 15).

MS Project can apply only the last two methods listed in the table; it cannot handle any of the other methods that are often more effective to level the workloads. Therefore, we have to conclude that you must level the workloads by hand if you want the tightest schedule possible.

MS Project can also reassign resources across tasks and even across projects (similar to methods number 1 and 2). For this to work, it needs to know what skill is needed on each assignment and what skill(s) each resource has. In the enterprise resource pool from Project Server you could capture the skills of the resources and enter the skill requirements on all assignments in a customized enterprise field. MS Project could then reallocate using its *automatic resource substitution* features (see page 390). Capturing the skills and maintaining them requires quite a bit of work, but the gains can be substantial in terms of resource utilization.

Use the Gantt Chart: Leveling Workloads on a Few Tasks

As we mentioned before, Project 2010 will alert you to harmless overallocations of just one minute or serious overallocations of 35 hours of work in one day for one person depending on the following setting: ribbon **Resource**, Leveling Options, **Look for overallocations on a … basis**. We recommend you choose this setting by relating it to your overall project duration; for example, if you are in a 6-month project, we would recommend a **Day by Day** setting.

If you then only see a few icons in the indicators column of the Gantt Chart, you may be able to level the workloads quickly by using some new features in Project 2010. You can do this task-by-task by right-clicking on the task and selecting **Reschedule to available date** from the popup menu. To do this for multiple, overallocated tasks:

1. Insert the field **Leveling Delay** – this is where MS Project will enter values.
2. Select the tasks with an icon in the indicators column. If there is more than one, click on the first one and hold down the Control key while clicking on the rest to select them.
3. Click ribbon **Task** and find its section **Task**, click  and select **When Resources are Available** from the drop-down menu – MS Project has entered a value in the field **Leveling Delay** (for one of the selected tasks) to solve the overallocation.

This feature enters the elapsed days to slip the task in the task field **Leveling Delay**. If you selected both tasks involved in one overallocation, MS Project will only delay one of the two – the one with the most *slack* (*buffer*) by default. The view Leveling Gantt will display the before and after leveling task bars side-by-side. You can apply this view by clicking ribbon **View**, Other Views, item **More Views** and selecting **Leveling Gantt** from the list.

Use the Team Planner View to Level Workloads

To switch to the Team Planner view, click ribbon **View** and click .

The *Team Planner* view indicates with the color red if there are *overallocations* (see page 362 for screenshots):

- If a resource name is red, that resource has an overallocation.
- Red lines above and below a task bar in the timescale indicate when the overallocation occurs.

The Team Planner is the only view that clearly displays when an individual resource planned some time off work; those days are colored gray in the timescale. If you have a challenge scheduling around the vacations, this view may be best. Double-clicking on the nonworking time displays the **Change Working Time** dialog where you can see the details.

There are many ways in which you can resolve overallocations in the Team Planner view. If you activate the **Task Inspector** (ribbon **Task**, section **Task**, button **Inspect**, item **Inspect Task**) and then perform the actions below, you can check what each feature does. Try these things in the **Team Planner** view:

- *Dragging task bars* in time or between resources – this creates constraint dates.
- Ribbon **Task**: button **Move**, move task to **When Resources are Available** (discussed on page 476 in more detail) – this enters **Leveling Delay**.
- Ribbon **Resource:** button **Level Selection**:
  Select two tasks that cause one overallocation and click the button **Level Selection** on the **Resource** ribbon – this enters **Leveling Delay**.
- Ribbon **Resource:** button **Level Resource**: right-click on an overallocated resource (red), select **Level resource –** this enters **Leveling Delay**.
- Ribbon **Resource:** button **Level all –** this enters **Leveling Delay**.
- Ribbon **Format**, **Prevent overallocations** – this enters **Leveling Delay**.

We recommend using **Level Resource** in this view in particular. Even though it is quick, we recommend against dragging task bars (first item in the list) because it creates constraint dates – you are using a static solution for a dynamic problem. All other methods enter **Leveling Delay** to resolve overallocations, which is specifically designed to deal with workload problems and provides a more dynamic solution. After you have re-assigned resources, you can easily wipe out all leveling delay and level again. It will take much more time to find and remove the constraints you created by dragging task bars.

9

Use the Resource Allocation View When You Level

1. Click ribbon **View**, [Other Views], **More Views** – the **More Views** dialog appears:

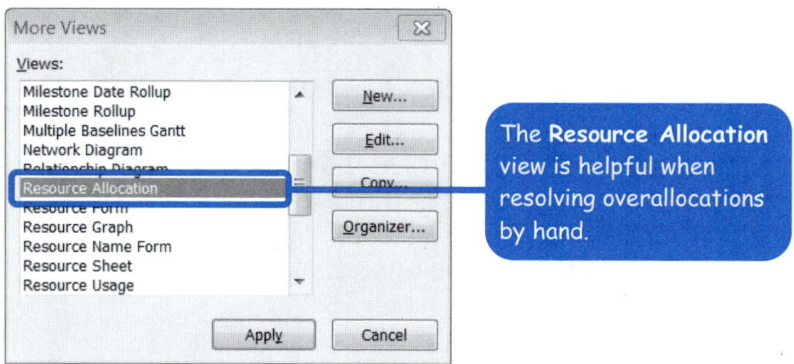

2. Select the **Resource Allocation** view and click [Apply] – a combination view appears with the **Resource Usage** view in the top pane and the **Leveling Gantt** in the bottom pane. The top view shows the overallocated resources by showing the **Resource Name** in red. When you click on an overallocated resource, the bottom view shows only the tasks assigned to that resource. Some of these tasks are contending for this resource.

3. Having both views helps in resolving the overallocation:

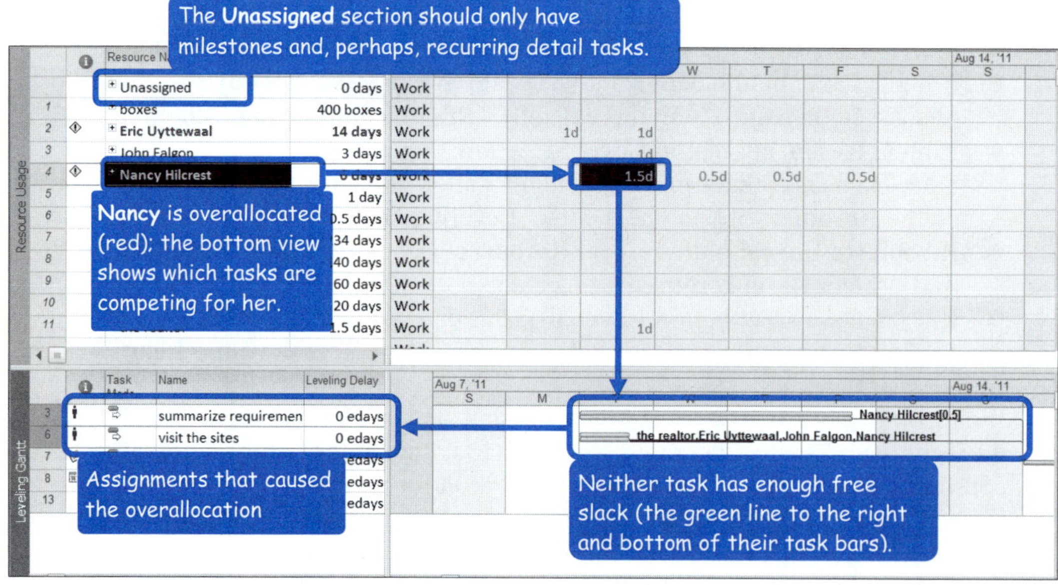

Project 2010 does a better job than previous releases of highlighting with red in the timescale when there is a real overallocation. Project 2010 establishes if there is an overallocation dependent on the time unit displayed in the Leveling Options dialog (ribbon **Resource**). So, it is important to first select the right time unit in this dialog:

4. First, select the time unit by which you want to check for overallocations. Click ribbon **Resource**, and click Leveling Options and select the time unit in the **Look for overallocations on a <time unit> basis** field.
5. Adjust the time unit displayed in the timescale accordingly by selecting the right time unit in the Timescale: Weeks list on the **View** ribbon.
6. Check to see if you forgot any *assignments*; if you did, there is little use starting the workload leveling. The heading ⊞ **Unassigned** at the top contains the unassigned tasks. Click on the button ⊞ to expand them, and click ⊟ to hide them again. Typically only the *milestones* and perhaps the *recurring detail tasks* should be listed in the **Unassigned** category. If you have not assigned resources to all detail tasks, you have not captured all the workloads, and you should not start leveling the workloads. If assignments are incomplete, manual leveling is a lot of wasted effort.
7. If needed, hide all assignments in the top view by clicking on any column heading and clicking ribbon **View**, Outline and selecting item **Hide Subtasks**.
8. The overallocated resources are shown in red, and they also have an icon in the indicators column.

Go to the first overallocation by clicking Next Overallocation on the **Resource** ribbon. MS Project searches forward in time to find the next overallocation; it does not stay with the selected resource. Note that, unlike the red highlighting, this tool stops on all overallocations even if they are not overallocations based on the time unit you chose in the first step! Also, the tool does not want to start over again at the start date of the project; switching away from this view and then back to it helps (sometimes!). These are bugs in the original release of Project 2010; they may be resolved in later service packs.
OR
You can browse for overallocations by clicking on the shaft of the horizontal scroll bar (between the scroll box and the scroll arrow) to move the timescale one screen forward starting at the start date of the project. Look for red numbers.

9. Determine if the overallocation is serious enough that it needs resolution. We think you need to resolve overallocations when they exceed 150% of a person's

availability on a day-to-day basis and 120% on a week-by-week basis. Thresholds like these will exist or should be established within your organization. Please consult with your team members and your project management office.

10. Resolve the serious overallocations one-by-one by applying one of the methods provided on page 473. This view is particularly suitable to re-assign tasks (by dragging them to another resource) or delay a task (by entering a number in the **Leveling Delay** field).

In the next illustration, you can see how the overallocation is solved by delaying one of the tasks that was competing for the same resource:

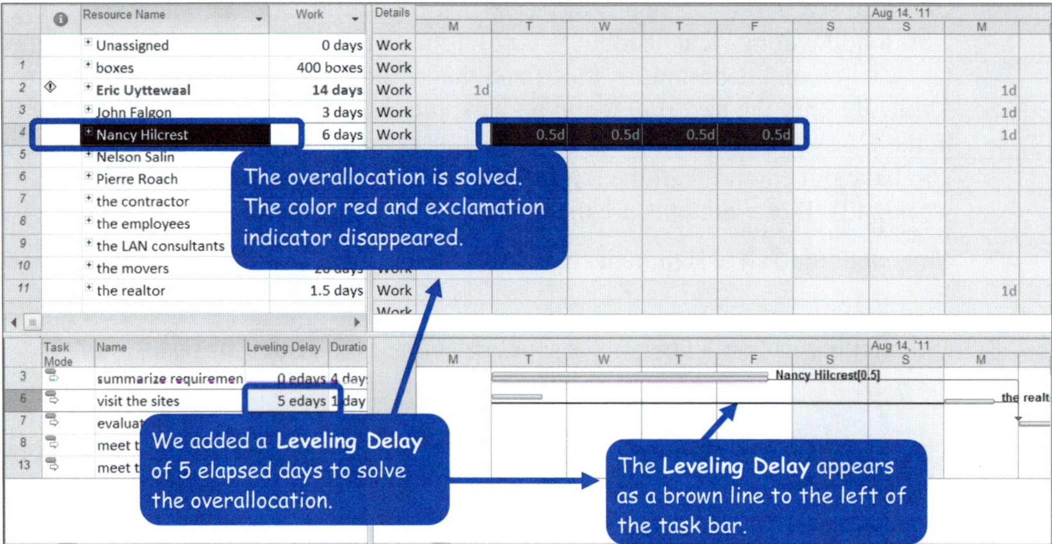

We can improve the bottom view by displaying a line for the *total slack* as well (see page 421 for an explanation on the two types of slack). If the *free slack* is not large enough, the total slack may provide possibilities to resolve the overallocation. We will have to add a colored line for total slack to each task bar. Click in the bottom view and click ribbon **Format,**  , **Bar Styles** – the **Bar Styles** dialog appears.

Scroll down until you see the **Slack** line item, which depicts free slack. Cut the **Slack** line and paste it back in twice. Change the **Name** of the first one to **Total Slack**, then change the color to **Lime** (light green); under **To,** select **Total Slack** from the list.

Change the name of the second one to **Free Slack** and change the **Shape** to the second to last item in the list (bar that is, vertically seen, in the middle).

You can see all these changes in the following screenshot: [60]

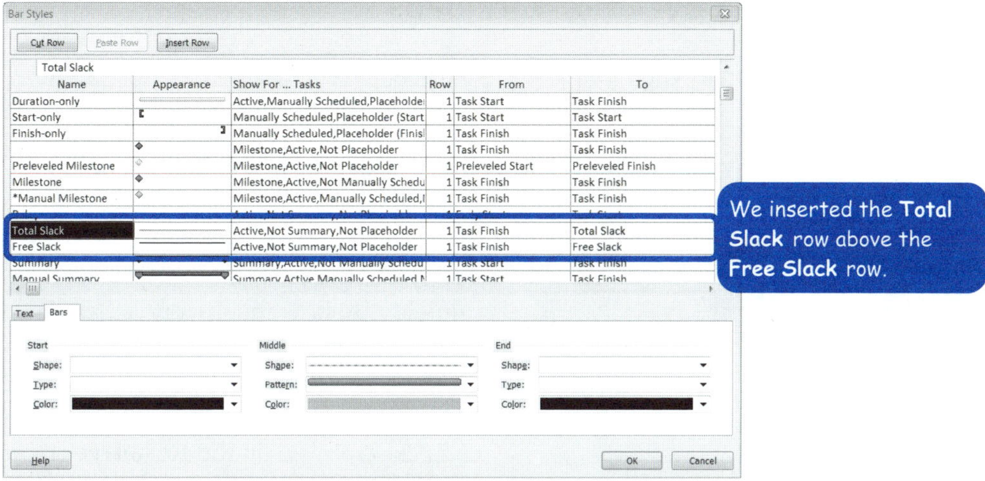

If you keep the same **Shape**, the lines will fall on top of one another and the shorter **Free Slack** line could be covered. With the free slack item listed under the total slack, the shorter free slack line will be superimposed on the total slack line. MS Project creates the bars in the order they are listed.

With the **Total Slack** you can see how far you can delay tasks without affecting the next constraint date or the project end date. If a task does not have enough *free slack* to solve overallocations, you can use its *total slack* to solve the work overload. The total slack is always greater than or equal to the free slack. In the illustration, task *A* does not have enough free slack to solve the overallocation, but it does have enough total slack. If you go beyond the total slack, you are violating a constraint date or increasing the project duration. In the

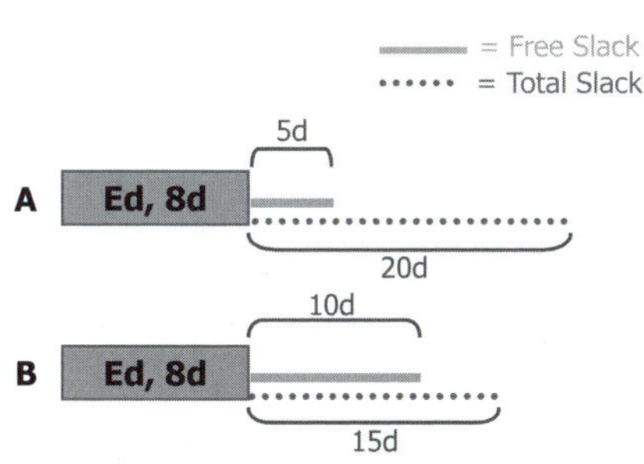

---

60 We have created this view for you in the file *09 Resource Allocation view – ProjectPro.mpp* that is available for download. See page iv for the procedure to access these files.

illustrated example, I would prefer to delay task B in a large schedule, since it resolves the overallocation within the free slack and no other task is affected. I would prefer to slip task A if my deadlines are very hard, since A has more total slack.

Have MS Project Level the Workloads

We explained already that when you ask MS Project to level the workloads, it will typically delay tasks (see page 475). The result will usually be a schedule that is extended as shown in the illustration. The automatic leveling feature may not help in finding the tightest schedule possible, but its real benefit is telling you quickly by how much your schedule will slip when all workloads are leveled. MS Project also allows you to go back to the original schedule with a feature called Clear Leveling on the **Resource** ribbon.

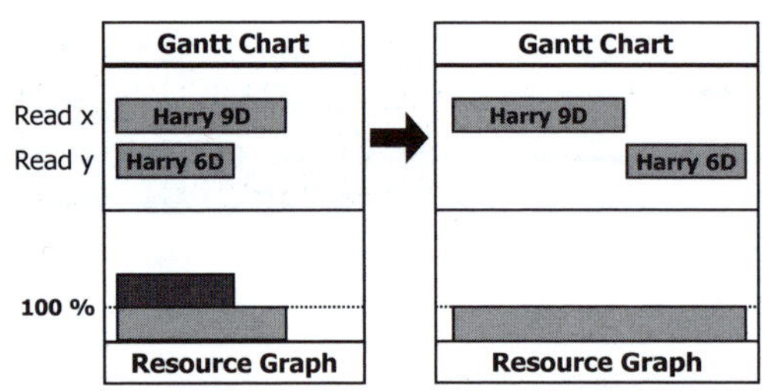

Human resources can do more than one task at a time, which is also known as *multi-tasking*. Whether this affects the productivity is a separate discussion. To level human resources, you fill the workload up to the limit of their availability. If someone is only used 80% of their time, another small part-time task could be added without over allocating. I call this *percentage leveling*, since you try to fill availability up to 100%.

In Project 2010, you can now see in the Gantt Chart if you have overallocations; tasks with an icon in the indicators column are involved in an overallocation. Where two tasks scheduled concurrently have the same resource assigned, the workloads can exceed its availability. Note that the number of icons you will see is driven by the following setting in ribbon **Resource**, Leveling Options, setting **Look for overallocation on a … basis**.

Leveling of Facility and Machine Resources

In general, facilities and machines are either occupied or not and need *yes/no leveling*. Unfortunately, MS Project does not consider facilities and machines as distinct types of resources. You could make facilities and machines **Work** resources (field **Type**) and assign only at 100% to emulate yes/no leveling. Perhaps it is better to enter facilities and machines as **Material** resources and create a reservation system for board rooms and training rooms in Outlook, for example.

Materials are consumable and do not need leveling. MS Project excludes materials by automatically setting the resource field **Can Level** to *No* as soon as you set the resource **Type** to **Material**.

Choosing the Leveling Options

Click ribbon **Resource**, button **Leveling Options** to access the *leveling options* when you are resolving *overallocations*.

We will discuss the options in the dialog box section by section:
Leveling calculations

- We recommend ⦿ **Manual** (see page 469). You can still have MS Project level the current overallocations by clicking [Level All] at the bottom of the same dialog. You can also delete any traces of leveling by clicking [Clear Leveling...] in this dialog, which will change all values in the task field **Leveling Delay** to zero.
- In the list **Look for overallocations on a … basis,** you can choose the granularity with which MS Project combs through the data to find overallocations. A double workload on Monday with a total workload of 16 hours in that same week constitutes an overload on a day-by-day basis, but not on a week-by-week basis. The setting is about the granularity of leveling. We recommend using **Day by Day** or **Week by Week** for most projects. This setting drives the red highlighting.
- Select ☑ **Clear Leveling values before leveling** if you want to start fresh and clear the field **Leveling delay** of values left by previous leveling. Clear it if you want MS Project to only add to the leveling delay values; this often leads to unnecessarily long project durations.

9

Leveling range for <name of project>

- Select ⦿ **Level entire project**. You normally would level the entire project, but you can also indicate a date range.

Resolving overallocations

- Select or clear **Level only within available Slack**.
  You can select this option to develop a scenario that will tell you how many of the overallocations MS Project can resolve within the total slack of the project. If you create a *Must Finish On* constraint date on the project finish milestone you create a certain amount of total slack, a certain time frame within which MS Project can solve as many overallocations as possible (see page 487 for detailed procedure). Clear this option if you want MS Project to resolve all your overallocations; if you have minimized the number of hard constraint dates as we recommended, it will definitely solve them all.

- ☑ **Leveling can adjust individual assignments on a task**
  Select this option if you want to find the shortest leveled schedule. If you have more than one person assigned to a task, this option will reschedule the individual *assignments* rather than all assignments as a group. The result is that task bars are often split into multiple parts connected by dots (see illustration), because each assignment on the task will be scheduled separately. You cannot allow this for tasks on which people are supposed to work together (i.e., *collaborate*, for example for meetings, trainings, joint application development sessions). If you want to use this leveling option, make sure that for those collaborative tasks you enter **No** in the task-related field **Level Assignments**. If you set it to **No,** MS Project will schedule the task only on dates when the whole group is available. Notice that MS Project sets this field by default to **No** for *Fixed Duration* and *recurring detail tasks*; **Yes** is the default setting for all other tasks. MS Project acts smartly here because meetings and trainings will normally be Fixed Duration tasks, if you followed our recommendations on page 361.

- ☑ **Leveling can create splits in remaining work**
  Check this option if you want to allow MS Project to split task bars (see illustration). Splitting may generate a tighter schedule, because if you allow splitting, MS Project can schedule around tasks that have fixed dates. The drawback is that task bars become fragmented. If you want to exclude certain tasks from being split, clear their task-related field **Leveling can split**.

☑ Leveling can create splits in remaining work

In Project 2010, there are now many buttons to level the workloads. You need to realize that, regardless of which button you use, the options selected in this dialog stay in effect and, therefore, you should always review them first.

Three Automatic Leveling Scenarios

Before we ask MS Project to create scenarios, we must first check whether we have completed the network logic and assigned resources to all detail tasks:

- Without complete logic, MS Project will produce ridiculous schedules when it levels the workloads in your schedule (see page 239).

- If we forgot to assign some tasks to resources, not all workloads are entered and there is no use asking MS Project to level the workloads. It is important to complete the assignments (see page 396).

There are three scenarios you can develop with MS Project. It is easy to switch back and forth among them. Each scenario provides some useful information for a negotiation about the project target date. In your negotiation it will help to know what you will first propose, at what point you will gracefully decline to be the project manager and what a reasonable compromise is. The illustration shows all three scenarios. The dark workloads are the overallocations. If you never leveled the workloads, you currently have the first scenario of *No leveling*. The more the workloads are leveled, the fewer overallocations, but the longer the schedule. The three scenarios are:

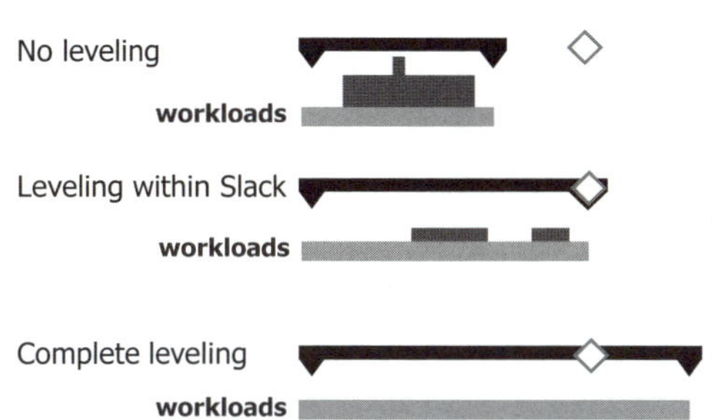

- **No leveling**
  This scenario answers the question: *What is the project duration when the workloads are not leveled?* It tells us the minimum duration for the project.
- **Leveling within the slack of the project**
  If you create a milestone with a Must Finish On constraint on the proposed target date, you can level within the slack this hard constraint date creates. This scenario answers the question: *What workload will critical resources have while meeting a compromise target date for the project?* It tells you how many extra resources you should hire in order to meet the compromise target date.
- **Complete leveling**
  This answers: *What is the end date of the project if the workloads of all resources are entirely leveled?* This shows a comfortable deadline for the project and the team and could serve as your initial bid in a negotiation.

All three scenarios provide useful information when negotiating deadlines with upper management or clients:

- The no-leveling date from the first scenario is your resistance point in negotiations; you should not commit to an earlier date. You will still have to resolve all overallocations if you commit to this date without delaying the project finish date, which can be challenging depending on how many overallocations you have. This scenario tells you the absolute earliest date to which you could commit if you could get all the resources you might need (*unlimited resources*).
- The proposed target date from the second scenario provides the common ground in your negotiations with the client. You can ask MS Project to resolve as many

overallocations as it can while staying within that proposed target date. You can then easily find out how many extra resources you need to hire to meet the target date and calculate what that would cost. If the client is willing to pay for these extra resources, you may have a date that meets your mutual needs. You could propose to increase the budget of the project so you can hire the resources. This scenario tells you what a feasible compromise looks like. Trading time for money is also known as *crashing*.

- The finish date of the third scenario of complete leveling is the date we recommend you first quote to your client. It is a date that is nice to have (no overallocations), and that you will likely not get. It could be your starting position in negotiations.

For each of these scenarios, it is nice to see what changes MS Project has made to the schedule; and the **Leveling Gantt** will tell you exactly that. To apply this view, click ribbon **View, Other Views, More Views**, select **Leveling Gantt** from the list and click [Apply].

The Leveling Gantt view looks like this:

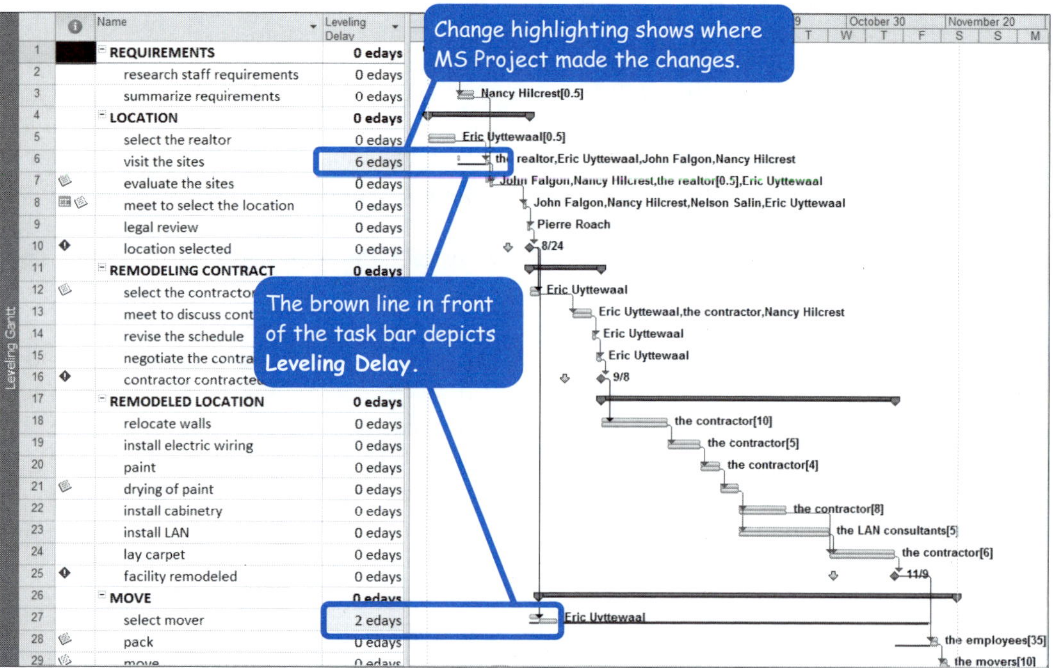

This view includes the field **Leveling Delay** as one of the columns. It also shows the delay graphically with a brown line to the left of any task bars that were delayed.

You can even make the three scenarios show up side-by-side in one Gantt Chart, which we will explain in detail on page 490.

No Leveling or Clearing the Leveling

1. If you have leveled workloads before, the task field **Leveling Delay** will have entries. To check if this is the case, make sure you insert this column.
2. To remove all leveling delay, click ribbon **Resource** and click Clear Leveling.
3. The numbers in the task field **Leveling Delay** should all be zero.
4. If you want to compare all three scenarios in one Gantt Chart (see page 490), you should at this point save the dates of this scenario. Click ribbon **Project** and find its section **Schedule**, click button **Set baseline**, item **Set baseline** and select ⦿ **Set interim plan** and **Copy** the **Scheduled Start/Finish into Start1/Finish1**. Click OK when done.

You now know the minimum duration for your project; note that there may be overallocations in the schedule that need to be taken care of.

Leveling within the Slack of the Project

1. Make sure you have a project finish milestone at which all dependencies come together. For this scenario we must set a *Must Finish On* constraint on the project finish milestone at the proposed date; a Finish No Later Than constraint does not work here. Ensure that the number of other constraint dates is kept to minimum (as we recommended earlier), because they hinder MS Project's workload leveling.
2. If needed, insert the column **Leveling Delay** by right-clicking on a column heading, clicking **Insert Column** and selecting the field **Leveling Delay** from the list. This field allows you to see the result of the MS Project's leveling.

3. Click ribbon **Resource**, Leveling Options – the **Resource Leveling** dialog appears:

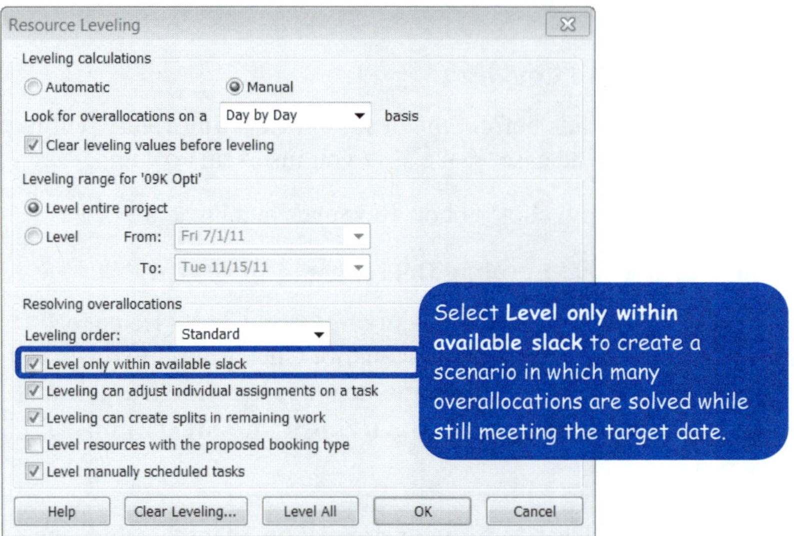

4. From the list **Look for overallocations on a … basis,** choose the granularity of the leveling by selecting the time unit in which MS Project should find overallocations. We recommend **Day by Day** or **Week by Week** for most projects.

5. Select ☑ **Clear leveling values before leveling** to clear the field **Leveling delay** of old leveling values; MS Project will make a fresh start with the leveling.

6. Select ☑ **Level only within available slack**.

7. Clear ☐ **Level resources with the proposed booking type** unless you also want to level the workloads of resources that are *proposed* for but not *committed* to potential projects.

8. Select ☑ **Level manually scheduled tasks** to include them as well.

9. Click Level All MS Project may alert you that it cannot resolve certain overallocations, which is what is expected, since we gave it a fixed time frame. Click Skip All to skip all overallocations it cannot resolve.

10. Click OK.

11. If you want to compare all three scenarios in one Gantt Chart (see page 490), you should at this point save the dates of this scenario. Click ribbon **Project**, button **Set baseline**, item **Set baseline** and select ◉ **Set interim plan** and **Copy** the **Scheduled Start/Finish into Start2/Finish2**.

Check the workloads of the resources in the Resource Usage view; the overallocations you skipped are left. You could analyze how much extra expense you would incur by hiring temporary workers to solve the remaining overallocations, or, you could explore other methods to make those workloads reasonable (see page 473).

Complete Leveling

1. Check whether you have hard constraint dates in your schedule because they will hinder this process of complete leveling. In the column, look for the icon with a red dot.
2. If needed, insert the column **Leveling Delay** by right-clicking on a column heading, clicking **Insert Column** and selecting the field **Leveling Delay** from the list. This field allows us to see the result of MS Project's leveling.
3. Click ribbon **Resource,** Leveling Options – the **Resource Leveling** dialog appears:

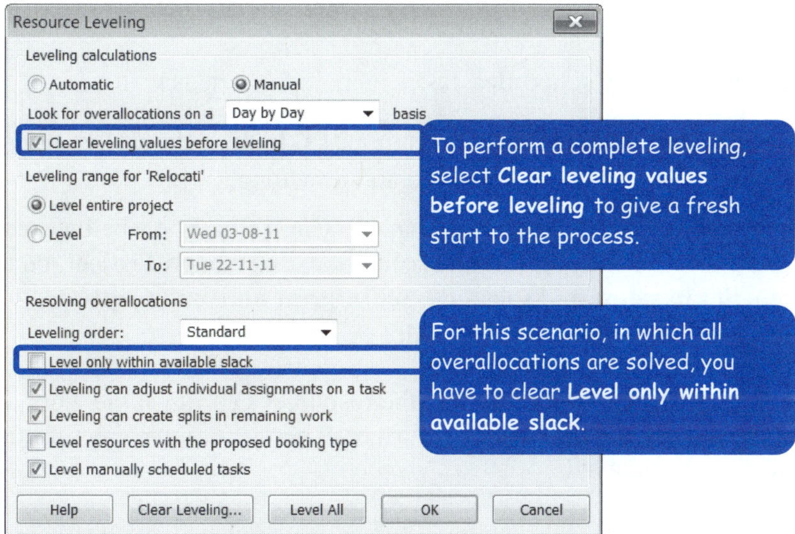

4. From the list **Look for overallocations on a … basis,** choose the granularity of the leveling by selecting the time unit in which MS Project should find overallocations. We recommend **Day by Day** or **Week by Week** for most projects.
5. Select ☑ **Clear leveling values before leveling** to clear the field **Leveling delay** of old leveling values.
6. Select ◉ **Level entire project**.

7. Clear ☐ **Level only within available slack**; otherwise MS Project may not solve all overallocations.

8. Select ☑ **Leveling can adjust individual assignments on a task** if you want to find the shortest leveled schedule. MS Project schedules the assignments individually instead of as a group, and you may end up with split task bars. To address this, you can redo the leveling and clear the option to prevent task bar splits, or you can set the task field **Level assignments** to *No* for task bars that you do not want split.

9. Select ☑ **Leveling can create splits in remaining work** if you want to allow MS Project to split task bars. The drawback is that the task bars become fragmented. If you want to exclude certain tasks from being split, set their task field **Leveling can split** to *No*.

10. Clear ☐ **Level resources with the proposed booking type**, unless you also want to level the workloads of resources that are *proposed* on potential projects but not *committed.*

11. Select ☑ **Level manually scheduled tasks** to include them as well.

12. Click Level All. MS Project delayed certain tasks. In the column **Leveling Delay**, you can see which tasks have been delayed and how long.

13. If you want to compare all three scenarios in one Gantt Chart (see below), you should at this point save the dates of this scenario. Click ribbon **Project**, button **Set baseline**, item **Set baseline** and select ◉ **Set interim plan** and **Copy** the **Scheduled Start/Finish into Start3/Finish3**.

The schedule is now realistic in the sense that the resources can finish the work assigned to them without the project end date slipping further. Check the finish date of the project; it has likely been delayed.

Comparing the Three Scenarios in One Gantt Chart

In order to compare the three scenarios in terms of dates on the different milestones, you should create a new view and select separate bar styles for the Start1/Start2/Start3 scenarios. These steps assume that you have already captured the three scenarios as shown in previous procedures and have already executed the last step of all three procedures. We have prepared this view for you; you can find it in the file *Comparing Three Scenarios - ProjectPro.mpp* available for download from our website (see page vi for the procedure to access these files). If you download it, you can skip this procedure.

1. Click ribbon **View,** Other Views, **More Views…** – the **More Views** dialog appears:

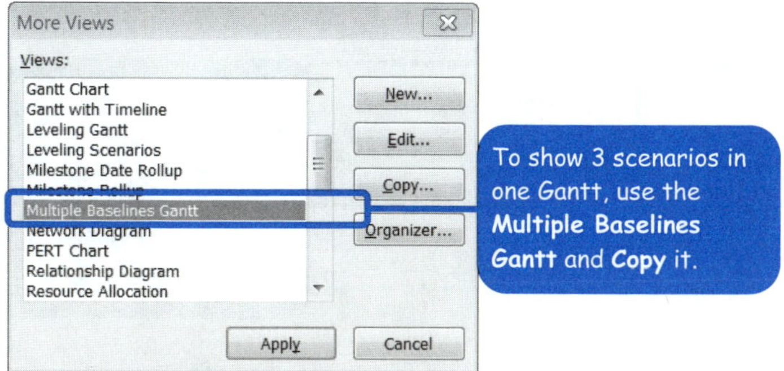

2. Select **Multiple Baselines Gantt** and click Copy... .
3. The **View Definition** dialog appears:

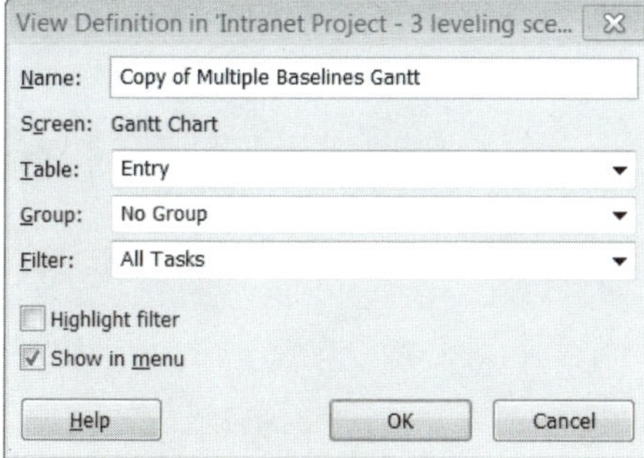

4. Change the name of the new view to *Comparing Three Scenarios* or something that is descriptive.
5. Check ☑ **Show in menu**; the view will be available with only two mouse clicks.
6. You can keep the rest of the settings and click OK – you are now back in the **More Views** dialog. Click Apply.
7. Click ribbon **Format,** Format, **Bar Styles**, then change the settings in the **From** and **To** field so that:
Baseline dates are replaced by the *Start1/Finish1* dates,
Baseline 1 dates are replaced by the *Start2/Finish2* dates, and
Baseline 2 dates are replaced by the *Start3/Finish3* dates.

9

You also need to make changes in the **Show for … Tasks** field. All changes you need to make are shown in the following dialog:

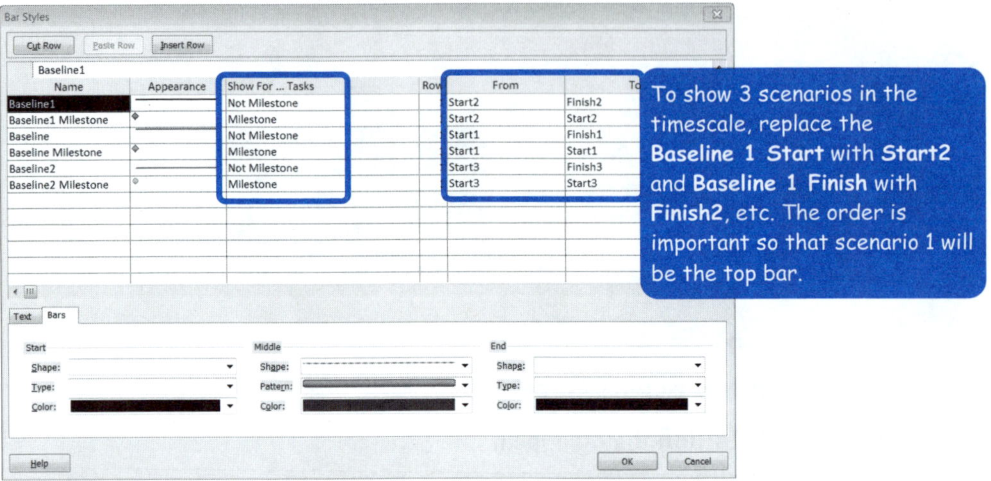

8. Click [OK] once done.

9. You should now see the three task bars for each task and have the three scenarios next to each other in the timescale with scenario 1 (no leveling) as the top bar, scenario 2 (leveling within slack) as the middle bar and scenario 3 (complete leveling) as the bottom bar for each task:

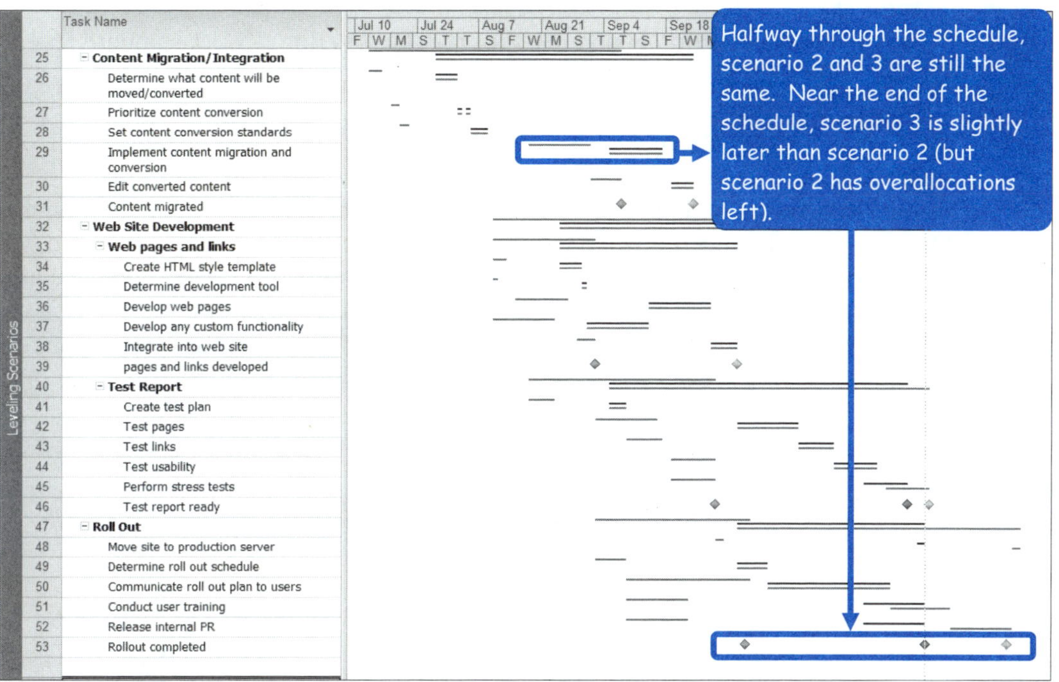

Influencing MS Project's Leveling

How can you predict which tasks will be postponed when resources are overallocated? When you ask MS Project to level your schedule, it will try to intelligently choose which tasks to delay. It looks at the amount of slack on both tasks that compete for the same resource and will delay the one task that has the most slack. This is smart, because the tasks with most slack are least likely to affect your project end date. However, it does not always delay the task you would prefer. MS Project offers you three choices to influence which tasks are delayed. You will find these in the **Resource Leveling** dialog (ribbon **Resource**, button Leveling Options)

The options to look at are in the **Leveling order** list. Here are some suggestions on when to use each:

- **ID Only**
  MS Project will level tasks based upon their ID numbers. It will give priority to the task higher up in the list of tasks. Use this setting to prioritize multiple projects in a

consolidated schedule, for example for scheduling small *maintenance projects*. Put your highest priority projects at the top of the list and then level your consolidated schedule using this option. Dragging projects up and down the list is less effort than maintaining priority numbers.

- **Standard**
  This is the default setting and is used for regular leveling. Under standard leveling, the task with the most slack will be delayed, which makes sense.
- **Priority, Standard**
  When you are not entirely happy with MS Project's leveling, you can enter a priority number for certain tasks in the field **Priority**. In this way you can influence which task is delayed in the leveling. This involves a fair bit of work if you do it on a task-by-task basis; if you fill down a priority number for all tasks of a deliverable, you may be finished a lot faster. Priority numbers can range from 0 to 1000. The higher the number, the higher the priority, and the more likely it will be that the task keeps its current dates. MS Project will not delay the higher priority task when you level using the leveling setting **Priority, Standard**.

Another way to influence leveling is to exclude certain tasks or resources as candidates for leveling.

Excluding Tasks from MS Project Leveling

If the priority number is set to *1000*, MS Project will not delay the task and will effectively exclude it from the leveling process. This is even the case if you use the **ID Only** or **Standard** setting in the **Resource Leveling** dialog. MS Project sets a priority of 1000 automatically on recurring detail tasks.

Excluding Resources from MS Project Leveling

For example, you would typically exclude subcontractor resources from leveling, because the workload of people external to your organization is not usually your problem.

You can exclude human resources by entering **No** in the resource-related field **Can Level**.
OR

1. In Project 2010 you can now easily select certain resources to level their workloads and you can even start this from any view.

2. Click the **Resource** ribbon and then 

– the **Level Resource** dialog appears:

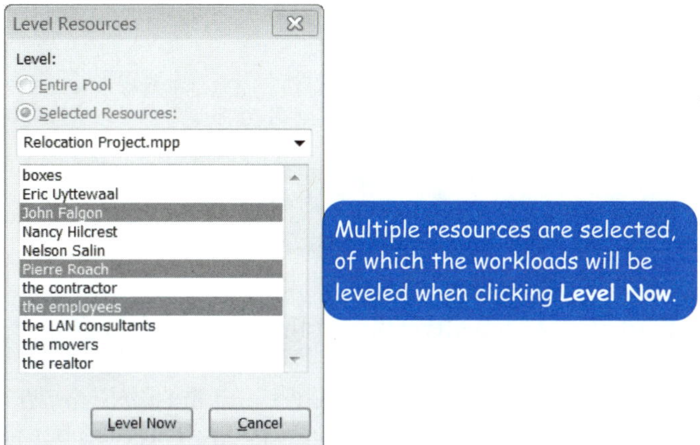

3. You can select multiple resources by clicking on the first one and holding down the Control key while clicking on the rest.

4. Click Level Now – the resources you leveled will no longer be red (unless MS Project alerted you it could not resolve all their overallocations and you skipped some).

9

How Leveling Affects the Critical Path

In the illustration, there are two tasks *write X* and *write Y* (another unrelated document).

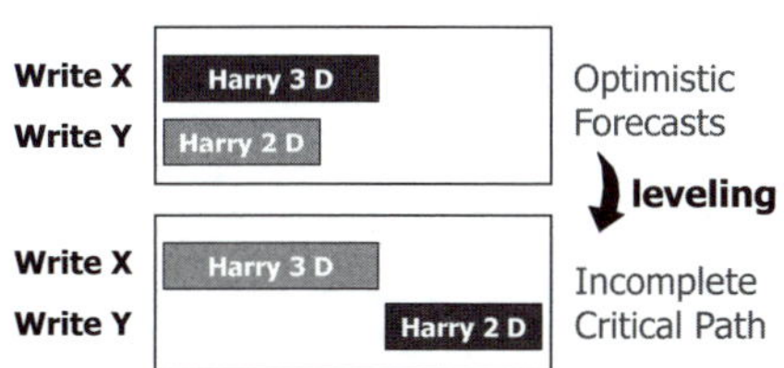

The tasks are not logically dependent upon each other; Harry can choose to do them in any order. Before workload leveling, the Critical Path is the task *write X*. The Critical Path in the unleveled schedule forecasts optimistic finish dates, because there is an overallocation for Harry. After leveling, *write Y* is the only critical task, which is an incomplete Critical Path. Try this out in MS Project! Do not worry, there is nothing wrong with your software; this is how the Critical Path algorithm is supposed to work and how it works in any other scheduling software. The Critical Path theory assumes that you have access to unlimited resources and does not take the *resource dependency* between *write X* and *write Y* into account.

In MS Project, the leveled mini-schedule looks as follows:

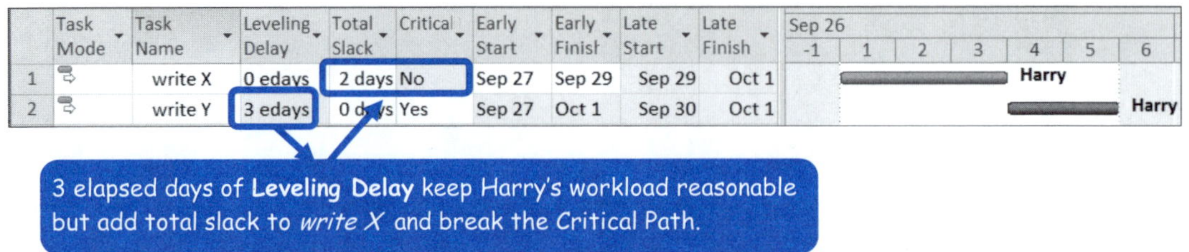

	Task Mode	Task Name	Leveling Delay	Total Slack	Critical	Early Start	Early Finish	Late Start	Late Finish
1		write X	0 edays	2 days	No	Sep 27	Sep 29	Sep 29	Oct 1
2		write Y	3 edays	0 days	Yes	Sep 27	Oct 1	Sep 30	Oct 1

Let me first explain the mathematics of the algorithm in this simple example (see the timescale in the screenshot):

- On the *forward pass*, the *early start* for *write X* is day 1 and the *early finish* is day 3 given the duration of 3 days. For *write Y* the early start is day 1; remember that there is no dependency between the tasks, and the early finish is at the end of day 5, given the delayed start date of day 4.
- On the *backward pass*, the *late finish* for *write Y* is also day 5; the *late start*, therefore, is day 4. *Write X* has to be finished on the project finish date; the late finish date is day 5, since there is no dependency between the two. It has to start, at the latest, on day 3 to meet this date.

Total slack can be calculated by subtracting the early finish date from the late finish date. The total slack of the task *write Y* is 5 – 5 = 0 days; the task is critical and highlighted in red (the light bar in the screenshot). The total slack for *write X* is 5 – 3 = 2 days; the task is not seen as critical by the algorithm. However, common sense dictates that there really is no slack on the task *write X*, because it competes for the same resource, *Harry*. And if the task *write X* takes longer, the task *write Y* will be moved out. This example demonstrates the weakness of the Critical Path algorithm. The algorithm does not take resource dependencies into account.

Resource Dependencies Differ from Logical Dependencies

A *logical dependency* imposes the sequence in which you perform the tasks. For example, if you create a Finish-to-Start dependency between *dig foundation* and *build walls*, you tell MS Project to always schedule *dig foundation* before *build walls*.

A *resource dependency* is a relationship between two tasks that does not impose sequence. The relationship is caused by sharing the same resource to perform these tasks. The only impact of a resource dependency is that both tasks cannot be scheduled in parallel because this would cause an overallocation. Resource dependent tasks need to be scheduled in serial in any sequence.

In the example where Harry had to work full-time on *write X* and *write Y*, there is no logical dependency; he can do them in any order, but he cannot do them at the same time. A resource dependency is different from a logical dependency because a logical dependency imposes sequence, whereas a resource dependency does not. This is also the reason why we do not recommend that you model resource dependencies by entering extra logical dependencies. In the illustration we used, therefore, dotted arrows instead of solid arrows to distinguish a resource dependency from a logical dependency. Logical dependencies impose the sequence and will result in suboptimal schedules after you re-assign tasks or when tasks start slipping.

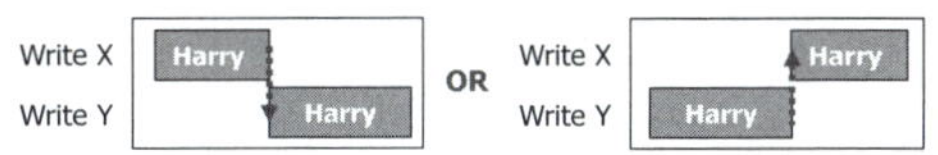

9

Who Has Access to Unlimited Resources?

The Critical Path theory was built on the assumption that you have access to *unlimited resources*. Assuming unlimited resources is unrealistic for most organizations. Companies that use their resources well gain a competitive edge. This is particularly true for those that compete with companies located in countries with lower wages. Resources are often stretched to their limits and drive the project end date. A company that does not optimize the usage of its resources will soon notice this in its bottom line. In other words, more organizations find themselves having to level the workloads of their resources. Upon doing so, the Critical Path often becomes incomplete and only partially explains the duration of the project. The leveling of tasks can make the calculated total slack value of tasks meaningless and therefore the Critical Path as well. In fact, tasks with total slack may be driving the project end date in reality, as is the case with the task *write X* in the previous example. If *write X* slips, it will move *write Y,* because of the resource dependency through *Harry* being assigned to both tasks. The slack is false slack on the *write X* task.

There are some types of companies that schedule as if they have access to unlimited resources. Construction companies that can easily find any number of carpenters in any skill level are in a situation of unlimited resources. They will not let their schedule be driven by the availability of resources. Consulting firms that hire or relocate their resources all across the country or the world may treat resources as unlimited. These companies can apply the Critical Path Method. and that is all they need. Other companies need to observe how their limited resources affect the forecasts in their project schedules that are *resource-constrained.*

Critical Path or Resource-Critical Path?

We need a smarter Critical Path that takes resource dependencies as well as logical dependencies into account. Such a path is called the *Resource-Critical Path (RCP),* which is a concept we first published in 1999 in PM Network.[61]

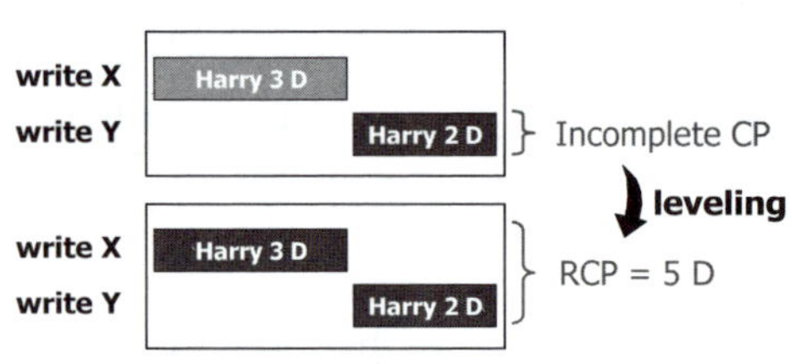

Given the example in the illustration, which should a project manager monitor, the incomplete *Critical Path (CP)* or the *RCP*? The answer is obvious; both tasks drive the project end date. They are resource-critical, because Harry is assigned to both tasks which creates the *resource dependency* between the tasks. One should try to find the RCP in *resource-constrained* projects, rather than the Critical Path. Only the RCP provides a complete explanation of the project duration. It shows what drives the project end date at any time during the project duration, just like the Critical Path in projects not constrained by resources. The RCP is helpful in a completely leveled schedule.

Can we give the *CPM* a well-deserved retirement? The answer is no, because there are situations that are not resource-constrained, and situations in which organizations will not allow (a lack of) resources to drive out the schedule. In those situations, the RCP is not needed and CPM will do.

---

[61] *Take the Path That Is Really Critical*, Eric Uyttewaal, PM Network, PMI, December 1999.

In general, any project that uses *expert resources* tends to be a *resource-constrained* or *resource-limited* project. *Experts* are by definition scarce; otherwise, you would not call them "expert". Examples of projects in which resources are typically scarce are pharmaceutical, information technology, defense, R&D and biotechnology. If you are the project manager of such a project, you should find and monitor the Resource-Critical Path in your schedule instead of the Critical Path.

The Resource-Critical Path (RCP)

Let us first define this new concept of RCP. An *RCP* is the longest path through the logical dependencies and resource dependencies in a workload-leveled schedule. Notice the definition is not very different from the Critical Path definition (see page 418) except that resource dependencies are also taken into account. In the example we just discussed, the task *write x* has slack, but still drives the project end date and is, therefore, as critical as *write y*. Both are *resource-critical tasks*, however, because the same resource works on them. When two tasks compete for the same resource, those tasks have a *resource dependency*.

The RCP, in other words, is the chain of tasks that drives the project end date while taking into account that resources have limited availability. When you have few resources relative to the work to be done, you should focus on the RCP instead of the Critical Path. Any project manager who has experts on the team may need to find the RCP instead of the Critical Path. An easy way to find out if you are in a resource-constrained situation is by leveling the workloads completely; if your project end date slipped when the overallocations are gone, you are in a *resource-constrained* project. On page 414 we discussed a detailed procedure on determining this.

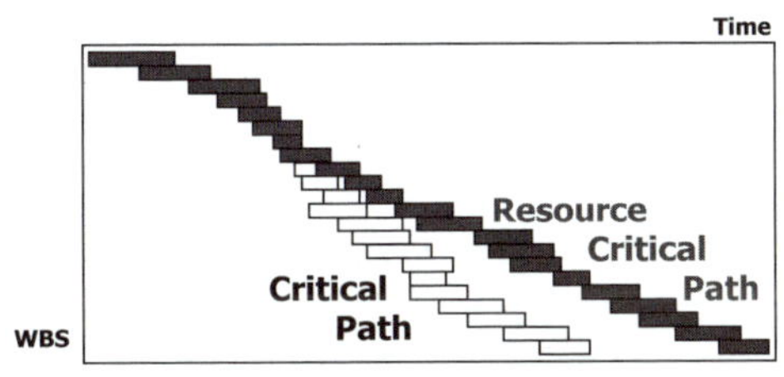

You can see in the illustration that the RCP often is the same as the Critical Path early in the schedule. Later in the schedule you will find that tasks are delayed because of leveled workloads of the limited resources. All those tasks drive the project end date. *Resource-critical tasks* are tasks that, when delayed or extended, make the project end date slip. I would like to introduce an acronym here to help you remember this fundamental message for resource-constrained projects: **ERIC** (**E**ach **R**esource **I**mplies

Criticality). In a leveled schedule, any resource can be so limited in availability, or needed so much, that it could drive the project finish date. I propose calling this the ERIC-principle. [62]

Identify the Resource-Critical Path

At this point the resource workloads should be entirely leveled. The next steps in the process (see step 2 and 3 in the process chart) are to identify the RCP and the most critical resources. In order to optimize the schedule, it is imperative that you find and highlight the RCP. If you do not know whether a task is resource-critical or not, you do not know if optimizing the task will shorten your project. We will discuss two methods to find the RCP: a manual process and an automatic process. There is no feature in Project 2010 that highlights the RCP for you, like with the Critical Path. We have developed an add-in to MS Project, called *Complete Critical Paths* that will automatically find your RCP. [63] If you manage *resource-constrained* projects, it will make your life much simpler.

1. Check the workloads and level them
2. **Identify the Resource-Critical Path (RCP)**
3. **Find the most critical resources**
4. Record the current project duration and cost
5. Optimize the RCP
6. Consider impacts on quality, scope, time, cost and resources
7. Decide whether to keep the change
8. Repeat steps 1 – 8

There are two ways in which you can find the RCP:

- **Manual process**
  We recommend this process for learning to understand the concept of RCP. If you can identify the RCP in a schedule by hand, you truly understand it. When you first learned the Critical Path concept, you were also challenged to find it first by hand in several schedules before you started to rely on automated tools. Therefore, we recommend you try this manual process first to enhance your understanding of the RCP concept.
- **Automatic process**
  After you understand the concept of RCP, you can use our add-in, which identifies the RCP in your schedule very quickly.

Please note that before identifying the RCP, the workloads in the schedule need to be completely leveled. You can have MS Project perform a complete leveling first by

---

[62] Hey, that's my first name!

[63] See www.ProjectProCorp.com and click on *Products* in the side pane.

clicking the **Resource** ribbon, [Leveling Options], selecting ◉ **Level entire project**, clearing ☐ **Level only within available slack** and clicking [Level All].

Pro

We do not recommend automatically leveling a single enterprise schedule in Project Server with all workloads from other schedules aggregated in it. Instead we recommend prioritizing all schedules of a business unit and entering these priority numbers in the **Project Information** dialog (ribbon **Project**, button **Project Information**). You can then level them as a group using the project priority numbers (ribbon **Resource**, [Leveling Options], under **Leveling order** use **Priority, Standard**) in such a way that the high priority projects get the resources first. [64] After this, the RCP can be identified in each enterprise schedule.

Manual Process

First, make sure the workloads are completely leveled (see page 489 for steps). It is easiest to identify *resource-critical tasks* by starting at the project finish milestone and working backward through a schedule. You look for driving predecessors or driving resources shared between the tasks. Tasks that are resource-critical have either a logical dependency or a resource dependency with earlier tasks. A logical dependency, as you know, is shown as an arrow between the task bars in the Gantt timescale and is easy to find. A resource dependency occurs when two tasks are competing for the same resource. In the Gantt Chart view, you can see in the timescale to the right of the task bars which resources are assigned. There is a resource dependency when another task with the same resource ends just before the start date of the task you are analyzing.

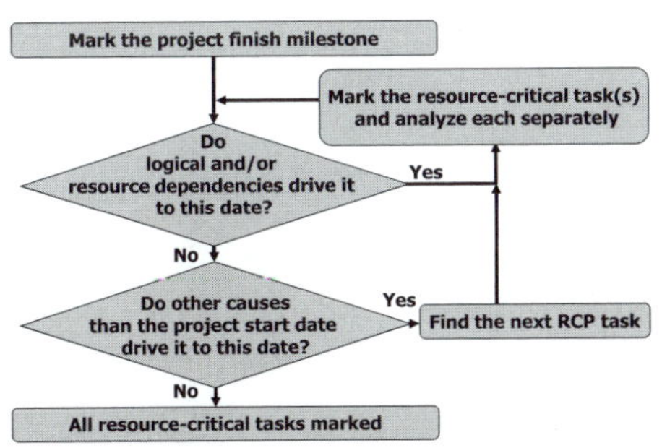

The flowchart in the illustration gives an overview of the process. You will work backward starting with the project finish milestone. This milestone is by definition resource-critical, so mark it right away. Then ask yourself for this milestone: *Do logical and/or resource dependencies drive it to this date?* Check all the predecessors of the project milestone and determine which ones are driving it to the date on which it

[64] We discuss this in detail in our *Managing Portfolios* course, see www.ProjectProCorp.com and click on *Courses 2010* in the side bar.

9

starts. You will find at least one predecessor that has a finish date that is just before the start date of the final milestone. (Milestones always have driving logical dependencies but never driving resource dependencies, because there is no work on milestones.) Once you have found the driving predecessor, you mark it as a resource-critical task and continue with that task as the next task to analyze.

Ask the same question again for this next task to find all tasks that drive it to its start date through logical dependencies. Check all of its predecessors to find the predecessor that finishes just before the resource-critical task starts; this is most likely the driving predecessor. You may have to check for *lags* on dependencies to determine if the link is driving. If you find a driving predecessor, mark it. Continue to check all predecessors because there can be more than one parallel path (just like with parallel critical paths). Mark all predecessor tasks that explain the start date of the task in question. You need to continue the analysis separately for each task you marked.

Also check if resource dependencies explain the start date of the task observed. This is often the case for detail tasks in a *resource-constrained*, fully leveled schedule. Look at the resources that are assigned to the task, and look for other tasks using the same resource that finish just before it. Once you have found the resource dependency and the driving task, mark the task as resource-critical. Look for other resource dependencies in case there are multiple parallel paths. If there are more, mark them as well. You need to continue the analysis separately for each task you marked.

You continue until you have arrived at the project start date, at which point all resource-critical tasks are marked.

Once you understand this manual process, you can use it to find the RCP in a 100-task schedule within minutes. If you need to do this often and in larger schedules, we recommend you use the automatic process instead.

We recommend the following Gantt Chart view for finding the RCP:

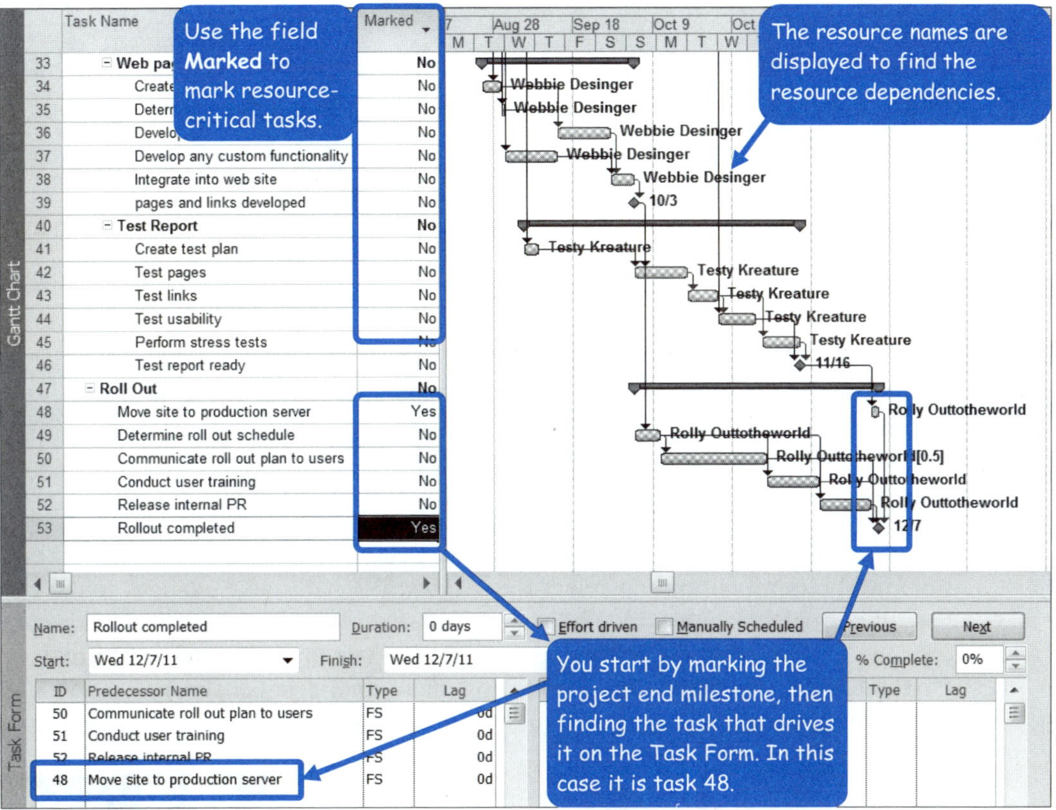

As you can see in the screenshot, the **Gantt Chart** is in the top pane and the **Task Form** in the bottom. Make sure you insert the task field **Marked** to tag the tasks that you find to be resource-critical.

The steps to identifying the RCP in your schedule are:

1. Perform a complete leveling in your schedule, see page 489 for the steps.

2. Click ribbon **View** and click the bottom part of Gantt Chart ▾ and select **Gantt Chart**.

   This view displays the resource names next to the task bars, which is useful for finding resource dependencies.

3. Click ribbon **View,** Details to display the **Task Form** with the dependencies and their lag.
4. Click ribbon **Format** and then select Critical Tasks to color critical tasks red. Notice that the Critical Path has gaps and is incomplete; it does not explain the entire project duration. The RCP will do this.
5. Insert the field **Marked** and enter **Yes** for those tasks that you identify as resource-critical tasks. Mark all resource-critical tasks using the process explained.
6. We will now make changes to the bar styles of the view, but we probably want to preserve the original Gantt Chart view as well. Therefore, we will copy the view first. While still in the Gantt Chart view, click ribbon **Views,** Other Views and select **Save View**. The **Save View** dialog appears, select ⦿ **Save as New View** (this option appears only in Project 2010 standalone – not when connected to Project Server) and **Name** it *Resource-Critical Path Chart* and click OK. You are now back in the main screen with the new view displayed.
7. We will make the RCP look the same as our good old Critical Path. Click ribbon **Format**, button **Format** and select **Bar Styles.** We will make changes to the bars so that all normal tasks have blue bars and all marked tasks have red bars. These changes are circled in the following screenshot (we moved the items **Critical** and **Critical Split** higher up in the list to show them in one screenshot):

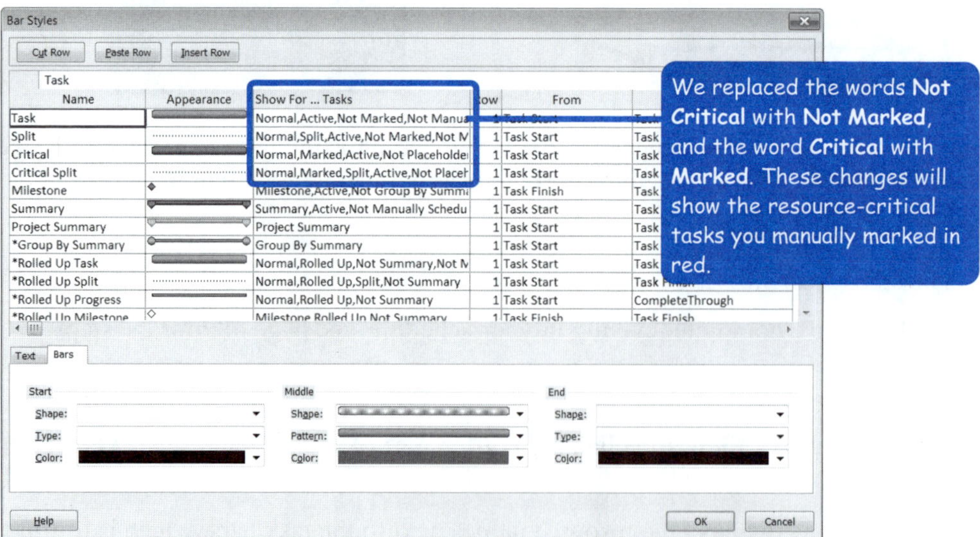

8. Click OK – you can now color task bars red if you change their field **Marked** to **Yes**, or you can change them back to blue by entering **No** in the **Marked** field. This is useful if you need to make corrections to your RCP.

9. In the column heading **Marked,** click the button, click item **Filters** and select **Yes** from the list that appears while clearing the others. This filters the tasks and displays the resource-critical tasks only. Notice that the button changed to as a reminder that the task list is filtered.
10. Make the dependency arrows disappear by clicking **Format, Layout...** and under **Links**, select the first option.

If you follow these steps and the process for identifying the RCP in the exercise on page 536, the schedule should at this point look like the next screenshot:

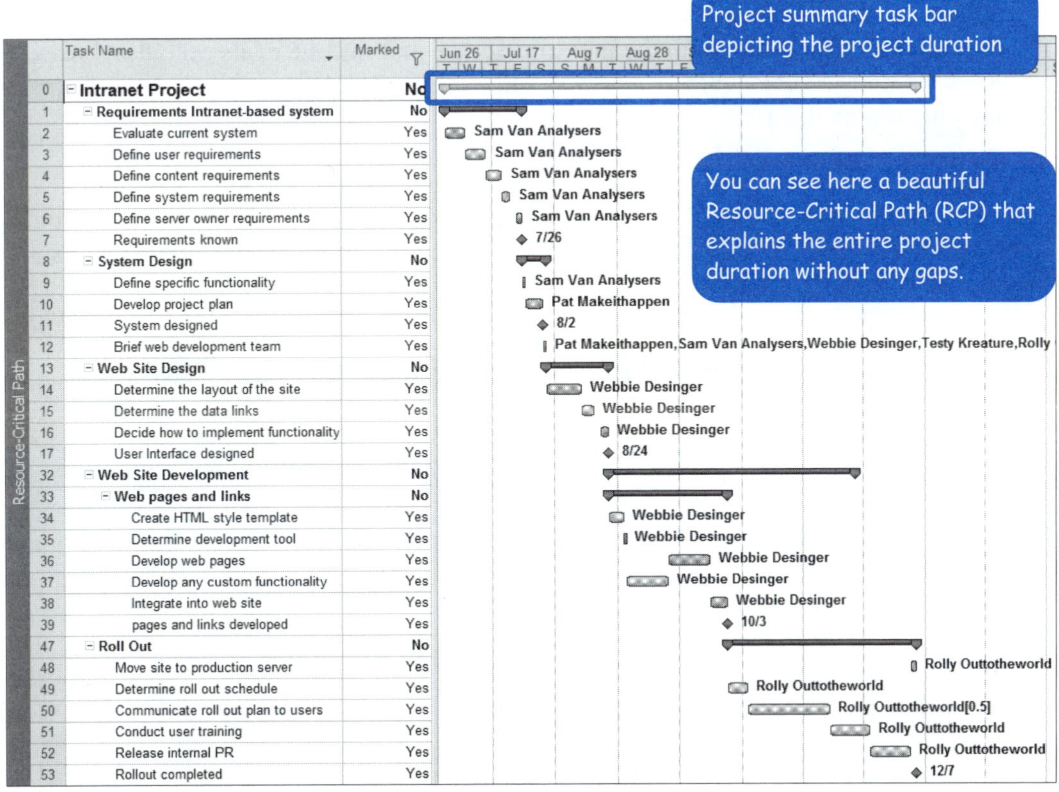

To the uninitiated, the schedule now looks as if the regular Critical Path is shown in red, except that it really is the RCP. The RCP drives the project end date, just like the Critical

Path. The RCP provides a complete explanation for the project duration in a *resource-constrained schedule*, just like the Critical Path would in a project not constrained by resources. You could present this as your "Critical Path" to people who are not familiar with the concept of the RCP. They will not argue about the correctness of it, because you can easily prove that all red tasks drive the project end date. After all, if any of the tasks on the RCP slips or extends, the project will take longer.

Automatic Process

Identifying the RCP should eventually be done in an automated fashion, because when you are making changes to the schedule during optimization, you need to find the new RCP over and over again. This is just like finding the good old Critical Path again, after you have optimized it.

ProjectPro provides an add-in to MS Project, called *Complete Critical Paths* that can automatically identify the RCP in your workload-leveled schedule. Our add-in produces the view exactly as shown in the previous screenshot (as one of its outputs). Please visit our website *www.ProjectProCorp.com* and click on **Products** in the sidebar for more information on this tool.

Optimizing for time, cost and resources is challenging enough, and being able to automatically find the RCP is a great help to project managers. It allows you to quickly find what drives the project end date in a resource-constrained schedule, and to start optimizing such a schedule.

Why Should I Care About the Resource-Critical Path?

Since understanding the RCP-approach requires some effort, we feel compelled to raise your motivation. There are five reasons why applying the RCP-approach is worthwhile in any resource-constrained schedule:

- The RCP drives the project end date.
- The RCP reveals the critical resource(s).
- The RCP allows for finding domino effects.
- The RCP allows workload smoothing.
- The RCP facilitates smarter fast-tracking.

We will discuss each of these reasons.

The RCP Drives the Project End Date

Somewhere along the Critical Path, the resources typically start to constrain the schedule more than the logic, and the RCP overtakes the Critical Path. If that happens, the RCP drives the project end date, not the Critical Path. As you can see in the illustration, the white tasks constitute the regular Critical Path, but workload leveling delayed many of them. The result of leveling is shown as black tasks. The RCP is the combination of the critical tasks early in the schedule and all the resource-dependent tasks later on. If any of these tasks slip, the project will finish later; the resource-critical tasks drive the project end date.

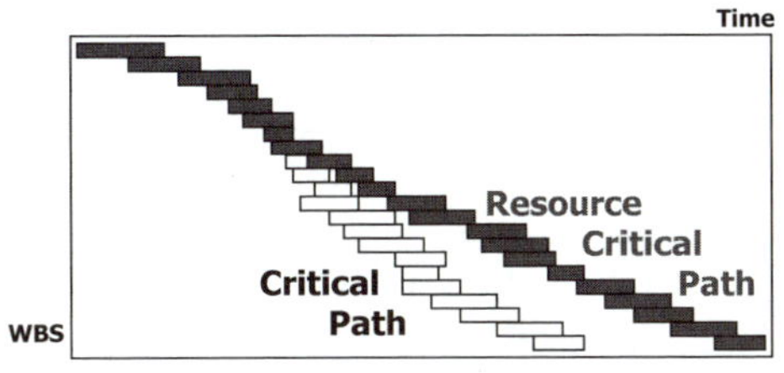

The RCP Reveals the Critical Resource(s)

The RCP identifies the *critical resources* and when they are critical. It is important for the project manager to know at any time which resource determines the speed of progress of the entire team. Project managers need to know who is critical and provide them a work environment that is free of interruptions and disruptions. If critical resources bring up an issue, the project manager should deal with it right away. Better yet, the project manager will know who is critical week by week, and could ask the team to give them uninterrupted work time. The project manager could even ask the team for full and immediate cooperation when critical resources call for help. Having been a critical resource myself at times, I can speak from experience that my productivity is much higher if colleagues help me out immediately. Project success becomes a team effort instead of individual heroism (or *burn-out*!).

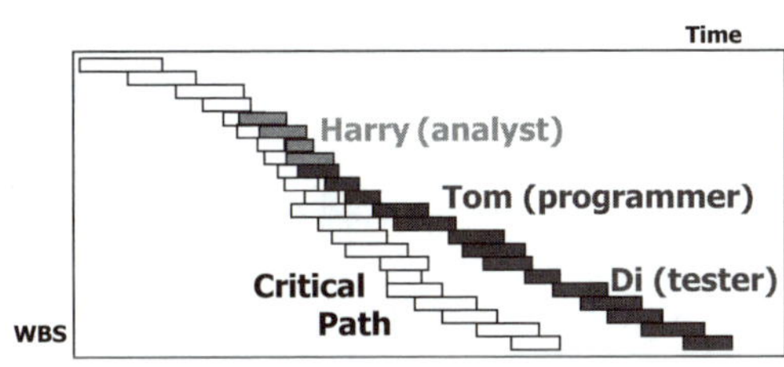

Managers are people who get things done through others. The RCP identifies those resources that should receive special attention from project managers. The RCP allows project managers to focus on people again instead of on tasks. A renewed focus on people frees project managers from the image that they force reams of tasks down team members' throats, like farmers stuff their turkeys.

The RCP Allows Finding Domino Effects

Have you ever experienced an avalanche of changes after you made one small change? If you make one change to a schedule, you may trigger a disastrous *domino effect*. The illustration shows that when *John* became sick, his task *write* slipped. Mary had planned to finish *edit* just before her holiday. By the time John finished late, *Mary* had left for her holiday, so her part slipped even more. When she returned, finished her part and handed off to *Gord*, he was temporarily reassigned to another project and would not be available for three weeks. You decide not to wait for *Gord*, and so assign a new person. The new person will need one week of introduction and training, and so forth and so on… One little slip that seems innocuous can cause big delays as it compounds through the resource dependencies – the domino effect. The RCP makes the critical resource dependencies visible. If you can see them, you can make changes to the schedule in a more educated fashion. If you monitor only the conventional Critical Path, you will not realize that you are creating an avalanche of changes. Minimizing the turbulence is often the art of project management.

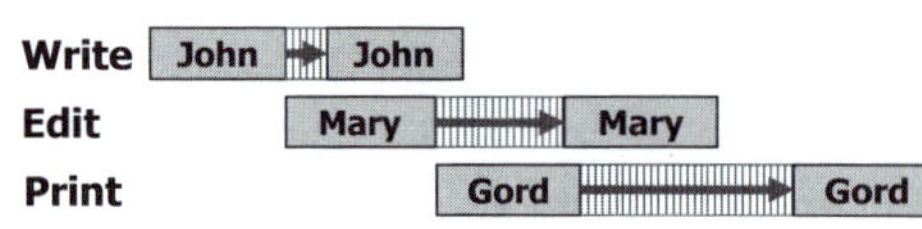

The RCP Allows Workload Smoothing

There is often a huge amount of cost involved with erratic workloads, as shown in the illustration and discussed on page 465. How much does Ed's workload cost before and after smoothing? He has periods when he can twiddle his thumbs and other periods when he is overloaded (and may be wishing he had another job). I often see companies *burn out* their most *critical resources*, especially in time-to-market organizations. If a critical resource burns out, the individual and the organization are severely hurt. Burn outs have expensive consequences for organizations in terms of dissatisfied employees, demoralized work culture, sick leave, attrition, and, not to be forgotten, the cost of finding new, highly specialized people. Burn outs also cost extra when deadlines are missed or contracts are lost.

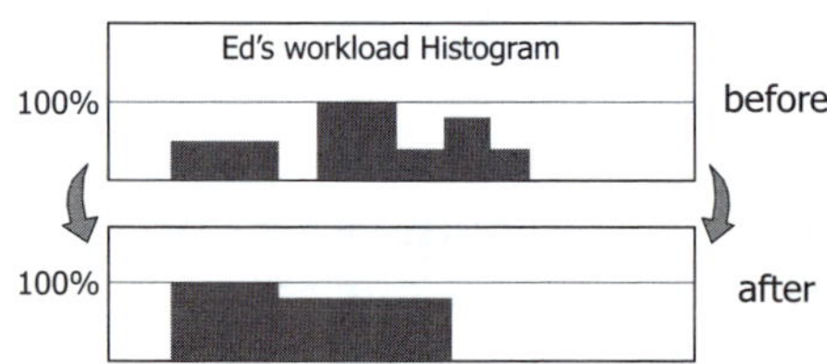

The RCP allows you to better monitor and manage the workloads of your most important resources. Keeping a continuous eye on their workloads is essential because their progress drives the RCP.

The RCP Facilitates Smarter Fast-Tracking

You may create workload problems if you focus only on the Critical Path when fast-tracking your schedule. You may work a long time to create a shorter schedule, only to find you have replaced time problems with workload problems. In the illustration on the left, the dependency was cut, and this created a new overallocation for Harry. The schedule is now infeasible. If you ignore the resource dependencies and just focus on logical dependencies, you may create short schedules, but these schedules may not be feasible.

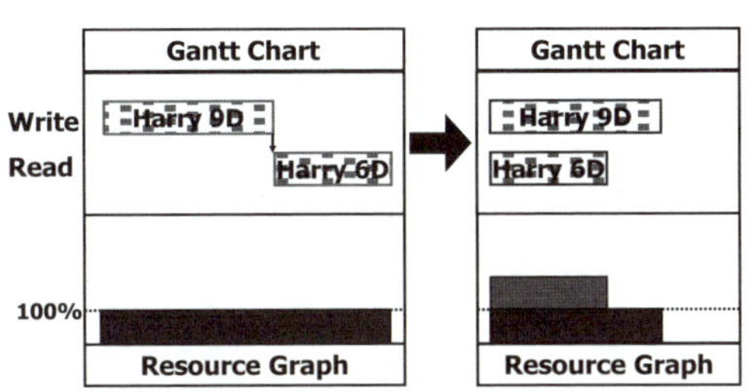

An Incomplete Resource-Critical Path: Possible Causes

Just like the Critical Path, a Resource-Critical Path (RCP) can have gaps. Some gaps may be legitimate and some gaps indicate that resource-critical tasks are missing.

The Resource Critical Path can have legitimate gaps that are caused by:

- Actual progress: Completed tasks always have zero Total Slack. MS Project will not highlight any completed tasks in red; the Critical Path does not explain the completed portion of the project duration.
- Lags on dependencies between resource-critical tasks
- Nonworking time on the calendars between resource-critical tasks

Analyzing if a gap is legitimate requires some effort or you can use our automated tool, *Complete Critical Paths* (see page 434), which will explain these situations to you.

The following factors can cause resource-critical tasks to be missing (the list is the same for the Critical Path, see page 427):

- *Incomplete network logic*
  If you have not checked the dependencies to see if you entered them all, you may see a fragmented RCP. See page 239 for how to check the dependencies.
- *Constraint dates*
- *Elapsed durations* and *elapsed lags*
- *Resource calendars*: unavailability of resources
  This may stretch task bars or appear as a gap in the RCP.
- *Task calendars*
- *External predecessors*

9

- *Workload leveling*
  Leveling delay from a complete leveling by MS Project is not an issue, but manually entered **Leveling Delay** numbers may break the RCP.

Our add-in, *Complete Critical Paths*, can handle most of these situations. Below you can see another view this add-in produces to explain any gaps in the RCP, so you will always have a complete explanation for the project duration:

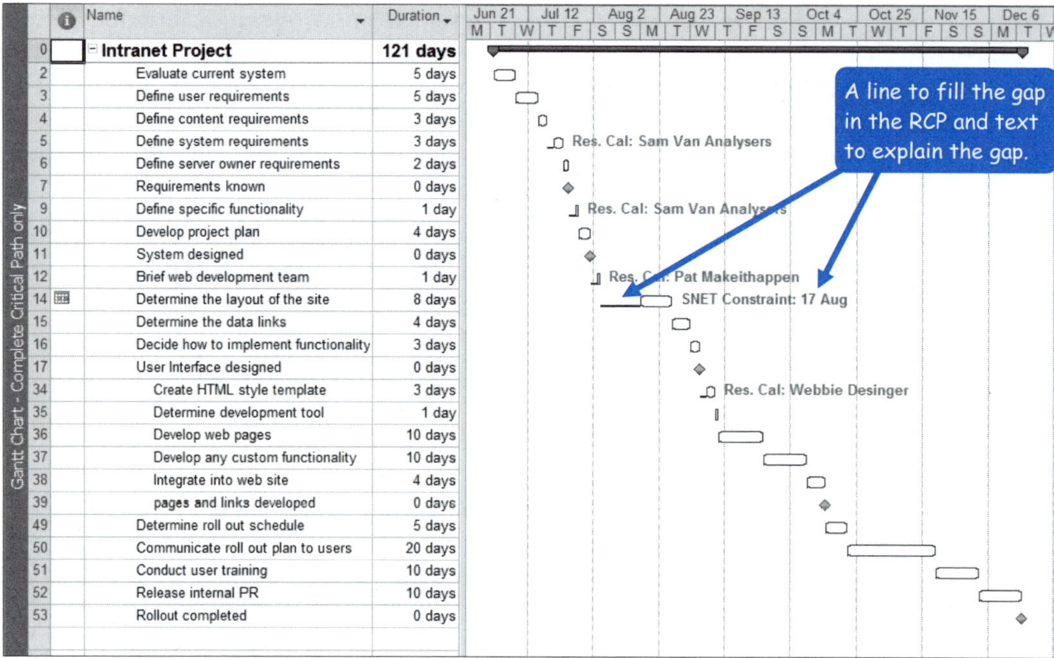

The screenshot shows that the add-in *Complete Critical Paths* has identified several gaps in the RCP and explained them. In this schedule, resource calendars (abbreviated to *Res.Cal.)* of several resources explain most gaps (weekends!) except for one caused by a Start-No-Earlier-Than (SNET) constraint on task 14.

For situations our add-in would not handle, you can select the next resource-critical task and run the add-in again to find the RCP into that task. The add-in allows you to keep marked the tasks that were already identified as resource-critical up to that point. So, you can incrementally find your complete RCP quickly enough.

Record the Current Project Duration and Cost

1. Check the workloads and level them
2. Identify the Resource-Critical Path (RCP)
3. Find the most critical resources
4. **Record the current project duration and cost**
5. Optimize the RCP
6. Consider impacts on quality, scope, time, cost and resources
7. Decide whether to keep the change
8. Repeat steps 1 – 8

Next we record the current situation, step 4 in the process chart. The *project statistics* dialog is the best way to find the current project duration and cost, see page 439 for how to display it. If you have added it to the Quick Access Toolbar (QAT), it is just one click away (see page 440).

Optimize the Resource-Critical Path (RCP)

1. Check the workloads and level them
2. Identify the Resource-Critical Path (RCP)
3. Find the most critical resources
4. Record the current project duration and cost
5. **Optimize the RCP**
6. Consider impacts on quality, scope, time, cost and resources
7. Decide whether to keep the change
8. Repeat steps 1 – 8

We are now finally at the step in the process chart where we will make changes to the resource-critical tasks. We would like to shorten the project and lower the cost while keeping the workloads reasonable. To shorten the project, the resource-critical path needs to be shortened. The best methods are those that make the *quality* (Q) go up (↑), the *scope* (S) go up (↑), the *time* (T) go down (↓), the *cost* (C) go down (↓) and the *resource workload* of *critical resources* (R) go down (↓). Unfortunately, there are no such ideal methods. The next table indicates what the effect of each method would be in a typical project (Q=Quality, S=Scope, T=Time, C=Cost, R=Resource workload):

	Method	**For**	Q	S	T	C	R
1.	Change sequential dependencies into partial dependencies (fast-tracking)	resource-critical tasks	0	0	↓	0	?
2.	Create parallel paths from a sequential path (fast-tracking)	resource-critical tasks	?	0	↓	0	?
3.	Split tasks with long durations	resource-critical tasks	0	0	↓	?	?

9

	Method	For	Q	S	T	C	R
4.	Change constraint dates	resource-critical tasks	0	0	↓	0	?
5.	Shorten *lags* (waiting periods)	resource-critical tasks	0	0	↓	0	?
6.	Split task bars around a short Must Start On task	resource-critical tasks	0	0	↓	0	?
7.	Decrease estimates	resource-critical tasks	↓	?	↓	↓	↓
8.	Reduce the scope or delete tasks	resource-critical tasks	↓	↓	↓	↓	↓
9.	Reallocate the best resources to the most critical tasks	resource-critical tasks	0	0	↓	?	↓
10.	Remove a critical resource when multiple resources are assigned	resource-critical tasks	?	0	↓	↓	↓
11.	Increase assignment units to full-time assignments for critical resources	resource-critical, auto scheduled, fixed work tasks	0	0	↓	0	?
12.	Assign overtime hours to critical resources	resource-critical, auto scheduled, fixed work tasks	↓	0	↓	?	↑
13.	Add noncritical resources	resource-critical, auto scheduled, fixed work tasks	0	0	?	↑	?
14.	Replace critical resources with noncritical resources	resource-critical, fixed work tasks	?	?	↓	?	↓
15.	Postpone vacation of critical resources to after the deadline	resource-critical tasks, fixed work or fixed units tasks	0	0	↓	?	?

Even though we indicate what the impact might be in a typical project, you have to ask yourself what the possible impacts might be in your own project, particularly where we entered a question mark (?). We now have limited human resources, and we should assess each method for its impact on the resource workload in the project. Where a question mark (?) appears in the resources column (R), you need to check on new overallocations after applying the method. Where a zero (0) is shown, no impact is expected. We ranked the actions in order of overall effectiveness to reduce the duration of the project. We recommend starting at the top of the table with the two fast-tracking methods. After exhausting the fast-tracking, go to the next method in the table. We recommend you make changes on multiple tasks before going to the next method in the table. For example, you can apply method 9 and lower on each of the critical resources. Then you level all workloads again and identify the RCP again. We have found this to be the fastest way to realize gains.

Some remarks about optimizing an RCP:

- The *Optimizing for Time* actions discussed on page 442 are repeated in this table as actions 1-8, because they are also valid in situations with limited resources. The only difference is that these actions will now work only on resource-critical tasks instead of critical tasks.

- *Fast-tracking* is changing the dependencies in such a way that more tasks take place concurrently. Fast-tracking on the RCP is not as effective as it was on the Critical Path. However, it is still the preferred action to start with, because it is *quality*, *scope* and *cost* neutral. Fast-tracking is less effective on the RCP, because:
  - There are fewer logical dependencies between resource-critical tasks, because the RCP often has resource dependencies instead.
  - You cannot fast-track two tasks if the same resource is working on both linked tasks. In this case there is a logical dependency and a resource dependency! When you overlap these tasks, you create a new overallocation. Fast-tracking has to be applied with greater care. The RCP will show you which tasks have the same resources assigned that will cause new overallocations when you overlap them. You should focus your fast-tracking efforts on tasks that are linked but done by different resources. For example, when you remodel an office, the tasks of carpenters and electricians can overlap each other, as long as the carpenters start a few days ahead and finish a few days earlier. Fast-tracking on the RCP is typically effective at hand-off points between critical resources.

- Actions 11 through 15 can shorten the durations of resource-critical tasks. These actions will work for all task types except **Fixed Duration** tasks. Before using one of these methods, you have to change its task type to *Fixed Work*, assuming that you want the total effort and, hence, the quality to stay the same.

- Overhead tasks or support tasks have effort involved but should never be on the RCP. Overhead tasks support the real work on the deliverables and should not drive the project end date. If you see the project manager, team leaders, technical support or administrative support people on resource-critical tasks, you may have found an easy way to shorten your project. In most cases these people can and should be removed from the RCP. After all, they are managing or supporting the real critical resources (or at least that is what they are supposed to do!).

We discussed the first eight methods on page 442 and following pages; we will discuss the remainder of them next.

9

Reallocate the Best Resources to the Most Critical Tasks

This is the best and most basic principle to apply when trying to find the shortest schedule possible while maintaining quality and cost. The Resource-Critical Path reveals which tasks are driving your project duration. You should ask yourself: *Have I assigned my best resources to these most critical tasks?* Check whether the resources who are working on your resource-critical tasks are the best and fastest at creating quality deliverables. If not, you have an opportunity to shorten your project duration by moving your best resources to these tasks. In the illustration, the project manager has reassigned his best resources, *Jack*, *Paula* and *Rino*, to the resource-critical tasks. The project is now as short as it can be.

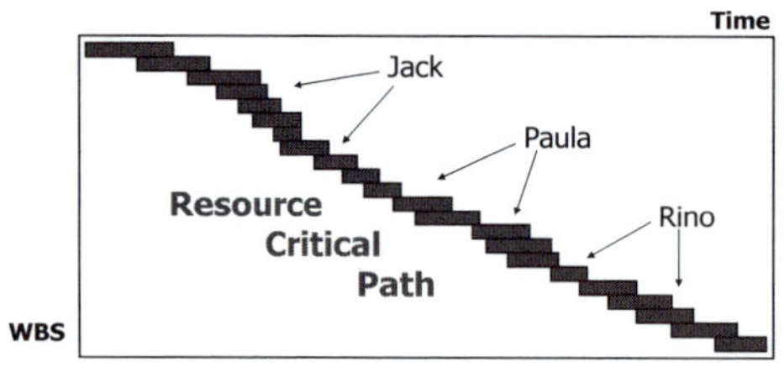

Remove a Critical Resource When Multiple Resources Are Assigned

If there are multiple people working on a task, and one of them is a critical resource who has a lot of other work at the same time, you should ask yourself how important the involvement of the critical resource is on this task. If the other people could do without the critical resource, you should consider removing the critical resource from the task. Again, a *critical* resource does not mean that the resource is important for the successful completion of the task. In the illustration, *Harry* is removed from the task, which shortens the RCP. Make sure you think about the task **Type** before removing a resource; you are changing the units, so use **Fixed Duration** if you can or **Fixed Work** which will make the **Duration** increase and may reduce the gain. If you do a complete leveling (**Tools, Level resources…**) you will see that the schedule is shorter.

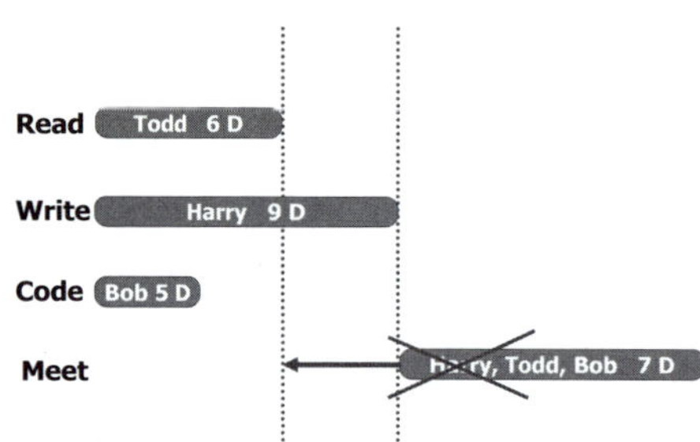

Increase Assignment Units

When you notice that a resource is working half-time on a critical task, you can finish the task earlier if you can get the resource to temporarily work full-time on it. Again, the right task type has to be applied if you want the duration to decrease. The task type has to be **Fixed Work**. For example, if the work takes 10 person days and Harry could work on it full-time instead of half-time, he would finish the task twice as fast, as depicted in the illustration. If you are concerned that getting Harry full-time will be difficult if you need to ask another project manager, remember that when Harry is done on your task, he will be available on a full-time rather than a half-time basis to that other project manager and his project will still end at the same time.

1. In the Gantt Chart, select a resource-critical task with a part-time assignment.
2. Click ribbon **View,** [Details] – the **Task Form** appears at the bottom of the screen:

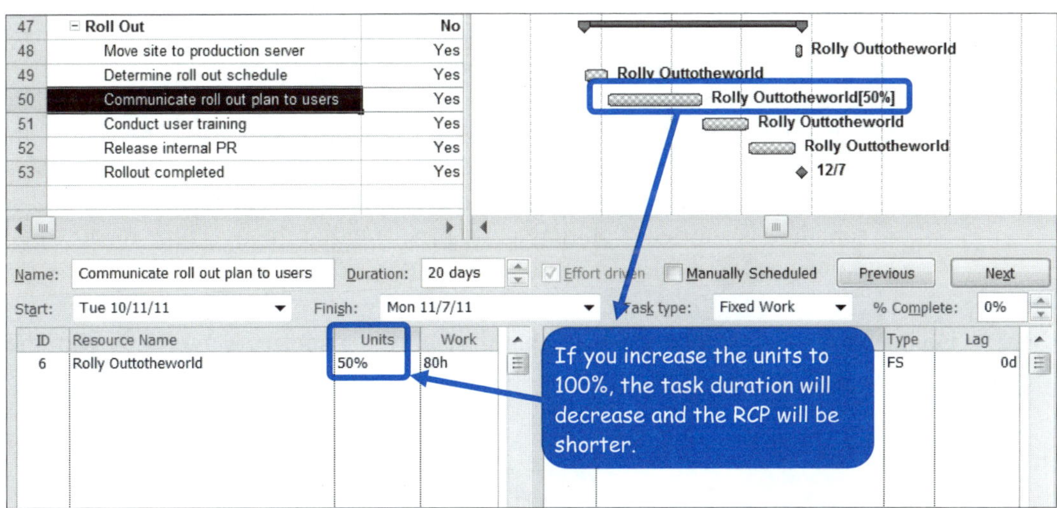

3. If more than one resource is assigned to the task, check if the part-time assignment is driving the task duration. If not, it will not result in a gain and you can stop here.
4. On the **Task Form** from the list **Task type** select the type **Fixed Work** and click [OK]. This assures that MS Project will shorten the duration when you increase the resource units.

5. Increase the resource **Units** on the task so that the resource works full-time on the resource-critical task. Click OK – the task duration should be less.
6. If you do a complete leveling (ribbon **Resource**, button **Level All**) you will see that the schedule is shorter.

Assign Overtime Hours

If you can get resources to put in overtime, critical tasks can often be finished earlier. In the illustration, the second bar shows a shorter duration. Asking your team members to work overtime is often unpopular, and you are trading off against the resource dimension of the project and may lose some goodwill with your team.

Two situations can arise:

- If overtime will not be charged to the project, then change the resource calendar of that particular resource. You can increase the working hours or change holidays or weekend days to working days. You can compensate by giving the resource time off later. We discussed changing the resource calendar on page 314.
- If overtime will be charged to the project at a higher overtime rate, you enter overtime in the overtime field (**Ovt. Work**) in the Task Form. The cost of the project will increase. We discussed the detail steps for this on page 326. Then you need to do a complete leveling (ribbon **Resource, Level All**), and you will see that the schedule is shorter. You may get a message that the overtime resource is assigned with more units than available; click Skip All.

Do not lower the original work estimate; MS Project subtracts overtime from the original work estimate before calculating the new duration.

Add Noncritical Resources

Two resources can normally finish a task faster than one resource. When you add a resource, the duration will decrease, but it will only decrease if you have the right task type applied to the task before adding. When you add a resource to a fixed work task, the same amount of work is now performed by two resources and can be done twice as fast. MS Project will calculate this for you on auto scheduled tasks.

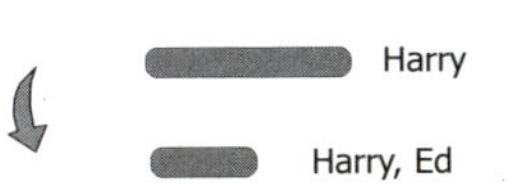

Let us think about what happens in practice. First of all, you need to find the right resources. When you do find new resources, you have to train them. You would typically remove your best resources from their crunching to train the new ones. At first you will see a short-term decrease in the rate of progress hoping that, in the longer term, the progress accelerates. For this reason we have marked this method with a "?"for the *Time* dimension in the table. Look carefully at your situation to see if adding resources would indeed help.

1. Select a resource-critical task. Check in the **Task Mode** field if it is **Auto Scheduled**.
2. Click ribbon **View,** [✓ Details] – the **Task Form** appears at the bottom of the screen:
3. Determine which resource drives the duration of the task and needs help.
4. From the list **Task type** select the type **Fixed Work**; this ensures that MS Project will shorten the duration when a resource is added. Click [OK].
5. Assign another resource and click [OK] – the task **Duration** should decrease.
6. If you do a complete leveling (ribbon **Resource**, button **Level All**) you will see that the schedule is shorter.

9

Replace Critical Resources with Noncritical Resources

If you replace a *critical resource* with a noncritical resource, it may be possible to schedule more tasks in parallel. In the illustration, *Ted* replaces *Harry* on the second task, which can now be done in parallel with the first one. The gain in time equals the duration of the second task.

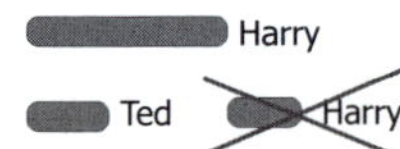

Some people argue that you cannot substitute critical resources; otherwise they would not be critical (as in "important"). Remember that the word *critical* has a different meaning for project managers. *Critical* does not mean that the resource is important to the task. It merely means that the resource is driving the project duration. In fact, the resource could be a second-choice resource, but it is not a good idea to have your project duration be driven by second-choice resources if you are working against time. Your project will take long enough with first-choice resources. That is why we started by having you check if you applied your best resources to your most critical tasks.

You can use the **Assign Resources** on the **Resource** ribbon and use its 

button.
OR

1. In the Gantt Chart, select a resource-critical task on which you can replace a critical resource.
2. Click ribbon **View,** Details – the **Task Form** appears at the bottom of the screen.
3. In the Task Form click on the name of the critical resource – its list button appears. Select the substitute resource from the list.
4. Click OK – the duration should still be the same (unless the resource calendars were different).
5. If you do a complete leveling (ribbon **Resource, Level All**) you will see that the schedule is shorter.

Postpone Vacations to After the Deadline

If you can convince your resource to postpone a vacation until after a critical deadline, you may be able to meet the deadline. In the illustration, the deadline appears as a diamond. The vacation happens to be scheduled just before the deadline. If it can be moved, the deadline can be met. It is not uncommon for vacations to happen just before deadlines, since projects tend to shift back and forth, whereas vacations do not. Also, some resources seem to have a talent for planning their vacations just before deadlines.

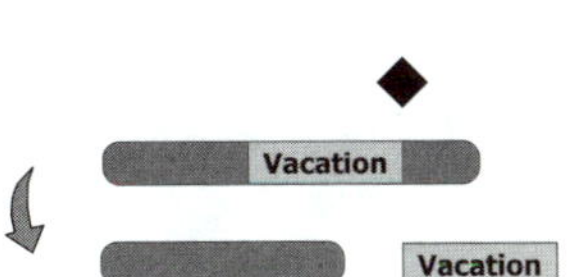

On page 314 we mentioned that **Fixed Duration** tasks ignore resource calendars; so if you apply this method to a Fixed Duration task you will see no time gain. Instead you will see the **Work** go up and the cost as well, but the schedule may also be more realistic and feasible.

To postpone vacations:

1. Check the task **Type**; you can expect gains on **Fixed Work** and **Fixed Units** tasks, but not on Fixed Duration tasks.

2. Click ribbon **Project,** 

– the **Change Working Time** dialog appears:

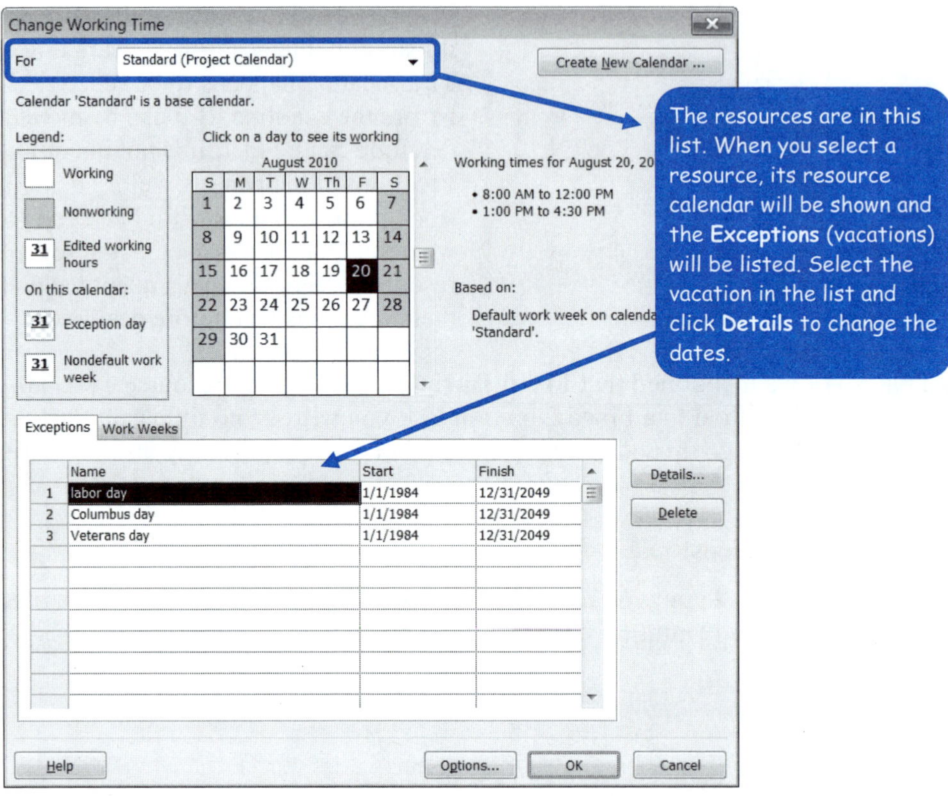

3. From the list **For**: Standard (Project Calendar) select the resource.
4. On the tab **Exceptions** all vacation days are now listed for the resource. Select the vacation to postpone by clicking on it and click Details... and change the dates of the vacation under **Start** and **End by**. Click OK and you are back in the **Change Working Time** dialog.
5. Click OK. You will see right away that the schedule is shorter. We recommend you identify the Resource-Critical Path again after moving a vacation; it may be different.

Consider the Impacts and Decide

After optimizing the RCP, you have to consider the impacts on *quality*, *scope*, *time*, *cost* and *resource workload* of the critical resources (see step 6 in the process box on the left). Whenever you make a change to a resource-critical task, the workloads may move or change. In order to make sure all workloads are still leveled, we recommend a complete leveling at this point: click ribbon **Resource, Level All**. The impact on time and cost can be concluded from the project statistics dialog; see page 439 for the steps to display it. You can now see how much time and/or cost you have gained, and whether it is worth any sacrifices you may have made on the scope of the project or the quality of the deliverables.

1. Check the workloads and level them
2. Identify the Resource-Critical Path (RCP)
3. Find the most critical resources
4. Record the current project duration and cost
5. Optimize the RCP
6. **Consider impacts on quality, scope, time, cost and resources**
7. **Decide whether to keep the change**
8. Repeat steps 1 – 8

You can identify the new RCP by running our *Complete Critical Paths* add-in again (see page 506) or by finding it manually (see page 500). In the latter case, we recommend that you first unmark all resource-critical tasks. To unmark all, click on the column heading **Marked** and press [Control] + [Delete] OR click ribbon **Task**, section **Editing**, [Clear ▾] and select item **Clear All**. Then enter **Yes** for each task that you find to be resource-critical in the optimized schedule.

9

Simulation of the Resource-Critical Path

We discussed *Monte Carlo simulation* of the *Critical Path* on page 452. You can also simulate Resource-Critical Paths in *resource-constrained* schedules. The only thing you need to do in this case is change the leveling to continuous automatic leveling so that the simulation software does not forget to keep the workloads reasonable in each scenario it creates. Click ribbon **Resource**, [Leveling Options], select ◉ **Automatic**, clear ☐ **Level only within available slack** and keep ☑ **Level manually scheduled tasks** selected. This ensures that for each scenario of the schedule the workloads are entirely leveled before the project duration is calculated. As you can imagine, simulating RCPs requires major computing power, so make sure you run this on the fastest computer in your office, or enjoy a nice, long coffee break…

The reasons to consider simulating RCPs are similar to those for simulating the Critical Path. The RCP is crippled by the following assumptions:

- Durations are more likely to extend than shrink. Estimates do not follow a normal distribution, but have a distribution that is typically skewed to the pessimistic side (see page 454 for more explanation)
- The more parallel paths you have, the more delays will compound at the merge points (*path convergence* or *merge bias*) of the logical dependencies and, additionally, the resource dependencies (see page 455 for more explanation of path convergence).

If you simulate the *RCP*, you have taken care of all three assumptions that cripple the utility of the traditional *Critical Path*: the previous two assumptions plus the idea that the Critical Path assumes access to unlimited resources.

Apart from these assumptions, there are extra factors that are quantified when you simulate resource-constrained schedules:

- Simulation of the RCP will quantify the *domino effects* we discussed on page 508:
  - ◇ The effect on the project duration of personal vacations that happen on fixed dates. It is hard to predict how much the project end date will change when some tasks are moved a little bit around hard vacation dates. The simulation software will run many scenarios, calculate and average the impact of the hard-date vacations.
  - ◇ The effect on the project duration of asynchronous working hours of resources: *What overall delay will you experience from some resources working a regular workweek and some a compressed workweek?* This effect is also hard to predict, other than through simulation.
- Simulation of the RCP will quantify the overall effect of probabilities with regard to resource availability. You can identify those activities where exact resource availability is not entirely certain. You consider this uncertainty when you decide what range estimate and what distribution curve you need on those tasks. When you simulate that, you will get a better idea of how uncertain resource availability affects your forecasts.

The s-curve output from the Monte Carlo simulation (see page 453 for an example) will indicate the probability by date for a range of project finish dates. Our experience is that most people tend to underestimate the overall effect of all the factors discussed. We prove this over and over again in classes where we ask participants to estimate the outcome of a simulation on a tiny project while showing them the exact inputs of the simulation. Our students always underestimate the compounded effect. We, therefore, recommend you quantify the impact of the factors that can throw off your schedule from its baseline by simulating your schedules. After all, it is prudent for you to minimize surprises from so-called *known unknowns*. You will still have to deal with enough *unknown unknowns*.

Checks on the Optimized Schedule

Here are checks to verify if you have applied best practices when optimizing your schedule. The numbering corresponds to the complete checklist in the summary chapter, see page 711. The filters mentioned in the checks can be found in the file *ProjectPro tools to check project schedules.MPP* available for download at www.ProjectProCorp.com (see page vi for the procedure to access these files).

9 Optimizing

Optimizing Resource Workloads

9.1. Is the total effort within the person hour budget of the project (if a person hour or person day budget is available)?
You can find the total effort of the project in the **Project Statistics** (see page 439 for steps to display it) in column **Work,** row **Current**.

9.2. Are the workloads for the resources reasonable?
First, select the time unit by which you want to check for overallocations in the **Look for overallocations on a <time unit> basis** field (ribbon **Resource,** Leveling Options dialog). Adjust the timescale in the view accordingly using the **View** ribbon, section **Zoom**, list **Timescale**. Check for overallocations in the **Resource Allocation** view (for more detail, see page 473):

- ◇ The workload limits for individuals may differ from organization to organization. For schedule certification purposes, we often use the following limits: the workload for individuals should not exceed 150% of their regular availability on a day-by-day basis. On a week-by-week basis, the workload for individuals should not exceed 120%. We think that exceeding these maximums will cause a dramatic loss of productivity, and perhaps even burnout and attrition. The maximums may differ for your organization, in which case you should use yours.
- ◇ The workload of *team resources* (consolidated resources) should not exceed their availability.
- ◇ The workload for facilities and machines should be within their availability.
- ◇ The workloads should be fairly smooth for resources dedicated to your project, since there are hidden costs involved with erratic workloads

9

(see page 465). If resources are used elsewhere when not busy in your project, you do not need to be concerned about erratic workloads.

Optimizing Costs

9.3. Is the total cost within the budget of the project (if a cost budget is available)?
You can find the total cost of the project in the **Project Statistics** dialog (see page 439 for steps to display it) in column **Cost,** row **Current**.

Optimizing Time

9.4. Are there as many parallel paths as logically possible in the network of dependencies?
Novice schedulers tend to schedule all tasks in one long sequential chain. In that situation there are many *soft dependencies* that make the duration of the project unnecessarily long. If two things can logically happen at the same time, it is important to schedule them in parallel when optimizing for time. Focusing on creating true cause-and-effect dependencies instead of simply sequencing tasks will help with this. As we discussed on page 208, dependencies should reflect *practical necessities* or *mandatory processes*.

9.5. Are all conflicts between the task calendars and resource calendars resolved?
If there are conflicts, the forecasts may be too optimistic. You can find the conflicts by looking in the indicators column for the icon (see page 273). You can find the tasks with a task calendar by applying the out-of-the-box filter **Tasks with a Task calendar assigned**.

9.6. Are the tasks with a task calendar and resource calendar scheduled appropriately?
If the task and resource calendars have very few hours in common, the task will only be scheduled during those few common hours, and the task bar may become very long. You may want to look for a long bar on any task with a **Task Calendar** by applying the out-of-the-box filter **Tasks with a Task calendar assigned**.

9.7. Are all deadlines and constraint dates met in the schedule?
You can check this by applying filter
9.7 Deadlines or Constraints not met. It displays tasks with deadlines or constraints that have negative slack. If you have any of these, then you are planning to miss deadline or constraint dates. In addition you have a project end date that is too optimistic.

9.8. Does the schedule have a complete Critical Path or Resource-Critical Path?
A solid (Resource) Critical Path explains the entire project duration, has

only legitimate gaps in it and should only show tasks as critical if they are on thc longest path in the network (see page 425 and 499 for details). If a schedule is extended when the workloads are completely leveled, a Resource-Critical Path needs to be identified instead of a Critical Path (see page 414). Then you check the *Critical Path*: You can display the Critical Path in a Gantt Chart view by selecting [✓ Critical Tasks] on the **Format** ribbon. You can check the completeness by checking whether the Critical Path has gaps. If the Critical Path has gaps, you need to determine if critical tasks are missing or if the gaps are legitimate. (See page 427 for legitimate gaps in a Critical Path and how to find missing critical tasks.) You can manually raise the threshold for criticality (see page 429) to complete the Critical Path, or you can use our add-in, *Complete Critical Paths* (see page 506) to present a complete critical path to you and explain any legitimate gaps.

9.9. *Resource-Critical Path*: Resource-constrained schedules need to have their Resource-Critical Path marked and highlighted. Resource-critical tasks can be found manually (see page 501) or by our add-in *Complete Critical Paths* (see page 506). You can check the completeness by displaying the Resource-Critical Path and then checking whether it has gaps. If you find any gaps, you need to determine if resource-critical tasks are missing or if the gap is legitimate, see page 509. Our add-in, *Complete Critical Paths* (see page 506), will present a complete Resource-Critical Path to you and explain any legitimate gaps. The only gaps allowed in a complete Resource-Critical Path are:
– positive lags (waiting times) on critical dependencies
– vacations of critical resources during their resource-critical tasks
Our add-in, *Complete Critical Paths,* will explain any legitimate gaps to you and indicate the reason for the gap. See page 509 for causes of an incomplete Resource-Critical Path.

9.10. Does the (Resource) Critical Path make sense?
There are tasks that we do not expect to appear on the (Resource) Critical Path:

- ◇ *Summary tasks*
  The (Resource) Critical Path can only consist of detail tasks and milestones. Summary tasks cannot be on the (Resource) Critical Path if you followed our recommendation to keep the dependencies and the resources on detail tasks only (see page 236).
- ◇ *Overhead tasks*
  Tasks like *technical support* and *project management* are tasks with start and finish dates determined by other activities, which is why they

9

are also called *hammock tasks*. Overhead tasks cannot be critical, and if they are, their duration needs to be shortened.

◇ *Recurring tasks*
Regularly scheduled tasks like *status meetings* should not be on the Critical Path. Any recurring detail tasks, similar to *status meetings*, that appear on the Critical Path should be removed from the schedule.

◇ Tasks that normally have large time buffers
For example, *write test plan* in a software development project normally has a big buffer.

Exercises

Review

1. We distinguished three optimization approaches in this chapter: optimizing for time, optimizing for time and cost, and optimizing for time, cost and resources.
   a. What are the main differences between these approaches?
   b. Describe the situations in which you should apply each.
   c. What are common techniques used in each approach?

2. Choose one of the following four answers. Total slack is:
   a. The amount of time a task can move freely without affecting its successors.
   b. The difference between the late finish date and early finish date of the task.
   c. The amount of time the resource has in which to complete the task.
   d. The difference between the early start of the earliest successor and the early finish date of the task.

3. You receive a schedule and notice that the project finish milestone has a negative **Total Slack** of *–10 days*. In your own words, what does this mean?

4. There are six possible causes for fragmentation of the Critical Path; list four of those six causes.

5. When optimizing for time:
   a. What are the seven process steps for shortening the Critical Path?
   b. What are at least six of the nine possible methods to shorten the Critical Path?

6. One of your team leaders suggests that the duration of one of her critical tasks can be decreased if you provide her with more people to do the work. What factors should you consider?

7. What is Monte Carlo simulation? What benefits can project managers derive from simulating their schedules?

8. What methods are available to decrease the cost of a project? Give at least four of the eight methods discussed.
9. Will the eventual actual cost of smooth workloads be higher or lower than erratic workloads? Why?
10. If MS Project levels the workloads in your schedule, would the project duration be longer or shorter than if you leveled the workloads yourself? Why?
11. There are many ways to level workloads manually. Name at least eight ways.
12. What three scenarios can MS Project create for you when leveling the workloads? What is the "nice-to-know thing" from each scenario when negotiating with a client? Why?
13. In your own words, how does MS Project's workload leveling affect the calculation and the display of the Critical Path?
14. Describe one of the two processes used to identify the Resource-Critical Path. What is the major disadvantage of this process?
15. We discussed five reasons why finding the Resource-Critical Path might be a good idea. Name three.
16. There are 15 methods with which you can shorten the Resource-Critical Path. Name as many as you can.
17. Why is the s-curve of a Monte Carlo simulated Resource-Critical Path the most reliable information you can present to executives about resource-constrained projects?
18. A project is experiencing a lack of progress during execution:
    a. How would you determine which resources to ask to work overtime in order to make up the slippage (assuming they will not be paid a higher overtime rate)?
    b. What ribbon buttons do you need to click to enter overtime into MS Project?

Relocation Project — Understanding the Gantt Chart

The goal of this exercise is to understand the slack numbers that MS Project calculates.

1. Open the file *09A Optimal Schedule — Time.mpp* available for download at www.ProjectProCorp.com (see page vi for the procedure to access these files).
2. Display the field **Total Slack** in the spreadsheet of the Gantt Chart. Is the total slack expressed in calendar days, business days or person days?
3. Highlight the critical tasks red by clicking ribbon **Format** and selecting [✓ Critical Tasks].

4. Tasks 5 and 6 are highlighted red by MS Project. Are they on the longest path? Is this path more or less critical than the path of tasks 2 and 3? Should you optimize task 5 and 6?
5. Why does the negative slack change from task *7 evaluate the sites* to task *8 meet to select the location*? Hint: there is a constraint date on task 8.
6. Why does the negative slack change from task *13 meet to discuss the contract* to task *14 revise the schedule*? Hint: Nancy is on holiday in the third full week of August, which affects the **Late Start** date for task 13. (This is the most difficult question.)
7. Is task *22 install cabinetry* on the longest path? Is it more or less critical than task *23 install LAN*? Should you optimize it?
8. Why does the negative slack change from task *20 paint* to task *23 install LAN*? Hint: there is a task with an elapsed duration between them.
9. Why does the negative slack change from task *25 facility remodeled* to task *29 move*? Hint: the movers only work weekends.
10. Why does the negative slack change from task 29 *move* to task 30 *unpack*? Hint: the movers only work on the weekend.
11. Close the file without saving.

Relocation Project — Shorten the Critical Path

The goal of this exercise is to be able to apply the optimizing for time approach.

1. Open the file *09A Optimal Schedule — Time.mpp* available for download at www.ProjectProCorp.com (see page vi for the procedure to access these files). The forecasted finish date is currently mid-November, but your CEO insists that the office should be moved by November 1.
2. Display the Critical Path in your schedule in a Gantt view by clicking ribbon **Format** and selecting ☑ Critical Tasks. Make sure you understand all the total slack numbers on each task. If you do not understand the total slack numbers, first do the previous exercise *Relocation Project — Understanding the Gantt Chart.*
3. Look at the parallel paths and the **Total Slack** numbers and determine which tasks that are highlighted red by MS Project are the most critical tasks; these are the tasks on the longest path through the network, see page 426 for an example.
4. Find and record the duration of the project before optimizing; it is ……….. days.

5. The objective of this exercise is to decrease the duration (time) of the project as much as possible. Use the process as discussed on page 436:
   - ◇ Focus on the longest critical tasks first.
   - ◇ Use the methods in the table on page 442 and start at the top of the table.
   - ◇ Determine if you can apply the first method to any of the longest critical tasks in this project. Then go to the second method in the table, and so forth.
   - ◇ See how much time you gain with each change and decide if you want to keep it. Notice that the task *move* is tied to a resource that works on weekends only and will only reschedule to the previous weekend if you have shortened the project enough. You may not see the project duration decrease on every change. Instead, look at the **Total Slack** numbers on the tasks you changed to track progress.
   - ◇ If you keep a change, write down what you changed in order to compare your measures with other students and with our solution. If you want to throw it out, use the **Undo** list on the Quick Access Toolbar to undo one or more changes.
6. Decrease the duration of the project as much as you can, but be prepared to defend the changes you made in the schedule to other students.
7. Notice that the Critical Path may become incomplete after any change. You have to make sure that you continue making changes to critical tasks only. Therefore, you may have to find the missing critical tasks so that you see the complete Critical Path in the schedule again. We discussed this on page 425.
8. Find and record the duration of the project after optimizing; it is .... days.
9. Save the file and compare your results with the ideas we will discuss in the next exercise.

Relocation Project — Shorten the Critical Path — Guided

The goal of this exercise is to be able to apply the optimizing for time approach.

1. To illustrate how a schedule can be optimized, we will explain a complete optimization that will bring the project duration down to less than half the original duration! A similar reduction can be achieved in many projects by applying all of the techniques discussed in this chapter.
2. Open the file *09B Optimal Schedule — Time.mpp* available for download at *www.ProjectProCorp.com* (see page vi for the procedure to access these files).
3. Find and record the current duration of the project; it is .... days.

4. Find the longest critical tasks. Since the tasks *drying of paint, install LAN, relocate walls* and *lay carpet* are the longest critical tasks, these are the most critical tasks (looking at the **Total Slack** numbers) and suggest a good starting point for finding time in the schedule.

Enter the changes in the following steps to shorten the relocation project. Notice that the Critical Path may become incomplete at any step. You have to make sure that you continue making changes to critical tasks only. You may have to repair a fragmented Critical Path so that you see the most critical tasks in the schedule again.

5. Create an overlap in the dependency on *relocate walls*, so that *install electric wiring* is done mostly in parallel with relocating the walls. Overlap *relocate walls* and *install electric wiring* with a finish-to-finish plus 1 day dependency. The electricians can start on a wall as soon as the carpenters have it up.
   The duration of the project is now: .... days.
6. We will schedule *lay carpet* in parallel with *install cabinetry* and *install LAN.* Cut the dependency between *install cabinetry* and *lay carpet* and cut the dependency between *install LAN* and *lay carpet.* Instead, make *lay carpet* dependent on *drying of paint.* Create new dependencies from *install cabinetry* and *install LAN* to *facility remodeled* to get rid of the loose ends in the network. You can lay carpet in parallel with installing cabinets and installing the LAN.
   The duration of the project is now: .... days.
7. Change the type of dependency between *install electric wiring* and *paint* to finish-to-finish plus 1 day. The painters can start on a wall as soon as electricians finish it.
   The duration of the project is now: .... days.
8. Change the type of dependency between *paint* and *drying of paint* to finish-to-finish plus 1 elapsed day (eday). The paint starts drying as soon as the first wall is painted.
   The duration of the project is now: .... days.
9. Change the type of dependency between *facility remodeled* and *pack* into finish-to-finish. The packing should ideally be ready when the facility is ready.
   The duration of the project is now: .... days.
10. Cut the dependency between *location selected* and *select the contractor*, and make *select the contractor* dependent on *evaluate the sites.* Create a new dependency between *location selected* and *meet to discuss contract.* You can select the contractor when you have an idea which location will be chosen. Answer OK if any prompts pop up.
    The duration of the project is now: .... days.
11. Change the Start No Earlier Than constraint into As Soon As Possible on task 8 *meet to select the location* and arrange for a conference call or internet meeting with the CEO, who is abroad.

The duration of the project is now: ……….. days. There are very few critical tasks left; by how, much do you need to raise the threshold for criticality to see a complete Critical Path again? Make this change by clicking ribbon **File,** Options , tab **Advanced**, and changing the field **Task are critical if slack is less than or equal to … days** at the bottom of the dialog. Threshold: ……… days

12. Overlap *summarize requirements* and *research staff requirements* finish-to-finish plus 1 day. You can start summarizing as soon as you receive some completed questionnaires. Answer OK if any prompts pop up.
    The duration of the project is now: ……….. days.

13. Get rid of the lag on the dependency between task 12 *select the contractor* and task 13 *meet to discuss contract*. Make sure that you give advance notice of 5 days to the participants expected at the meeting, so the 5-day time frame for calling the meeting is not needed anymore.
    The duration of the project is now: ……….. days.

14. Change the task *install LAN* into a summary task by adding the following subtasks:
    install LAN cables (20 d of Fixed Work, predecessor *relocate walls),*
    install LAN hardware (20 d of Fixed Work, predecessor *install LAN cables),* and
    install LAN operating system (20 d of Fixed Work, predecessor *install LAN hardware,* successor *facility remodeled).*
    Cut the dependencies between *drying of paint* and *install LAN* and between *install LAN* and *facility remodeled.* Keep the assignment units at 5 units for all subtasks; remove the *LAN consultants* from the summary task. The result is a more refined and shorter schedule.
    The duration of the project is now: ……….. days.
    The threshold for criticality should be raised to: ……… days

15. Increase the assignment units of the *contractor* for the task *lay carpet* from 6 to 12. This decreases the duration of *lay carpet* to 5 days, which is now done entirely in parallel with *install cabinetry*.
    The duration of the project is now: ……….. days.

16. You decide to ask the *LAN consultants* to work with 8 consultants instead of 5. Change all assignments of the *LAN consultants* to 8 units on the subtasks of *install LAN*. This will reduce the duration of the subtasks to 2.5 days.
    The duration of the project is now: ……….. days.

Please answer the following questions:

17. We have reduced the project duration to less than half of the original duration! Most changes are quite defendable. You have seen here an example of how you can easily find time in your project schedule if you create a dynamic model of your project in

9

the first place. Could you apply similar methods to your own project schedule? Which ones?

18. Were trade-offs made against the scope or quality of this project? What were they? Would you undo some proposed changes? Why?

19. Save your file and compare it to the solution file *09C Optimal Schedule — Time.mpp* available for download at www.ProjectProCorp.com (see page vi for the procedure to access these files). See page 697 of this book for an automated way of comparing and reporting differences between two versions of one schedule.

Relocation Project — Lower the Cost

The goal of this exercise is to be able to apply the optimizing for time and cost approach.

1. Open the file *09D Optimal Schedule — Time Cost.mpp* available for download at www.ProjectProCorp.com (see page vi for the procedure to access these files).

2. Find and record the cost and duration of the project before optimizing.
   The cost is ....
   The duration is ....

3. The objective of this exercise is to decrease the cost of the project as much as possible while maintaining or decreasing the duration. Use the process as discussed on page 459:
   ◇ Focus on the most expensive tasks first.
   ◇ Use the methods in the table on page 461 and start at the top of the table.
   ◇ Determine if you can apply the first method to any of the most expensive tasks in this project. Then go to the second method in the table, and so forth.
   ◇ See how much cost each change saves and then decide if you want to keep it.
   ◇ If you keep a change, write down what you changed in order to compare your methods with other students. If you want to throw out the change, use the list of **Undo** to undo one or more changes.

4. Find and record the cost and duration of the project before optimizing.
   The cost is ....
   The duration is ....

5. Save your file.

6. Compare the changes you made with the ideas that we will discuss in the next exercise.

Relocation Project — Lower the Cost — Guided

The goal of this exercise is to be able to apply the optimizing for time and cost approach.

1. Open the file *09E Optimal Schedule – Time Cost.mpp* available for download at www.ProjectProCorp.com (see page vi for the procedure to access these files).
2. You found some new resources and asked them for quotes. The result is shown in the next table. Enter these new resources in the Resource Sheet view.

Name	Type	Position	Function	Max. Units	Std. Rate	Accrue at
Carpeteers	Work	contractor	External	20	$140/d	End
cablers	Work	contractor	External	5	$40/h	End
students	Work	contractor	External	5	$80/d	End

3. The current cost of the project is: ....
   The current cost for the task *lay carpet* is: ....
   The current duration of the project is: ....
4. A specialized carpet company, *Carpeteers*, is willing to do the job. Carpeteers estimates the work will take 30 person days, and they will do it with 10 employees. Reassign the task *lay carpet* to the new resource *Carpeteers*:
   The new forecasted cost for *lay carpet* is: ....
   How much did we save on this task? ....
   The new total cost of the project is: ....
5. The new total duration of the project is: ....
   Why is it lower?
6. What consequences does this change have for the scope and quality of the project? Why?
7. Would you keep the reassignment to *Carpeteers*? Why?

Enter the following additional changes to lower the cost of the relocation project:

8. Delete the task *revise the schedule;* it is a nice-to-have task. Is there a possible trade-off in doing this?
   The total cost of the project is now: ....
9. Delete the task *select the realtor* and hire the one you know. Is there a possible trade-off in doing this?
   The total cost of the project is now: ....

9

10. Delete the task *select the contractor* and hire the one you know. Is there a possible trade-off in doing this? Add a new dependency to keep the original logic.
    The total cost of the project is now: ....

11. Make the task *install LAN* a summary task by adding the following subtasks:
    install LAN cables (20 d of Fixed Work, predecessor *relocate walls),*
    install LAN hardware (20 d of Fixed Work, predecessor *install LAN cables),* and
    install LAN operating system (20 d of Fixed Work, predecessor *install LAN hardware,* successor *lay carpet).*
    Keep the resource units at 5 units for all subtasks; remove the *LAN consultants* from the summary task. Cut the dependencies between *drying of paint* and *install LAN.*
    You ask the LAN consultants to use cheaper resources to do the cabling. They offer you specialized *cablers*, as shown in the table at the beginning of this exercise.
    Reassign the task *install LAN cables* to the cheaper resource *cablers*. Is there a possible trade-off in doing this?
    The total cost of the project is now: ....

12. You ask the contractor to come up with sharper estimates to save cost. He offers to provide students who can help the carpenters relocate walls. He proposes to replace half of the carpenters with *students*; remove the contractors and then re-assign 5 contractors and 5 students. Are there possible trade-offs on time, scope or quality?
    The total cost of the project is now: ....

13. In your search to save cost you decide that the same 35 employees should pack all of their stuff in 1 day instead of 2 days to decrease the effort (**Work**) and cost. Are there possible trade-offs on time, scope or quality?
    The total cost of the project is now: ....

14. The labor cost should now be within the budget of $100,000. Compare your schedule with the solution file *09F Optimal Schedule – Time Cost.mpp* available for download at www.ProjectProCorp.com (see page vi for the procedure to access these files). See page 697 of this book for an automated way of comparing and reporting differences between two versions of one schedule. Make sure you insert column **Cost** before comparing.

15. What is the forecasted duration for the project now?
    The total duration of the project is: ....

16. Would you use this lower-cost version of the schedule in real life? Why?

17. Save your file.

Relocation Project — Leveling Manually

The goal of this exercise is to be able to level the workloads manually as part of the optimizing for time, cost and resources approach.

1. Open the file *09G Optimal Schedule – Time Cost Resources.mpp* available for download at www.ProjectProCorp.com (see page vi for the procedure to access these files).
2. Display the **Leveling Options** dialog by clicking the ribbon **Resource**, button Leveling Options :
   Set **Leveling Calculations** to ◉ **Manual** and
   Set **Look for overallocations on a Day by Day basis**.
3. Which view do you recommend to check the overallocations?
4. You find that a few resources are overallocated: *Nancy Hilcrest* and *You*. We discussed many ways to resolve overallocations manually on page 473; use these to answer the following questions:
   a. What changes would you recommend to level the workloads manually for *Nancy*?
   b. What changes would you recommend to level the workloads manually for *You?*
5. Save your file and compare it with the solution file *09H Optimal Schedule – Time Cost Resources.mpp* available for download at www.ProjectProCorp.com (see page vi for the procedure to access these files). See page 697 of this book for an automated way of comparing and reporting differences between two versions of one schedule.

9

Relocation Project — Leveling Automatically

The goal of this exercise is to be able to level the workloads automatically as part of the optimizing for time, cost and resources approach.

1. Open the file *09I Optimal Schedule – Time Cost Resources.mpp* available for download at www.ProjectProCorp.com (see page vi for the procedure to access these files).
2. What is the current duration of the project? It is ….. business days.
3. Which view do you recommend for analyzing the results of MS Project's workload leveling (see page 484 and following if you need help)? Apply this view.

4. Click ribbon **Resource**, button [Leveling Options] and set the following options:
   ◉ **Manual**
   Look for overallocations on a Day by Day basis.
   ☑ **Clear leveling values before leveling**
   ◉ **Level entire project**
   ☐ **Level only within available slack**
   ☑ **Leveling can adjust individual assignments on a task**
   ☑ **Leveling can create splits in remaining work**
   Leave the other options set to their default. Use the [Level All] button to have MS Project resolve all overallocations.
5. Which field does MS Project change when leveling automatically?
6. Which tasks were delayed? By how much?
7. Has MS Project increased the duration of the project? Why?
8. Are there any trade-offs in scope or quality?
9. Would you keep the solution proposed by MS Project? Why?
10. Save your file and compare it with the solution file *09J Optimal Schedule – Time Cost Resources.mpp* available for download at www.ProjectProCorp.com (see page vi for the procedure to access these files). See page 697 of this book for an automated way of comparing and reporting differences between two versions of one schedule. Make sure you insert the column **Leveling Delay** before comparing.

Intranet Project — Identify the Resource-Critical Path

The goal of this exercise is to be able to identify the Resource-Critical Path (RCP) in a resource-constrained schedule as part of optimizing for time, cost and resources.

1. Open the file *09K Optimal Schedule – Time Cost Resources – Intranet Project.mpp* available for download at www.ProjectProCorp.com (see page vi for the procedure to access these files). [65]

---

[65] We will use a different project here, because we saw in the previous exercise that the workload leveling did not affect the project end date; the Critical Path was identical to the RCP.

2. How many resources of the different roles do you need by month? Are there serious overallocations?
3. Would you level the workloads in this schedule manually? Why?
4. What is the current duration of the project? The duration is ....
5. Level all workloads entirely and use the same settings as in the previous exercise in the **Resource Leveling** dialog (**Resource**, button **Leveling Options**). Use the Level All button to level all workloads. What is the duration now?
   The duration is ....
6. Check the Critical Path in the schedule. Does it explain the entire project duration?
7. Mark the RCP by entering **Yes** in the field **Marked** for each resource-critical task using the manual process as explained on page 501. Set the settings in the **Bar Styles** dialog as explained in the pages after page 501. You should now see an RCP that explains the entire project duration without any gaps, with red task bars for all tasks on the RCP.
8. Compare your file against the file *09L Optimal Schedule – Time Cost Resources – Intranet Project.mpp* available for download at www.ProjectProCorp.com (see page vi for the procedure to access these files). See page 697 of this book for an automated way of comparing and reporting differences between two versions of one schedule.

9

Intranet Project — Shorten the Resource-Critical Path

The goal of this exercise is to be able to shorten the Resource-Critical Path (RCP) in a resource-constrained schedule as part of optimizing for time, cost and resources.

1. Open the file *09L Optimal Schedule – Time Cost Resources – Intranet Project.mpp* available for download at *www.ProjectProCorp.com* (see page vi for the procedure to access these files). All workloads in this schedule are leveled and the resource-critical tasks are flagged with **Yes** in the field **Marked**.
2. Find and record the duration of the project before optimizing; it is .... days.
3. The objective of this exercise is to decrease the duration (time) of the project as much as possible, while maintaining or lowering the cost and keeping the workload reasonable (resources). Use the process as discussed on page 468:
   - ◇ Focus on the most critical resources first.
   - ◇ Use the methods in the table on page 511 and start at the top of the table. Apply the first method from the table to the longest RCP tasks and their most critical resources.
   - ◇ Go to the next method in the table and apply it, and so forth.

- ◇ See how much time you gain with each change, and then decide if you want to keep it.
- ◇ If you keep a change, write down what you changed in order to compare your measures with other students. If you want to throw out the change, use the list of **Undo** [undo button] to undo one or more changes.
- ◇ Make several changes before you identify the new RCP.

4. Decrease the duration of the project as much as you can, but be prepared to defend the changes you made in the schedule to the other students.
5. Find and record the duration of the project after optimizing; it is ……….. days.
6. Save your file. Compare your changes with the ideas that we will discuss in the next exercise.

Intranet Project — Shorten the RCP — Guided

The goal of this exercise is to be able to shorten the Resource-Critical Path (RCP) as part of the Optimizing for Time, Cost and Resources approach.

1. Open the file *09M Optimal Schedule – Time Cost Resources – Intranet Project.mpp* available for download at www.ProjectProCorp.com (see page vi for the procedure to access these files). All workloads in this schedule are leveled and the resource-critical tasks are flagged with **Yes** in the field **Marked**.
2. What is the current duration and cost of this project schedule?
   The total duration of the project is: …………
   The total cost of the project is: …………
3. It is somewhat peculiar that the project manager is on the RCP on task 10. We should be able to take him off the RCP. In general, a project manager should never be on the Critical Path, except, perhaps, in very small projects where he does tasks as a resource as well. Cut the dependency between task *9 Define specific functionality* and task *10 Develop project plan*. Give the task *10 Develop project plan* a new predecessor task *3 Define user requirements*. Give task *9 Define specific functionality* a new successor, task *11 System designed*. Is task 10 still resource-critical? If not, set **Marked** to *No*. Are there new work overloads? If there are, level the workloads again. Determine the new RCP.
   The total duration of the project is: …………
   The total cost of the project is: …………
4. Notice that the *Roll-out manager* is working only 50% on task 50 *Communicate roll out plan to users*. Increase this to 100% while keeping the work on the task the same. Level the workloads in the schedule again using the option ☑ **Clear leveling**

values before leveling; the Resource-Critical Path explains the entire project duration again. Are there new overallocations? Is the task still on the RCP?
The total duration of the project is: ....
The total cost of the project is: ....

5. You see that the longest resource-critical tasks are tasks *36 Develop web pages* and 37 *Develop any custom functionality*. Together they take 20 days in the current schedule. If you can find a substitute web designer for task 37 *Develop any custom functionality*, you can schedule those two tasks in parallel. You ask the resource manager for an extra designer, and you get one. Create a new resource, *Ann Webweaver*, with the same rate as the other designer and substitute her on task 37 *Develop any custom functionality*. Set a new dependency between task 35 *Determine development tool* and 37 *Develop any custom functionality*. Are tasks 36 and 37 still resource-critical? Are there new work overloads? Level the workloads again. Determine the new RCP.
The total duration of the project is: ....
The total cost of the project is: ....

6. We shortened the schedule by about 25% without increasing the cost and without overallocations. Does the current RCP make sense? Why?

7. Compare your file with the solution file *09N Optimal Schedule – Time Cost Resources – Intranet Project.mpp* available for download at www.ProjectProCorp.com (see page vi for the procedure to access these files). See page 697 of this book for an automated way of comparing and reporting differences between two versions of one schedule.

8. Save your file.

9

Chapter 10 Creating Reports for Project Stakeholders

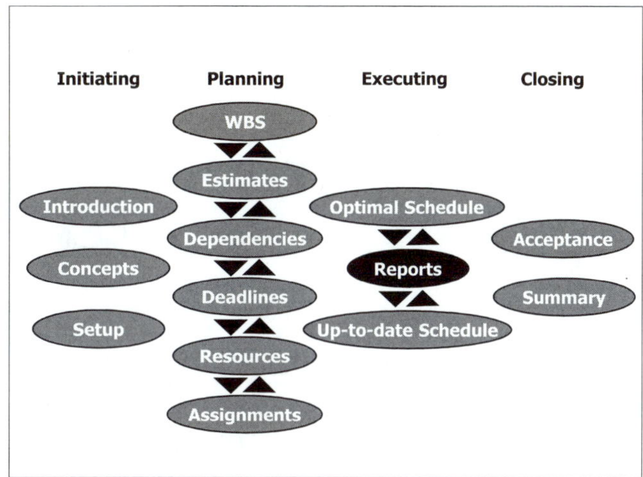

In the previous chapter, we found the optimal schedule that meets the project deadline and stays within the budget and availability of resources. You are now ready to show the schedule to your executives and other project stakeholders by creating *reports* (see the black ellipse above). Hopefully, the executive or customer will approve the project schedule and you can start project execution. You will then need to create reports again at every status cycle.

After reading this chapter you will:

- realize that you need to explicitly display the buffer in your schedule (except for in-firm, fixed price project proposals)
- know the standard views, tables, groupings and filters of MS Project
- be able to customize views for reporting with custom tables, filters and groupings
- realize that one-page reports are important and know your options to create them
- be able to format, lay out and print your schedule efficiently
- know how to use the organizer to copy custom report objects between projects
- be able to check if you used scheduling best practices for project reporting

My Buffer is my Buddy

Bob holds a presentation for the client and has invited Lena along as the technical expert on his team. As they leave the meeting, Lena mentions something that bothered her during the meeting. "Hey Bob, why did you show the client a schedule with a finish date in April? You told us we should be done early March."
Bob recognizes the explosive nature of this question and responds: "It gives me a time buffer of one month to compensate for time lost to unforeseen things."
Lena pleads: "Why don't you just give us more time? We're very stressed!"
Bob: "I've asked you and the others for estimates, and I created a schedule from those estimates that showed we could finish in March. Are you saying you can't stick to the estimate you gave me?"
Lena sounds assertive: "It's a tight schedule!"
Bob is relaxed. "Don't worry, I inserted a time buffer at the end and I own it. If you find that you need extra time, drop by my office and show me why you need more time."
"Bob, how do you handle two different schedules of the same project? It's like double bookkeeping isn't it?"
"Not really Lena, because I show the early-dates schedule to the team and the late-dates schedule to the client. It's still one and the same project file. I just apply a different view!"
"That's smart!" Lena admits.

Project Communications Management

Scheduling software is efficient in reporting. The software behaves like a database in that you can pull data from it to focus on any deliverable, any period or any resource you want. The type of information in a report can be changed as well; you can report scheduled dates, cost figures or calculated values, like *Earned Value*. Reports allow you to compare actual against planned progress (*baseline*) and to establish performance. Indicators for performance typically are: *Was the project delivered on time and within budget?*

Is This a Peak Performance?

Performance measurement by itself is impossible! Of course, you can measure the quality of the performance, but you are always measuring the quality of the originally approved schedule (the *baseline schedule*) at the same time. Both the baseline and the performance relative to the baseline are the products of the project manager. For example, if a project manager deliberately pads his baseline schedule by 50% and then boasts that he delivered his project in 30% less time, is this peak performance or poor planning? Does this project manager deserve a raise? In my view, he should be scolded, because he could have saved his organization money and time!

Executives cannot measure performance only; they need to assure the quality of their measuring stick first, the baseline schedule. Executives, or the project management office on their behalf, need to be involved in the planning and the baselining of the project. At least, they need to do an evaluation of the quality of the proposed baseline schedule and make sure it is complete and realistic, but challenging. If it is, the quality of the baseline is assured. The executive can then delegate the *execution* of the project entirely to the project manager and truly measure the performance of the project, instead of the quality of the baseline.

Do Project Managers Need a Time Buffer?

The answer is yes! A project is a temporary endeavor by definition, and all projects have a deadline attached (often a monetary budget as well) that is often firm. With a firm deadline, the project manager needs a time buffer to accommodate for unforeseen events that happen in every project. The real question a project manager needs to deal with then becomes: *Will I make my time buffer visible or shall I hide it?*

Should Project Managers Make Their Time Buffer Visible?

When we optimized the schedule, you may have found a healthy amount of time as a buffer to accomplish the deadline. The dilemma of whether or not to hide the buffer can be one of the most difficult choices. As a project manager, you may think you are in a double bind here. If you show the buffer, you may lose it. If you hide the buffer, you are not showing the true situation to your stakeholders. You enter into a dark game of secrecy, and you may have to do double bookkeeping with your schedule.

We recommend that you consider the following when faced with this dilemma: *Is this project performed on a fixed price basis or on a time and materials basis? Fixed price* is when you agree with the client on a fixed amount of money and a hard delivery date. *Time and materials* is getting paid for all hours that you spent and all materials you used on the project.

We also need to make a distinction here between projects with a customer who is external to the organization, and projects with a customer internal to the organization (i.e., another department or division).

If you are a manager of projects with *external customers*, the crucial question is whether you will provide a quote with a firm fixed price or not. In dealing with an external client, it is important to be aware of the type of contract that is established with the client. With a time and materials contract, the client will be looking over your shoulder, and you will not need a buffer at all; you will get paid for every hour spent. If the contract is a firm fixed price contract, you will need a buffer that you do not need to show to the client. You are even expected to hide it, just as you hide your profit margin. But you still need to show the true cost of the project to your executives. Construction and consulting companies, for example, have mostly external customers and often use fixed price contracts.

Even in projects where the customer is within the same organization (*internal customers*), the cost of the project may be *charged back* to the business unit of the customer. The type of contract would still be relevant, even though most internal projects are charged back on a time and material basis. If you have an internal customer that engaged you with a time and materials agreement, you will have to make your time buffer visible.

Some project managers choose to hide the time buffer in their schedule even if they are not in a fixed price situation. For those of you who do this, please note that it is not in line with PMI's *Code of Ethics and Professional Conduct* that applies, among others, to every PMI member and anyone who holds one of the PMI certifications. Specifically, it violates chapter 5 on *Honesty* in the mandatory standard: *We do not engage in or condone behavior that is designed to deceive others* as well as the following sections in the aspirational standard: *We are truthful in our communications and in our conduct*, and *We provide accurate information in a timely manner.*[66]

Methods to Hide the Time Buffer

If you have an *external customer* engaged with a firm fixed price contract, you may hide your time and cost buffer from the client, but not from your own executives. The following are methods to hide a buffer. Most of them are the opposite methods to the optimizing methods we discussed (see page 511). Most will increase the overhead cost of the project, because they increase the project duration. They are ranked in order of ascending sophistication. The likelihood that a buffer will stay hidden from examining eyes increases as you move down the list:

1. **Overestimate lags**
   Lags are gaps between task bars of dependent tasks. You can use lags to model waiting time that is out of your control, as when you are waiting to receive a construction permit. It is smart to estimate these lags on the (very) safe side. For how to enter lags, see page 214. However, they can easily be noticed in the Gantt Chart. Lags are cost neutral except for overhead cost.

2. **Insert extra holidays in the project calendar**
   You can insert extra common holidays in the project calendar. The task bars that span these days will simply stretch. This can be noticed in the Gantt Chart by sharp analysts. For the steps to insert extra holidays, see page 105. The method is cost neutral except for overhead cost.

3. **Decrease the working hours in the project calendar**
   This is frequently applied. Managers know that resources are not focused and productive 8 hours a day, even though their workday is 8 hours. In the project calendar, start the business day later or finish it earlier. For the how-to, see page 102. This may make the calendar inconsistent with the **Hours per day** and **Hours per Week** setting (ribbon **File**, Options, tab **Schedule**). Durations may start to show decimals and will be obvious. Therefore, adjust these settings accordingly. The method is cost neutral except for overhead cost.

10

---

[66] *Project Management Institute Code of Ethics and Professional Conduct*, 2006, PMI, Newtown Square, PA, USA.

4. **Ignore the benefits of learning curves**
   If you have repetitive activities in your schedule, you will likely benefit from the decreasing learning time with every repeat. Your estimate should be lower with every repeat. If you ignore this effect of the learning curve, you are, in fact, keeping a buffer in your schedule (see page 189). The cost of the project will also be overstated with this method.

5. **Introduce ramp-up and wind-down factors**
   If your resources are involved in more than one project at a time, they will be less productive, because of setting up and closing down work when moving from project to project. You can include this time in your estimates, which will also affect the cost (see page 181).

6. **Introduce distraction factors for high-focus tasks**
   Certain tasks require your full focus, but the world around will not stop spinning. Writing a report or a book is a situation in which most people need to concentrate fully and need consecutive, uninterrupted time. (This is why you always get my voicemail when I am writing the next edition of this book.) Increase the estimate on these tasks with a distraction factor, which will affect the cost as well.

7. **Introduce extra revision cycles**
   Every revision cycle has two tasks: *revise* and *modify*. For writing, you could add tasks like *edit* and *rewrite*. You might even get away with another cycle of *re-edit* and *re-re-write*, but you may want to call it something else. For the how-to of inserting tasks, see page 148. Inserting extra revision cycles increases the cost as well, but could have a positive impact on quality.

8. **Keep maximum units or the working hours of resources low**
   In a resource-constrained schedule you can influence the forecasted project end date by changing the availability of resources through working hours on the resource calendar or in the resource-related field maximum units (**Max Units**). You can create a time buffer in your schedule if you lower the working hours on the resource calendars (see page 314). The effect on the schedule will be immediate. Or, you can keep their maximum units on the low and safe side (see page 318). When you assign these resources to **Fixed Work** tasks, their durations will become artificially long, since they are being represented as working fewer hours per day than they are actually working. These methods will affect the duration of the project and, hence, the overhead cost.

9. **Insert extra holidays for your critical resources**
   Determine who the most critical resources are in your schedule and insert extra holidays in their resource calendar. For the how-to, see page 314. This cannot be easily seen in the Gantt Chart, but you can easily find the extra holidays on the resource calendars (ribbon **Project**, button **Change Working Time**, list **For**, select

a resource and click tab **Exceptions**) since Project 2007. This method is cost neutral except for overhead cost.

10. **Assign one scarce expert to more tasks than needed**
If one expert is in great demand, she will likely be a *critical resource* and drive the project finish date. If you *assign* her to more tasks than strictly needed and delay tasks to level her workloads, she will drive out the forecasted finish date even further, thus creating a time buffer for you. It is hard to argue with using the best resource on many tasks, which makes this an effective method. For the how-to, see page 361 and following. If the expert is paid at a higher rate than other resources, you are also increasing the cost.

11. **Create extra tasks that are inconspicuous**
One of my students once confided that he always creates the task *Find alternative resources* in the task list, wherever it is remotely appropriate; I will not mention his name so as not to spoil his fun. Other good additions are *Apply quality check* or *Update the project plan*. Who will argue about those? These extra tasks increase the cost as well.

12. **Pad the duration and work estimates**
As a project manager once put it, *To pad or not to pad* is similar to the Shakespearian *To be or not to be* in fixed price situations. If you asked for range estimates (optimistic, pessimistic) instead of single-point estimates, you could build your schedule based on the pessimistic estimates. Padding also increases cost.

13. **Do not use overtime yet**
If you know you can count on your resources working some overtime, do not enter it into the schedule during the planning of the project. When your team members work a weekend, the 2 days will be pure gain. For the how-to, see page 516. Be careful with this method if you pay a higher rate for overtime, since the planned cost of the project may be understated in such a schedule, because it is calculated based on regular rates. You may gain time but run over budget.

14. **Set extra dependencies that are soft by nature**
Soft dependencies are dependencies that are not absolutely needed, but you can defend them with an argument such as: "*We prefer to do it like this, because it has the following advantage ...*" and give your rationalization. This method is cost neutral except for overhead cost. For how to enter dependencies, see page 221.

15. **Be pessimistic about material delivery dates**
When you are dependent upon receiving a shipment before you can do your work, create a delivery milestone on a date that is later than the date you were promised by the supplier. In this way you create some buffer on the performance of other people upon whom you depend. You now face a new dilemma: *Will you tell your supplier?*

This method is cost neutral except for overhead cost. For more on modeling delivery dates, see page 234.

16. **Name it something that nobody understands**
Name the time buffer line item *TCR*, for example, and wait to see if anybody asks what that means. (Between you and me, it means *Time Contingency Reserve*.) If your colleagues do not understand it, they may be too afraid to ask, which is typical for professional organizations where nobody wants to look dumb.

17. **Split the big buffer into smaller ones**
You can split the big buffer at the end of your schedule into smaller ones that you spread across your schedule. Visually, this will look more reasonable and, thus, acceptable.

18. **Report only high-level schedules**
If all else fails, you can try providing reports on such a high level only that buffers are not visible at all. For example, one-page milestone reports do not reveal buffers (see page 595).

As you may have noticed, most of these methods boil down to not fully optimizing your schedule. If you do not use all the methods of optimization or if you do not apply them to their fullest, you have buried the time buffer in your schedule. We recommend you try to optimize your schedule to the maximum first, so you will be sure of the true buffer you have. Then you could hide it again in hard-to-find places if you are in a fixed price contract situation.

Why You Should Make Buffers Visible and Explicit

We recommend that project managers make their time buffer explicit and visible in their schedule (except to an external client engaged in a fixed price contract). In addition to PMI's *Code of Ethics and Professional Conduct* already mentioned, there are other reasons for this:

- **It is generally accepted practice**
It is generally accepted that when executives ask project managers to commit to hard deadlines, project managers are allowed to own time buffers to accommodate for unforeseen events. If an executive ever questions the need for it, ask: *Don't you put a contingency line item for unforeseen events in your financial budget?* Contingencies in financial budgets are generally accepted practice. Hence, contingencies should be accepted in the time budgets of project managers.
- **It prevents secrecy and creates trust**
The big drawback of hiding time buffers from executives is that it creates a *culture of secrecy*. If the different levels of management stop communicating openly with each other, the situation may worsen over time. Ideally, the time and money buffers

should be on the table instead of under it. If a project manager habitually hides time buffers and an executive happens to find out, the executive may start cutting time off future schedules for this project manager. In turn, the project manager will then hide bigger buffers in harder-to-find places. As soon as the executive finds out, she may start slashing the schedules more, resorting to arbitrary cuts. The situation deteriorates in a downward spiral. As a consultant, I have been witness to organizations that continuously play this game, instead of conducting projects in an open and professional manner. Openness is greatly preferred over a culture of secrecy that can spiral downward.

- **It sets the right example for your team members**
  If you show your buffers, your team members will show theirs too. Whether you like it or not, you are leading by example in everything you do. If you hide your buffers from your executives, your team members will follow your example and start hiding their buffers from you. They will start padding their estimates and their timesheets as they report to you, since you also pad your schedule when you report to executives. When team members own most of the buffer instead of you as the project manager, it is impossible to come out ahead of schedule, because your team members will fill up the time given (or risk exposing their secretive padding).
  At best, you will finish on time. More likely, you will always finish a little late. From a statistical point of view, it is abnormal if your internal projects always run a bit late, but this is typical for a culture of secrecy that may have developed within an organization slowly over many years. In contrast, it is statistically normal if several projects run over and several under, some much over and some much under. This is typical for a healthy organization where a culture of openness and integrity reigns.

How to Defend Visible Buffers

10

There are several ways for project managers to defend buffers that are explicitly visible in the schedule:

- **Reserves are common in monetary budgets**
  Monetary budgets have financial reserves as a generally accepted budgeting practice. These line items are often called *management reserve* or *contingency reserve*. If monetary budgets always have money reserves, why cannot schedules have time reserves?
- **Calculate the buffer you need with schedule simulation**
  A *Monte Carlo simulation* is an entirely scientific method that will prove that you need a reasonable amount of time buffer in your schedule (discussed on page 452). You can use simulation to create a probability curve of project end dates. When you have the curve, you can decide which probability you feel comfortable with and find the corresponding end date. This will dictate the size of the buffer you need in your schedule. Alternatively, you can ask executives for the level of probability with

which they feel comfortable; then, quote the corresponding date from the *s-curve* as the date to which you commit. You then add a buffer as a line item in the WBS that makes the schedule extend to the commitment date.

- **Show in the schedule that you own the buffer**
  Create a separate line item for the time buffer in the task list, instead of leaving it as an undefined, gaping hole in your schedule. As the project manager, you can *assign* yourself as the resource on this line item, so it becomes clear to everybody that you own it. (This also adds a buffer of effort and cost.) Make sure you hook up the line item to the end of the network and set the project end milestone as its sole successor.
- **Hand back responsibility when the buffer is taken away**
  If executives still try to steal your time buffer, you may start to feel that you cannot be held responsible any longer for meeting the non-buffered deadline. If that is the case, make it clear that you do not accept this responsibility any longer and you will only do your best. If deadline accomplishment is an item in your performance appraisal, state clearly that you do not want to see missing this particular deadline brought up in your performance appraisal, and ask for agreement on this. If a verbal understanding did not work in the last project, ask for a written confirmation this time. This will make it perfectly clear that you do not appreciate being held accountable for something that you know is impossible. Your family and friends do not appreciate it either, by the way.

Choosing the Options

There are some MS Project options to explore in order to make good reports. For example, you may have noticed questions marks in the duration column of **Auto Scheduled** tasks. These question marks signify that you did not enter the duration yourself, but had MS Project enter the default duration (*1 day?*) or a calculated duration based on the formula **Duration = Work / Peak Units**. MS Project calls these *estimated durations*. Executives typically do not appreciate seeing question marks next to all your estimates in the schedule; it decreases their level of confidence, and they may start asking questions of their own.

You can make the question marks in the duration column disappear by clicking ribbon **File**, Options and on the tab indicated in the next table:

Tab	Option
Schedule	Section **Scheduling options for this project**: ☐ **Show that scheduled tasks have estimated durations** Clear it if you want to hide the question marks in the duration field. Executives may start asking questions if you leave question marks in your reports.
	☐ **New scheduled tasks have estimated durations** Clear if you do not want to see question marks for any new tasks you create.
Advanced	Section **Display options for this project**: You can change the time units for **Minutes, Hours, Days, Weeks, Months, and Years** to one character to save space on the screen.

Communication Features in Project 2010

The word *report* refers to a specific feature in MS Project (i.e., the ribbon **Project**, button **Reports**). All reports are table-like, with precise, numeric information; we will not discuss this feature in detail. There are newer features for communication in MS Project, so when we use the word *report* in this chapter we do not necessarily refer to the **Reports** button only.

2007 You can print a view to publish your schedule. There is also a feature called *Visual Reports* on the **Project** ribbon. In Project Server, project managers can publish their schedule on a website with restricted access. We will discuss the following reporting vehicles in more detail:

- **Visual Reports** (see page 553)
  2007 This feature can provide three specific types of useful reports: *pivot tables* and *pivot charts* in *Excel 2010* and *pivot diagrams* in *Visio 2010*. Pivot diagrams are tree-like charts. MS Project creates the visual reports as separate files that can be manipulated further in their native applications; you will need these applications, of course, to do so. You can email them in their native formats or as PDF files to your stakeholders.
- **Views** (see page 556)
  A view is what you see on the screen when you apply a view from the **View** ribbon;  MS Project always has a view applied. When you print a view, it will show on paper whatever you created on the screen: MS Project comes close to the principle of WYSIWYG (What You See Is What You Get). Rarely will you see differences between screen and paper. You can print any view except for the form views (Task Form, Resource Form and Relationship Diagram), which display very little

information anyway. Charts like the Gantt Chart, Network Diagram and Resource Graph can be printed only through views. We will discuss the new *Timeline view* separately, see page 582.

Pro

- **Project Server** (see page 582)
  Project Server is the companion application for Project Professional, even though when you realize the magnitude of Project Server you would state it the other way round. Essentially, Project Server is middleware that makes many applications talk to each other: MS Project, SQL Server, SharePoint Server, Internet Explorer and Outlook, among others. It allows you to communicate with stakeholders via a central website and is, therefore, the way of the future. Project Server goes beyond communication and also facilitates two-way *collaboration*, *delegation* and *updating* of schedules.

The following table provides a summary of our previous discussion and further specifics. This table may help you determine which option is best for you:

Visual Reports	**Views**	**Project Server**
Separate electronic files	Paper-based output	Online access to views
One-way communication	One-way communication	Two-way collaboration
Edits possible	Edits possible	Some edits possible
Customizable	Highly customizable	Highly customizable
Drill down or up in dimensions that are out-of-the-box	Drill down or up through WBS or custom grouping	Drill down or up in many custom dimensions
Slice and dice	Slice and dice	Slice and dice
Little effort	More effort	Most effort
Pivot tables and charts and pivot diagrams only	Tables and timescale charts	(Pivot) tables and all charts

In this chapter, we will discuss in detail how to customize Visual Reports and Views. Each group of stakeholders needs a custom report, and the project manager needs to be good at customizing reports to suit them. We will also give an overview of the vast online reporting possibilities in Project Server.

Using MS Project Visual Reports

The *visual reports* address specific reporting needs. There are three types of visual reports: *pivot tables* and *pivot charts* in Excel 2010, and *pivot diagrams* in Visio 2010. We will discuss them in that order.

Pivot Tables in MS Excel

The strength of pivot tables is the capability to slice and dice data (group and aggregate), and to drill down into the details and back out to the overview. An example of a useful pivot table is:

A filter button indicates that only some items are shown.

Baseline Cost Report - Focus Group Product Implementation Project				
		Data		
Project	Tasks on Outline Level 1	Baseline Cost	Cost	Actual Cost
⊟Focus Group Product Implementation	⊞Develop Customer Feedback Collection Processes	$ 4,308,363.08	$ 4,319,132.31	$ 551,570.77
	⊞Design Customer Feedback Monitoring Process	$ 3,025,750.00	$ 3,027,903.85	$ 31,153.85
	⊞Deploy Feedback Program	$ 47,692.31	$ 47,692.31	$ 47,692.31
	⊞Monitor Customer Feedback	$ 163,230.77	$ 148,615.38	$ 4,615.38
Focus Group Product Implementation Total		$ 7,545,036.15	$ 7,543,343.85	$ 635,032.31
Grand Total		$ 7,545,036.15	$ 7,543,343.85	$ 635,032.31

Totals

Plus button for drilling down into detail.

Click the plus button ⊞ to drill down into detail. The button will then change into a minus button ⊟ to drill back up to the overview. The steps to create this pivot table are:

1. Click ribbon **Project** and 

.
2. Clear ☐ **Microsoft Visio** to hide the *Visio* pivot diagrams.
3. From the list select the report you want and click View – the pivot chart appears in Excel 2010.
4. To see the pivot table, click the worksheet tab **Assignment Usage** at the bottom left of your screen.

You may have to further manipulate the pivot table in Excel 2010 to make it look the way you want it to.

Pivot Charts in MS Excel

Excel 2010 immediately creates a *pivot chart* from the *pivot table* data. An example of a useful pivot chart is:

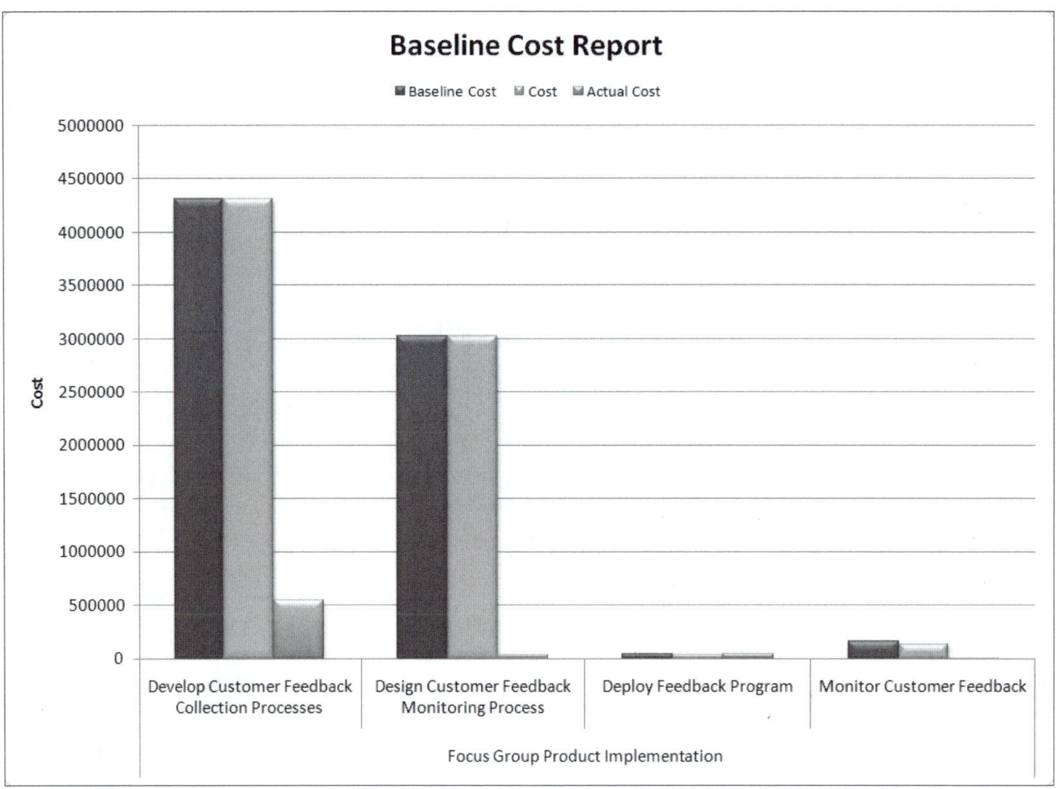

The steps to create this pivot chart are the first three steps in the previous procedure for pivot tables.

Pivot Diagram in MS Visio

Pivot diagrams in Visio 2010 are like breakdown charts, similar to a visual WBS chart. An example of a useful pivot diagram is:

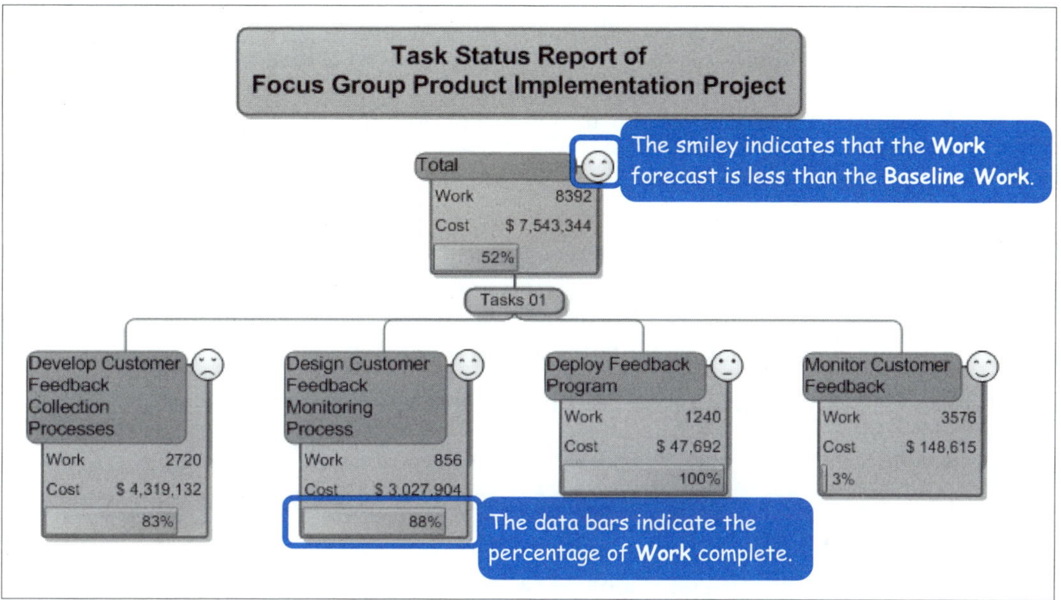

The steps to create this pivot diagram are:

1. Click ribbon **Project** and [Visual Reports].
2. Clear ☐ **Microsoft Excel** to hide the *Excel* pivot tables and charts.
3. From the list select the report you want and click [View] – the pivot diagram appears in Visio 2010.
4. You may have to manipulate the chart further in Visio 2010 to make it look the way you want.

10

Using Custom MS Project Views

Views provide more options for customization than **Visual Reports** and often allow you to create the output that your clients expect. The steps to tailoring views to your reporting needs are given next. It may seem like an elaborate process, but there are advantages to customizing views:

- You will use them regularly, and the custom views are only two mouse clicks away.

- You may be able to re-use custom views in other projects. You could even forward your successful custom view to the project management office to have it considered across the enterprise as a standard view in Project Server.

The process for customizing views is:

1. Customize **Fields**: what data do you want to show?
2. Design a new **Table**, which fields do you want?
3. Design a new **Filter**, which tasks or resources do you want to show?
4. Create a new **Group** to list the tasks or resources in custom categories.
5. Create a new **View** that displays the newly created **Table** (including any customized fields)**, Filter** and **Group**.
6. Sort the records through ribbon **View**, button **Sort**.
7. Apply any formats through the **Format** ribbon.
8. Choose the **Page Setup** settings.
9. Draw objects in the timescale using the **Format** ribbon.

A view applies a table (that may contain custom fields), a filter and a group. The view refers to a table, filter and group object to apply; therefore, it is best to create those first. The view object itself actually contains the remaining settings: sort order, formats applied, page setup settings, and any objects created with the drawing tools on the **Format** ribbon. Because these settings and drawing objects are stored in the **View** object, we recommend creating the new view before doing the sort, format, page setup and drawing; otherwise, they end up in both view objects, one of which is then messed up.

The **Fields, Table, Filter** and **Group** also exist as separate objects in the **Organizer** dialog (ribbon **File**, tab **Info**, button **Organizer**). If you want to create a new view, for example, a one-page *Executive Overview*, you can customize a field and call it *Executive Overview,* then create a table called *Executive Overview*, a filter called *Executive Overview* and a group called *Executive Overview*. When you apply the view, it will apply all of its *Executive Overview* components; if they have the same name, it is clear that they all belong together. This helps when you want to give the view to somebody else with the **Organizer** (see page 580); you can easily see which objects belong together.

To shuffle the names of certain objects to the top of the list, start them with an * (asterisk) or a number. You can also use an acronym to indicate that they are customized for your organization (at ProjectPro, for example, we use PP).

New views can be created using a *single view* or a *combination view*. A combination view applies two other views, one in the top pane and one in the bottom. Combination views are useful for analyzing projects, because what you select in the top view is shown in more detail in the bottom view.

You can print the row and column totals in the timescale of the **Task** or **Resource Usage** views by clicking ribbon **File,** tab **Print**, hyperlink **Page Setup**, tab **View**, ☑ **Print row totals for values within print date range** and ☑ **Print column totals**. The print date range is set in the ribbon **File**, tab **Print** backstage screen under **Dates ... To**.

Fields

MS Project has many extra fields in the project database that are called **Text1-Text30**, **Flag1-Flag20**, **Number1-Number20** or **Outline Code1-Outline Code10** among others. You can claim and rename these extra fields. You can create lists in them, called *lookup tables*, that display custom-made pick lists in the cell to facilitate data entry. In the **Text** fields you can create single-level lists, and in the **Outline Code** fields you can create multi-level lists (indented, tree-like lists). In the **Number** fields, you can enter Excel-like formulas so that they calculate values of interest to you, like performance indicators. You can design performance metrics specific to your organization. You can go one step further and choose graphical indicators (like red/yellow/green) to represent the calculated metrics and quickly reveal the health of any task or project as a whole. In the illustration, the **Number1** field was changed to traffic light indicators for the *Status* of the tasks. Executives tend to like traffic lights, because they point out the problem areas. There are many fields in MS Project that can be customized, but this does not mean you should go wild with it.

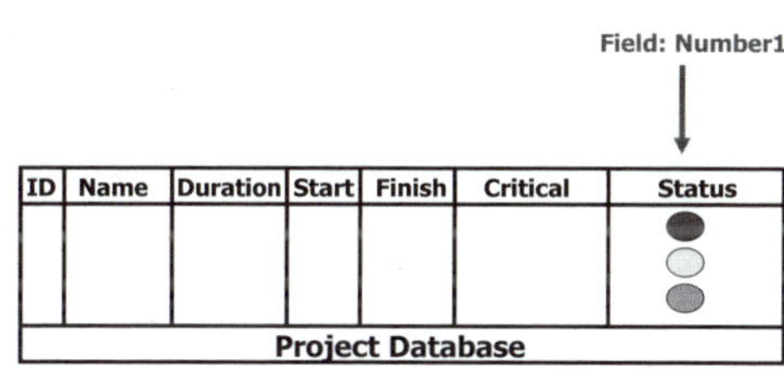

Pro

Project Server has many additional *enterprise fields* available for projects, tasks and resources. [67] In this book we focus on the non-enterprise fields in the MS Project application.

The steps to customize Project 2010 fields are:

1. Click ribbon **Project,**  ; the **Custom Fields** dialog appears:

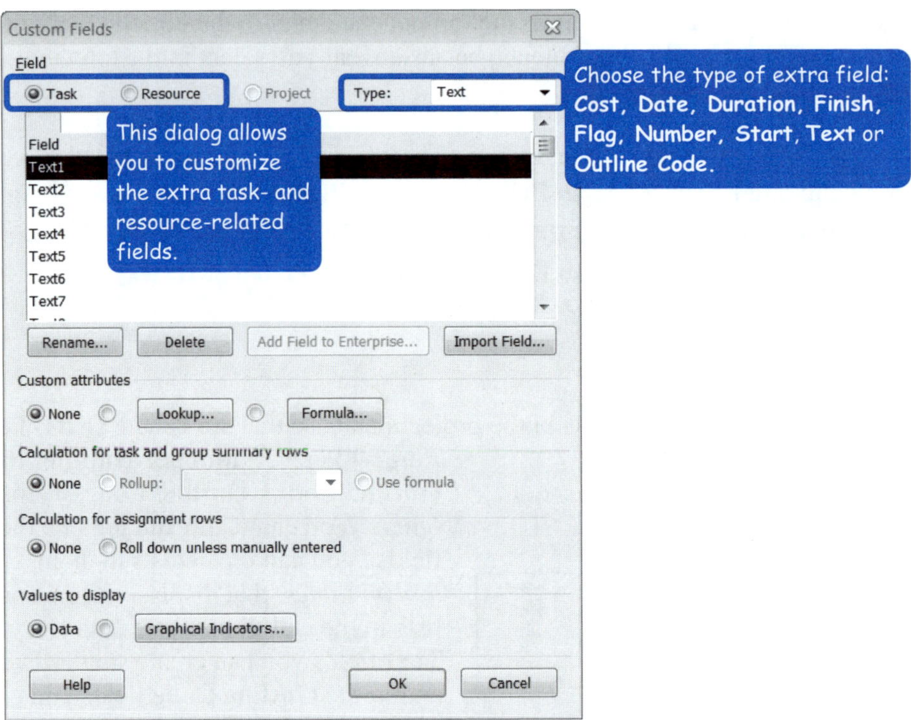

2. First, decide if you want to customize a ◉ **Task** or a ◉ **Resource** related field.

---

[67] We discuss customizing the *enterprise fields* and *enterprise lookup tables* in the *Configuring Microsoft Project Server* course. For more information, visit www.ProjectProCorp.com.

3. From the list **Type**, select the type of field. There are a total of 130 task-related fields and 130 resource-related fields to customize:
   - ◇ **Cost1 - Cost10** fields can capture extra dollar information like *committed cost*, which is useful if you have a budget from which to commit dollars. Project managers may need to track the dollars committed from their budgets in order to determine the dollars they can still spend. You could use a second cost field to calculate the amount of *available budget* – the total budget minus the committed amount. The accounting system is typically too slow in producing these numbers, because it becomes aware of expenditures only when invoices are received.
   - ◇ **Date1 - Date10** can be used for performance indicator formulas or for filters. If you enter the project status date in a task-related **Date** field with the formula **[Status Date]**, you can then develop filters that compare task start and finish dates to this status date. With a second **Date** field you can calculate the end date of a look-ahead window – the status date plus two months, for example. This would allow you to filter tasks that fall within the two-month look-ahead window, and the window will automatically move when you update the **Status Date**.
   - ◇ **Duration1 - Duration10** fields can be used to store durations of interim plans. You have to copy them yourself, since saving an *interim plan* (ribbon **Project,** button **Set baseline**, item **Set baseline,** ⦿ **Set interim plan**) only saves the start and finish dates.
   - ◇ **Finish1 - Finish10** fields are used to store finish dates in interim plans. We used Start1 - Start10 and Finish1 - Finish10 to display the three workload leveling scenarios in one Gantt Chart (see page 490).
   - ◇ **Flag1 - Flag20** fields are used to save *yes/no* type of information, for example, to indicate if a milestone is a major milestone in a large schedule, or if a resource is willing to travel.
   - ◇ **Number1 - Number20** fields are often used to enter formulas that calculate with input from other numeric fields. For example, you create a formula that calculates the time performance with an under/over percentage; this formula could look like: **Duration Variance / Baseline Duration** * 100%.
   - ◇ **Outline Code1 - Outline Code10** fields allow you to create breakdown structures other than the deliverable-oriented Work Breakdown Structure (WBS) which you entered in the **Task Name** column. First create the custom **Outline Code** with a multi-level lookup table and code all tasks. Then, apply a **Group** that sorts the records on that custom **Outline Code** field. See the section starting on page 569 for an example of how this would look. You can also use these fields to create coding structures for accounting or responsibility chart purposes.
   - ◇ **Start1 - Start10** and the corresponding Finish1 - Finish10 fields are used to store start and finish dates in interim plans. They can also be used to make a

10

schedule *impact analysis* when you receive project *change requests* from clients (see page 614).

◇ **Text1 - Text30** fields are used to store extra textual information, like the *performing organization* for tasks, or the *skills* or *department* for resources. Text fields can be enriched with a pick list, known as a **Lookup Table** in MS Project.

4. The list of fields is refreshed when you choose the **Type** of field. Select the field to customize in the list.

5. Click [Rename...] to give the field a more descriptive name that reveals its purpose. Click [OK]. Eventually you will see that the field is now listed under both names in the database. For example, if you changed the name *Cost1* to *Committed Budget*, you will see that the field is listed as *Cost1 (Committed Budget)* and *Committed Budget (Cost1)* in the **Insert Column** list among others.

6. Set **Custom attributes**:
   ◇ You can create a *pick list* or *lookup table* for the field. Click [Lookup...], or
   ◇ You can enter an Excel-like formula in the field. Click [Formula...].

7. Decide if you want MS Project to calculate values on summary tasks or on group headings by selecting your preferences under **Calculation for task and group summary rows**. We recommend using ⦿ **Use Formula** if you have a formula in the field.

8. Under **Values to display** you can click [Graphical Indicators...] to replace the calculated values with images by specifying a **Test** for the **Value(s)** you enter and choosing a cute **Image**. You can add tests and images for multiple ranges of values. Summary and detail tasks will use the same tests by default, but you can create separate tests, values and images for:
   ◇ **Nonsummary rows** ("*nonsummary*" is Microsoft's addition to the English vocabulary)
   ◇ **Summary rows**, if you clear the option:
   ☑ **Summary rows inherit criteria from nonsummary rows**
   ◇ **Project summary**, if you clear the option:
   ☑ **Project summary inherits criteria from summary rows**

9. Click [OK] – the field is now customized. You can display it by right-clicking on any column heading and selecting **Insert Column**.

MS Project has some unique functions that can be very useful when creating formulas. For example, the **ProjDateDiff** function can give you the number of business days between two dates and even base it on a *base calendar* of your choice. These functions (which use business days) are better than using your own arithmetic, like

[Baseline Finish] – [Finish], since the latter produces calendar days instead of business days. This function is also better than the **DateDiff** function you may know from Excel for the same reason. Most data in MS Project are expressed in business days.

When you develop formulas, you have to stay within the type of data that corresponds to the **Type** of field you choose to customize (i.e., you can neither put letters in number fields, nor put numbers in flag fields).

You can also rename columns in the field **Title** of the **Field Settings** dialog (right-click a column heading and select **Field Settings**). If you do this, MS Project will only rename the field in the active table, since the column titles are stored in the table object instead of in the database. Alternatively, using **Custom Fields** (ribbon **Project**) renames the field in the entire database. This process also lists the field under its old and new name(s) in every column pick list in every view. Obviously, the latter is a better practice.

There are also **Enterprise fields** available for customization by the Project Server administrator . Enterprise fields are fields reserved for standardization across all projects in the entire enterprise, or by *department* (new in Project 2010). The use of enterprise fields is typically determined centrally by the *Project Server administrators*, since they are a means of standardizing data capture and performance evaluation across the enterprise. Organizations usually standardize on project performance reports. When we discuss reporting using Project Server, we will elaborate further (see page 582).

Because the number of possibilities for customizing fields is almost limitless, a detailed discussion is beyond the scope of this book, which is meant for project managers, not Project Server administrators.[68]

10

Tables

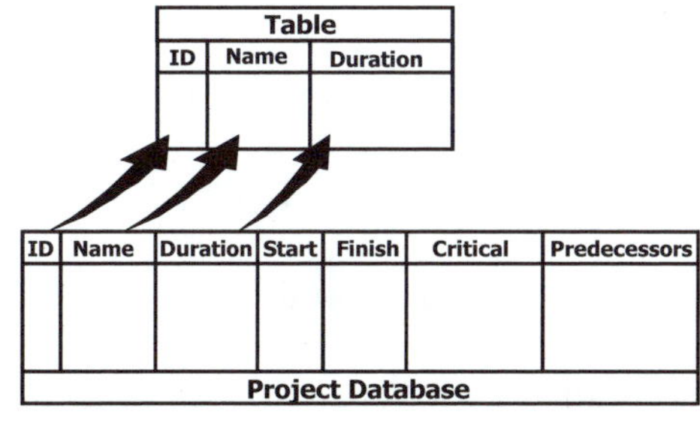

A *table* is a selection of fields from the project database, including their order of display. A table in MS Project is what one would call a *query* in a relational database. You can display your customized fields in the table. A table does not contain project data; it is only a layout of columns.

[68] We discuss them in great detail in the *Configuring Microsoft Project Server* course, visit www.ProjectProCorp.com for a course outline.

MS Project differs from other applications in this sense, because tables in MS Word or MS Excel do contain data. In the illustration, the table displays only the fields *ID, Name* and *Duration* out of all the fields present in the MS Project database.

Using an Existing Table

1. Make sure you are in one of the table views; a table view has a spreadsheet with columns and rows, like the *Gantt Chart* and *Resource Sheet*. The *Network Diagram* and the *Resource Graph* do not use tables. There are also views that are fill-in forms such as the *Task Form* view; forms do not use tables either.
2. Click ribbon **View,** Tables and select the table you want to apply. The currently displayed table (if listed) has a check mark in front of it.
   OR
   Right-click on the select-all area where the column headings intersect with the row headings in the spreadsheet. A popup menu appears with the same pick list, and you can click the table you wish to apply.
3. The layout of columns is now replaced by a new layout as defined in the table object you applied.

You can rearrange the columns very quickly (provided the option in ribbon **File**, Options, tab **Advanced**, section **Edit**, option ☑ **Allow cell drag and drop** is selected). Click on a column heading and release the mouse. As soon as you see the mouse pointer, drag the column to its new place.

Some worthwhile tables that ship with MS Project are:

- **Cost** table contains the **Fixed Cost** fields that are handy for when you have subcontracts for certain *deliverables*.
- **Schedule** table contains all the early and late date fields related to the *Critical Path Method***.**
- **Summary** table brings together date, duration, cost and effort data in one table. Most other tables have either cost or schedule data.
- **Tracking** table will be used when we start updating the schedule (see page 601).
- **Work** table is useful when you track the work (effort) completed, rather than the task duration completed.
- **Export** table that allows you to export all fields to MS Excel or other applications.

There are more tables available if you click ribbon **View**, button **Tables**, item **More Tables…**. Some extra ones in this list are:

- **Baseline** table shows all baseline fields.
- **Constraint Dates** table shows the fields **Constraint Type** and **Constraint Date**, which allow you to view any constraints you might have in your schedule.
- **Earned Value** table if you use *Earned Value Management* as your *performance measurement* system.

Designing a New Table

The **Entry** table is shared between the Gantt Chart and the Tracking Gantt view. Instead of constantly changing this **Entry** table in the Gantt Chart view and then back again in the Tracking Gantt view for custom reports, there are advantages to creating a separate table object for each view so you will not have to reinvent the wheel every time.

1. Click ribbon **View**, Tables, **More Tables…**; the **More Tables** dialog appears:

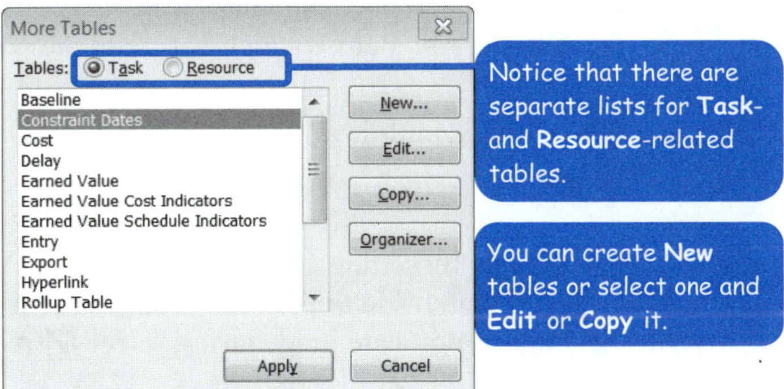

2. To list the task tables, select ◉ **Task**; for resource tables select ◉ **Resource**.
3. Select the table in the **Tables** list that is closest to what you want, and click Copy... to create a duplicate for customization.

10

4. The **Table Definition** dialog appears:

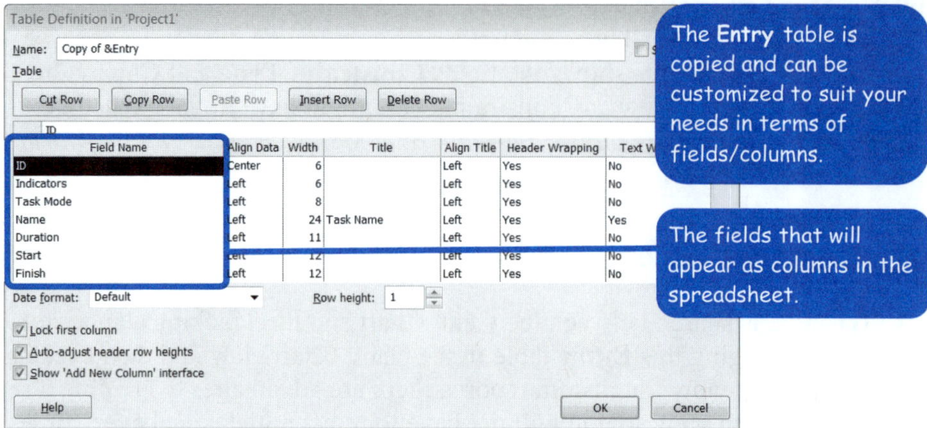

5. In the **Name** box, type a new name for the table.

6. If you want to list the new table in the ribbon, check ☑ **Show in menu** in the top right.

7. To delete a field in the table, click the row to delete and click Delete Row.
   To insert a new field in the table, click the row before which you want the new field to appear and click Insert Row.
   To replace a field, click on its field name; a pull-down list button appears. Display the list and select the new field.

8. Text wrap:
   - ◇ Wrap the text in each column heading by setting **Header Wrapping** to **Yes**
   - 2010 ◇ Wrap the text in each cell of the column by setting **Text Wrapping** to **Yes**; if you also want the row heights to accommodate long entries, select ☑ **Auto-adjust header row heights**.

9. If you want to lock the first field, check ☑ **Lock first column**. There are advantages to having a locked first column; it allows you to select an entire task or resource record in the database, plus the locked title will not scroll off the screen. The data cannot be edited in the locked column, which is just fine for ID numbers, which are maintained by MS Project anyway.

10. Click OK – you are now back in the **More Tables** dialog.

11. Click Apply – the fields you chose are now displayed.

Filters

A *filter* displays records from the project database that meet the criteria that you set and hides the rest. You can filter tasks or resources. MS Project allows you to create criteria that look in any field in the database. The filter is applied to data from the project database; it does not contain the data. An MS Project filter works the same as a selection *query* in a relational database. In the illustration, the tasks with a duration greater than 5 days have been filtered from the database, which renders only two records from the database.

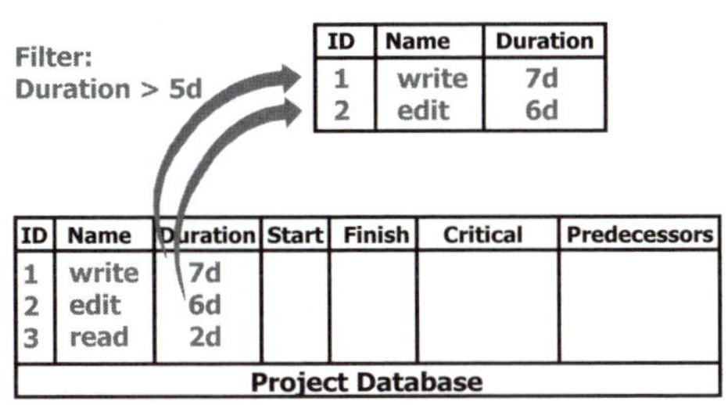

A filter does not display any detail tasks that are collapsed and are invisible under their summary task, even if they meet the filter criteria. If you find that a filter does not display all the tasks you expected, they were probably collapsed under their summary. Expand all summary tasks first by clicking the **View** ribbon, button **Outline** and selecting **All Subtasks**, before applying a filter. As you can see, collapsing and filtering interfere with each other.

To get rid of a filter in a view, press [F3] or reapply the **[No filter]** "filter" or click **Clear Filter**.

Applying an Existing Filter

1. Click ribbon **View**, and click the list button [▾] of [Filter: [No Filter] ▾] – a list of filters appears.
2. Select a filter from the list. Only the records that meet the criteria in the filter definition are now displayed. If you want to see the definition of the filter, click the list button [▾] of [Filter: [No Filter] ▾] again, and select **More Filters...**, select a filter from the list and click [Edit...].

There are some very useful filters included with MS Project out-of-the-box such as these task filters:

- **Critical** displays all tasks that drive your project end date. Note that the word "*critical*" does not necessarily imply that the task is important. This filter looks for **Yes** in the calculated field **Critical**.

- **Date Range...** displays tasks that fall in whole or in part within the period you indicate. This allows you to focus on the tasks in the coming weeks.
- **Milestones** displays all important events in your schedule (e.g., the delivery dates for the deliverables in your project). It looks for **Yes** in the calculated field **Milestone**.
- **Slipping Tasks** displays all tasks that are forecasted to finish later than their baseline.
- **Summary Tasks** displays all summary tasks and gives you a high-level view of the project. It looks for **Yes** in the calculated field **Summary**.
- **Using Resource...** displays tasks assigned to a resource of your choice. This allows you to create simple to-do lists. It looks for tasks that contain the name of the resource that you chose in the **Resource Names** field. For some reason this filter cannot be edited or copied.
- **Using Resource in Date Range...** displays tasks assigned to a resource of your choice and within a date range of your choice. This filter can be edited and copied!
- **Work Overbudget** displays tasks that have actual effort exceeding the approved amount of (baseline) effort.

Some useful resource-related filters that you can use in any resource views are:

- **Overallocated Resources** displays resources with more work than their availability. Realize, however, that it will display resources that may only have an overallocation during one hour in the project. It normally displays more resources than you need to worry about. It looks for resources with **Yes** in the calculated field **Overallocated**.
- **Slipping Assignments**, when applied in the Resource Usage view, displays those resources with assignments that are late.

Just as with tables, there are advantages to creating a new filter object for each reporting need, so that you will not have to change or recreate your filter every time.

Designing a New Filter

1. Click the **View** Ribbon

2. Click the list button ▾ of Filter: [No Filter], and select **More Filters…** – the **More Filters** dialog appears:

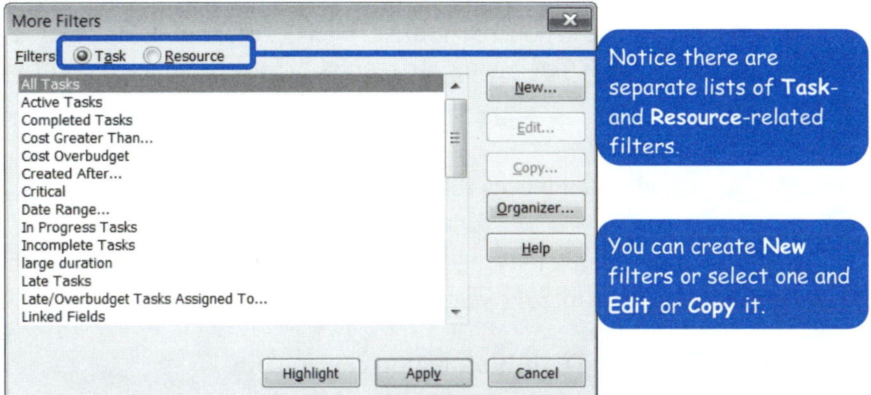

3. Select ◉ **Task** to see a list of task-related filters or ◉ **Resource** for resource-related filters.

4. Click on a filter that is close to what you want and click Copy... – this will keep the original intact. The **Filter Definition** dialog appears:

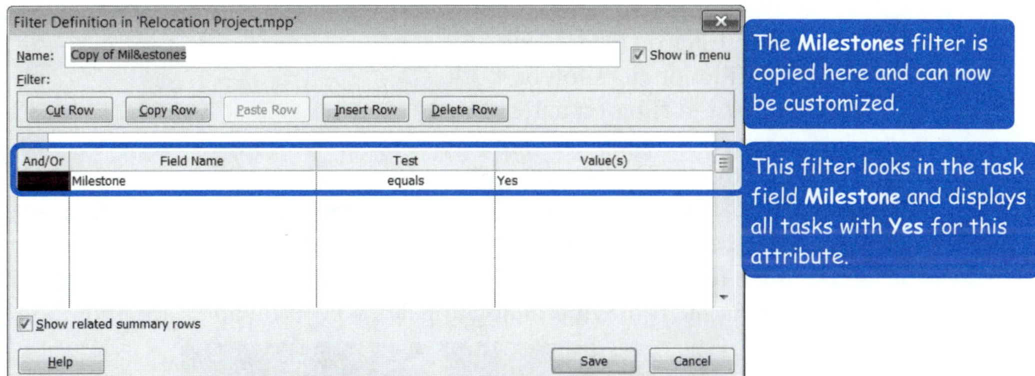

10

5. Enter a name for the filter; keep it the same as the name of the table you created.

6. To list the new filter in the ribbon, check ☑ **Show in menu**.

7. Change the filter definition:
   In the column **Field Name,** select the field from which to filter data. Click in an empty cell and a list button appears. Display the list and select the field on which to filter.
   In the column **Test**, select the type of comparison from the list.

Enter the **Value(s)**; for an explanation of your many options in this field, see after this procedure.

8. You can add more conditions by adding **And** or **Or** in the **And/Or** field on the second line and entering the second condition. Please note that using **And** results in fewer displayed records, whereas using **Or** results in more displayed records.

9. Click Save.

10. Click Apply – only the records that meet the filter condition are displayed.
    or
    click Highlight – the records that meet the filter condition are colored with a yellow background color, while the rest are displayed in the original color.

The **Value(s)** field in the **Filter Definition** dialog can contain:

- Other field names that you select from the list
  This allows you to make comparisons between fields and, for example, display all tasks that slipped. The definition of such a filter would be: *Finish is greater than [Baseline Finish]*. Notice that in the field **Value**, field names are enclosed in square brackets. This is to distinguish field names from literal values that you can enter.
- Literal values that you type in, for example:
  - *Yes* to filter on a flag field
  - *$10,000* to filter on a cost field
  - *5 days* to filter on duration or work
  - *Jan 15, 2012* to filter on dates
- Prompts for the user to enter a value
  This creates a totally customized and interactive filter. You have to enter the prompt in the syntax: "<text of the prompt>"? where <text of the prompt> is the question to display to the user. An example is *"Enter the minimum duration"?*. Notice that you need to put the text between quotation marks and append the question mark at the end. As a result, the following dialog appears when you apply the filter:

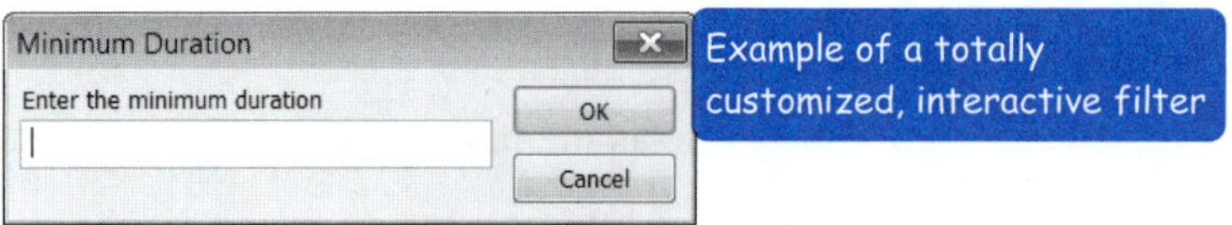

Enter the value, click OK and the desired records are displayed.

Groups

Groups allow you to categorize all tasks (or resources) on the values in a field. When you apply a grouping to the task list, the original structure of the WBS will be temporarily hidden and the new breakdown structure (grouping) will be displayed. In the illustration you can see that the tasks are categorized on the field *Critical* in two groups of *Yes* and *No*. The task-related field *Critical* is a calculated yes/no field that indicates whether or not a task is critical. When you apply [**No Group**], the grouping will disappear, and the *Work Breakdown Structure* will re-appear.

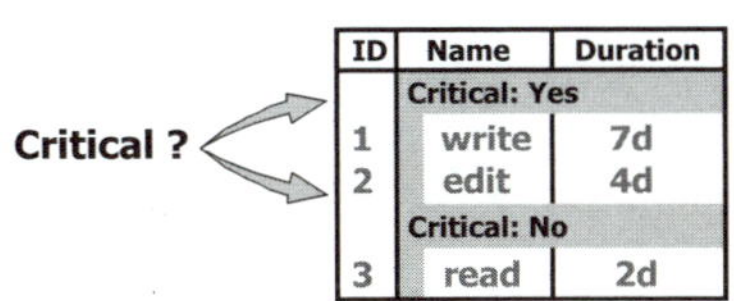

ID	Name	Duration	Start	Finish	Critical	Predecessors
1	write	7d			Yes	
2	edit	4d			Yes	
3	read	2d			No	
Project Database						

You can create alternative breakdown structures by grouping on one field or multiple fields. Grouping on multiple fields will create a multi-level breakdown structure. You can even create multi-level breakdown structures that are an alternative to the WBS using just one special field, an outline code field (e.g., **Outline Code1**). You code all tasks with their outline levels of the new breakdown, similar to what you will find in the **WBS** and **Outline level** field for the WBS grouping.

For example, your finance department may request a breakdown of tasks by *accounting codes* for *Team member (code 1.1)*, *Manager (code 1.2)* and *Subcontractors (code 1.3)*: [69]

Accounting Code	Task Name	Baseline Cost	Actual Cost	Remaining Cost	Cost	Cost Variance
1	⊟ **Labor Cost**	**$129,125.00**	**$12,062.50**	**$118,662.50**	**$130,725.00**	**$1,600.00**
1.1	⊟ **team member (employee)**	**$35,093.75**	**$8,518.75**	**$28,175.00**	**$36,693.75**	**$1,600.00**
1.1	research staff requirements	$1,125.00	$2,000.00	$0.00	$2,000.00	$875.00
1.1	summarize requirements	$525.00	$525.00	$0.00	$525.00	$0.00
1.1	select the realtor	$1,125.00	$1,300.00	$0.00	$1,300.00	$175.00
1.1	meet to select the location	$2,175.00	$2,500.00	$0.00	$2,500.00	$325.00
1.1	legal review	$281.25	$281.25	$0.00	$281.25	$0.00
1.1	select the contractor	$1,125.00	$1,350.00	$0.00	$1,350.00	$225.00
1.1	revise the schedule	$562.50	$0.00	$562.50	$562.50	$0.00
1.1	contractor contracted	$0.00	$0.00	$0.00	$0.00	$0.00
1.1	select mover	$1,125.00	$562.50	$562.50	$1,125.00	$0.00
1.1	pack	$13,925.00	$0.00	$13,925.00	$13,925.00	$0.00
1.1	unpack	$13,125.00	$0.00	$13,125.00	$13,125.00	$0.00
1.2	⊟ **Manager (overhead)**	**$4,106.25**	**$3,543.75**	**$562.50**	**$4,106.25**	**$0.00**
1.2	visit the sites	$1,312.50	$1,312.50	$0.00		
1.2	evaluate the sites	$1,181.25	$1,181.25	$0.00		
1.2	location selected	$0.00	$0.00	$0.00		
1.2	meet to discuss contract	$1,050.00	$1,050.00	$0.00		
1.2	negotiate the contract	$562.50	$0.00	$562.50	$562.50	$0.00
1.2	facility remodeled	$0.00	$0.00	$0.00	$0.00	$0.00
1.2	new location opened	$0.00	$0.00	$0.00	$0.00	$0.00
1.3	⊟ **subcontractor (external)**	**$89,925.00**	**$0.00**	**$89,925.00**	**$89,925.00**	**$0.00**
1.3	relocate walls	$22,500.00	$0.00	$22,500.00	$22,500.00	$0.00
1.3	install electric wiring	$5,625.00	$0.00	$5,625.00	$5,625.00	$0.00
1.3	paint	$1,800.00	$0.00	$1,800.00	$1,800.00	$0.00
1.3		$0.00	$0.00	$0.00	$0.00	$0.00
1.3		$9,000.00	$0.00	$9,000.00	$9,000.00	$0.00
1.3		$33,750.00	$0.00	$33,750.00	$33,750.00	$0.00
1.3		$13,500.00	$0.00	$13,500.00	$13,500.00	$0.00
1.3		$3,750.00	$0.00	$3,750.00	$3,750.00	$0.00

[69] This screenshot was created using the *Relocation Project* exercise files. We discuss custom lookup tables in the *Configuring Microsoft Project Server* course, see www.ProjectProCorp.com.

As you can see in the screenshot, the original WBS is entirely hidden and all detail task records are placed into a new breakdown structure with new group headings (comparable to *summary tasks* in a WBS).

The grouping feature even calculates new totals on the group headings, similar to the summary tasks, which makes it a very useful feature.

This grouping feature almost gives MS Project the power of a relational database. An example of a grouping of resources is shown in the following screenshot. You can try to reproduce this screenshot by doing the exercise on page 598:

	Resource Name	Position	Function	Cost
	⊟ Function: employee			**$28,500.00**
3	John Falgon	employee representative	employee	$675.00
4	Nancy Hilcrest	planner	employee	$1,575.00
8	the employees	employees	employee	$26,250.00
	⊟ Function: external			**$90,825.00**
6	Pierre Roach	lawyer	external	$281.25
7	the contractor	contractor	external	$52,650.00
9	the LAN consultants	LAN consultants	external	$33,750.00
10	the movers	movers	external	$3,750.00
11	the realtor	realtor	external	$393.75
	⊟ Function: manager			**$9,000.00**
2	Eric Uyttewaal	project manager	manager	$7,875.00
5	Nelson Salin	CEO	manager	$1,125.00
	⊟ Function: material			**$800.00**
1	boxes		material	$800.00

The resources are grouped by **Function** (resource-related field).

Group totals provide total expenses per resource category.

10

Applying an Existing Grouping

1. Click ribbon **View** and click the list button ▾ of Group by: [No Group] ▾ – a drop-down menu appears.
2. Select a grouping from the list; MS Project categorizes the task or resource records and displays them within their group headings.

Just as with tables and filters, there are advantages to creating a new group object for each reporting need, so you will not have to recreate your group every time.

Some worthwhile out-of-the-box *Groups* that are available are:

- **Active v. Inactive**, which separates the *active tasks* from the tasks marked as inactive.
- **Complete and Incomplete Tasks**, which separates the past tasks from future tasks.

- **Critical**, which separates the critical tasks from noncritical ones.
- **Milestones:** many people want the milestones at the top of the list, and this grouping does that for you in two clicks. If you need more sophistication, for example, only hand-picked milestones, you will have to mark them in one of the extra **Flag** fields and develop a custom filter, see page 595 for more.

Designing a New Grouping

1. Click ribbon **View**, click the list button [▾] of [Group by: [No Group] ▾] and select **More Groups** – the **More Groups** dialog appears:

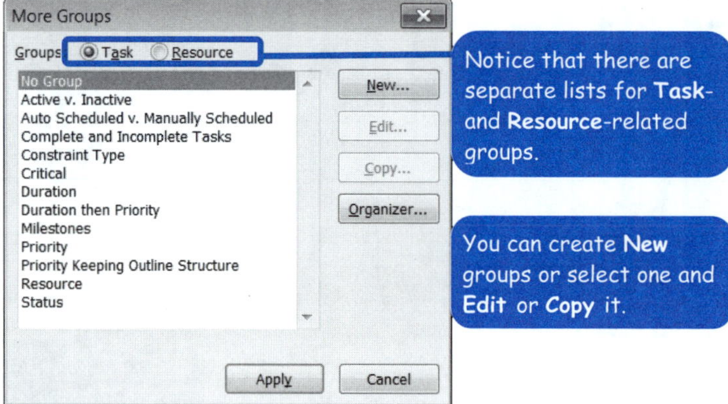

2. Select ◉ **Task** to see a list of task-related groupings or ◉ **Resource** for resource-related groupings.

3. Click on a group that is close to what you want and click [Copy...] – this will keep the original intact. The **Group Definition** dialog appears:

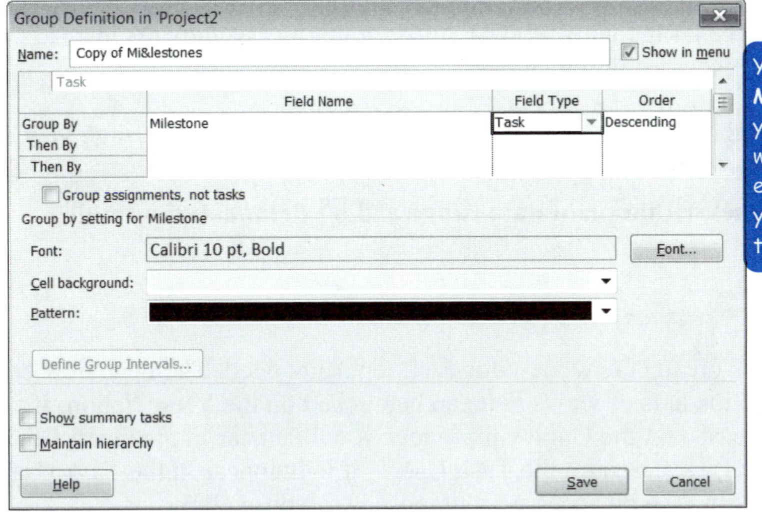

You can group the **Milestones** at the top of your task list. Executives will be able to quickly establish the status of your project by looking at the group of milestones.

4. Enter a name for the group; keep it the same as the name of the table you created.

5. To list the new group in the ribbon, check ☑ **Show in menu** in the top right.

6. Change the group definition:
   Under **Field Name**, select the field by which to group; click in an empty cell and a list button appears. Select the fields by which to group from the list.
   Select **Descending** or **Ascending** from the list under **Order**.
   In either the Task Usage or the Resource Usage view, you can select ☑ **Group assignments, not tasks** to categorize the assignments; see remarks below these steps.
   If you choose a field that contains numbers, it is important to select the intervals as well by clicking [Define Group Intervals...]. If you skip this, MS Project will group on each value in the field, which is useless most of the times.

7. Click [Save] – you are now back in the **More Groups** dialog.

8. Click [Apply] – the records are now sorted under their respective group headings.

In the Task Usage or Resource usage views, assignments are shown and you can group on them. If you group assignments instead of tasks in the Task Usage view, the tasks will disappear temporarily. Instead of grouping on the task-related **Cost** field, for example, you can group the *assignments* on their **Cost** instead. In the **Group Definition**

dialog, check ☑ **Group assignments, not tasks** – this enables the list under **Field Type**. From this list, select **Assignment** instead of **Task**. The grouping will now use the assignment-related rows instead of the task-related rows and will hide the task-related rows. In the Resource Usage view, you can also group the assignments instead of resources, and the resources will be hidden.

You can also print the row and column totals in the timescale of the **Usage** views by clicking ribbon **File,** tab **Print**, hyperlink **Page Setup**, tab **View**, and selecting ☑ **Print row totals for values within print date range** and ☑ **Print column totals**.

Views

We recommend you create a new view for each reporting need. The new view can be added as an item to the lists of views that can be clicked on the **View** ribbon; if you create a new view based on the Gantt Chart view, it will appear in the Gantt Chart list. If you create a new view based on the Task Usage, it will appear in the Task Usage list. Each custom view can then be accessed with only two mouse clicks.

A view object contains:

- A reference to the table object it uses, and the table can contain custom field objects
- A reference to the filter object it applies
- A reference to the group object that categorizes all filtered records
- Any drawing objects created with the drawing tools on the **Format** ribbon
- The **Page Setup** settings
- Any formats applied through the **Format** ribbon
- The sorting order applied via ribbon **View**, button **Sort**

The following illustration depicts this:

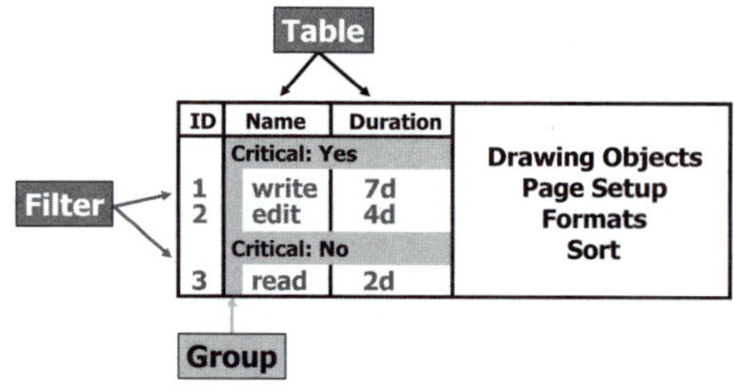

Perhaps you noticed that the **Format** ribbon shows different buttons in each view; for instance, the Calendar view provides different options than the Gantt Chart view. Even the **Page Setup** dialog contains different options for each view. The fact that this ribbon and dialog change when you switch views can be confusing to occasional users of MS Project. It also makes the MS Project interface very rich and large. The context-sensitive Format ribbon provides options that are specific to each view, and the settings are stored in the view object itself. Thanks to this, each view provides a consistent format of the data; its look persists.

Creating a New View

1. Click ribbon **View, More Views…** – the **More Views** dialog appears:

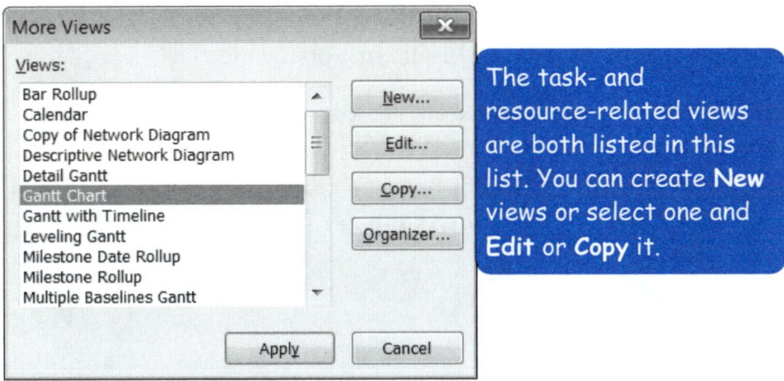

2. Choose the view that is closest to what you want and click [Copy...].
   OR
   Click [New...] – the **Define New View** dialog appears, which allows you to choose between creating a ◉ **Single view** or a ◉ **Combination view**.
   A combination view consists of two views: a top view and a bottom view. We will focus on a single view in the rest of the steps. Click [OK].
3. The **View Definition** dialog appears:

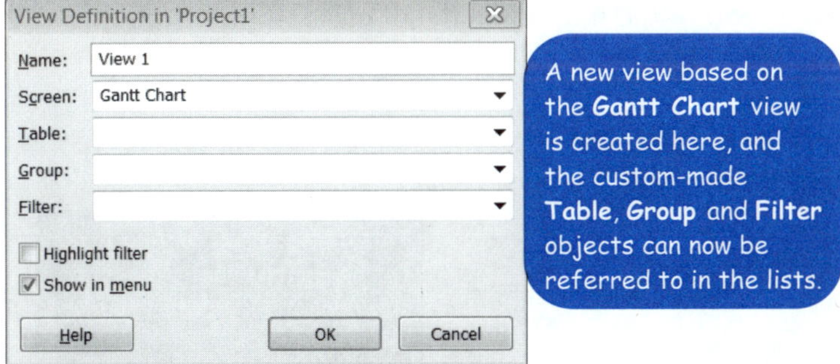

4. Notice under **Screen** you can see on which type of view you based your new view. If you clicked [New...] in step 2, you can still change this, but if you copied a view, you cannot change it.
5. Fill in the name of the new view and select the **Table**, the **Group** and the **Filter** from the lists. It helps if all the components of the view have the same name, as we

10

recommended before; with identical names, it is obvious they belong together. You can still return to the definition dialogs for table, group and filter to rename them.

6. If you want this view to show in the ribbon, check ☑ **Show in menu**; the view will be available with only two mouse clicks.
7. Click [OK] – you are now back in the **More Views** dialog.
8. Click [Apply] – the view appears and, on the left-hand side of your screen, you can read the name of the current view displayed in vertical text.
9.  After switching to another view, you can re-apply the new view by clicking the **View** ribbon and clicking on the list button of the view on which you based this view (see step 2 and 4); for example, if you based the new view on the **Gantt Chart** view, you will find the new view in the **Gantt Chart** list that you can display by clicking the bottom part of .

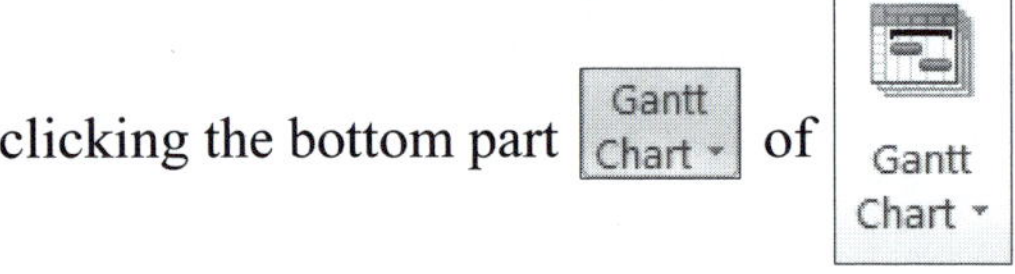

Sort the Records

When customizing the sort order, make sure you are in a *task view* to sort tasks and in a *resource view* to sort resources. In the steps that follow, we will explain sorting tasks.

Click ribbon **View** and find its section **Data**. Click button **Sort** and pick one of the listed sort orders; the sort will be applied immediately. However, you will find that it sorts the summary task families instead of the individual detail tasks. If you want to sort the individual detail tasks, follow the OR steps below.

OR

1. Click ribbon **View**, button **Sort, Sort by...** – the **Sort** dialog appears:

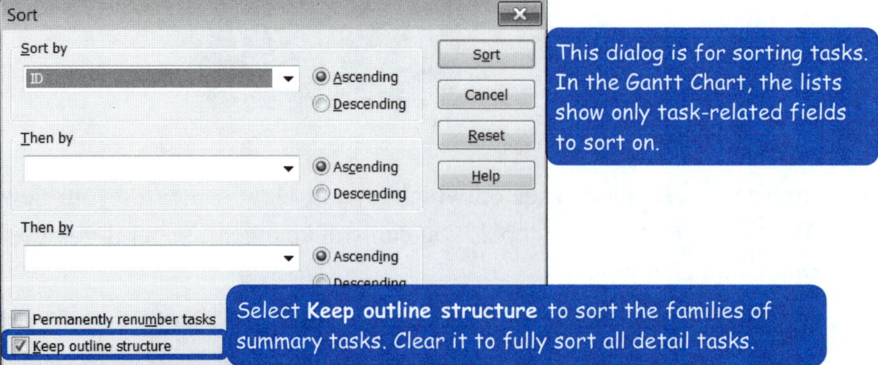

2. Select the first sort order key from the **Sort by** list; if you think you will need a second sort key to break any ties, select it from the list **Then by**.

3. Be careful to never select ☐ **Permanently renumber tasks**; this is the quickest way to wreck the structure of your WBS entirely.

4. An important choice is whether you want to ☐ **Keep outline structure**. If you do, MS Project will only sort the summary tasks that will take their subtasks with them. If you do not keep the outline structure, MS Project will do a complete and continuous sort of all detail task line items, ignoring the WBS.

5. Click [Sort] and the sort will be applied.

6. To reset the sort order (if you did not permanently renumber), simply resort by ID number by clicking ribbon **View**, button **Sort, By ID**.
   OR

   If you did accidentally renumber, click **Undo** on the Quick Access Toolbar to get your WBS back. (Thank you, Bill Gates, for multiple levels of undo in MS Project!)

The sort order is stored in the view object in which you applied the sort. Each view can have a different sort order.

Apply Any Formats

MS Project offers many options on the **Format** ribbon to improve the appearance of the output. Any change you make through the Format ribbon will be stored in the view object that you have on the screen at the time.

10

The Format ribbon changes when you apply another view. For example, when you are in a view without columns (e.g., Network Diagram), you will not see a button titled **Insert Column**. When you realize that each view has its own Format ribbon, you understand that MS Project has many more features than it first appears to have.

We reviewed the different format options when we discussed printing each view:

- Printing the Gantt Chart was discussed starting on page 277.
- Printing the Tracking Gantt view will be discussed on page 672.

The important choices are summarized here:

- What text formats do you want in Gantt views?

  You could customize the text for individual tasks by right-clicking on the task and selecting the font from the mini toolbar that pops up. We recommend you instead

apply a style to each type of task by clicking ribbon **Format**, button **Text Styles**. Use the text styles first before overriding the styles for single tasks.

- What bar formats do you want in Gantt views?
  You could format an individual bar by right-clicking on the task bar and selecting **Format Bar…**. Again, we recommend you use the **Bar Styles** dialog (ribbon **Format**, button **Format**, item **Bar Styles**) first and then format some individual bars, if needed.
- Which date formats do you want in any view?
  First of all, choose the default date format for all date fields in MS Project by clicking ribbon **File,** [Options], tab **General**, field **Date Format**.
  If you want to change the date order (e.g., from mmddyy to ddmmyy) in Windows 7, click the start menu, **Control Panel, Clock Language and Region, Region and Language**.
  To override the date format in the spreadsheet of a task-related view, click ribbon **View**, button **Tables, More Tables…**, click [Edit...] and select the format you want from the **Date Format** list at the bottom.
  To override the default date format in the timescale of a Gantt view when you display dates next to the task bars, click ribbon **Format**, button **Layout** and select the date format from the list **Date Format**.
- Do you want to show dependencies in a Gantt view?
  Make your choice using the ribbon **Format**, button **Layout**, under **Links**. You can also choose between straight and hooked arrows.
- What time-phased fields do you want to show in the timescale of the **Task Usage** and **Resource Usage** views? You can select fields other than the default **Work** field. Click ribbon **Format** and in the **Details** section you will find several check boxes or click **Add Details** for a complete list; better yet, right-click in the timescale and a menu will pop up that allows you to quickly pick a field or select **Detail Styles** for the complete list.

Choose the Page Setup Settings

MS Project stores the page setup settings in the view object that you have on the screen when you click to the page setup dialog. This allows you to have different page setup choices for each view you print regularly. If you create a separate view for each reporting need as we suggest, it will always come out the same.

You can access the page setup dialog by clicking ribbon **File,** tab **Print**, hyperlink **Page Setup** – the **Page setup** dialog appears:

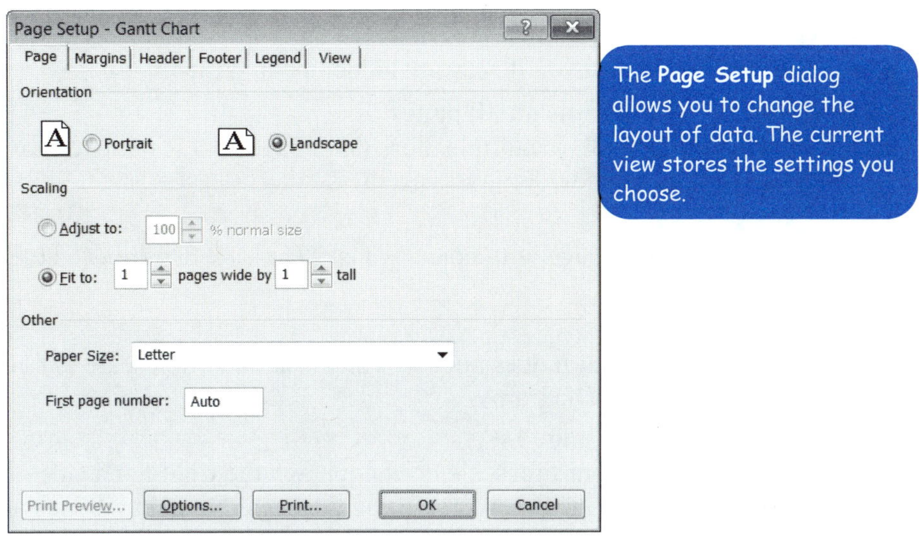

We will only summarize the important options in the **Page Setup** dialog, since we discussed many of them in previous chapters:

- **Page** tab
  - **Orientation**: when you print views with a timescale, it is often best to change from ⦿ **Portrait** to ⦿ **Landscape**. This will allow you to keep the entire timescale on one page and prevent you from having to tape pages together.
  - The **Scaling** option will shrink or enlarge the print image, but it is only available if your printer can handle scaling; the range for **Adjust to** is from 10% to 500%. Instead of guessing the scaling percentage, you may as well use the **Fit to** option and check how it comes out in print preview.
- **Header, Footer, Legend** tab

  Choose the position first; click tab **Left, Center** or **Right**. You can enter in any header text, or better, use the lists **General** or **Project Fields** at the bottom of the dialog to select standard phrases. Select the item from the list and then click [Add] – this will add a cryptic code, like *&[View]* for the **View Name**, in the header, footer or legend box. The items in the **General** list refer to entries you made in the ribbon **File**, tab **Info**, list **Project Information**, item **Advanced Properties** dialog. If you make changes in that dialog, all headers of all views will be updated automatically.

  The font size of a header is small by default. To increase it, select the text of the cryptic codes by dragging and clicking [A] – the **Font** dialog appears, wherein you can choose the font, style and size. When done, click [OK].

- **View** tab
  The important options for *task views* (except the Calendar task view, which has its own set of options) are:
  - ◇ ☐ **Print all sheet columns**
    This will print all columns, even if they are hidden behind the timescale.
  - ◇ ☐ **Print first** 3 **columns on all pages**
    This option will help you align multiple, horizontal pages but is not necessary if your report is only one page wide.
  - ◇ ☑ **Print Notes**
    This will create a separate page with notes by task. The task IDs are used to relate the notes to the tasks.
  - ◇ ☑ **Print blank pages**
    This will print a page even if it does not show any task bars (timescale of Gantt Charts) or nodes (Network Diagram).
  - ◇ ☑ **Fit timescale to end of page**
    This is only useful when your timescale does not reach the right-hand side of the page. This option stretches the timescale, filling the page. Note that it does not shrink the timescale; it only stretches.
  - ◇ Available in Task Usage or Resource Usage views only:
    ☑ **Print row totals for values within print date range**
    ☑ **Print column totals**
    These options allow you to add the row totals to the timescale of the usage views on the right-hand side and column totals at the bottom by day, by week or by month, depending on the current time unit.

Copying Views Between Projects

Once you have changed an existing view or created a new view object and formatted it, you can use it in all your other projects by putting it in your *Global.MPT* file. You can even share it with other people by giving them an MPP file containing the view object and all its components: fields, table, filter and group objects.

1. Open the schedule that contains the object, and open the schedule into which you want to copy the object. You do not need to open the Global.MPT, as it is always open when MS Project is running.

2. Click ribbon **File**, tab **Info**, button **Organizer…** – the **Organizer** dialog appears:

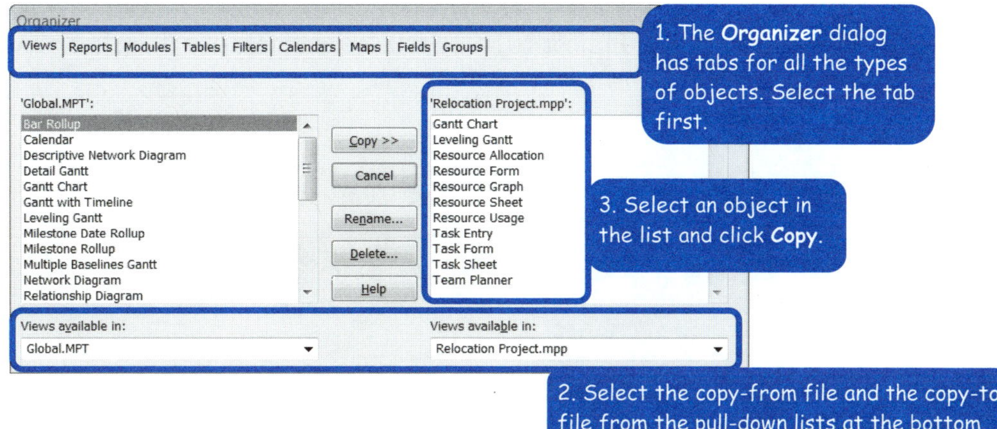

3. Activate the tab **Views** as the type of object to copy.
4. In the list **Views available in** on the left at the bottom of the dialog, select the schedule from which to copy the object; in a similar list on the right, select the schedule to which to copy.
5. Then select the view object to copy and click Copy >>.
6. Click the tab **Fields** and copy the fields the view uses in its table.
7. Click the tab **Tables** and copy the table that the view uses.
8. Click the tab **Filters** and copy the filter object that the view uses.
9. Click the tab **Groups** and copy the group object that the view uses.
10. Click Close when done or Cancel.

It is much easier to see which objects are the components of one view if they all have the same name. That is why we recommend naming them the same.

The organizer allows you to copy objects into the *Global.MPT* file. Any objects you put into this global template are visible in all of your projects, unless there is already an object in the project schedule that has the same name. We recommend, therefore, that you give new objects unique names if you want to see them in any schedule to which you copy them.

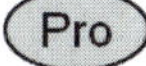

If you use Project Server, the Project Server administrator can easily make successful views available to every project manager by creating *enterprise views*. Ask your administrator to add them to the *Enterprise Global*.

Timeline View

The *Timeline view* is new in Project 2010. Here is an example of a Timeline view:

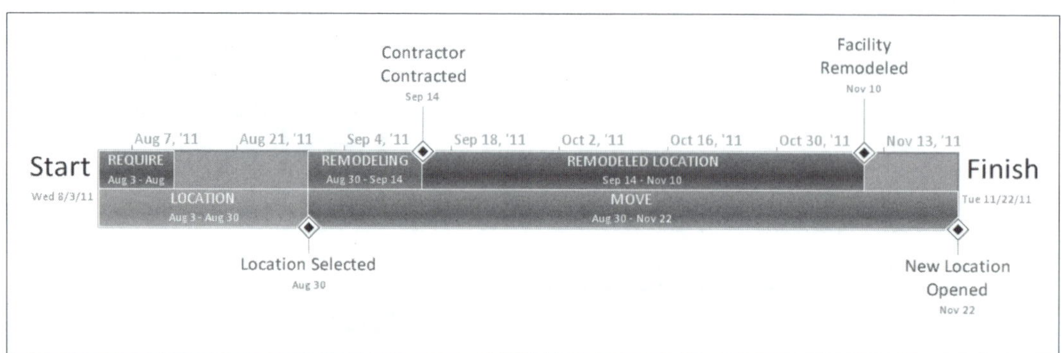

You can see that the deliverables appear as bars inside the big timeline bar and the milestones as callouts. In order to create a Timeline view, we recommend the following process:

1. Switch to the Gantt chart and display the Timeline view by clicking the **View** ribbon, finding its **Split View** section and selecting ☑ Timeline.
2. Identify the milestones to display on the timeline by applying the out-of-the-box **Milestones** filter (**View** ribbon). You can then select all of them by dragging, including their summary tasks if you have fewer than 20. If you have more than 20, handpick them by clicking on the first one and, while holding down the Control key, clicking on the rest. Then right-click anywhere inside the selected area and select **Add to Timeline** from the popup menu.
3. Identify other summary tasks, like phases or deliverables, you want to display on the timeline as bars. You can easily identify them by applying the out-of-the-box **Summary Tasks** filter (**View** ribbon). Again, you select them all or handpick them. Then right-click anywhere inside the selected area and select **Add to Timeline** from the popup menu.
4. Refine your selection with ribbon **Format** and the Existing Tasks button. Select the tasks.
5. The milestone names easily overlap each other, and you may have to drag some milestones to above the timeline bar to untangle them.

6. Format the dates, colors and fonts using the view-specific **Format** ribbon.

The timeline view is great for several reasons:

- It allows you to zoom and pan a project timescale as we discussed on page 78.
- It is a great *one-page report* that summarizes the project concisely.
- It is easy to create and maintain. Notice that if you make any changes to the schedule, the timeline view is immediately updated, keeping the timeline in sync with the schedule.
- The view can easily be copied into a PowerPoint slideshow (ribbon **Format**, button **Copy Timeline**). In PowerPoint, you can continue to format because the timeline view appears as an editable PowerPoint graphic.

There is one weak point: the timeline view can display neither baseline nor progress information. So, it can only be used to report on the project if the schedule is an entirely dynamic model of the project that is kept up-to-date and built to forecast the project (*forecast scheduling*).

Using Project Server Views

The Project Center views in Project Server aggregate data across multiple projects, creating the *project portfolio* for executives. Executives can also drill down into individual projects in Project Server. In this book, we focus on managing a single project and will, therefore, provide only an overview of the reporting capabilities of Project Server without delving into the steps to create them.[70]

In order to create informative views in Project Server, you need to capture organization-specific information about all projects. Fortunately, you can capture any type of data in custom enterprise fields. First, determine what type of data you want to collect, then create a custom enterprise field for it using Project Web App (PWA). If, for example, you want to report on the number of projects in the enterprise that are in each life-cycle phase (initiating, planning, executing and closing), you need to create a custom field in which the project managers can indicate the current phase of their project.

---

[70] In the courses *Managing Programs*, *Managing Portfolios* and *Managing Resources*, we focus on managing multiple projects with Project Server, see www.ProjectProCorp.com.

You can create fields that relate to projects, tasks and resources. The fields come in six types in Project Server: cost, date, duration, flag, number and text. When you customize a field, you can do one of the following:

2007

- In the text fields only, you can make a single or multi-line field or attach a *lookup table*. The lookup table can have one level (simple list) or multiple levels of items (tree-like list). Multi-level fields allow you to drill into the data on more than one level of aggregation, for example, projects by country, by state (province) or by city. All fields with lookup tables allow you to enter multiple values. One multi-level, multi-value field is, therefore, able to capture all skills of each resource and facilitate *skill-based scheduling*.
- In any type of field, you can create a *formula,* which are Excel-like formulas. Formulas are often used to calculate metrics indicating project performance. Formula fields often display traffic-light colors as output (called *graphical indicators*) for good, medium and bad performance.

Once you have customized the fields you can incorporate them into views. These views can be views in PWA used by executives and resource managers or views in Project Professional used by project managers. Project Server allows organizations to standardize custom-made views across the enterprise, called *Enterprise views*. This makes comparing projects and their performance much easier.

The Project Server administrators within your organization consider what views will benefit project managers, resource managers and executives and create these views as *Enterprise* Views. Only people with Project Server administrative privileges can create and change the enterprise views. As a project manager you can, of course, request extra views to be added.

New in Project Server 2010, views can be made specifically for each *department* or *line of business*, but there can also be overall views. This provides the best of both worlds: *standardization* on the enterprise level and *customization* on the levels below.

Enterprise views that are centrally designed provide several benefits for your organization:

- The project management office can capture and disseminate best-practice reports. Project Server provides a vehicle to capture and implement best practices.
- Executives can analyze faster.
  With a standard format, executives will be able to analyze portfolios faster, particularly when traffic light colors are used.
- Executives can compare more accurately.
  The metric will be applied to all projects in the view, so executives will be comparing apples with apples in one view and oranges with oranges in another.

- Project managers and resource managers can save time on project reporting. Standard reports prevent project managers and resource managers from having to spend time and energy developing appropriate report formats for each new project. They do not need to reinvent the wheel over and over again.

We will now discuss a selection of Project Server views for resource managers, portfolio managers and executives. We will discuss views for team members later on page 662.

Resource Manager Workload View

In this out-of-the-box view in Project Web App (PWA), a *resource manager* can assess the workloads and find any *overallocations* across all projects, both on the level of the team and for individual members of the team.

In the next screenshot the team workload looks reasonable, apart from some peaks exceeding the availability. However, if you look more closely at individual workloads, you will see that *Ben Spain* is heavily overallocated. In certain months he has more than 600 hours of scheduled work, whereas mere mortals typically only have 160 hours per month. It is likely that all projects in which Ben is involved will slip.

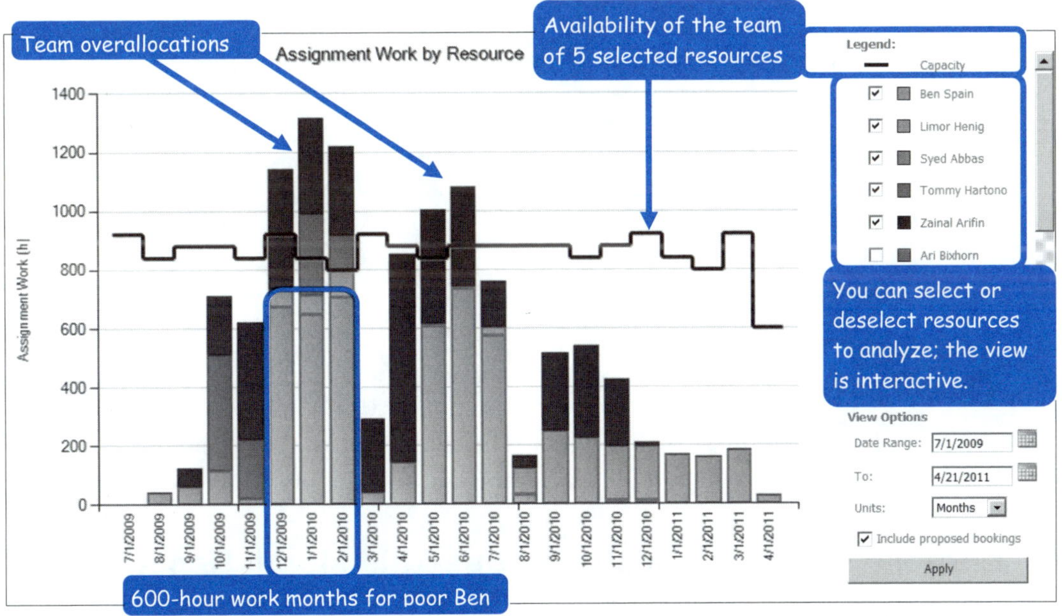

Notice that the resource manager can use the check boxes on the right-hand side to zoom in on one resource; the view is interactive. In this way, the resource manager can easily

10

find any overallocations and the projects that cause the problems. More detailed tabular information is available below this view in PWA.

Resource Manager Resource Utilization View

The following view shows the resource utilization for the different roles within the company. This is an out-of-the-box view in PWA for *resource managers* that pulls data from the *OLAP*-cube. *OLAP* stands for *Online Analytical Processing* and refers to the capability of slicing and dicing data without having to wait an eternity. OLAP also allows you to drill down into the detail data and back up to the overview.

The next view provides an overview of resource utilization by role and allows drilling down to find the roles that are very busy and others that are not:

2010 Resource Demand Planning

	Work (hrs)	Capacity (hrs)
Accounting	1441	13328
Analyst	6490	20944
Creative	256	7616
Customer	164	2094
Developer	3584	19040
Manufacturing Engineer	4545	7616
Marketing	7080	17136
Procurement	1200	5712
Product Engineer	12635	11424
Project Manager	10446	13328
Sales	112	5712
SME	2792	13328
Tester	6888	7616
Trainer	2248	7616
Grand Total	**59881**	**152510**

Under-utilization of most resource roles

This is a small overallocation for the product engineering team.

As you can see, the utilization has a lot of room for improvement, and this company should look into taking on more projects in order to better utilize available capacity.

Portfolio Manager Milestones-Due-This-Month Report

Portfolio managers who monitor many projects at arm's length may have an interest in finding out which milestones should be accomplished in the next month by their team of project managers. The report below was custom-made in MS Excel by using data from the *OLAP*-cubes that Project Server generates. The report is posted in the SharePoint site, so it can be accessed through PWA. It is served up by *Excel Services*. The portfolio manager can open it for viewing in PWA or open it for editing in MS Excel.

You see in the next screenshot that this portfolio manager has about 15 milestones to monitor with their latest forecast dates:

Milestones Due This Month

Project Name	Task Name	Task Finish Date
Acquisition Target	Due Diligence Assessment Complete	10/11/2010
	Valuation and Due Diligence Complete	10/11/2010
	Initial Selection Complete	10/13/2010
	Complete Transaction	10/20/2010
	Merger & Acquisition Transaction Complete	10/20/2010
Asset Tracking System	Pilot complete	10/13/2010
Asset-Change Ownership	Scope complete	10/8/2010
Automated Software	Analysis complete	10/28/2010
	Identify Target Areas for Improvement	10/14/2010
	Review current market solution vendors	10/21/2010
Catalog Publishing	Development complete	10/8/2010
	Unit testing complete	10/29/2010
	Documentation complete	10/15/2010
Corporate Web Site	Scope complete	10/19/2010
Data Exchange and	Development complete	10/22/2010

Milestones Due report created in Excel and accessible through PWA.

The portfolio manager can check in with the project manager to see the deliverables and inspect them or have them demonstrated, if needed.

Portfolio Manager Earned Value Reports

The *Earned Value Management* system has several performance indicators for both schedule and cost performance reporting.[71] These indicators are widely accepted in government, defense and construction circles. Earned Value Management provides three main indicators to *portfolio managers*:

10

[71] For more information on Earned Value Management, see:
- *PMBOK® Guide*, Fourth Edition, PMI, 2008.
- *Practice Standard for Earned Value Management*, PMI, 2005

- *Planned Value* (*BCWS*): the value you have planned to earn at each time interval. This is calculated from the baseline schedule by cumulating the Baseline Cost values up to that point. BCWS stands for Budgeted Cost of Work Scheduled.
- *Earned Value* (*BCWP*): the value of the work completed at each time interval. This is what you have actually "earned". BCWP stands for Budgeted Cost of Work Performed.
- *Actual Cost* (*ACWP*): the value you have actually incurred to make the progress. The incurred value consists of amounts spent and amounts owed. You typically get these values from the accounting system. ACWP stands for Actual Cost of Work Performed.

As you can see, all these values are time-phased values that can be charted over time. The format of an Earned Value chart typically looks like this for a project:

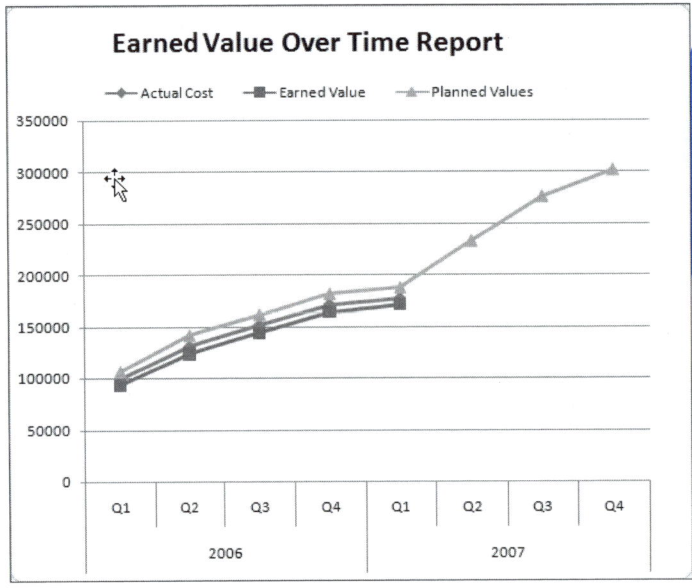

Earned Value charts indicate how the progress and the spending compare to the original plan (baseline). This project is close to its target: its **Earned Value** is close to the **Planned Value** (on schedule) and **Actual Cost** (on budget).

The chart shows that the value earned by the project team (*Earned Value* or *BCWP*) is slightly below the value that was planned to be earned at this point in time, the *Planned Value* (*BCWS*). This means that the progress is slightly behind schedule. The Earned Value is a little below the *Actual Cost* (*ACWP*), which means that the project is slightly over budget.

From the three main indicators you can calculate differences (a.k.a. variances):

- *Schedule Variance* (*SV*) = Earned Value – Planned Value
- *Cost Variance* (*CV*) = Earned Value – Actual Cost

If the variances are positive, life is good. If they are negative, the project is in trouble. The variances are shown in the next bar chart:

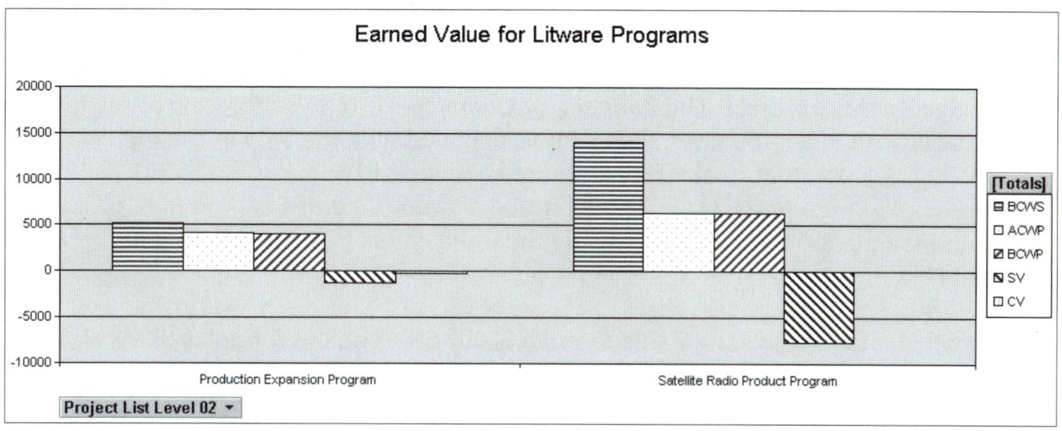

The previous screenshot shows two programs, each consisting of several subprojects; one of them, the *Satellite Radio Product Program*, is in trouble in terms of progress. Both are doing well in terms of cost.

You can also divide and calculate *indices* from the three main indicators of Planned Value, Earned Value and Actual Cost:

- *Schedule Performance Index* (*SPI*) = Earned Value / Planned Value
- *Cost Performance Index* (*CPI*) = Earned Value / Actual Cost

If the indices are greater than 1, you are doing fine. If they drop below 1, you are in trouble. Fleming and Koppelman report that the CPI becomes stable within 10% as early as 15-20% into the project duration based on empirical research (looking at factual data) from many projects.[72]

Within MS Project itself you can create a one-page report in a **Task Sheet** view that displays all Earned Value indicators. It could look like this:

	Task Name	Planned Value (BCWS)	Earned Value (BCWP)	Actual Cost - (ACWP)	Schedule Variance (SV)	Cost Variance (CV)	Estimate at Complete (EAC)	Budget at Complete (BAC)	Variance at Complete
0	⊟ Relocation Devom Inc.	$30,150.00	$16,217.00	$17,775.00	($13,933.00)	($1,558.00)	$141,530.30	$129,125.00	($12,405.30)
1	⊟ Requirements	$1,650.00	$1,650.00	$1,650.00	$0.00	$0.00	$1,650.00	$1,650.00	$0.00
4	⊟ Location	$6,075.00	$6,075.00	$6,075.00	$0.00	$0.00	$6,075.00	$6,075.00	$0.00
11	⊟ Remodeling Contract	$3,300.00	$3,300.00	$3,300.00	$0.00	$0.00	$3,300.00	$3,300.00	$0.00
17	⊟ Remodeled Location	$16,875.00	$5,192.00	$6,750.00	($11,683.00)	($1,558.00)	$112,034.14	$86,175.00	($25,859.14)
26	⊟ Move	$1,125.00	$0.00	$0.00	($1,125.00)	$0.00	$31,925.00	$31,925.00	$0.00

[72] *Earned Value Project Management*, Fleming, Quentin W. and Koppelman, Joel third edition, PMI, Newton Square, PA, USA, 2005.

If you look at how the indices develop over time, it will give you an idea whether the situation is deteriorating or ameliorating. If an index drops below 1 and keeps dropping, the trend is bad.

Budget at Complete (*BAC*) is the same as the Baseline Cost of the entire project, or the "budget" for the project. The *Estimate at Complete* (*EAC*) is a forecast of the total cost of the project when it is over and can be calculated with the help of the indices:
$EAC_{optimistic}$ = Actual Cost + (BAC-Earned Value)/CPI
$EAC_{pessimistic}$ = Actual Cost + (BAC-Earned Value)/(CPI x SPI)
You calculate the EAC typically while the project is in progress to predict the eventual total cost.

Note that since Project 2007 this *formula* is aligned with the formulas that PMI suggests for calculating EAC.[73]

Earned Value reports are powerful because:

- They can summarize the performance of a project in one page. It does not matter if your project is small or very large; you just need the ten indicators we discussed and a chart or two.
- They are relentless in revealing the state of progress. Even if project managers update their project schedules in a sloppy fashion (leaving work-to-be-done scheduled in the past and leaving completed work scheduled in the future), Earned Value reports will provide an accurate view on the progress and reliable forecasts on where the project will likely end up. Sometimes, I quip that the *Earned Value* technique was developed for lazy project managers, because if project managers do their job and update their schedule well, the schedule by itself will forecast the project accurately. This is the central message we are trying to get across in this book, hence the title *Forecast Scheduling*. Since Earned Value requires tight integration with the accounting system, it is easier to forecast with the schedule itself. It is certainly also much faster than waiting for the numbers you need from the accounting department.

There are other things to be aware of when working with the Earned Value feature as Microsoft implemented it:

- Microsoft is still using the old terms: *BCWS = Planned Value*, *BCWP = Earned Value*, *ACWP = Actual Cost*.

---

[73] *Practice Standard for Earned Value Management*, PMI, 2005

- You have to set a baseline and you must enter a **Status Date** (on the **Project** ribbon) before MS Project will calculate Planned Values and Earned Values. The status date must be later than the project start date. It is odd that the status date is needed for the Planned Values.
- The **Planned Values** (BCWS) are only calculated up to the status date, whereas you need planned values to the project end date to create a complete *performance baseline*, the target. As a workaround, you can take the time-phased **Baseline Cost** values and cumulate them yourself in MS Excel and chart them.
- You will not get any Earned Value (BCWP) from MS Project for tasks you completed ahead of schedule (i.e., with baseline dates that are after the status date). This is an error from Microsoft that tends to understate the real value you earned in your project. You should, of course, get paid (earn value) when you completed work, regardless when the work was supposed to be completed.

ProjectPro is working on a solution to these problems and will publish an evaluation copy as one of the files available for download on our website (see page vi for the procedure to access these files). You can also purchase the full version of this Earned Value add-in for MS Project on our website, see www.projectprocorp.com and click *Products* in the side bar.

Executive Traffic Light Portfolio View

The following screenshot shows a portfolio view for *executives* with cost and schedule traffic lights for all projects the organization currently has. Two fields are shown that were customized with formulas:

- The *Schedule Health* field on the left calculates the percentage with which the forecasted duration has extended over or shrunk under the baseline duration. The red minus signs allow the executive to quickly find the troubled projects.
- The *Schedule Health* field on the right translates the percentage into easy-to-understand text, like *17% over baseline duration*. This field displays the exact percentage and allows the executive to assess the magnitude of the trouble.

Executives can see the baseline schedule in the Tracking Gantt view (bottom gray bar for each project) in the next screenshot:

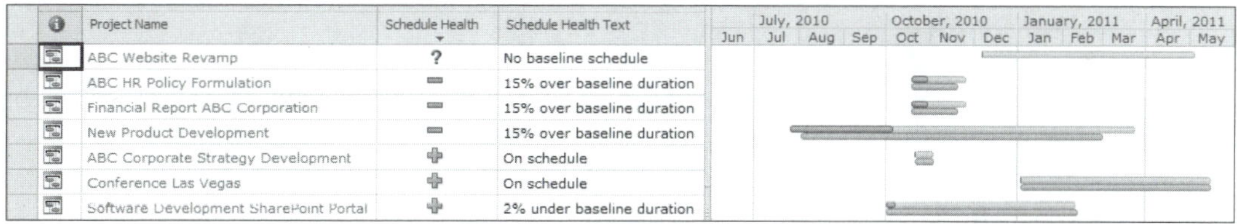

Project Name	Schedule Health	Schedule Health Text
ABC Website Revamp	?	No baseline schedule
ABC HR Policy Formulation	−	15% over baseline duration
Financial Report ABC Corporation	−	15% over baseline duration
New Product Development	−	15% over baseline duration
ABC Corporate Strategy Development	+	On schedule
Conference Las Vegas	+	On schedule
Software Development SharePoint Portal	+	2% under baseline duration

The thresholds used in the screenshot for red, yellow and green are: more than 10% over (red minus), between 0 and 10% (yellow diamond) and at or under 0 (green plus). If your executives do not need the baseline, you could present a report similar to this:

	Project Name	Schedule Health	Schedule Health
	Asset-Change Ownership	?	No Baseline
	Auditing Services Training		17% over baseline duration
	Acquisition Target Analysis		15% over baseline duration
	Content Filtering Firewall Design		13% over baseline duration
	Apparel ERP Upgrade		4% over baseline duration
	Audit Tracking Solution		4% over baseline duration
	Automated Software Installation		3% over baseline duration
	Automated Software Design		On schedule
	Catalog Publishing		On schedule
	Company Portal Database Migration		On schedule
	Compliance Database System Implem		On schedule
	E-CRM Solution		On schedule
	Asset Tracking System		5% under baseline duration
	Data Exchange and Integration		5% under baseline duration

Executives can easily gauge the performance of each project with this view. The list is sorted on the **Schedule Health** metric and puts the worst performers at the top of the list. The exact explanation of each health icon is provided in the next column.

This view would be ideal for executives as input for portfolio reviews. The graphics used in this report speak for themselves:

- ? Purple question mark means the project does not have a baseline yet and its performance cannot be assessed.
- Red minus means bad performance: the currently forecasted project duration is more than 10% over its originally approved (baseline) duration in the example above.
- Yellow diamond means medium performance: between 0 and 10 % over the baseline duration in the example above.
- Green plus means good performance: the currently forecasted project duration is at or under the approved (baseline) duration in the example above.

Notice that the metrics and the thresholds chosen above do not indicate if the project meets the dates in the schedule; they only reveal if the project will stay within its original (baseline) duration. Similar metrics can be developed on dates and entered as formulas customized for the organization, showing, for example *14 days behind schedule* as output.

Notice that the progress (hatch marks) is visible inside the current forecasts (white bars). The original schedule, the baseline, is also visible as the black bar, which helps in assessing the status. Executives can even drill down into each project to have a look at the cause of slippages.

If you want to do traffic light reporting with red, yellow and green indicators to give a quick impression of the health of a project or portfolio, you have to think about the metrics and the thresholds that determine which of the three colors is shown for each project, deliverable and task.

You can use traffic light colors for:

- *Budget performance*: what are the threshold values for well within budget (green), close to the original budget (yellow) and running dangerously over budget (red)? You can do this also for the effort budget or person-days budget.
- *Schedule performance*: what are the threshold values for well within schedule (green), close to on schedule (yellow) and slipping dangerously (red)? Instead of dates, you can also opt for metrics on if the approved project duration is met as shown in the example above. You have to determine if dates or duration is more important for you.
- *Quality performance*: Project Server does not have features for quality management. You will need a separate quality management system to determine or to calculate the quality values. In software development projects, you could develop a quality indicator that, for example, reveals if one or more must-have requirements are not met (red), one or more nice-to-have requirements are not met (yellow) and all requirements are met (green). In *Project Server*, you can definitely present these quality indicators next to schedule and budget indicators in a project portfolio view. Executives would probably be very grateful.
- *Risk performance*: are the risks adequately mitigated? From the risk register in Project Server, metrics can be calculated such as what percentage of the identified risks have been closed, are still active but have a risk response identified, and are still active but no response identified. If most are closed, risk status would be green. If most are active but have responses, risk status would be yellow. If most have no response, risk status would be red.

10

The metrics and thresholds typically differ from organization to organization; even within an organization they can, and perhaps even should, differ from business unit to business unit. It is not uncommon for business rules to even differ from one department to the next; the IT department can have different standards for healthy projects than the engineering department. This is particularly true if the average budget for IT projects is $50,000 and for engineering projects it is $1 million. In Project Server 2010, you can now easily set up views specific to the department. You can assign each project to a department and each resource as well. This facilitates portfolio and resource management by department.

No matter what criteria you use, it should be clear to everybody what a red light means, just like when driving a car. If red traffic lights were not clearly understood by everybody, the streets would not be very safe …

Executive Portfolio Bubble Chart

The following chart is a very nice view for *executives* to analyze the health and balance of a project portfolio. Portfolio management is concerned with making sure that the investments in projects generate strategic value for the organization. The diameter of the bubble represents the total amount of money to be invested in the project (*project cost*). The y-axis shows the level of expected revenues, the *Financial Benefit of Project* in Million dollars. The x-axis shows the percentage that the project contributes to realizing the corporate strategy, the *Strategic Value of Project*. Maximizing the revenues and strategic value is the objective of for-profit organizations. Executives can assess which projects are their stars and which ones just eat the money without ever producing revenues (which is why I call them *black holes*). In the next chart, the stars are in the top right quadrant:

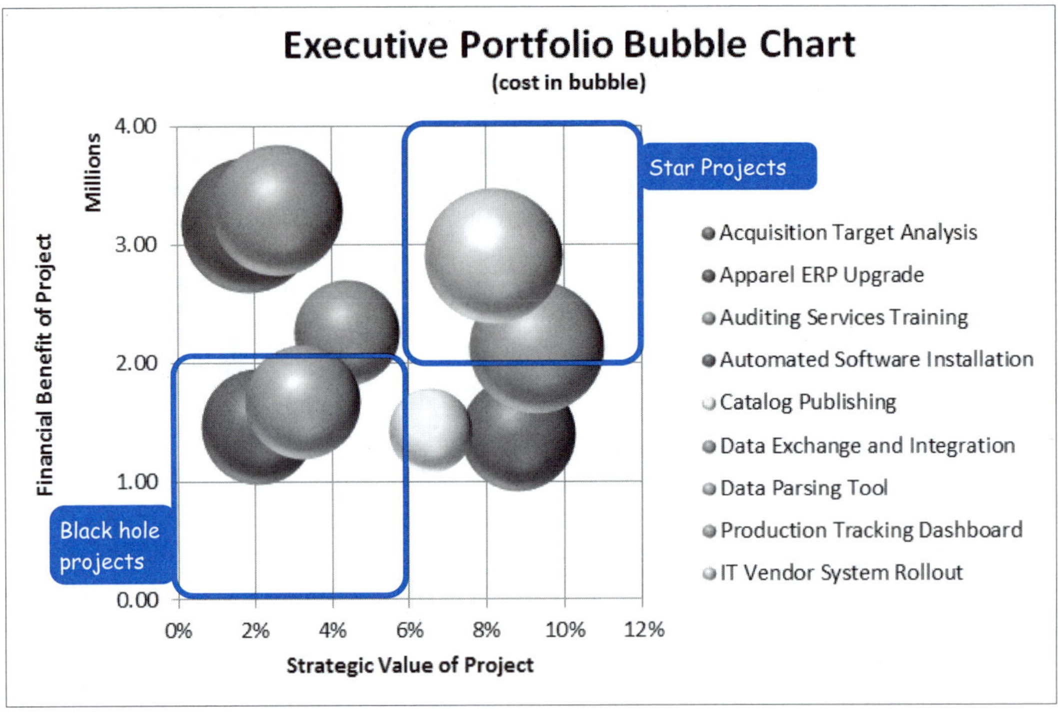

This custom-made view required several customizations of enterprise fields, views and *OLAP-cube* (*Online Analytical Processing)* in Project Server.

Creating One-Page Reports ... Always!

This heading may seem pretentious if you are juggling a schedule with thousands of tasks. Regardless of the size of the project, you can always pleasantly surprise your executives and clients with one-page project reports. There is a simple technique for doing this, and it will make your stakeholders happy, if not euphoric. Executives typically do not have the time to dig through pages and pages of schedules, and they will surely never tape a large Gantt Chart together from many pages. They expect you to provide concise information, not a mountain of data. One-page reports are concise, and since you limit yourself to one page you really need to think what you are going to show on it. The one-page report could, for example, only show the major milestones. That is all you need if all the milestones are on schedule. Where a milestone is off its *deadline* or *baseline* date, you need to provide more detail that explains the discrepancy.

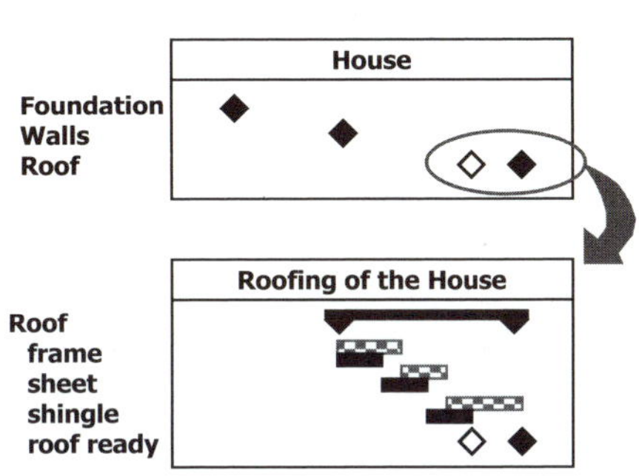

In the illustration, the milestone chart at the top shows slippage on the *Roof* milestone. In the bottom, the cause of the slippage is shown in detail. With a *one-page report*, you should be able to give an adequate impression of your project, regardless of size.

If you use this option, we prefer that the milestones are filtered by this view instead of listed together in the WBS. Many project managers put the major milestones at the top of their schedule to create a one-page milestone overview of the project. This makes the network of dependencies very complex in the Gantt Chart, because the dependencies run up and down with long arrows. Long dependency arrows make it very difficult to understand the network and to check if the network of dependencies is complete. Instead, we advocate using a separate view that displays all milestones using (a copy of) the out-of-the-box **Milestones** filter, see page 556 for creating a custom view with a custom filter. We recommend you use one of the extra **Flag** fields (Flag1 – Flag20) to mark all major milestones.

You will have to master the filter feature of MS Project to accomplish this (see page 565) or another technique that summarizes succinctly, like *Earned Value* (see page 587). The new *Timeline* view also summarizes well, but it cannot display the original baseline dates. It reports the project well if its schedule is an entirely dynamic schedule created with the purpose to continuously forecast (see page 582).

10

Checks on Reporting

We would like to suggest the following checks to verify if you used best practices for project reporting. The checks pertain to which custom view objects you developed in your schedule. We discussed creating custom views on page 556. The numbering corresponds to the complete checklist in the summary chapter, see page 711:

10 Reports

10.1. Is there a one-page status report for the schedule that is readily available as a separate **View** object? This can be one of the following:

- ◇ View that supports *Earned Value Management*. The view should report at least the *Planned Value* (*BCWS*), *Earned Value* (*BCWP*) and *Actual Cost* (*ACWP*) for the schedule. For some examples, see the section starting on page 587.
- ◇ View that displays only major milestones with their forecast dates relative to their baseline dates. See page 595 for more detail.
- ◇ The new *Timeline view* in Project 2010 cannot display progress or baseline data. It is only suitable to present as a status or forecast report if it is based on a dynamic and up-to-date schedule created with the purpose of forecasting (see page 582).

10.2. Does the one-page report give an appropriate impression of the health of the project?

- ◇ If you used the *Earned Value* view, you can verify if the schedule supports the Earned Value values. For example, if the **Schedule Variance** is positive, the schedule should show that the deadlines are easily met. If the **Schedule Variance** is negative, the schedule should show that deadlines are missed. For this comparison of the Earned Value indices with the schedule, it is important to make sure that all actuals are scheduled in the past and all remaining durations in the future.
- ◇ If you used one of the major milestone charts, you have to ask this question: are the right milestones chosen to represent the health of a large project? If you have many milestones, you may end up with multiple pages. Instead of reporting on all milestones, work with your client to identify certain milestones as your major milestones. Then you can mark them using a flag field (**Flag1** - **Flag20**) and add a filter to the view that displays all milestones with the flag set to **Yes**.
- ◇ If you used the *Timeline view*, it needs to be based on a dynamic and up-to-date schedule created to forecast.

Exercises

Review Questions

1. Is it possible to create a one-page report for a 1,000-task schedule? The report should reflect the performance of the project. Would you recommend doing this? Why?
2. We discussed many ways to hide a time buffer in your schedule. In what specific circumstance should you consider hiding your buffer? Why?
3. What are the communication features in MS Project?
   What are their main differences?
4. What other objects does a view object apply?
   What other settings are stored inside the view object?
5. How can you transfer an object to another project schedule?

Relocation Project — Reporting an Executive Overview

The goal of this exercise is to be able to create custom, one-page reports targeted at executives.

1. Open the file *10A Reports.MPP* available for download at www.ProjectProCorp.com (see page vi for the procedure to access these files).
2. Click ribbon **View**, button **Tables**, item **More Tables…** and create a new task table named *Executive Overview*. Use the columns **ID, Name, Duration** and **Cost**.
3. Click ribbon **View**, list **Filter**, item **More Filters…** and create a new filter, *Executive Overview*, to display milestones plus summary tasks.
4. Click ribbon **View**, Other Views, **More Views…** and create a new view, *Executive Overview*, which is based on a Tracking Gantt view. Select ☑ **Show in menu** to display it as an item in the list of **Gantt Charts** on the **View** ribbon. Make sure that when you apply the view *Executive Overview*, the corresponding table and filter that you created are both applied.
5. Hide the question marks in the **Duration** column by clicking ribbon **File**, Options, tab **Schedule** and clearing the options ☐ **Show that scheduled tasks have estimated durations** and ☐ **New scheduled tasks have estimated durations**.

10

6. Click ribbon **View**, find its section **Zoom** and click the button [▾] of the list **Timescale**, and select item **Timescale**: Apply the following settings in the **Timescale** dialog:

		Middle Tier	Bottom Tier
Field	**Units**	Months	Days
	Label	Jan, Feb, …	1, 2, …
	Count	1	7
	Align	Center	Center
	Size	100 %	100 %

7. In the **Page Setup** dialog (ribbon **File,** tab **Print**, hyperlink **Page Setup**), format the **Header, Footer** and **Legend** as follows:

		Section	Set to	Font
Tab	**Header**	Center	&[View] &[Project Title]	Arial, Bold, 20
	Footer	Left	&[Manager] &[Company]	Arial, Regular, 8
		Right	&[Date]	Arial, Regular, 8
	Legend	Legend on	⦿ None	

8. Save your file and compare the view you created with the view called *Executive Overview* in the solution file *10B Reports.MPP* available for download at www.ProjectProCorp.com (see page vi for the procedure to access these files).

Relocation Project — Reporting Cost by Function

The goal of this exercise is to be able to create a custom cost report.

1. Open the file *10B Reports.MPP* available for download at www.ProjectProCorp.com (see page vi for the procedure to access these files).
2. Switch to the **Resource Sheet** view.
3. Click ribbon **View**, button **Tables**, item **More Tables…** and create a new resource-related table named *Cost by Function* that shows the fields **ID, Name** (the title of this column will appear as **Resource Name**), **Position**, **Function** and **Cost**.
4. Click ribbon **Project**, list **Group by**, item **More Groups…** and create a grouping *Cost by Function* so that you can easily read the total cost by resource function of the project.
5. Click ribbon **View**, button **Other Views** and select item **More Views…** and create a new view based on the resource sheet that is named *Cost by Function* (select

☑ **Show in menu**). The view should apply the corresponding table and grouping that you created.

6. Best fit the column widths (see page 279).
7. In the **Page Setup** dialog (ribbon **File,** tab **Print**, hyperlink **Page Setup**), enter the following settings:

Tab	**Section**	**Set to**
Page	Orientation	◉ Portrait
	Scaling	**Fit to:** 1 page wide by 1 tall
Margins	top, bottom, left, right	1 inch or 2.5 cm
	Borders Around	every page
Header	Center Arial, Bold, 20	&[View] &[Project Title]
Footer	Left	&[Manager] &[Company]
	Center	none; delete the default entry
	Right	&[Date]

8. Save your file and compare the view you created with the screenshot on page 571 or the view called *Cost by Function* in the solution file *11A Up-to-date Schedule.MPP*. This file is available for download at www.ProjectProCorp.com (see page vi for the procedure to access these files).

10

Chapter 11 Keeping the Schedule Up-to-date

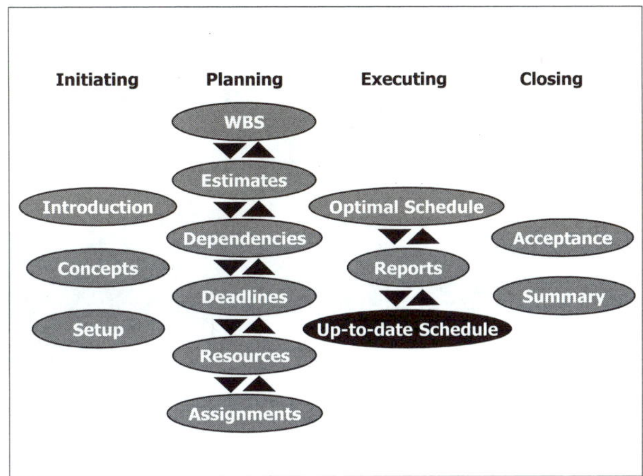

When the schedule is approved, you capture that version in the baseline. You can then start the first tasks in your project. As team members make progress, you will be *updating* your schedule regularly to maintain an up-to-date schedule (see the black ellipse above). In this chapter we will discuss how you can approach the ideal situation where you keep your schedule alive and up-to-date during project execution in order to continuously forecast the project.

After this chapter you will be able to:

- Prepare your schedule for updating.
- Set and preserve the baseline.
- Assess the impact of a change request on the schedule and the cost.
- Maintain the baseline when change requests are approved.
- Choose the appropriate way of updating your schedule:
  - Updating the tasks (using live status meetings or paper turn-around reports).
  - Updating the assignments (using electronic timesheets).
- Update on the task level using actual and remaining duration and, perhaps even actual start and actual finish dates using MS Project or SharePoint.
- Update on the assignment level using timesheets in Project Web App or Outlook.
- Handle the wide variety of update situations that occur in practice.
- Communicate the status and forecasts of the project to stakeholders.
- Verify whether the schedule is updated properly using best practices.
- Optimize the schedule after updating to compensate for slippages.

To Timesheet or Not To Timesheet?

Nob enters Bob's office and starts a tirade: "Our captains upstairs now want us to start filling in timesheets; I can't believe this!" "What's your problem with that?" Bob calmly inquires. Nob: "Well, I already have enough to do and now I also have to keep track of where I spend my time all day." Bob turns to face Nob: "Yeah, it is more work, but it will allow them to compare estimates to actuals and learn from it to become better estimators. It also gives them insight into how much time we spend on admin and maintenance stuff versus billable work. Don't you think that information is important for management to know?" Nob: "Do you really think they'll get truthful data? I think people are desperately going to cram 40 hours into their timesheet simply because they are supposed to work 40 hours per week." Bob: "If we make sure we have the right line items in the timesheets, it will be easy entering the hours." Nob: "Timesheets take all initiative, innovation and creativity out of the job. If it's not a line item in your timesheet, you aren't supposed to do it!" "Yes, work life will get more regimented, but right now I find sometimes that my team members aren't very focused and waste time horsing around," counters Bob.

Nob: "I just like the way my life is right now. I don't like having to account for every minute I spend at work." Bob: "You get paid a nice salary and you don't agree that management has the right to see what they bought for that?" Nob's smile is mildly sarcastic: "Big Brother is watching you!" Bob: "Yes, but only for 40 hours out of 168 hours in a week." Nob throws his hands up while retreating in search of a more willing ear for his grief.

Project Execution

Executing a project is often a more chaotic experience than anticipated in the project plan:

- Team members discover that they were too optimistic when they said they could handle a task.
- The progress runs behind on some tasks relative to the baseline schedule. When critical tasks slip, the schedule needs to be optimized further.
- Team members find ways to work on future tasks ahead of schedule.
- Clients throw new requirements at you or insist on cumbersome review processes.
- A new understanding emerges about what the client really wants.
- Extra approval cycles for certain deliverables are imposed on the project.
- Sudden budget cuts or unexpected expenses may require adjustments in the project.
- People become sick, or worse, sick people who hand over deliverables to healthy people pass on their bugs as well…

In other words, no project is ever executed exactly as planned! Optimizing methods are important when you plan a project, but even more so when you execute a project.

Forecast Scheduling

Forecast scheduling is the theme of this book. The principle of *forecast scheduling* is built on three premises:

- Project managers will use *deadline* dates (see page 256) or the *baseline schedule* to capture promised and committed dates. Too many schedulers use the schedule itself to reflect their promises or commitments and then want to keep their schedule static. With that decision, they kill the dynamic nature, the schedule needs to continually forecast the project. In our approach, the schedule will be a dynamic model that reflects the living and changing nature of a project at all times. The commitments can be captured using deadlines and the baseline schedule, and will reflect the static nature of those promises made at all times. We must separate active, forecast scheduling from the act of entering deadlines or setting a baseline. The set of deadlines or the baseline schedule reflects the static nature of the promises and commitments made at all times.
- Project managers want to minimize the time spent on scheduling. They can do this by setting up the schedule in the right way with all dependencies and as few date constraints as possible (which we introduced as the principle of *Dynamic Scheduling* in previous books).

- Project managers will update their schedules with revisions to forecasts. Many project managers just enter actual progress. In order to forecast, you need to capture revised forecasts from your team members as well. As team members start tasks, they learn what the tasks really take to complete. Project managers need to reflect those new insights in their schedule in order to get a real sense of how long the project will take. Of course, you may have to re-optimize your schedule to stay within the dates promised.

Updating a project schedule is entering revised estimates-to-complete in order to refine the future part of the project schedule. The amazing paradox is that everybody enters actuals, even though entering the actuals is not necessary for forecasting as far as we are concerned. Updating actuals only serves to draw lessons learned from the project, which is of some value for forecasting the current project but of most value for future projects. Updating the estimates-to-complete is what really counts for forecasting the current project. Once team members have started working on a task, they have a much better idea how long the remainder of the task will take. Updating forecasts is of immediate benefit for the current project.

The Process for Updating Schedules

The process steps for updating schedules can be summarized as follows:

- Switching to Auto Scheduled Tasks (see next section).
- Baseline the schedule: set it once for the entire schedule and preserve it by making an extra copy. Once the baseline is set, you need to maintain the baseline when change requests are approved (see page 605).
- Choose the reporting period (see page 617).
- Choose the update strategy (see page 620).
  - Tasks update:
    Updating tasks is collecting progress information on the task level. It is less effort than updating assignments (see page 623).
  - Assignments update:
    Updating assignments is collecting actual hours worked by day, by resource. When you update assignments, you will likely work with electronic timesheets (see page 646).
- Update the schedule: enter the actual values and remaining estimates. This is discussed separately for each strategy.
- Check if the schedule is updated correctly (see page 677).
- Prepare the status and forecast report (see page 672).
  You may need to re-optimize your schedule before reporting on it.

Switching to Auto Scheduled Tasks

We recommend switching all tasks in your schedule to Auto Scheduled at this point. You may have already done so when we first recommended it in chapter 5 (see page 218), and later in chapter 8 (see page 360) and chapter 9 (see page 417). When you update your schedule, there are two reasons to switch to auto scheduled tasks:

- You will not see the impacts of your updating efforts if you continue to work with *manually scheduled* tasks; they are not rescheduled by the *network logic*. Only if you switch all tasks in your schedule over to **Auto Scheduled** (field **Task Mode**) will you see the impact of the updates on the forecast finish date of the project. If you apply *rolling wave* scheduling, we recommend you switch all tasks that fall within the detailed planning window over to auto scheduled. See page 220 for the how-to steps.
- We do not think it makes sense to baseline *manually scheduled* tasks. These are the reasons:
  - ◇ Tasks that have missing data (**Duration, Start** or **Finish**) would create an incomplete *baseline schedule*.
  - ◇ Tasks that have *schedule conflicts* (field **Warning** equals **Yes**) would create an optimistic baseline schedule. Schedule conflicts happen when manually scheduled tasks bend dependencies out of shape; manually scheduled start and finish dates are stronger than dependencies!
  - ◇ If the task bars of manually scheduled tasks have gaps between them (*schedule gains*) that were not removed by the as soon as possible scheduling of auto scheduled tasks, it would create a pessimistic baseline schedule.
- A schedule built on manually scheduled tasks likely has scheduling conflicts that are normally taken care of by dependencies. Such a schedule may be forecasting optimistically; if you baseline it, you will end up with a baseline schedule that is too optimistic and impossible to meet. Creating baseline schedules that can never be met is a poor career choice.

Therefore, please change all tasks to **Auto Scheduled** – for how-to steps, see page 218.

The Baseline Schedule

The *baseline schedule* is a frozen copy of the approved schedule. It is the target you work towards and compare progress against.

Some people do not realize that the approved schedule can be copied to and isolated as the baseline schedule. Others do not realize that there is a feature in MS Project that allows you to do this very easily. All these people treat the schedule itself as a collection of promised dates that need to stay the same, which is the role of the baseline schedule. These people become reluctant to make any changes to the schedule once it has been approved and stop using the schedule as a tool to explore the impact of changes and suggest ideas for solutions. This is similar to being the doctor of a dead patient; there is no need to monitor or intervene any longer. Instead, project managers need to treat the schedule as a living body to be constantly updated with the latest available data. Now, the doctor has a live patient and will need a thermometer to measure the temperature of the patient and a standard of reference to determine if the temperature is reasonable. For project managers, the live schedule is the thermometer, and the baseline schedule (or the set of deadlines) is the standard of reference. Together they will reveal how much the project is behind or ahead.

We hope you recognize that the baseline feature in MS Project is a major feature – very beneficial and very important. It allows you to actually monitor and control your *living project*. Alternatively, you should have at least a set of deadlines to work towards (see page 255 for more on deadlines).

In the illustration, you can see that each task bar is split into two parts once the baseline is set. The top part (with the gray shade) is the current schedule — the *forecast model* of the project. The bottom part (solid black) is the static *baseline* — the target schedule. The latest moment at which you need to set the baseline for the schedule is when the day's date is just before the start date of the first task in your project, as in the illustration. The day's date comes from the system date on your computer. This date is updated automatically each day. MS Project calls it the *current date*, and some people refer to it as *time now*.

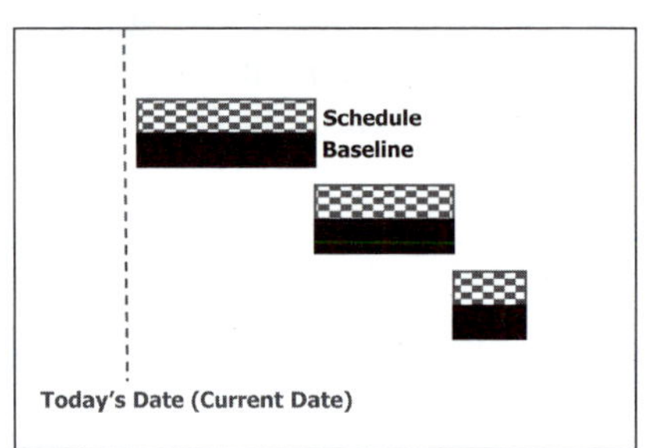

The baseline is an important artifact that should be handled with care; the baseline is essentially the contract between you as the project manager and the *external customer*, or between you and the *internal sponsor* of the project. The baseline should remain the same throughout the project unless there is a valid reason to change it. Like every contract, it requires careful control of change, as explained in PMI's *Practice Standard*

for Project Configuration Management.[74] Our recommendations and procedures in this chapter are consistent with this new standard.

Viewing the Baseline Schedule

1. Click ribbon **View** and click the bottom part of 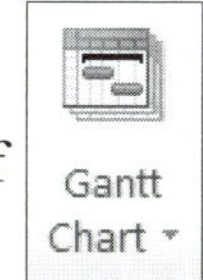 and select **Tracking Gantt**

   – a special type of Gantt chart appears that displays the baseline schedule next to the current schedule in the timescale. Each task has two task bars in this view: the bar for the live schedule at the top and the bar for the (static) baseline schedule, if it is present, at the bottom.

2. Click ribbon **View,** 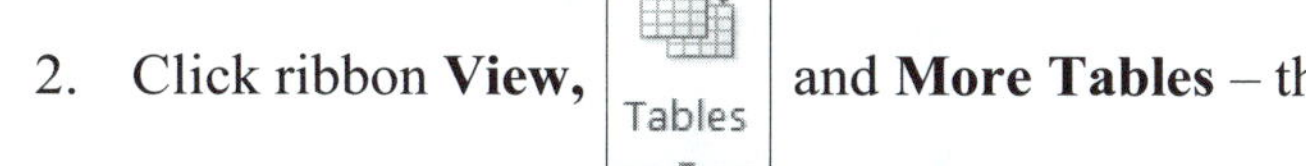 and **More Tables** – the **More Tables** dialog appears.

3. Select the table **Baseline** in the list.

4. Click Apply.

Notice that the cells in the baseline date columns display **NA** when the baseline is not yet set for the tasks.

Setting the First Baseline Schedule

1. Make sure you have opened the approved version of your schedule. The approved version is your target schedule that you should capture in the *baseline schedule.*

2. We need to make sure the baseline schedule does not have any scheduling conflicts from manually scheduled tasks. Check if all tasks are **Auto Scheduled**: you can check if any tasks have a push pin icon in the **Task Mode** field OR you can apply a filter: click ribbon **View** and find its **Data** section. Click the list button of Filter: and select **More Filters** from the drop-down list, then select **Manually Scheduled Tasks** from the ⦿ **Task** filter list presented. Click Apply.

---

[74] Published by PMI, USA, 2007

If the filter displays any manually scheduled tasks, then select them, right-click and select **Auto Scheduled** from the pop-up menu. You may want to check the highlighted changes to make sure the schedule has not shifted significantly. Now you are ready to baseline.

3. Click ribbon **Project,** 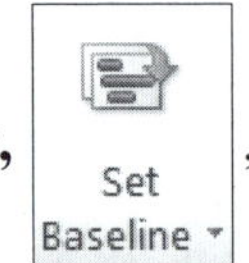

, item **Set Baseline** – the next dialog appears:

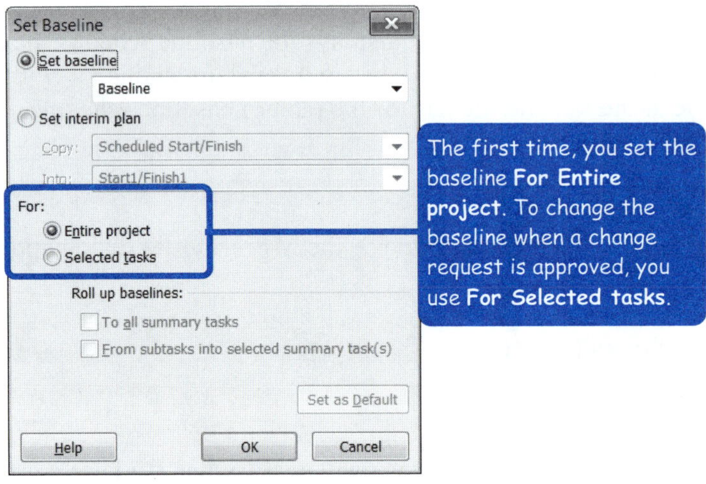

4. Select ◉ **Set Baseline**.
5. To set the baseline for all tasks, select ◉ **Entire Project**.
   If you apply *rolling wave* scheduling, you need to cancel this dialog and select the tasks within the detailed planning window first; after you redisplay this dialog, you use the ◉ **Selected tasks only** option.
6. Click OK – the current schedule is copied to the **Baseline** fields. You will see that black bars are added just below the other bars in the timescale of the Tracking Gantt view. If you receive notification that you do not have the rights to save a baseline in the *Project Server* environment, then your administrator has not granted you permission to save baselines. You need to find the people who have the privileges to baseline; most likely these are *Project Server administrators* or the *project management office*.

7. If you suspect that you will receive change requests that will result in multiple baselines, it is a good idea to preserve the current baseline by copying it also into **Baseline1**. See the next procedure on page 610.

Some remarks about the baseline feature in MS Project:

- Make sure you set the baseline after you have substituted *generic resources* with real people, because if you still have generic resources (with unlimited availability) in your schedule, you have not performed a workload feasibility check on your schedule. The dates in the schedule may turn out to be unfeasible once you start assigning real people to the tasks.

- When you first baseline your schedule, you may actually see small discrepancies between the baseline bar and the task bar of the live schedule. Microsoft has acknowledged this as an issue in the originally released version of Project 2010. The bug is caused by the fact that the Start and Finish date fields are text fields in Project 2010 and in the conversion to dates, small discrepancies come up. You can work around this and always get exact matches if, in the **Bar styles** dialog (ribbon Format, button **Format**, item **Bar Styles**), you replace all occurrences of **Baseline Start** with **Baseline Estimated Start** and all occurrences of **Baseline Finish** with **Baseline Estimated Finish**. All baseline bars should then be aligned with the schedule bars.[75]
- MS Project captures the date in the name of the baseline. The date on which you set the baseline is visible in the dialog ribbon **Project**, button **Set baseline**, item **Set baseline**. The **Set Baseline** list at the top will reveal the dates for each baseline that was set. Notice that the other lists **Copy** and **Into** do not reveal the date on which the baseline was set!

- Note that the baseline version of the schedule contains only five task-related fields: *baseline start* and *baseline finish* dates, *baseline duration*, *baseline work* and *baseline cost*. It also saves the time-phased data for these same fields. Similar fields are also baselined for resources and assignments. You can see that a baseline is not a complete version of the schedule; many task-related fields are not captured in the baseline fields. Most notably, the baseline does not contain who does what (the resource assignments). Do not use baselines if what you really need is a complete version of the schedule. You can click **File, Save As** to create a complete version of the schedule.
- Apart from eleven baselines, there are also ten interim plans (*Start1/Finish1* through *Start10/Finish10*). In each of these you can store a complete set of start and finish dates for all tasks. Be aware that the interim plans only contain the start and finish dates; unlike baselines, they do not hold duration, work or cost data. Interim plans are an even less complete version of the schedule than a baseline. The interim plans are useful for a quick comparison before and after a series of changes. We used them

[75] Our download file, called *11 Tracking Gantt - ProjectPro.mpp*, that comes with this book contains an improved Tracking Gantt view. See page iv for the procedure to access these files.

on page 490 to compare the three different leveling scenarios in one Gantt Chart. You can also use them when change requests come your way to perform a *time impact analysis* (see page 614).

- While you can change parts of the baseline, you should not set the baseline for the entire project more than once, because comparing to a baseline that moves constantly is not meaningful and is not a generally accepted practice of project management. If you change your baseline schedule, it becomes a target-seeking missile trying to catch up with a constantly moving target. Instead, your live schedule should be the target-seeking missile with the baseline schedule as a static target.
  - Treat the baseline as a contractual agreement, even if it was not formalized with signatures. Contracts should always and only be amended through a formal process that involves the stakeholders.
  - Insist that changes to the baseline be brought forward as formal change requests that go through a formal change control process.
  - Assess any impacts of the change requests in your live schedule only.
  - Incorporate the changes in your baseline schedule only after they are formally approved by the stakeholders.
  - Pay attention to creating a clear and smooth change request process and communicate it to all stakeholders of your project before your project starts.
- A solid baseline schedule is necessary for *Earned Value Management*, since MS Project calculates the *Planned Values* (*BCWS*) from the baseline.

Preserving a Baseline Schedule

Change requests will necessitate changing the baseline. It is prudent to preserve every steady-state baseline that was in effect at some time. You can preserve up to ten baselines in MS Project. To copy the current baseline into an extra baseline:

1. Click ribbon **Project,** 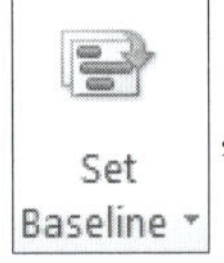

, item **Set baseline**; the **Set Baseline** dialog appears.

2. Check what the next available baseline is in the ◉ **Set Baseline** list; baselines that are currently in use have a date behind their name in the pull-down list.

3. Select ◉ **Set interim plan** and, from the list **Copy**, select the current **Baseline** and, from the list **Into,** select the next available baseline schedule. The first time you preserve your baseline the next available baseline will be **Baseline1**. In that case, the dialog should now look like:

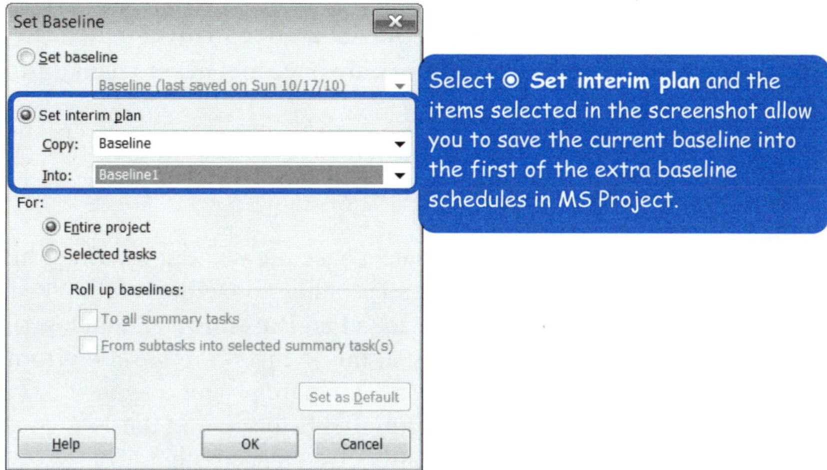

4. Click [OK] – that day's date is captured in the name of the baseline schedule you used. This will help you manage multiple baselines.

Re-baseline Entire Project or Selected Tasks Only?

After you have baselined the entire project for the first time, you should <u>never</u> re-baseline the entire project again! You should certainly not use the ◉ **Entire Project** option again after you have entered any actuals into the schedule. MS Project's feature for baselining projects has a weakness: it re-baselines even the tasks that are already 100% complete. For example, it would re-baseline the completed tasks *Design* and *Write Specs* in the illustration below, as well as the in-progress tasks *Code* and *Develop screens*. In doing so, it wipes out any discrepancies between your originally approved schedule and actual delivery. The discrepancies can be seen in the illustration. The schedule will start to show perfect performance because the baseline will be adjusted to be in line with the actuals. You are rewriting the history book to make yourself look good — a no-no in the modern world. When the discrepancies are gone, you cannot learn from past mistakes, and the lessons

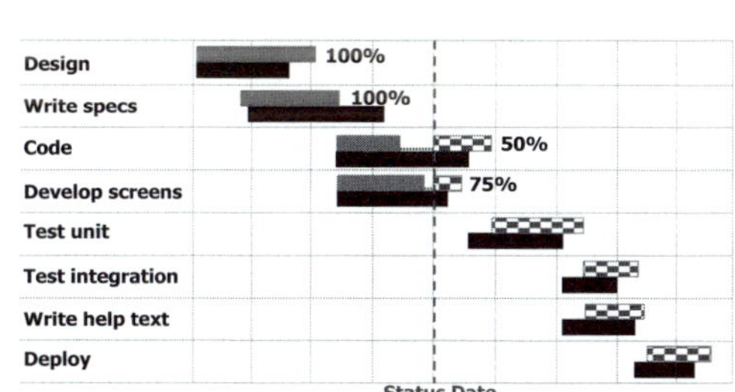

learned are compromised. I am in shock every time I encounter project managers who simply re-baseline their entire project over and over again! At the end of the project, their schedule looks like they have delivered the project exactly according to the baseline schedule, a pleasure I have never had … and never will have, I am afraid!

Therefore, you should use the ⦿ **Set Baseline** for ⦿ **Entire Project** option (ribbon **Project**, button **Set baseline**, item **Set baseline)** only once and never again during project execution!

Managing Multiple Baseline Schedules

We need to explore how you can properly update a baseline without rewriting history in the schedule. MS Project has fields for ten extra baselines (**Baseline1** through **Baseline10**), but MS Project only displays the so-called **Baseline** (without a serial number) in the *Tracking Gantt* view. We will call this the *working baseline* from now on. If you want to display a previous baseline and compare progress against it, you need to copy that baseline back into the active **Baseline** fields to see it in the Tracking Gantt view. You can copy baselines back and forth and between each other. This allows you to compare against any of your ten steady-state baselines, which are all versions of the active contract at some point in time.

Before you copy a particular baseline back into the working baseline, make sure you preserve your most current baseline in the next available set of baseline fields. We recommend you document what each baseline represents in a separate document or in the **Notes** field on the project summary task. If you preserve baselines immediately after you created them, the baseline date shown in the list of baselines may be enough documentation to identify each baseline. Would it not be nice if Microsoft added a description field for each baseline?

If you maintain the baselines as we explained, you will do it properly. Proper baseline change control is needed if you plan to use *Earned Value* reporting. The *Planned Values* **(***BCWS***)** are calculated from the time-phased *Baseline Cost* values. In fact, the planned values are the **Baseline Cost** values cumulated over time. If the baseline cost numbers are not reliable, the earned value analysis cannot be done.

The Earned Value calculations can be based on any of the 11 baselines by clicking ribbon **File,** [Options], tab **Advanced**. In the section **Earned Value options for this project**, you can select the baseline from the list **Baseline for Earned Value calculation**. If you want to compare against another baseline, for example *Baseline3*, you need to switch the earned value calculation to be based on **Baseline3**. If you also want to see the **Baseline3** bars in the timescale of the Tracking Gantt view, you need to copy *Baseline3* back into the **Baseline** (assuming you have preserved the current baseline already) following similar steps as for preserving the baseline, see page 610.

Real World Changes and Project Change Requests

The baseline is considered to be a contract between the project manager and the internal sponsor or the external client of the project. There are situations in which you need to maintain and adjust the *baseline schedule*:

- *Errors* turn up unexpectedly in the baseline or in the current schedule that was recently baselined. You would need to submit a project change request to get formal approval to re-baseline the affected tasks. Yes, it is hard to admit to errors.
- Changes are formally approved <u>after</u> you have set the first baseline. These changes could be:
    - *Scope* changes: this type of change entails addition or removal of requirements or deliverables
    - Changes in the budget of the project
    - Substantial additions or removals of *tasks*
    - Substantial additions or losses of *resources*
    - Substantial changes in resource *rates* or *fixed costs*
- Changes in the organization's strategy have been approved that force you to rethink and re-baseline your schedule, like budget increases, changes of deadline, or availability of crucial or *critical resources*. In this case, as the project manager, you would write a project change request yourself and propose it for approval.
- The economy suddenly turns down, or up for that matter. Either change could affect the validity of the schedule and its baseline. If the economy suddenly turns up, resources may demand higher rates. If news media suddenly turn their spotlight onto some resources or skills you use, these people may soon appear in your office to negotiate for higher rates.
- A strike on one of your sites, one of your supplier's sites (like air travel) or in public services (like public transport). If workers start a strike anywhere in your *supply chain*, it may affect their ability to deliver to you on time. If this affects your schedule significantly, you could submit a change request to re-baseline.
- Exceptional circumstances or "*Acts of God*" affect your project schedule or any of your suppliers' ability to deliver. These can be: fire, flood, tornado, hurricane, earthquake, landslide, tsunami, volcanic eruption, and so forth. Even if these happen far away, shipments with supplies for your project may be affected in today's global economy.

In each of these cases, a change request should be submitted to the decision-makers requesting approval to adjust the baseline of any affected tasks. Typically change requests:

- Describe the cause of the impacts on the schedule.
- Explain these impacts in terms of scope, quality, cost, time and risk.
- Contain a signature block for sign-off.

If the change request is approved, you should only re-baseline those tasks that are affected. These are, of course, the tasks that are new and inserted, but also their dependent tasks downstream (*successors*). Do not forget them!

If you baseline the ⦿ **Entire project** for a second time, you overwrite the values in the **Baseline** fields for all tasks. This is a problem for: tasks that are completed already, tasks that are in progress and future tasks that are not related to the change request through dependencies. When you re-baseline these, the new baseline will follow any actuals and will show perfect past performance (which may be the reason it is still so common!). All slippages and gains will be wiped out, and you lose historic data that are valuable contractual information. After you have set the first baseline, every subsequent change to the baseline should be only for selected tasks (i.e., those that are impacted by the change as captured in the change request).

Identifying the Tasks Impacted by a Change Request

The question now arises: how can you easily identify the tasks that are affected?

- In a small schedule, you can easily find the tasks that are impacted by a change request. When you make the change, you follow the chain of dependencies downstream. All tasks that are dependent are typically affected and will need to be re-baselined.
- In a large schedule, this would be too much work. Instead, we will have MS Project find the affected tasks for you. You can do this by first saving the current dates, then making the change and, finally, filtering the tasks that have new dates. This allows you to do a *time impact analysis* for the change request.

We will only discuss the steps for a time impact analysis in detail, but an *effort* and *cost impact analysis* are also needed. The process for an effort and cost impact analysis is essentially the same as for the time impact analysis: save the original numbers, insert the change and compare the new numbers to the old ones. You can save original work (effort) and cost values by right-clicking on their column headings and selecting **Copy**. You can then paste the work values into any of the extra text fields (**Text1-Text30**) and cost into any of the extra cost fields (**Cost1-Cost10**).

The detailed steps for a thorough time impact analysis are easier:

1. Save the schedule as it is. If you want to perform the impact-analysis without saving any changes to your schedule, you need to be able to revert to this saved version.

2. Copy the current **Start** and **Finish** dates; click ribbon **Project**, 

, item **Set baseline** – the **Set Baseline** dialog appears.

3. Select ◉ **Set interim plan** and in the list **Copy** select the current **Scheduled Start/Finish** and under **Into** select the item **Start1/Finish1** – the dialog should now look like:

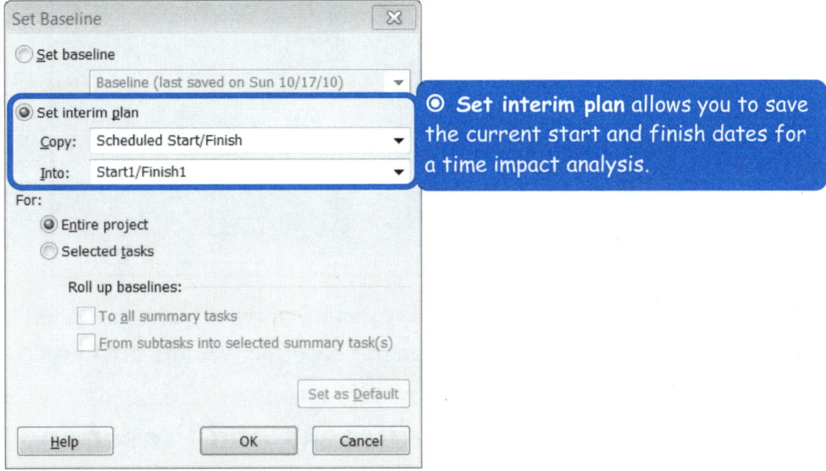

4. Click OK – the dates are now saved.

5. Now enter the change(s). Read the change request carefully and incorporate the changes:
   - ◇ Insert the new deliverables or new tasks. Make sure you create new dependencies with the existing network to capture how the new ones affect the old ones. This will cause the **Start** and **Finish** dates of the affected tasks to change.
   - 

◇ Mark the tasks that need to be removed as inactive using the Inactivate button on the **Task** ribbon. Make sure that the successors of inactive tasks are still scheduled where they should be, because the feature inactivates all dependencies on the task. You may need to create a new dependency. This button toggles the selected tasks between active and inactive status.

11

6. By filtering on what tasks have new **Start** and **Finish** dates, we can easily find the ones affected by the change request. Click ribbon **View**, [▾] of [Filter: [No Filter] ▾], **More Filters** – the **More Filters** dialog appears. Make sure ⦿ **Task** is selected. Click [New...] – the **Filter Definition** dialog appears. Please enter the following settings in this dialog:

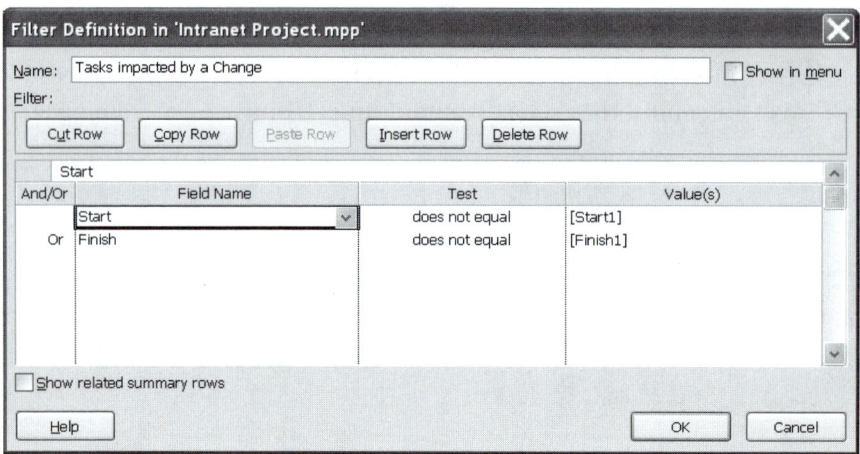

7. Click [OK] and [Apply] – MS Project displays all tasks affected by the change request. You can now easily change the baseline; see the next procedure.

Updating the Baseline of Impacted Tasks and Preserving It

The baseline data of completed tasks should never be changed. Only tasks that have not been started yet and that are affected by change requests through dependencies can be re-baselined.

1. If you have not preserved the current baseline, called **Baseline**, we recommend that you copy and preserve it first by following the steps on page 610.
2. You will now adjust the current baseline. Filter the tasks in the Gantt spreadsheet affected by the change request as explained in the previous procedure. Select all tasks that the filter displays.
3. Click ribbon **Project**, [Set Baseline ▾], item **Set baseline** – the **Set Baseline** dialog appears.

4. Select the option **For:** ◉ **Selected tasks**.
5. Under **Roll up baselines**, we recommend you select:
   ☑ **To all summary tasks** to update baseline information on all the higher-level summary tasks of the detail tasks selected.
   ☐ **From subtasks into selected summary task(s)** to update the baseline information of only the summary tasks that you selected. If you want to update specific summary tasks, you can always do so later by selecting those summary tasks only, and then selecting this option.
6. Click OK.
7. Preserve the new baseline, called **Baseline**, by following the steps on page 610.

Can I Delete Tasks in a Baselined Schedule?

The answer is *no* if you need *Earned Value* reports and you do not have an approved change request for deleting the tasks. Be careful with deleting tasks that you do not need any longer. If you simply delete them, you will compromise the integrity of the baseline the next time you update the baseline for selected tasks. Before you delete tasks, the baseline on the summary tasks and project summary task still include the baseline values of the deleted tasks. When you update the baseline and roll up to the summary tasks after deleting tasks, the total *baseline work* and *baseline cost* decrease on the summary tasks and on the project summary task.

Instead of deleting tasks, we recommend you make baselined tasks *inactive* (new feature in Project Professional 2010) by selecting the tasks you wanted to delete and clicking Inactivate on the **Tasks** ribbon or by setting the **Active** field to **No**. When you adjust the baseline, you should turn the inactive tasks back to active again and then maintain the baseline. After maintaining the baseline, you can turn them back to inactive. In this way, you maintain the integrity of the *Planned Values* (*BCWS*) and your Earned Value system. Once you get a formal approval to delete the tasks and change the baseline accordingly, you can remove the inactive tasks entirely and then re-baseline the affected parts of the project (see page 612 and following for the proper procedure).

The Client Reporting Period

As we discussed on page 137, ten reporting periods is the minimum for giving your client enough possibilities for corrective action; otherwise, your project may be spinning out of control without your client's knowing it. Clients will often prescribe the reporting interval to you.

You do not want too many reporting periods, because each progress report takes time and effort to prepare and discuss. Each report, therefore, adds to the overhead cost of managing the project. With too many reporting periods, overhead becomes too heavy a burden for the project budget. It can run up to 25% of the total cost, which can be a lot of money. We have the opinion that you should not have to report more than 30 times to executives or to clients on *projects* that are not *programs*; programs may require more than 30.

What does this mean for our projects? The next table shows what it means for projects of different durations.

Project Duration	**Minimum Client Reporting Frequency**	**Maximum Client Reporting Frequency**
1 month	Every other business day	Every business day
3 months	Weekly	Twice a week
1 year	Monthly	Every two weeks
2 years	Every two months	Every month
5 years	Every half year	Every two months

As the project manager you should ask your team to report status to you at least as frequently as the client needs reports. In practice, team members report much more frequently to you as the project manager than you report to the client. If you manage by walking around and interacting with your team members, you will have many more feedback cycles.

Showing Progress

Graphically

The progress can best be seen in the **Tracking Gantt** view. This view shows the task bars as shown in the illustration. The scheduled task will slowly but surely fill in with solid dark blue/red (*Actual*) to indicate how much progress has been made: field *Actual Duration*. Notice that the actual duration represents the number of days a team member has worked on the task so far — even though many people only think of it as the number of days the task took once it is completed.

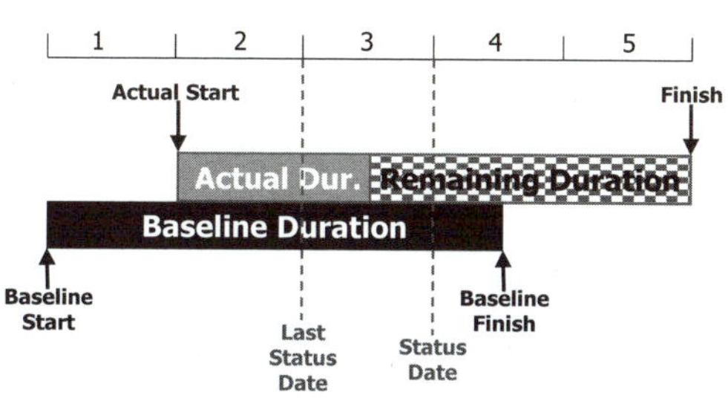

Ideally, the actual duration runs up to the *status date*, indicating that the task is progressing as scheduled. In the **Project, Project Information** dialog, you will find the **Status Date** field. If you display the status date also as a line in the timescale, you have all you need to visually assess the status of a project. The **Current Date** is updated every day by your computer, whereas the **Status Date** is manually entered. The PMBOK Guide® from PMI calls MS Project's **Status Date** the *Data Date*, which is defined as: *The date up to or through which the project's reporting system has provided actual status and accomplishments.*

In the illustration you can see that the progress (*Actual Dur.*) has fallen behind (perhaps because of sickness, under-estimation, or other tasks that took priority). The rest of the bar represents the *Remaining Duration*. The remaining duration is how many days the task will still take from the current status date to completion. Actual Duration plus Remaining Duration equals the Duration. This *formula* works behind the screens of MS Project to recalculate the duration when you enter an actual duration or revise a remaining duration that causes deviations from the baseline duration.

The black *Baseline* allows us to analyze slippages. In the illustration, you can see that:

- The task started 1 week later (Actual Start) than scheduled (Baseline Start).
- The task duration was already revised from 3.5 (Baseline Duration) to 4 weeks (current Duration); this is a 0.5-week increase in duration.
- The progress is still behind; the task is also progressing 0.5 weeks more slowly, because the Actual Duration (progress) is 0.5 weeks behind the status date. This

0.5 week of work to be done should be rescheduled to the future. It is likely the slippage will further increase; since the rate of progress was about half of the expected rate in the last update period, the remaining duration may need to be increased again.

Mathematically

The *% Complete* and *% Work Complete* are calculated indicators of progress. In addition to the formula in the illustration, there is a second *formula* for durations: *Actual Duration + Remaining Duration = Duration.*

$$\% \text{ Complete} = \frac{\text{Actual Duration}}{\text{Duration}}$$

$$\% \text{ Work Complete} = \frac{\text{Actual Work}}{\text{Work}}$$

For work (effort), the formula is very similar: *Actual Work + Remaining Work = Work.* Again, MS Project only needs two values and it will calculate the other two. It can even calculate the Actual Duration and Remaining Duration on the task level and update the tasks accordingly. Entering Actual Work (often in hours) is more precise than entering Actual Duration (often in days). You can also update the work on the lower level of assignments.

Updating Strategies

There are two different strategies for updating your schedule: *updating tasks* or *updating assignments*. An *assignment* is always a combination of one task and one resource, as discussed on page 353. Since one task can have one or more assignments, assignments are on a more detailed level than tasks.

- **Updating tasks**
  The strategy of updating the tasks is quick and easy. You have to enter only actual and remaining durations, and in most cases, you can do that with the mouse. MS Project arbitrarily calculates and spreads the *actual hours* in the timescale. Because of its arbitrary nature, this method is less precise than updating assignments by entering actual hours worked from timesheets, but if you update regularly, it is precise enough, even for *Earned Value Management.* As you go along, the precision increases because differences average out. If you are concerned about accuracy, you could enter actual work and remaining work instead of actual duration and remaining duration. Furthermore, there are options that can improve the precision of the automatic spreading; see page 631 or the section **Calculation options for this project** (in ribbon **File,** Options, tab **Advanced**).

- **Updating assignments**
  When you update assignments, you typically update every assignment of the resource. This is a lot of data and you would need an electronic timesheet to capture and transfer the data into the schedule. We recommend you collect:
  - ◇ *Actual hours by day* to be entered into the timescale field *Actual Work*
    Note that there is also an **Actual Work** field in the spreadsheet, that displays the total of all the timescale entries; we are not referring to that field here.
  - ◇ *Remaining hours* by assignment to be entered into the field *Remaining Work* in the spreadsheet.

The illustration summarizes the two ways of updating the schedule. If you *update tasks*, MS Project can update the assignments for you. If you update the assignments from the timesheets, MS Project can update the tasks. MS Project will do this for you if you select the following option: ribbon **File,** Options, tab **Schedule**, section **Calculation options for this project**, option ☑ **Updating task status updates resource status**. If you clear this option you can update both tasks and assignments in parallel, if you so desire. We think that is too much work.

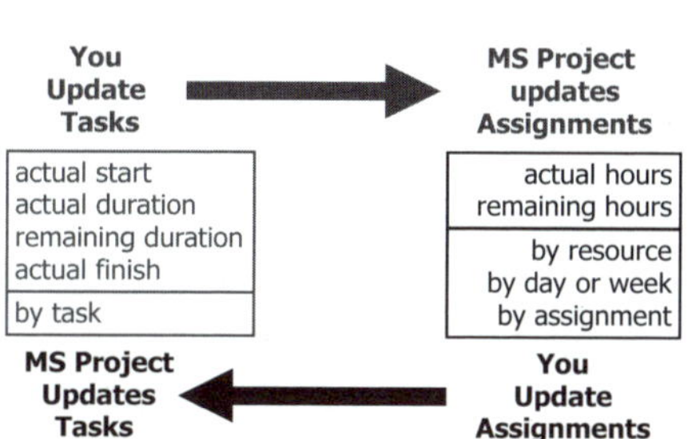

Updating assignments requires more numbers to process and, therefore, more work during the busy project execution. To illustrate this, consider the following situation. You have a schedule with 300 tasks and 10 weekly reporting periods, which means that every week you must update an average of 30 tasks, 20 of which are typically completed in that week. If you do a task update:

- For the 20 completed tasks, you collect their actual duration – 20 actual durations.
- For the 10 tasks in progress, you collect actual duration and remaining duration – 10 actual durations and 10 remaining durations.

The grand total for updating tasks therefore is 20 + 20 = 40 pieces of data.

For a day-by-day assignment update common with timesheets, we will have to make more assumptions. We will assume that the average task duration is 4 days and the average number of resources per task is 1.5:

- For the 20 completed tasks: 20 tasks * 4 days * 1.5 resources = 120 pieces of data
- For the 10 tasks in progress:
  - ◇ 10 tasks * average of 2 days progress * 1.5 resources = 30 pieces of data
  - ◇ 10 tasks * 1.5 resources = 15 remaining work estimates

The grand total for updating assignments is: 120 + 30 + 15 = 165 pieces of data.

As you can see, if you choose to update assignments instead of tasks, you will process about four times as much data during project *execution*, when you are already very busy managing the project!

We recommend you use the strategy of updating tasks in the following instances:

- If you do not have an electronic timesheet system in place. Paper timesheets will drown you in data. Data entry takes (too) much effort, and often project managers cannot keep up, even if they need to review the data only on a weekly basis. We have not even mentioned the double data-entry and the likelihood of errors that will need to be sorted out.
- If your timesheet system does not allow you to automatically transfer both actual hours worked and remaining work estimates back into your project schedules. Most in-house developed timesheets and many vendor timesheet systems do not allow automatic transfer into the schedules.

We have observed that too many project managers stop updating their schedules sometime during the project *execution*, because:

- They fail to get enough information from their team members,
- They drown in the flood of data, or,
- They waste a lot of time sorting out the errors in the timesheet data. Some people seem to take pleasure in entering garbage data, if only to test if the data are ever reviewed. No one likes to enter data that are never looked at (and rightfully so!).
- They cannot get the resource managers to approve the timesheet data promptly so they can use that same data to update their project schedules and report project status in a timely fashion.

If you, as a project manager, abandon updating your schedule, you lose the model that provides you with up-to-date forecasts and allows you to create what-if scenarios to determine the best course of action. Slowly but surely, you lose your grip on the project. It is better to have a less precise grip than no grip.

Project Professional with *Project Server* provides an electronic timesheet system that supports updating assignments. Project Server's electronic timesheet offers the following benefits:

- It makes collecting status updates from your team members much easier. Project Server can automatically send out reminders by email to team members that their tasks are coming up and again that their tasks need updating.
- It allows you to automatically transfer the numbers back into your MS Project schedule, thereby preventing double data entry.
- It makes submitting performance reports to executives and clients much easier.

If you have Project Server, or an equally efficient electronic timesheet system from another vendor (for a list, see the section starting on page 646), we recommend you use our strategy of updating assignments.

We recommend you consider carefully which update strategy fits your situation best. We will now discuss both updating strategies in more detail:

- Updating tasks, see the next section
- Updating assignments, see the section starting on page 646.

Updating Tasks

Here are the things you need to do when *updating tasks*:

- Collect the update information by task
- Choose the **Options** on the **File** ribbon (see page 631)
- Prepare the view (see page 633)
  - Change the view to **Tracking Gantt**
  - Apply the **Tracking** table
  - Display the **Tasks** ribbon
- Set the task **Type** of the tasks you will update to **Fixed Units** (see page 636)
- Set the **Status Date** for updating (see page 635)
- Enter the update information (see page 638)
- Check whether the schedule is updated correctly (see page 677)
- Prepare the status and forecast report (see page 672)
  You may need to re-optimize your schedule before reporting on it.

The first four things you normally need to do once; the rest are done regularly at every status cycle.

What Data to Collect? Percent Complete?

The ideal type of progress data to collect is *factual* or *objective* data, but objective progress measurements are not always possible. If they are not, the next best are progress measurements that independent assessors would easily agree upon, also known as *intersubjective* data. Avoid collecting *subjective* data, where progress is in the eye of the beholder, much like beauty.

Construction project managers typically collect percent complete and enter these into MS Project to update their schedule. In construction projects you can often easily see or measure objectively the percent complete. From the architectural drawings you can derive that you need to pour 100 cubic yards of concrete; if you have poured 50, you are at 50% complete. This is a visible and measurable percent complete, or *physical percentage complete* (MS Project calls the field **Physical % Complete**). In construction projects, the physical % complete is factual and (fairly) objective, and can be used as an indicator for *Earned Value*. We recommend entering **Physical % Complete** on construction tasks.

In all other projects, like *software development*, establishing the percentage complete is much more difficult, and we recommend you do not collect percent complete but treat it as a value calculated by MS Project. In those projects, you can easily and objectively count the number of days the resource has worked on the task up to the status date. This number can be entered as the **Actual Duration**, which is an indicator for *Earned Value*. With the following formula, MS Project will calculate the percent complete:
% Complete = Actual Duration / Duration

In non-construction projects, you need to ask yourself whether it makes sense to ask your team members for percentages complete. What does it mean if a team member tells you, *I am at 90% complete?* Does it mean:

- *I am almost finished!* (this is what we would like it to mean, of course), or
- *I have spent 90% of the time I was supposed to spend on this task* (quite defendable, but detrimental if you forget to ask for the remaining duration as well), or
- *I have just figured out how to do this, and now I will do it,* (programmers often think like this, I have found) or
- *I did all the easy stuff, now I will start the difficult stuff!* or
- *Last week it was 80% complete, so this week it must be 90%,* or
- *I want the project manager to think that I am at 90% complete!* or
- *I pulled the percentage from the breakfast cereal box this morning,* or
- *Leave me alone, so I can do my work; I am busy enough!* or
- *I have now started to work on the task!*

As you can see, the answers became more devious as we went down the list. In polls that we take during our classes, we have found that *90% complete* can mean any of the above (in non-construction projects)! We, therefore, recommend you ask for factual actuals instead of perceived percentages. Ask for **Actual Durations** instead of **% Complete** when collecting update information; you are then asking for facts rather than fiction. Using **% Complete** is less objective than entering the actual number of business days that people worked on a task (**Actual Duration**). The number of days somebody really worked on a task can easily be counted and is factual information. For example, if the resource worked on the task on Wednesday, Thursday and Friday the **Actual Duration** is 3 days, so far. If you find the time unit of days too rough and you need more precision, you can collect the **Actual Work** instead in terms of hours actually worked on the task. Defining the **Actual Duration** or **Actual Work** like this also provides an indicator for what is earned on the task (a.k.a. the *Earned Value* of the task).

If you still want to enter **% Complete** instead of the **Actual Duration** or **Actual Work**, this more complex method requires a longer, two-step process that follows the formulas in the illustration on the left. First you enter the **% Complete** (step 1 in illustration), but when you revise the **Remaining Duration** (step 2) or **Actual Work**, MS Project recalculates the **% Complete** that you first entered. You may not like that. Why would you want to enter a number that will change in most cases? For *construction project* managers, this is not acceptable, since the percent complete is objectively assessed and should not be changed. That is why we recommend they use the **Physical % Complete** instead of **% Complete**.

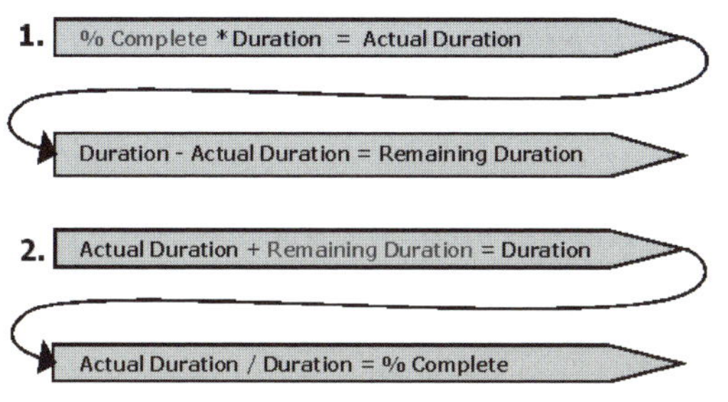

If you nevertheless choose to enter **% Complete** instead of having MS Project calculate it as we suggest, we recommend:

- You still ask for **Remaining Duration** updates, since they will keep your forecasts accurate. If you only enter **% Complete** your forecasts will be inaccurate. You cannot afford not asking for revisions to remaining durations (*Forecast Scheduling*!).
- You allow fairly rough increments in **% Complete** only. We suggest increments such as 0%, 25%, 50%, 75%, 100% as shown on the **Tracking** ribbon, or perhaps only 0% and 100%. In the latter case, you can simply ask: *Are you finished with it, or not?* This question does not leave much room for wishful thinking (or outright manipulation!). However, you need to have a fairly detailed schedule in order to get good results with rough percentages. The durations of the detail tasks should be closer to the 1% minimum rather than the 10% maximum in the *1%-10% rule*; see our discussion on page 135. If you create tasks that are small enough, you can get to the facts more easily.

- You consider the options that will influence how MS Project will spread the *actual hours* worked when entering **% Complete**. Click ribbon **File,** Options **,** tab **Advanced**, section **Calculations options for this project**; the main options are (see page 631 for more detail):
  ☑ **Move end of completed parts after status date back to status date** which moves the actual durations to before the status date.
  ☑ **Move start of remaining parts before status date forward to status date** which moves the remaining durations to after the status date.
  ☑ or ☐ **Edits to total task % complete will be spread to the status date.** If you change a % complete, MS Project can calculate the actual hours and spread them out to the status date when this option is on. When it is off, the actual hours will be

11

entered where they were scheduled or from the **Actual Start** date onward. Splits will often appear in the task bars with this option on.

In summary, we recommend the following for:

	Collect and Enter	**Have MS Project calculate**
Construction projects	*Physical % Complete* *Actual Start,* *(Actual) Finish*	*Actual Duration, Remaining Duration, Earned Value, SV, CV, SPI, CPI, EAC* (see page 587 and following for an explanation of these indicators)
Non-construction projects	*(Actual Start)* *Actual Duration* *Remaining Duration* OR *(Actual Start)* *Actual Work* *Remaining Work*	*% Complete* *Duration* *Finish*

The process for updating construction schedules is straightforward: enter **Physical % Complete**, **Actual Start** dates and the **Actual Finish** dates if it is in the past. If a task takes longer than originally planned, you can update the **Finish** date to the new date when the work is promised to be finished. Then you make sure that MS Project calculates the Earned Value based on the **Physical % Complete**: click ribbon **File**, Options, tab **Advanced**, scroll to the bottom and find section **Earned Value options for this project** and from the list **Default task Earned Value method** select the item **Physical % Complete**. MS Project will then calculate the indicators listed in the previous table. That is all we will say about updating *construction schedules*. We will elaborate on what the rest of the world (i.e., non-construction project managers) should do. By the way, construction project managers could also adopt the methods we will discuss next, if they so desire; it will work well for them as well and they can still do Earned Value. In highly specialized or one-off construction projects where **Physical % Complete** becomes as nebulous as it is for the rest of the world, it may even be a better way to go.

So, What Data Should I Collect?

The answer to this question depends on:

- The level of cooperation you can get from your team members for updating the project schedule.

The typical excuse from team members for not cooperating with updates is: *You have given me too many tasks and too little time to do them already — and now you are also asking me to do what!!??* If your team members do not have time for your requests for update information, you will have to minimize the amount of data you need from them and insist that you get at least that. At the absolute minimum, you need revisions to **Remaining Duration** or **Remaining Work** on all tasks that are in progress.

- The importance of receiving feedback on your original estimates.
  How important is it to be able to compare estimates to actuals? If this is as important as getting the project done, you need to collect **Actual Duration** or **Actual Work** as well.
- The likelihood that you may end up in a contractual dispute where you may need to reconstruct all events on their exact dates.
  If a dispute is likely (and particularly if the contract has penalty clauses for late delivery), you may have to capture actual dates. This is often needed in construction projects.

When you update the tasks in your project, you should keep the formulas shown in the illustration on the left in the back of your mind. They explain the values that MS Project calculates and displays when you enter your updates. In a task update, you enter the **Actual Duration** and allow MS Project to calculate the **Remaining Duration** and the **% Complete** using the formulas shown in the illustration. Once resources have started working on a task, they often have a much better idea how long it will take, and when you ask them for updates, you may find that the remaining duration calculated by MS Project may be too little or too much time. If so, you should update the **Remaining Duration** field with a more precise estimate. MS Project will then recalculate the total **Duration** (**Actual** plus **Remaining**) and change the **% Complete** accordingly. The forecast dates will be accurate at this point, and the % Complete will be accurate as well as an indicator for *Earned Value*.

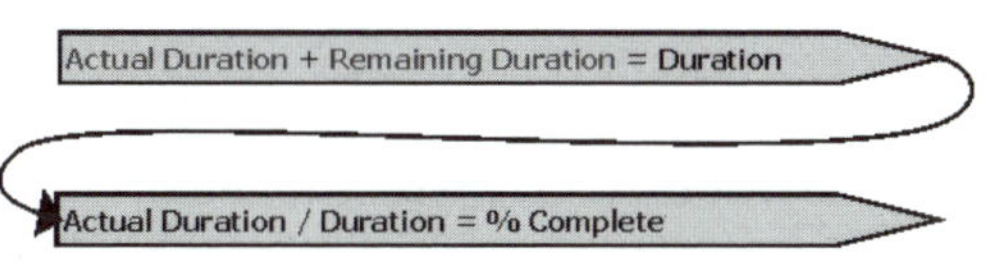

We recommend you collect at least the **Remaining Duration** (or **Remaining Work**) from your team members (we will explain the steps on page 629), and at most the following four data points (we will explain the steps on page 631). To do so, ask these questions:

- *On what date did you start the task?* (**Actual Start**)
  This question is only needed if accuracy of actual dates is important (e.g., in contractual disputes).

- *How many business days have you worked on the task as per the status date?* (**Actual Duration**) Defined in this way, Actual Duration becomes an objective measure for *Earned Value*; you only earn if you perform work on the task. It allows you to measure progress in non-construction projects where it is more difficult to agree on the percent complete. Note that we neither defined Actual Duration as the number of days that have passed, nor as the number of days a task took once the task is entirely completed, which would not be measures for Earned Value.
- *How many business days do you still need to finish the task after the status date?* (**Remaining Duration**) You need to ask this question only for tasks that are currently in progress.
- *On what date was the task finished?* (**Actual Finish**) This question is often not needed if you kept the remaining durations up-to-date in previous updates.

If you do not want to collect and enter this much information, we recommend you collect **Remaining Duration** (or **Remaining Work**) as the absolute minimum. If you can collect more data, we suggest adding **Actual Duration** (or **Actual Work**) as the next data point to collect. The added value of the **Actual Duration** data is that it allows you to compare your original estimates against the actuals. Since **Actual Work** is expressed in hours instead of days, it allows you to compare more precisely. You can often learn a lot from this comparison and enjoy the benefit in your next project.

Adding **Actual Start** dates provides the value that you can better trace when actual events happened. This may be important when contract disputes need to be sorted out in front of a judge.

In summary, these are your choices:

Actual Start	
Actual Duration	Actual Work
Remaining Duration	Remaining Work
Actual Finish	

How to Collect the Data

Two ways are commonly used to collect the data for task updates:

- Regular status meetings:
  In a short meeting of one hour at most, you quickly collect the data from each team member. You then enter it, or have it entered. Some project managers have it entered immediately during the status meeting, then display the schedule with a projector on

a screen to reveal new schedule conflicts that can be discussed and resolved right away with the team.

- Paper to-do list turn-around reports:
  You can distribute to each team member paper to-do lists with their tasks. The reports also contain empty fill-in fields for the status information. Ask the team members to enter the status information and return it to you by the end of the week. If you report weekly, we recommend you print a to-do list that covers two weeks ahead to show what is coming up, and to allow the resource to make progress ahead of schedule. Note that such a list is not as detailed as a timesheet.
- 2010 Pro In Project 2010, Microsoft has added the first release of synchronizing task lists to a *SharePoint Foundation* or *SharePoint Server* site. Team members can also enter updates on the SharePoint site that the project manager can sync back into the schedule, allowing two-way synchronizing between Project Professional 2010 and a SharePoint site. We were very excited about this new possibility (you do not need Project Server!) until we thoroughly tested the original release of Project 2010.
  At the time of writing this book (fall of 2010), we did not think the feature was user-friendly enough to deploy it. We think, however, that Microsoft will keep improving this feature very rapidly, and we want to keep you up-to-date in a document called *11 Updating through SharePoint - ProjectPro.doc* that you can download from our website. We will revise this document regularly with news on service packs or interim releases. The document will also explain the issues and the latest best practices for this feature. See page vi for the procedure to access these files.

The Quickest Way to Update Tasks in Your Schedule

The important goal of updating schedules is to keep your date forecasts accurate; remember the title of this book: *Forecast Scheduling*. To achieve accurate date forecasts, the minimum data that you need from your team members are revisions to the remaining durations for in-progress tasks. With just that information you can keep your forecasts up-to-date.

11

The quickest way to update your schedule is to first update it as if every task were running as scheduled (yes, this is not very accurate!), then enter the remaining duration estimates and schedule them all after the status date. Through the network of dependencies (that you carefully crafted and checked), all forecasts will be updated and as accurate as they need to be.

1. Click on a column heading to select all the tasks; then, on the **Tasks** ribbon, click Mark on Track ▾.

OR

Click ribbon **Project,** Update Project – the **Update Project** dialog appears:

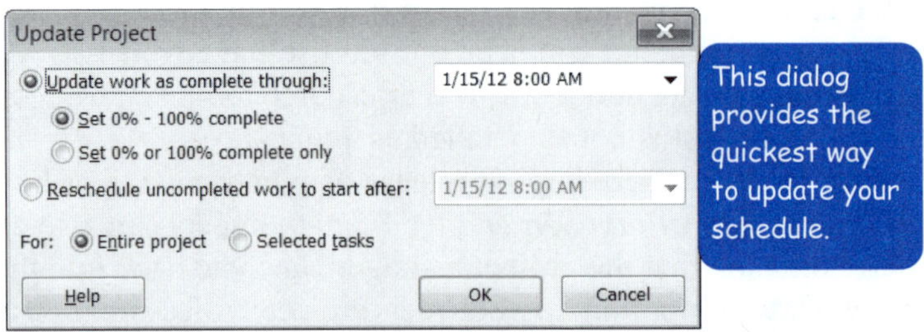

Select ◉ **Update Work as Complete Through** and enter the status date in the date field. Make sure it is the same date as the status date in the **Status Date** field on the **Project** ribbon.
Select ◉ **Set 0% - 100% complete** (or ◉ **Set 0% or 100% complete only** if you follow the 0%-100% updating of *Earned Value*)
Select ◉ **For entire project**.
Click OK.

2. Update any tasks that were started ahead of schedule by entering the number of days worked on them so far into the field **Actual Duration** or marking them with 100% (**Task** ribbon) if they are completed already.
3. In the field **Remaining Duration**, enter the remaining durations that you collected from your team members on all tasks that are in progress (not finished).
4. Now reschedule all remaining durations to the future after the status date. Click

ribbon **Project,** Update Project – the **Update Project** dialog appears.

5. Select the following options:
Select ◉ **Reschedule uncompleted work to start after** and in its date field enter the status date, if needed.
Select ◉ **Entire Project**.
Click OK.

If you do this, the forecasts in your schedule will be *accurate* and *valid*. If you update your schedule regularly in this way, you will spend the least amount of effort while producing accurate forecasts! You are applying the principle of *forecast scheduling*!

The Thorough Way to Update Tasks in Your Schedule

We will now explain how to update your schedule by collecting **Actual Duration** and **Remaining Duration**. The *Actual Duration* for in-progress tasks is the number of days that a person has worked on the task so far (until the **Status Date**). The *Remaining Duration* is the number of days still to go (from the status date forward to complete the task).

Instead of collecting Actual Duration and Remaining Duration, you can also collect *Actual Work* and *Remaining Work* on the task level. If most of your tasks are based on effort (Work), this may make more sense. This will function in a way similar to durations, except that you enter the actual and remaining work numbers into the fields **Actual Work** and **Remaining Work**, of course. We recommend you use the table **Work** if you want to do this. You may also request work update numbers expressed in hours instead of days for duration, thus adding a level of precision, but also difficulty. If you choose this route, we recommend you also change the visual progress indicator in the timescale from **% Complete** to **% Work complete**. You can do this by: clicking **Format**, button **Format**, item **Bar Styles**; replacing all entries **CompleteThrough** with **% Work complete**; and on the tab **Text** changing **% Complete** to **% Work complete** for all items that have percent complete to the **Right** of their task bar.

Choosing the Options for Updating Tasks

Here are the options we recommend for updating tasks using **Actual** and **Remaining Duration**. Click ribbon **File**, Options and click on the tab indicated in the table below where you want to change settings.

Tab	Option
Schedule	Section **Scheduling options for this project:** ☑ **Split in-progress tasks** Allows moving the uncompleted portion of a task to after the **Status Date** by splitting the task bar. With this option cleared, the options on the **Advanced** tab cannot split any task bars and will behave quite differently as a result. We recommend selecting it.

Tab	Option
Schedule	Section **Calculation options for this project** ☑ **Updating task status updates resource status** Updating the tasks will update the actual work of the assignments. We recommend you keep this option checked for task updates. Only clear it if you want to update the tasks and the assignments.
	☐ or ☑ **Actual costs are always calculated by Microsoft Project** Updating the tasks will update the *actual cost*. It is up to you whether you want MS Project to do that. If you clear this option, you can enter the actual cost.
Advanced	Section **Calculation options for this project**: ☑ **Move end of completed parts after status date back to status date** This moves the actual duration bar to before the status date; actual work done is moved into the past. We recommend you turn this on; it will help you keep the forecasts accurate. ☐ or ☑ **And move start of remaining parts back to status date** The remaining duration bar will cuddle up to the status date (unless there are dependencies that keep it where it is). The choice is up to you.
	☑ **Move start of remaining parts before status date forward to status date** This moves the remaining duration bar to after the status date; work still to be completed is moved to the future. We recommend you turn this on; it will help you keep the forecasts accurate. It has no effect on tasks that have not started yet, but should have started as per the status date. These tasks will still have to be rescheduled to after the status date to put them into the future where they belong, since work can only be done in the future. ☐ or ☑ **And move end of completed parts forward to status date** This moves the actual duration bar to cuddle up to the status date. The choice is up to you.
	☐ **Edits to total task % complete will be spread to the status date** If a task is falling behind, the progress entered will be evenly spread to the status date. This option is only relevant if you enter % Complete, which we do not recommend.

Tab	Option
Advanced	Section **General options for this project**: ☐ **Automatically add new resources and tasks** This prevents a typo in a resource name from accidentally adding a new resource, and works similarly for tasks. We recommend clearing it, particularly in a Project Server environment where resources should come from the enterprise resource pool.
	Section **Edit:** ☐ **Allow cell drag and drop**, which prevents accidentally dragging data on top of other data in your baselined schedule. We recommend clearing it.

As you can see, the options on the **Advanced** tab help when updating the schedule, but do not guarantee that your schedule will be entirely up-to-date.

Prepare the View for Updating

One of the download files that comes with this book contains an improved Tracking Gantt view and table. The file is called *Tracking Gantt - ProjectPro.mpp* with a view called *Tracking Gantt ProjectPro* and a table called *Tracking Table ProjectPro*. You need to transfer both the view and the table into your schedule using the organizer (ribbon **File**, tab **Info**, button **Organizer**). If you download this file, you can skip the following procedure. See page vi for the procedure to access these files.

11

1. Click ribbon **View**, click the bottom part of 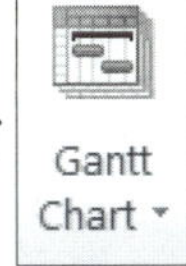

and select **Tracking Gantt** – the **Tracking Gantt** view appears. The current schedule is shown in the top half of the task bars (colored blue or red). The baseline is shown as the gray bottom half of the task bars.

2. Keep the critical tasks visible (ribbon **Format**, ☑ **Critical Tasks**); otherwise, the timescale pane misses the most important task bars and the schedule may look too optimistic. If you clear this option, the critical task bars disappear entirely, which is a bug in Project 2010 as originally released!

3. Click ribbon **View,** 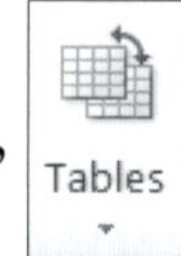

and **Tracking** – the tracking table appears.

4. The tracking table has all the fields in which to enter data for task updates. We recommend that you modify the table to make it look like the table in the following screenshot, because in complex update situations (e.g., a task that started late, is progressing slowly and will take longer, see page 643 for details), it is important to enter the information in the order in which the fields are displayed. This provides a visual reminder of the order of data entry:

	Task Name	Act. Start	Act. Dur.	Rem. Dur.	Act. Finish	Act. Cost
1	**Scope**	**NA**	**0 days**	**3.5 days**	**NA**	**$0.00**
2	Determine project scope	NA	0 hrs	4 hrs	NA	$0.00
3	Secure project sponsorship	NA	0 days	1 day	NA	$0.00
4	Define preliminary resources	NA	0 days	1 day	NA	$0.00
5	Secure core resources	NA	0 days	1 day	NA	$0.00
6	Scope complete	NA	0 days	0 days	NA	$0.00
7	**Analysis/Software Requirements**	**NA**	**0 days**	**14 days**	**NA**	**$0.00**
8	Conduct needs analysis	NA	0 days	5 days	NA	$0.00
9	Draft preliminary software specifications	NA	0 days	3 days	NA	$0.00
10	Develop preliminary budget	NA	0			

Enter actual progress and forecasts into a modified **Tracking** table.

If you want to collect effort (work) instead of durations, use the fields **Actual Work** and **Remaining Work** instead of the fields **Act.Dur.** and **Rem.Dur.**.

5. Display the **Tasks** ribbon. The Tasks ribbon contains several useful tools for updating schedules:

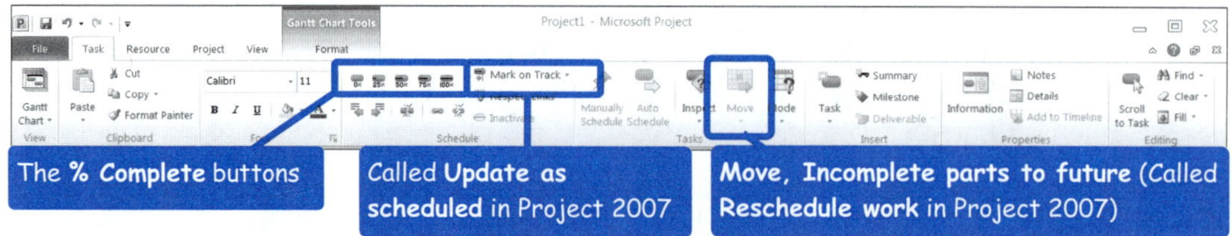

2010 The **Tasks** ribbon has all the handy tools for updating. Notice the **Reschedule Work** button is not on the **Task** ribbon. You can add it by customizing the ribbon (see page 73 for the how-to) or you can use the new **Move** button and its **Incomplete parts to future** item.

Setting the Status Date for Updating

If you do not enter the **Status Date**, Project 2010 will use the **Current Date** (that day's date) for the update. The Current Date is maintained by the clock in your computer. We recommend you use the Status Date, because then it is always clear:

- As per what date you updated your schedule, which may be a date in the near future, like next Monday. You need to prepare this report in the week before.
- When you last updated your schedule.

The steps are:

1. Click ribbon **Project** and click the bottom half of [Status Date: 10/19/10] – the **Status Date** dialog appears (the smallest dialog in Project 2010):

   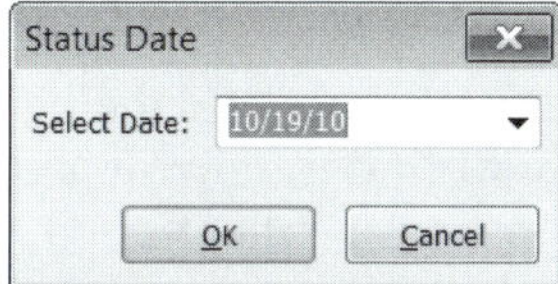

2. Change the **status date** to the date when you want to update tasks and compare the schedule against the baseline. Include the time as well if it should not default to the end of the working day.

3. The status date does not yet appear as a vertical line in the timescale. Click ribbon

   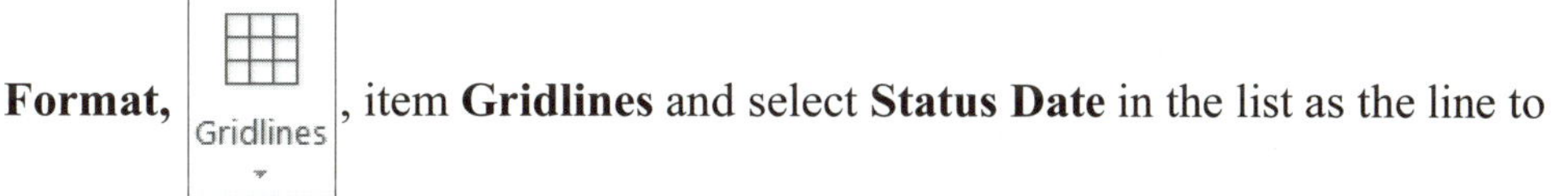

   Format, [Gridlines], item **Gridlines** and select **Status Date** in the list as the line to change. Choose a dashed line in **Type** and a bright **Color**. The dashed line makes it different from dependency lines (arrows). Click [OK].

4. The status line is now visible in the timescale, similar to:

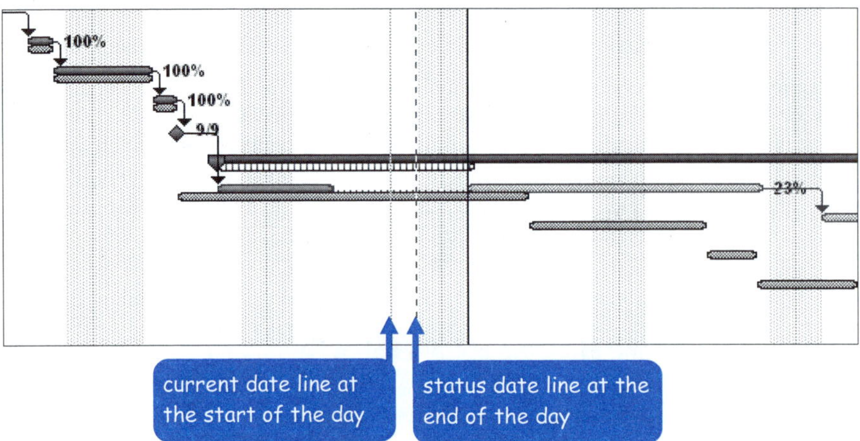

MS Project uses the system date of your computer to continuously update the *current date*. When you open your schedule again tomorrow, you will find tomorrow's date as the current date. The current date line is positioned at the start of the day by default. The *status date* stays the same since you last entered it and will refresh your memory about when your last schedule update took place. The status date line is displayed at the end of the day by default. In the previous screenshot the same date was entered for **Current Date** and for **Status Date**.

Set the Task Type for Tasks to Update

When you enter update information into MS Project, you will trigger recalculations in the *formula* **Duration * Peak Units = Work**. The task **Type** has to be set in such a way that it causes MS Project to perform the right unsolicited recalculations.

What is the best task Type for all tasks during Task Updates?

Duration changes often during updates!
D * U = W

When we update tasks, we change duration values. Therefore, **Fixed Duration** is not the task **Type** that will trigger the right recalculations. The type **Fixed Units** allows us to keep the number of resources assigned to the tasks the same while the duration changes. Essentially, you are telling MS Project that the resources (units) that are working on the task will continue. As a result, MS Project will recalculate the Work; the total work (effort) will decrease or increase. If that is your purpose, the **Fixed Units** type is appropriate. If instead you want the number of *resource units* to be recalculated when the duration changes, you could choose **Fixed Work**. We have often seen ridiculously high units in updated schedules, like 3300% for an individual. These allocated **Units** numbers are not easy to spot in Project 2010 and, therefore, we recommend **Fixed Units**.

1. Click on any column heading in the Tracking Gantt spreadsheet to select all tasks. OR
   Be more selective by selecting just those tasks that need to be updated.

2. On the **Task** ribbon click [Information] – the **Multiple Task Information** dialog appears. Click the **Advanced** tab; the dialog should now look like:

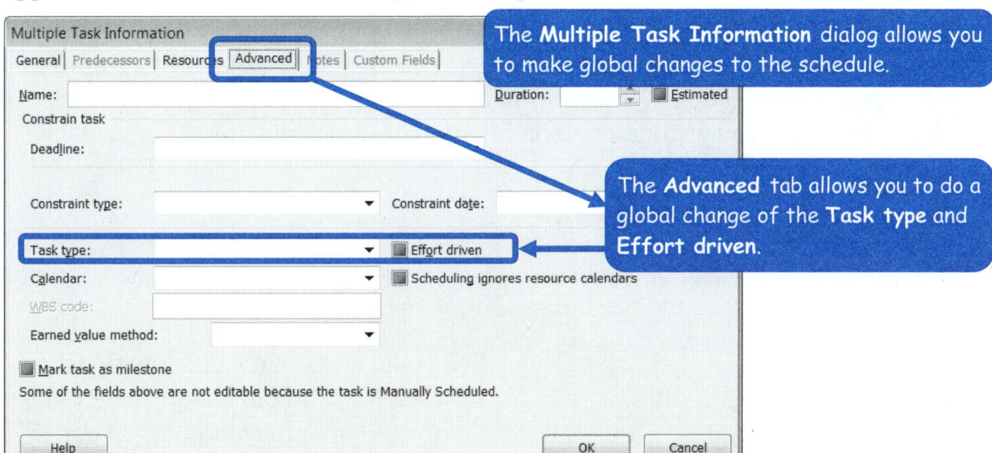

3. From the list **Task type**, select the item **Fixed Units**. Changing the task type does not trigger a recalculation, only a change of one variable will do that in the *formula*: **Duration * Peak Units = Work**.

4. Clear ☐ **Effort driven**; we recommended earlier that you keep effort driven turned off (see page 358 and following). Click [OK]. Please note that summary tasks continue to be **Fixed Duration**, which is okay since we will not update summary tasks.

Task Updating Situations in Practice

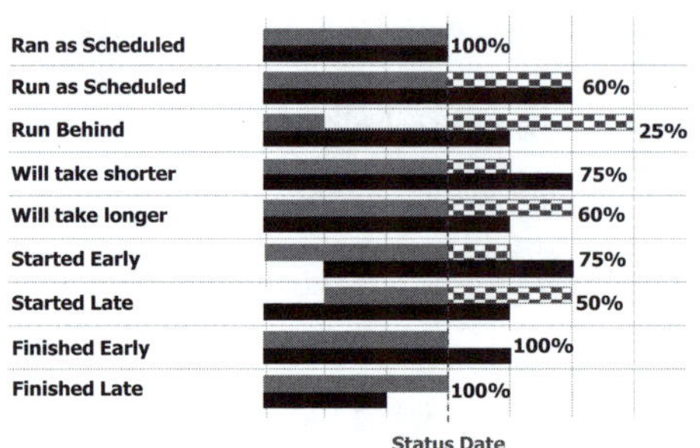

The following situations and combinations of them are the only ones that you will encounter when updating tasks:

- Tasks that Ran as Scheduled
- Tasks that Run as Scheduled
- Tasks that Run Behind
- Tasks that Will Take Longer (or Shorter)
- Tasks that Started Late (or Early)
- Tasks that Finished Late (or Early)

For each situation, there is a preferred way to enter update information. We will provide how-to steps for each situation, then address what to do when you encounter a combination of these situations (see page 643).

Tasks that Ran as Scheduled

Simply mark these tasks as 100% complete in the Tracking Gantt view, as shown in the illustration.

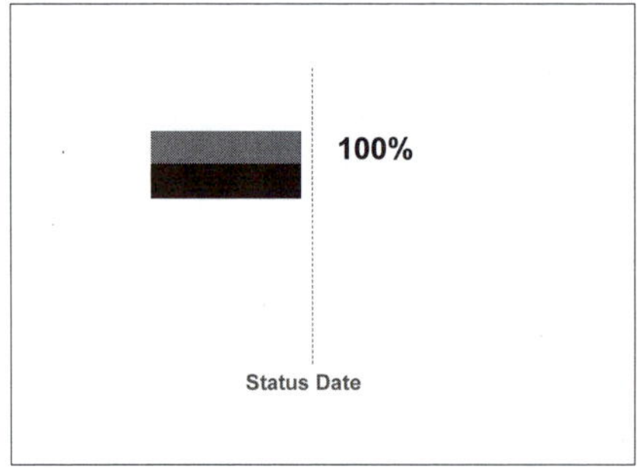

1. Select the tasks that were completed as scheduled by dragging over them or by clicking on the first and, while holding down [Control], clicking on the rest of the tasks.
2. On the **Task** ribbon, click [100%]
   OR
   In the **% Complete** field of the tracking table, enter 100%.
   OR
   in the **Actual Duration** field, enter a value equal to the **Remaining Duration**.

Tasks that Run as Scheduled

In this case you want to show actual progress up to the status date, as in the illustration.

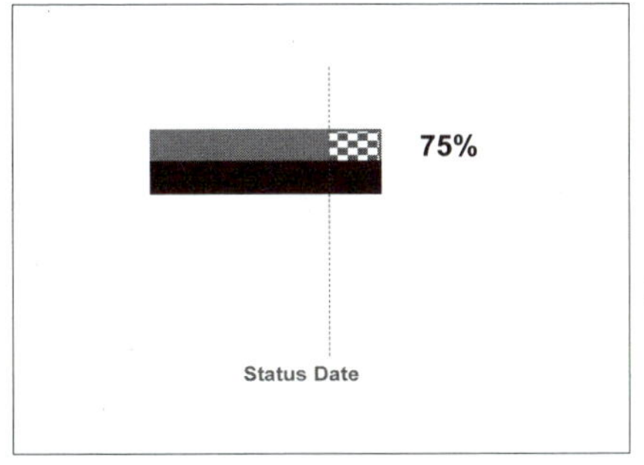

1. Select the tasks that are on schedule by dragging over them or by clicking on the first and, while holding down [Control], clicking on the rest of the tasks.
2. On the **Tasks** ribbon, click [Mark on Track] – this updates all selected tasks as if they progress on schedule as per the status date.

Tasks That Run Behind

This situation will require more updating effort. Observe bar A in the illustration; you can see that the progress is falling behind, because the solid color denoting actual progress does not run up to the status date in the task bar. You will need to capture the actual number of days the resource(s) worked on the task (**Actual Duration**), but, because the task is behind, you will also have to bring forward the incomplete portion of the task bar (**Remaining Duration**) to after the *status date*, as done for bar B in the illustration. You cannot leave work still to be done scheduled in the past (unless you have a time machine!). Progress falling behind may also require a revision of the remaining duration. If the number of actual days worked on the task is less than planned, the resources were interrupted by:

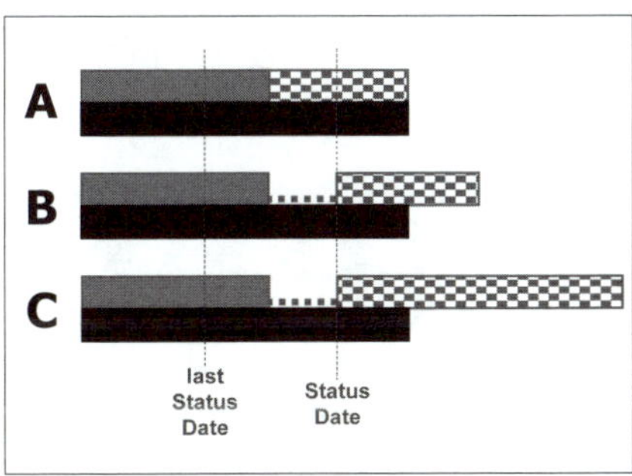

- work on other, higher priority tasks,
- Illness, or
- Other distractions.

The question is: Will this disruption continue?

- If the disruption(s) will stop, you could keep the remaining duration as shown by bar B in the illustration (calculated by MS Project); it has a split showing the incomplete portion of work rescheduled to after the status date without an increase.

11

◆ If the disruption(s) will continue, you need to revise the remaining duration; see how bar C in the illustration is doubled in length because the resource worked only half of the intended number of days on the task.

It could also be that all days were worked but the rate of progress was slower; we will discuss this as the next situation: *Tasks that will take longer*.

The steps to enter disruptions are:

1. In the Tracking Gantt view, enter the **Actual Duration** of the task (the number of days the resource has actually worked on the task); MS Project will calculate the new remaining duration.
2. Revise this calculated **Remaining Duration** (the number of business days still to go), and MS Project will calculate the **% Complete**.
3. The remaining durations are automatically moved to the future if you selected ☑ **Move start of remaining parts before status date forward to status date** (in ribbon **File**, Options, tab **Advanced**). If this option is off, the remaining durations will still be scheduled in the past; you will have to reschedule them to the future (i.e., after the status date). You can do this either by:
   - ◇ Selecting the task and clicking the **Task** ribbon, Move, and selecting **Incomplete Parts to Status Date** (This will split the task bar if the option ☑ **Split in-progress tasks** is in effect in ribbon **File**, Options, tab **Schedule**, section **Scheduling options for this project**)
   OR
   - ◇ Dragging that part of the task bar in the timescale to the right to after the status date. You have created a split task bar manually.
   OR
   - ◇ Add the button **Reschedule Work** to the **Task** ribbon in a new group (see page 73 for the how-to). Select the task and click this button.

You have to move the remaining duration out to the future, because you cannot schedule work-to-be-done in the past (if only we could…). This is the essence of updating the schedule when you want your schedule to forecast all the time (What was the title of this book again?). Only if you move remaining duration to the future, and revise it if needed, will the dependent successors be rescheduled. If you forget to do this, you will end up with a *status report* instead of a *forecast report*. A status report is like a report on today's weather. Most people find a weather forecast more interesting than a weather status, just like most executives will find a *project forecast* more interesting than a *project status*.

Tasks That Will Take Longer or Shorter

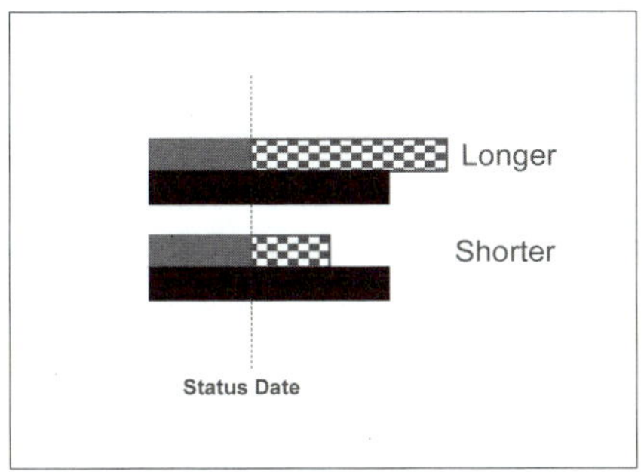

In this situation, the resource(s) worked all the days on the task as planned, but the realization sinks in that the remaining duration will not suffice; the task was underestimated. In this case, you need to increase the estimate for the **Remaining Duration**. If the task was overestimated, you may need to shorten it. (Hey, it has been known to happen!)

Since you are going to change the duration, you will trigger a recalculation through the *formula* **Duration** * **Peak Units** = **Work**. You should not leave the task type set to **Fixed Duration**, since MS Project might recalculate the units or the work. We recommended changing the task type to **Fixed Units** before you start updating. If you choose **Fixed Units**, the work will change. If you choose **Fixed Work**, the number of resources (units) working on the task will change.

1. If needed, set the **Type** of task to *Fixed Units* if you want to see where the project will finish if the same resource(s) continue (or *Fixed Work* if you want to see how many more resources you need to attract).

2. Click the Mark on Track button on the **Task** ribbon.
   OR
   Enter an **Actual Duration** for the task equal to the number of working days between the start of the task and the status date.
   As a result, the progress bar now runs up to the status date.

3. Revise the **Remaining Duration** for the task.
   OR
   Change the remaining duration with the mouse by pointing to the right side of its task bar. When you see the single-headed arrow mouse pointer, drag to the right to increase the remaining duration to compensate for the slippage. You may have to use the methods to optimize your schedule to compensate for the slipped finish date (see page 442). Drag to the left to decrease the remaining duration. If you cannot get it on the right date, zoom the timescale in first.

Tasks That Started Late or Early

In this situation, the task did not start on the day that was planned. The illustration on the left reveals that the top task started late, whereas the bottom task started early. In the *Late* situation, the actual start date (left side of top bar) is later than the baseline start date (the left side of its black bottom bar). If you updated your schedule regularly and had a dynamic schedule (with all dependencies and few constraints), the start date may have moved already to the right date and you do not need to change it. If that is not the case, you have to enter it.

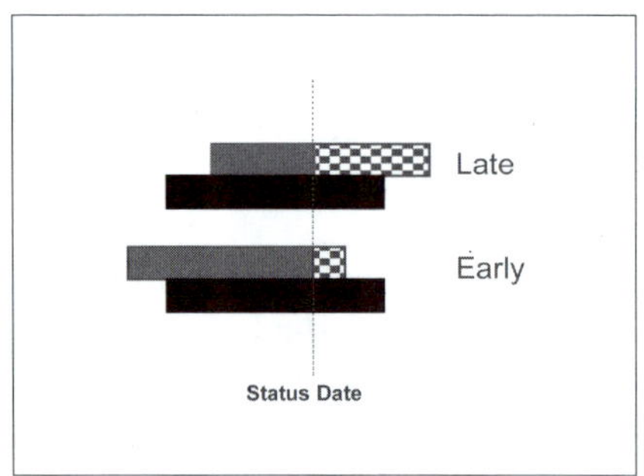

1. In the Tracking Gantt view, point to the middle of the blue task bar; when you see a four-headed arrow mouse pointer, drag the task bar to its new start date. If you cannot get it on the date you want, zoom the timescale in first. This does not enter an Actual Start date, but this will happen as you enter progress.
   OR
   In the **Actual Start** field of the tracking table, enter the date.
2. Click the Mark on Track button on the **Task** ribbon – the progress now runs up to the status date.
3. If the task slipped, you may have to use the methods to shorten your schedule as discussed in chapter 9 to compensate for the slipped finish date (see page 442).

Tasks That Finished Late or Early

In this situation, you need to enter the finish dates. In the illustration on the left, you can see that the top task finished late relative to the black baseline bar. The bottom task finished early. If you update your schedule regularly, however, you often do not need to enter finish dates; you just need to mark the task as 100% complete. When you revise the remaining duration, MS Project changes the finish date to the right date, or close to it. If it still is not the right date, you can enter the correct **Actual Finish** date into the project schedule.

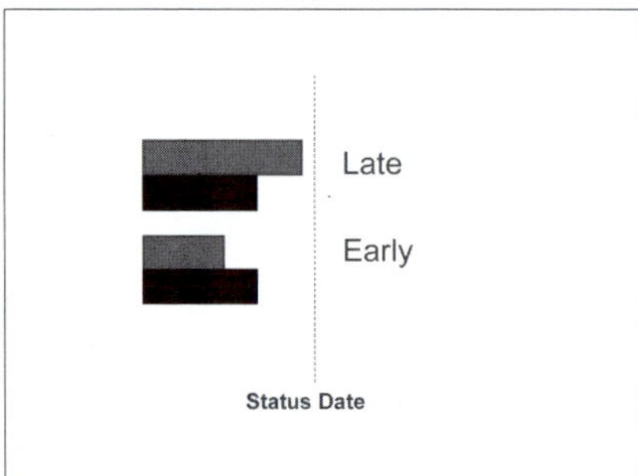

The steps are:

1. In the Tracking Gantt view, point to the right side of the blue or red task bar, and when you see a single-headed arrow mouse pointer – drag the finish to its new date. Set the task to 100% complete; click on the **Task** ribbon.
   OR
   In **Actual Finish** field of the tracking table, enter the date.
2. If the task slipped, you may have to shorten your schedule using the methods discussed in chapter 9 (see page 442).

"My Reality Is More Complex..."

There are certain situations that seem more difficult to update in your schedule:

- Combination of pure situations discussed previously
  What to do with a task that started late, runs behind and will take longer?
- Updating out of sequence
  What if tasks are done out of sequence? A task that is scheduled to begin in the future could be started before its planned date.
- New activities or new assignments on the fly
  What if you realize, while working on a task, that it actually consists of more tasks? What if you decide to reassign resources?

We will discuss each of these more complex situations in more detail.

Combination of Situations

Your situation could be a combination of the six situations previously discussed. For example, the start date is different from the baseline start date, the progress is behind and the task will take longer. This is a combination of three of the pure situations described previously. Let us say, on day 1 (Baseline Start) you started a 4-day task (Baseline Duration). At the end of the workday on day 4, the status on the task is:

- The Actual Start date is day 2
- The Actual Duration is only 2 days instead of 3 days. The resource had to work 1 day on something else.
- The Remaining Duration is revised from 1 day to 2 days; the disruption is expected to continue.

In situations like this one, we recommend you first update the **Actual Start**: (1) in the illustration. Then you update the **Actual Duration** (2), next the **Remaining Duration** (3) and finally the **Actual Finish** (4). Graphically speaking, you enter data going from left to right over the task bar. If you remember this, you will never see unexpected results in MS Project while entering complex updates. It will help if you put the columns in that order, as we recommended on page 633.

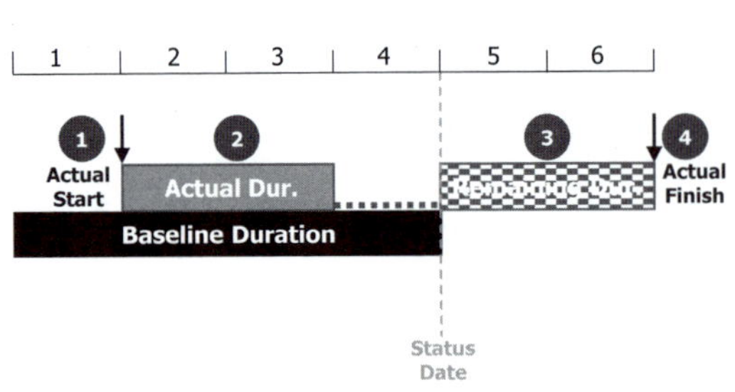

The resource worked on the task only on day 2 and 3; the Actual Duration is two days. The *% Complete* will be calculated at *67%*. Before entering the Remaining Duration, the schedule will look like:

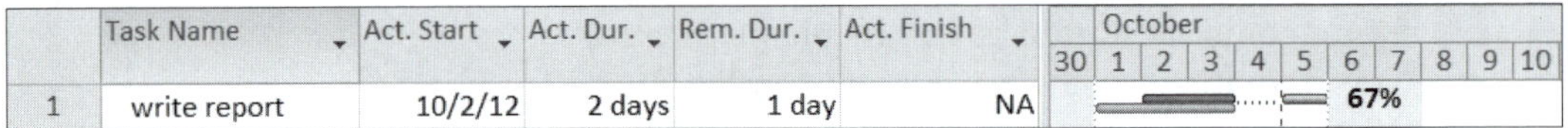

	Task Name	Act. Start	Act. Dur.	Rem. Dur.	Act. Finish
1	write report	10/2/12	2 days	1 day	NA

When you revise the Remaining Duration to 2 days, you trigger a recalculation of the *% Complete*, which will be *50%*; you have completed 2 days of what is now a 4-day task. The task carries over the weekend (day 6 and 7), so it finishes Monday (day 8) of the following week. See the next screenshot:

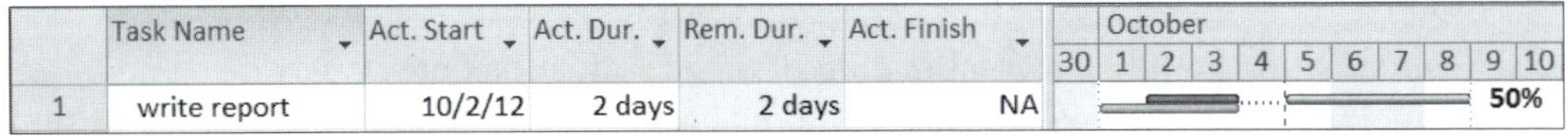

	Task Name	Act. Start	Act. Dur.	Rem. Dur.	Act. Finish
1	write report	10/2/12	2 days	2 days	NA

Updating Out of Sequence

Occasionally, you may need to show progress on a task that is scheduled in the future. The predecessors of the task may hold it in the future, but if work has started on it, you need to show progress on it, regardless of the logic of the dependencies. This is known as *out-of-sequence updating*. Normally, a task can only start when its predecessors are finished.

Out-of-sequence progress often occurs in practice. For example, authors have to wait until they receive the research results before they can start writing the research report. The research takes longer than planned, and the authors decide to start developing the outline of the report and creating the format styles for the layout of the document. They even start writing, describing their research approach. They do not need to have the results of the research for any of this.

Updating out of sequence is actually simple, because actuals are stronger than any other scheduling feature in MS Project. Actuals override the logic of the dependencies and even date constraints, so you can go ahead and update in the regular way. However, you need to pay attention to how you want the schedule to function. You will need to select the option ☑ **Move end of completed parts after status date back to status date** (ribbon **File,** [Options], tab **Advanced**). With this on, another option called **Split in-progress tasks** (ribbon **File,** [Options], tab **Schedule**) will affect the result in out-of-sequence situations:

- With ☑ **Split in-progress tasks** selected, the remaining duration stays where its dependencies kept the task. This is called *retained logic*, because the dependency still works, albeit on the remaining duration only.
- With ☐ **Split in-progress tasks** cleared, the remaining duration is scheduled to start on the status date, which pulls the successors back to the status date. This is called a *logic override*, also known as *progress override*, because the dependency is now overridden. With this option cleared, MS Project does not allow the bar to split and the remaining duration is, therefore, pulled back to the status date.

You need to check the resulting schedule to determine whether it is better to retain or override the logic. Often, retaining the logic is better when there is a *hard dependency*, like between *construct walls* and *build roof*. When there is a *soft dependency*, like between *install cabinetry* and *lay carpet*, overriding the logic may make more sense. You need to look at your situation and decide.

11

New Activities on the Fly

When you are executing the project, you may realize that you omitted some tasks. You may have forgotten certain activities that involve discrete effort, or you may find better approaches to create the deliverables. Generally speaking, it is better to add new activities to show changes rather than modifying existing activities. This is particularly true if you have already reported any progress on the activities. For example, if progress is lagging, you could decide to reassign a portion of a task to somebody else. In that case, this is clearer in the schedule if you leave the baselined activities as they are and create new activities for this extra resource. The new activities end up without a baseline and are thus clearly marked as new activities inserted on the fly during project execution. These new activities capture how the project was executed in fact. In the case of contract disputes, you must be able to explain what the plan was and how the project unfolded in reality. Some experts go as far as capturing all impacts by creating new line items; the resulting schedule is called the *as-built schedule*. This technique is particularly useful when a contract dispute erupts and escalates to litigation, but it also allows you to learn more from your past projects. These new line items should only be in the past or present (i.e., before the status date), and not in the future. They should not be baselined, because then you will no longer be able to determine if it was an original activity or an activity added on the fly.

This concludes our discussion of updating tasks, except for reporting on project status and forecasts, see page 672.

Updating Assignments

An MS Project schedule is accessible read-write to only one concurrent user. Some project managers would like multi-user access in order to allow resources to update the project schedule. Giving my team members access to my schedule never seemed like a good idea to me; they often do not know MS Project well and can easily wreck my sophisticated, forecast model of the project. The timesheet features in Project Web App (Project Server) facilitate updating by all team members without giving them read-write access to your project schedule.

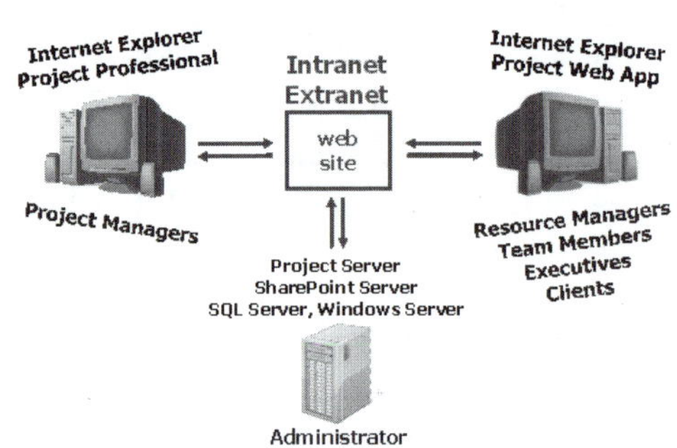

Take the following steps when *updating assignments*:

- ◆ Collect the data using Project Web App (see next).
- ◆ Set the options:
  - ◇ In MS Project click ribbon **File,** [Options] – set the correct options (see page 649)
  - ◇ In Project Server, click **Server Settings**
- ◆ Prepare the view **Resource Usage** with table **Work** (see page 652) and know the formulas behind the screen (see page 656)
- ◆ Set the **Status Date** for this update (see page 657)
- ◆ For all tasks to be updated, set the task **Type** to **Fixed Units** (see page 658)
- ◆ Publish the assignments (see page 660)
- ◆ The team members fill in and submit their updates in Outlook (see page 662) or in PWA (see page 662)
- ◆ Accept and transfer the update data into the schedule (see page 669)
- ◆ Check whether the schedule is updated correctly (see page 669)

- Prepare the status and forecast report (see page 672)
  You may need to re-optimize your schedule before reporting on it.

You could work with paper timesheets; however, paper systems often turn out to be too laborious and are abandoned during the busy time of project execution. If you do not have an electronic timesheet system, we recommend updating tasks instead (see the section starting on page 623).

Timesheets that are developed in house often do not transfer the timesheet information back into the MS Project schedule. If the only purpose of your current timesheet system is to bill clients or administer salaries (HR), then you are not well served as a project manager. We recommend updating tasks instead (see page 623). The Project Server timesheet system sets itself apart in this respect, because it allows you to electronically transfer the update information back into your project schedule.

For electronic timesheets, you can use the *Project Web App* or *Outlook 2010* timesheets that come with *Project Server*, or third party timesheets that integrate well with MS Project. There are third-party timesheet applications that can also transfer the update information into MS Project. These are:

- *PSA Solution* by Tenrox (www.tenrox.com)
  This timesheet system targets the *Professional Services Automation* (*PSA*) market, like consulting firms or service departments within large organizations.
- *TimeControl* by HMS Software (www.hmssoftware.ca)
  This system seems particularly strong in integrating with accounting systems and any project scheduling software.
- *WorkEngine* by EPMlive (www.workengine.com)

  EPMlive set itself apart, in that it built the first work management and timesheet application entirely inside SharePoint. The popularity of SharePoint itself has helped their success.

11

If you are currently looking for a timesheet system, HMS published a useful timesheet buyers guide evaluation worksheet in Excel that will help you identify the right type of timesheet for your organization. With their permission, we provide that to you as the file *11 Timesheet System Evaluation Worksheet - HMS.xls* in the download files that come with this book. See page vi for the procedure to access these files.

In this book we will focus on electronic timesheets only, not paper ones, and we will only discuss the Project Server timesheets in PWA and Outlook.

Collect the data using Project Web App

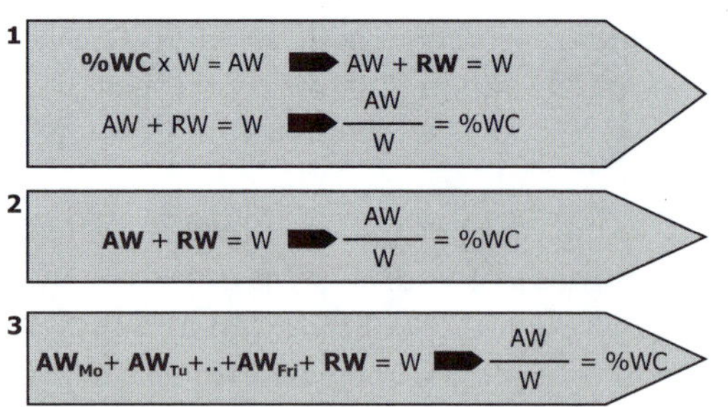

You can collect the following data from your team members using *Project Web App*. The illustration displays your three options. A fourth option, called *free form*, allows the resources instead of the project manager to choose the method they prefer. The bolded variables are the ones you enter; the formulas explain what the application will calculate with the numbers that team members enter. We will discuss each in more detail:

- **Percent of work complete** *(%WC)*
  Resources report the percentage of work complete and enter a percentage between 0 and 100%. The *% Work Complete* is an ambiguous metric to collect from team members, as explained on page 623. This is perhaps why team members like it so much. Also, you still have to collect the remaining work (RW), which will force MS Project to recalculate the % Complete as per the formulas in the illustration. Therefore, we do not recommend using this.
- **Actual work done** *(AW)* **and work remaining** *(RW)*
  For each assignment ,resources report the running total of actual work done and the work remaining to be done. This option has the advantage that it requires little data entry, just two numbers for each assignment at every status cycle. The disadvantage is that, because these numbers are running totals, the team members must do the addition themselves before entering the numbers. For example, if the field displays 17 hours up to last week, and if 15 hours were worked this week, then the resource needs to enter 17 + 15 = 32 hours. People can easily make mistakes doing this. Also, when the data are transferred into the schedule, MS Project has to spread these hours arbitrarily over the days, since you did not ask the team members on which days the 15 hours were worked. This spread will not be precise, and the Actual Start will not be precise even with options chosen in MS Project that control this in ribbon **File**, Options, tab **Advanced**:

  ☑ **And move start of remaining parts back to status date**, and

  ☑ **And move end of completed parts forward to status date**.
- **Hours of work done per period** and **remaining work** *(RW)*
  In the *traditional timesheet,* resources report the hours worked daily on each assignment; this is the most common type of timesheet. When team members enter their actual hours, the **Remaining Work** for the assignment is automatically

calculated: RW = W – AW. Just before sending the timesheet back to the project manager, the resource reviews the calculated **Remaining Work** number. After having worked on the task, the team member has a much better idea how much longer the task will take and adjusts the time, if necessary. We recommend you use this type of timesheet; it is the most precise and least prone to errors.

- **Free form**
  Resources can choose to report in any of the three methods explained previously. Normally, the project management office or project manager decides which of the three will be used.

Project Server has to be configured for the type of data you want to collect from your team. If you want to use the traditional timesheet, the Project Server administrator needs to change this configuration setting (**Server Settings**, section **Time and Task Management, Task Settings and Display**); otherwise, the actual work fields are grayed out and not editable.

Even though we recommend you use the third option (i.e., the traditional timesheet), we would like to emphasize that using another type of timesheet (or updating tasks, for that matter) is still preferred to not updating your schedules at all. The remainder of this chapter focuses on the option we recommend, the traditional timesheet.

Set the Options in MS Project for Assignments Update

Below you will find our recommended update options for assignments. Click ribbon **File**, Options and click on the tab indicated in the table below where you want to change settings. Realize that your schedule will have many tasks on which resources work and submit timesheets, but also some tasks for which you will not receive update information through the timesheet system (milestones,

11

Tab	Set to:
Schedule	Section **calculation options for this project:** ☑ **Updating task Status updates Resource Status** We recommend you check this option so that MS Project calculates the **% Complete** on the task level after receiving timesheet data. We also recommend you protect the timesheet numbers by locking them in; otherwise, you can change the timesheet numbers within MS Project by entering a **% Complete**. The Project Server Administrator can lock in actuals by closing periods that should be final (**Server Settings, Time Reporting periods**, column **Status**). OR ☐ **Updating task Status updates Resource Status** If you turn it off, you will not see calculated **% Complete** on tasks. Having this option turned off allows you to update both tasks and assignments simultaneously. Doing both types of updates is a lot of work. We advise against clearing this option or doing those updates.
	☑ **Actual costs are always calculated by Microsoft Project** If you keep it on, MS Project will calculate the *actual costs* based upon *actual hours* worked. If you want to enter actual cost numbers yourself (a lot of work!) or import them from your accounting system (a data migration challenge!), you should turn it off.
Schedule	Section **Scheduling options for this project**: ☑ **Split in-progress tasks** Selecting this allows you to split the task bar and move the remaining duration to after the status date. We recommend keeping this option on, see also page 644 for *progress override* as opposed to *retained logic*.
Advanced	Section **Calculation options for this project:** ☑ **Move end of completed parts after status date back to status date** This option has no effect for tasks that you update with traditional timesheets. However, there are always tasks for which nobody will fill in a timesheet (external resources, for example). Therefore, we recommend selecting this feature so you can more easily update those tasks in MS Project. See also after this table. ☐ or ☑ **And move start of remaining parts back to status date** This option has no effect when you work with traditional timesheets. See also after this table.

Tab	Set to:
Advanced	☑ **Move start of remaining parts before status date forward to status date** This option has no effect when you work with traditional timesheets, but we recommend you turn it on because you will always have to update some other tasks in MS Project itself. See also after this table. ☐ or ☑ **And move end of completed parts forward to status date** This option has no effect when you work with traditional timesheets. See also after this table.
	Section **General**: ☐ **Automatically add new resources and tasks** Turning this off prevents accidentally adding resources during updating and re-optimising. Most, if not all, project *team members* should come from the *enterprise resource pool*.
	Section **Edit**: ☐ **Allow cell drag and drop** This option cleared prevents accidentally dragging data on top of other data in your baselined schedule. We recommend turning it off at this point.

Notice that, in ribbon **File,** Options, tab **Advanced**, section **Calculation options for this project**, the *Move* options have no effect on tasks that you update with traditional timesheets. When a team member enters 8h on December 11 as the first *actual hours* worked on that task, December 11 will become the **Actual Start** date for the task. These *Move* options only make a difference:

- When you update tasks and enter **Actual Durations** or **Actual Work**.
  There are always some tasks in a schedule that will not be updated through somebody's timesheet. These tasks are:
  - ◇ Milestones (that have no effort and will not appear in any timesheet),
  - ◇ Tasks with external resources, such as client contributors, vendors or subs (people who are typically not allowed into the timesheet system),
  - ◇ Tasks without resources assigned — a questionable practice
  - ◇ Recurring detail tasks without resources assigned.

  You will have to update these tasks in MS Project by using our Updating Tasks process, which we explained starting on page 623.
- When you use the first or second type of timesheet discussed on page 648. Since these types of timesheets do not indicate on which dates the work actually took place, MS Project does so. The calculation options control the distribution of the

11

actual hours across the days. When you leave it to MS Project, the resulting spread will be fairly rough.

Set the Options in Project Server for Assignment Update

The Project Server administrator and the project management office need to review the configuration settings for the *timesheet* interface in PWA. If you change the configuration after some weeks of filling in timesheets (for example, from weekly to daily timesheets), you will see that the completed weekly timesheets will persist in their weekly format, but from the date of changing onward, the new timesheets you create (by clicking **Next**) will be daily timesheets. This can be very confusing. It is, therefore, essential to think carefully about what the timesheets should look like before creating any. The configuration is done in **Server Settings**, section **Time and Task Management**, item **Timesheet Settings and Defaults**. Without attempting to be complete, [76] we will discuss some major items:

- Whether or not to allow team members to add line items to the timesheet:
  - ◇ project tasks (**Insert Task**),
  - ◇ suggest new task to the project manager (**New Task**),
  - ◇ assign yourself to a task (**Add Yourself to a Task**),
  - ◇ assume responsibility for tasks assigned to your team (**Insert Team Tasks**),
  - ◇ add administrative line items, like vacation (**Insert Administrative Tasks**), or
  - ◇ allow adding free form items (**Insert Personal Task**).

  Generally speaking, we recommend allowing team members to report on everything they do, so they can get a complete overview of their workload and a handle on all their commitments. I will admit I have personally refused to fill in a timesheet where my boss only wanted to see a small portion (billable hours only) of what I really contributed. A complete list of employee activity will be a great discussion piece for performance reviews and allows the manager to become aware of initiative taken, and to redirect or focus the employee.
- Whether you want the **Tasks** and the **Timesheet** interface to automatically be synchronized all the time: ☑ **Single entry mode**. Notice that even though they are kept in sync, only the Timesheet interface displays the admin line items like *Sick, Leave, Vacation*, so we recommend you use the **Timesheet** interface. If a team member enters actual hours in both the Tasks and Timesheet interface in *Single*

[76] For a complete overview of configuration options and decisions to make, please review our **Configuring PS** (*Configuring Microsoft Project Server 2010*) course. See www.ProjectProCorp.com and click *Courses 2010* in the sidebar.

Entry Mode, the Tasks interface prevails and sends the hours into the MS Project schedule. Therefore, we recommend removing the Tasks interface entirely from PWA in single entry mode (**Server Settings**, section **Look and Feel, Quick Launch**). In this book, we recommend and will only discuss single entry mode because it provides unity of data and prevents double data entry.

- Allowing the resource to request vacation, days off and leave through the timesheet interface (☑ **Allow future time reporting**).

We recommend you think carefully about your choices here and discuss them vigorously. If not, the cost of receiving and sorting out erroneous timesheet data from resources will soon drown you in work; the amount of data is staggering. It will also destroy any remaining, reluctant willingness from resources to continue filling in their timesheets. Would you like to have your entire professional life captured with 15-minute precision? Most people prefer to fly under the radar if their executives let them. This discussion often unfolds in the way Bob and Nob argued in the story at the start of this chapter. Personally, I think it is reasonable to expect employees to report how they spent their work time, because their organization pays them a significant salary. Paradoxically, timesheets really help the busiest resources by making their towering *workload* visible to management, but the challenge is to get the *critical resources* to fill in their timesheets on top of their crushing workload.

Prepare the View Resource Usage with Table Work

In the Resource Usage view in MS Project, you can see the timesheet data after you have transferred them into your schedule. If the timesheet numbers are not locked in, you can even make corrections. We are about to create a custom Resource Usage view, but this view can also be found in the file *11 Update Assignments - ProjectPro.mpp* as the view object named *Update Assignments - ProjectPro* and its table object called *Update Assignments - ProjectPro*. You need to copy both the view and table into your own schedule (ribbon **File**, button **Organizer**). The file is available for download from our website (see page vi for the procedure to access these files). If you download it, you can skip the following, tedious procedure.

1. Click ribbon **View** and find its section **Resource Views**, click 

.

11

2. Create a new table by clicking **View,** 

, item **More Tables...** – the **More Tables** dialog appears:

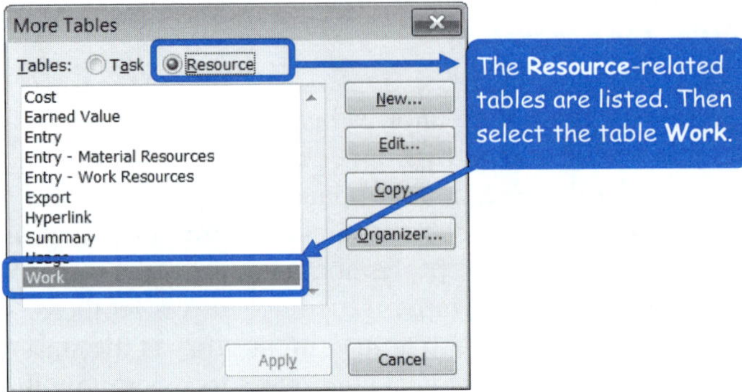

3. Select the table **Work,** and click Copy... – the **Table Definition** dialog appears:

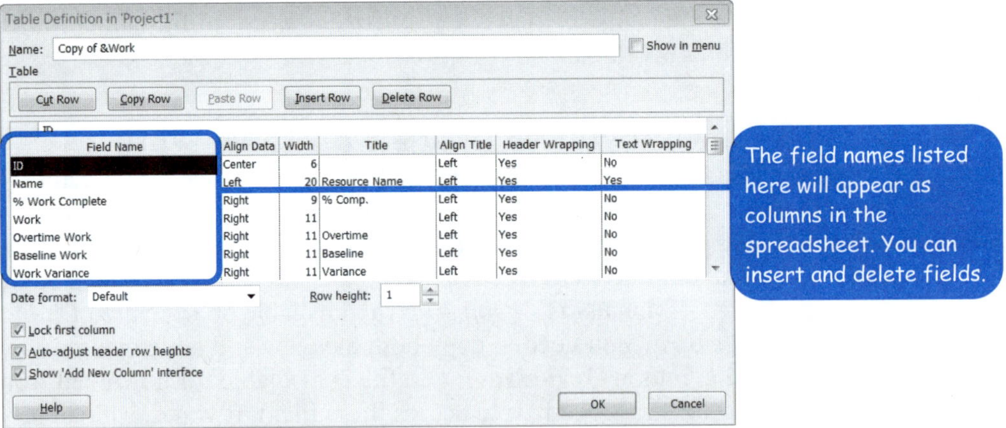

4. Give the table a name, for example *Update Assignments*. After the field **Name,** insert the fields **Baseline Work, Work, Actual Work, Remaining Work** and **% Work Complete**. In the field **Title** abbreviate the column titles to, for example, *Base. Work, Work, Act. Work, Rem. Work* and *% Work Compl.,* respectively, to save some space. Click OK and Apply.

5. In ribbon **File,** Options, tab **Advanced,** under **Display options for this project**, change the time unit label to one character to save space. Click OK

6. In the timescale, only the field **Work** is shown. Right-click anywhere in the timescale and from the popup menu select **Detail Styles...** – the **Detail Styles** dialog appears:

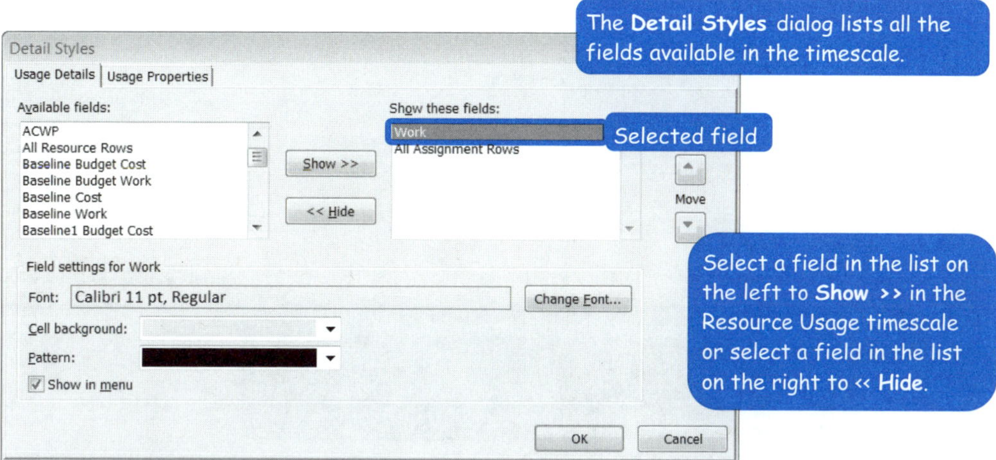

7. In the list **Available Fields,** select **Baseline Work** and click Show >>. Do the same for the field **Actual Work,** which will be the input field. Perhaps you should even give this field a different **Cell background** color, like white, to make it stand out as an input field. Select the item **All Assignment Rows** in the list on the right and << Hide it. Rearrange the fields so that the **Baseline Work** field is at the top. Click OK.

8. Format the spreadsheet in such a way that the input cells are white and the rest are gray. The input cells in the spreadsheet are the assignment-related **Rem. Work** cells. Click ribbon **Format**, button **Text Styles**, under **Item to change** select **All** and under **Background Color** select the lightest shade of gray. Under **Item to change** select **Assignment Row** and select under **Background Color** white. Click OK.

9. Drag over the column headings **Resource Name, Bas.Work, Work** and **Act.Work** and right-click in selected area to display the mini toolbar:

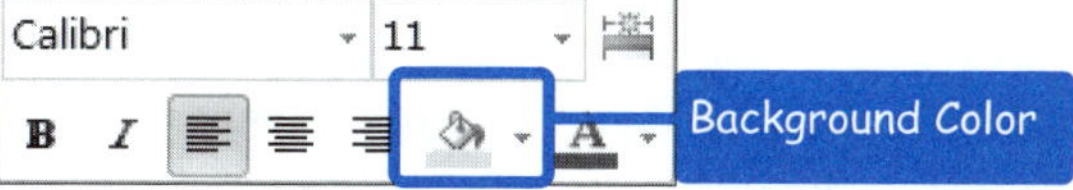

and select as the background color the same lightest shade of gray. Do the same for the column *% Work Compl.*.

The view should now look like:

View ready for checking and correcting assignment updates.

	Resource Name	Base. Work	Work	Act. Work	Rem. Work	% Work Compl.	Details	October 24 S	M	T	W	T	F	S
1	- Harry	32 h	32 h	0 h	32 h	0%	Base. Work		8h	8h	8h	8h		
							Work		8h	8h	8h	8h		
							Act. Work							
	write	*32 h*	*32 h*	*0 h*	*32 h*	*0%*	Base. Work		8h	8h	8h	8h		
							Work		8h	8h	8h	8h		
							Act. Work							
2	- Ed	32 h	32 h	0 h	32 h	0%	Base. Work		8h	8h	8h	8h		
							Work		8h	8h	8h	8h		
							Act. Work							
	read	*32 h*	*32 h*	*0 h*	*32 h*	*0%*	Base. Work		8h	8h	8h	8h		
							Work		8h	8h	8h	8h		
							Act. Work							

White cells: Timesheet information can be reviewed and corrected in the **Rem. Work** in the spreadsheet and the **Act. Work** fields of the assignments (*with italic text*) in the timescale (unless actuals are protected).

Unfortunately, this view cannot display the status date line. Instead, you can click on that date on the timescale. This selects the entire column for that day and can act as a surrogate for the status date line.

The Formulas behind the Screens

The illustration shows the *formulas* that Project Web App will use when you update the assignments with timesheets. You should keep these formulas in the back of your mind, because they explain the values that Project Web App calculates and displays. The formulas define the relationships between the four variables: *Actual Work*, *Remaining Work*, *Work* and *% Work Complete*. If you enter only two out of the four variables, Project Web App will calculate the rest using the formulas shown.

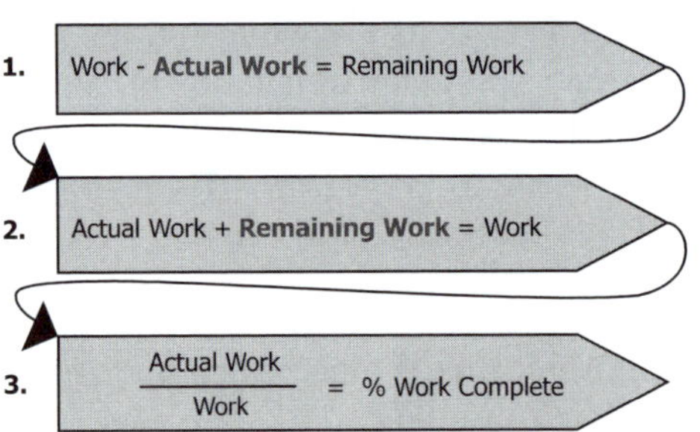

Typically, the team member first enters the **Actual Work** hours and PWA will subtract this from **Work** to calculate the **Remaining Work** for each assignment (step 1 in the illustration). This will immediately be visible in the **Tasks** screen, but in the **Timesheet** screen only after the actual hours have been approved. At the end of the week, the team members revise the **Remaining Work** number, and PWA will recalculate and revise the total **Work** forecasted on the task (step 2 in the illustration). The team member sends the timesheet off for approval. The project manager reviews the numbers and transfers the accepted ones into the schedule; MS Project calculates the **% Work Complete** (step 3 in the illustration).

Setting the Status Date for Updating

If you do not enter the **Status Date**, Project 2010 will use the **Current Date** (that day's date) for the update. The **Current Date** is kept up-to-date by the clock in your computer. We recommend you use the **Status Date** so the date of your last schedule update will always be clear. Also, the status date line will appear at the end of the day, in contrast to the current date line, which will show at the start of the day.

1. Click ribbon **Project** and click the bottom half of Status Date: 10/19/10 – the **Status Date** dialog appears (this must be the smallest dialog in Project 2010):

   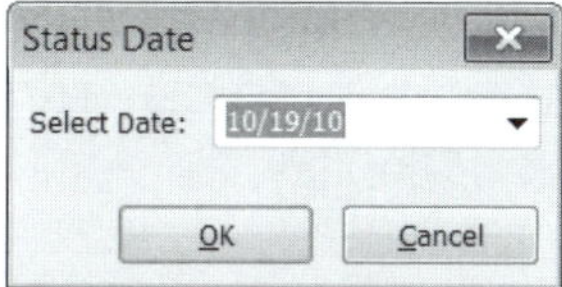

2. Change the **status date** to the date when you want to update tasks and compare the schedule against the baseline.
3. Unfortunately, the status date line does not appear by default so we need to add it as a highly visible, vertical, dashed line in the timescale. Click ribbon **Format,** 

   , item **Gridlines** and select **Status Date** in the list as the line to change. Choose a dashed line in **Type** and a bright **Color**. The dashed line makes it different from dependency lines (arrows). Click OK.

4. The status line is now visible in the timescale, similar to:

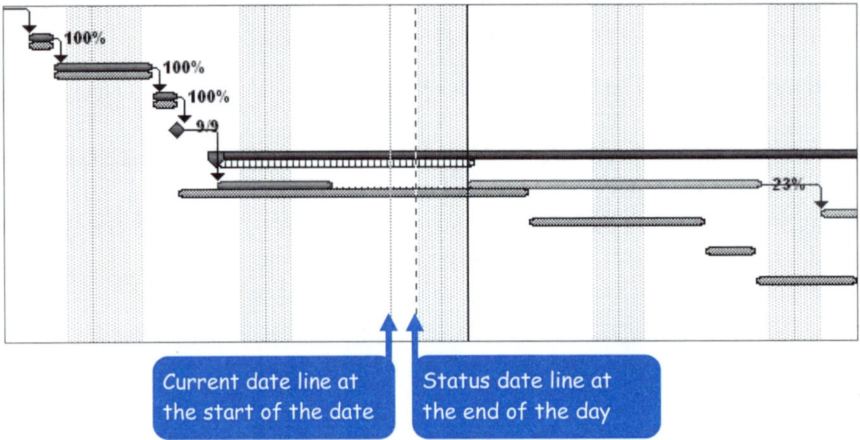

In the screenshot above, the same date was entered without a time for **Current Date** and for **Status Date**, but the line for the status date is displayed at the end of the day, whereas the line for the current date is displayed at the start of the day.

Set the Task Type for All Tasks to Update

The task field **Type** has to be set in such a way that it controls the recalculations in MS Project. When working with timesheets, we will be entering **Actual Work** and **Remaining Work** values that cause the **Work** value to be recalculated as shown in the illustration: *Actual Work + Remaining Work = Work.* Fixed work is, therefore, not the right type of task, because we will not control what MS Project recalculates; will it recalculate the units or the duration? Remember that you protect one value, change another and have MS Project calculate the third one. When the **Work** value changes while updating assignments, you usually want to see the effect on the **Duration** of the task to get an accurate forecast, while keeping the same resources on the task (**Fixed Units**).

Work changes often during updates!
D * PU = W

Fixed Units seems to be the most appropriate type of task for updating assignments. Essentially, you are telling MS Project to first show you the resulting schedule if you ask the same resources to continue their crunching. If the task duration extends too far in the forecast model, then you can consider corrective actions and re-optimize the schedule.

If you use **Fixed Duration** instead, you are asking MS Project to recalculate the number of allocated **Units** on every task; you are essentially asking the tool to tell you how many resources you need, which is a management decision, not something a tool should do. Aside from that philosophical argument, adding resources is a last resort corrective action, as we explained on page 451, because it does not work unless you do it early enough. Finally, we have often seen impossibly high numbers in the **Units** field caused by **Fixed Duration**. The highest number I have seen was a single individual assigned at 33,100% (yes, thirty-three thousand one hundred percent!); in other words, 330 clones of this person were needed to finish on time. For these reasons, we recommend **Fixed Units** instead of **Fixed Duration** (or **Fixed Work**).

The steps to switch to Fixed Units are:

1. Click on any column heading in the Tracking Gantt spreadsheet to select all tasks.
   OR
   Be more selective by selecting just those tasks that need to be updated.

2. On the **Task** ribbon click [Information] – the **Multiple Task Information** dialog appears. Click the **Advanced** tab; the dialog should now look like:

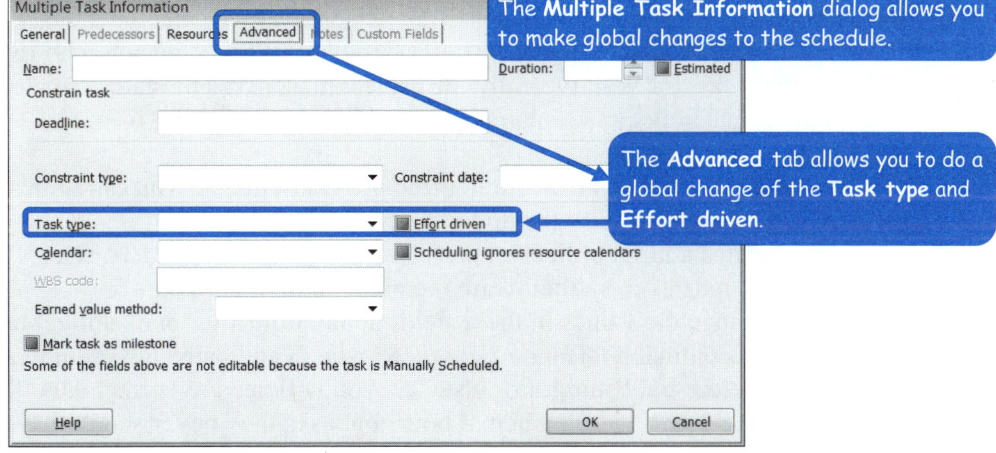

3. From the list **Task type**, select the item **Fixed Units**. Changing the task type does not trigger a recalculation; only a change of one variable will do that in the *formula*: **Duration * Peak Units = Work**.

4. Clear ☐ **Effort driven**; we recommended earlier that you keep effort driven turned off (see page 358 and following). Click [OK]. Please note that summary tasks

11

continue to be **Fixed Duration**, which is okay since we will not update summary tasks.

Publishing the Assignments to Project Server

Upon saving the schedule, the data end up in the draft database (called ⦿ **Working** in MS Project) for your eyes only as the project manager. When you have finalized the schedule, you can publish it from within *Project Professional 2010* to Project Web App (PWA). It is replicated and ends up in the database called ⦿ **Published** in MS Project. Upon publishing a schedule, it becomes automatically visible to your project stakeholders in PWA; executives can see the project in the Project Center, resource managers can see the new workloads of the team members in the Resource Center, and the team members can see their assignments in their timesheet or tasks screen. Project Server has a very robust *security module* that allows the *Project Server administrator* to give specific people access to specific data in the database.

Before you publish you should review and revise the following fields for each task:

- **Assignment Owner** or *surrogate resource* that fills in the timesheet information on behalf of the resource. By default, the assignment owners are the resources themselves. In some cases, a surrogate resource fills out timesheets; for example, workers in a plant often have admin staff enter their timesheets.
- **Status Manager**. The status manager is the person who will receive the task updates from the resources working on the task. By default, this is the person who first publishes the tasks to PWA, typically the project manager. The status manager reviews the actual hours and remaining hours before transferring them to MS Project. This is useful:
  - If you are about to go on vacation as the project manager; you can indicate in this field who will review the updates while you are gone.
  - If you manage a large project where you work with team leaders, who will review the updates from their team members rather than you.

You can always change the values in these fields at any time after publishing, but you can prevent a lot of confusion (*Why do I get these tasks?*) and data correction if you think about them before publishing. For instance, you will need to correct data if eager resources immediately start entering actual hours on tasks they never should have seen in their timesheet (wrong Assignment Owner).

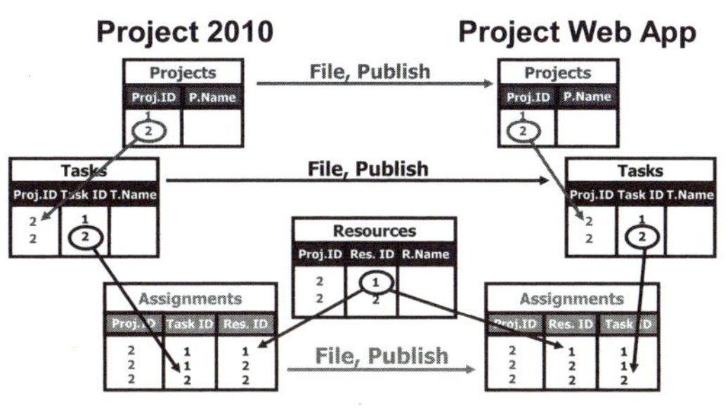

The steps for *publishing* your project are: Click ribbon **File,** Publish. At the bottom right of the screen in the status bar, Project 2010 will update you on how far the publishing has progressed until it displays **Publish completed successfully.** When you publish the project, you publish all information in it: the project, tasks (including progress and latest forecasts), and the resources on the team and their assignments (workload and progress). When assignments shift, you must again publish the project to post the new assignment dates in the resource timesheets. You need to do this every time assignments change, such as a change to the start date or amount of work, or in case of a cancellation. MS Project will immediately tag the tasks with changes as candidates to be published. To communicate the changes to the team members, you click ribbon **File,** Publish again – MS Project will find all the tasks tagged for republication and publish them again.

If you want to unpublish tasks, you can set their field **Publish** back to *No* and click ribbon **File,** Publish again. This will effectively remove them from all future timesheets of all assigned resources. Unfortunately, you can only set the field **Publish** on a task-by-task basis, not on an assignment-by-assignment basis, which would be better yet. If an unpublished task already has actuals from the resources, the task will stay in their timesheets, but resources can no longer report actual hours on them. If the resource does anyway, PWA displays an error message to the user: the status bar located between the timesheet and its ribbon turns red and displays the (not so very helpful message) **Status: Error**. The error will also block any later timesheets from being processed.

If you add a button to your ribbon, you can remind team members to complete their timesheets. Select the tasks in MS Project and click **Request Progress Information**. The indicators column in MS Project will display the request progress icon. Project Server sends out an email to remind the appropriate team members to submit progress information. *Project Web App* will mark the tasks in the timesheet with the message Update Requested in the Process Status column in the **Tasks** screen only. To add the button **Request Progress Information** to your ribbon, please follow the steps provided on page 73.

The Team Members Fill in Task Status in Outlook

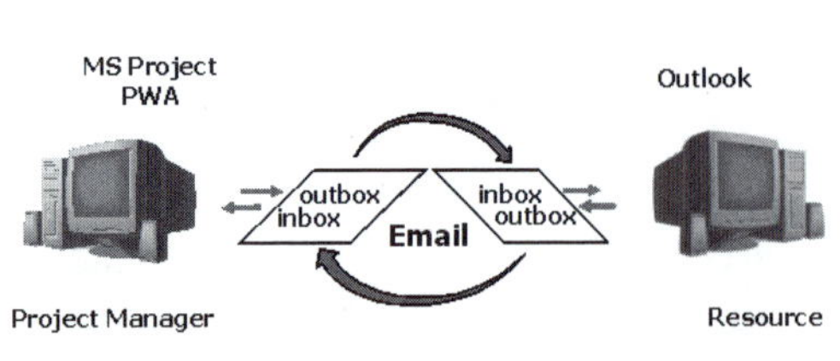

Instead of using Project Web App, team members can also enter their task progress in Outlook. In the 2010 release, the integration between Project Server and Outlook runs through Exchange Server, whereas in the 2007 release, each team member needed to install an ActiveX control. The new integration with Exchange Server has some benefits:

- The tasks appear now also in *Outlook Web Access 2010*, the web-based Outlook version, as well as in the rich Outlook client, of course.
- There is no need to import the tasks from PWA into Outlook; they will appear automatically in Outlook as soon as the schedule is published by the project manager. Exchange Server pushes them into people's Outlook, which saves many clicks.
- Almost all of the functionality is now native to Outlook instead of injected into Outlook by the MS Project developers, which is expected to increase stable.

The tasks appear in the **My Tasks** view, the **To-Do** list and on the **Calendar** in Outlook. Team members can enter the status of their tasks but only **% Complete** or the running total of **Actual Work** and **Remaining Work**, and not in a traditional weekly timesheet day-by-day view as was possible in 2007 with the ActiveX. These status updates are then automatically submitted to the task project manager (or **Status Manager**) when the tasks are updated in Outlook.

To Enter the Progress Information in Outlook

1. Display the **Tasks** view in Outlook by clicking Tasks in the navigation pane (if this button is not visible in Outlook, click the button on at the bottom of the navigation pane and select **Add or Remove Buttons** and then **Tasks**).

2. Double-click on a task in the list, and the **Task** window appears where you can select one of the pre-defined status items in the list **Status**:

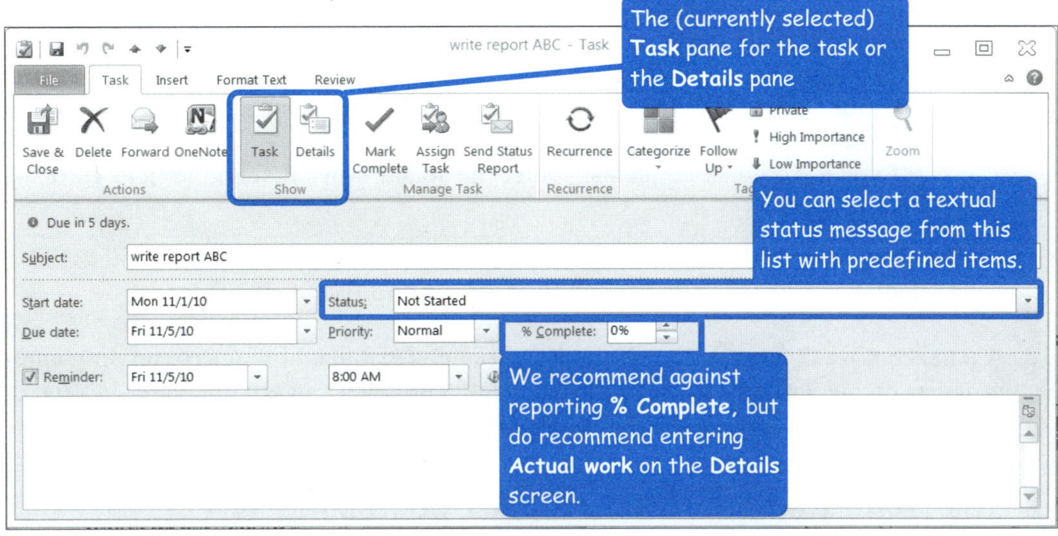

3. Click Details to display the screen where you can enter the **Actual work**:

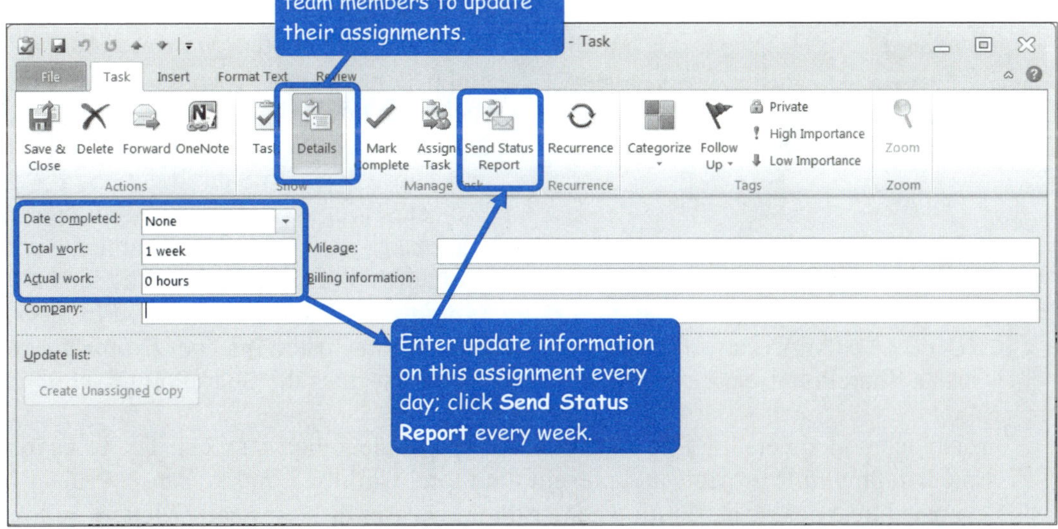

4. Enter the **Actual work** hours at the end of every day by adding the day's hours worked on this assignment to the running total currently displayed in the field

Actual work and entering the sum as the new running total. For example, if **Actual work** displays *1.5 days* and you worked another half day on the task today, you enter *2 days*.

5. At the end of every week:
   - ◇ If the task is not finished yet: Revise the **Total Work** estimate with the current **Actual Work** plus how many hours you still need on the task before submitting to the project manager.
   - ◇ If you have finished the task, enter the actual finish date in the field **Date completed**.
6. To send the actual hours worked, revised work estimate and date completed to the project manager for review, click the button **Send the Status Report**.

A persistent weak point in the Outlook interface is that team members can only enter progress on one task at a time. In Project Web App, they can see the entire list and can more easily enter progress on multiple tasks.

The Team Members Fill in Their Updates in PWA

Many organizations will opt for having the resources provide updates on their tasks through PWA. The *Project Web App* (*PWA*) website is the single interface for project team members and all other stakeholders in the project. Project Server stores the timesheet data in an *SQL Server* database and puts the right data on the web page for each stakeholder based on their Windows login identity (Active Directory synchronizes access privileges to SharePoint and PWA). Project Server acts as so-called *middleware* that makes SQL Server communicate with *Project 2010*, *PWA* and *Outlook 2010* among others. All users of PWA will need a PWA *Client Access License* (*CAL*), a *SharePoint Standard CAL* and a *SharePoint Enterprise CAL* (*eCAL*). PWA is a web-based application that runs inside *Internet Explorer*. PWA is also a SharePoint *service application*, which necessitates the SharePoint CALs.

Project team members log into Project Web App to view their task list. The tasks may come from multiple projects and present their total workload. In that sense, Project Server is like a postal distribution center that processes tasks instead of letters and sends them to the right people, the team members. The team members can access their timesheets by browsing to the website with PWA and logging in. When they fill in their timesheets, they can send them back to the project manager for approval. The project manager then logs into the Project Server site using PWA, reviews timesheet information, rejects or accepts the numbers, and transfers the accepted numbers into the MS Project schedule. As you can see, the project managers completely control what ends up in their schedules.

New since the 2007 version, Microsoft has separated the timesheet from the task update interface. The **Timesheet** interface is for:

- *Attendance recording* and *salary administration* by HR
- Billing for *professional services* for the accounting department, specifically *Accounts Receivable*.
- *Compliance*: Many countries, like USA and Canada, give huge incentives to private companies that perform research and development (*R&D*). These companies need to carefully record which hours were spent on R&D tasks (for which they will receive *subsidies* or *tax deductions*) and which hours were spent on *normal operations*.

The **Tasks** interface, on the other hand, is only for project managers to keep their schedules up-to-date.

The main difference between the two interfaces is that the **Timesheet** screen only shows one update period and lists only the tasks that have scheduled work during this period plus the admin line items (vacation, sick time etc.), whereas the **Tasks** screen shows by default all tasks the resource is assigned to and does not show admin line items. The **Tasks** screen provides rich grouping and filtering capability to deal with the long list. In 2010, you can even create your own custom filter in **Tasks** and multiple views that remember their settings, so it always re-appears on your screen the way you last saw it.

New in the 2010 release, Microsoft provides a *single entry mode* to prevent double data entry and enforce one version of the truth. We recommend this. Single entry in combination with a weekly timesheet that must be filled in day-by-day is the only configuration we will discuss in this book.[77]

11

[77] For a discussion of other configurations, please refer to another course on *www.ProjectProCorp.com*: click *Courses 2010* in the sidebar and *Configuring PS* in the chart.

The **Timesheet** screen in PWA looks like this:

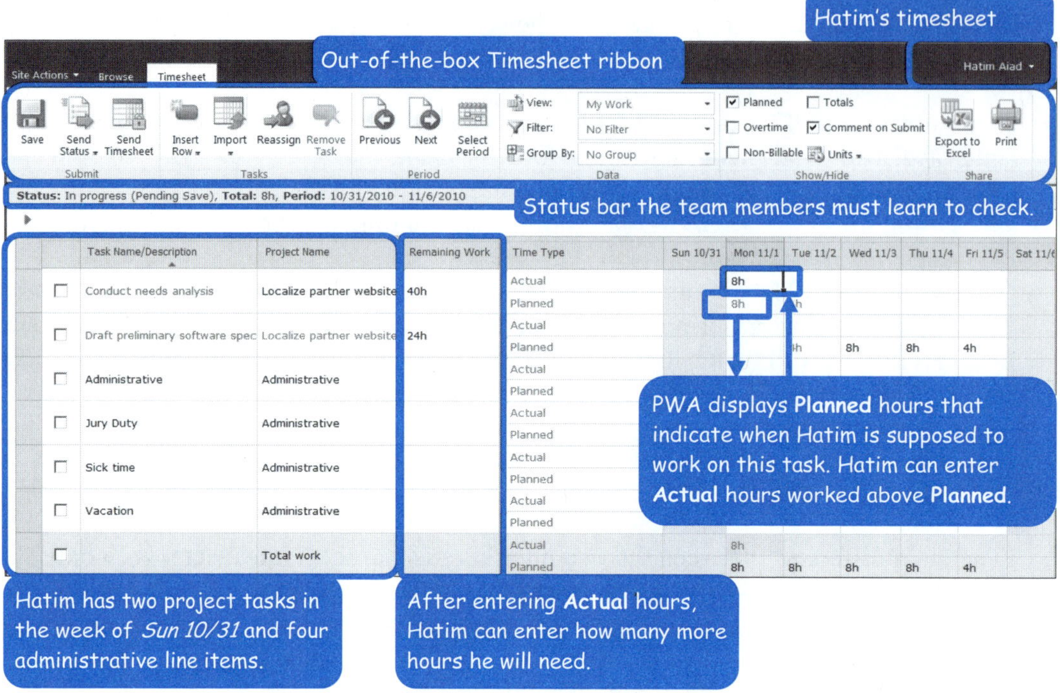

Microsoft is working towards a unified interface for the **Tasks** and **Timesheet** screens and has come very close to it in this release. Here are some tips that now apply to both the **Task** and **Timesheet** interface in PWA (unless otherwise indicated):

- The **Timesheet** and **Task** interfaces always display the period containing the current date (the system date of your computer).
- Click **Select Period** once and the screen will remember the number of days when you click **Previous** or **Next**. We recommend entering a period of one full week, but you can start the week on the day you want (Saturday, Sunday or Monday).
- By clicking **Next** you automatically create the timesheet for the next week (if you report every week). unlike the previous release of Project 2007. Changes are not automatically saved, but PWA is nice enough to prompt for saving. Microsoft told me there was strong objection against saving automatically in usability studies – an outcome that surprised me.
- In PWA 2010, you can now choose the time unit for **Duration** and **Work** separately by clicking the **Units** button. This button also allows selecting a **Date** format you prefer!
- The 2010 timesheet will now display tasks that were published after creating the timesheet, which was an issue in 2007. It even shows tasks that are late and originally did not fall into the time period of the current timesheet.

- If you click on a cell in the spreadsheet on the left or in the timescale on the right, the background of the cell will:
  - turn gray, which means you cannot enter data into this cell, or
  - stay white, which means you can enter data into this cell.
- For Timesheet screen only: You can speed up entering actual hours:
  - By using the **Import** button, with which you can **Replace Actual with Planned** hours. This will decrease tedious data entry, particularly if you tend to work according to the plan. Select the task first and then click **Import**, **Replace Actual with Planned**. The hours shown in the **Planned** row will be copied to the **Actual** row. Then you just make minor adjustments, and you are ready to enjoy the weekend!
- For **Tasks** screen only: You can speed up entering actual hours:
  - By entering numbers in the **Period Total** field and letting PWA distribute the hours across all days. In most weeks, people can simply enter 40h in the period total field, and PWA will enter 8h on each weekday. Minor adjustments can be made if necessary.

- The **Tasks** interface automatically recalculates and decreases the **Remaining Work** field after entering actual hours worked; in contrast, the **Timesheet** interface does not do this, which is too bad.
- Make sure you re-arrange the columns so that you can easily access the editable field **Remaining Work**: Click and hold down on the column heading of the field **Remaining Work,** and drag it to the left next to the **Project Name** field.
- The colored status bar located between the grid and the ribbon changes color depending on what you did:
  - It will turn yellow when you entered new numbers but did not save them (Timesheet: **Status: In Progress (Pending Save)** or Tasks: **Status: There are unsaved updates**).
  - It will turn blue if you click the **Save** button and PWA saved your data. You have not submitted the hours yet for approval (Timesheet: **Status: Processing (Pending Send Timesheet)** or Tasks: **Status: Updates have been saved**),
  - It will stay blue when the hours are sent; click button **Send Timesheet** to resource manager or **Send Status** to project manager (**Status: Updates have been sent for Approval**).
  - It will stay blue when hours are approved, but the text will change to: **Status: Approved (Final)**. The column **Process Status** will also inform the user if hours have been approved.
  - It will turn red when the timesheet gets stuck in the queue and displays **Status: Error**. Team members should learn to monitor the color and the messages on this status bar!
- Apart from the status bar, a field called **Process Status** will report the status on the task and shows extra messages on a task-by-task basis. For example, when the project manager requests an interim status update, the field in the Tasks view will

show: **Update Requested**. You may want to drag this field to the left to keep it in sight.

- You can click on the name of the task in the **Timesheet** or **Tasks** interface and see a screen with additional details on the assignment as well as features where you can add detail, including:
  - You can see **Recent Task Changes** with a complete archive of all work submitted and what was approved. This is very handy for reviewers.
  - You can attach issues, risks and documents to the "task" (assignment really!).
  - You can view **Related Assignments**: predecessors (from whom to get information about your task or draft work products) and successors (to whom you forward your work product). This feature can enhance collaboration between team members!
  - You can add any **Notes**.
- Team members can ask Outlook to remind them via email of upcoming tasks by setting alerts in **Personal Settings**. We recommend this to help create the habit of filling out timesheets. Alternatively, the reminders and hours can be entered in Outlook itself, see page 662.
- Manually scheduled tasks with only a duration do not have a Start and Finish date and will, therefore, not have any Planned values in the Timesheet screen; you can only update them by entering a % Work Complete. All other cells will turn gray.

Overall, the **Timesheet** and **Tasks** interfaces have greatly improved and are much more reliable in PWA 2010. Finally, the 2007 era of endless service packs and cumulative updates will be behind us!

Standard Operating Procedure for Timesheets in PWA

It is important that team members develop a (new) habit of entering their hours in Project Web App. If the status cycle is weekly, we recommend the following *standard operating procedure*:

- At the end of each day, the team member enters the actual hours worked that day in the **Timesheet** screen in PWA and clicks **Save**. We recommend using the **Timesheet** screen because only this screen has line items for *administrative*, *sick time* and *vacation* and allows for checking the total actual hours entered per day as a sanity check.
- At the end of each week:
  - The team member checks the totals for the week and then clicks **Send Timesheet** ; the timesheet goes to the timesheet approver, normally the team member's resource manager.
  - The team member switches over to the **Tasks** screen in PWA and reviews the calculated **Remaining Work** hours on tasks that are still in-progress and revises them where needed. We recommend using the **Tasks** screen for revising the

Remaining Work because only in this view is the Remaining Work decreased by the Actual Hours entered for the week! It is important that team members revise the Remaining Work, because they often have a much better idea how much longer the task will take after having worked on the task. Revised estimates are important for the project manager because these revisions will, in turn, keep the forecasts in the project schedule as accurate as possible. In fact, without collecting revisions to the Remaining Work, you are not applying the main message of this book: *Forecast Scheduling*!

◇ The team member clicks **Send Status**, and the hours go to the project manager (or **Status Manager** if the project manager delegated this). Once the project manager approves, the hours are automatically transferred into the schedule.

We recommend that you train your team members on applying this standard operating procedure. Encourage them to develop it as their new habit – a good working habit.

Accept the Timesheet Data and Transfer into the Schedule

As soon as the team member submits the timesheet data, the project manager will receive the data in Project Web App and can review it in the **Approval center**.

1. In PWA, click **Approval Center** in the Quick Launch side pane on the left – the **Approvals** screen appears:

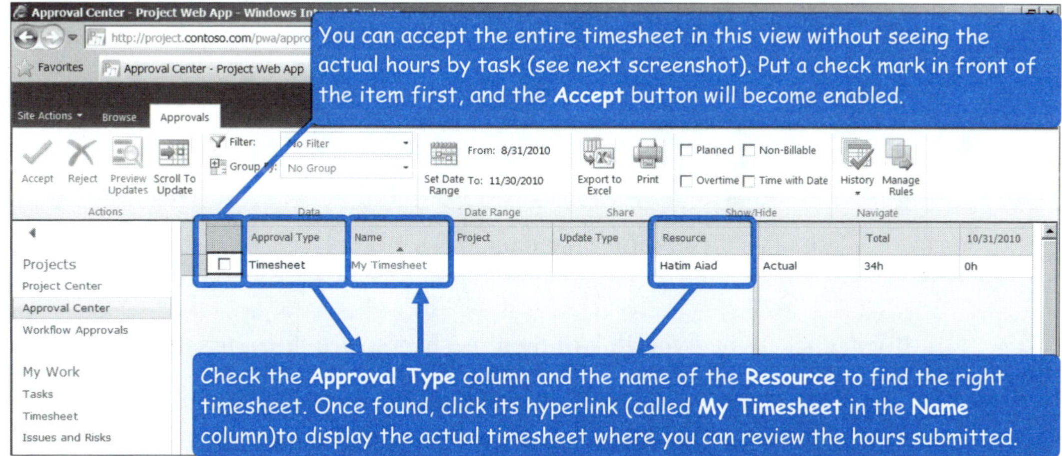

2. Notice that in this screen the numbers in the timescale are totals aggregated from all the tasks in the submitted timesheet. You can do one of two things at this point:
   ◇ Click on the hyperlink in the **Name** column of one of the timesheets to look at lower level of detail: actual hours by task by day. Continue with step 3.

◇ Review the update on this aggregate screen and approve or reject here. You have the following options on this screen:

Click Scroll To Update to scroll the numbers into view that were sent to you for review.

2007 Click Preview Updates to see how the schedule will look in the Gantt Chart if you decide to accept the updates as they are. This is a very powerful feature for you, as a project manager, because it allows you to keep garbage out of your schedule instead of having to clean up the mess later (which has not been easy in the past!). Notice that the selected tasks are highlighted in blue in preview.

Click Manage Rules to create automatic approval and rejection rules to make the tedious reviewing of the weekly wheelbarrow of numbers as efficient as possible. Certain team members may always submit very reliable timesheets, and rules will eliminate mindless clicking. You can have the tool apply these rules automatically; they are truly "automatic" since 2007.

Click Approve to approve the entire timesheet.

Click 

to refuse the data.

3. If you clicked the hyperlink of the timesheet to see the hours per task, the timesheet screen appears where you can approve hours. Click the button in the top of the *quick launch* side pane to make the pane disappear so that all days of the week are shown in the timescale.

4. The result can be seen in the following screenshot:

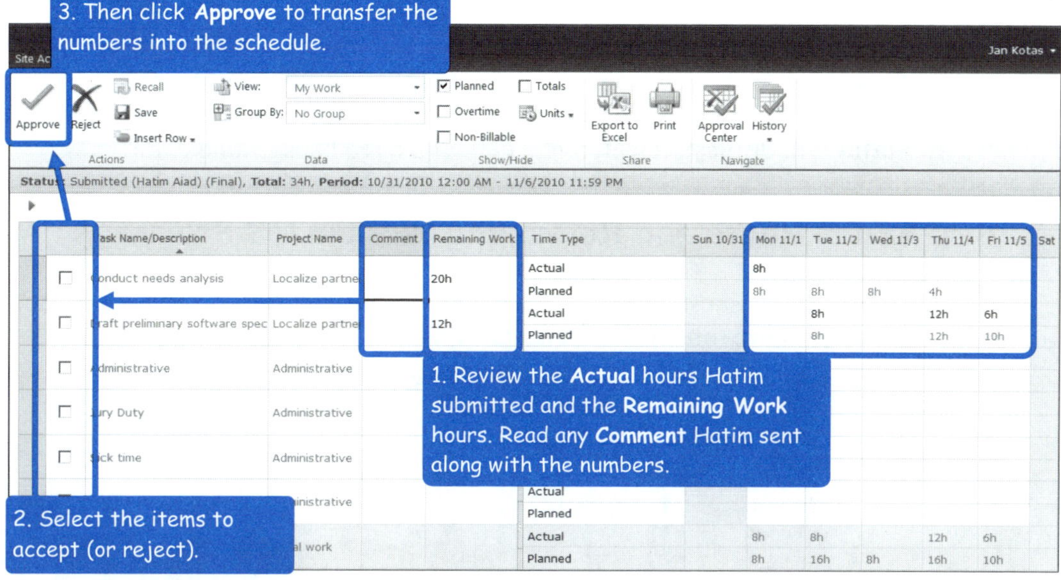

4. You can leave the task in this screen and decide to accept or reject later. If you are ready to process the updates, first review the hours submitted and select the tasks to be approved:
   - ◇ You can select single tasks or quickly click the list button above the column of check boxes as shown in the following screenshot:

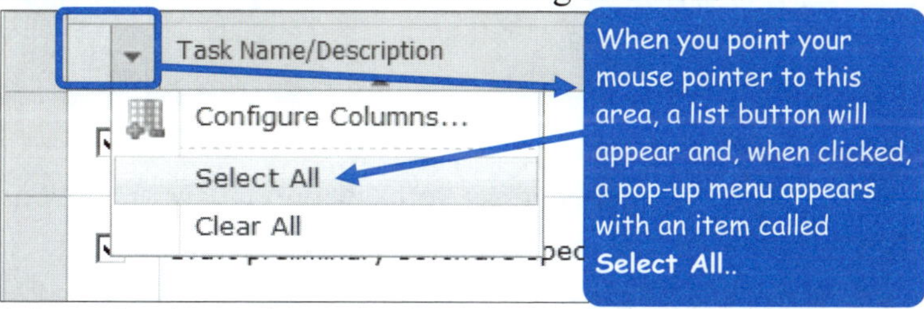

   - ◇ After selecting tasks, you will see that the following buttons are automatically enabled at the top:
   - ◇ Click Approve to approve the line item. An **Approve Timesheet** prompt appears, in which you can write comments to yourself. Enter any notes and click OK to confirm.

◇ Click  to refuse the data. You should enter an explanation in the **Reject Timesheet** prompt and get in touch with the team member to resolve the issue. The team member will see a rejection indicator in PWA: the field **Process Status** will display **Rejected** in a cell with a red background color.

View Actual Hours and Remaining Work in MS Project

After transferring the timesheet hours, you can view the *actual hours* entered in the **Resource Usage** view with the assignments expanded. Click ribbon **Format, Details, Actual Work** to see the exact numbers typed in by the resources, as illustrated in the next screen:

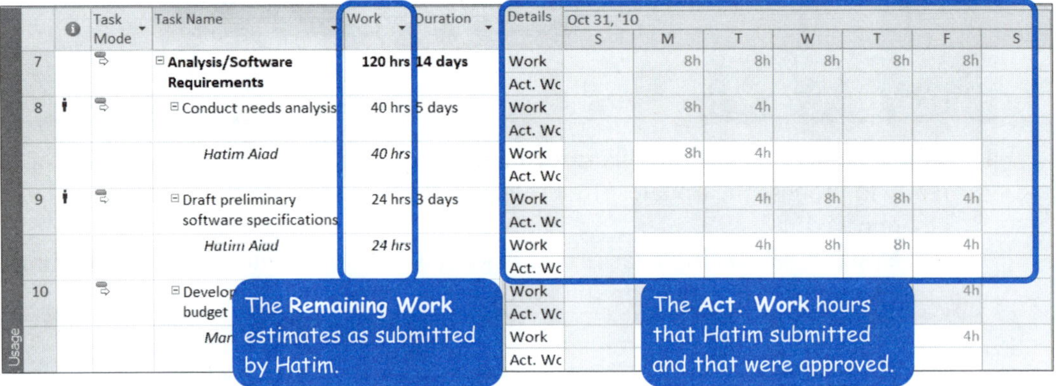

You should see the identical numbers here as you saw previously on the **Task Updates** page in Project Web App.

Prepare the Status and Forecast Report

Regardless of whether you chose to update *tasks* or *assignments*, the *Tracking Gantt* chart is good for monitoring and for reporting progress and new forecasts.

1. Click ribbon **View**, click the bottom portion Gantt Chart of 

and select **Tracking Gantt** from the pull-down menu – the **Tracking Gantt** view appears.
2. Click ribbon **View**, button **Tables** and item **Variance** to see where the *forecast schedule* is relative to the *baseline schedule*.
3. The screen should now look similar to:

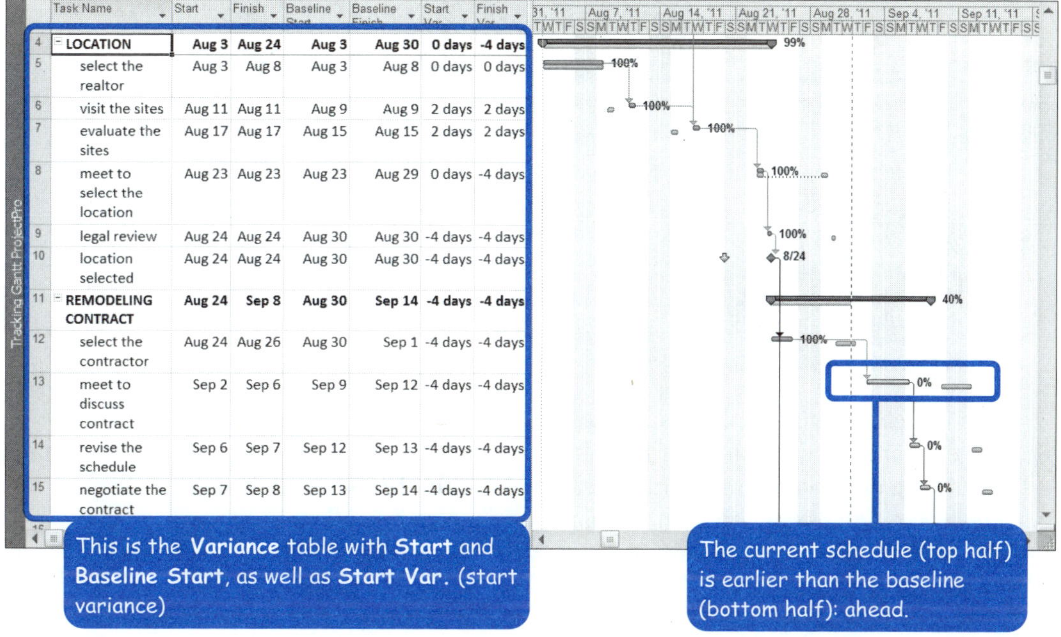

	Task Name	Start	Finish	Baseline Start	Baseline Finish	Start Var.	Finish Var.
4	- LOCATION	Aug 3	Aug 24	Aug 3	Aug 30	0 days	-4 days
5	select the realtor	Aug 3	Aug 8	Aug 3	Aug 8	0 days	0 days
6	visit the sites	Aug 11	Aug 11	Aug 9	Aug 9	2 days	2 days
7	evaluate the sites	Aug 17	Aug 17	Aug 15	Aug 15	2 days	2 days
8	meet to select the location	Aug 23	Aug 23	Aug 23	Aug 29	0 days	-4 days
9	legal review	Aug 24	Aug 24	Aug 30	Aug 30	-4 days	-4 days
10	location selected	Aug 24	Aug 24	Aug 30	Aug 30	-4 days	-4 days
11	- REMODELING CONTRACT	Aug 24	Sep 8	Aug 30	Sep 14	-4 days	-4 days
12	select the contractor	Aug 24	Aug 26	Aug 30	Sep 1	-4 days	-4 days
13	meet to discuss contract	Sep 2	Sep 6	Sep 9	Sep 12	-4 days	-4 days
14	revise the schedule	Sep 6	Sep 7	Sep 12	Sep 13	-4 days	-4 days
15	negotiate the contract	Sep 7	Sep 8	Sep 13	Sep 14	-4 days	-4 days

The Tracking Gantt view depicts progress using the calculated date field **Complete Through**. You can see this field listed in the **Bar styles** dialog (ribbon **Format**, button **Format**, item **Bar Styles**) and looking under **To**. The **Complete Through** field:

- Follows closely the **Actual Duration** that was entered if you did task updates, but it is adjusted for weekends and holidays.
- Is the number of days on which actual hours were entered if you used timesheets.

Notice that the Tracking Gantt does not show progress on the tasks (**% Complete** and **Actual Durations**) if you work with timesheets and you cleared the option ☐ **Updating Task Status updates Resource Status** (ribbon **File,** Options**,** tab **Schedule**).

11

With the option off, the **% Complete** and **Actual Duration** are not calculated at all for tasks.

Pro

In *Project Professional 2010* with *Project Server*, reporting progress is as simple as can be. As the project manager, you just need to keep your schedule up-to-date and save it. Executives can view the status and forecasts online at any time, even Saturday night at 10 o'clock.

Executives will see their entire portfolio of projects in *Project Web App*:

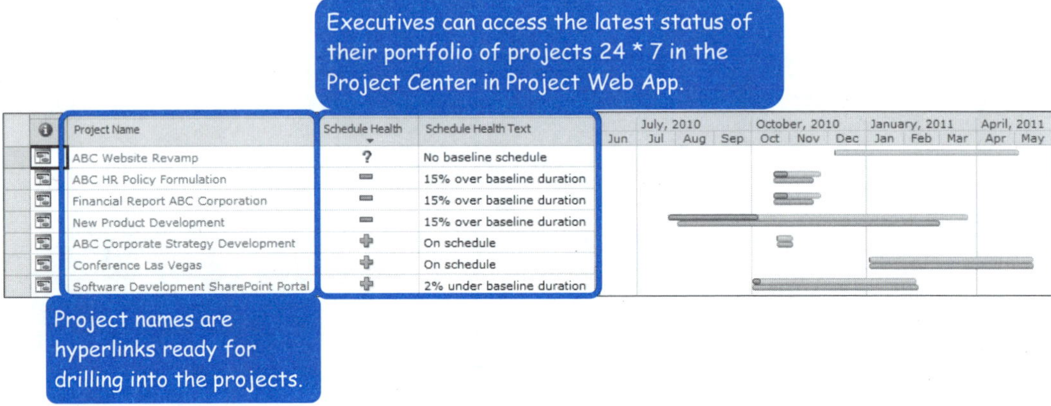

The Project Center displays one line item for each project. The line item states the project name, and it is a hyperlink. In case executives wonder how current the data are, your Project Server administrators can add the field **Last modified** to the Project Center view. Executives can click on the name of the project and drill down into the details of the project schedule, all inside Project Web App (no need to know MS Project or have a license for it).

If executives would drill into the last project listed in the previous screenshot, they would see this:

From the Project Center, we drilled down into this **Software Development** project. An executive could drill down to find the cause of a schedule slip or learn from schedule gains.

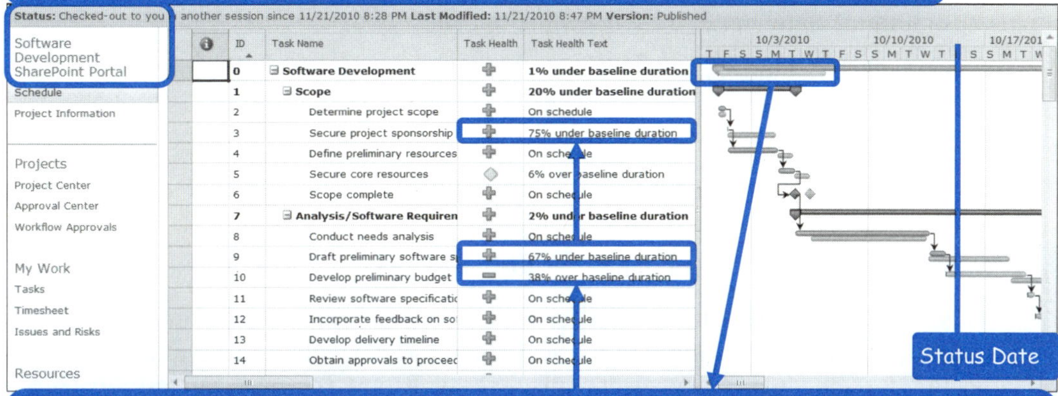

The executive should first check if the progress bar on the project summary task (task 0) runs up to the status date; the schedule is out-of-date. Then (s)he can analyze where the discrepancies are and find out how this project managed to get 1% ahead of its baseline duration and learn valuable lessons.

Executives can visually determine if the schedule is current; if the schedule is up-to-date, the gray progress bar of the project summary task (second bar of task 0) should run all the way up to the *status date*. If you put all actuals are in the past and all remaining durations in the future as we recommended, the progress bar always runs up to the status date. If this is not the case, the schedule is either out-of-date, or it has been updated incorrectly.

The executive can identify the source of problems in the schedule by finding the problem tasks and the resources working on them. If needed, the executive can take action or (s)he can sit back and rely on the project manager to do the right thing. A little chat might clarify things.

Reporting on the Differences since the Last Update

Executives who try to be efficient with their time sometimes ask for reports that only show the differences since the last update. To create such a report, you need to take a snapshot immediately after each schedule update:

1. Save all start and finish dates by setting an interim plan before entering any update information; click ribbon **Project**, [Set Baseline], **Set baseline** – the dialog appears.
2. Select ◉ **Set interim plan** and ◉ **Entire project**. Click [OK].

Taking this step immediately after each update is better than just before the next update, because it catches any changes in the schedule other than changes resulting from updating the schedule. The project manager may also re-assign resources, revise to-complete estimates or even add new tasks.

To create the differential report:

1. Enter the task update information and apply a custom view that highlights the tasks with changes in bold. For more on how-to create new views, see page 556. Click ribbon **View**, click [Other Views] and click **More Views**. In the **More Views** dialog, select the **Tracking Gantt** view and click [Copy...]. **Name** the view *Tracking Gantt delta since last update*. Furthermore, have this view:
   - ◇ Apply a table with the fields **Baseline Start**, **Start1** (before), **Scheduled Start** (after), **Baseline Finish**, **Finish1** (before) and **Scheduled Finish** (after). We recommend that you change the titles of the columns in the **Table Definition** dialog, so that they are more descriptive; for suggested titles, see our screenshot below.
   - ◇ Apply a filter that displays all tasks that have changed since the last update; you need to enter the following filter definition:
     Start1 does not equal Scheduled Start
     or Finish1 does not equal Scheduled Finish.
   - ◇ Apply the filter as a highlight filter by clicking ribbon **View**, [Other Views] **More Views...**, select the newly-created view and click [Edit...] – select ☑ **Highlight filter**. Click [OK] and [Apply].
   - ◇ Make the highlighted tasks appear in bold font: click ribbon **Format**, button **Text styles**; from the list **Item to change**, select **Highlighted tasks**; and, from the list **Font style**, select **Bold**.

The result will look like this:

The project manager updated the schedule, and the view bolded all tasks that were affected by the update.

	Task Name	Baseline Start	Start before	Start after	Baseline Finish	Finish before	Finish after
15	negotiate the contract	Tue 9/8/09	Tue 9/8/09	Tue 9/8/09	Wed 9/9/09	Wed 9/9/09	Wed 9/9/09
16	contractor contracted	Wed 9/9/09	Wed 9/9/09	Wed 9/9/09	Wed 9/9/09	Wed 9/9/09	Wed 9/9/09
17	**REMODELED LOCATION**	**Wed 9/9/09**	**Fri 9/11/09**	**Fri 9/11/09**	**Fri 11/6/09**	**Wed 11/18/09**	**Tue 11/17/09**
18	**relocate walls**	**Wed 9/9/09**	**Fri 9/11/09**	**Fri 9/11/09**	**Wed 9/23/09**	**Fri 10/2/09**	**Wed 10/7/09**
19	**install electric wiring**	**Wed 9/23/09**	**Mon 10/5/09**	**Mon 10/5/09**	**Wed 9/30/09**	**Fri 10/9/09**	**Thu 10/8/09**
20	**paint**	**Wed 9/30/09**	**Tue 10/13/09**	**Mon 10/12/09**	**Fri 10/2/09**	**Wed 10/14/09**	**Wed 10/14/09**
21	**drying of paint**	**Fri 10/2/09**	**Wed 10/14/09**	**Thu 10/15/09**	**Tue 10/6/09**	**Sun 10/18/09**	**Mon 10/19/09**
22	**install cabinetry**	**Tue 10/6/09**	**Mon 10/19/09**	**Mon 10/19/09**	**Wed 10/14/09**	**Fri 10/23/09**	**Mon 11/2/09**
23	**install LAN**	**Tue 10/6/09**	**Mon 10/19/09**	**Mon 10/19/09**	**Fri 10/23/09**	**Tue 11/3/09**	**Mon 11/2/09**
24	**lay carpet**	**Fri 10/23/09**	**Wed 11/4/09**	**Tue 11/3/09**	**Fri 11/6/09**	**Wed 11/18/09**	**Tue 11/17/09**
25	**facility remodeled**	**Fri 11/6/09**	**Wed 11/18/09**	**Tue 11/17/09**	**Fri 11/6/09**	**Wed 11/18/09**	**Tue 11/17/09**
26	**MOVE**	**Tue 8/25/09**	**Mon 9/21/09**	**Wed 10/21/09**	**Tue 11/17/09**	**Tue 11/24/09**	**Tue 11/24/09**
27	**select mover**	**Tue 8/25/09**	**Mon 9/21/09**	**Wed 10/21/09**	**Thu 8/27/09**	**Tue 9/22/09**	**Thu 10/22/09**
28	pack	Thu 11/12/09	Thu 11/19/09	Thu 11/19/09	Fri 11/13/09	Fri 11/20/09	Fri 11/20/09
29	move	Sat 11/14/09	Sat 11/21/09	Sat 11/21/09	Sun 11/15/09	Sun 11/22/09	Sun 11/22/09
30	unpack	Mon 11/16/09	Mon 11/23/09	Mon 11/23/09	Tue 11/17/09	Tue 11/24/09	Tue 11/24/09
31	new location opened	Tue 11/17/09	Tue 11/24/09	Tue 11/24/09	Tue 11/17/09	Tue 11/24/09	Tue 11/24/09

Checks on an Updated Schedule

Next, proceed to the **Tracking Gantt** chart to apply the checks to verify if the schedule is updated correctly. The following checks reflect best practices on updating schedules. A schedule has to be updated if that day's date has moved past the project start date as indicated in the **Project information** dialog (ribbon **Project**). If the project should have started, the schedule needs to show actuals and also revisions to the forecasts. The latter is important if you want to implement the principle of *forecast scheduling*.

The following questions help determine if the best practices of updating schedules were applied. The numbering corresponds to the complete checklist in the summary chapter, see page 711. The filters mentioned in the checks can be found in the file *ProjectPro tools to check project schedules.MPP* available for download at www.ProjectProCorp.com (see page vi for the procedure to access these files).

11

11 Updating

11.1. Is the *baseline schedule* present, complete, correct, relevant and challenging?

The schedule needs a good baseline, because it will be the standard of comparison used to measure progress.

◇ Is a baseline schedule present?

Note that projects planned far into the future and not yet approved do not necessarily need a baseline.

◇ Is the baseline schedule complete?

You can verify the presence and completeness by applying the filter **11.1 Tasks with missing baseline info.** The filter displays any tasks without entries in the fields **Baseline Start, Baseline Finish, Baseline**

Duration or **Baseline Work**. When *assignments* are created after the baseline is set, the **Baseline Work** field is still empty. Note that the filter does not check on the field **Baseline Cost**, because not every project has a monetary budget. If your project does have a budget, **Baseline Cost** values should be present for all tasks.

- ◇ Is the baseline schedule correct?
  The baseline cannot be changed without formal approval of the appropriate project stakeholders. Does the current baseline reflect the schedule as originally approved, plus all approved change requests?
- ◇ Is the baseline schedule relevant?
  If the project has deviated too far from the baseline, a new baseline needs to be negotiated. The baseline should provide a meaningful *standard of comparison* for the current schedule. You can check this by looking at how far the current schedule is removed from the baseline. Does the project have a fighting chance to catch up with the baseline again, or is it a lost cause? If it is a lost cause, you should submit a change request to move the baseline schedule. If your project was subjected to *acts of God*, there may be a valid reason to update the baseline schedule.
- ◇ Is the baseline schedule challenging?
  As we discussed on page 543, if project managers buffer their schedule before baselining to such a degree that it will be very easy to meet the baseline schedule, the performance of these project managers and their teams will always look good.

11.2. Are the appropriate options selected in ribbon **File,** Options for the chosen updating strategy?

- ◇ For task updating (i.e., revising the task-related **Actual Duration** and **Remaining Duration** fields), the options should be set as follows:
  Tab **Schedule**:

  ☑ **Split in-progress tasks**

  ☑ **Updating task status updates resource status**

  Tab **Advanced**:

  ☑ **Move end of completed parts after status date back to status date**

  ☑ **Move start of remaining parts before status date forward to status date**
- ◇ For assignment updating (entering numbers from the timesheets into the assignment-related **Actual Work** and **Remaining Work** fields), the options should be set as follows:
  Tab **Schedule**:

☑ **Split in-progress tasks**

☑ **Updating task status updates resource status**

If you keep this option selected, you should not enter **% Complete** on tasks, because this may override timesheet data. The *Project Server administrator* can prevent overriding by locking in timesheet periods.
Tab **Advanced:**

☑ **Move end of completed parts after status date back to status date**

☑ **Move start of remaining parts before status date forward to status date**

◇ We do not recommend updating both the tasks and the assignments for two reasons: it is a lot more work and the datasets can get out-of-sync, in which case you are telling two different stories about your project instead of providing one version of the truth. If you want to update both tasks and assignments regardless, the options should be set as follows:
Tab **Schedule**:

☑ **Split in-progress tasks**

☐ **Updating task status updates resource status**: you cannot enter both types of information unless you clear this option.
Tab **Advanced:**

☑ **Move end of completed parts after status date back to status date**

☑ **Move start of remaining parts before status date forward to status date**

11.3. Is the **Status Date** set to an appropriate date?
The **Status date** in the **Project, Project Information** dialog should be set to a date that is within one reporting period from that day's date. If it is too far in the past, the schedule is out-of-date. If it is too far in the future, the project manager is guessing the progress instead of entering factual progress.

11.4. Is the task type for soon-to-be-updated tasks set to **Fixed Units** and non **Effort-driven**?
When you update the schedule, you change the durations (task updates) or the work (assignment updates). For both updating strategies, we recommended Fixed Units and non Effort-Driven, because typically you would like to see how the schedule looks when the same resources continue to work on the task. You can always re-optimize the schedule after that (see page 407) and re-allocate resources.

11

11.5. Are all actual durations (actual work / actual hours worked) scheduled in the past when they actually happened?
This is an important check to make sure the schedule forecasts accurately by itself: *forecast scheduling*. The actuals are scheduled in the past if their dates are before the status date. If that is not the case, the forecasts in the schedule have not been updated. When you bring actual durations to the past, all their dependent tasks may be rescheduled earlier as well, which improves the accuracy of the forecasts. This is why rescheduling actuals is important. You can perform this check by applying the filter
11.5 Reschedule Actual Durations… You should move the tasks displayed by this filter by using **Tasks** ribbon, button **Move**, and item **Completed Parts to Status Date.**

11.6. Are all remaining durations (remaining work numbers) scheduled in the future when they will happen?
This is an important check to make sure the schedule forecasts accurately by itself: *forecast scheduling*. The remaining estimates are scheduled in the future if their start date is later than the status date. You cannot leave unfinished work scheduled in the past, because the past is done and gone. The work should be moved to the future to update the forecast dates of all their dependent tasks. Otherwise, the schedule does not reflect up-to-date forecasts, and you have created a *status report*, instead of a *forecast report*. You can perform this check by applying the filter
11.6 Reschedule Remaining Durations... Then move the tasks by using **Tasks** ribbon, button **Move**, item **Incomplete Parts to Status Date**.

11.7. Are the to-complete estimates revised?
This is an important check to make sure the schedule forecasts accurately by itself: *forecast scheduling*. If remaining duration or remaining work values are not revised, the schedule may not reflect up-to-date and accurate forecasts. If team members do revise the remaining durations of their detail tasks, the forecasts will be more accurate. You can display the tasks with a revised duration by applying the filter
11.7 Remaining Durations revised. This filter is different from the other filters in the sense that if it displays tasks, the schedule is good because its forecasts are more accurate. If the filter does not display any tasks, it is an indication that the project managers are not revising their to-complete estimates while updating.

11.8. Are the workloads of the resources still reasonable?
Updates to the schedule may have increased or decreased workloads, or shifted them and caused new *overallocations*. If workloads decreased, there are new opportunities to shorten the schedule.

11.9. Is the latest forecast finish date still before the project deadline date or before the baseline schedule finish date?

If the project update slipped the schedule and extended it beyond its promised and agreed-upon finish date, you have a responsibility to re-optimize the schedule in such a way that it finishes on time. If your current project finish date is later than the baseline schedule finish date, you are planning to finish late, which is unacceptable. You need to develop what-if scenarios with the dynamic model of the project to find a scenario that finishes on time. If you do not succeed in finding an on-time scenario of the dynamic model, you need to ask for permission to finish the project later by filing a change request to change the baseline. Once this change request is approved, the baseline finish can be moved to the agreed-upon date. In other words, the latest forecasted finish date should never be later than the baseline schedule finish date, since it indicates project managers are not doing their job.

11.10. If you used overtime to compensate for slippages, are the overtime rates filled in for those resources?

You can check this by switching to the Resource Sheet and applying the resource filter **11.10 Overtime rates entered**. This filter displays all resources with overtime hours assigned, but without an overtime rate.
If the overtime rates are not filled in (zero rate) and you assign work in overtime, the cost of the project will actually decrease instead of increase. MS Project will multiply the overtime effort with a zero rate. The cost should stay the same if you pay the same rate for overtime, or increase if you pay more for overtime.

11.11. Is the latest forecasted total cost (or effort) of the project still within the budget of the project?

You may need to re-optimize the schedule to find ways to get within budget. If you cannot find a way to get within budget, you need to submit a change request for more money. The forecast model of the project will allow you to quickly develop a variety of what-if scenarios to find one that works. The cost may run out of hand: If you are using resources with higher rates than in the original plan, if the resources are spending more effort than they estimated, or if the prices for raw materials, equipment, and facilities are higher than expected.

Exercises

Review

1. What are the process steps for updating schedules?
2. a. What benefit can you gain from having a baseline in your schedule?
   b. How do you set the first baseline in MS Project?
   c. How often do you set it for the entire project?
3. What are legitimate reasons for changing your baseline?
4. Describe in your own words the meaning of the following indicators:
   - ◇ Actual Duration
   - ◇ Remaining Duration
5. How do the following indicators relate to each other? Please describe their relationship using formulas.
   - ◇ Actual Duration
   - ◇ Remaining Duration
   - ◇ Duration
   - ◇ % Complete
6. There are two main strategies for updating schedules. What are they and what are the main differences between them?
7. When collecting update data, you could ask your team members for percentages complete. What are the weaknesses of this metric?
8. a. What ribbon buttons do you need to click to set the status date?
   b. Why do you need a status date?
9. a. What task type do you recommend when updating tasks?
   b. How can you change multiple tasks or all tasks in your schedule to this task type?
10. There are six different update situations in practice. Please mention four.

11. A team leader submits the schedule update report shown in the illustration below. Dark gray is Actual Duration; light gray is Remaining Duration; black is baseline or summary task bar. Would you accept this report:
    - ◇ As a status report? Why?
    - ◇ As a forecast report? Why?

    If you would not accept it, indicate what needs to be changed.

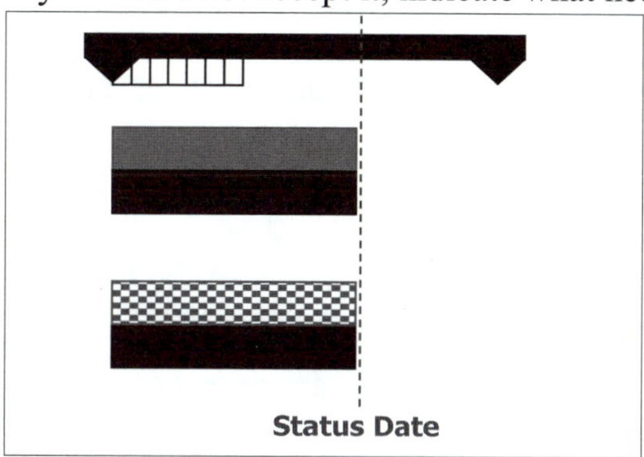

12. Identify the pieces of data that you need to collect when you want to update assignments?
13. Which vehicles are available to collect timesheets? What requirements do project managers have for a good timesheet application?
14. What do you look at when verifying whether your schedule is properly updated?
15. What do the following progress situations mean? Describe the project status in your own words. Top black bar is Actual Duration, top gray bar is Remaining Duration and bottom gray bar is Baseline Duration.

a.

	Task Name	Bas. Dur.	Dur.	Act. Dur.	Rem. Dur.
1	Project OpTijd	20 d	20 d	11 d	9 d
2					

Month 1 / Month 2: 29 01 04 07 10 13 16 19 22 25 28 | 01 04 07

b.

	Task Name	Bas. Dur.	Dur.	Act. Dur.	Rem. Dur.
1	Project LaatBegonnen	20 d	20 d	6 d	14 d
2					

Month 1 / Month 2: 29 01 04 07 10 13 16 19 22 25 28 | 01 04 07 c.

	Task Name	Bas. Dur.	Dur.	Act. Dur.	Rem. Dur.
1	Project MeerTijd	20 d	25 d	11 d	14 d
2					

d.

	Task Name	Bas. Dur.	Dur.	Act. Dur.	Rem. Dur.
1	Project AchterLoper	20 d	20 d	5 d	15 d
2					

16. What is the status of the following portfolio of projects?

	Task Name	Bas. Dur.	Dur.	Act. Dur.	Rem. Dur.	Actual Start
1	Project AAAA	20 d	22 d	8 d	14 d	Mon 06-04-09
2	Project BBBB	20 d	21 d	10 d	11 d	Mon 30-03-09
3	Project CCCC	20 d	18 d	6 d	12 d	Fri 03-04-09
4						

Relocation Project – Updating Tasks – First Update

The goal of this exercise is to be able to update a schedule and to get accurate forecasts.

1. Open the file *11A Up-to-date Schedule.MPP* available for download at www.ProjectProCorp.com (see page vi for the procedure to access these files).
2. This schedule is the optimized version of the schedule, which easily meets its deadline of November 1. We will manage our project with this schedule and update it as we go along. Change to the **Tracking Gantt** view.
3. Click ribbon **View**, click button **Table**, item **Tracking** to apply the Tracking table. Remove the columns **% Comp. (% Complete**) and the **Phys. % Comp. (Physical % Complete**). Move the column **Act. Finish** (**Actual Finish**) to after **Rem. Dur.** (**Remaining Duration**). The order of the columns is the order in which to enter update information and is a memory bridge for updating.
4. Using ribbon **Project**, button **Set baseline**, item **Set baseline…** – set the baseline for the entire project. The baseline schedule will be the challenging target schedule for the project.
5. Click ribbon **Project** and set the **Status Date** to *August 28, 2012 5:00 p.m.* and create a gridline for the status date in the Tracking Gantt timescale using ribbon **Format**, button **Gridlines**, item **Gridlines…**(see page 635 for more details).

6. Set the following options in ribbon **File,** Options, tab **Schedule**:
   ☑ **Updating Task status updates resource status**
   ☑ **Actual costs are always calculated by Project**

7. Set the following options in ribbon **File,** Options, tab **Advanced:**
   ☑ **Move end of completed parts after status date back to status date**
   ☑ **Move start of remaining parts before status date forward to status date**

8. Switch the task type to **Fixed Units** and non **Effort-Driven** for all tasks (see page 636).

9. Update the tasks in the project schedule. As of the status date the situation is:
   - ◇ All the tasks until *Contractor Contracted* ran as scheduled.
   - ◇ The contractor started early because he finished his previous contract early. He supplied the following update on the first and only task he started: *relocate walls*:

Task	**Started**	**Actual Duration**	**Remaining Duration**
relocate walls	August 20, 2012	7 days	3 days

10. Check whether the schedule is updated correctly (see page 677):
    a. Check whether there are any remaining durations scheduled before the status date. Reschedule these after the status date.
    b. Check if there are actual durations after the status date and reschedule these before the status date.

11. Describe the status of the project in your own words.

12. Do you need to take corrective action?

13. Save your file and compare it with the solution file *11B Up-to-date Schedule.mpp* available for download at www.ProjectProCorp.com (see page vi for the procedure to access these files). See page 697 of this book for an automated way of comparing and reporting differences between two versions of one schedule.

Relocation Project – Re-optimizing After First Update

The goal of this exercise is to be able to improve a schedule so that it is closer to its baseline schedule again.

1. Open the file *11B Up-to-date Schedule.mpp* available for download at www.ProjectProCorp.com (see page vi for the procedure to access these files).

2. You find that your project may run late relative to the baseline. You want to take corrective action by making the following changes in your schedule:

Task name	Action
relocate walls	Change the task type back to **Fixed Work**, then change the number of units to 15 for the balance of the activity: add 5 resources to help complete the activity. The result is a gain of 1 day.
install electrical wiring	Enter an **Ovt. Rate** for the Contractor of $45 per hour (150%). Change the task type back to **Fixed Work**, then change the number of units to 8 for the activity. Have the resources work overtime to a total of 32 overtime hours (see page 326). The duration shortens to almost 2.6 days.
install cabinetry	If the painters start their painting in the area where the cabinets will be installed, the paint in that area should be dry by the time the painters are finished painting. Delete the dependency from *drying of paint* to *install cabinetry* and replace it with a dependency from *paint* to *install cabinetry*. *Install cabinetry* should be on schedule.
install LAN cables	The task *install LAN cables* does not have to wait for all of the walls to be relocated. Change the dependency from *relocate walls* to *install LAN cables* to Finish-to-Finish with a 1.5 day lag. The *Install the LAN* activities should be on schedule.

3. Save your file and compare it with the solution file *11C Up-to-date Schedule.mpp* available for download at www.ProjectProCorp.com (see page vi for the procedure to access these files). See page 697 of this book for an automated way of comparing and reporting differences between two versions of one schedule.

Relocation Project – Updating Tasks – Second Update

The goal of this exercise is to be able to update a schedule and get accurate forecasts.

1. Open the file *11C Up-to-date Schedule.mpp* available for download at www.ProjectProCorp.com (see page vi for the procedure to access these files).

2. If needed, do the following:

◇ Display the **Tracking Gantt** view.
◇ Apply the **Tracking** table. Remove the columns **% Comp.** (**% Complete**) and the **Phys. % Comp.** (**Physical % Complete**). Move the column **Act. Finish** (**Actual Finish**) to after **Rem. Dur.** (**Remaining Duration**).

3. On the **Project** ribbon, set the **Status Date** to *September 4, 2012* and, if needed, create a gridline (ribbon **Format**, button **Gridlines**, item **Gridlines...**) for the status date in the Tracking Gantt timescale.

4. Verify if the following options are set:
   In ribbon **File,** Options, tab **Schedule**:
   ☑ **Updating Task status updates resource status**
   ☑ **Actual costs are always calculated by Microsoft Project**
   In ribbon **File,** Options, tab **Advanced**:
   ☑ **Move end of completed parts after status date back to status date**
   ☑ **Move start of remaining parts before status date forward to status date**

5. Switch the task type to **Fixed Units** and non **Effort-Driven** for the tasks needing update (see page 636).

6. Update the tasks in the project schedule. The contractor supplied the following table with update data for the status of the project as of the status date. Tasks that are not listed in the table have not started yet:

Task name	Actual Start	Act. Duration	Rem. Duration
relocate walls	Aug 20, 2012	9 days	0 days
install electric wiring	Aug 31, 2012	2.6 days	0 days
Paint	Sep 2, 2012	2 days	0 days
drying of paint	Sep 2, 2012	2 elapsed days	0 elapsed days
install cabinetry	Sep 4, 2012	1 day	4 days
install LAN cables	Sep 1, 2012	2.5 days	0 days
install LAN hardware	Sep 3, 2012	1.5 days	1 day
select mover	Aug 31, 2012	2 days	0 days

7. Check whether the schedule is updated correctly (see page 677):
   a. Check whether there are any remaining durations scheduled before the status date. Reschedule these after the status date.

11

   b. Check if there are actual durations after the status date and reschedule these before the status date.

8. Describe the status of the project in your own words.
9. Do you need to take corrective action?
10. Save your file and compare it with the solution file *11D Up-to-date Schedule.mpp* available for download at www.ProjectProCorp.com (see page vi for the procedure to access these files). See page 697 of this book for an automated way of comparing and reporting differences between two versions of one schedule.

Relocation Project – Re-optimizing After Second Update

The goal of this exercise is to be able to improve a schedule so that it meets its baseline finish date.

1. Open the file *11D Up-to-date Schedule.mpp* available for download at www.ProjectProCorp.com (see page vi for the procedure to access these files).
2. You find this current schedule too risky; there is little buffer left. You decide to explore whether working overtime offers solutions. Enter the following overtime rates in the Resource Sheet:

Name	Std. Rate	Overtime Rate
Employees	$ 25/h	$ 50/h
Contractor	$ 30/h	$ 50/h
LAN consultants	$ 75/h	$ 100/h
Realtor	$ 35/h	$ 45/h

3. What is the cost of the project currently? The cost is: ....
4. Who would you ask first to work overtime to meet the project baseline? Why?
5. You want to explore whether overtime by the contractor can solve the schedule conflict. To meet the deadline, how many overtime person hours would you propose for which task(s)?
6. You will enter overtime on the task *lay carpet*. You promised to pay the contractor the overtime rate. Because the area will be overcrowded if more carpet layers are used on the activity, the contractor has agreed to work overtime for the balance of this activity. Schedule 90 hours of the work on this task as overtime (see page 326).

7. How much does your project cost if you pay the overtime rate for the contractor? The cost is: .... The extra cost for the overtime is: ....
8. With what arguments could you negotiate the payment of regular rates instead?
9. How would you enter the overtime work if you paid the regular standard rate (see page 325)?
10. Save your file and compare it with the solution file *11E Up-to-date Schedule.mpp* available for download at www.ProjectProCorp.com (see page vi for the procedure to access these files). See page 697 of this book for an automated way of comparing and reporting differences between two versions of one schedule.

Relocation Project – Updating Tasks – Third Update

The goal of this exercise is to be able to update a schedule and get accurate forecasts.

1. Open the file *11E Up-to-date Schedule.mpp* available for download at www.ProjectProCorp.com (see page vi for the procedure to access these files).
2. If needed:
   - ◇ Change to the **Tracking Gantt** view.
   - ◇ Apply the **Tracking** table. Remove the columns **% Comp.** (**% Complete**) and the **Phys. % Comp.** (**Physical % Complete**). Move the column **Act. Finish** (**Actual Finish**) to after **Rem. Dur.** (**Remaining Duration**).
3. On the **Project** ribbon, set the **Status Date** to *Friday September 11, 2012* and, if needed, create a gridline (ribbon **Format**, button **Gridlines**, item **Gridlines...**) for the status date in the Gantt timescale.
4. Verify if the following options are set:
   In ribbon **File,** Options, tab **Schedule:**
   ☑ **Updating Task status updates resource status**
   ☑ **Actual costs are always calculated by Microsoft Project**
   In ribbon **File,** Options, tab **Advanced**:
   ☑ **Move end of completed parts after status date back to status date**
   ☑ **Move start of remaining parts before status date forward to status date**
5. If needed, switch the task type to **Fixed Units** and non **Effort-Driven** for the tasks needing update (see page 636).
6. Your executives requested that you provide a report that displays the exact impact of this third update relative to the second update. Please follow the steps of the procedure on page 676 to create this report.

11

7. Update the tasks in the project schedule. The contractor supplied the following table with update data for the status of the project as of the status date. Tasks that are not listed in the table have not started yet:

Task name	Actual Start	Act. Duration	Rem. Duration
install cabinetry	Sep 4, 2012	5 days	0 days
install LAN hardware	Sep 3, 2012	2.5 days	0 days
install LAN operating system	Sep 9, 2012	2.5 days	0 days
lay carpet	Sep 8, 2012	4 days	0 days
facility remodeled	Sep 11, 2012	0 days	0 days
pack	Sep 10, 2012	2 days	0 days

8. Check whether the schedule is updated correctly (see page 677):
   a. Are any remaining durations scheduled before the status date? Reschedule these after the status date.
   b. Are actual durations after the status date? Reschedule these before the status date.
9. Describe the status of the project in your own words.
10. Do you need to take corrective action?
11. Save your file and compare it with the solution file *11F Up-to-date Schedule.mpp* available for download at www.ProjectProCorp.com (see page vi for the procedure to access these files). See page 697 of this book for an automated way of comparing and reporting differences between two versions of one schedule.

Chapter 12 Acceptance by Client or Sponsor

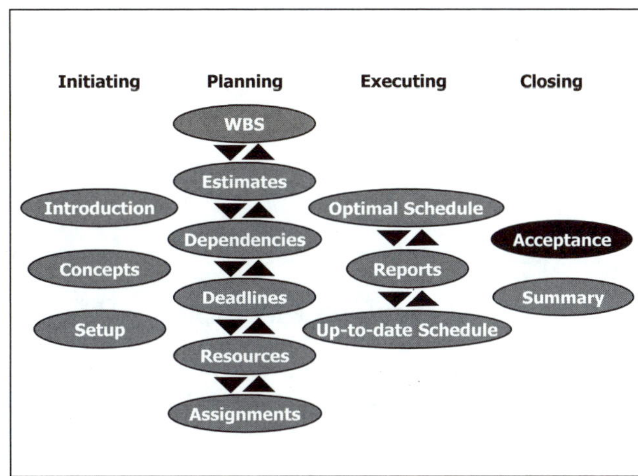

In this chapter, we will review gaining *acceptance* from the client or the sponsor and how you can become a better project manager on future projects by *evaluating* the one you just completed.

After this chapter you will:

- Understand customer acceptance as the most important deliverable in the life cycle of the project
- Know why project evaluation is important to become a better project manager or team member.
- Have a list of questions that will help you learn from a finished project
- Know what to capture in lessons learned
- Be able to compare two versions of one project schedule

"Can We Go Now …?"

Nob and his team members sit down at lunch with a pizza to look back at the project they just finished. The pizza is almost finished when Nob kicks off the meeting by asking: "What did we learn from this project?"

Harry says: "Well, I learned that I am not going to work with Chris again … ever!"

Chris fires back immediately with: "Likewise, man!"

Nob straightens his body and asks again: "Folks, we're here to learn from our mistakes and our successes. What did we learn?"

Mary: "I found out that I'm always too optimistic in my estimates! Next time I won't give estimates unless I'm forced to."

Nob: "Did you ask yourself how you could get more accurate estimates?"

Mary: "I don't like estimating; it's too hard."

Vern: "Yeah, I agree."

Nob makes a big gesture to interrupt this exchange and summarizes: "So, all you've learned from this project is that you don't want to provide estimates to project managers anymore?"

Vern: "That sums it up pretty well!"

Nob: "What else did we learn?"

Veronica: "I learned that filling in timesheets takes a lot of time. The timesheets were a nuisance, particularly when we were crunching!"

Nob has grown slightly irritated by the negativity that befalls him in this meeting and remarks sarcastically: "I guess you learned you don't want to fill in timesheets either?"

Then Harry poses the deadly question: "Can we go now?"

Gaining Acceptance from Client or Sponsor

So, you spent all the effort and money to create the project product. The team members did their best, and everybody believes they created a wonderful product. The project now reaches its climax when the product is presented to the *customer* for *approval*. It is an apocalyptic moment of truth. If the customer accepts the product, and accepts the date on which it was delivered as well as the price she will have to pay for it, the project is a success. Then, the project will soon be over. If she rejects, the project can become a failure and will continue. With a *rejection* from the customer, the project is a failure even if every deliverable was completed on time and within budget up to that moment. The customer can also state something like: *I will approve it if you fix this and that!* This is like a *pending approval* for the project. Pending approvals are very common in project management. Most projects on which I have been involved have received a pending approval when the project product was presented to the *client* or *sponsor*.

There are several things that may happen at this point in the *project life cycle*. We have listed them from harmless to horrible:

- **Venting Frustrations**
  The client needs to vent *frustrations* that built up during the process of the project. A meeting is called in which the client gives you an earful and then proceeds to accept the product anyway. A project is part process and part product; if the process was painful, the client will vent at some point. It is always better to release the client's frustrations earlier in the project than at the project acceptance stage. If the client accumulates frustration, she will certainly vent at the end. The project product is accepted reluctantly. Process events that cause frustration are, for example, phone calls not returned or late, missed conference calls, late arrival at meetings, lack of attention to detail, lack of attention to emotional needs of client, or forgetting to ask formal approval for seemingly small things. Generally speaking, any disrespect shown to the client will eventually backfire on you. The challenge is to keep calm in such a situation and not engage in a "*Yes, but ...*" argument.
- **New Negotiations**
  The client may invite you and the executive sponsor of the project for a new round of *negotiations* in an attempt to remedy the situation:
  - How to meet new, additional requirements and their deadline.
  - How to be compensated financially for missed requirements.
  - How to remedy missed requirements.

  Optimistic project managers might call such a project an "*almost-success*" at this point depending on the outcome of the negotiations.
- **Written Notice with Modifications and Holdback**
  Written notices often mean trouble. The client may send a written notice in which:

12

  - ◇ The client suggests what modifications to make. She will hold back a certain amount of money until her requirements are met.
  - ◇ The client terminates the contract and claims that she will not pay at all.
- ◆ **Written Notice of Default**
  The client or the court serves you papers for a lawsuit. The client may go to court in order to:
  - ◇ Claim damages
  - ◇ Claim the cost of a missed opportunity

  Particularly in the case of a lawsuit, the schedule will become an important source of information for sorting out the differences. *The project is not over until the project product is accepted!*

Project Evaluation

Evaluating a project when it is completed is often seen as a waste of time. The reason seems to be that the evaluation is generally experienced as unpleasant and can even explode into an atmosphere of animosity. When things did not go the way they should have, pointing fingers tend to appear. Evaluations conducted like that are indeed a waste of time. The little story of Nob on the previous page shows a perfect example, albeit a bit extreme, of time wasted on an evaluation meeting.

Evaluation is useful when the focus is stays on the future. Why would you want to dish up pain from the past and serve it again in the present? This only makes sense if the pain is meant to improve the future. Only by learning from the past can you become better prepared for the future. Lessons learned can lead to improvements to the WBS, the accuracy of estimates, the use of dependencies, the use of resources and the appropriateness of assignments in the schedule. The meeting must be facilitated in such a fashion that people focus on gain for the future instead of pain from the past. If managed well, the meeting can become a source of valuable information and personal growth. Evaluating prevents running into the same troubles again.

If you, as the project manager, want to prevent finger pointing, you should start each question with: "*What could I have done to …?*" Or, second best, "*What could we have done to …*?"

Of course, many projects run well. Even when a project ran well, evaluating it is important, because it is the only way to become an even better project manager. There will always be room to deliver projects better. When you stop asking yourself the question: *What could we have done better?*, you stop learning from your experiences and you are getting mentally ready to retire from the job. In this age, in which the only constant seems to rapid change, nobody can afford to stop learning. *Life-long learning* is the motto for success.

Evaluation Points

After the project is over, you can pose some questions to your team. These are some suggestions for questions about using the schedule as a tool for managing and controlling the project:

1. Was the schedule clear to all stakeholders? How can we make it clearer in future projects?
2. Was the WBS complete? Did people understand it? Was it easy to understand? Did it function as a tool for delegation? Were the deliverables clearly formulated in it, or did some deliverables cause confusion? How can we improve the WBS for similar projects in the future?
3. Were the estimates optimistic or pessimistic? What factors caused the estimates to be optimistic or pessimistic? How can we better forecast these factors in future projects?
   You can determine the *personality factors* of each estimator by comparing the resource-related fields **Actual Work** with **Baseline Work**. These numbers are aggregates and will give a good impression of whether someone tends to be optimistic or pessimistic in estimating. People tend to be amazingly consistent over time unless a mirror is held up in front of their face and they become aware of their *natural tendency*. We discussed this in more detail on page 168.
4. Was there enough of a time *buffer* in the schedule to compensate for unforeseen events? Which tasks consumed most of the buffer? Why? On page 490, we discussed how up to three versions of the schedule can be shown next to each other in the timescale of the Gantt Chart; a view like this would be very helpful for this analysis. What can we do in the future to prevent similar tasks from slipping again?
5. Was the schedule easy enough to maintain during project execution? Was the network of dependencies complete, and did it update the forecasts automatically? Could accurate status and forecast reports be generated at each reporting period? How can we produce the reports more easily in future projects?
6. Were the right resources available at the right times? How can we better predict or more successfully ensure the timely availability of resources in future projects?

We recommend that you capture these findings in *lessons learned* on the project.

To prevent learning painful lessons in the school of hard knocks, we recommend you use a checklist to ensure the quality of your schedule. In the next chapter, we will provide such a checklist with which you can evaluate the quality of your schedule. This list can be used to check the quality as soon as the schedule is created. This checklist allows you to be more proactive in your next project.

Comparing Two Versions of One Project Schedule

In order to create the lessons learned for a project, you may have to compare two version of the same schedule to analyze how it got from one version to the next. MS Project can easily find the differences between two schedules. This can be useful in the following situations:

- Learning from the exercises in this book
  To check your results in the Relocation Project exercises, you can compare your MPP file with the solution file available for download at www.ProjectProCorp.com (see page vi for the procedure to access these files).
- Checking what changes subcontractors made to their schedules before you incorporate them into your *master schedule.*
- *Troubleshooting* a schedule by comparing it to a previous *version.*

You can ask MS Project to create a report showing the differences between two versions of one schedule:

1. Switch to the most recent version of the schedule, and display it on the screen.
2. Click the **Project** ribbon and click  .
3. The dialog **Compare Project Versions** appears with your latest version as the schedule to compare:

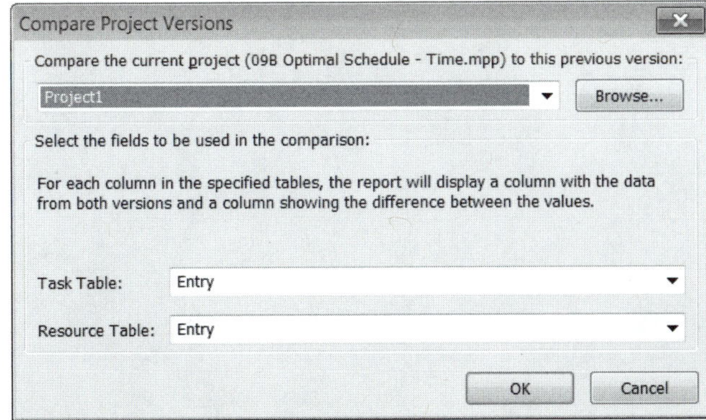

4. Under **Task Table** select the table **Entry** from the list. If you suspect that the table in the most recent version does not have all the fields that you want to compare,

12

select the right table from the list (if you cannot find one, cancel the dialog and insert the columns first into a table or create a new table). To find differences in:

- ◇ Duration estimates use table **Entry** or insert the column **Duration**
- ◇ Duration estimates use table **Work** or insert the column **Work**
- ◇ Dependencies use table **Entry** or insert the column **Predecessors** or **Successors**,
- ◇ Constraint dates use table **Constraint Date** or insert columns **Constraint type** and **Constraint Date**,
- ◇ Deadlines insert column **Deadline**, and/or
- ◇ Assignments use table **Entry** or insert column **Resource names**.

5. If you want to compare resource information as well, select a **Resource Table**. The resource table called **Entry** will often meet your needs.

6. Click [OK] – the comparison starts and the screen will flash a few times. Notice that you have now a new ribbon called **Compare Projects.** MS Project has created a new project file that displays data and difference columns.

8. You can zoom in on the differences. From the respective lists on the **Compare Projects** ribbon, in the list **Items**, select the **All differences**. In the list **Columns**, select **Differences Columns Only**. This will display only the records that are different and only the **Diff** columns. After you have found the differences, you might like to see the data columns from the schedules again by selecting **All items** from the **Items** list.

Once you are done with your analysis, you can close the report schedule by clicking the button **Close Comparison** or save it for future reference.

Chapter 13 Summary

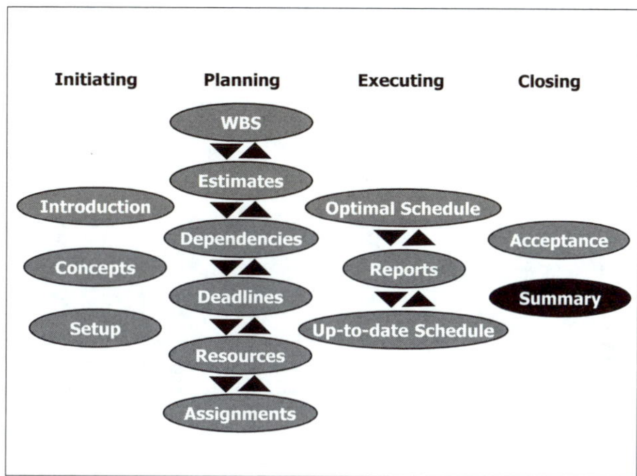

As you can see in the illustration, we have discussed a project throughout its entire life cycle from *Setup* to closing out a project with the *Acceptance* from the client to the legacy of lessons learned.

Throughout the book we have made many recommendations that reflect best scheduling practices. We will bring these recommendations together by providing two checklists in this summary chapter:

- Checklist for Troubleshooting MS Project Schedules (see page 701)
- Checklist for Dynamic Project Models (see page 703)

Check It Out Before You Check It In

"Creating a good schedule is more difficult than I thought. I've been working on it for days and I still find places to improve.", Nob exclaims. Bob adds: "Yeah, there are so many things to think of!" Nob: "I think I'm finally done now." Bob smiles broadly when he says: "Do you REALLY want to know if your schedule is good? I have a checklist from this book called *Forecast Scheduling*. It always gives me more ideas to improve my schedule." Nob takes on the challenge, and they sit down to go over the checks.

Bob: "The WBS looks solid and well formulated! What about the level of detail? Let's apply this filter that comes with the checklist. Oh, I see several tasks are much longer than 10% of your project duration. You may need to split them into multiple tasks!" Nob: "The line item says 'Reports'; I guess I can list them individually."

Bob: "Here is a filter to check if all dependencies are there; oops ... you can see that there are several open ends!" Nob: "Okay, those are tasks I added yesterday; I will hook 'em up."

Bob: "Oh, I found several overallocations. You may want to do something about that!" Nob: "How did you find that so quickly?" Bob: "My checklist tells me the quickest way to do a check. Let's see if the baseline is complete. There's a filter for that as well!" Nob: "I set the baseline already!" Bob: "Did you do that a while ago because there are still tasks without a baseline!" Nob: "Oh, those are some tasks I added recently! Man, you saved my neck with this check! I would have a made a fool of myself."

Checklist for Troubleshooting MS Project Schedules

The new *Task Inspector* will help you understand your schedule. When there are multiple predecessors, the Task Inspector will indicate which predecessor is the driving predecessor. When a resource calendar affects the scheduling, it will tell you. You can invoke the Task Inspector in this way:

1. Click ribbon **Task** and find its section **Tasks**.
2. Click the top part of Inspect to display the **Task Inspector** side pane.

   It appears in the left of the screen and will provide an explanation of the start date of the selected task.
3. Select a task to analyze and read the **Task Inspector** pane, which will provide buttons to solve problems, if any, with one click.
4. In order to make the Task Inspector even more useful, request it to make suggestions

   as well. Click the Inspect bottom part of Inspect and select **Show suggestions**.

   (This turns on the option ☑ **Show task schedule suggestions** in ribbon **File,** Options, tab **Schedule** and section **Schedule Alerts Options**. You could even turn on **Show ignored problems**.
5. The suggestions are particularly useful if you have many **Manually Scheduled** tasks.

If you do not understand why MS Project has scheduled a task on the dates it has, go down the following *checklist*. The questions are ranked in terms of precedence: the higher on the list, the stronger the effect. Start at the top of the list and work your way down. As soon as you find the reason, you do not need to go down the list further.

13

1. In Project 2010, there are still instances where the schedule was not recalculated after making a change. Press F9 to force a recalculation and a refresh of the screen. Even if automatic recalculation is turned on, we have found that the schedule is not always freshly calculated. Check to see if this solves the problem.

2. Does the task have an actual start date? Or, does one of its predecessors or successors have an actual start date?
   Insert the column **Actual Start** to check this.

3. Check the field **Task Mode**: Is the task **Manually Scheduled** or **Auto Scheduled**? Manually scheduled tasks do their own thing and do not necessarily adjust to constraints or dependencies.

4. Is there a *hard date constraint* on the task or on its predecessors or successors? Insert the column **Constraint Type**.

5. Is there a task calendar on the task or on its predecessors or successors?
   Insert the column **Task calendar**. To see what the task calendar has in terms of nonworking days, click ribbon **Project**, button **Change Working Time**, then select the task calendar from the list at the top under **For**.

6. Is there a leveling delay on the task (or on its predecessors) from workload leveling? Insert the column **Leveling Delay**. If the task is delayed by MS Project for the purpose of leveling the workload of resources, there will be an entry in this field.

7. What predecessors does the task have?
   Insert the field **Predecessors**. Is there a *lag* on the dependency?
   If there is more than one predecessor, usually only one of them drives the start date of the task you are checking.

8. Are there vacation days set on the calendar of the resource working on the task? Notice that, when there is a resource vacation, *Fixed Units* and *Fixed Work* tasks will extend in duration and schedule around the resource vacation, which may explain a finish date you did not understand.
   Project 2010 protects the duration on *Fixed Duration* tasks and, thus, it simply does not schedule work for that resource when there is a resource vacation; as a result, the amount of Work on the task decreases.

9. Are there trailing dots after a task bar?
   Task bars can have trailing dots following them that are left over from task bar splits. You can often get rid of these dots by changing the task **Type**, or, as a last resort, by manually editing the **Resume** date task field that contains the date on which the task resumes after that split; you can set this date to the end date of the first bar of the task, which will remove the trailing dots.

10. Are there leading dots before a task bar?
    Leading dots in front of a task bar can have one of two causes:
    - ◇ A delay on one of the assignments on the task. The delay may have been entered manually or automatically by MS Project when leveling workloads. You can see the assignment-related delay field by clicking on the Task Form, click ribbon

Format and button Schedule – the fields on the Task Form change and display the field **Delay**.

◇ A vacation for one of the resources working on the task. Check the resource calendars (see page 314 for how-to steps).

11. Task-specific constraint tendencies (ASAP or ALAP):
    If you have an ALAP task constraint in an ASAP schedule, it tends to move dependent ASAP tasks out to later dates while staying within the **Total Slack** of the ASAP tasks.

12. Default constraint tendencies (ASAP or ALAP):
    You can check the default constraint in the dialog you can display by clicking ribbon **Project**, button **Project Information**. If you **Schedule from** the **Project Start Date**, the default is ASAP. If you **Schedule From** the **Project Finish Date**, the default is ALAP. Under ASAP scheduling, tasks will tend to stay close to the project start date, unless one of the previous factors overrides this. Under ALAP scheduling, tasks will tend to stay close to the project finish date.

Building Project Forecast Models

As a summary of this book, we will provide a *checklist* of criteria for good schedules. What is a good schedule? A good schedule is a model of the project that provides *valid* forecasts and is easy to maintain. Only dynamic and robust models of a project are easy to maintain. We would like to see project managers create valid, dynamic and robust models to forecast their projects.

Let us break down *valid, dynamic* and *robust model* that are built to *forecast* into its five components:

Valid

The model has to produce forecasts that are *valid*. The criteria for a model that will produce valid forecasts are:

- It contains all deliverables required or expected and no more than that. Deliverables that will not be produced as agreed upon with the client are explicitly excluded.
- The hours per day setting (ribbon **File**, Options, tab **Schedule**, section **Calendar options for this project**) must be aligned with the working hours as indicated on the project calendar (the **Standard (Project Calendar)** by default).
- The basis for estimates (*pure work time* versus *gross work time*) is consistent with the working times captured on the project calendar and on resource calendars.
- The time estimates seem reasonable for the work to be done.

13

- The schedule produces accurate forecasts.
  The last criterion can be verified to a certain degree during project execution, but it is best verified after the project is over.
- Assigned overtime work to be paid at overtime rates has been included. If you assign overtime work but forget to fill in required overtime rates, the cost forecast will be understated and invalid.

Dynamic

A schedule has to be *dynamic*. The ideal, totally dynamic model works as follows: If one thing changes in the reality of your project, you should have to change only one field in your model in Project 2010. Even though this ideal is hard to attain, you can get very close to it if you set up your schedule the right way. A schedule is dynamic if it is easy to maintain so that it can be kept alive during project execution. The criteria for a dynamic schedule are:

- The schedule has as few constraints as possible without compromising its validity. If you really need a constraint to make the schedule valid or robust, enter one; otherwise, do not.
- The schedule has a complete and correct network of dependencies.
- The schedule is up-to-date all the time and correctly updated with all completed work in the past and all remaining work scheduled in the future.
- The schedule is in electronic format and accessible online.

Robust

A schedule has to be robust. A robust model of a project can handle a variety of changes and situations without needing to change the structure of the model. The structure of a project model is the list of tasks, the set of estimates, the network of dependencies, the set of constraint dates and the system of calendars. The criteria for a robust schedule are:

- The schedule continuously provides accurate and reliable forecasts when a change is entered.
- A wide variety of changes can be entered, and the model still produces accurate forecasts.
- You never have to change the structure of the model while entering regular updates of the schedule. Only when re-optimizing the schedule may you have to change the structure of the model.

Model

A schedule has to be a model of the project. A schedule is only a model of the project if the following criteria are met:

- The model is a deliberate simplification of the reality.
  We use the criterion that if you cannot or will not explain the model to your stakeholders, the model is too complex. A model should be a deliberate simplification of the complex reality of the project. When simplifying, the acts of averaging out and omitting details are allowed. Simplification also allows the making of assumptions in order to complete the model. You always need to provide these assumptions in conjunction with the model.
- The simplification of the project reality has to be effective.
  When leaving things out of your schedule, the danger exists that you remove the things you need to keep or, conversely, you keep the things you need to remove. For example, if you only have phases, but do not have *deliverables* in your WBS, your simplification efforts are ineffective from a scheduling point of view.
- The purpose of a project model is to provide accurate and reliable forecasts of the project. Any simplification measure should be applied in such a way that the purpose of forecasting is never compromised. The purpose is more important than the simplification.

Forecast

The model of the project has to be built to forecast the project. People build schedules for a variety of reasons. The following reasons should not be the main reason for building a schedule (see page 49 for more detail on these purposes):

- To sell the project within the organization in order to acquire a budget for the project.
- To delegate work to project team members.
- To be able to present the status or progress to project stakeholders.
- To present as the static, target schedule to the project team.

Throughout the book we have made many recommendations for making your schedule a valid, dynamic and robust model of a project. These recommendations are compiled in the checklist that follows. The list can be used to evaluate the quality of your project schedule and to check for the use of best practices with Project 2010. Several organizations are using the checklist for schedule quality assurance. Some organizations require that the schedule first must pass all the checks on the list before the schedule is allowed to be published to Project Server.

If your schedule passes all checks on the checklist, then you have created a valid, dynamic and robust model of your project that will serve as a tool to help you bring the project to a successful completion. This is especially true for managing a large schedule. Executing and controlling a large project is a nearly impossible task if its schedule does not meet the requirements of the checklist. The schedule needs to meet all the requirements of the checklist if:

- You expect that you will have a lot of turbulence during project execution. Turbulence can be caused by unreliable suppliers, volatile resource availability, hectic progress or many change requests from stakeholders. A valid, dynamic and robust model of your project is your best preparation for a turbulent project execution.
- You want to monitor and level the workloads of the individual resources across all projects. If you apply the checklist to all the projects that are sharing resources, the checklist will make sure that all workloads are accurately modeled and that the aggregated workloads are true.
- If you are managing multiple projects. The more projects you have, the more important it is to work efficiently with MS Project.
- You need to create an *integrated program schedule* from subschedules for a large endeavor. In this case, you need to apply the checklist on all subschedules. For example, if the subschedules have too many constraints, you cannot perform what-if analyses on the program schedule.
- You want to optimize the portfolio of projects. This often starts with developing what-if scenarios with the *portfolio* of projects by using *Microsoft Project Server.* With Project Server, you can also optimize your portfolio using the *Efficient Frontier* technique. If new projects are properly modeled, you can explore how many new projects you can take on (given limited resource availability) and what their impact will be on existing projects.
- You want to apply *Monte Carlo simulation* to your schedules. Simulation requires that all dependencies are entered and few constraints are present.

Applying the checklist to your schedules will provide several benefits:

- It ensures that you will work as efficiently with Project 2010 as is possible.
- It ensures that you can keep your schedule up-to-date during project execution when you are busy.
- You will get more accurate and more reliable forecasts from your schedule.
- You will be able to provide better information to decision-makers and other project stakeholders.
- Application of the checklist creates repeatability in project management processes, which will advance the project management maturity within your organization.

In the Appendix you will find a list of about one hundred examples of schedules that reflect these best practices of scheduling with MS Project. These schedules are valid, dynamic and robust models of real-life projects. We recommend you look at the schedules in this list that are relevant for your business.

We also provide tools with the checklist to help you check your schedules easily and efficiently.

Filters to Check Project Schedules

We provide several filters that make it easier to check your schedules. You will find them in the file *13A ProjectPro filters to check Project Forecast Models.MPP* available for download at www.ProjectProCorp.com (see page vi for the procedure to access these files).

The following filters will help you check if you have created a valid, dynamic and robust model of your project. The numbering of the filters corresponds to the chapter numbers. You can use ribbon **File**, button **Info**, button **Organizer** to copy the following filters into your schedule or into your *Global.MPT*.

The filters are:

- **3.5 One Milestone per Deliverable**
  This filter will display all summary tasks and also all milestones so you can determine if each deliverable has a milestone associated.
- **3.6 Milestones Only**
  This filter allows you to display the milestones without the summary tasks, which makes this filter different from the out-of-the-box **Milestones** filter. With our filter you can more easily copy milestones into an email to provide feedback to the scheduler.
- **3.8 Level of Detail > 10% of Proj Dur…**
  This is an interactive filter that prompts for the maximum duration of detail tasks to check if the WBS is on the right level of detail. The filter is based on the *1%-10% rule*. The filter displays neither summary tasks nor recurring tasks.
- **3.9 Level of Detail < 1% of Proj Dur...**
  This is an interactive filter that prompts for the minimum duration of detail tasks to check the level of detail in the WBS using the *1%-10% rule*. The filter displays neither summary tasks nor recurring tasks.
- **4.1 All Estimates Entered?**
  This filter will display all *unscheduled tasks*, which are tasks that have duration, start or finish date missing and is just a placeholder task with its field **Placeholder** set to **Yes**. The estimates need to be completed on these tasks.
- **5.2 Summary Tasks with Dependencies**
  This filter displays all summary tasks that have a predecessor or successor. If there are many summary tasks with dependencies, it makes checking the completeness of

the network logic and tracing the Critical Path too difficult. We recommend keeping the logic on detail tasks as much as possible.

- **5.3 Detail Tasks without Predecessors**
  This filter displays all detail tasks without any predecessors, in order to find the starting points of the network of dependencies. Detail tasks without predecessors may start on the project start date or have a Start No Earlier Than constraint (SNET). The network of dependencies can have multiple starting points but only one ending point. This filter displays all starting points of the network. You can then see if there are starting points in the network that should have a predecessor instead. Recurring tasks are not shown by this filter. Use the filter to copy all the IDs and task names into the feedback e-mail to the project manager.
- **5.4 Detail Tasks without Successors**
  This filter displays all detail tasks without any successors, in order to find tasks that are not incorporated into the network of dependencies (*loose ends*). There should be only one ending point in the network of dependencies, otherwise Critical Path and slack calculations are not likely to be correct. Recurring tasks are not shown. Use this filter to copy all the IDs and task names into the feedback e-mail to the project manager.
- **5.5 Detail Tasks with SS in Successors**
  This filter displays all tasks with an SS dependency in the successors field. These tasks also need to have an FS or FF successor to hook up their end, otherwise they are a loose end in the network.
- **5.6 Detail Tasks with FF in Predecessors**
  This filter displays all tasks with an FF dependency in the predecessors field. These tasks also need to have an FS or SS predecessor to hook up their start, because otherwise they could be a loose starting point in the network.
- **6.2 All Milestones and Deadlines**
  This filter will display all milestones that have an associated deadline date.
  We recommended capturing dates promised to clients and dates agreed upon with your team as deadline dates in MS Project. If this filter displays several milestones, the project manager is following this recommendation.
- **6.4 Constraints other than ASAP**
  This filter displays any tasks with a constraint other than As Soon As Possible (ASAP). A dynamic model should have as few constraints as possible without compromising the accuracy of the forecasts of the schedule. Recurring tasks are not shown, because they should have constraint dates.
- **8.1 Non default task Type**
  The default task type is **Fixed Units** with **Effort Driven** set to **No** in Project 2010. This filter displays all tasks that do not have these default settings any longer.
  We expect that people manipulate the task **Type** and **Effort Driven** field to make MS Project do what it needs to – add value in forecasting the project.

- **8.2 Effort Driven tasks**
  This filter displays all **Fixed Duration** and **Fixed Units** tasks that have the **Effort Driven** attribute set to yes. This combination protects two values in the formula **Duration** * **Peak Units** = **Work** and makes it hard to predict what MS Project will recalculate when you make a change to the **Units** (in some places called **Assignment Units)**. We recommend keeping **Fixed Duration** and **Fixed Units** tasks non effort driven.
- **8.3 Summary Tasks with Resources Assigned**
  This filter displays all summary tasks with resources assigned. We recommend re-assigning these resources from the summary tasks to their detail tasks.
- **8.4 Detail tasks without Resources Assigned**
  This filter displays all detail tasks without any resources assigned. You can also check this by looking under **Unassigned** section at the top of the **Resource Usage** view, but this filter allows you to copy the task IDs and names into the feedback e-mail. With that information, you can find the tasks without *assignments* easily. If assignments are forgotten, workloads are omitted and the forecasted dates may be too optimistic.
- **8.6 Tasks with Elapsed Durations**
  This filter displays all tasks with an elapsed duration. The elapsed durations should be less than one day when there are human resources assigned because they continue day and night, seven days a week.
- **9.6 Deadlines or Constraints not met**
  This filter displays items with deadlines or constraints that have negative slack. These deadlines or constraint dates have not been met, and the schedule may forecast dates that are wrong. You can copy the task IDs and names into the feedback e-mail.
- **11.1 Tasks with missing baseline info**
  This filter displays any tasks that do not have baseline information in Baseline Start, Baseline Finish, Baseline Duration or Baseline Work. This filter will display all tasks that were created since the baseline was set. Also, when new assignments are created after the baseline is set, the Baseline Work field would still be empty on these tasks and the filter will display them. Notice that the filter does not check the field Baseline Cost.
- **11.5 Reschedule Actual Durations…**
  This is an interactive filter that prompts you twice for the status date and displays tasks with an Actual Start or Actual Finish date later than the status date. All actual dates should be in the past (i.e., earlier than the status date), when they actually happened. With this filter, you can determine if there are actuals in the future, which does not make sense. There should be no Actual Start or Actual Finish dates later than the status date; how can you present something that has yet to occur as a fact? The filter shows if the schedule is updated properly and, thus, if the forecasted dates are accurate and reliable.

- **11.6 Reschedule Remaining Durations...**
  This is an interactive filter that prompts you twice for the status date and displays tasks with remaining durations scheduled in the past (earlier than the status date). Remaining durations should be scheduled in the future when they will happen. With this filter you can determine if the schedule is updated properly and if the forecasted dates are accurate and reliable.
- **11.7 Remaining Durations revised**
  This filter displays all detail tasks for which the latest, forecasted duration is not equal to the baseline duration. If the filter displays any tasks, it would indicate that you are revising the **Remaining Durations**, which is what we would like you to do, so this filter displays the good side of your schedule instead of exposing the bad side. If the filter does not display any tasks, you are not revising the remaining durations, which is bad. Regular revision of remaining durations is important to ensure that the forecasted dates are as accurate and reliable as they can be.

Also copy the following resource-related filter into your schedule or into your *Global.MPT*:

- **11.10 Overtime rates entered**
  You need to apply this filter in the Resource Sheet or Resource Usage view. This filter displays all resources that have scheduled **Overtime Work** but do not have their **Overtime Rate** entered. MS Project will understate the cost of the project, because the overtime hours are now charged at a zero rate instead of the regular rate or a higher overtime rate.

Press [F3] to stop a filter and display all tasks (or resources) again.

Copyright of Filters and Checklist

The filters and checklist are copyrighted: © 2010 ProjectPro Corp.
If you just bought this book, this checklist and the filters are provided for your personal use only. If you would like to use this checklist or the filters for commercial purposes within your organization:

- Please contact ProjectPro to purchase a license for these tools; our telephone number is 613-692-7778 (Canada) or email *sales@ProjectProCorp.com*.
- Register for and attend our *Forecast Scheduling* course (see *www.ProjectProCorp.com*) and you will receive one free, named license to use the checklist for business use (instead of for personal use only) as a take-away from this course.

Checklist for Project Forecast Models

The following checklist is essentially a succinct summary of this entire book.

This checklist is meant for detail schedules. *Detail schedules* are schedules created after the *project charter* is approved. Detail schedules are meant to help the project manager manage and control the project. The entire checklist is applicable to detail schedules. The checklist is not meant for:

- *High-level schedules* that are created only to estimate the duration and cost of a project and to gain approval for it. Only a few checks in the checklist that follows are applicable to high-level schedules.
- *Schedule templates* that are created for a project that will be repeated and run in a similar fashion. Some construction and consulting firms have several types of projects they run over and over again. Many checks do apply to schedule templates, but there are also many that need to be applied in an entirely different manner; for example, a template schedule should not have a *baseline schedule* at all, but a detailed schedule needs to have a complete baseline schedule.
- *Rolling wave schedules* that are typically used in very long projects (several years long). The checklist can be applied in its entirety on the portion of the schedule that falls within the detailed planning window (the detailed portion of the rolling wave schedule). Only certain checks should be applied to the rest of the schedule.
- *Subproject schedules* in an integrated program schedule need a modification to some checks. For example, the network of dependencies in one subproject schedule can have loose ending points, as long as they all tie into the other schedules involved in the integrated program schedule.

The checklist starts with a section of questions to gather important background information; we have labeled this section as number 1. The remaining sections are categories of checks that are numbered to correspond to the chapters in which these checks were first discussed. The section headings of this checklist are:

1. Background (see next section)
2. Setup (see page 713)
3. Work Breakdown Structure (WBS) (see page 714)
4. Estimates (see page 717)
5. Dependencies (see page 718)
   - Checking the completeness of the network of dependencies
   - Checking the correctness of the network of dependencies
   - Other checks on the network of dependencies
6. Deadlines (see page 723)
7. Resources (see page 724)
8. Assignments (see page 727)

9. Optimal schedule (see page 728)
   - ◇ Checking the resource workloads in the schedule
   - ◇ Checking the costs in the schedule
   - ◇ Checking the time in the schedule
10. Reports (see page 731)
11. Up-to-date schedule (see page 732)

We have numbered all the checks so you can more easily refer to a specific check when working with your colleagues. In many checks, we refer to and recommend applying a filter. All filters can be found in the file *13A ProjectPro filters to check Project Forecast Models.MPP* available for download at www.ProjectProCorp.com (see page vi for the procedure to access these files).

Make sure that all summary tasks are expanded before applying any of these filters, since filters never display detail tasks that are collapsed and hidden under their summary tasks. Click ribbon **View**, 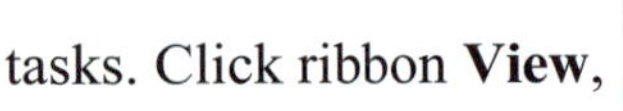 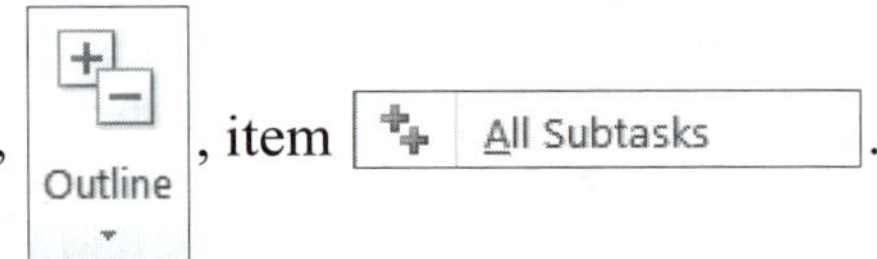

, item .

In the checklist, we have used the words "*summary task*" and "*detail task*" very carefully. A *summary task* is any task with subtasks indented and listed beneath it. A *detail task* is any task without indented subtasks in the WBS. It is important that these words are used with these meanings for the checks to make sense.

1 Background Information About the Project

You need to know the answers to the following questions in order to make a thorough evaluation of the schedule:

1.1. Is the schedule a high-level schedule or a detailed schedule?
If you created a small schedule to estimate the total duration and cost of the project, you may have a high-level schedule instead of a detailed schedule. You can only apply certain checks on a high-level schedule.
If the schedule is a detailed schedule that is created to manage and control the project, you can apply the entire checklist.

1.2. What is the objective or final product of the project
The objective can be present in:
- A note on the *Project Summary task* (see page 90).
- The project-related field **Comments** (ribbon **File**, tab **Info**, button **Project Information**, item **Advanced Properties**, tab **Summary**).

1.3. What is the *deadline* date of the project
(if not already entered as a deadline date in the schedule)?

1.4. Does the project have a cost budget? If yes, how much?

1.5. Does the project have a person hour *budget* (effort)?
If yes, how many person hours, person days, person weeks, person months or person years do you have in your budget?
1.6. Did the project manager gather *pure work time estimates* or *gross work time estimates*? For an explanation of these terms, see page 181.
1.7. Did the project manager apply the *rolling wave* approach in the schedule? If so, what is the duration of the *detail planning window*?
For an explanation of rolling wave, see page 187.
1.8. Will the project manager update the tasks (task fields **Duration** or **Work**) or update the assignments (using timesheets) or both (not recommended)? See page 620 for a description.
1.9. How many hours does a full-time resource work as per the standard labor contract in your organization?

2 Setup

2.1. Does your schedule contain a succinct description of the objective or final product of the project?
We recommend you use the field **Comments** (ribbon **File**, tab **Info**, button **Project Information** on the right side of screen**, Advanced Properties**, **Summary** tab), which makes it visible as a **Note** on the project summary task. It does not hurt to have a one-liner on your project ready for when you need to explain to an executive what your project is all about, for example, if you are only with this person in an elevator for one minute between the third and fifth floor.
2.2. Do the business days, the working hours and holidays (corporate and national) on the project calendar align with a typical, full-time resource on the project?
2.3. Do the working hours on the **Standard (Project Calendar)** (ribbon **Project**, button **Change Working Time**) correspond to the **Hours per day** option (ribbon **File**, Options, tab **Schedule)**?
For example, working times of 8:00 AM - 12:00 PM and 1:00 PM - 5:00 PM are consistent with 8 hours per day and 40 hours per week. If these settings are inconsistent, your forecasts are either too optimistic or too pessimistic. Also, you might see decimals in the durations of tasks.
The quickest way to check consistency is by clicking ribbon **Project**, button **Change Working Time**. If you click Options... the **Project Options** dialog will appear (ribbon **File,** Options, tab **Schedule**).
If the hours-per-day setting is wrong, see page 95 for a trick to align these two settings. If the working hours on the calendar are wrong, you can correct them with the steps on page 102.

3 WBS

3.1. Are there deliverables in the task list?
If there are not, the schedule does not have a WBS. Deliverables should be captured using nouns (perhaps with adjectives, but without verbs). Verbs change a deliverable into an activity. If there are no nouns (without verbs) in the task list, there are no deliverables and the list is not a *WBS*.
See page 116 for a detailed discussion.

3.2. Is the list of deliverables *complete*, but *lean*? See page 116 for details.
- ◇ Are all expected deliverables explicitly included in the WBS?
  The WBS should also include significant reporting items, like monthly status reports and test reports.
- ◇ Are the project management deliverables, like schedule and budget, included in the WBS (or modeled as overhead tasks)?
- ◇ Are there only deliverables in the WBS that were explicitly agreed upon with the *client* or *project sponsor*? There should not be extra deliverables in the WBS.
- ◇ Are *out-of-scope* deliverables that the client may expect explicitly excluded from the WBS? We recommend you capture exclusions in the **Notes** field on the project summary task (task 0) or the **Project Information** dialog (ribbon **File**, tab **Info**, button **Project Information**, list item **Advanced Properties,** tab **Summary, Comments** field).

3.3. Is the breakdown of the WBS *deliverable-oriented*?
The breakdown is deliverable-oriented if the deliverables are entered as summary tasks. Alternatives for a deliverable-oriented breakdown are a phase-oriented breakdown, a chronological breakdown or an organizational breakdown. From a project control perspective, these alternatives are less effective; see page 118 for a detailed discussion.
Apply the filter **Summary Tasks (View** ribbon) to display all summary tasks. See also page 122.

3.4. Does the WBS have a *logical hierarchy*?
If you do not have a logical hierarchy, you may report the wrong cost or duration by phase or by deliverable. You can perform the next checks by expanding the outline structure to the right level using the **Outline** button on the **View** ribbon. See page 123 for a detailed discussion.
- ◇ Is the WBS an indented list with multiple hierarchical levels instead of one long list without structure?
- ◇ Are the most important items on the highest levels in the WBS?
  - Are the phases, if present, on a higher level than the deliverables?
  - Are the tasks, if present, on a lower level than the deliverables?
- ◇ Does each summary task have at least two subtasks?
- ◇ Is there no duplication or logical overlap between deliverables?

- ◇ Does each group of sub items capture all the work of its summary item (top-down check)? Check if the deliverable would be completed if all the activities are done.
- ◇ Does each lowest-level item logically relate to all of its higher-level items (bottom-up check)? Check if (a sample of) the detail tasks relate to all their summary tasks.
- ◇ Is the feature ☑ **Project Summary Task** on the **Format** ribbon of the Gantt chart used instead of a physical project summary task? MS Project's project summary task has ID number 0 (zero) in the first column.

3.5. Is there one *milestone* for each deliverable?
Milestones typically capture when the deliverable is completed, approved, sent, signed-off, published or shipped. Those events will have dependencies to other activities and allow you to keep the logic on the detail tasks (milestones) instead of on summary tasks (deliverables). You can check this by applying the filter **3.5 One Milestone per Deliverable** and verifying if most summary task deliverables have a corresponding milestone, see page 140 for more.

3.6. Are the WBS elements properly formulated?
If you use the following guidelines you will ensure that everybody can understand the WBS (see page 130 for more explanation):

- ◇ Phases are formulated using the *present continuous tense* (-ing).
- ◇ Deliverables are formulated using a *noun* (perhaps with an adjective, but without a verb).
- ◇ Detail tasks are formulated using a *present tense* verb except for *fixed duration* tasks with no resource assigned (like *backing up server*) or a group of resources assigned (like *training*), which can have the *–ing* ending.
- ◇ Milestones are formulated using the noun of the deliverable and a verb in *past perfect tense* that typically has an *-ed* ending in English. Instead of a verb, the words *ready*, *complete* or *sign-off* can be used. You can apply our filter **3.6 Milestones Only** to display only milestones without summary tasks, which allows you to copy the milestones into a schedule evaluation report.

3.7. Are the names of the deliverables, tasks and milestones used consistently in the WBS?

3.8. Does the WBS have enough *detail*?
Too little detail does not provide enough control on your project, see also page 133. There may be too few levels in the WBS:

- ◇ If you cannot estimate the duration or work on the detail tasks.
- ◇ If you have difficulties finding the dependencies between the detail tasks.

- ◇ If you often *assign* more than one resource per detail task or more than one department per deliverable.
- ◇ If there are detail tasks with a duration longer than a reporting period.
- ◇ If there are detail tasks with durations longer than 10% of the project duration (1%-10% rule). You can check this by applying the filter **3.8 Level of Detail > 10% of Proj Dur…** The filter prompts you to enter a duration equal to 10% of the project duration. You can find the project duration by looking at the **Duration** field of the project summary task (task 0). The filter will display all detail tasks that are longer than 10% of the project duration. We recommend you break down all these tasks into smaller ones.
  There are two exceptions to this 10% maximum:
  - *overhead tasks* (like *project management* or *technical support*), and
  - tasks in *high-level* schedules that are created only to estimate duration and cost of the entire project and to gain approval for the project.

3.9. Does the WBS have too many items, too much detail?
Too much detail will cause you to spend too much effort updating your schedule during project execution, see also page 134. There may be too many levels in the WBS:

- ◇ If you think there are too many levels or if you think the task list is too long.
- ◇ If you cannot guarantee you will be able to keep all detail tasks updated in the schedule during project execution.
- ◇ If there are items that do not contribute to deliverables of value that someone expects to receive.
- ◇ If you added reminders, to-do items or acceptance criteria into the task list. Transfer these to the **Notes** field.
- ◇ If there are tasks with durations shorter than 1% of the project duration (1%-10% rule). You can keep a few tasks that are shorter than 1%, but if you keep many, you will spend too much effort on updating your schedule during project execution. You then risk letting your schedule become obsolete at some point.
  You can check how many you have by applying the filter **3.9 Level of Detail < 1% of Proj Dur...** The filter prompts you to enter a duration that is equal to 1% of the project. You can find the project duration by looking at the **Duration** field of the project summary task. The filter will display all detail tasks that are shorter than 1% of the project duration while skipping milestones and recurring detail tasks.
  Two exceptions to the 1% minimum are: *Milestones* and *Recurring detail tasks*, that are typically short and can be shorter than 1%.

3.10. Is the WBS clear to all project stakeholders?
All stakeholders — customers, suppliers, executives, team members and support staff — need to fully understand the WBS. If you do not understand it as a project manager, nobody will. If an outside reviewer does not understand it, chances are other stakeholders will not either. Ideally, a total stranger should be able to understand your WBS without further explanation.

3.11. Do project management overhead tasks (see page 143), if present, cover the entire duration of the project? It does not make sense to stop managing the project halfway.
- ◇ Do the long task bars representing overhead tasks (like *project management)* extend over the entire duration of the project?
- ◇ Do the *status meetings*, as recurring tasks, continue over the entire duration of the project?

3.12. Are task bar splits in the schedule kept to a minimum during the *planning* phase of the project?
Task bar splits often require extensive maintenance and should be applied with restraint (see page 129). During project *execution* you will see enough splits appear when updating your schedule with actuals.

4 Estimates

4.1. Do all detail tasks have an estimate?
When the **Task Mode** is **Manually Scheduled**, one of the essential pieces of schedule data may be missing: duration, start or finish. If one piece is missing, the task is called *unscheduled* and is just a placeholder with its field **Placeholder** set to **Yes**. By filtering on this field you can easily check if you have entered all estimates. **Auto Scheduled** tasks always have all three pieces of information, because MS Project will enter default durations of 1 day, if needed, and dates (the project start date as the default start date). You can perform this check by applying the filter
4.1 All Estimates Entered?

4.2. Are the estimates that you collected consistent with the working hours entered in the **Standard (Project Calendar)**?
If they are not consistent the schedule will be too long or too short.
- ◇ Gross working time estimates should be entered in a schedule with gross working hours on the project calendar (typically 8:00 AM - 5:00 PM). This is what most organizations use, see page 183 for the reason why.
- ◇ Pure working time estimates should be entered in a schedule with pure working hours on the project calendar – a shorter working day. If you estimate that the productive hours are 70% of the time spent at work, the working hours should be 70% * 8h = 5.6 hours,

13

rounded to 5.5 hours. Working hours that correspond to this are, for example, 9:00 AM - 12:00 PM and 1:00 PM - 3:30 PM.
We recommend that you set working hours like these on the project calendar if you want to work with pure work time estimates.
See page 185 for more details. For the steps to enter working hours, see page 102. If you adjust the working times, you also need to adjust the conversion factors, see page 95.

4.3. Are the *estimates* reasonable given the work that needs to be performed?
  - ◇ Some types of tasks are easily underestimated; for example, writing documents takes a lot of time (I sigh deeply while writing this), at least 2 hours per page. For other tasks, you will need some technical expertise to verify if the estimates are reasonable. If you do not have this technical expertise, you could review the schedules of similar, completed projects. You can ask your team members who have the technical knowledge to review each other's estimates (peer review) or you can ask a *subject matter expert* (*SME*) to review the estimates.
  - ◇ Sometimes tasks are overestimated. Some project managers incorporate waiting time into the duration estimates, such as when they have to wait two weeks for approvals or one week for a review by the end user. Waiting time is more appropriately modeled as a lag on the dependency; see page 235 for how to enter lags. Any review or approval cycle includes waiting time.

4.4. Is the amount of effort on overhead tasks reasonable compared to the total amount of effort (Work)?
The percent of overhead effort needs to be between 10% (construction projects) and 30% (research projects) of the total effort in the project.

5 Dependencies

Checking the Completeness of the Network of Dependencies

5.1. Have you turned the **Task Mode** of all linked tasks to **Auto Scheduled**?
What is the use of dependencies if you do not take advantage of them?
See page 218 for the detailed discussion on why switching tasks to Auto Scheduled is important.
You can perform this check by applying the out-of-the-box filter **Manually Scheduled Tasks** (ribbon **View**, list button **Filter**, item **More Filters**, item in list **Manually Scheduled Tasks**). If you find any, please refer to page 220 for the steps to switch them to **Auto Scheduled**.

5.2. Is the logic set only on detail tasks and milestones (not on summary tasks)?
If some dependencies run through summary tasks and others through detail

tasks, it is too hard to check if the network is complete. It is also too hard to trace the Critical Path and understand it. Only with a complete network can the schedule be a fully dynamic model of the project. Therefore, we recommend that you keep the logic on the detail tasks and milestones only. We discussed this point in more detail on page 236. You can check if there are dependencies on summary tasks by applying the filter **5.2 Summary Tasks with Dependencies**.

5.3. Are all the starts of the detail tasks and milestones linked to at least one other detail task or milestone?
You can verify if all starts are linked by applying the filter **5.3 Detail Tasks without Predecessors**. Note that if the project manager used SS or FF dependencies, the filter is not conclusive. There will be another check we need to do on those dependencies.
Exceptions for having a predecessor are:
- ◇ *Summary tasks* (see page 232).
- ◇ All tasks that can start independently from each other when the project starts.
- ◇ All tasks or milestones driven by deliveries from suppliers outside the project team (*external dependency*) rather than by hand-offs within the project. We recommend you create extra milestones for delivery events. You can put a **Start No Earlier Than** constraint date on these delivery milestones (see page 234).
- ◇ *Recurring tasks* (see page 141).
- ◇ *Overhead tasks* (see page 143).

5.4. Are all the ends of the detail tasks and milestones linked to at least one other detail task or milestone?
A detail task that does not have its end tied to another task is a *loose end*, *hanger* or *dangling task*. In any project there should only be one loose end: the project finish milestone (ignoring the summary, recurring and overhead tasks). You can verify whether all ends are linked up by applying the filter **5.4 Detail Tasks without Successors**. Note that if the project manager used SS or FF dependencies, the filter is not conclusive. There will be another check that we need to apply on those.
Exceptions are:
- ◇ The project end milestone
- ◇ *Summary tasks* (see page 232)
- ◇ *Recurring tasks* (see page 141)
- ◇ *Overhead tasks* (see page 143)

5.5. Do you have SS dependencies properly linked up?
Project managers often forget to link a task bar on both ends when they use SS or FF dependencies. People often forget to set a dependency on the finish of the predecessor involved in an SS dependency (see the question

marks in the illustration at the left). The finish of the predecessor task must also be linked; otherwise, it could still continue even though the project is already finished. If you just check that each detail task has a successor, you will not find these loose ends.
You can display the tasks with an SS dependency by applying the filter **5.5 Detail Tasks with SS in Successors**. Then insert the column **Successors**. Does a task with SS in the **Successor** field also have, in the same cell, an FS or FF entry that ties up its end? Note that MS Project does not display the label *FS* since it is the default type of dependency; it will only display the ID-number. For example, if you see "*33*", you know this is an FS dependency with task 33.

5.6. Do you have FF dependencies properly linked up?
Also, project managers often forget to set a dependency on the start of the driven task in an FF dependency.
You can display the tasks with an FF dependency by applying the filter **5.6 Detail Tasks with FF in Predecessors**. Then insert the column **Predecessors** and check if the task with *FF* in the predecessor cell also has an SS or FS entry that ties up its start in the same cell. Again, MS Project does not display the label FS. If you cannot create a link to other detail tasks in your schedule, you should create a link to the project end milestone. If you do not have a project end milestone, you should create one even if this only serves the purpose of hooking up all your loose ends. Certain tasks can be linked only to the project end milestone. For example: Tasks to inform other organizations or tasks that create entirely independent parts of a system, which can be assembled with very little effort.

Checking the Correctness of the Network of Dependencies

5.7. Do all tasks have a reasonable amount of *Total Slack*?
For now, you can treat the Total Slack on a task as the *time buffer* on that task. For an explanation of total slack, please refer to page 421. Insert the **Total Slack** field by right-clicking on a column heading and selecting **Insert Column**. You can check if the total slack is reasonable by doing a sort on **Total Slack**. Click ribbon **View**, button **Sort**, item **Sort by...** and select **Total Slack** from the **Sort by** list. Select ◉ **Descending** to display the tasks with the most Total Slack at the top of the list. Also, clear ☐ **Keep outline structure** because this sorts only the summary task

families instead of all detail tasks.
Check whether you expected that much slack on the tasks listed at the top comparing their slack amount to the project duration. If not, you have found missing or incorrect logic. [78] In a healthy project, most tasks should have slack that is less than 25% of the project duration. This check is very effective in catching missing or incorrect logic even in large schedules. Remember that if you miss just one essential dependency, your Critical Path is wrong, your forecasts are not *valid* and your model is not *dynamic*.

5.8. Are there no circular dependencies?
There should be no *circular dependencies*, because a schedule with circular dependencies will not be dynamic, but entirely static. As soon as a circular dependency is created, MS Project can no longer recalculate and maintain a schedule. How could it schedule two tasks over time where A drives B, but B also drives A? The application will warn you if you try to create circularity in the logic within a single schedule. When you set dependencies across multiple schedules (*cross-project dependencies*), circular dependencies can still easily occur. They will manifest themselves in the *master schedule* that contains all *subschedules*. This topic ventures into *program management*, which is the subject of another course.[79]

5.9. When a change is entered into the schedule, does it update the rest of the schedule automatically and appropriately through dependencies?
This check is a matter of trial and error, but we recommend you try some likely what-if scenarios. Is the entire schedule still *valid* after you made a change? Where the schedule is not valid, an essential dependency might be missing. If you always have to check the entire schedule after each change, you do not have a dynamic model. You should be able to rely on the logic to always produce valid scenarios of the schedule, whatever change you throw at it, see page 210 for a detailed discussion. Remember, the logic should be helpful, especially during project execution when you update your schedule regularly.

---

[78] This check was contributed by Frank Walker, TWG Project Management, LLC.
[79] Visit www.ProjectProCorp.com for more information on the courses *Forecasting Programs* or *Managing Programs*.

Other Checks on the Network of Dependencies

5.10. Are there dependencies that leapfrog each other? Dependencies that skip over the back of other dependencies within a chain are indirect relationships that you can remove.

5.11. Are there dependencies that run in parallel on detail tasks and their summary tasks? If that is the case, keep the detail task dependency and remove the dependency on the summary task. See page 236 for why logic should be kept to the detail level.

5.12. Can you, as the project manager, explain the network to your project team? If you cannot explain it, the network is too complex. If you can explain the network, you can immediately show team members who else will be affected if their tasks slip. In this way the network diagram becomes a powerful tool for team members to coordinate their activities and act as a team.

A clear network also allows you to do a quick *impact analysis* of suggestions made by team members or executives. Imagine that the project sponsor of your software development project comes to you during the *execution* of the project and asks: *What if we wait for the new release of this operating system?* or *What if we use this new line of more powerful computers?* With a simple network, you will be able to easily indicate the impacts by following the dependency arrows from the components that will be affected by such a change in direction. You may be able to stem unwanted turbulence, or immediately negotiate for more time or money when superiors throw *what-if scenarios* at you.

5.13. Does the Resulting High-Level Schedule Make Sense?

If you followed our recommendations, the start and finish dates of all tasks are entirely driven by the network of dependencies. If the network is complete and correct, the high-level schedule should make sense. You can check the high-level schedule by showing only the first few outline levels of the Work Breakdown Structure. You will then check if the dates of the deliverables (or phases) make sense relative to one another. You can use the **Outline** button on the **View** ribbon to display **Outline level 1, Outline level** 2 or **Outline Level 3**, depending on the size of your project. Even though you may not be an expert in the field of this project, with your common sense you will check if the *walls* are scheduled before the *roof*, *writing* before *publishing*, and so forth. If the schedule does not make sense on its higher levels, you probably overlooked an essential dependency.

This check is important because your executives will look at the high-level schedule. We recommend that you catch any anomalies before sharp executive eyes pry into it.

5.14. Have you turned off *Autolink* after checking the network?
After you have done all the previous checks and have ensured that you now have a complete network of logical dependencies between all detail tasks and milestones, it is time to turn this option back to off: click ribbon **File**, Options, tab **Schedule**, section **Scheduling options for this project**, ☐ **Autolink Inserted or Moved Tasks**. You have just crafted your network very carefully, and you do not want MS Project to change any dependencies you deliberately created. See page 211 for a discussion on what this option does.

6 Deadlines

6.1. Is the project deadline date captured in the schedule?
It can be set using the **Deadline** feature date or using the **Constraint** feature in MS Project. The deadline or constraint date needs to be set on the project finish milestone. Only use a constraint if the project target finish date is a very hard date, see page 266.

6.2. Are deadlines used to capture target dates on milestones that are promised to clients? Are deadlines used to capture agreed-upon dates?
If you promised a date to a client, we recommend you capture it in the schedule using the **Deadline** date feature. If you agree with your team on certain target dates, we recommend you capture these as deadlines as well. Interim deadline dates help you meet the project deadline, see page 256.
You can check this by applying the filter **6.2 All Milestones and Deadlines**.

6.3. When task calendars are used, are they used to create *windows of opportunity* to schedule certain tasks?
Task Calendars are useful when you want to create recurring periods when certain tasks can happen (see page 273). Examples are: evening tasks (office demolition), night tasks (back up computers), weekend tasks (move), seasonal tasks (road construction in Russia).

6.4. Does the schedule have as few *constraint dates* as possible?
Constraints should be used only when they increase the validity of the schedule apart from increasing the rigidity of the schedule, see page 263 for detailed discussion. Constraint dates are maintenance-hungry. Constraints can fragment the *Critical Path.* Constraints are stronger than dependencies and will bend dependencies out of whack, thus jeopardizing the forecasts downstream. However, constraints are useful when they improve the schedule's ability to forecast. When you enter a constraint, we recommend explaining why you use it in the task's **Notes** field. You can display all tasks that have constraints by applying the filter
6.4 Constraints other than ASAP. The filter will not display recurring

detail tasks; they should have constraints.
Exceptions to this rule are:

◇ *Recurring detail tasks*, like *status meeting 1, status meeting 2, etc.*
◇ External dependencies, such as *delivery of supplies* or *arrival of materials*.
◇ Group activities that have to take place on a hard, agreed-upon date, like *deliver presentation* and *conduct training*. These are activities for which a group of people needs to get together.
◇ Do-or-die-by dates: e.g., when you represent your company at a conference, you need to have the booth, marketing materials and demonstrations ready; the conference date will not move.
◇ Activities affected by (winter) weather conditions; i.e., in most of Canada asphalting streets can only start in April, because of the cold. Alternatively, you can use **Task Calendars** for these situations in MS Project (see page 273). Task Calendars are better for creating *windows of opportunity* in a multi-year planning.

7 Resources

7.1. Are all resources identified in the Resource Sheet?
This is the case if all resources that could have a potential impact on the project schedule are entered into the Resource Sheet. Resources can have an impact on *scope*, *quality*, *duration* or *cost* of the project. If you expect an impact, you should enter those resources and assign them to the tasks in the project to create a *resource-loaded schedule*:

◇ Where you expect that limited resource availability or huge workloads will affect the forecasted end date of the project, see page 294.
◇ Where you expect that significant differences in the productivity of resources will affect the forecasts. In programming computer applications, for example, it is well known that one programmer can finish a module in hours, whereas another needs days.
◇ If you have a *cost budget* for the project and you are responsible for staying within that budget.
◇ If you have an *effort budget* expressed in *person months* or *person days* and you have to stay within this effort budget. This is quite common in government IT projects.
◇ If you foresee a *quality* or *scope* impact on the project depending on which resources you will get.

7.2. Are all resources named consistently using a naming convention like *<first name> <last name>* or *<last name>-<first name>*?
Note that a comma as a separator between last name and first name is not allowed because MS Project uses this as its default *list separator* for when there are multiple values shown in one cell. We do not recommend

changing this list separator in the Control Panel because the setting is machine-dependent and will not allow you to give your schedule to someone else.

7.3. Are there no overlaps between the resources or duplication of resources?
If there are overlaps or duplications of resources, the workload and availability numbers will be useless when you start checking on overallocations. For example, if *Bill Tan* is listed twice as a resource (*Bill Tan* and *William Tan*), you would have to sum all time-phased workloads of *Bill Tan* and *William Tan* in order to determine if he is overallocated. There is also duplication if *Bill Tan* is listed individually and also as part of a *consolidated resource*. When there are overlaps or duplications, the workloads appear to be smaller and the availability greater than they really are. This may affect the validity of the forecasts in the schedule; it can make the forecasts too optimistic.

7.4. Is the availability of the resources appropriately modeled?
The limited availability of expert resources often affects forecast dates. Check if the availability is modeled properly by asking yourself the following questions:

- ◇ Does the availability of individuals not exceed 48 hours per week in the working times on the resource calendar, or 120% in the resource field **Max Units (**or in the **Resource Availability** profile in the **Resource Information** dialog, tab **General)**? See page 318 for the reason why.
- ◇ If the **Max Units** are less than 100%, is there a valid reason for this? The only valid reason is if the resource has other work or other projects. In any other case including part-time resources, we recommended adjusting the working times on the resource calendar instead, see page 322 for why.
- ◇ Are the working times on the resource calendar appropriate? The working times need to be adjusted, if the project manager collects *pure work time* estimates from the team members (see page 181) instead of *gross work time* estimates, or if the resource is a part-time resource instead of a full-time resource, see page 322.
- ◇ Are the vacations of individual resources captured in their resource calendar?
Vacations need to be entered, particularly when there are important deadlines close to the vacations. To check whether they are entered, click ribbon **Project**, button **Change Working Time**; select the resource name from the list labeled **For**. Click the tab **Exceptions** and you will see individual vacations listed that are departures from the **Base calendar** for the resource. The bias in the forecasts can be as much as10% if you do not capture individual vacations, since

13

resources in Europe typically have 5 weeks of vacation in 52 weeks per year.

- ◇ If the project resources are located and working in multiple countries, are base calendars created for each country? Do all resources have the proper country calendar entered in their field **Base Calendar** (see page 311)?

7.5. Do all resources have their **Type** field set right?

- ◇ Are human resources entered as **Work** resources in the resource field **Type**?
- ◇ Are resource-related fixed costs captured using the type of **Cost** resources?

- ◇ Are facilities, machines and materials entered as **Material** resources, see our discussion on page 338?
- ◇ Do *consumable* or *bulk resources* have an appropriate **Material Label** to indicate their unit of measure? The *material label* should reflect the unit of measure, for example, the material label for cables could be *feet, yards* or *meters*.

7.6. Are the rates entered in the appropriate fields?

- ◇ Time-related costs for **Work** resources in the **Std. Rate** column **(Standard Rate** field)
- ◇ Unit-related cost for **Material** resources in the **Std. Rate** column **(Standard Rate** field)
- ◇ Time-related cost for facilities and machines as **Material** resources using two fields: in the **Std. Rate** column **(Standard Rate** field) you enter the per-unit cost, and in the assignment-related **Units** field you enter the number of units used per time unit (as the *consumption rate),* see page 338.
- ◇ Use-related costs in the column **Cost/Use** (field **Cost per Use**).
- ◇ Overtime costs in the **Ovt. Rate** column (**Overtime Rate** field), but only if the overtime is paid and also paid at a higher rate than the standard rate (see page 326 for more detail).
- ◇ Rates that vary over time in the **Cost Rate Tables** (see page 339).
- ◇ Multiple rates per resource in the five **Cost Rate Tables** and the appropriate cost rate table (A, B, C, D or E) selected for each assignment, see page 339.
- ◇ Resource-related fixed costs in the assignment-related **Cost** field that is visible in the **Assign Resources** dialog (see page 340)?
- ◇ Task- or deliverable-related fixed costs in the task-related **Fixed Cost** field in the Gantt Chart view (see page 341 for more).

7.7. Is the cost scheduled when it will occur?
This is important for managing the cash-flow of the project: Can bills be paid when they are supposed to be paid?

- ◇ Does the resource-related field **Accrue At** reflect when the cost occurs: at the **Start** or at the **End**, or **Prorated** with the time-phased amount of work?
- ◇ Does the task-related **Fixed Cost Accrual** field reflect when the fixed cost will be incurred?

8 Assignments

8.1. Are you using the task-related field **Type** for **Auto Scheduled** detail tasks?
Your choices in the field **Type** are: **Fixed Duration, Fixed Units** or **Fixed Work**. With this field, you can control what MS Project recalculates on **Auto Scheduled** tasks: duration, units or work. If you do not monitor the field **Type**, you are not controlling what MS Project changes in the schedule. You are using a software tool, but you are using it in a trial-and-error fashion. This is similar to having a carpenter's stud finder, but not knowing how to use it. Instead you start drilling many holes in the drywall to find the studs by trial and error. This can result in the wall looking like it was hit by a machine gun. If you do not use the field **Type**, you are not controlling MS Project. We expect that people learn to use the field **Type** in MS Project. Only then will they master the tool. If we see the default task type **Fixed Units** and **Effort Driven** set to *No* (default setting) for all tasks in the schedule, we know people are not using this powerful feature in MS Project that makes it a pleasant tool to work with. You can check if the user has changed the **Type** of some **Auto Scheduled** detail tasks by applying the filter **8.1 Non default task Type**.

8.2. Is **Effort Driven** off for **Fixed Duration** and **Fixed Units** tasks (**Auto Scheduled**)?
Effort Driven tries to keep the work value constant. **Fixed Duration** and **Fixed Units** tasks that have **Effort Driven** on as well, have two out of the three variables fixed in the formula **Duration * Peak Units = Work**. It is then very hard to predict what MS Project will do when you change one variable. You can check this easily by applying the filter **8.2 Effort Driven tasks**.

8.3. Are there no assignments on the summary tasks?
As discussed on page 384, there are several reasons not to have assignments on summary tasks and to strictly keep assignments on detail tasks only. You can check if there are resources assigned to summary tasks by applying the filter **8.3 Summary Tasks with Resources Assigned**.

8.4. Do all detail tasks have a human resource assigned?
If there are activities without human resources assigned, you have not yet captured all the workloads in your project and not assigned responsibility. If workloads are missing, the schedule may be too optimistic, since

leveling workloads often leads to longer schedules and later forecasts.
An exception to this rule is that *recurring detail tasks* do not require that resources be assigned to them.
You can check if all detail tasks have a human resource assigned in one of two ways:

- ◇ In the **Resource Usage** view, there should be no detail tasks with effort listed under the first category **Unassigned**.
- ◇ In the **Gantt Chart** view, you can also apply filter **8.4 Detail tasks without Resources Assigned**. The filter allows you to easily copy the tasks, including their ID number, into a schedule evaluation report to send back to the project manager.

Note that there may still be detail tasks with only material resources assigned, if you check the **Unassigned** category or apply the filter, so neither check is bullet proof.

8.5. Do detail tasks have just one human resource assigned?
As a guideline (not a hard check), we recommend that you formulate the tasks in the WBS in such a way that each task will have one resource assigned. This makes very clear who is responsible for the work and will avoid confusion and finger-pointing. There are exceptions to this guideline:

- ◇ Where people are supposed to meet to make decisions, or collaborate on tasks or work together as a group, there should obviously be more than one person assigned to the task.
- ◇ When you have a high-level schedule, you will often have multiple resources per detail task.

8.6. Are the workloads on long, elapsed duration tasks reasonable?
Elapsed duration tasks continue 24 hours a day, 7 days per week and could easily create unreasonable workloads for human resources. The elapsed durations should be less than one day when there are human resources assigned. You can apply the filter **8.6 Tasks with Elapsed Durations** to display all tasks with an elapsed duration.

9 Optimizing

Checking the Resource Workloads in the Schedule

9.1. Is the total effort within the person hour budget of the project (if a person hour or person day budget is available)?
You can find the total effort of the project in the **Project Statistics** (see page 439 for steps to display it) in column **Work,** row **Current**.

9.2. Are the workloads for the resources reasonable?
First, select the time unit by which you want to check for overallocations

in the **Look for overallocations on a <time unit> basis** field (ribbon **Resource,** Leveling Options dialog). Adjust the timescale in the view accordingly using the **View** ribbon, section **Zoom**, list **Timescale**. Check for overallocations in the **Resource Allocation** view (for more detail, see page 473):

- ◇ The workload limits for individuals may differ from organization to organization. For schedule certification purposes, we often use the following limits: the workload for individuals should not exceed 150% of their regular availability on a day-by-day basis. On a week-by-week basis, the workload for individuals should not exceed 120%. We think that exceeding these maximums will cause a dramatic loss of productivity, and perhaps even burnout and attrition. The maximums may differ for your organization, in which case you should use yours.
- ◇ The workload of *team resources* (consolidated resources) should not exceed their availability.
- ◇ The workload for facilities and machines should be within their availability.
- ◇ The workloads should be fairly smooth for resources dedicated to your project, since there are hidden costs involved with erratic workloads (see page 465). If resources are used elsewhere when not busy in your project, you do not need to be concerned about erratic workloads.

Checking the Cost in the Schedule

9.3. Is the total cost within the budget of the project (if a cost budget is available)?
You can find the total cost of the project in the **Project Statistics** dialog (see page 439 for steps to display it) in column **Cost,** row **Current**.

Checking the Time in the Schedule

9.4. Are there as many parallel paths as logically possible in the network of dependencies?
Novice schedulers tend to schedule all tasks in one long sequential chain. In that situation there are many *soft dependencies* that make the duration of the project unnecessarily long. If two things can logically happen at the same time, it is important to schedule them in parallel when optimizing for time. Focusing on creating true cause-and-effect dependencies instead of simply sequencing tasks will help with this. As we discussed on page 208, dependencies should reflect *practical necessities* or *mandatory processes*.

9.5. Are all conflicts between the task calendars and resource calendars resolved?
If there are conflicts, the forecasts may be too optimistic. You can find the

conflicts by looking in the indicators column for the icon (see page 273). You can find the tasks with a task calendar by applying the out-of-the-box filter **Tasks with a Task calendar assigned**.

9.6. Are the tasks with a task calendar and resource calendar scheduled appropriately?
If the task and resource calendars have very few hours in common, the task will only be scheduled during those few common hours, and the task bar may become very long. You may want to look for a long bar on any task with a **Task Calendar** by applying the out-of-the-box filter **Tasks with a Task calendar assigned**.

9.7. Are all deadlines and constraint dates met in the schedule?
You can check this by applying filter **9.7 Deadlines or Constraints not met**. It displays tasks with deadlines or constraints that have negative slack. If you have any of these, then you are planning to miss deadline or constraint dates. In addition you have a project end date that is too optimistic.

9.8. Does the schedule have a complete Critical Path or Resource-Critical Path?
A solid (Resource) Critical Path explains the entire project duration, has only legitimate gaps in it and should only show tasks as critical if they are on the longest path in the network (see page 425 and 499 for details).
If a schedule is extended when the workloads are completely leveled, a Resource-Critical Path needs to be identified instead of a Critical Path (see page 414).
Then you check *Critical Path*: You can display the Critical Path in a Gantt Chart view by selecting ☑ Critical Tasks on the **Format** ribbon. You can check the completeness by checking whether the Critical Path has gaps. If the Critical Path has gaps, you need to determine if critical tasks are missing or if the gaps are legitimate. (See page 427 for legitimate gaps in a Critical Path and how to find missing critical tasks.) You can manually raise the threshold for criticality (see page 429) to complete the Critical Path, or you can use our add-in, *Complete Critical Paths* (see page 506) to present a complete critical path to you and explain any legitimate gaps.

9.9. *Resource-Critical Path*: Resource-constrained schedules need to have their Resource-Critical Path marked and highlighted. Resource-critical tasks can be found manually (see page 501) or by our add-in *Complete Critical Paths* (see page 506). You can check the completeness by displaying the Resource-Critical Path and then checking whether it has gaps. If you find any gaps, you need to determine if resource-critical tasks are missing or if the gap is legitimate, see page 509. Our add-in, *Complete Critical Paths* (see page 506), will present a complete Resource-Critical Path to you and

explain any legitimate gaps. The only gaps allowed in a complete Resource-Critical Path are:
– positive lags (waiting times) on critical dependencies
– vacations of critical resources during their resource-critical tasks
Our add-in, *Complete Critical Paths,* will explain any legitimate gaps to you and indicate the reason for the gap. See page 509 for causes of an incomplete Resource-Critical Path.

9.10. Does the (Resource) Critical Path make sense?
There are tasks that we do not expect to appear on the (Resource) Critical Path:

- ◇ *Summary tasks*
The (Resource) Critical Path can only consist of detail tasks and milestones. Summary tasks cannot be on the (Resource) Critical Path if you followed our recommendation to keep the dependencies and the resources on detail tasks only (see page 236).
- ◇ *Overhead tasks*
Tasks like *technical support* and *project management* are tasks with start and finish dates determined by other activities, which is why they are also called *hammock tasks*. Overhead tasks cannot be critical, and if they are, their duration needs to be shortened.
- ◇ *Recurring tasks*
Regularly scheduled tasks like *status meetings* should not be on the Critical Path. Any recurring detail tasks, similar to *status meetings*, that appear on the Critical Path should be removed from the schedule.
- ◇ Tasks that normally have large time buffers
For example, *write test plan* in a software development project normally has a big buffer.

10 Reports

10.1. Is there a one-page status report for the schedule that is readily available as a separate **View** object? This can be one of the following:

- ◇ View that supports *Earned Value Management*. The view should report at least the *Planned Value* (*BCWS*), *Earned Value* (*BCWP*) and *Actual Cost* (*ACWP*) for the schedule. For some examples, see the section starting on page 587.
- ◇ View that displays only major milestones with their forecast dates relative to their baseline dates. See page 595 for more detail.
- ◇ The new *Timeline view* in Project 2010 cannot display progress or baseline data. It is only suitable to present as a status or forecast report if it is based on a dynamic and up-to-date schedule created with the purpose of forecasting (see page 582).

10.2. Does the one-page report give an appropriate impression of the health of the project?

◇ If you used the *Earned Value* view, you can verify if the schedule supports the Earned Value values. For example, if the **Schedule Variance** is positive, the schedule should show that the deadlines are easily met. If the **Schedule Variance** is negative, the schedule should show that deadlines are missed. For this comparison of the Earned Value indices with the schedule, it is important to make sure that all actuals are scheduled in the past and all remaining durations in the future.

◇ If you used one of the major milestone charts, you have to ask this question: are the right milestones chosen to represent the health of a large project? If you have many milestones, you may end up with multiple pages. Instead of reporting on all milestones, work with your client to identify certain milestones as your major milestones. Then you can mark them using a flag field (**Flag1** - **Flag20**) and add a filter to the view that displays all milestones with the flag set to *yes*.

◇ If you used the *Timeline view*, it needs to be based on a dynamic and up-to-date schedule created to forecast.

11 Updating

Quality of the Baseline Schedule and Options Chosen

11.1. Is the *baseline schedule* present, complete, correct, relevant and challenging?

The schedule needs a good baseline, because it will be the standard of comparison used to measure progress.

◇ Is a baseline schedule present?
Note that projects planned far into the future and not yet approved do not necessarily need a baseline.

◇ Is the baseline schedule complete?
You can verify the presence and completeness by applying the filter **11.1 Tasks with missing baseline info.** The filter displays any tasks without entries in the fields **Baseline Start, Baseline Finish, Baseline Duration** or **Baseline Work**. When *assignments* are created after the baseline is set, the **Baseline Work** field is still empty. Note that the filter does not check on the field **Baseline Cost**, because not every project has a monetary budget. If your project does have a budget, **Baseline Cost** values should be present for all tasks.

◇ Is the baseline schedule correct?
The baseline cannot be changed without formal approval of the

appropriate project stakeholders. Does the current baseline reflect the schedule as originally approved, plus all approved change requests?

- ◇ Is the baseline schedule relevant?
  If the project has deviated too far from the baseline, a new baseline needs to be negotiated. The baseline should provide a meaningful *standard of comparison* for the current schedule. You can check this by looking at how far the current schedule is removed from the baseline. Does the project have a fighting chance to catch up with the baseline again, or is it a lost cause? If it is a lost cause, you should submit a change request to move the baseline schedule. If your project was subjected to *acts of God*, there may be a valid reason to update the baseline schedule.
- ◇ Is the baseline schedule challenging?
  As we discussed on page 543, if project managers buffer their schedule before baselining to such a degree that it will be very easy to meet the baseline schedule, the performance of these project managers and their teams will always look good.

11.2. Are the appropriate options selected in ribbon **File,** [Options] for the chosen updating strategy?

- ◇ For task updating (i.e., revising the task-related **Actual Duration** and **Remaining Duration** fields), the options should be set as follows:
  Tab **Schedule**:

  ☑ **Split in-progress tasks**

  ☑ **Updating task status updates resource status**

  Tab **Advanced**:

  ☑ **Move end of completed parts after status date back to status date**

  ☑ **Move start of remaining parts before status date forward to status date**
- ◇ For assignment updating (entering numbers from the timesheets into the assignment-related **Actual Work** and **Remaining Work** fields), the options should be set as follows:
  Tab **Schedule**:

  ☑ **Split in-progress tasks**

  ☑ **Updating task status updates resource status**

  If you keep this option selected, you should not enter **% Complete** on tasks, because this may override timesheet data. The *Project Server administrator* can prevent overriding by locking in timesheet periods.
  Tab **Advanced:**

  ☑ **Move end of completed parts after status date back to status**

13

date

☑ **Move start of remaining parts before status date forward to status date**

◇ We do not recommend updating both the tasks and the assignments for two reasons: it is a lot more work and the datasets can get out-of-sync, in which case you are telling two different stories about your project instead of providing one version of the truth. If you want to update both tasks and assignments regardless, the options should be set as follows:

Tab **Schedule**:

☑ **Split in-progress tasks**

☐ **Updating task status updates resource status**: you cannot enter both types of information unless you clear this option.

Tab **Advanced:**

☑ **Move end of completed parts after status date back to status date**

☑ **Move start of remaining parts before status date forward to status date**

Quality of the Update of the Schedule

11.3. Is the **Status Date** set to an appropriate date?
The **Status date** in the **Project, Project Information** dialog should be set to a date that is within one reporting period from that day's date. If it is too far in the past, the schedule is out-of-date. If it is too far in the future, the project manager is guessing the progress instead of entering factual progress.

11.4. Is the task type for soon-to-be-updated tasks set to **Fixed Units** and non **Effort-driven**?
When you update the schedule, you change the durations (task updates) or the work (assignment updates). For both updating strategies, we recommended Fixed Units and non Effort-Driven, because typically you would like to see how the schedule looks when the same resources continue to work on the task. You can always re-optimize the schedule after that (see page 407) and re-allocate resources.

11.5. Are all actual durations (actual work / actual hours worked) scheduled in the past when they actually happened?
This is an important check to make sure the schedule forecasts accurately by itself: *forecast scheduling*. The actuals are scheduled in the past if their dates are before the status date. If that is not the case, the forecasts in the schedule have not been updated. When you bring actual durations to the

past, all their dependent tasks may be rescheduled earlier as well, which improves the accuracy of the forecasts. This is why rescheduling actuals is important. You can perform this check by applying the filter **11.5 Reschedule Actual Durations...** You should move the tasks displayed by this filter by using **Tasks** ribbon, button **Move**, and item **Completed Parts to Status Date.**

11.6. Are all remaining durations (remaining work numbers) scheduled in the future when they will happen?
This is an important check to make sure the schedule forecasts accurately by itself: *forecast scheduling*. The remaining estimates are scheduled in the future if their start date is later than the status date. You cannot leave unfinished work scheduled in the past, because the past is done and gone. The work should be moved to the future to update the forecast dates of all their dependent tasks. Otherwise, the schedule does not reflect up-to-date forecasts, and you have created a *status report*, instead of a *forecast report*. You can perform this check by applying the filter **11.6 Reschedule Remaining Durations...** Then move the tasks by using **Tasks** ribbon, button **Move**, item **Incomplete Parts to Status Date**.

11.7. Are the to-complete estimates revised?
This is an important check to make sure the schedule forecasts accurately by itself: *forecast scheduling*. If remaining duration or remaining work values are not revised, the schedule may not reflect up-to-date and accurate forecasts. If team members do revise the remaining durations of their detail tasks, the forecasts will be more accurate. You can display the tasks with a revised duration by applying the filter **11.7 Remaining Durations revised**. This filter is different from the other filters in the sense that if it displays tasks, the schedule is good because its forecasts are more accurate. If the filter does not display any tasks, it is an indication that the project managers are not revising their to-complete estimates while updating.

11.8. Are the workloads of the resources still reasonable?
Updates to the schedule may have increased or decreased workloads, or shifted them and caused new *overallocations*. If workloads decreased, there are new opportunities to shorten the schedule.

11.9. Is the latest forecast finish date still before the project deadline date or before the baseline schedule finish date?
If the project update slipped the schedule and extended it beyond its promised and agreed-upon finish date, you have a responsibility to re-optimize the schedule in such a way that it finishes on time. If your current project finish date is later than the baseline schedule finish date, you are planning to finish late, which is unacceptable. You need to develop what-if scenarios with the dynamic model of the project to find a scenario that

finishes on time. If you do not succeed in finding an on-time scenario of the forecast model, you need to ask for permission to finish the project later by filing a change request to change the baseline. Once this change request is approved, the baseline finish can be moved to the agreed-upon date. In other words, the latest forecasted finish date should never be later than the baseline schedule finish date, since it indicates project managers are not doing their job.

11.10. If you used overtime to compensate for slippages, are the overtime rates filled in for those resources?
You can check this by switching to the Resource Sheet and applying the resource filter **11.10 Overtime rates entered**. This filter displays all resources with overtime hours assigned, but without an overtime rate.
If the overtime rates are not filled in (zero rate) and you assign work in overtime, the cost of the project will actually decrease instead of increase. MS Project will multiply the overtime effort with a zero rate. The cost should stay the same if you pay the same rate for overtime, or increase if you pay more for overtime.

11.11. Is the latest forecasted total cost (or effort) of the project still within the budget of the project?
You may need to re-optimize the schedule to find ways to get within budget. If you cannot find a way to get within budget, you need to submit a change request for more money. The forecast model of the project will allow you to quickly develop a variety of what-if scenarios to find one that works. The cost may run out of hand: If you are using resources with higher rates than in the original plan, if the resources are spending more effort than they estimated, or if the prices for raw materials, equipment, and facilities are higher than expected.

In Closing

If you have any further questions, do not hesitate to contact me, I always enjoy hearing from you. Obviously, I enjoy it when your feedback is positive. But, perhaps surprisingly, I also enjoy when the feedback is negative. At least, you provide me with an opportunity to redeem myself in the next edition of the book. So, if you have any feedback on this book (good or bad), please visit our online database of errata and comments at: *www.projectprocorp.com/fs.php.* I would like to remind you that we reward you for submitting errors and omissions in this book. We will pay $20 to the first person who reports each technical error or serious omission to us.

This book contains the entire content for our two courses:

- *Fundamentals of Microsoft Project 2010*
  The course binder for this course is a subset of this book. It contains carefully selected parts of this book suitable for novice users, with the goal of building their confidence in scheduling with Project 2010.
- *Forecast Scheduling with Microsoft Project 2010*
  In this course, we use this book you have in your hands as course material. The aim of this course is to review how you scheduled your current project and improve that schedule. We will comb through your schedule by applying all the checks from the checklist. If you register for this course, you will receive a full, named license for commercial purposes to apply the filters that accompany the checklist.

Please visit our Web site, *www.ProjectProCorp.com*, for detailed, topical outlines of these courses and for our other course offerings. I hope to personally welcome you into one of these courses.

At our website *www.ProjectProCorp.com* you will find the files available for download. In the sidebar on the left, click the **Log in** button at the bottom, and you will be prompted for your **Log in** data. If you bought the book on our website, you have your log in account already. If you bought the book elsewhere, you will need to create a new log in account. As soon as you do this, you are taken to the **My Account** page with the **My Download Page** section where you can find the links to the download files. The following files are available to all readers of this book (subject to modification without prior notice):

- Solution files for the *Relocation Project* exercises that will allow you to check if you have done the exercises correctly
- Additional files with views, tables, groups and filters we explained and recommended in the chapters:
  - *02 Ribbon bar reference guide for Project 2007 users - Microsoft.xls*

  - ◇ *04 Entry Table - ProjectPro.mpp*
  - ◇ *09 Resource Allocation view - ProjectPro.mpp*
  - ◇ *11 Timesheet System Evaluation Worksheet - HMS.xls*
  - ◇ *11 Tracking Gantt - ProjectPro.mpp*
  - ◇ *11 Update Assignments - ProjectPro.mpp*
  - ◇ *11 Updating through SharePoint.doc*
- Filters with which you can check the quality of your own schedule in the file *13A ProjectPro filters to check Project Forecast Models.MPP*
- Approximately one hundred certified schedules as real-life examples of project forecast models

Professors who use this book as required reading for their students can request from us a solutions manual that provides the solutions for all other questions raised in this book: all review questions and several questions posed in the hands-on exercises for the Relocation Project.

I thank you for all the hours you have spent reading this book if you made it this far. I hope you found it worth your valuable time. If you did, please tell others. If you did not, please let me know at *EricU@ProjectProCorp.com*. I am in a perpetual search for ways to make this book better.

Eric Uyttewaal, PMP, MCITP, Microsoft MVP for Project
President ProjectPro Corporation
www.ProjectProCorp.com

Appendix: Files Available to Readers

The download files are available for every rightful owner of this book. In addition, a solutions manual for college professors (PDF file) contains all answers to the review questions and the open questions in the Relocation Project exercises. This solutions manual will be given only to professors who require this book as required reading in their courses.

We have created a download page on www.ProjectProCorp.com for buyers of this book (see page vi for the procedure to access these files). You will find the following files:

- **Filters to check the quality of your own schedule**
  (MPP file: *13A ProjectPro filters to check Project Forecast Models.MPP*)
  These filters can be used to evaluate the quality of schedules. You can use these same filters for your personal benefit. Please contact ProjectPro about licensing these tools if you want to use them for business purposes within your organization. Call 613-692-7778 (North America) or email *sales@ProjectProCorp.com.*
- **Relocation Project - Solution Files** (MPP files)
  This download contains the exercise files for the Relocation Project that is featured throughout the exercises at the end of each chapter. This case-study project is taken through a complete project life cycle from inception to updating and closing. The exercise files include the files to start exercises and the solution files with which to compare your results.
- **Best Practice Schedules** (about one hundred MPP files in total)
  ProjectPro certifies schedules. You will find many of the schedules we certified here, published with permission, in several different ZIP files for downloading. Each ZIP file contains the certified schedules for a particular industry vertical or type of project. Feel free to download as many as you want to explore. The files are a selection of excellent schedules that have proven valuable to the individuals who created them and their organizations. The criteria we use to select the schedules to be published are:
  - The schedules are passed for certification by our organization, ProjectPro. We certify schedules if they meet the requirements of the checklist discussed in the summary chapter, which contains an overview of all the scheduling best practices discussed throughout the book.
  - The schedules display a wide variety of projects and come from many different industries in which MS Project and our best practices are implemented.
  - The schedules may have value for you personally for your own projects. We did not publish schedules that are so specialized that few people may benefit.

A

Thanks to all the individuals and organizations that were so kind in allowing us to share their schedules with you. These schedules provide insight into how the corporate world uses MS Project to deliver projects successfully. The next table lists the names of all the individuals, their organizations (if allowed) and the MPP file.

CREATOR	FILE NAME
AUTOMOTIVE PROJECTS	
Aytekin Bozkan	Aytekin Bozkan – TEHCM DV testing Automotive parts
Patty Amsden EPW, Inc., USA	Patty Amsden – Dew Model
Carl Koerschner Simpson Industries, Inc., USA	Carl Koerschner – Steering Knuckle Design
Steve Magee Dura Automotive, USA	Steve Magee – Recliner
Construction Projects	
Sandra J. Perko GS XXI, Inc.	Sandy Perko – Expansion of Suite101a
Dale Dawson Central Lincoln PUD, USA	Dale Dawson – Transformer House
Alberto Alcala General Services Administration, Auburn, WA, USA	Alberto Alcala – Phased Construction
Eric Marois Algonquin College, Canada	Eric Marois – Voice and IP Installation
HARDWARE PROJECTS	
Jim McCluskey	Jim McCluskey – EDI links for Pharmacies
Dick Lane WeBeGeeks, Inc.	Dick Lane – Network Installation
Wayne Broich	Wayne Broich – Install PCs
Bill Reinhart SBC/Ameritech, USA	Bill Reinhart – Router Installation
Tim Schell	Tim Schell – Install Web Hardware
Eddie Perez	Eddie Perez – Office Move
Charlie Milstead	Charlie Milstead – IT Infrastructure
Robertson Young	Rob Young – PC Deployment
HOME AND GARDEN PROJECTS	
Nancy Tighe	Nancy Tighe – Master Bathroom
Larry Smith	Larry Smith – Landscape yard

CREATOR	FILE NAME
Kenny Liss, PMP La-Z-Boy Incorporated	Kenny Liss – Building a Deck
Karel Swinnen EDS	Karel Swinnen – Garden works
Ken Taylor, PMP	Ken Taylor – Build Log Home
	Windows Restoration
Dohn Kissinger, PMP	Dohn Kissinger – Backyard Landscape Project
Ann Hardie	Ann Hardie - Summer 2001 Cleanup
Joy Barnitz	Joy Barnitz – House sale
John Rouster	John Rouster – Vacation
Tom Cappel	Tom Cappel – First Floor Remodel
John Koepke	John Koepke – Build Fence
Kevin Gore	Kevin Gore – Build Deck
NEW PRODUCT DEVELOPMENT PROJECTS	
Chris Benson	Chris Benson – Autonomous Lawn Mower
Lisa James Pharmacia	Lisa James – Design and build air compressor
PLANT DEVELOPMENT & MAINTENANCE PROJECTS	
Todd A. Daily PCT Engineered Systems, LLC	Todd Daily – PCT Shop Test for Mill
	Refurbishing a Plant
	Installation Remstar equipment for comp tooling
David Peeters, PMP Alliant Energy	David Peeters – Facility Center Database
Steven Stricklin	Steven Stricklin – Heat Rolls Rebuild
Daniel Zook	Daniel Zook – Process Plant
Donald Martin Walker & Associates, Inc., USA	Donald Martin – Plant Development
PROJECT MANAGEMENT	
Roy L. Ragsdale	Roy Ragsdale – Time-Keeping Project
Stephanie Ghingher AEGON USA	Stephanie Ghingher – PMO Software Selection
Kristin Horhay	Kristin Horhay – Establishing a PMO
Derek Scoble, PMP SGR Inc.	Derek Scoble – Montana State PMO
Greg Callahan	Greg Callahan – Planning Process Development
	Project Portfolio Management
Stephanie Iverson Marriott Vacation Club International, USA	Stephanie Iverson – Project Management System Implementation

CREATOR	FILE NAME
Daniel Vitek	Daniel Vitek – Hardware & Software Purchase Process
Linda Lawlor Linda Lawlor Consulting, Canada	Linda Lawlor – Automated Project Office
Ann Russell	Ann Russell – Project Charters
SOFTWARE DEVELOPMENT PROJECTS	
Alan Bearder	Alan Bearder – W2K Active Directory SMS Schedule
Allie Darr	Allie Darr – Insurance Software development
Allie Fairfax	Allie Fairfax – AEF Data Application
Amy Schoenherr ProjectSavvy	Amy Schoenherr – Proposed Citrix Schedule
Beth Devroy Access Business Group	Beth Devroy – Skin Care System-COGS
Chas Eddingfield	Chas Eddingfield – Software Modification
Darrell Little North American Mortgage Company	Darrell Little – MERS TOSR software development
Doug Winters, PMP	Doug Winters – Data Retrieval
Frank A. Stillo, PMP OneWorld Inc.	Frank Stillo – Software Development Concert
Isabella M. Stengele Marsh	Isabella M Stengele – RMX Enhancements
James P. Crowell Marsh	James P Crowell – Detailed Analysis of Placement Repository
Joanne M. Greene-Blose Eastman Kodak Company	Joanne M Greene-Blose – ReMan release 4 Reprinted with permission from Eastman Kodak Company
	Full Flight Simulator Upgrade for Company XYZ
	Sales Forecasting Database
Carla Carter Levi, Ray & Shoup, USA	Carla Carter – Monthly checkwriting
Kathy Convery Levi, Ray & Shoup, USA	Kathy Convery – Database
	Requirements and Specifications
	Software Development
David Kempster Centrefile, Ltd. UK	David Kempster – Customer Database
Charlotte Mensah	Charlotte Mensah – Develop Cube

CREATOR	FILE NAME
Centrefile, Ltd. UK	
Ron Ainsworth Centrefile, Ltd. UK	Ron Ainsworth – Software Development
Michael Jordan Great American Insurance, USA	Michael Jordan – Claims Software
SOFTWARE IMPLEMENTATION PROJECTS	
Brad Jones Mount Carmel Health	Brad Jones – Software Installation
Bonnie Heinecke Fortis, Inc.	Bonnie Heinecke – Cognos suite deployment
Bob Herman	Bob Herman – Software Transition
	Beta Testing
Carol A. Ergen, PMP	Carol A Ergen – SuperMontage Implementation
Dino Nosella SAP Canada Inc.	Dino Nosella – SAP Performance and Balancing
Jim Schuster, PMP Fortis, Inc.	Jim Schuster – Implementation of DB2
Larry Wentzel	Larry Wentzel – Automate Benefit Enrollment
Len Maland, PMP HP Consulting & Integration Services	Len Maland – Computer-Aided Dispatch System
Mark Cimon Cognos	Mark Cimon – Logistics Software
Nicholas Scott	Nicholas Scott – PROMPT Implementation Project Seven
Ronald Sonnabend	Ronald Sonnabend – SAP Upgrade Workplan
	Software Selection and Procurement
Beth Pollard	Beth Pollard – Emulation Evaluation
TRAINING AND ORGANIZATION PROJECTS	
Tommie G. Cayton, Ph.D.	Tom Cayton – Incentive Standardization
Tara T. Miller	Tara Miller – training
Peter Avery Capital Defender Office, NY	Peter Avery – Newsclips for Capital Defender Office
	Translation Japanese
Gail Angel Cognos	Gail Angel – Document Writing
Chris Baeten EDS	Chris Baeten – MS Project training
Caroline Robison EDS	Caroline Robison – Communications Project

A

CREATOR	FILE NAME
Annie Nuyts EDS	Annie Nuyts – Security Organization and Governance delivery
Michael Starkey	Michael Starkey – Training Process Development
REGULATION IMPLEMENTATION PROJECTS	
Chetna Mathur	Chetna Mathur – Health regulation implementation

Glossary

Activity See *task*. In this book, the terms *task* and *activity* are used interchangeably.

Actuals The actuals is the subset of schedule data that represents how the project ran. It consists of the final duration (*Actual Duration*), the hours that were spent (*Actual Work*), the real start date (*Actual Start*), the real finish date (*Actual Finish*) and the final cost (*Actual Cost*) of each task.

Assignment An assignment is a combination of a task and a resource. It is either a resource scheduled to work on a particular task or a task assigned to a specific resource. Assignments have their own specific fields, such as start and finish, work, units, work contour and cost rate table.

Bar Chart See *Gantt Chart*.

Baseline Schedule The baseline schedule is the originally approved schedule, plus the approved changes. The baseline schedule is the standard of comparison to measure progress. The baseline contains the start and finish dates, durations, work and cost numbers and their time-phased spread. The baseline values do not change unless you baseline again. See also *interim plan*.

Base Calendar The Base Calendar is any calendar that can be used as the project calendar, a task calendar or as a starting point for a resource calendar. See also *project calendar* and *resource calendar*.

Business Day A business day is a working day, normally a weekday, with certain working hours. See also *person day* and *calendar day*.

Calendar day A calendar day is a 24-hour day. Unlike a business day, a calendar day disregards nonworking time. See also *business day* and *person day*.

Critical Path The *Critical Path* is the longest path through the network of logical dependencies of the project. See also *Resource-Critical Path*.

Critical Path Method (CPM) The Critical Path Method is an approach for optimizing schedules that is based on identifying the Critical Path in a schedule. The method is based on the assumption that the availability of resources is unlimited. See also *Critical Path* and *resource-critical path*.

Critical Resource A critical resource is a resource that drives the duration of the project because of its limited availability. A critical resource is assigned to a (resource) critical task and drives the duration of the task. See also *Critical Path* and *resource-critical task*.

G

Critical Task A critical task is a task on the Critical Path. See also *Critical Path* and *resource-critical task*.

Delaying is rescheduling one of two tasks that compete for the same resource to a later date, in order to resolve a resource overallocation. The overallocation is caused by the concurrent scheduling of both tasks and the use of the same resource. See also *leveling*.

Dependency A dependency is a relationship between two tasks. The relationship can be one of these:

- A logical dependency between two tasks that reflects a cause-and-effect relationship.
- A resource dependency between two tasks that have one or more assigned resources in common and that compete for the limited availability of the resource.

See also *logical dependency* and *resource dependency*.

Detail Task A detail task is a task on the lowest outline level. It is any task without subtasks. See also *summary tasks*.

Duration The duration is the number of business hours or business days estimated to complete a task or deliverable. See also *work*.

Earned Value The Earned Value is the value of the completed work. Earned value analyses are often made during execution of the project to evaluate the progress and to forecast the trend of the project duration and cost.

Effort See *work.*

Elapsed Duration Elapsed duration is the time it takes to perform a task expressed in calendar hours or calendar days (which includes evenings, weekends and holidays). See also *duration*.

Filter A filter is an object with a condition that determines which tasks (or resources) are displayed. The filter is an object that can be transferred among project schedules using the organizer. See also *organizer*.

Fixed Duration Task A fixed duration task has a duration that will stay the same regardless of how many additional resources are assigned to the task.

Fixed Units Task A fixed units task is a task that keeps the number of resources assigned the same when a change is made to the *duration* or the *work*. The duration will change if the work is changed, and vice versa.

Fixed Work Task A fixed work task has an amount of *effort* (*work*) that will stay the same when making changes to duration or number of resources assigned.

Float See *slack* and see also *free slack* and *total slack*.

Free Float See *free slack*.

Free Slack Free Slack is the time that a task can be delayed without influencing the start of any dependent tasks. On the *Critical Path* there is no free slack. Free slack is synonymous with *free float*.

Gantt Chart A Gantt Chart is a graphical presentation of tasks over time. Bars in a timescale represent the durations of the tasks. The chart is named after Henry L. Gantt, who invented it in the early 20th century. The Gantt Chart is also called a *bar chart*.

Global.MPT The Global.MPT file is the default template file that is always open when MS Project is running. It contains the default objects that are accessible in new and existing project schedules.

Group A group is an object that categorizes task or resource records in the MS Project database. A group is an object that can be transferred among project schedules using the organizer. There is also a resource-related field *group*, in which the department of a resource could be captured. See also *organizer*.

Interim Plan An interim plan is a set of start and finish dates that can be used to compare versions of a schedule. Interim plans only contain start and finish dates. Interim plans are different from the baseline. See also *baseline*.

Lag A lag is the duration of a dependency. In a finish-to-start dependency, it is the time you have to wait after the independent task is finished before the dependent task can start. Lag shows as a gap between task bars in the timescale of a Gantt Chart.

Lead A lead is a negative duration of the dependency. In a finish-to-start dependency, it is the amount of time by which the dependent task starts earlier than the finish of the independent task. The two task bars will overlap in the timescale and create a partial dependency. See also *partial dependency*.

Leveling the workload of resources means bringing workload peaks down within the availability of resources or increasing workload valleys to the availability. Resources can have too much work when they happen to be assigned to two tasks scheduled at the same time. See also *delaying*.

Logical dependency A logical dependency is a cause-and-effect relationship between two tasks. If a task cannot start until another task is finished because of a practical necessity, it is "logically dependent" on the completion of the other task. A logical dependency requires a strict sequence in the scheduling of the two tasks, unlike a resource dependency. See also *dependency* and *resource dependency*.

Milestone A milestone is an event with a zero duration. A milestone is an important point in time; it often represents a date on which a deliverable is completed, approved or shipped. Milestones appear as diamonds in the timescale of the Gantt Chart as visual reminders of these important dates.

Model A model is a representation of a reality. The representation is deliberately simplified and built for a particular purpose. For example, a schedule is a model of a project built to forecast the project.

Network Diagram The network diagram shows the logical dependencies between the tasks. Dependencies are shown in the network diagram as arrows between task boxes. Each arrow depicts a dependency and points from the driving task to the driven task. See also *dependency*.

Object Objects are things (e.g., views, reports, modules, tables, filters, calendars, maps, fields, groups) that change the appearance of the schedule data or Visual Basic for Applications modules. All objects can be seen in **File, Info**, button **Organizer**. See also *organizer*.

Organizer The organizer is a feature in MS Project through which objects can be transferred between project schedules and *Global.MPT* file. Examples of objects are tables, filters, groups, views and calendars.

Outline Structure The outline structure refers to the indentation of detail tasks under their summary task. See also *work breakdown structure*.

Person Day A person day is one person working for one full business day. See also *business day* and *calendar day*.

Predecessor The predecessor is the independent or driving task in a dependency relationship. In the example of *writing* and *printing*, the task *writing* is the predecessor of *printing*, and *printing* is the successor of *writing*. See also *successor*.

Project Calendar The project calendar is the calendar on which you specify which days are working days and which are nonworking days for everybody involved in the project. It restricts the scheduling by MS Project. See also *base calendar* and *resource calendar*.

Project Database The project database is the container for all data relating to the project, including all project artifacts, like documents, budget, and schedule. The *schedule database* is a subset of the project database. See also *schedule database*.

Project Summary Task The project summary task is the project title at the top of the task list that displays summarized totals for the entire project. Its task ID number is zero, and all other tasks are indented below it, so that it summarizes the duration, work and cost for the entire project.

Project Template A project template is a standardized schedule that is typical of a kind of project run often by an organization. It contains a standard WBS with dependencies; generic resources are often assigned to the tasks.

Recalculation A recalculation is a refresh of the entire schedule after a change is made to the schedule.

Resource Calendar A resource calendar is a calendar with the working days and times defined for one individual. See also *project calendar* and *base calendar*.

Resource-Critical Path A Resource-Critical Path is the longest path through the logical dependencies and resource dependencies in a workload-leveled schedule. The Resource-Critical Path is based on having access to limited resources, unlike the Critical Path. See also *Critical Path, logical dependency* and *resource dependency*.

Resource-Critical Task A resource-critical task is a task on the resource-critical path. See also *resource-critical path* and *critical task*.

Resource Dependency A resource dependency is a relationship between two tasks through a shared resource assigned to both tasks. If the resource needs more time to finish the task that is scheduled first, it will cause the other (resource-dependent) task to start later. A resource dependency does not prescribe a strict sequence between the tasks, unlike logical dependencies. See also *logical dependency*.

Resource A resource is a person, team, facility, machine or material used in a project to accomplish tasks. Anything that can influence the timing, cost or quality of tasks should be defined as a resource in the project.

Resource Leveling, see *leveling*.

Responsible A responsible person is the person who is accountable for deliverables of the project. Responsible people only become resources to the project if they work on any tasks in the project. See also *resource*.

Schedule A schedule is a set of (start and) finish dates of the deliverables (or their milestones) of the project.

Schedule Data The schedule data are the data entered into a scheduling software application that can produce a schedule. The schedule data usually consist of: WBS, estimates, dependencies, deadlines, constraints, task calendars, resources, resource calendars and assignments.

Schedule Database The schedule database is the file (or set of files) created by the scheduling software application that contains all the schedule data.

Schedule Report The schedule report is a selection of data from the schedule database represented in such a way as to meet a particular need from a stakeholder for information on the project. The primary schedule report is the list of deliverables and their finish dates, the *schedule*. Secondary schedule reports can be, for example, milestone chart, bar chart, workload histogram and network diagram.

Slack see *float, total slack* and *free slack*.

Sort A sort is a ranking of tasks or resources based on one or more fields in the project database.

Standard (Project Calendar) The Standard (Project Calendar) is the default project calendar. See *project calendar*.

Successor The successor is the dependent task or driven task in a dependency relationship. In the example of *writing* and *printing,* the task *writing* is the predecessor of *printing*, and *printing* is the successor of *writing*. See also *predecessor*.

Summary Task A summary task is an item in the WBS that has subtasks. A summary task summarizes the duration, total cost and total amount of work of all its subtasks. Summary tasks are used to make a schedule easier for stakeholders to understand by grouping detail tasks. See also *detail tasks*.

Table A table is a selection of task- or resource-related fields that appear as columns in the spreadsheet of a view. A table is an object that can be transferred among project schedules using the organizer. See also *organizer*.

Task A task is a concrete package of work that has to be done and that can be assigned to a resource. In this book, the word *task* is used interchangeably with *activity*. See *activity*.

Task bar A task bar is a bar in the timescale of the Gantt Chart. The length of the task bar represents the duration of the task.

Total Float See *total slack.*

Total Slack Total slack is the total amount of time a task can be delayed without influencing the end date of the project (or any earlier deadline or constraint date). Total slack is synonymous with *total float*.

Tracking progress Tracking progress is comparing the current schedule to the baseline. Comparisons can be made on the start and finish dates, duration, work, and cost.

Updating The updating of a project schedule is entering what happened in the past (the *actuals*) and what you forecast for the future of the project. See also *Actuals*.

View A view is an arrangement of project data in MS Project. A view applies a table, filter and group object, and also contains the sort order, format, page layout choices and drawing objects. A view is an object that can be transferred among project schedules with the organizer. See also *organizer*, *table*, *filter* and *group*.

Work Breakdown Structure or *WBS* is a deliverable-oriented hierarchical decomposition of the work to be executed by the project team to accomplish the project objectives and create the required deliverables. [80] See also *outline structure*, *summary tasks* and *detail tasks*.

---

[80] See the *PMBOK® Guide*, Fourth Edition, published by the PMI.

What-If Analysis A what-if analysis is a way of finding a better schedule by means of trial and error.

Work The work is the estimated number of person hours or person days a resource spends on a task or deliverable. In MS Project, *work* is synonymous with *effort*. See also *duration*.

Work Breakdown Structure See *WBS*.

Workload leveling See *leveling*.

Index

If an index item is the name of a field (object), you will see one of the following appended behind the index entry:

- (task field) if it is the name of a task-related field
- (task field value) if it is a value you can see in a task-related field
- (resource field) if it is the name of a resource-related field
- (resource field value) if it is a value you can see in a resource-related field
- (assignment field) if it is the name of an assignment-related field
- (assignment field value) if it is a value you can see in an assignment-related field

If an index item is the name of another type of object, you will see the following labels appended:

- (table) if it is the name of a table object
- (filter) if it is the name of a filter object
- (group) if it is the name of a group object
- (view) if it is the name of a view object

This will help you decide if you want to read up on the *earned value (table)* or the *earned value* concept.